The Legal Environment of Insurance

The Legal Environment of Insurance

Karen Porter, JD, CPCU, ARP
Director of Curriculum
American Institute for CPCU/Insurance Institute of America

First Edition • Fifth Printing

American Institute for Chartered Property Casualty
Underwriters/Insurance Institute of America
720 Providence Road, Suite 100
Malvern, Pennsylvania 19355-3433

First Edition · Fifth Printing · June 2009

Library of Congress Control Number: 2005929301

ISBN 978-0-89463-242-6

Foreword

The American Institute for Chartered Property Casualty Underwriters and the Insurance Institute of America (the Institutes) are not-for-profit organizations committed to meeting the evolving educational needs of the risk management and insurance community. The Institutes strive to provide current, relevant educational programs in formats that meet the needs of risk management and insurance professionals and the organizations that employ them.

The American Institute for CPCU (AICPCU) was founded in 1942 through a collaborative effort between industry professionals and academics, led by faculty members at The Wharton School of the University of Pennsylvania. In 1953, AICPCU coordinated operations with the Insurance Institute of America (IIA), which was founded in 1909 and remains the oldest continuously functioning national organization offering educational programs for the property-casualty insurance sector.

The Insurance Research Council (IRC), founded in 1977, is a division of AICPCU supported by industry members. This not-for-profit research organization examines public policy issues of interest to property-casualty insurers, insurance customers, and the general public. IRC research reports are distributed widely to insurance-related organizations, public policy authorities, and the media.

The Institutes' new customer- and solution-focused business model allows us to better serve the risk management and insurance communities. Customer-centricity defines our business philosophy and shapes our priorities. The Institutes' innovation arises from our commitment to finding solutions that meet customer needs and deliver results. Our business process is shaped by our commitment to efficiency, strategy, and responsible asset management.

The Institutes believe that professionalism is grounded in education, experience, and ethical behavior. The Chartered Property Casualty Underwriter (CPCU) professional designation offered by the Institutes is designed to provide a broad understanding of the property-casualty insurance industry. Depending on professional needs, CPCU students may select either a commercial or a personal risk management and insurance focus. The CPCU designation is conferred annually by the AICPCU Board of Trustees.

In addition, the Institutes offer designations and certificate programs in a variety of disciplines, including the following:

- Claims
- Commercial underwriting
- Fidelity and surety bonding
- General insurance
- Insurance accounting and finance
- Insurance information technology
- Insurance production and agency management
- Insurance regulation and compliance

- Management
- Marine insurance
- Personal insurance
- Premium auditing
- Quality insurance services
- Reinsurance
- Risk management
- Surplus lines

You can complete a program leading to a designation, take a single course to fill a knowledge gap, or take multiple courses and programs throughout your career. The practical and technical knowledge gained from Institute courses enhances your qualifications and contributes to your professional growth. Most Institute courses carry college credit recommendations from the American Council on Education. A variety of courses qualify for credits toward certain associate, bachelor's, and master's degrees at several prestigious colleges and universities.

Our Knowledge Resources Department, in conjunction with industry experts and members of the academic community, develops our trusted course and program content, including Institute study materials. These materials provide practical career and performance-enhancing knowledge and skills.

We welcome comments from our students and course leaders. Your feedback helps us continue to improve the quality of our study materials.

Peter L. Miller, CPCU
President and CEO
American Institute for CPCU
Insurance Institute of America

Preface

The Legal Environment of Insurance is the textbook for CPCU 530, one of the five foundation courses required of students pursuing the CPCU designation. If you are planning to take the CPCU 530 examination, you should make sure that you have the current CPCU 530 study materials by checking the Institutes' Web site or calling the Institutes' Customer Service Department.

The following summarizes the fifteen chapters in The Legal Environment of Insurance:

Chapter 1 describes the United States legal system, including the classifications and sources of law, the structure and procedures of courts and administrative agencies, and alternative dispute resolution. The regulation of insurance is examined within the broader context of the U.S. legal system.

Chapters 2 through 5 cover various aspects of contract law, starting with contract formation and types of contracts in Chapter 2 and presenting the four necessary elements of contracts in Chapters 2 and 3. Chapter 4 examines a variety of contract issues, including interpretation, discharge, performance issues, breach of contract, and damages for breach. Finally, Chapter 5 applies the contract principles and concepts of the previous chapters to insurance contracts, noting the distinguishing features of insurance contracts. Issues that apply specifically to insurance contracts, such as representations and warranties and waiver, estoppel, and election, are presented with examples of how they might arise in insurance transactions.

Chapter 6 introduces commercial law, focusing on the Uniform Commercial Code (UCC) provisions relating to the sale of goods, negotiable instruments, commercial paper, and security interests. The chapter also examines other legislative enactments relating to commercial law, including bankruptcy provisions.

Chapter 7 examines property law concepts relating to both personal property—including intellectual property and bailments—and to real property—including various kinds of land interests, the sale of real property, and landlord-tenant rights and obligations.

Chapters 8 through 10 cover the law of torts, starting with an examination of the broad unintentional tort of negligence in Chapter 8 and continuing with intentional torts against persons and property in Chapter 9. Chapter 10 presents some special tort issues, including products liability, toxic torts and environmental damage claims, and absolute liability. The chapter also covers tort litigation and remedies.

Chapters 11 and 12 provide an overview of agency law, introducing the basic concepts of agent-principal relationships, agency creation and termination, the rights and responsibilities created by agency relationships, and the rights of third parties in relation to agencies. Chapter 12 applies these agency law concepts to agency relationships in the insurance business with particular emphasis on insurance producers and claim representatives.

Chapter 13 summarizes employment law, including specific laws affecting employment relationships, and discusses the collective-bargaining process.

Chapter 14 introduces the various types of business entities, discussing the features of corporations, partnerships of several kinds, and unincorporated associations and describing how each type of corporation is created, operated, and terminated.

Chapter 15 adds a topic not presented in the previous CPCU 530 textbook: international law. This chapter applies and expands the legal principles presented in the first fourteen chapters of the textbook to the international arena. It examines legal issues affecting businesses that establish operations in other countries or that engage in foreign trade, including multinational corporations (MNCs). It also provides an overview of the various types of legal systems and various forms of government found throughout the world, as well as treaties affecting international business generally. Finally, it describes the international legal environment of insurance and discusses various international insurance markets.

By providing an overview of the legal environment of insurance, this textbook is designed to acquaint insurance professionals with general business law and to give them an understanding of insurance legal issues within that broader context.

The Institutes are deeply indebted to the following individuals who reviewed one or more chapters, or who advised about the content of this book:

Robin E. Aronson, CPCU
Thomas M. Bower, CPCU
Austin J. Bowles, CPCU
Elizabeth Brinkman, CPCU, AIM, ARe
Diane Burns, AIS
David Edwards, CPCU
Eric A. Fitzgerald, JD, CPCU, ARe

Kurt Foerster, CPCU, ARM, AMIM

Catherine H. Hanson, CPCU, AIC, AIS

Joanne Hirase-Stacey, JD, CPCU, AIM

Dennis M. Hughes, JD, CPCU, ARe

John D. Kearney, JD, AIC

Chris Kendall, CPCU, AIM, ARM

Penny J. Kilberry, CPCU, ACP, AIS

Richard Kline, CPCU, AIM, AU

David Lewis, JD, CPCU, AIC

Stanley Lipshultz, JD, CPCU

James A. Sherlock, MBA, CPCU, CLU

Michelle St. Jane, JD

Craig F. Stanovich, CPCU, CIC, AU

Dennis Stauffer, CPCU

Robert P. Suglia, CPCU, CLU

Storm Wilkins, JD, CPCU

Richard C. Yarbrough, CPCU

Their thoughtful review of the material has contributed to making this text accurate and relevant to current insurance business conditions. The Institutes remain equally thankful to individuals who contributed to the development of earlier texts for this course, although they are too numerous to name here. This revised text still reflects the valuable insight of these insurance professionals. Kevin M. Quinley, CPCU, ARM, AIC, deserves additional thanks for updating Chapter 13, "Employment Law."

For more information about the Institutes' programs, please call our Customer Service Department at (800) 644-2101, e-mail us at customerservice@cpcuiia.org, or visit our Web site at www.aicpcu.org.

Karen Porter

Contributing Author

The American Institute for CPCU, the Insurance Institute of America, and the author of this text acknowledge, with deep appreciation, the work of Joseph E. Tornberg, JD, as contributing author.

Contents

Chapter 1

Direct Your Learning

Introduction to U.S. Law and Insurance Regulation

After learning the content of this chapter and completing the corresponding course guide assignment, you should be able to:

■ Describe the U.S. civil-law and common-law systems and classifications.

■ Describe the role of each of the following sources of U.S. law:
- Constitutions
- Legislative bodies
- Courts
- Executive branches
- Administrative agencies

■ Given a case, explain how each of the following U.S. Constitutional provisions applies:
- Congressional powers
- Commerce Clause
- Due Process Clause
- Equal Protection Clause

■ Given a case, explain how conflicts of law principles apply.

■ Given a case, apply court procedural and evidentiary rules.

■ Describe the forms of alternative dispute resolution (ADR).

■ Summarize administrative agency functions and powers and the judicial review of agency activities.

■ Describe the Privacy Act and Freedom of Information Act (FOIA) provisions.

■ Describe the roles of federal and state law in insurance regulation, and explain how those roles would apply in a case.

■ Define or describe each of the Key Words and Phrases for this chapter.

Develop Your Perspective

What are the main topics covered in the chapter?

The chapter introduces the structure of the U.S. legal system and sources of law, court and administrative agency structure and procedure, and the roles of federal and state laws in insurance regulation.

Identify the sources of legal power in the United States.

- How does the U.S. Constitution lay the legal groundwork for the law?
- How do legislative bodies and courts enact and enforce laws?

Why is it important to learn about these topics?

Insurance professionals must be familiar with legal principles of insurance and with general legal principles to understand the bases of liability, the reasons insurance policies include certain provisions, and the contractual obligations of insureds and insurers.

Consider your organization's involvement in the legal system, both in courts and in administrative agency matters.

- What are the most common kinds of lawsuits your organization is involved in, and in what courts?
- What current administrative agency processes or decisions are affecting your organization?

How can you use what you will learn?

Evaluate the costs of court procedures to resolve conflicts.

- How might your organization decrease the costs of lawsuits at each step in the legal process?

Chapter 1
Introduction to U.S. Law and Insurance Regulation

Today's insurance professionals must be familiar with legal principles of insurance, as well as with many other general legal principles. Knowing insurance-specific and general legal principles provides the foundation for understanding the following:

- Legal bases of liability
- Reasons that insurance policies contain certain provisions
- Contractual obligations of insureds and insurers

Although insurance professionals need not understand all facets of insurance law, they should understand its general principles. This course examines general law within the insurance and risk management context and gives industry professionals an overview of many legal principles that affect their business and personal lives.

THE U.S. LEGAL SYSTEM

Ever since ancient people first gathered in groups, people have adopted rules to govern their relations with one another. These rules were handed down orally to succeeding generations and eventually recorded in writing.

In Europe, two basic legal systems developed over hundreds of years: the Roman Empire's civil-law system, adopted by continental European countries, and Great Britain's common-law system.

These two systems differ significantly in origin and in form, and both systems exist in the United States. The civil-law system is the basis of law in some states, such as Louisiana and California, but the common-law system is the foundation of the U.S. legal system.

Civil-Law System

The **civil-law system**, one of the two basic western legal systems, is the foundation of law in continental Europe, Latin America, Scotland, the state of Louisiana, and some other parts of the world. Civil-law systems, such as the French Code of Napoleon, have comprehensive codes of written laws,

Civil-law system
A basic legal system that relies on scholarly interpretations of codes and constitutions rather than court interpretations of prior court decisions, as in common-law systems.

or statutes, that apply to all legal questions. These systems rely on scholarly interpretations of their codes and constitutions rather than on court decisions, the basis of the common-law system.

Common-Law System

The common-law system is the body of law derived from court decisions as opposed to statutes or constitutions. Beginning as unwritten customs that eventually came to be recognized and enforced by local courts, the common-law system arose in England after the Norman Conquest in 1066. The "law common to all England" developed out of a constantly expanding number of disputes, or cases, settled by English royal courts and tribunals. Over time, the English legal system expanded to include written laws as well as written court cases.

The English common law, brought by English colonists to North America, became the foundation for U.S. law. Today, U.S. law consists of that common-law foundation, the written laws passed by Congress and state legislatures, and the decisions resulting from thousands of U.S. court cases.

Doctrine of *stare decisis*
A method of case resolution in which courts follow earlier court decisions when the same issues arise again in lawsuits.

The U.S. common-law system relies on prior case rulings, or precedents. Using this method of resolution, the **doctrine of *stare decisis*** ("to stand by things decided"), courts follow earlier court decisions when the same issues arise again in lawsuits. This common-law doctrine gives a degree of certainty to the law on which citizens can rely in conducting their affairs. Courts do not necessarily decide all similar cases exactly the same as previous courts have, but they must provide strong reasons to depart from precedents.

This example illustrates how the U.S. common law evolves: If an insured sues an insurer in state court over a disagreement about a policy provision's meaning, the court analyzes prior cases in which courts have ruled on the meaning of the same or similar provisions. The court first seeks similar cases in its own state; then the court seeks similar cases in other states. If no such cases apply, the court might analyze general contractual principles and court rulings in somewhat similar cases. The court also analyzes the facts of the current case for distinctions among and similarities to prior cases. This process of analyzing prior cases and their related statutes, if any, and applying previous law to a new case is called synthesis (see Exhibit 1-1).

Courts often encounter situations for which they can find no prior case or previous law that directly applies. Such unprecedented situations are called "threshold cases" because they present new legal questions. When encountering threshold cases, judges summon all applicable law in an attempt to arrive at fair decisions.

Judicial Influence on Common Law

Methods of selecting judges, as well as individual judges' views and values, can influence judicial decisions. Judicial selection methods include election and

EXHIBIT 1-1

Synthesis

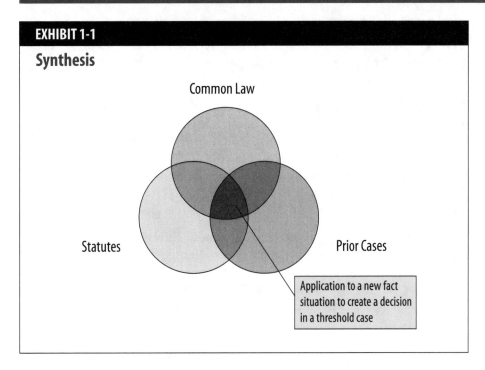

Common Law

Statutes

Prior Cases

Application to a new fact situation to create a decision in a threshold case

appointment, and they vary by state. In some states judges are elected, while in other states elected officials either appoint judges or choose other officials to appoint them.

Although courts strive for objectivity in their decisions, individual judges' political beliefs, views, values, and biases can affect decisions. Newly elected judges can change the direction of a court. Appointed judges can reflect the positions of the political party in power, and court composition can change when the party in power changes. However, some judicial appointments, particularly at the federal level, are for life. For example, U.S. Supreme Court justices are appointed by the president for life terms. Through judicial appointments, a president can influence the law for many years into the future.

The legal system has built-in controls for promoting fair outcomes in disputes. For example, a party that loses in trial court can appeal the decision to a higher court, in some cases all the way to the U.S. Supreme Court. Because the Supreme Court is the country's highest court, the views of the court's justices have a profound influence on the law, particularly when justices decide threshold questions.

The Evolution of Common Law

The common law is not an absolute; it reflects the evolution of society's values and attitudes. What was acceptable law in the U.S. a century ago can, in many instances, be unacceptable today. A court can find a prior decision clearly wrong and discard it as precedent. Courts generally do not follow precedent when the earlier rule of law has lost its usefulness or when the original reasons for the rule no longer exist. Absent those reasons, courts may overrule prior decisions only for sound judicial reasons. This approach helps prevent legal capriciousness and gives stability to society and business. The U.S. Congress or a state legislature can pass new legislation that changes a common-law principle.

The common law also changes through landmark decisions, historic court rulings that significantly change or add to prior law with far-reaching societal effects. One of the most well-known examples is the U.S. Supreme Court decision in *Brown v. Board of Education*,[1] which overruled previous cases condoning racial segregation in schools. Another example is *Miranda v. Arizona*,[2] which requires police to inform suspects in criminal cases of their constitutional right against self-incrimination before questioning them.

The Supreme Court made a landmark decision in 1869 affecting insurance regulation. *Paul v. Virginia*[3] established that insurance is a contract delivered locally and governed by state law rather than federal law. That decision was modified by another landmark insurance decision in 1944, the *South Eastern Underwriters* case,[4] in which the Supreme Court ruled that federal law applies to insurance in some cases.

Equity

Common-law courts historically determined legal rights and remedies and awarded money damages. Courts of equity arose in England because of the failure of courts of law to provide adequate remedies in some cases. **Equity** means fairness, or in the legal context, a body of principles constituting what is fair and right. Courts of equity complemented law courts by recognizing many rights that common law courts did not recognize.

Equitable remedies seek fair solutions beyond what traditional legal remedies can offer. For example, the usual legal remedy for breach of a contract for the sale of a unique item, such as a one-of-a-kind antique, would be money damages. However, a court of equity would consider money damages inadequate as a remedy because the item, being unique, cannot be replaced. A court of equity might order the breaching party to perform the contract by transferring the antique to the injured party.

Although some states still have separate law and equity courts, many states have unified them into a single system. In some states, one court might sit as a court of equity on one occasion and as a court of law on another. In the federal system and some state systems, the same courts provide both equitable and legal remedies. A U.S. citizen is entitled to a trial by jury on questions of law, but equity court decisions are made by judges.

Classifications of U.S. Law

The U.S. legal system of civil law and common law is subject to classification based on several other factors. Three of the most common ways to classify U.S. law, which can overlap, are the following:

Equity
Fairness, or a body of principles constituting what is fair and right.

1. Classification as either criminal or civil law
2. Classification by subject matter
3. Classification as either substantive or procedural law

Classification as Criminal or Civil Law

Criminal law applies to acts that society deems so harmful to the public welfare that government is responsible for prosecuting and punishing the perpetrators. This body of law defines offenses; regulates investigating, charging, and trying accused offenders; and establishes punishments for convicted offenders. **Civil law** applies to legal matters that are not governed by criminal law. Civil law basically protects rights and provides remedies for breaches of duties owed to others. The term civil law is not, within this classification context, the same as the civil-law system discussed previously.

Another distinguishing factor between civil and criminal law is the burden of proof. A party to a lawsuit has the duty to prove a charge or an allegation. The extent of the proof varies depending on the type of case. The prosecution in a criminal case must establish guilt beyond a reasonable doubt, that is, proof to a moral certainty. The burden of proof in a civil case is less strict. The injured party must establish the case only by a preponderance of the evidence, that is, the evidence supporting the jury's decision must be of greater weight than the evidence against it.

Criminal law covers offenses ranging from major crimes, such as murder, to minor offenses, such as traffic violations. A felony is a major crime involving long-term punishment. A misdemeanor is a minor crime punishable by a fine or short-term imprisonment. Summary offenses are crimes that are neither felonies nor misdemeanors under state law; they usually result in fines but not imprisonment. Written laws, such as statutes and ordinances (local laws), specify the nature of crimes and their punishments, whether imprisonment or fines or both. In criminal law, the government acts as the prosecutor, representing the public.

Civil law protects rights and provides remedies for breaches of duty other than crimes. In a civil action, the injured party usually seeks reimbursement, in the form of money damages, for harm. Cases in equity courts, or those having equitable remedies, also fall under civil law. In a civil equity case, a court can order a specific action, for example, directing an insurance company to honor policy terms.

A single act can be both a crime and a civil wrong. In such a case, an injured party can bring a civil suit for money damages, while the government can prosecute a criminal case and seek fines or imprisonment. Suppose an insurance agent has defrauded an insured with misleading information about coverage. This action can constitute both a civil misrepresentation and the crime of fraud and could result in separate civil and criminal trials. The injured party sues for the civil wrong, and the government prosecutes for the crime.

Criminal law
A classification of law that applies to acts that society deems so harmful to the public welfare that government is responsible for prosecuting and punishing the perpetrators.

Civil law
A classification of law that applies to legal matters not governed by criminal law and that protects rights and provides remedies for breaches of duties owed to others.

In criminal law, the government decides whether it is in society's best interests to press charges and prosecute on society's behalf.

Classification by Subject Matter

Beyond classification as either civil or criminal law, U.S. law can be classified by subject matter. Criminal law is also a subject-matter classification. Subject-matter classifications group cases by type, defined by parties' rights and liabilities. Examples of subject-matter classifications, in addition to criminal law, are contracts, torts, agency, and property law, all of which also fall into the civil law classification. Each type of law has its own rules and precedents.

Subject-matter classifications fall under another classification, substantive law, discussed next.

Classification as Substantive or Procedural Law

Substantive law
A classification of law that creates, defines, and regulates parties' rights, duties, and powers.

Procedural law
A classification of law that prescribes the steps, or processes, for enforcing the rights and duties defined by substantive law.

Within the classifications of law as civil or criminal, U.S. law is also either substantive or procedural. **Substantive law** creates, defines, and regulates parties' rights, duties, and powers. It includes the subject-matter classifications, such as crimes, contracts, torts, agency, and property law. **Procedural law** prescribes the steps, or processes, for enforcing the rights and duties defined by substantive law. These two classifications are closely intertwined and are often difficult to distinguish.

Substantive law governs the merits of a case, which are based on the facts giving rise to the lawsuit or criminal case. It includes rules of legislative and judicial law that specify what constitutes an enforceable contract, who can own and transfer property, and what forms of conduct are criminal. For example, substantive law is involved in how contract law applies to an insurance policy.

Procedural law involves the procedures, or mechanics, of court processes and the methods used to enforce substantive law. Criminal and civil actions follow different procedures, called civil procedure and criminal procedure, which specify steps that parties to actions must follow.

Procedural law also specifies the means by which courts can apply substantive law. For example, a state can set a maximum period within which a criminal defendant must come to trial, a procedural rule that enforces a criminal defendant's right to a speedy trial. Substantive law would describe the crime itself and establish the criteria for determining the defendant's guilt. An example of procedural law would be the question of in what court (federal or state, and in which state), an insured should sue an insurer.

Regardless of how laws are classified, all U.S. laws arise from the U.S. Constitution or one of the three branches of government.

SOURCES OF U.S. LAW

Jurisdiction is a court's, or a government's, power to exercise authority over all persons and things within its territory. The U.S. has fifty-one separate and distinct legal systems, each with its own respective jurisdiction. They include the following:

- The U.S. federal legal system
- The separate legal system of each of the fifty states

Each of the fifty-one legal systems has the following five sources of law:

1. A constitution, which establishes fundamental rights and creates the other branches of government
2. The legislative branch—Congress and state legislatures, for example—which enact statutes
3. The judicial branch—courts—which decide cases
4. The executive branch—the president and state governors, for example—which enforces law
5. Administrative agencies—in reality, part of the executive branch—which make and enforce regulations

The sources of U.S. law are numerous and complex. Each system has its own statutory, case, and regulatory law. Exhibit 1-2 summarizes the sources of U.S. law.

Constitutions

In the U.S., constitutions lay the groundwork for the legal systems of both state and federal governments. The U.S. (federal) Constitution defines itself as the "supreme Law of the Land." Each state has its own constitution, which is the supreme law of that state, subservient only to the U.S. Constitution. In the case of a conflict, the U.S. Constitution always prevails over a state constitution. Any law that violates the U.S. Constitution, whether state or federal, is void. Since its adoption in 1789, the Constitution has survived many significant social and economic developments to become the oldest constitution in the world today. In more than 200 years of U.S. history, the Constitution has undergone few changes. A copy of the U.S. Constitution appears in the Appendix to this volume.

A constitution, whether federal or state, specifies a government's powers and the limitations on those powers. Not all countries have constitutions (England, for example, does not); some countries are developing constitutions. In democratic countries, constitutions not only define governmental powers but also specify individual rights. The U.S. Constitution has served as a model for many countries in specifying individual rights.

Jurisdiction
The power of a court to decide cases of a certain type or within a specific territory.

EXHIBIT 1-2

Sources of U.S. Law (Federal and State)

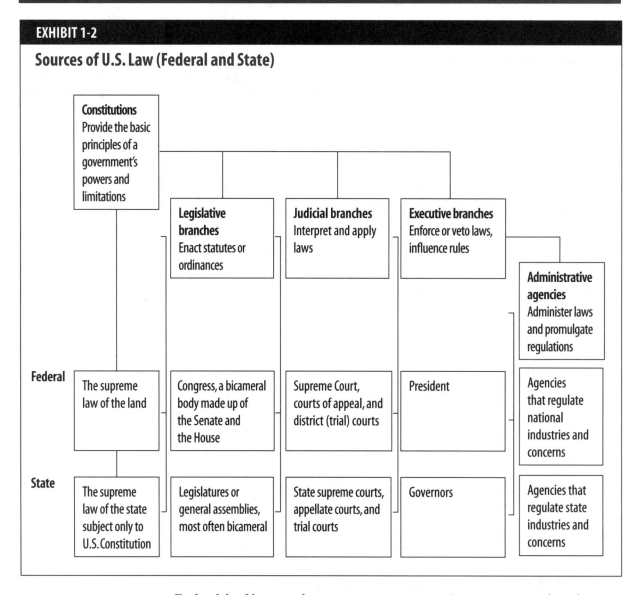

Each of the fifty states has its own constitution. A state can grant broader rights to its citizens than those that federal law or the U.S. Constitution grants as long as the state does not violate the federal Constitution. For example, although the U.S. Constitution does not contain an amendment explicitly prohibiting gender-based discrimination, some state constitutions do.

The U.S. Constitution provides for separation of powers among three coequal branches of government: legislative, judicial, and executive. State constitutions, and most local government charters, follow this model. Inherent in the U.S. legal system is the concept of checks and balances, designed to ensure that no single branch of government can become too powerful. The branches, their powers, and how they check and balance the other branches, are summarized as follows:

- The executive branch (led by the president on the federal level and governors on the state level) has power to recommend, approve, or veto laws and to administer and carry out many laws through administrative agencies. This branch's checks on the other two branches include the power to appoint some judges (those who are not elected at the state level) and the power to veto laws passed by the legislative branch.

- The legislative branch (the federal Congress and state legislatures) has the power to pass laws. This branch's checks on the other two branches include its power to approve or deny many of the executive's appointments (judges and heads of administrative agencies, for example) and its ability to pass constitutional laws negating judicial opinions.

- The judicial branch (the courts) interpret, affirm, or negate laws passed by the legislative branch. Supreme courts at both the federal and state levels also interpret their respective constitutions. The judicial branch's checks on the other two branches include the power to declare laws, and sometimes actions or regulations of the executive branch, unconstitutional or unlawful.

Administrative agencies are part of the executive branch of government, although some may be independent of executive oversight. These agencies are created by law, and they often develop and enforce regulations to carry out the law. As discussed, the chief executive is responsible for appointing the heads of most administrative agencies, often with the legislature's approval, and through that appointment power, has some influence over the agency. For example, a state governor appointing the state insurance commissioner might choose someone who agrees with the governor's political philosophy.

In addition to checks and balances, the U.S. Constitution has several other provisions relevant to the insurance business. They include the following:

- Delegation of powers to Congress
- Commerce Clause
- Due Process Clause
- Equal Protection Clause

The Constitution establishes the express powers of Congress, including the power to regulate commerce, levy and collect taxes, borrow money, and establish uniform laws on bankruptcy. The Constitution also establishes the implied powers of Congress to pass laws necessary to implement all of Congress's express powers. The Constitution delegates to states any powers that it does not specifically reserve for the federal government or forbid states to exercise.

The Constitution's **Commerce Clause** gives Congress the power to regulate commerce (trade) with foreign nations and among the states (interstate commerce). Interstate commerce includes any commercial activity, whether interstate or intrastate, that has any appreciable direct or indirect effect on trade among states. Any state law or action that interferes with interstate commerce is, therefore, unconstitutional. Commerce includes such activities as underwriting and selling insurance, distributing movies, transacting real estate, gathering news, and playing professional sports. For example, an insurer that conducts business in more than one state would be subject to a federal law.

Commerce Clause
The provision of the U.S. Constitution that gives Congress the power to regulate commerce (trade) with foreign nations and among the states (interstate commerce).

Due Process Clause
The Fifth Amendment to the U.S. Constitution, guaranteeing notice and a hearing before the federal government can deprive any person of life, liberty, or property; and the Fourteenth Amendment's extension of these same requirements to state government actions.

The Fifth Amendment **Due Process Clause** guarantees notice and a hearing before the federal government can deprive any person of life, liberty, or property. The Fourteenth Amendment extends the same protection in state government actions. An example of a state due process case is an insurer's complaint against the department of insurance for attempting to lower the insurer's premium without notifying the insurer or giving the insurer an opportunity to be heard. The insurer charges that it was adversely affected because it had no opportunity to protect its interests.

Equal Protection Clause
A part of the Fourteenth Amendment to the U.S. Constitution prohibiting state laws that discriminate unfairly or arbitrarily, and requiring equal treatment to all persons under like circumstances and conditions.

The Fourteenth Amendment's **Equal Protection Clause** also addresses individual rights by prohibiting state laws that discriminate unfairly or arbitrarily and requiring equal treatment to all persons under like circumstances and conditions, in terms of both privileges and liabilities. It protects both individuals and corporations. Many state constitutions contain equal protection clauses.

Guest statute
A law requiring a passenger who has been injured in a vehicle accident and is seeking to recover damages to establish that the accident resulted from the driver's gross negligence.

State automobile guest statutes are a good example of how equal protection clauses can work. Guest statutes relate to people injured in vehicle accidents who are passengers in, not drivers of, a vehicle. **Guest statutes** usually require that a guest passenger who is injured in a vehicle accident and is seeking to recover damages from a driver must establish that the accident resulted from the driver's gross negligence. Proof of ordinary negligence is normally required in vehicle injury cases. Willful misconduct or gross negligence is much more difficult to prove than ordinary negligence. Many courts have stricken guest statutes as unconstitutional under equal protection clauses because they impose unequal burdens of proof on guest passengers as opposed to other vehicle accident victims.

Legislative Bodies

Constitutions delegate the power to make laws to legislative bodies. At practically every level of government, legislative bodies enact laws, or statutes. Major U.S. legislative bodies are Congress and the fifty state legislatures. Local governments also have legislative bodies, for example, city councils, which enact laws, usually called ordinances.

The U.S. Congress is bicameral, that is, it has two chambers: the Senate and the House of Representatives. Each state has two senators and a number of representatives in the House based on that state's population. Only Congress can enact legislation regarding any powers granted exclusively to the federal government by the Constitution. In the areas that are primarily the concern of the individual states, only the respective states' legislatures can enact legislation.

Most states have bicameral legislatures, or assemblies, mirroring the federal Congressional structure. A few states and U.S. territories have unicameral— single house—legislatures. At the city, county, township, and village levels, thousands of local legislative bodies enact written ordinances governing their citizens. A state or local legislative body can clarify or change the common law and can proscribe unacceptable conduct as long as the laws it enacts do not violate either the U.S. Constitution or federal law or the state constitution and laws.

Questions about whether Congress or a state legislative body has the power to enact a law must be decided by the courts. Courts also interpret statutes and ordinances.

With the federal, state, and territorial governments, as well as thousands of local governments, enacting laws, confusion and conflict can result. Business law can be complicated by laws that vary by state and by local government. To minimize such difficulties, many states have adopted uniform laws. For example, all states except Louisiana have adopted the Uniform Commercial Code (UCC), which regulates the sale of goods and other commercial transactions. The UCC has resulted in uniformity in commercial transactions throughout the country.

Efforts to promote uniformity among state laws have also been made in insurance law. Insurance companies are subject to a multitude of statutes, rules, and regulations in the states. As early as 1871, states recognized the need to establish an organization to promote uniformity in regulation among the states and to exchange regulatory information, resulting in the creation of the **National Association of Insurance Commissioners (NAIC)**. The NAIC pools information to help regulators coordinate responses to changing conditions in the insurance marketplace. The NAIC also develops model laws, regulations, and guidelines.[5]

National Association of Insurance Commissioners (NAIC)
An organization established to promote uniformity in regulation among states, exchange regulatory information, and coordinate responses to changing conditions in the insurance marketplace.

Courts

In addition to constitutions and legislative bodies, courts are another source of laws. The federal government has its own court system, as does each of the fifty state governments. These fifty-one court systems are separate in most respects. A party can appeal from a state to a federal court, but only in cases involving a violation of the U.S. Constitution or a federal statute.

Federal courts have jurisdiction over such cases. Jurisdiction is the power of a court to decide cases of a certain type or within a specific territory. For example, a state trial court has territorial jurisdiction over cases involving state law. Jurisdiction related to types of cases is called subject matter jurisdiction. Courts in which cases are initiated have **original jurisdiction**. Courts that hear appeals from other courts have **appellate jurisdiction**. Courts that hear a variety of types of cases have **general jurisdiction**.

Original jurisdiction
The power of a court in which cases are initiated to hear those cases.

Appellate jurisdiction
The power of a court to hear appeals from another court.

Federal Court System

The U.S. Constitution provides that "the judicial power of the United States shall be vested in one Supreme Court, and in such inferior courts as Congress may from time to time ordain and establish." Congress has provided for many U.S. circuit courts, which are federal trial courts, and for courts of appeal in twelve multi-state judicial circuits and a federal circuit. Special federal courts,

General jurisdiction
The power of a court to hear a variety of types of cases.

including the U.S. Customs Court, Bankruptcy Courts, Patent Appeals Court, and the Court of Military Appeals, hear particular kinds of cases. Exhibit 1-3 summarizes the federal court system structure.

Federal courts handle cases raising federal questions, such as those involving the U.S. Constitution, federal laws, and the United States as either plaintiff or defendant. Original jurisdiction also rests with federal courts in the following kinds of cases:

- Cases involving admiralty and maritime law
- Lawsuits in which citizens of different states claim land under grants by different states
- Cases involving a legal minimum amount in damages between citizens of different states or between citizens of one state and of a foreign state

The U.S. District Courts (see Exhibit 1-3) are the trial courts of the federal system. For example, a person accused of a federal crime stands trial in a U.S. District Court. District courts hear lawsuits for damages involving federal law and also try cases involving diversity jurisdiction, such as a case between an insured in one state and an insurer in another state. **Diversity jurisdiction** is a federal court's authority to hear cases involving parties from different states that involve amounts in controversy over a legal minimum.

A small state, such as Maine, may have one federal district court. Larger states have more than one. Pennsylvania, for example, has three federal district courts; the state of Washington has two, and California has four.

Diversity jurisdiction
The authority of federal district courts to hear cases involving parties from different states that involve amounts in controversy over a legal minimum.

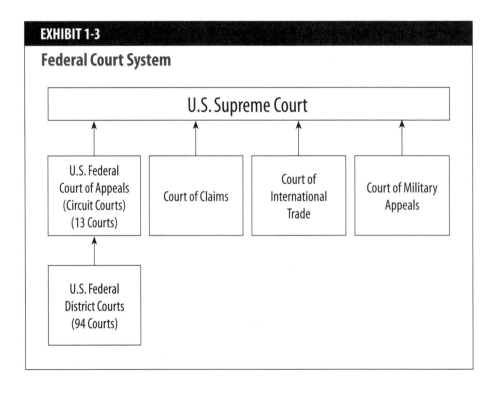

EXHIBIT 1-3

Federal Court System

- U.S. Supreme Court
  - U.S. Federal Court of Appeals (Circuit Courts) (13 Courts)
    - U.S. Federal District Courts (94 Courts)
  - Court of Claims
  - Court of International Trade
  - Court of Military Appeals

The losing party in a case before a federal district court can appeal to the appropriate U.S. Circuit Court of Appeals. For example, a party who loses a lawsuit in the U.S. District Court in Maine can appeal to the U.S. Circuit Court of Appeals for the First Circuit, which serves as the federal appellate court for Maine, Massachusetts, New Hampshire, Puerto Rico, and Rhode Island. There are eleven circuits, each covering more than one state or territory, a circuit for the District of Columbia, and a federal circuit, which has nationwide jurisdiction to hear appeals in specialized cases. In early U.S. history, federal appeals judges "rode the circuits" on horses or in carriages over a large area, holding court in different places. The federal appeals courts have retained the name "circuit courts." Appeals courts at any level of government are also called **appellate courts**.

Appellate court
An appeals court at any level of government.

The losing party on appeal in a circuit court of appeals can take the case to the U.S. Supreme Court by filing a petition for a writ of *certiorari*, a request for the Supreme Court to consider a case. The **writ of *certiorari*** is an appellate court's order directing a lower court to deliver its record in a case for appellate review. The U.S. Supreme Court grants review solely within its discretion, and it is not required to explain its reasons for granting or denying a petition for a writ of *certiorari*. Today, the Court's caseload exceeds more than 7,000 cases per year, a constantly increasing number, ranging from 1,460 in 1945 and 2,313 in 1960. The Court chooses only about 100 cases to review and writes formal decisions, totaling about 5,000 pages, in only 80 to 90 of the chosen cases annually.

Writ of *certiorari*
An appellate court's order directing a lower court to deliver its record in a case for appellate review.

The Supreme Court is the final avenue of appeal in the U.S. legal system for the parties involved in a case. Because the Court does not consider most cases, the Circuit Courts' decisions usually stand as the law for their circuits.

State Court Systems

The state court systems are similar to the federal court system. However, no uniformity exists in the use of court names at various levels among the states and territories. Lawyers must learn the court system in each state in which they might practice.

The highest appellate court in each state is usually called the supreme court. Exceptions include the highest Massachusetts court, which is the Supreme Judicial Court, and the highest New York court, the New York Court of Appeals.

Most states have an intermediate appellate-level court, which hears appeals from trial courts. For example, Pennsylvania has two intermediate appellate courts: the Commonwealth Court, which hears all appeals involving the state, and the Superior Court, which hears appeals involving all other parties. Cases can be appealed from either of these courts to the Pennsylvania Supreme Court.

A state's trial courts in which most litigation starts are courts of general jurisdiction. States have various names for this court, including court of common pleas, superior court, and district court. The term "superior court" can mean a trial court in some states but an appellate court in others.

A state's trial court system also includes courts of limited jurisdiction, which hear specific types of cases. Examples are probate courts, county courts, and municipal courts. Probate courts hear primarily estate cases; municipal courts might hear cases involving only limited amounts of money. The lowest courts may be called municipal, small claims, or mayors' courts, depending on local custom. Judges in these courts can be justices of the peace or magistrates. Exhibit 1-4 shows the general structure of most state courts.

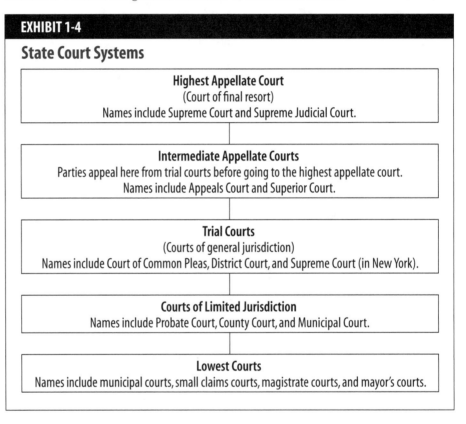

EXHIBIT 1-4

State Court Systems

Highest Appellate Court
(Court of final resort)
Names include Supreme Court and Supreme Judicial Court.

Intermediate Appellate Courts
Parties appeal here from trial courts before going to the highest appellate court.
Names include Appeals Court and Superior Court.

Trial Courts
(Courts of general jurisdiction)
Names include Court of Common Pleas, District Court, and Supreme Court (in New York).

Courts of Limited Jurisdiction
Names include Probate Court, County Court, and Municipal Court.

Lowest Courts
Names include municipal courts, small claims courts, magistrate courts, and mayor's courts.

Conflicts of Law

Conflicts of law
A body of law that resolves questions when states' laws conflict.

Questions often arise about which states' law should apply in given cases. The body of law known as **conflicts of law** resolves such questions when states' laws conflict. For example, cases about insurance contracts often involve people living or traveling in different states. A resident of Georgia may obtain insurance with an insurer in Illinois to cover property located in Oregon. Which state's law would apply in the event of loss to the Oregon property depends on the state laws that govern such cases, and the laws of each state can vary.

In tort cases (cases that involve wrongs between parties), the law in force where the injury occurred generally applies. Suppose a person living in

Mississippi purchases automobile insurance. While driving in Michigan, the policyholder has an accident that injures another person. The two states' laws might vary considerably regarding this accident. If the injured person sues in the policyholder's state of residence, Mississippi, the Mississippi court would apply Michigan substantive law to the accident. However, Mississippi's procedural law would apply because the state in which a party sues, or the **forum state**, applies its own procedural law.

Forum state
The state in which a party sues.

Courts in contract cases, in contrast, use the center of gravity rule, applying the law of the state with the most significant relationship to the case. In determining the state, courts consider the following:

- Where the parties to the contract live
- Where the parties entered into the contract
- Where the parties are to perform the contract

To avoid conflicts of law, the parties to a contract may include in their contract an agreement on which state's laws will apply if a dispute arises.

Conflicts of law problems also arise between the federal and state court systems. Federal courts apply federal procedural law in every case and also apply federal substantive law in matters involving a federal law dispute. However, in a diversity of citizenship case, a dispute between residents of different states, a federal court might apply the substantive law of the state in which the court is located.

Executive Branches

An additional source of law, along with constitutions, legislative bodies, and courts, are executive branches of government, which include chief executives, such as the U.S. president and state governors, and administrative agencies. A president, governor, or mayor can either recommend, approve, or veto laws after the legislative body enacts them but before they become effective. The executive can also appoint the heads of administrative agencies to assist in enforcing the laws. Some of these appointments require legislative approval.

The executive branch can influence the numerous rules and regulations that administrative agencies issue. For example, a state governor appoints the insurance commissioner. Through this appointment power, a governor can influence insurance industry activities.

Administrative Agencies

Administrative agencies, although part of the executive branch, can be considered a separate source of law. The legislative branch, whether Congress or a state legislature, creates administrative agencies by statute. These agencies implement and enforce governmental functions. At the federal level, more than 150 regulatory agencies administer laws affecting thousands of organizations and all citizens.

The federal regulatory system arose to regulate certain large and powerful industries, such as railroads and banks. The federal government has since created agencies to regulate particular functions across all industries, such as equal employment, financial disclosure, worker health and safety, and environmental concerns. Agencies regulate specific areas, such as taxation, health, and labor, and they vary in the scope of their functions, purposes, and powers. However, they all generally have the power to make rules and to prescribe behavior.

Administrative law

The body of law, including agency rules, regulations, and adjudicatory rulings, created by government agencies.

Agency rules, regulations, and rulings have the full force of law and comprise the body of **administrative law**. Federal agencies promulgate thousands of rules every year; that is, they initiate and finalize formal rules and make them known through formal public announcements. The legislative delegation of rulemaking power to an administrative agency is constitutional as long as it meets the following three conditions:

1. The legislation carefully defines the scope of the delegated power.
2. The agency exercises its rulemaking power within the defined scope.
3. The rules are subject to court (judicial) review.

Few businesses, if any, escape administrative agency supervision. To be valid, business regulations must apply uniformly to all members within the same business class. The federal government can impose regulations on any aspect of business necessary for the nation's economic needs. The states can regulate business as long as they do not impose unreasonable burdens on interstate commerce or on any federal government activity.

LEGAL PROCEDURES

Legal procedures are the steps by which legal rights or duties are enforced or legal disputes are resolved. They include court procedures, alternative dispute resolution, and administrative agency procedures.

Court Procedure

When individuals or businesses cannot resolve their differences privately, they can go to court for resolution. At any point in litigation (the process of carrying on a lawsuit), parties can settle a case by agreeing to terms. The legal system encourages out-of-court settlements. Litigation is extremely costly and time-consuming and often proceeds for several years. It involves a complex legal process, such as meticulous pre-trial preparation by lawyers, carefully plotted trial tactics, and procedural complexities.

Suppose, for example, that Mary's estranged husband set fire to her house. Does Mary's insurance policy cover the fire damage? Mary's case involves both substantive and procedural issues. The substantive insurance and contract law of the state in which Mary, the plaintiff, sues determines the answer. Another issue is whether Mary is suing the insurance company in the right court, a procedural law question.

Procedures are prescribed for every stage of the legal process. While jurisdictions vary in procedure and terminology, the following discussion gives a general picture of pretrial, trial, and post-trial procedures in most federal and state courts.

Pretrial Procedure

Although trials are the most prominent stage of the legal process, lawyers do substantial pretrial preparation to gather as much information as possible about all allegations and evidence the party's might present. **Allegations** are claims that parties to a lawsuit assert and that they expect to prove. Exhibit 1-5 shows basic pretrial procedure.

A party, whether an individual or an organization, starts a lawsuit by filing a **complaint** containing the party's allegations in the court that has jurisdiction over the dispute. The party who files the complaint is the **plaintiff**, and the party against whom the plaintiff files a complaint is the **defendant**. The complaint is the first **pleading**, or formal written statement, filed with the court. The complaint sets out the plaintiff's allegations; explains why the plaintiff has a **cause of action**, or legal grounds to sue, against the defendant; and states what remedy the plaintiff requests. The complaint also tells the court why it has jurisdiction over the matter.

In small claims or municipal courts, which handle cases involving small amounts of money damages, parties can usually file a complaint without a lawyer's assistance. In courts of general jurisdiction, lawyers are usually needed to file pleadings. Pleadings follow prescribed forms that have developed over many years, and lawyers have pleading forms that they can adapt to individual cases.

After a complaint is filed, the court issues a summons notifying the defendant of the lawsuit, with a copy of the complaint attached. The summons specifies how long the defendant has to file an answer to the complaint. In the **answer**, the defendant explains why the plaintiff should not win the case. The answer can include **counterclaims**, complaints against the plaintiff in connection with the case. Alternatively, the defendant can file an entry of appearance, which neither admits nor denies any allegations in the complaint but only states that the defendant will appear in court.

After receiving the defendant's answer, the plaintiff files a reply. Taken together, all pleadings—the complaint, the answer, and the reply—comprise a written dialogue between the parties that informs the court about the substance of the dispute. Given that information, the parties can respond by filing motions. A **motion** is a party's formal request for a particular action from the court. For example, the defendant might move to dismiss the case because the plaintiff has failed to state a claim for which the court can grant relief. In a **motion to dismiss**, the defendant admits the truth of the plaintiffs allegations but asks the court to end the lawsuit because the allegations are not sufficient to justify a legal action.

Allegation
A claim that a party to a lawsuit asserts and expects to prove.

Complaint
Allegations made by the party starting a lawsuit.

Plaintiff
The party who starts a lawsuit by filing a complaint.

Defendant
The party in a lawsuit against whom a complaint is filed.

Pleading
A formal written statement of a party's claims filed with a court as part of a lawsuit.

Cause of action
A plaintiff's legal grounds to sue a defendant.

Answer
A document filed in court by a defendant responding to a plaintiff's complaint and explaining why the plaintiff should not win the case.

Counterclaim
A complaint filed by a defendant against a plaintiff in a lawsuit.

Motion
A party's formal request for a particular action from a court.

Motion to dismiss
A defendant's formal request to a court admitting the truth of the plaintiff's allegations but asking the court to end a lawsuit because the allegations are not sufficient to justify legal action.

EXHIBIT 1-5

Pretrial Procedure

Action	Acting Party	Purpose/Result
Complaint	Plaintiff	• Sets out allegations. • States cause of action. • Requests remedy.
Summons	Court	• Notifies defendant of lawsuit. • Contains copy of complaint. • Sets out time frame for defendant to answer.
Answer	Defendant	• States why plaintiff should not win. • May include counterclaims. • In the alternative, may be only "entry of appearance," which neither admits nor denies allegations.
Reply	Plaintiff	• Responds to defendant's answer.
Motions		
• To dismiss	Defendant	• Asserts that plaintiff has failed to state a claim for which the court can grant relief.
• For judgment on the pleadings, or summary judgment	Defendant	• Admits the allegations but questions whether the law provides a remedy. Granted motion ends lawsuit.
Pretrial conference	Both parties, with judge	• Parties may stipulate some or all of the facts. • Judge encourages settlement. Settlement ends lawsuit.
Discovery	Both parties	• Parties elicit evidence, using depositions, interrogatories, and motions to produce evidence.

Motion for judgment on the pleadings, or motion for summary judgment
A request made to a court before a lawsuit goes to trial in which one party accepts the other party's statement of facts but questions whether the law provides a remedy; if request is granted, the lawsuit ends.

A **motion for judgment on the pleadings,** or **motion for summary judgment,** which is similar to the motion to dismiss, is a request made to a court before a lawsuit goes to trial in which one party accepts the other party's statement of facts but questions whether the law provides a remedy. In effect, the motion is saying "I admit all the facts, but the law is on my side." Many cases end at this stage, when the court grants the motion, and never go to trial.

Another pretrial option for either party is to request a pretrial conference with the judge, at which the plaintiff and defendant stipulate, or agree, to the truth of some or all of the facts in the pleadings. Courts use pretrial conferences to encourage settlements—agreements between both parties to end a case—rather than to proceed to trial. Stipulations can also shorten a trial by reducing the amount of evidence presented.

The pretrial stage also includes **discovery**, the often lengthy and involved process by which each party elicits the other party's evidence. In cases involving complex business questions, such as insurance antitrust cases, discovery can span months or even years and can involve tedious examination of thousands of documents and records.

Parties to lawsuits use three discovery tools:

1. **Depositions**—oral examinations of witnesses, transcribed by a stenographer to produce a written verbatim record
2. **Interrogatories**—written questions to the opposing party, requiring written answers
3. **Motions to produce**—motions requesting that the court order the opposing party to produce documents or physical evidence

Parties must provide everything requested in discovery. A party can object to a request for discovery and ask the court to rule on whether the evidence is required. Discovered information enables the parties to know as much as possible before trial and prevents surprises. If testimony at trial contradicts an earlier deposition or an answer to a written interrogatory, attorneys can use the pre-trial evidence to challenge the evidence presented at trial. Discovery can sometimes lead to settlement; once the parties know all the evidence, they may decide to settle rather than go to trial.

Trial Procedure

Although the legal system encourages settling disputes at each step of litigation, many cases still go to trial. Trials are costly but often provide the best means to determine truth and provide justice. A trial gives a judge or jury the opportunity to observe witnesses, to hear subjective arguments, and to evaluate those factors, in addition to written or other tangible evidence, in reaching a decision. Exhibit 1-6 shows basic trial procedure.

A jury is a group of people who hear and consider the evidence in a case and decide what facts are true. The jury is unique to the Anglo-American justice system. In a jury trial, the jury decides all questions of fact and the judge decides all questions of law. If the parties choose not to have a jury, the judge makes all decisions about both facts and law. For example, a question of law in an insurance coverage case is whether the insurance policy covers the loss. A question of fact in the same case might be whether the insured actually bought the policy.

Discovery
The pretrial process by which each party elicits the other party's evidence.

Deposition
A pretrial discovery tool involving oral examination of a witness to produce a written verbatim record.

Interrogatories
A pretrial discovery tool consisting of written questions directed to the opposing party, requiring written answers.

Motion to produce
A pretrial discovery tool requesting that a court order the opposing party in a lawsuit to produce documents or physical evidence.

EXHIBIT 1-6

Trial Procedure

Action	Acting Party	Purpose/Result
Jury selection (if parties choose to have a jury)	Both parties	• Parties' lawyers select jury members.
Swearing-in of jury	Judge	• Jury members take oath.
Opening statements	Plaintiff, followed by defendant	• Presents summary of what the party expects to prove.
Direct examination	Plaintiff	• Questions witnesses to establish allegations.
Cross-examination	Defendant	• Questions witnesses to challenge testimony or to bring out evidence favorable to defendant.
Direct examination	Defendant	• Questions witnesses to establish defense.
Cross-examination	Plaintiff	• Questions witness to challenge testimony or bring out evidence favorable to plaintiff.
Closing arguments	Plaintiff, then defendant	• Summarizes evidence.
Instructions to jury	Judge	• Instructs the jury about applicable law.
Deliberation and delivery of verdict (if no jury, judge delivers verdict)	Jury	• Confers to reach a verdict and delivers it to court.
Alternatively, judge can end trial at any point by declaring one of the following:	Judge	
• Directed verdict		• Tells the jury what verdict to reach.
• Mistrial		• Ends trial because of error or event that would make it impossible for the jury to reach a fair verdict, or because the jury cannot reach a verdict.
• Nonsuit		• Ends trial because the plaintiff has failed to present a sufficient case or has not complied with a court order.

The parties to a case decide whether to have a jury trial. Many considerations influence this decision. For example, a large insurer involved in a lawsuit against an individual might decide against a jury trial because some juries favor individuals over businesses. Geography also can be a factor in deciding whether to have a jury trial. Juries in some geographic areas are less likely than those in other areas to award plaintiffs large judgments.

Parties to a lawsuit (usually their lawyers) select jurors from a pool. Each party can exclude potential jurors by using challenges. A challenge for cause can be used to exclude any number of jurors for apparent bias. Each party also has a specified number of peremptory challenges to eliminate jurors for no stated cause.

After the jury is selected and sworn in, or in trials before a judge, the trial begins with opening statements. First, the plaintiff's lawyer summarizes the facts of the case and explains why the plaintiff should prevail. The defendant's lawyer follows with an opening statement summarizing the defendant's position.

Next, the lawyers present the evidence, starting with the plaintiff's case. The plaintiff's attorney calls and examines witnesses to present the facts to establish the case against the defendant. Questioning of witnesses is called **direct examination** (questioning one's own witnesses). The defendant's attorney can then conduct **cross-examination** of each of these witnesses to bring out information favorable to the defendant or to challenge the witness's testimony. When the plaintiff finishes presenting evidence, the defendant follows the same procedure to establish the facts of the defense.

Direct examination
Questioning one's own witness during a legal proceeding.

Cross-examination
Questioning an opposing party during a legal proceeding to bring out information favorable to the questioner's own position or to challenge the witness's testimony.

The attorneys follow the rules of evidence in presenting their evidence and in challenging the evidence and testimony presented by the opposing party. Lawyers must be alert during trials to recognize when evidence might violate evidentiary rules and to object immediately. Rules of evidence require that evidence be relevant, material, and competent. Trial courts exclude evidence that does not meet these conditions; that is, the evidence cannot be considered either by the judge or the jury when reaching a decision in the case.

Relevance describes evidence that relates directly to the matter at issue. For example, evidence of the dollar limits of a defendant's liability insurance, or even the existence of such an insurance policy, is irrelevant to determining whether a defendant was negligent in an auto accident case. Insurance coverage is not relevant to whether an accident occurred, whether the defendant was at fault, or whether the plaintiff suffered damages.

Relevance
Referring to evidence, the quality of relating directly to the matter at issue in a case; required for evidence to be admissible in a court proceeding.

Evidence also must be material, a concept closely related to relevance. **Materiality** means that the evidence has significance and consequence in the case. A fact can be relevant but might have no importance in a case, rendering it immaterial. For example, evidence that the car in an automobile accident was a recent model is immaterial unless that model had a defect that might have caused the accident.

Materiality
Referring to evidence, the quality of having significance and consequence in a case; required for evidence to be admissible in a court proceeding.

Evidence also must have **competence**; that is, it must appear to have a reliable source and must be adequate enough to justify admission in court. Many objections related to competence are based on the **hearsay rule**, which generally prevents the admission at trial of out-of-court statements not made under oath by a person who is unavailable to testify. Such evidence is presented by witnesses who repeat the statement but who have no personal knowledge of whether the statement is true. Hearsay can be either a spoken statement repeated or a written document containing the statement.

Competence
A quality of evidence that suggests the source is reliable and the evidence is adequate to justify admission in court.

Hearsay rule
The rule of evidence that prevents the admission of out-of-court statements not made under oath by a person who is unavailable to testify.

For example, Wilma testifies about actuarial figures in a book that someone else prepared and about which Wilma has no personal knowledge. John testifies about a conversation he overheard. Both witnesses' testimony is inadmissible hearsay unless it falls under one of the many exceptions set out in the rules of evidence.

At common law, courts excluded all hearsay. However, many exceptions to the hearsay rule have developed, to the point of almost eliminating the rule. A lawyer who perceives hearsay testimony during a trial must object and provide a sound reason for that objection for the court to rule that the evidence is not admissible.

Opinion evidence, in general, can also be challenged on the basis of competence. An expert in a particular area can give opinion testimony within that area of expertise. For example, an expert in insurance might testify about underwriting practices or policy coverage. First, however, the expert's credibility as an expert witness must be established in court. This process usually involves detailed questioning about the witness's background and qualifications.

After both sides have presented their evidence, they make closing arguments to the jury to summarize their evidence. The judge instructs the jury about the law applicable to the case, and the jury retires, that is confers, to reach its final decision, or verdict. Jurisdictions may allow one or both of the following two kinds of verdict:

General verdict
A kind of verdict that entails a complete finding and a single conclusion by a jury on all issues presented.

1. With a **general verdict**, the jury makes a complete finding and a single conclusion on all issues presented.
2. With a **special verdict**, the jury makes findings of fact by answering specific questions posed by the judge. The judge then applies the law to the facts as the jury has found them.

Special verdict
A kind of verdict reached by a jury that makes findings of fact by answering specific questions posed by the judge. The judge then applies the law to the facts as the jury has found them.

At any time during the trial, the judge can decide to take the case from the jury by any one of the following actions:

- Issuing a directed verdict telling the jury how to decide the case
- Declaring a mistrial because of an egregious error, an extraordinary event, or the jury's inability to reach a decision
- Declaring a nonsuit if the plaintiff has failed to present a sufficient case or has not complied with a court order

As discussed in the next section, all lower court decisions can be appealed to higher courts. However, parties cannot relitigate claims in the lower courts based on transactions or on issues already decided by a lower court. The following two doctrines evolved in the common law to prevent parties from relitigation:

Res judicata
A doctrine that bars parties to a lawsuit on which final judgment has been rendered from bringing a second lawsuit on the same claim or on related transactions.

- The doctrine of **res judicata** bars parties to a lawsuit on which final judgment has been rendered from bringing a second lawsuit *on the same claim or on related transactions*. The doctrine prevents parties from raising in a subsequent lawsuit issues or facts that could have been, but were not, included in the first lawsuit. For example, if judgment was against Marie in her lawsuit against Danford Plumbing for negligence that caused damage to her kitchen, she cannot bring another lawsuit against Danford for the same act of negligence that caused damage to her living room at the same time the kitchen was damaged. Nor can she sue Danford Plumbing for intentional destruction of property, having failed on the negligence claim.

- **Collateral estoppel** bars parties from relitigating *an issue* on which a court has already ruled, even if the second lawsuit differs significantly from the first. For example, if a court has ruled that Marco's insurance policy did not cover fire damage to his outbuilding, Marco cannot sue the insurer for loss from a later fire in the same building under the same policy.

Appeals

An **appeal** is a request to a higher court for review of a case. The **appellant,** party who appeals, is the party that lost the original lawsuit whether plaintiff or defendant. The nonappealing party, usually the winner of the original lawsuit, is the **appellee.** Appeals must be filed to the appropriate court within a prescribed period. Appeals courts do not conduct new trials but decide whether law has been applied appropriately to a case in the lower court. To decide whether the trial court's decision was correct, the appeals court relies on a transcript of the lower court proceedings and on briefs and arguments made by the lawyers for both parties. A brief is a lawyer's written statement submitted on appeal to establish legal and factual arguments and provide supportive authorities, such as statutes and case precedents. Briefs are mandatory in appeals, and courts prescribe their format and content. Many appellate courts base their decisions on the briefs in most cases; they hear oral arguments only in a few cases.

Any objection by either party before, during, or after a trial and overruled by the court is a potential ground, or basis, for appeal. An appellate court can affirm the trial court outcome, reverse it, or send the case back (remand it) to the trial court for a new trial. For example, if an appellate court finds that the trial court improperly admitted evidence prejudicial, or harmful, to the appellant's case, the court can send the case back to the lower court for a new trial. On the other hand, an appellate court might determine that evidence, although improperly admitted at trial, did not prejudice the appellant.

A new trial is not necessarily a victory for the appellant because it can reach the same result as the first trial. The time involved in the appeal process also can jeopardize the appellant's case by making testimony stale or unavailable. Losing parties in lawsuits often decide not to appeal after they weigh the probability of an ultimate victory against the high costs of appeal.

Collateral estoppel
A doctrine that bars parties from relitigating an issue on which a court has already ruled, even if the second lawsuit differs significantly from the first.

Appeal
A request to a higher court for a review of a case.

Appellant
The losing party in a court case who appeals the case to a higher court.

Appellee
The winning (nonappealing) party in a court case, against whom the losing party appeals to a higher court.

Alternative Dispute Resolution

As the number of lawsuits filed in the U.S. continues to increase, congested court dockets (calendars), long delays, and additional costs result. While the judicial system handles thousands of disputes, most controversies are resolved by compromise or settlement agreements. Out-of-court settlements offer the advantages of economy, greater speed of resolution, less hostility between the parties, and some degree of privacy. **Alternative dispute resolution (ADR)** procedures, including arbitration, mediation, and negotiation, are methods that help settle disputes without litigation.

Alternative dispute resolution (ADR)
Procedures to help settle disputes without litigation, including arbitration, mediation, and negotiation.

Arbitration

One ADR method, **arbitration**, involves taking a dispute to an impartial third party (an arbiter or arbitration panel) for a decision the parties agree will be final and binding. Arbitration has become a major means of dealing with disputes in contracts, labor-management relations, and insurance. Some states' laws and court rules mandate court-administered arbitration for some types of cases.

Arbitration
An alternative dispute resolution (ADR) procedure that takes a dispute to an impartial third party (an arbitrator or arbitration panel) for a decision the parties agree will be final and binding.

Arbitration is frequently used for settling insurance disputes. Many insurance policies specifically provide for arbitration. For example, uninsured motorist coverage in automobile policies uniformly includes a provision requiring arbitration of policy disputes. Insurers use special arbitration agreements to allocate costs of settlements when coinsurers are involved and to resolve disputes resulting from overlapping coverages. Use of arbitration has also increased under no-fault automobile statutes, under which people involved in automobile accidents seek benefits payments from their own insurers.

Most states have enacted laws that cover all aspects of arbitration procedures. Both the Uniform Arbitration Act, drafted by the National Conference of Commissioners of Uniform State Laws, and the Federal Arbitration Act, passed in 1925, provide specific remedies if one of the parties refuses to arbitrate or denies the existence of an arbitration agreement.

The American Arbitration Association, which provides arbitration services, designs arbitration systems, and provides training about ADR, has developed the following procedure for selecting an arbitrator: Each party receives a list of proposed arbitrators and has ten days to select several preferred arbitrators from the list. The association then appoints an arbitrator acceptable to both parties. Alternatively, each party can appoint an arbitrator, and those arbitrators, in turn, can appoint a third arbitrator.

Most states allow parties to call witnesses in arbitration proceedings, but strict adherence to rules of evidence and procedure is not required. An arbitrator's award or judgment is filed with the appropriate court and is as valid and enforceable as any court judgment. Parties have limited grounds for appealing an arbitrator's award and must do so within a legally prescribed period.

Mediation

Another ADR procedure, **mediation**, uses an impartial intermediary, usually selected by the parties, to assist them in reaching a decision. The mediator is a neutral third party who acts as a catalyst to help parties analyze their dispute, consider possible solutions, and devise a compromise formula. Mediation is nonbinding. Judges often try to mediate during settlement conferences in court cases, but formal mediation involves submitting a dispute to an outside mediator. Mediators are often experienced trial lawyers or retired judges.

Mediation

An alternative dispute resolution (ADR) procedure that uses an intermediary, usually selected by the parties, to assist them in reaching a decision.

Negotiation

Using the ADR procedure of negotiation, parties to a dispute discuss all issues and determine a mutually satisfactory resolution. Negotiation is often the most direct route to dispute resolution. Because negotiations can end at any time, they do not limit opportunities to pursue other dispute resolution methods.

Private mini-trials and court-sponsored mock summary jury trials can lead to negotiation of major disputes. In a mini-trial, lawyers or others familiar with the dispute present evidence and arguments to a panel that may include business executives or other professionals. A neutral party, such as a retired judge or another expert, can act as mediator or issue an advisory opinion after the presentation of evidence and arguments. Because the mini-trial presents the issues to both parties in a dispute, it can encourage negotiation and settlement. Summary jury trials are brief mock trials before juries. The parties can accept the jury's advisory verdict, or the verdict can provide the basis for further negotiations toward settlement.

Administrative Agency Procedure

Administrative law is pervasive in the activities of people and organizations. The legislative output of administrative agencies far exceeds that of legislatures, and the number of administrative decisions far exceeds the thousands of court decisions.

Legislators at the federal and state levels delegate responsibilities to administrative agencies in much the same way that a supervisor delegates responsibilities to an employee. Legislators do not have the time to pass all the rules and regulations necessary to implement legislation; to develop expertise in every area regulated; or to settle disputes arising from legislation, rules, and regulations. For example, a state legislature that passes a law prohibiting excessive insurance rates delegates the power to administer and enforce the law to its state department of insurance (DOI), which has the insurance expertise to set standards for and examine insurance rates.

Courts generally have upheld legislative delegation to administrative agencies. Although legislators cannot delegate their ultimate power and responsibility, they can delegate the duty to fill in the details of legislation by allowing agencies to make rules and regulations and to resolve disputes. "Enabling legislation" creates an administrative agency and states its purpose.

Administrative agencies have two primary functions: rulemaking and adjudication. Rulemaking is the process by which agencies promulgate rules to implement legislative policies. Adjudication is the process by which agencies decide cases and settle disputes.

To illustrate DOI rulemaking and adjudication, after a state legislature passes a law prohibiting excessive insurance rates, the DOI makes rules about insurance rate review and creates guidelines to determine whether rates are excessive. The insurance commissioner, a private citizen, or a group of citizens might contest an insurance rate as excessive. The DOI then holds a hearing to adjudicate the rate in question. This adjudication affects only the insurer involved and the insureds who would pay the new rate.

Agencies' Rulemaking Function

Agencies promulgate the following three types of rules:

Legislative rule

A type of substantive administrative agency rule that comes from a statutory delegation of authority and that has the same force as a law enacted by Congress or a legislature.

Interpretative rule

A type of administrative agency rule that interprets statutes, providing guidance for agency staff or regulated parties, but that lacks the force and effect of law and therefore is not binding on individuals.

Procedural rule

A type of administrative agency rule that prescribes procedures for agency operations, legislative rulemaking, and adjudication proceedings.

1. **Legislative rules** (substantive rules) come from a statutory delegation of authority and have the same force as a law enacted by Congress or a legislature. The development and passage of legislative rules require adherence to rulemaking procedures.

2. **Interpretative rules** interpret statutes providing guidance for agency staff or regulated parties. However, these rules lack the force and effect of law, and, therefore, are not binding on individuals.

3. **Procedural rules**, primarily internal, prescribe procedures for agency operations, for legislative rulemaking, and for adjudication proceedings.

The Administrative Procedure Act (APA) prescribes the procedure for administrative agency rulemaking at the federal level. Most states follow the rulemaking procedures of the Model State Administrative Procedure Act (MSAPA), which requires agencies to adhere to the following three basic steps:

1. Publish a notice of intent to adopt a regulation

2. Provide opportunity for public comment

3. Publish the final regulation

Federal agencies publish notices of proposed regulations in the weekly Federal Register. States usually have similar publications for state agency notices. Notice in one of these official publications usually suffices as official notice to all interested parties that the agency is considering an action that will affect them. For example, a state DOI notice of its plan to adopt a regulation about an aspect of the insurance business, published in the state's official publication for agency notices, is legally sufficient notice to insurers and consumers.

Typically, the published notice of a proposed regulation invites comments by a certain date, usually within a month. Public hearings are required for some, but not all, proposed regulations. The MSAPA requires a public hearing if either a governmental agency or twenty-five interested individuals request it. If no hearing is required, interested organizations and individuals can submit written comments on a proposed regulation.

Interested individuals and representatives of organizations can speak at public hearings; comments can also be submitted in writing. A presiding hearing examiner usually has discretion about who testifies. If large groups of people attend, the examiner can require that only their chosen representatives testify. If the proposed regulation is controversial, the examiner can require advance registration of those who will testify.

After the agency has reviewed all comments about the proposed rule, it can do one of the following:

* Adopt the originally proposed rule
* Make minimal or extensive changes
* Nullify the proposed rule

If the agency decides to adopt the rule, it must publish the final version. A rule usually becomes effective thirty days after publication, giving affected parties time to conform to the new rule or to challenge its legality. Agencies can publish emergency rules with immediate effective dates when necessary for the public health and welfare.

Agencies' Adjudicatory Function

In addition to rulemaking, agencies have an adjudicatory function. Adjudicatory proceedings are similar to court cases. They affect the rights of an individual or a limited number of people. As in court, people in an agency adjudicatory process have a constitutional right to due process of law. The specific requirements for due process can vary by the nature of the proceeding.

The Due Process Clause of the U.S. Constitution grants parties whose rights are affected by an agency decision the right to be heard. Not every case requires a hearing. However, the agency must provide reasonable notice of the opportunity for a fair hearing. If the party does not waive the right to a hearing, the agency must hold a fair hearing and must render a decision supported by the evidence. Denying due process can be grounds for reversing a decision if the party was harmed by denial.

Appropriate notice is essential to due process, and improper notice can result in nullification of an entire proceeding. Appropriate notice requires the following:

* Statement of the hearing time, place, and nature
* Statement of the hearing's legal authority and jurisdiction
* Reference to the particular statute or rule involved
* A short, clear statement of the matters at issue

The test of appropriate notice is whether it informs the interested party fairly and sufficiently about the case so that the party can respond adequately at the hearing.

Many disputes, such as pension or Social Security claims, do not warrant full hearings and are too numerous to make formal proceedings practical. However, any party faced with deprivation of an alleged property or liberty right can demand a hearing before action is taken. Such hearings are often informal. Agencies can use informal hearings when time, the nature of the proceedings, and the public interest permit. Adjudication, complete with a full hearing, is necessary only if the law specifically requires it or if either party demands one. A hearing examiner or an administrative law judge (ALJ), who is usually both an agency employee and a lawyer, presides.

Generally, any person compelled to appear before an agency and every party to a dispute have the right to counsel. Counsel need not be a lawyer but can be a qualified representative, that is, any trusted person. The government is not required to provide counsel to a party for an administrative hearing.

As in court proceedings, expert witnesses can testify in agency cases. Generally, the rules governing witnesses in court proceedings apply in agency hearings, but agency rules are not as strict. Agency cases do not have juries; the hearing examiner decides factual and legal matters. Generally, evidence in an agency hearing must be relevant, but the rules of evidence are much more relaxed than in a court trial.

Counsel in an adjudicatory hearing can make arguments relating to both fact and law. Most arguments are relatively short and often written instead of oral. Parties have no inherent right or duty to present formal written briefs arguing the law. The hearing examiner or ALJ considers the parties' arguments and makes findings of fact and law. Such decisions may accept, reject, or modify the parties' arguments.

To illustrate an adjudication, a hearing examiner's findings in a case challenging an insurer's rates might be as follows:

- The insurer kept statistics properly.
- The insurer interpreted those statistics properly.
- The statistics indicated the insurer had a loss ratio of 35 percent.
- Insurers can make a profit with a loss ratio of 50 percent.

From these facts, the hearing officer could conclude that the 35 percent loss ratio was too low and that the proper loss ratio should be 50 percent. The hearing officer's decision, based on a statute prohibiting excessive rates, could be to require the insurer to lower rates by a stated percentage to produce a 50 percent loss ratio.

Agencies can impose fines or grant, revoke, or suspend licenses. Enabling legislation for an agency usually defines appeal rights and whether they involve a court or the agency. Most agencies have at least one, and sometimes three or four, tiers of appeal. Once a case has gone through all levels of the agency adjudication and appeals process, the party has exhausted all administrative remedies and can seek judicial review in a court of law.

Administrative agencies can give advisory opinions, unlike courts which, with very limited exceptions, do not indicate in advance how they would decide a case based on a given set of facts. Although agency advisory opinions are not binding either on the agency or on any parties, the recipient of an advisory opinion can usually rely on it.

Agencies' Investigative Powers

Many federal and state laws contain provisions authorizing agency investigations, which typically relate to rulemaking, ratemaking, adjudicating, licensing, prosecuting, establishing general policy, or recommending legislation. Agencies may need information and evidence for administrative proceedings and may use subpoenas to gather such information. A **subpoena** is a legal order to a witness to appear at a certain place and time to testify or to produce documents. Those who disobey subpoenas are subject to penalties.

Agencies receive the power to use subpoenas from legislation. Not all agencies are given the power. If authorized by law, an agency can issue a subpoena on its own behalf or at a party's request. For example, a policyholder alleging an insurer's discriminatory practice can request the DOI to subpoena the insurer's records for a hearing that resolves the dispute.

A party to a dispute has the right not only to testify personally, but also to obtain relevant testimony and records from others. If the other parties refuse to cooperate, then due process requires compelling them to cooperate by subpoena. A subpoena to compel a witness to testify is a subpoena *ad testificandum* (command to testify), usually termed, simply, a subpoena. A subpoena to compel production of documents or records is a subpoena *duces tecum* (literally, a command to "bring things with you").

Violations of constitutional rights can defeat an investigation. The U.S. Constitution places the following limitations on agency investigations:

- Fourth Amendment protection against unreasonable searches and seizures
- Fifth Amendment protection against self-incrimination

In administrative law, the Fourth Amendment prohibition against unreasonable searches and seizures applies primarily to inspecting records. Records demanded must be relevant to the investigation. However, the connection between the requested records and the subject of the investigation can be slight; courts usually find such records relevant and require their production. For example, a government agency may ask an insurer for all automobile insurance accident records for the past twenty years, even though these records might be voluminous and might require many hours to produce, as long as the agency demonstrates a need for the records. Some courts have held that, when record retrieval and production are very expensive, the

Subpoena
A legal order to a witness to appear at a certain place and time to testify or to produce documents.

burden is on the agency to establish the records' relevance. Sometimes a regulatory agency has no specific purpose but is "fishing" through the records for a possible legal violation.

The Fifth Amendment states that no person "shall be compelled in any criminal case to be a witness against himself." Court decisions have broadened the term "criminal case" to mean almost any type of investigation or proceeding from which legal sanctions might arise. The term "witness" includes not only oral testimony but also the production of records and documents.

A legislative body can require firms to keep certain records and can delegate the power to enforce this requirement to an agency. Inspection power is not limited to records required by law but extends to other relevant records. Agencies do not have a general unlimited right to investigate beyond what is necessary, and any agency request must be reasonably relevant to the investigation.

Judicial Review

Generally, federal courts review actions of federal agencies, and state courts review actions of state agencies. As the actions of agencies increasingly affect personal interests, the courts seek to protect those interests more vigorously by insisting on strict judicial scrutiny of agency action. Judicial review is available as long it is not precluded by statute or as long as the action reviewed is not left by statute solely to administrative agency discretion. Judicial review is not limited to agency adjudications but also can apply to agency rulemaking.

Standing to sue
A party's right to sue, as one who has suffered or will suffer a legal wrong or an adverse effect from an action.

To take an administrative action to a court for judicial review, a plaintiff must have **standing to sue**; that is, the plaintiff must be the person who has suffered or will suffer a legal wrong or an adverse effect from the agency action. A party who seeks judicial review of a rulemaking procedure must show that the rule or its application would impair or interfere with that party's legal rights or privileges. If an adjudicatory hearing is involved, the party usually must be "aggrieved," that is, the order has substantially affected his or her personal rights.

Final order
An administrative agency's final conclusion or disposition of any material private right of a party, terminating an agency proceeding.

Judicial review of a case can occur only after the following two requirements have been met:

1. The agency has issued a final order in the case. This **final order**, which concludes or disposes of any material private right of a party and terminates the agency proceeding, is the basis of the appeal.

Exhaustion of administrative remedies
The completion of all possible administrative procedures and appeals in a case; required before a party can appeal an agency action to a court.

2. The doctrine called **exhaustion of administrative remedies** must apply: a party can appeal to the courts only after having taken the case through all possible administrative procedures and appeals. A court will make exceptions to this doctrine only when the available administrative remedy is inadequate or when it would be futile to require the party to exhaust administrative remedies.

A court can set aside agency action on the following grounds:

- The action was arbitrary and capricious, an abuse of discretion, or otherwise unlawful.
- The action was unconstitutional.
- The action violated statutory authority.
- The action violated agency procedural rules or was the result of illegal procedures.
- The action is unsupportable by substantial evidence in the record.

A court can review the law and substitute its own interpretation for the agency's interpretation, just as appellate courts review lower court decisions. Courts review facts only to determine whether substantial evidence supports an agency's action. Courts do not set aside agency actions unless they are clearly erroneous.

On appeal, parties often allege that an administrative agency's action was arbitrary and capricious or an abuse of discretion. An action is arbitrary and capricious if it is so clearly erroneous that it has no rational basis or if it is willful and unreasonable. Generally, courts give great deference to agency conclusions on questions of fact because of the agencies' assumed special knowledge and expertise. If a reviewing court determines that it needs more facts to make a judgment, it can send a case back (remand it) to the agency for another hearing.

Privacy and Freedom of Information Acts

Two pieces of federal legislation address issues of privacy and individuals' access to information held by government agencies. These acts affect the insurance business, which accumulates massive amounts of information about individuals.

The federal Privacy Act of 1974[6] responded to a growing concern over the increasing potential for the invasion of individual privacy in the name of information collection. The act applies to records maintained by an agency from which information about an individual is retrievable by some identifying mark or number. The act prescribes requirements for maintaining records and methods of collecting the information for the records. The records can contain only information that is relevant to the agency's purpose. Individuals have the right to access their personal records, and agencies are prohibited from disclosing records without an individual's permission. Agencies are permitted to issue compilations of statistics or records as long as they do not reveal information identifying a single company or an individual.

The Freedom of Information Act (FOIA)[7] of 1966 first established a statutory right of access to agency information. Its goals were to ensure an informed citizenry, to prevent criminal misuse of information, and to hold government accountable to the governed. These goals sometimes conflict with other goals, such as the right of privacy, national security, and criminal investigations. Therefore, the act prohibits access to the following:

- Properly classified security information
- Law enforcement investigation records
- Trade secrets
- Confidential commercial or financial information
- Records of financial institutions

Any person can request agency records for a fee and need not give a reason for the request. If the agency denies the request, the person can ask for agency review and, ultimately, for court review of the denial.

INSURANCE REGULATION

Insurance is a highly regulated area, mostly at the state level. Insurance regulatory law consists of state insurance statutes and regulations promulgated by state insurance agencies. An insurance company doing business in more than one state must comply with the statutes and with state DOI rules and regulations in each state, as well as with federal regulations. Additionally, many other state and federal agencies oversee various aspects of the insurance industry, such as employment practices, unfair competition, postal regulations, and tax matters.

Generally, no insurer or insurance producer (agent or broker) can solicit an application, quote a premium, issue a policy, or pay a claim without considering applicable state insurance laws. The frequency and scope of changes in the regulatory and judicial environments in which insurers work require that insurance professionals keep abreast of legal changes, especially those that signal massive industry changes. Most insurers have in-house legal departments, but many small insurers do not have staff whose primary responsibilities are to monitor legal developments. Consequently, many insurance professionals must have at least a working knowledge of the law in order to appreciate the effects of legal developments that they might read about or hear about from colleagues.

Federal Regulation

Although the federal government does not directly regulate the insurance industry, except in specific areas in which it regulates all other business (such as securities), federal law is becoming increasingly important in insurance.

One of the most important federal laws related to insurance is the McCarran-Ferguson Act,[8] passed in 1945. The law returned insurance regulation to the states, negating the Supreme Court's earlier decision in the *South Eastern Underwriters* case, discussed earlier in this chapter. McCarran-Ferguson permits each state to regulate the business of insurance conducted within its borders.

The McCarran-Ferguson Act states that the business of insurance is subject to the laws of the states relating to the regulation and taxation of the insurance business. Since passage of McCarran-Ferguson, federal laws have governed insurance only when one of the following applies:

- A federal law applies *only* to the business of insurance.
- A federal law affects insurers' activity that falls outside the business of insurance.
- The state has no law that regulates an aspect of the business of insurance covered by a federal law.

The question of which level of government—state or federal—should regulate insurance is far from settled. Suggestions for revising McCarran-Ferguson include the following:

- Eliminate McCarran-Ferguson altogether
- Modify McCarran-Ferguson's scope to increase federal involvement
- Expand the federal government's role in insurance while leaving McCarran-Ferguson intact

Proponents of federal regulation present the following arguments:

- *Federal regulation would provide regulatory uniformity across the states.* Insurers doing business in more than one state are confronted with differing laws, regulations, and administrative rules. Federal regulation would be uniform.
- *Federal regulation would be more efficient.* Insurers doing business nationally would deal with only one government agency instead of fifty different ones. Also, a federal agency might be less likely to yield to pressure from local or regional insurers. Federal regulation might also be less expensive than state regulation.
- *Federal regulation would attract higher-quality personnel.* If the federal agency were adequately funded under the federal budget versus individual state budgets, higher salaries and prestige would likely attract higher-quality personnel who would do a superior job of regulating insurers.

Opponents of federal regulation present the following arguments:

- *State regulation is more responsive to local needs.* Conditions vary widely among states, and state regulators can respond quickly to local problems and needs. In contrast, federal regulation and government bureaucracy would result in considerable delay in solving local problems.
- *Uniformity of state laws can be attained through the NAIC.* As a result of the NAIC's model laws, regulations, and guidelines, current state laws are reasonably uniform, with consideration given to local circumstances and conditions.
- *Greater opportunities for innovation are possible with state regulation.* An individual state can experiment with a new approach to regulation. If that approach fails, only that state is affected. In contrast, if a new approach to federal regulation fails, the entire country might feel its effects.

- *State regulation already exists, and its strengths and weaknesses are known.* In contrast, the benefits and possible adverse consequences of federal regulation on the insurance business and consumers are unknown. Moreover, some local regulation is inevitable; thus, increased federal involvement would result in increased dual regulation.

- *State regulation results in a desirable decentralization of political power.* In contrast, federal regulation would increase the power of the federal government and would dilute states' rights.

The debate over state versus federal insurance regulation will persist. The increasing role of electronic commerce raises challenging questions about the regulation of transactions that occur in cyberspace. And the changing role of banks (traditionally federally regulated) in marketing insurance (traditionally state-regulated) raises additional questions.

National concerns about insurer insolvencies have from time to time caused Congress to consider a more active role in licensing and monitoring insurance companies.

State Insurance Regulation

State insurance regulation is an administrative agency function emanating from state statutes that give state DOIs the power to develop and enforce regulations and to adjudicate disputes. This state insurance regulation overview is only an introduction to the way insurance regulation fits into the U.S. legal system. State insurance regulation is a complex and constantly evolving area of administrative agency law and practice.

DOIs operate under the supervision of commissioners of insurance, who receive their authority from state law. In some states, commissioners are appointed by the governor. In other states, they are elected. Even an appointed DOI commissioner can change when the appointing governor leaves office. Therefore, commissioners have a limited period in which to influence insurance operations in their states.

The state's insurance code is the systematic collection of all insurance statutory law in that state. DOIs enforce the code not just by promulgating insurance regulations but by issuing bulletins and other communications to the insurance industry. These publications explain the DOI's expectations for compliance with statutory requirements. DOIs operate under state administrative procedure acts and are subject to due process requirements just as other government agencies are. They follow the same rules and procedures for rulemaking and adjudication.

A DOI commissioner's responsibilities include the following:

- Licensing insurers
- Monitoring insurer solvency
- Reviewing insurer investments

- Approving policy forms
- Setting or approving rates
- Regulating insurer marketing
- Acting as liquidator and operating guaranty funds
- Operating government-mandated programs
- Reviewing insurers' annual reports
- Investigating complaints against insurers and producers
- Promulgating regulations and proposing legislation

Commissioners require periodic reports on insurer financial conditions, a recurring and time-consuming task for regulators. In addition, states establish minimum capital and surplus levels based on the types of insurance an insurer writes. Commissioners also closely scrutinize insurer financial investments.

National Association of Insurance Commissioners (NAIC)

The NAIC includes the insurance commissioners of all states, as well as of the District of Columbia, Puerto Rico, Guam, U.S. Samoa, and the U.S. Virgin Islands. The NAIC produces and adopts uniform reporting requirements, standardized procedures for financial examinations, and uniform regulatory procedures, facilitating the regulation of insurers operating in more than one state. The NAIC achieves a major purpose of promoting uniform insurance regulation among the states by developing model laws. Hundreds of active model laws are available, although all or most states have adopted only a few of them. Most states have adopted uniform laws covering the following areas:

- Competitive rating
- Reinsurance credit
- Unfair trade practices
- Unfair claim settlement
- Producer licensing
- Holding companies
- Insurance fraud
- Insurer rehabilitation and liquidation
- Asset valuation
- Redomestication

Some states adopt entire model laws. In other states, model laws serve as guidelines for drafting similar laws.

An insurer that operates in all states and U.S. territories must comply with the laws of each of those jurisdictions. Even among states with identical model laws, commissioners and courts can interpret them differently. Insurers must be aware of local interpretations of model laws to ensure that their compliance actions are consistent with those interpretations.

Regulation of Insurers

Insurers that operate in a state must receive express DOI permission in the form of a license, or certificate of authority. The relative ease or difficulty of obtaining a license in a particular state reflects the DOI's and legislature's attitudes toward the entry of new insurers into the state market. If an applicant is a subsidiary or an affiliate of an insurance group already doing business in the state, the licensing of one more member of the group can be easy to accomplish. However, an insurer that is unaffiliated with an experienced group of licensed insurers may find that getting a license is more difficult. An insurer applicant that is either newly formed or inexperienced in a particular type of insurance can experience difficulty obtaining a certificate of authority in a new state for the particular line of business.

The licensing process involves submitting an application package, which varies in size and complexity based on state requirements. Typically, the application package must include the following:

- Description of insurer management
- Insurer history
- List of states in which the insurer is licensed
- Types of insurance the insurer has written

The insurer's operating plans for writing business in the new state are subject to close scrutiny, particularly if the insurer belongs to a group of affiliated insurers who are already licensed in the state. The group might need to explain how an additional affiliate will serve the citizens of the state that the other already licensed affiliates cannot serve.

In addition to operating plans, an incorporated insurer must provide a copy of its articles of incorporation and confirmation from its state of origin, or domiciliary state, that the insurer's finances are adequate.

To be approved for a license, an insurer must show that it will abide by the state's laws and regulations and must respond to all questions and concerns a DOI raises. A DOI can ask an insurer applicant about previous regulatory examinations in other states, including examinations of both financial and market conduct. In some cases, an insurer must change its plans to satisfy regulatory concerns.

Other documents an insurer must submit in an application package include the following:

- Biographical information and affidavits of all senior officers and directors
- Copies of any reinsurance contracts transferring the insurer's liability or assuming another insurer's liability
- A copy of the contract authorizing the insurer's operation through a parent organization's employees
- Financial statements for recent years

After insurers are licensed, DOIs have both the right and the responsibility to make periodic financial audits and market conduct examinations to verify the contents of annual statements and to verify regulatory compliance generally. Several states are in zones for financial audits. In a **zone examination**, one state DOI conducts a financial audit of an insurer on behalf of all states in a zone in which the insurer holds a license. This arrangement reduces the number of reviews required from an insurer licensed nationwide so that its financial records need not be reviewed separately by each of the fifty states.

Zone examination
A state insurance department's financial audit of an insurer on behalf of all states in a zone in which the insurer holds licenses.

The broad authority that commissioners have under state insurance codes is not unlimited. It is subject to state administrative procedure acts and to the same constitutional due process requirements applying to other administrative agencies. As discussed, due process of law requires an agency to provide notice and the right to a hearing to any person or organization whose interests might be affected by an agency act or decision.

In a case before the DOI, the commissioner or another administrative hearing officer conducts the hearing. The legal question usually concerns a property right, for example the insurer's right not to have a state regulator compromise its potential profits. As a matter of state administrative law, state insurance codes prohibit the insurance commissioner from exercising authority that is arbitrary or capricious. A court can review a commissioner's acts or orders.

Insurance Producer Regulation

States regulate not only insurers but also insurance agencies and brokerages. States regulate licensing and renewal of licenses, banks engaged in the insurance business, managing general agents, and surplus lines brokers.

Licensing and License Renewal

To be licensed, producers must satisfy educational requirements and background checks. In a few states, not just the individual producer, but the agency or brokerage in which the producer works, must be licensed. This process raises additional revenue for the state and permits states to exercise some control over the actions of producers who move from one agency or brokerage to another.

An insurance producer can receive a license in one or more of the following types of insurance, among others:

- Life insurance
- Sickness and accident/health
- Credit life
- Fire and allied lines
- Automobile
- Personal and general liability

- Marine and transportation
- Workers' compensation
- Credit and mortgage guarantee
- Burglary and theft
- Crop
- Bail bonds
- Fidelity and surety bonds
- Homeowners and farm owners
- Commercial multiperil

The agency or brokerage activities that create a requirement for producer licenses usually include the following:

- Soliciting policy sales
- Negotiating policy terms
- Issuing policies
- Delivering policies

Several states license producers or agency brokerages, by type of insurance business. Often these types are divided, for example, into auto, homeowners, workers' compensation, surety, credit, property-casualty, life, and accident and health.

To qualify for a license, an applicant must fulfill the following requirements:

- Be of at least a minimum age
- Have an appointment from a licensed insurance company
- Have completed the requisite application forms
- Have satisfactorily completed the examination requirement

In many states, the Chartered Property and Casualty Underwriter (CPCU) designation satisfies part or all of the licensing exam requirement. States frequently require continuing education for the licensed producer to renew a license.

The insurer's role in the licensing process for agents and brokers is substantial. In many states, the insurer must send notice to the DOI confirming that it has appointed a producer to represent it. Such a notice must be on a prescribed form, usually accompanied by a filing fee. The producer cannot represent the insurer until the commissioner has approved the form, although approval is frequently implied if no disapproval has arrived within a reasonable period of time.

Managing general agent (MGA)
An independent business organization that functions almost as a branch office for one or more insurers and that appoints and supervises independent agents and brokers for insurers using the independent agency and brokerage system.

Managing General Agents (MGAs)

Another type of agency that has received increasing regulatory attention is the managing general agent. A **managing general agent (MGA)** is an independent business organization that functions almost as a branch office for one or more insurers and that appoints and supervises independent agents and brokers for insurers using the independent agency and brokerage system.

The reason for regulatory attention to MGAs is the increasing concern about the role that some MGAs have played in major insurer insolvencies. Under the NAIC Model MGA Act[9], the state must license an MGA. In addition, the DOI can require a bond, or monetary guarantee, from the MGA. Finally, the DOI can require the MGA to maintain an errors and omissions (E&O) insurance policy to cover damages resulting from the MGA's mistakes.

To control the MGA's activities and to address regulators' concerns, the model law not only dictates the minimum provisions of the written contract between the insurer and the MGA, but also imposes on the insurer the following duties:

- To have on file an independent financial exam of each MGA with which the insurer does business
- To obtain an annual actuarial opinion of the adequacy of any loss reserves established by the MGA
- To conduct periodic on-site reviews of the MGA's underwriting and claim-processing operations

The NAIC model law requires the contract between insurer and MGA contain certain minimum provisions, including the MGA's duty to report to the insurance company. The MGA must follow underwriting guidelines regarding the following:

- Maximum annual premium volume the MGA can write
- Types of loss exposures the MGA can insure and the basis for rates charged to these loss exposures
- Maximum policy limits
- Applicable exclusions
- Territorial limitations
- Policy cancellation provisions
- Maximum policy period

Surplus Lines Brokers

To place any contract of insurance through a nonadmitted insurer, the producer must have a surplus lines insurance license issued by the commissioner. Under the NAIC model act, to qualify for the license, the producer must pass a DOI-approved exam and post a bond of a specified amount.

Thereafter, the producer must keep in an office in the licensing state a complete record of each surplus lines policy placed, including a copy of the policy or other evidence of insurance. These records must be made available for DOI inspection for a specified period after policy termination. Further, the surplus lines broker must submit a quarterly report to the commissioner showing premiums written, amount of taxes paid, and return premiums.

SUMMARY

Insurance professionals need to be familiar with legal principles of insurance and general legal principles as a foundation for understanding legal bases of liability, reasons for insurance policy provisions, and contractual obligations of insureds and insurers. The U.S. legal system had its origins in the English common-law system. The foundation of the common-law system is the doctrine of *stare decisis*, the application of precedents to current court cases. The common-law system differs from the European civil-law system, founded exclusively on codified laws rather than case law.

U.S. law can be classified several ways, including the following:

- As either criminal or civil law
- In subject matter classifications
- As either substantive and procedural law

Sources of U.S. law include the following:

- Constitutions
- Legislative bodies
- Courts
- Executive branches
- Administrative agencies

The U.S. Constitutional provisions that most affect the insurance industry include the following:

- Congressional powers, express and implied
- Commerce Clause
- Due Process Clause
- Equal Protection Clause

Each of the fifty-one court systems in the U.S. (the federal and state systems), includes both trial and appellate courts. The names and methods of operation of each of the fifty-one court systems vary widely. Special rules govern conflicts of law between states and between the state and the federal systems and vary according to whether disputes involve tort or contracts cases.

Administrative agencies are part of the executive branch of government. The legislative branch of government creates administrative agencies to implement and enforce governmental functions. Insurance is a highly regulated area, subject primarily to state, but sometimes federal, regulation.

Congress passed the McCarran-Ferguson Act to place the power to regulate the business of insurance with state governments, with minimal federal interference.

Court legal procedures fall into different phases: pretrial, trial, post-trial, and appellate procedures. Evidence at trial must be relevant, material, and competent. Complex rules of evidence govern the admission of evidence at trial and, among other things, exclude hearsay evidence, with many exceptions. Alternative dispute resolution (ADR) methods, such as arbitration, mediation, and negotiation, are ways to resolve disputes more efficiently than through the overloaded court system.

Administrative agencies have investigatory powers but are also subject to Constitutional limitations. Administrative agencies promulgate legislative, interpretive, and procedural rules. Agency adjudicatory procedure is similar to court procedures, requiring notice, hearing, and adjudication. Judicial review of agency decisions involves issues of standing to sue and exhaustion of administrative remedies, as well as standards of review, such as determining the existence of agency abuse of discretion.

The Privacy Act and Freedom of Information Act protect the public from agency misuse of the vast amounts of information they collect, including insurance information. The Privacy Act prohibits the government and its agencies from releasing any information that would violate individual privacy. The Freedom of Information Act guarantees public access to some government and agency records and documents to prevent abuse of information collection.

At the federal level, the government regulates the insurance business in areas in which it regulates all other businesses. At the state level, state departments of insurance (DOIs) regulate the insurance industry. Among other things, DOIs regulate insurer, agent, and broker licenses, as well as policy forms and premium rates. They also conduct examinations to ensure compliance with regulatory law. DOIs are subject to the constitutional requirement of due process of law with regard to all functions.

The National Association of Insurance Commissioners (NAIC) promotes uniform insurance regulation among the states by developing model laws. Most property-casualty insurers apply for licenses in multiple types of insurance. An insurer that does business in more than one state must be "admitted" to do business, or licensed, in each of those states. "Nonadmitted" insurers are usually insurers that transact insurance in a state but are not licensed as admitted insurers there.

CHAPTER NOTES

1. *Brown v. Board of Education*, 347 U.S. 483 (1954).

2. *Miranda v. Arizona*, 384 U.S. 436 (1966).

3. *Paul v. Virginia*, 8 Wall. 168 (1869).

4. *Southeastern Underwriters Association, et al.* 322 U.S. 533 (1944).

5. For examples of model laws, regulations, and guidelines, see the National Association of Insurance Commissioners Web site at www.naic.org.

6. 5 U.S.C., § 552a.

7. 5 U.S.C., § 552.

8. 15 U.S.C., §§ 1011–1015.

9. NAIC, *Model Laws, Regulations and Guidelines*, vol. II, Model Managing General Agents Act, pp. 225–226.

APPENDIX

CONSTITUTION OF THE UNITED STATES

Proposed by Convention September 17, 1787

Effective March 4, 1789

WE the people of the United States, in order to form a more perfect union, establish justice, insure domestic tranquility, provide for the common defense, promote the general welfare, and secure the blessings of liberty to ourselves and our posterity, do ordain and establish this Constitution for the United States of America.

Article I

SECTION 1.

All legislative powers herein granted shall be vested in a Congress of the United States, which shall consist of a Senate and House of Representatives.

SECTION 2.

1. The House of Representatives shall be composed of members chosen every second year by the people of the several States, and the electors in each State shall have the qualifications requisite for electors of the most numerous branch of the State legislature.

2. No person shall be a representative who shall not have attained to the age of twenty-five years, and been seven years a citizen of the United States, and who shall not, when elected, be an inhabitant of that State in which he shall be chosen.

3. Representatives [and direct taxes][1] shall be apportioned among the several States which may be included within this Union, according to their respective numbers, [which shall be determined by adding to the whole number of free persons, including those bound to service for a term of years, and excluding Indians not taxed, three fifths of all other persons.][2] The actual enumeration shall be made within three years after the first meeting of the Congress of the United States, and within every subsequent term of ten years, in such manner as they shall by law direct. The number of representatives shall not exceed one for every thirty thousand, but each State shall have at least one representative; and until such enumeration shall be made, the State of New Hampshire shall be entitled to choose three, Massachusetts eight, Rhode Island and Providence Plantations one, Connecticut five, New York six, New Jersey four, Pennsylvania eight, Delaware one, Maryland six, Virginia ten, North Carolina five, South Carolina five, and Georgia three.

4. When vacancies happen in the representation from any State, the executive authority thereof shall issue writs of election to fill such vacancies.

5. The House of Representatives shall choose their speaker and other officers; and shall have the sole power of impeachment.

SECTION 3.

1. The Senate of the United States shall be composed of two senators from each State, [chosen by the legislature thereof,][3] for six years; and each senator shall have one vote.

2. Immediately after they shall be assembled in consequence of the first election, they shall be divided as equally as may be into three classes. The seats of the senators of the first class shall be vacated at the expiration of the second year, of the second class at the expiration of the fourth year, and of the third class at the expiration of the sixth year, so that one third may be chosen every second year; and if vacancies happen by resignation, or otherwise, during the recess of the legislature of any State, the executive thereof may make temporary appointments until the next meeting of the legislature, which shall then fill such vacancies.

3. No person shall be a senator who shall not have attained to the age of thirty years, and been nine years a citizen of the United States, and who shall not, when elected, be an inhabitant of that State for which he shall be chosen.

4. The Vice President of the United States shall be President of the Senate, but shall have no vote, unless they be equally divided.

5. The Senate shall choose their other officers, and also a president pro tempore, in the absence of the Vice President, or when he shall exercise the office of the President of the United States.

6. The Senate shall have the sole power to try all impeachments. When sitting for that purpose, they shall be on oath or affirmation. When the President of the United States is tried, the chief justice shall preside: and no person shall be convicted without the concurrence of two thirds of the members present.

7. Judgment in cases of impeachment shall not extend further than to removal from office, and disqualifications to hold and enjoy any office of honor, trust or profit under the United States: but the party convicted shall nevertheless be liable and subject to indictment, trial, judgment and punishment, according to law.

SECTION 4.

1. The times, places, and manner of holding elections for senators and representatives, shall be prescribed in each State by the legislature thereof; but the Congress may at any time by law make or alter such regulations, except as to the places of choosing senators.

2. The Congress shall assemble at least once in every year, and such meeting shall be on the first Monday in December,[4] unless they shall by law appoint a different day.

SECTION 5.

1. Each House shall be the judge of the elections, returns and qualifications of its own members, and a majority of each shall constitute a quorum to do business; but a smaller number may adjourn from day to day, and may be authorized to compel the attendance of absent members, in such manner, and under such penalties as each House may provide.

2. Each House may determine the rules of its proceedings, punish its members for disorderly behavior, and, with the concurrence of two thirds, expel a member.

3. Each House shall keep a journal of its proceedings, and from time to time publish the same, excepting such parts as may in their judgment require secrecy; and the yeas and nays of the members of either House on any question shall, at the desire of one fifth of those present, be entered on the journal.

4. Neither House, during the session of Congress, shall, without the consent of the other, adjourn for more than three days, nor to any other place than that in which the two Houses shall be sitting.

SECTION 6.

1. The senators and representatives shall receive a compensation for their services, to be ascertained by law, and paid out of the Treasury of the United States. They shall in all cases, except treason, felony, and breach of the peace, be privileged from arrest during their attendance at the session of their respective Houses, and in going to and returning from the same; and for any speech or debate in either House, they shall not be questioned in any other place.

2. No senator or representative shall, during the time for which he was elected, be appointed to any civil office under the authority of the United States, which shall have been created, or the emoluments whereof shall have been increased during such time; and no person holding any office under the United States shall be a member of either House during his continuance in office.

SECTION 7.

1. All bills for raising revenue shall originate in the House of Representatives; but the Senate may propose or concur with amendments as on other bills.

2. Every bill which shall have passed the House of Representatives and the Senate, shall, before it becomes a law, be presented to the President of the United States; if he approves he shall sign it, but if not he shall return it, with his objections to that House in which it shall have originated, who shall enter the objections at large on their journal, and proceed to reconsider it. If after such reconsideration two thirds of that House shall agree to pass the bill, it shall be sent, together with the objections, to the other House, by which it shall likewise be reconsidered, and if approved by two thirds of that House, it shall become a law. But in all such cases the votes of both Houses shall be determined by yeas and nays, and the

names of the persons voting for and against the bill shall be entered on the journal of each House respectively. If any bill shall not be returned by the President within ten days (Sundays excepted) after it shall have been presented to him, the same shall be a law, in like manner as if he had signed it, unless the Congress by their adjournment prevent its return, in which case it shall not be a law.

3. Every order, resolution, or vote to which the concurrence of the Senate and the House of Representatives may be necessary (except on a question of adjournment) shall be presented to the President of the United States; and before the same shall take effect, shall be approved by him, or being disapproved by him, shall be repassed by two thirds of the Senate and House of Representatives, according to the rules and limitations prescribed in the case of a bill.

SECTION 8.

The Congress shall have the power

1. To lay and collect taxes, duties, imposts, and excises, to pay the debts and provide for the common defense and general welfare of the United States; but all duties, imposts, and excises shall be uniform throughout the United States;

2. To borrow money on the credit of the United States;

3. To regulate commerce with foreign nations, and among the several States, and with the Indian tribes;

4. To establish a uniform rule of naturalization, and uniform laws on the subject of bankruptcies throughout the United States;

5. To coin money, regulate the value thereof, and of foreign coin, and fix the standard of weights and measures;

6. To provide for the punishment of counterfeiting the securities and current coin of the United States;

7. To establish post offices and post roads;

8. To promote the progress of science and useful arts, by securing for limited times to authors and inventors the exclusive right to their respective writings and discoveries;

9. To constitute tribunals inferior to the Supreme Court;

10. To define and punish piracies and felonies committed on the high seas, and offenses against the law of nations;

11. To declare war, grant letters of marque and reprisal, and make rules concerning captures on land and water;

12. To raise and support armies, but no appropriation of money to that use shall be for a longer term than two years;

13. To provide and maintain a navy;

14. To make rules for the government and regulation of the land and naval forces;

15. To provide for calling forth the militia to execute the laws of the Union, suppress insurrections and repel invasions;

16. To provide for organizing, arming, and disciplining the militia, and for governing such part of them as may be employed in the service of the United States, reserving to the States respectively, the appointment of the officers, and the authority of training the militia according to the discipline prescribed by Congress;

17. To exercise exclusive legislation in all cases whatsoever, over such district (not exceeding ten miles square) as may, by cession of particular States, and the acceptance of Congress, become the seat of the government of the United States, and to exercise like authority over all places purchased by the consent of the legislature of the State in which the same shall be, for the erection of forts, magazines, arsenals, dockyards, and other needful buildings; and

18. To make all laws which shall be necessary and proper for carrying into execution the foregoing powers, and all other powers vested by this Constitution in the government of the United Stales, or in any department or officer thereof.

SECTION 9

1. The migration or importation of such persons as any of the States now existing shall think proper to admit, shall not be prohibited by the Congress prior to the year one thousand eight hundred and eight, but a tax or duty may be imposed on such importation, not exceeding ten dollars for each person.

2. The privilege of the writ of habeas corpus shall not be suspended, unless when in cases of rebellion or invasion the public safety may require it.

3. No bill of attainder or ex post facto law shall be passed.

4. No capitation, or other direct, tax shall be laid unless in proportion to the census or enumeration hereinbefore directed to be taken.[5]

5. No tax or duty shall be laid on articles exported from any State.

6. No preference shall be given by any regulation of commerce or revenue to the ports of one State over those of another: nor shall vessels bound to, or from, one State be obliged to enter, clear, or pay duties in another.

7. No money shall be drawn from the treasury, but in consequence of appropriations made by law; and a regular statement and account of the receipts and expenditures of all public money shall be published from time to time.

8. No title of nobility shall be granted by the United States: and no person holding any office of profit or trust under them, shall, without the consent of the Congress, accept of any present, emolument, office, or title, of any kind whatever, from any king, prince, or foreign State.

SECTION 10.

1. No State shall enter into any treaty, alliance, or confederation; grant letters of marque and reprisal; coin money; emit bills of credit; make anything but gold and silver coin a tender in payment of debts; pass any bill of attainder, ex post facto law, or law impairing the obligation of contracts, or grant any title of nobility.

2. No State shall, without the consent of the Congress, lay any imposts or duties on imports or exports, except what may be absolutely necessary for executing its inspection laws; and the net produce of all duties and imposts laid by any State on imports or exports, shall be for the use of the treasury of the United States; and all such laws shall be subject to the revision and control of the Congress.

3. No State shall, without the consent of the Congress, lay any duty of tonnage, keep troops, or ships of war in time of peace, enter into any agreement or compact with another State, or with a foreign power, or engage in war, unless actually invaded, or in such imminent danger as will not admit of delay.

Article II

SECTION 1.

1. The executive power shall be vested in a President of the United States of America. He shall hold his office during the term of four years, and, together with the Vice President, chosen for the same term, be elected as follows:

2. Each State[6] shall appoint, in such manner as the legislature thereof may direct, a number of electors, equal to the whole number of senators and representatives to which the State may be entitled in the Congress: but no senator or representative, or person holding an office of trust or profit under the United States, shall be appointed an elector.

    The electors shall meet in their respective States, and vote by ballot for two persons, of whom one at least shall not be an inhabitant of the same State with themselves. And they shall make a list of all the persons voted for, and of the number of votes for each; which list they shall sign and certify, and transmit sealed to the seat of the government of the United States, directed to the president of the Senate. The president of the Senate shall, in the presence of the Senate and House of Representatives, open all the certificates, and the votes shall then be counted. The person having the greatest number of votes shall be the President, if such number be a majority of the whole number of electors appointed; and if there be more than one who have such majority, and have an equal number of votes, then the House of Representatives shall immediately choose by ballot one of them for President; and if no person have a majority, then from the five highest on the list the said House shall in like manner choose the President. But in choosing the President, the votes shall be taken by States, the representation from each state having one vote; a quorum for this purpose shall consist of a member or members from two thirds of the States, and a majority of all the States shall be necessary to a choice. In every case, after the choice of the President, the person having the greatest number of votes of the electors shall be the Vice President. But if there should remain two or more who have equal votes, the Senate shall choose from them by ballot the Vice President.[7]

3. The Congress may determine the time of choosing the electors, and the day on which they shall give their votes; which day shall be the same throughout the United States.

4. No person except a natural born citizen, or a citizen of the United States, at the time of the adoption of this Constitution, shall be eligible to the office of President; neither shall any person be eligible to that office who shall not have attained to the age of thirty-five years, and been fourteen years a resident within the United States.

5. In case of the removal of the President from office, or of his death, resignation, or inability to discharge the powers and duties of the said office, the same shall devolve on the Vice President, and the Congress may by law provide for the case of removal, death, resignation, or inability, both of the President and Vice President, declaring what officer shall then act as President, and such officer shall act accordingly, until the disability be removed, or a President shall be elected.[8]

6. The President shall, at stated times, receive for his services a compensation, which shall neither be increased nor diminished during the period for which he shall have been elected, and he shall not receive within that period any other emolument from the United States, or any of them.

7. Before he enter on the execution of his office, he shall take the following oath or affirmation:—"I do solemnly swear (or affirm) that I will faithfully execute the office of President of the United States, and will to the best of my ability, preserve, protect and defend the Constitution of the United States."

SECTION 2.

1. The President shall be commander in chief of the army and navy of the United States, and of the militia of the several States, when called into the actual service of the United States; he may require the opinion, in writing, of the principal officer in each of the executive departments, upon any subject relating to the duties of their respective offices, and he shall have power to grant reprieves and pardons for offenses against the United States, except in cases of impeachment.

2. He shall have power, by and with the advice and consent of the Senate, to make treaties, provided two thirds of the senators present concur; and he shall nominate, and by and with the advice and consent of the Senate, shall appoint ambassadors, other public ministers and consuls, judges of the Supreme Court, and all other officers of the United States, whose

appointments are not herein otherwise provided for, and which shall be established by law: but the Congress may by law vest the appointment of such inferior officers, as they think proper, in the President alone, in the courts of law, or in the heads of departments.

3. The President shall have power to fill up all vacancies that may happen during the recess of the Senate, by granting commissions which shall expire at the end of their next session.

SECTION 3.

He shall from time to time give to the Congress information of the state of the Union, and recommend to their consideration such measures as he shall judge necessary and expedient; he may, on extraordinary occasions, convene both Houses, or either of them, and in case of disagreement between them with respect to the time of adjournment, he may adjourn them to such time as he shall think proper; he shall receive ambassadors and other public ministers; he shall take care that the laws be faithfully executed, and shall commission all the officers of the United States.

SECTION 4.

The President, Vice President, and all civil officers of the United States, shall be removed from office on impeachment for and conviction of, treason, bribery, or other high crimes and misdemeanors.

Article III

SECTION 1.

The judicial power of the United States shall be vested in one Supreme Court, and in such inferior courts as the Congress may from time to time ordain and establish. The judges, both of the Supreme and inferior courts, shall hold their offices during good behavior, and shall, at stated times, receive for their services, a compensation, which shall not be diminished during their continuance in office.

SECTION 2.

1. The judicial power shall extend to all cases, in law and equity, arising under this Constitution, the laws of the United States, and treaties made, or which shall be made, under their authority;—to all cases affecting ambassadors, other public ministers and consuls;—to all cases of admiralty and maritime jurisdiction;—to controversies to which the United States shall be a party;—to controversies between two or more States;—between a State and citizens of another State;—between citizens of different States;[9]—between citizens of the same State claiming lands under grants of different States, and between a State, or the citizens thereof, and foreign States, citizens or subjects.

2. In all cases affecting ambassadors, other public ministers and consuls, and those in which a State shall be party, the Supreme Court shall have

original jurisdiction. In all the other cases before mentioned, the Supreme Court shall have appellate jurisdiction, both as to law and to fact, with such exceptions, and under such regulations as the Congress shall make.

3. The trial of all crimes, except in cases of impeachment, shall be by jury; and such trial shall be held in the State where the said crimes shall have been committed; but when not committed within any State, the trial shall be at such place or places as the Congress may by law have directed.

SECTION 3.

1. Treason against the United States shall consist only in levying war against them, or in adhering to their enemies, giving them aid and comfort. No person shall be convicted of treason unless on the testimony of two witnesses to the same overt act, or on confession in open court.

2. The Congress shall have power to declare the punishment of treason, but no attainder of treason shall work corruption of blood, or forfeiture except during the life of the person attained.

Article IV

SECTION 1.

Full faith and credit shall be given in each State to the public acts, records, and judicial proceedings of every other State. And the Congress may by general laws prescribe the manner in which such acts, records and proceedings shall be proved, and the effect thereof.

SECTION 2.

1. The citizens of each State shall be entitled to all privileges and immunities of citizens in the several States.[10]

2. A person charged in any State with treason, felony, or other crime, who shall flee from justice, and be found in another State, shall on demand of the executive authority of the State from which he fled, be delivered up to be removed to the State having jurisdiction of the crime.

3. No person held to service or labor in one State under the laws thereof, escaping into another, shall, in consequence of any law or regulation therein, be discharged from such service or labor, but shall be delivered up on claim of the party to whom such service or labor may be due.[11]

SECTION 3.

1. New States may be admitted by the Congress into this Union; but no new State shall be formed or erected within the jurisdiction of any other State; nor any State be formed by the junction of two or more States, or parts of States, without the consent of the legislatures of the States concerned as well as of the Congress.

2. The Congress shall have power to dispose of and make all needful rules and regulations respecting the territory or other property belonging to the

United States; and nothing in this Constitution shall be so construed as to prejudice any claims of the United States, or of any particular State.

SECTION 4.

The United States shall guarantee to every State in this Union a republican form of government, and shall protect each of them against invasion; and on application of the legislature, or of the executive (when the legislature cannot be convened) against domestic violence.

Article V

The Congress, whenever two thirds of both Houses shall deem it necessary, shall propose amendments to this Constitution, or, on the application of the legislatures of two thirds of the several States, shall call a convention for proposing amendments, which in either case, shall be valid to all intents and purposes, as part of this Constitution when ratified by the legislatures of three fourths of the several States, or by conventions in three fourths thereof, as the one or the other mode of ratification may be proposed by the Congress; Provided that no amendment which may be made prior to the year one thousand eight hundred and eight shall in any manner affect the first and fourth clauses in the ninth section of the first article; and that no State, without its consent, shall be deprived of its equal suffrage in the Senate.

Article VI

1. All debts contracted and engagements entered into, before the adoption of this Constitution, shall be as valid against the United States under this Constitution, as under the Confederation.

2. This Constitution, and the laws of the United States which shall be made in pursuance thereof; and all treaties made, or which shall be made, under the authority of the United States, shall be the supreme law of the land; and the Judges in every State shall be bound thereby, anything in the Constitution or laws of any State to the contrary notwithstanding.

3. The senators and representatives before mentioned, and the members of the several State legislatures, and all executive and judicial officers, both of the United States and of the several States, shall be bound by oath or affirmation to support this Constitution; but no religious test shall ever be required as a qualification to any office or public trust under the United States.

Article VII

The ratification of the conventions of nine States shall be sufficient for the establishment of this Constitution between the States so ratifying the same.

Done in Convention by the unanimous consent of the States present the seventeenth day of September in the year of our Lord one thousand seven hundred and eighty-seven, and of the independence of the United States of America the twelfth. In witness whereof we have hereunto subscribed our names.

[Names omitted] —————

[Articles in addition to, and amendment of, the Constitution of the United States of America, proposed by Congress, and ratified by the legislatures of the several States pursuant to the fifth article of the original Constitution.]

AMENDMENTS

First ten amendments (Bill of Rights) passed by Congress Sept. 25, 1789.

Ratified by three-fourths of the States December 15, 1791.

Article I

Congress shall make no law respecting an establishment of religion, or prohibiting the free exercise thereof; or abridging the freedom of speech, or of the press; or the right of the people peaceably to assemble, and to petition the government for a redress of grievances.

Article II

A well regulated militia, being necessary to the security of a free State, the right of the people to keep and bear arms, shall not be infringed.

Article III

No soldier shall, in time of peace be quartered in any house, without the consent of the owner, nor in time of war, but in a manner to be prescribed by law.

Article IV

The right of the people to be secure in their persons, houses, papers, and effects, against unreasonable searches and seizures, shall not be violated, and no warrants shall issue, but upon probable cause, supported by oath or affirmation, and particularly describing the place to be searched, and the persons or things to be seized.

Article V

No person shall be held to answer for a capital, or otherwise infamous crime, unless on a presentment or indictment of a grand jury, except in cases arising in the land or naval forces, or in the militia, when in actual service in time of war or public danger; nor shall any person be subject for the same offense to be twice put in jeopardy of life or limb; nor shall be compelled in any criminal case to be a witness against himself, nor be deprived of life, liberty, or property, without due process of law; nor shall private property be taken for public use without just compensation.

Article VI

In all criminal prosecutions, the accused shall enjoy the right to a speedy and public trial, by an impartial jury of the State and district wherein the crime shall have been committed, which district shall have been previously ascertained by law, and to be informed of the nature and cause of the accusation; to be confronted with the witnesses against him; to have compulsory process for obtaining witnesses in his favor, and to have the assistance of counsel for his defense.

Article VII

In suits at common law, where the value in controversy shall exceed twenty dollars, the right of trial by jury shall be preserved, and no fact tried by a jury shall be otherwise reexamined in any court of the United States, than according to the rules of the common law.

Article VIII

Excessive bail shall not be required, nor excessive fines imposed, nor cruel and unusual punishments inflicted.

Article IX

The enumeration in the Constitution of certain rights shall not be construed to deny or disparage others retained by the people.

Article X

The powers not delegated to the United States by the Constitution, nor prohibited by it to the States, are reserved to the States respectively, or to the people.

Article XI

Passed by Congress March 4, 1794. Ratified February 7, 1795.

The judicial power of the United States shall not be construed to extend to any suit in law or equity, commenced or prosecuted against one of the United States by citizens of another State, or by citizens or subjects of any foreign State.

Article XII

Passed by Congress December 9, 1803. Ratified July 27, 1804.

The electors shall meet in their respective States, and vote by ballot for President and Vice President, one of whom, at least, shall not be an inhabitant of the same State with themselves; they shall name in their ballots the person voted for as President, and in distinct ballots, the person voted for as Vice President, and they shall make distinct lists of all persons voted for as President and of all persons voted for as Vice President, and of the number of votes for each, which lists they shall sign and certify, and transmit sealed to the seat of the government of the United States, directed to the President of the Senate;—The President of the Senate shall, in the presence of the Senate and House of Representatives, open all the certificates and the votes shall then be counted;—The person having the greatest number of votes for President, shall be the President, if such number be a majority of the whole number of electors appointed; and if no person have such majority, then from the persons having the highest numbers not exceeding three on the list of those voted for as President, the House of Representatives shall choose immediately, by ballot, the President. But in choosing the President, the votes shall be taken by States, the representation from each State having one vote; a quorum for this purpose shall consist of a member or members from two thirds of the States, and a majority of all the States shall be necessary to a choice. And if the House of Representatives shall not choose a President whenever the right of choice shall devolve upon them, before the fourth day of March[12] next following, then the Vice President shall act as President, as in the case of the death or other constitutional disability of the President. The person having the greatest number of votes as Vice President shall be the Vice President, if such number be a majority of the whole number of electors appointed, and if no person have a majority, then from the two highest numbers on the list, the Senate shall choose the Vice President; a quorum for the purpose shall consist of two thirds of the whole number of Senators, and a majority of the whole number shall be necessary to a choice. But no person constitutionally ineligible to the office of President shall be eligible to that of Vice President of the United States.

Article XIII

Passed by Congress January 31, 1865. Ratified December 6, 1865.

SECTION 1.

Neither slavery nor involuntary servitude, except as punishment for crime whereof the party shall have been duly convicted, shall exist within the United States, or any place subject to their jurisdiction.

SECTION 2.

Congress shall have power to enforce this article by appropriate legislation.

Article XIV

Passed by Congress June 13, 1866. Ratified July 9, 1868.

SECTION 1.

All persons born or naturalized in the United States, and subject to the jurisdiction thereof, are citizens of the United States and of the State wherein they reside. No State shall make or enforce any law which shall abridge the privileges or immunities of citizens of the United States; nor shall any State deprive any person of life, liberty, or property, without due process of law; nor deny to any person within its jurisdiction the equal protection of the laws.

SECTION 2.

Representatives shall be apportioned among the several States according to their respective numbers, counting the whole number of persons in each State, excluding Indians not taxed. But when the right to vote at any election for the choice of electors for President and Vice President of the United States, representatives in Congress, the executive and judicial officers of a State, or the members of the legislature thereof, is denied to any of the male inhabitants of such State, being twenty-one years of age, and citizens of the United States, or in any way abridged, except for participation in rebellion, or other crime, the basis of representation therein shall be reduced in the proportion which the number of such male citizens shall bear to the whole number of male citizens twenty-one years of age in such State.

SECTION 3.

No person shall be a senator or representative in Congress, or elector of President and Vice President, or hold any office, civil or military, under the United States, or under any State, who having previously taken an oath, as a member of Congress, or as an officer of the United States, or as a member of any State legislature, or as an executive or judicial officer of any State, to support the Constitution of the United States, shall have engaged in insurrection or rebellion against the same, or given aid or comfort to the enemies thereof. But Congress may by a vote of two thirds of each House, remove such disability.

SECTION 4.

The validity of the public debt of the United States, authorized by law, including debts incurred for payment of pensions and bounties for services in suppressing insurrection or rebellion, shall not be questioned. But neither the United States nor any State shall assume or pay any debt or obligation incurred in aid of insurrection or rebellion against the United States, or any claim for the loss or emancipation of any slave; but all such debts, obligations, and claims shall be held illegal and void.

SECTION 5.

The Congress shall have power to enforce, by appropriate legislation, the provisions of this article.

Article XV

Passed by Congress February 26, 1869 Ratified February 3, 1870.

SECTION 1.

The right of citizens of the United States to vote shall not be denied or abridged by the United States or by any State on account of race, color, or previous condition of servitude.

SECTION 2.

The Congress shall have power to enforce this article by appropriate legislation.

Article XVI

Passed by Congress July 2, 1909. Ratified February 3, 1913.

The Congress shall have power to lay and collect taxes on incomes, from whatever source derived, without apportionment among the several States, and without regard to any census or enumeration.

Article XVII

Passed by Congress May 13, 1912. Ratified April 8, 1913.

The Senate of the United States shall be composed of two senators from each state, elected by the people thereof, for six years; and each senator shall have one vote. The electors in each State shall have the qualifications requisite for electors of the most numerous branch of the State legislature.

When vacancies happen in the representation of any State in the Senate, the executive authority of such State shall issue writs of election to fill such vacancies: Provided, That the legislature of any State may empower the executive thereof to make temporary appointments until the people fill the vacancies by election as the legislature may direct.

This amendment shall not be so construed as to affect the election or term of any senator chosen before it becomes valid as part of the Constitution.

Article XVIII[13]

Passed by Congress December 18, 1917. Ratified January 16, 1919.

After one year from the ratification of this article, the manufacture, sale, or transportation of intoxicating liquors within, the importation thereof into, or the exportation thereof from the United States and all territory subject to the jurisdiction thereof for beverage purposes is hereby prohibited.

The Congress and the several States shall have concurrent power to enforce this article by appropriate legislation.

This article shall be inoperative unless it shall have been ratified as an amendment to the Constitution by the legislatures of the several States, as provided in the Constitution, within seven years from the date of the submission hereof to the states by Congress.

Article XIX

Passed by Congress June 4, 1919. Ratified August 18, 1920.

The right of citizens of the United States to vote shall not be denied or abridged by the United States or by any State on account of sex.

The Congress shall have power by appropriate legislation to enforce the provisions of this article.

Article XX

Passed by Congress March 2, 1932. Ratified January 23, 1933.

SECTION 1.

The terms of the President and Vice President shall end at noon on the 20th day of January, and the terms of Senators and Representatives at noon on the 3d day of January, of the years in which such terms would have ended if this article had not been ratified; and the terms of their successors shall then begin.

SECTION 2.

The Congress shall assemble at least once in every year, and such meeting shall begin at noon on the 3d day of January, unless they shall by law appoint a different day.

SECTION 3.

If, at the time fixed for the beginning of the term of the President, the President-elect shall have died, the Vice President-elect shall become President. If a President shall not have been chosen before the time fixed for the beginning of his term, or if the President-elect shall have failed to qualify, then the Vice President-elect shall act as President until a President shall have qualified; and the Congress may by law provide for the case wherein neither a President-elect nor a Vice President-elect shall have qualified, declaring who shall then act as President, or the manner in which one who is to act shall be selected, and such person shall act accordingly until a President or Vice President shall have qualified.

SECTION 4.

The Congress may by law provide for the case of the death of any of the persons from whom the House of Representatives may choose a President whenever the right of choice shall have devolved upon them, and for the case of the death of any of the persons from whom the Senate may choose a Vice President whenever the right of choice shall have devolved upon them.

SECTION 5.

Sections 1 and 2 shall take effect on the 15th day of October following the ratification of this article.

SECTION 6.

This article shall be inoperative unless it shall have been ratified as an amendment to the Constitution by the legislatures of three-fourths of the several States within seven years from the date of its submission.

Article XXI

Passed by Congress February 20, 1933. Ratified December 5, 1933.

SECTION 1.

The Eighteenth Article of amendment to the Constitution of the United States is hereby repealed.

SECTION 2.

The transportation or importation into any State, Territory, or possession of the United States for delivery or use therein of intoxicating liquors in violation of the laws thereof, is hereby prohibited.

SECTION 3.

This article shall be inoperative unless it shall have been ratified as an amendment to the Constitution by conventions in the several States, as provided in the Constitution, within seven years from the date of the submission thereof to the States by the Congress.

Article XXII

Passed by Congress March 21, 1947. Ratified February 27, 1951.

No person shall be elected to the office of the President more than twice, and no person who has held the office of President, or acted as President, for more than two years of a term to which some other person was elected President shall be elected to the office of the President more than once.

But this article shall not apply to any person holding the office of President when this article was proposed by the Congress, and shall not prevent any person who may be holding the office of President, or acting as President, during the term within which this article becomes operative from holding the office of President or acting as President during the remainder of such term.

This article shall be inoperative unless it shall have been ratified as an amendment to the Constitution by the legislatures of three-fourths of the several states within seven years from the date of its submission to the states by the Congress.

Article XXIII

Passed by Congress June 16, 1960. Ratified March 29, 1961.

SECTION 1.

The District constituting the seat of Government of the United States shall appoint in such manner as the Congress may direct:

A number of electors of President and Vice President equal to the whole number of Senators and Representatives in Congress to which the District would be entitled if it were a State, but in no event more than the least populous state; they shall be in addition to those appointed by the states, but shall be considered, for the purpose of the election of President and Vice President, to be electors appointed by a state; and they shall meet in the District and perform such duties as provided by the twelfth article of amendment.

SECTION 2.

The Congress shall have power to enforce this article by appropriate legislation.

Article XXIV

Passed by Congress August 27, 1962. Ratified January 23, 1964.

SECTION 1.

The right of citizens of the United States to vote in any primary or other election for President or Vice President, for electors for President or Vice President, or for Senator or Representative in Congress, shall not be denied or abridged by the United States or any State by reason of failure to pay any poll tax or other tax.

SECTION 2.

The Congress shall have the power to enforce this article by appropriate legislation.

Article XXV

Passed by Congress July 6, 1965. Ratified February 10, 1967.

SECTION 1.

In case of the removal of the President from office or his death or resignation, the Vice President shall become President.

SECTION 2.

Whenever there is a vacancy in the office of the Vice President, the President shall nominate a Vice President who shall take the office upon confirmation by a majority vote of both houses of Congress.

SECTION 3.

Whenever the President transmits to the President pro tempore of the Senate and the Speaker of the House of Representatives his written declaration that he is unable to discharge the powers and duties of his office, and until he transmits to them a written declaration to the contrary, such powers and duties shall be discharged by the Vice President as Acting President.

SECTION 4.

Whenever the Vice President and a majority of either the principal officers of the executive departments, or of such other body as Congress may by law provide, transmit to the President pro tempore of the Senate and the Speaker of the House of Representatives their written declaration that the President is unable to discharge the powers and duties of his office, the Vice President shall immediately assume the powers and duties of the office of Acting President.

Thereafter, when the President transmits to the President pro tempore of the Senate and the Speaker of the House of Representative his written declaration that no inability exists, he shall resume the powers and duties of his office unless the Vice President and a majority of either the principal officers of the executive department, or of such other body as Congress may by law provide, transmit within four days to the President pro tempore of the Senate and the Speaker of the House of Representatives their written declaration that the President is unable to discharge the powers and duties of his office. Thereupon Congress shall decide the issue, assembling within 48 hours for that purpose if not in session. If the Congress, within 21 days after receipt of the latter written declaration, or, if Congress is not in session, within 21 days after Congress is required to assemble, determines by two thirds vote of both houses that the President is unable to discharge the powers and duties of his office, the Vice President shall continue to discharge the same as Acting President; otherwise, the President shall resume the powers and duties of his office.

Article XXVI

Passed by Congress March 23, 1971. Ratified June 30, 1971.

SECTION 1.

The right of citizens of the United States, who are eighteen years of age or older, to vote shall not be denied or abridged by the United States or any state on account of age.

SECTION 2.

The Congress shall have the power to enforce this article by appropriate legislation.

Article XXVII

Proposed by Congress September 25, 1989.

Ratified May 7, 1992.

No law, varying the compensation for the services of the Senators and Representatives, shall take effect, until an election of Representatives shall have intervened.

APPENDIX NOTES

1. See the 16th Amendment.
2. See the 14th Amendment.
3. See the 17th Amendment.
4. Modified by the 20th Amendment.
5. See the 16th Amendment.
6. See the 23rd Amendment.
7. This paragraph was superseded by the 12th Amendment.
8. See the 25th Amendment.
9. See the 11th Amendment.
10. See the 14th Amendment, Sec. 1.
11. See the 13th Amendment.
12. See the 20th Amendment.
13. Repealed by the 21st Amendment.

Chapter 2

Direct Your Learning

Contracts: Formation; Agreement and Capacity to Contract

After learning the content of this chapter and completing the corresponding course guide assignment, you should be able to:

■ Identify the elements of a legally enforceable contract.

■ Classify a contract presented in a case under one or more of the following types:

- Bilateral and unilateral contracts
- Executed and executory contracts
- Express and implied contracts
- Void contracts and voidable contracts

■ Apply the requirements of the following in a case:

- An offer
- An acceptance

■ Describe the contractual capacity of the following and apply the legal principles concerning their capacity in a case:

- Minors
- Insane people
- Intoxicated people
- Corporations

■ Describe the contractual capacity of the following:

- Insurers
- Insurance producers
- Insureds

■ Define or describe each of the Key Words and Phrases for this chapter.

Develop Your Perspective

What are the main topics covered in the chapter?

This chapter introduces the basics of contract formation, then addresses the first two (of four) required elements for legally enforceable contracts: agreement and capacity.

Identify the purpose of the required elements of a legally enforceable contract.

- How do the agreement and legal purpose define the actions of the parties?

- Why are competence and consideration necessary?

Why is it important to learn about these topics?

Insurance professionals must be familiar with basic contract law because insurance is based almost entirely on contracts, in the form of insurance policies, between insurers and insureds. The contractual relationships between insurers and insureds, between insurers and producers, and between producers and insureds give rise to most legal disputes involving insurance issues.

Consider the kinds of contracts your organization might have with others and the kinds of issues that could result in lawsuits.

- Aside from insurance policies, to what other kinds of contracts do you think your organization might be a party: With other organizations? With its employees? With employee benefits providers? With real estate owners? With suppliers?

- What is an example of a contract formation issue that might arise between an insurance producer and an insured?

How can you use what you will learn?

Examine the importance of contract formation in improving understanding of the promises made in insurance.

- How could producers improve contract formation with insureds?

- How could producers improve contract formation with insurers?

Chapter 2
Contracts: Formation; Agreement and Capacity to Contract

Contract law is one of the most important substantive law classifications, along with others, such as torts, property, and crimes. A contract is a legally enforceable agreement. People enter into agreements for many purposes, but not all agreements are legally enforceable contracts. Examples of contracts include agreements to purchase food, clothing, or insurance; to rent housing; to pay debts; and to buy property. Courts can enforce all of these agreements if they meet certain criteria. However, an agreement to have dinner with a friend is not legally enforceable because it does not meet those criteria. Understanding what circumstances give rise to legally enforceable agreements is essential to understanding contract law.

A contract must have each of the following four elements to be legally enforceable:

1. Agreement
2. Capacity to contract
3. Consideration
4. Legal purpose

This book devotes four chapters to contracts as follows:

*   Chapter 2—Contracts: Formation; Agreement and Capacity to Contract
*   Chapter 3—Contracts: Consideration and Legal Purpose; Genuine Assent
*   Chapter 4—Contracts: Formality, Interpretation, and Obligations
*   Chapter 5—Contracts: Insurance Contract Law

This chapter presents a general discussion of contract formation and then examines the first two elements of a contract. Chapter 3 covers the third and fourth elements.

CONTRACT FORMATION

A promise is an expression of intent to do or not to do something in the future, communicated in a way that assures another person of a firm commitment. Contract law concerns creating, transferring, and disposing of property and other rights through promises. When parties enter into a

Contract
A legally enforceable promise.

Promisor
The party to a contract making a promise.

Promisee
The party to a contract to whom a promise is made.

Third-party beneficiary
A person who is not a party to a contract but who benefits from it and has a legal right to enforce the contract if it is breached by either of the contracting parties.

Breach of contract
The failure of a party to a contract, without legal excuse, to perform all or part of the contract.

Privity of contract
The connection or relationship between parties to a contract because they have mutual interests.

Agreement
One party's offer and another party's acceptance of that offer.

Capacity to contract
A legal qualification that determines one's ability to enter into an enforceable contract.

contract, they establish their own terms and set limits on their own liabilities. In law, a liability is one person's legal responsibility to another person.

A **contract** is a legally enforceable promise. The party making the promise is called the **promisor**. The party to whom the promise is made is the **promisee**. Each party to a contract may be both a promisor and a promisee. For example, Spring Insurance Company (Spring) promises to provide Donna with homeowners coverage in return for her premium payment. Regarding coverage, Spring is the promisor, and Donna is the promisee. Regarding premium payment, Donna is the promisor, and Spring is the promisee.

Contracts frequently involve third parties' interests. A third party who is not a party to a contract but who benefits from a contract, called a **third-party beneficiary** of the contract, has a legal right to enforce the contract if it is breached by either of the contracting parties. A **breach of contract** is the failure of a party to a contract, without legal excuse, to perform all or part of the contract. For example, Bill agrees with Joe that he will pay Mary the money Joe owes her. Mary is a third-party beneficiary of the agreement between Bill and Joe. If Bill does not pay Mary, Mary may take legal action to enforce the contract.

The parties to a contract mutually agree to create and undertake obligations that did not previously exist. If one party does not fulfill the obligations, a breach occurs, and the other party can sue. The courts usually impose penalties consisting of money damages for failure to perform contractual obligations. Under some circumstances, such as a contract for the sale of a unique item—an antique, for example—a court can direct the breaching party to perform the contract by transferring the property in question. In contrast, courts generally do not order performance if the contract involves personal services, such as acting in a play, because it would be impossible for a court to supervise the performance. In such cases, courts are likely to order payment of money damages.

When two or more parties enter into a contract, they are said to be in privity of contract. **Privity of contract** is the connection or relationship between parties because they have mutual interests. Ordinarily, a party cannot sue for breach of contract without being in privity of contract with the other party. For example, a third party who is not a third-party beneficiary of a contract has no privity and therefore no right to sue under the contract if a breach occurs.

Elements are the constituent, or necessary, parts of a legal claim that a person bringing a lawsuit must prove in court to be successful. Each of the following four elements is necessary for a contract to be enforceable:

1. *Agreement.* An **agreement** consists of one party's offer and another party's acceptance of that offer. The parties must express real assent, which can be negated by fraud, duress, concealment, or mistake.

2. *Capacity to contract.* **Capacity to contract** is a legal qualification that determines one's ability to enter into an enforceable contract. Capacity involves the ability to understand the consequences of one's actions.

The parties to a contract must be legally competent, that is, they must have the capacity to enter into the contract. Competence is the basic or minimal ability to do something and the mental ability to understand problems and make decisions. Factors such as minority, insanity, or intoxication can restrict the parties' legal capacity.

3. *Consideration*. **Consideration** is something of value from the promisee that the promisor requested or bargained for in a contract. The price each party pays to the other, or what each party receives and gives up in the contract. For consideration to be valid, the promisor must receive a legal benefit or the promisee must suffer a legal detriment.

Consideration
Something of value or bargained for and exchanged by the parties to a contract.

4. *Legal purpose*. The contract must have a legal purpose that is consistent with sound public policy.

TYPES OF CONTRACTS

Contracts are categorized in a variety of ways, depending on their characteristics. Some common ways of categorizing contracts are the following:

- As either bilateral or unilateral contracts
- As either executed or executory contracts
- As either express or implied contracts
- Voidable contracts or void contracts

One contract can be more than one of these types.

Bilateral and Unilateral Contracts

A contract is either bilateral or unilateral. In a **bilateral contract**, each party promises a performance. Most contracts are bilateral because they involve exchanging mutual promises of future performances. For example, Jay's promise to pay Tony $500 in exchange for Tony's promise to paint Jay's garage creates a bilateral contract in which each party becomes both a promisor and a promisee. If a default occurs, either party may enforce the other's promise in a legal action.

Bilateral contract
A contract in which each party promises a performance.

In a **unilateral contract** only one party makes a promise or undertakes the requested performance. For example, Jay promises to pay $500 when Tony has completed painting the garage. A binding contract requiring Jay to pay Tony arises only when Tony has painted the garage. The performance of an act, painting, is required in exchange for the promise, payment. Tony does not breach a contract by failing to paint the garage. To "bind" means to impose legal duty on a party.

Unilateral contract
A contract in which only one party makes a promise or undertakes the requested performance.

Executed and Executory Contracts

A contract is either executed or executory. An **executed contract** is a contract that has been completely performed by both parties. For example, one party

Executed contract
A contract that has been completely performed by both parties.

has bought and paid for clothes that another party has delivered. The contract is executed, and nothing else is required of either party.

Executory contract
A contract that has not been completely performed by one or both of the parties.

In contrast, an **executory contract** is one that has not been completely performed by one or both of the parties. For example, if an insurance producer has contracted to find a business interruption policy for a client for a certain price, the contract is executory because the producer must find the policy and deliver it for the agreed-upon price. A fire insurance policy is another example of an executory contract. The insurer's promise to perform is an executory promise conditioned on the occurrence of a fire. As long as something remains undone, the contract is executory.

Express and Implied Contracts

Express contract
A contract that contains both the terms and the parties' intentions, either in writing or orally.

Contracts are either express or implied. **Express contracts** contain both the terms and the parties' intentions, either in writing or orally. For example, an insurance agent and insurance producer who agree either orally or in writing on an insurance premium rate of $1,000 per year create an express contract.

Implied-in-fact contract
A contract that is not express but that the parties presumably intended, either by tacit understanding or by the assumption that it existed.

Implied contracts can be either implied-in-fact or implied-in-law. An **implied-in-fact contract** is a contract the parties presumably intended, either by tacit understanding or by the assumption that it existed. For example, a person performs services for another, who can reject those services but fails to do so. A conscious accident victim who accepts the treatment of a doctor at the scene without comment might be liable to pay for the services under an implied-in-fact contract. In another example, if Bill, who has a credit account at the local hardware store, picks up an item, shows it to the storeowner without comment, and leaves the store with the item, he has made an implied-in-fact contract to pay for the item. Implied-in-fact contracts often arise through and are subject to trade customs, prior relations between parties, and community customs known to all parties.

Implied-in-law contract
An obligation that is not an actual contract but that is imposed by law because of the parties' conduct or some special relationship between them or because one of them would otherwise be unjustly enriched.

Implied-in-law contracts are not actual contracts and are sometimes called quasi-contracts. An implied-in-law contract is an obligation imposed by law because of the parties' conduct or some special relationship between them or because one of them would otherwise be unjustly enriched. These obligations do not arise from the parties' apparent intentions but from courts' notions of justice and equity in particular cases. For example, a parent who has not provided a child with the necessities of life might be liable under an implied-in-law contract to a third person who provides them. Even though the parties did not willingly or intentionally enter a legally enforceable contract, a court may determine that an implied contract exists based on justice and equity. Similarly, if a doctor has rendered professional services to an unconscious person unable to accept or refuse the services, then the law might obligate the patient to pay the reasonable value of the services based on an implied-in-law contract.

Voidable Contracts and Void Contracts

Some contracts are voidable, and some agreements are void because they are not contracts. A **voidable contract** is a contract that one of the parties can reject (avoid) based on some circumstance surrounding its execution. The right of avoidance is available only to an innocent or injured party. For example, a minor who has entered into a contract can avoid it any time during minority or within a reasonable time after reaching the age of majority, or legal age. If both parties to a contract are minors, then either or both can avoid the contract obligations. However, the contract is only voidable. It is not automatically void. A voidable contract is a valid contract that can continue in force, and the parties can execute it completely unless one of them chooses to avoid it.

The behavior of one of the contracting parties, such as fraud or illegal deceit, also can make a contract voidable. An example of fraud is a party's intentional misrepresentation of an important fact relating to a contract. Likewise, a party who has entered into a contract as the result of duress, a form of compulsion, can avoid the contract within a reasonable time. For example, if a salesperson has prevented a potential buyer from leaving the room until after signing a contract, the buyer later can avoid the contract.

An injured party can ratify, or affirm, a voidable contract. For example, if fraud or duress has occurred, the innocent party can elect to abide by the agreement and can hold the other party to the contract.

A **void contract** is an agreement that, despite the parties' intentions, never reaches contract status and is therefore not legally enforceable or binding. Even though the term void contract is contradictory because the parties never really create a contract in the first place, courts use it to describe agreements that the parties intend to be, but that never actually become, contracts. Void contracts are not legally enforceable or binding. An agreement to commit a crime, for example, is void and unenforceable because it is for unlawful purposes. An agreement between a sane person and a mentally incompetent person is void because the mentally incompetent person lacks the mental capacity to form a contract voluntarily.

Regardless of how contracts are classified, they are enforceable only if they include the four elements of a legally enforceable contract. The first two of those elements are presented next.

Voidable contract
A contract that one of the parties can reject (avoid) based on some circumstance surrounding its execution.

Void contract
An agreement that, despite the parties' intentions, never reaches contract status and is therefore not legally enforceable or binding.

FIRST ELEMENT OF AN ENFORCEABLE CONTRACT: AGREEMENT

The first element of an enforceable contract is an agreement between the parties. The parties to a contract must mutually assent, or agree, to the same terms. An agreement requires the following two steps:

1. The presentation of an offer
2. An acceptance of that offer

> ### First Element of a Contract: Agreement
>
> 1. Offer
>   - Intent to contract
>   - Definite terms
>   - Communication to offeree
> 2. Acceptance
>   - By offeree
>   - Unconditional and unequivocal
>   - Offeree's communication of acceptance

Offer

Offer
A promise that requires some action by the intended recipient to make an agreement.

An **offer** is a promise that requires some action by the intended recipient to make an agreement. The person who makes the initial offer is the offeror, and the person to whom the offer is made is the offeree. The following are the three requirements of a valid offer for contract purposes:

1. Intent to contract
2. Definite terms
3. Communication to offeree

If an offer meeting these three requirements is accepted, a contract is created. The contract becomes binding on both parties immediately upon the offeree's acceptance; consequently, the parties must fulfill the contract terms.

Intent to Contract

The first essential requirement of an offer is the intent to contract. The offeror must intend, or appear to intend, to create a legal obligation (contract) if the offeree accepts the offer. The offeror's language is the most important factor in determining whether a communication is an offer. Because an offer is a promise, words of promise indicate the offeror's intent to make an offer. Without specific words of promise, the communication is only a general statement of intention or an invitation for an offer.

A key question in each case involving contractual intent is whether, by words or conduct, a party has shown an intent to be immediately bound. The test of whether the intent has been shown is based on how a reasonable person would interpret the intent, not the party's actual intent.

This reasonable person's standard applies to many of the rules for forming contracts. To decide what is reasonable in each case, the judge or jury must weigh all the circumstances to determine how a reasonable person acting under the same or similar circumstances would react.

A general statement of intention that contains no inference of a promise is not an offer. If Anne says to Bob, "I am going to sell my car for $5,000," and Bob replies, "All right, I'll pay $5,000 for your car," Anne and Bob have not created a contract. The test is whether, under the circumstances, a reasonable person would conclude that Anne intended to promise to sell the car specifically to Bob. A reasonable person would not draw that conclusion in this case. Anne's statement only expressed an intention to sell the car in the future and did not make an explicit offer to Bob.

If Anne says to Bob, "I will not sell my property for less than $20,000," and Bob replies, "I accept your offer," no contract results. A reasonable person would not conclude that Anne's statement of a minimum price was a promise to sell at the figure mentioned.

Some communications are intended to induce others to respond with offers. These communications are not in themselves offers because they express no present intent to contract. Most advertisements, catalog, and sales letters meet this description; they are invitations to negotiate or to make an offer. For example, a store that advertises a camera at $495 is inviting offers from customers to purchase at that price. If the store sells all the advertised cameras, or if the advertisement mistakenly states a price of $4.95, the store is not bound to sell a camera at the stated price to a customer who responds to the ad. The usual advertisement or catalog does not define conditions so specifically that a customer's acceptance would make a contract.

However, some advertisements do constitute offers that would be bound by a customer's acceptance. For example, an advertisement that indicates that the first customer to enter the store can buy specific goods at a specific price has spelled out the conditions of acceptance. When the first person who enters the store agrees to buy the goods, a contract arises. In this case, the advertiser has used words of promise and described specific circumstances under which a customer could purchase the goods, giving rise to a contract based on the advertiser's legally enforceable contractual intention.

A party that asks for offers is free to accept them or reject them. In construction, for example, a project owner asking for bids can elect to accept one bid or to reject all of them. Any bidder can withdraw the bid at any time before its acceptance. A party calling for bids can accept any bid, whether or not it is the lowest one (unless acceptance of the lowest bid is required by law).

Following are some examples of statements that are not offers and that, if accepted, would not lead to valid contracts because they lack intent to contract:

- *Social invitations*. If a person withdraws an invitation or cancels a social event, the person who received an invitation has no legal remedy.
- *Predictions*. For example, a person mistakenly predicts favorable weather. A person who has relied on the prediction cannot sue for a loss resulting from bad weather. Similarly, if a doctor has predicted that a patient will be in the hospital only a few days, and the period of hospitalization turns out to be much longer, the doctor's prediction is not an enforceable promise.

- *Offers made in excitement or jest.* If a reasonable person would recognize that a statement was made in jest or in the heat of anger, then acceptance of the statement does not create a contract. However, whether a statement is made in excitement or jest is not always easy to recognize, and a contractual obligation can arise in some cases. Courts consider all of the circumstances in a case to determine whether a statement could reasonably be considered an offer.

Example: Statements Made in Excitement or Jest

Arthur offers to sell Bonnie a book for $50, in jest, intending to embarrass her into admitting that she does not have $50. If Bonnie accepts the offer and Arthur does not disclose that the offer was in jest, he is bound if a reasonable person would have believed that his offer was serious. Arthur's intention is not legally significant in this case. How a reasonable person would view Arthur's intent is the crucial test of contractual intent.

Joe's child is inside a burning building. Joe cries out, "Save my child, and I'll give you $1,000!" In response, Bill is able to rescue the child. Only if a reasonable person could have understood Joe's statement as an offer would Bill's actions create a binding contract. Particularly if Joe had cried "I'll give you a million dollars," and Joe is not a millionaire, a court would probably view Joe's statement as the result of excitement rather than an offer and would not require payment.

Definite Terms

The second essential requirement of an offer is definite terms. Definite terms make an agreement enforceable and make it possible to determine whether the parties have fulfilled their promises and to calculate damages.

An offer's terms must be stated with at least a reasonable degree of certainty. Reasonable certainty means generally identifying the contracting parties, the contract's subject matter, the price, and the time of performance. The absence of one or more of these terms, however, is not necessarily fatal to the offer.

To determine reasonable certainty, courts may ask whether the offer's terms are clear enough to provide a basis for a remedy if default occurs. If necessary and possible, the courts supply such missing terms as price or time of performance. For example, if the parties do not designate a time for performance, courts usually find an implication that performance is to occur within a reasonable time, considering the subject matter involved. If the offer is definite enough to determine the parties' intent, then a court will enforce the offer even though it might be necessary to imply some terms. However, inability to identify the parties to, or the subject matter of, an agreement, makes the offer indefinite and therefore impossible to accept.

Contracts to deal with one supplier, called requirement contracts, are usually enforceable even though the need for the goods might never arise. For example, Allen's promise to buy "all steel required" from Betsy is definite enough to enforce. Allen promises to buy all steel required from Betsy, and

Betsy promises to sell Allen the steel. In contrast, if Betsy promises to sell "all such steel as I want to supply" to Allen, then the agreement is illusory and too indefinite to provide a remedy in court. The indefiniteness stems from the possibility that Betsy might not wish to supply any steel.

Law also determines certainty. For contracts for sales of goods only, the Uniform Commercial Code (UCC) allows parties to agree, in a binding contract, to set terms in the future, including the price of the goods.[1] Most states have adopted the UCC to regulate the sale of goods and other commercial transactions. The UCC differs from the general common-law rule in contract law that the parties must specify the intended price when they form the contract unless the actual delivery and acceptance of the goods occur. In common law, delivery and acceptance imply a "reasonable" price.

Communication to Offeree

Along with intent to contract and definite terms, the third essential requirement of an offer is communication to the offeree. An offeree cannot accept a proposal before knowing about it. To illustrate, assume that Ruth has offered in a letter to sell her library to Jackie for $3,000. Before receiving the letter and without knowledge of Ruth's offer, Jackie sends a letter to Ruth stating that she will buy Ruth's library for $3,000. Jackie's letter is not an acceptance of Ruth's offer because Jackie did not know of that offer. The second letter was itself an offer, yet no contract existed because neither communication was in response to the other. No acceptance would occur until either party has responded to one of the two offers.

In another example, a newspaper advertisement offers "$100 to anyone who will enter the 100-yard dash on July 4 and beat David." Matt, unaware of the advertisement or offer, enters the race and beats David. No contract exists because Matt could not accept an offer of which he had no knowledge.

However, an offer can be valid if the offeree has begun performance before learning of the offer. For example, Jerry, a burglary victim, has offered a reward for information leading to the burglar's conviction. Paul has already investigated the burglary and has determined that Donna was the burglar. After learning about the reward, Paul reports Donna to the authorities. If Donna is convicted, Paul can collect the reward from Jerry even though part of his effort occurred before learning of Jerry's offer. The crucial fact is that Paul knew of the offer when he reported Donna as the burglar, that is, when he completed performance.

Duration and Termination

Duration and termination are key to determining whether an offer is binding. Factors considered include the following:

- Lapse of time
- Operation of law

- Offeree's rejection
- Counteroffers
- Offeror's revocation

Lapse of time. Offers do not remain open indefinitely. An offer ceases to be binding when the time the offer specifies expires or, absent a specific time, when a reasonable amount of time passes. What is reasonable depends on considerations such as the contract's subject matter and the general commercial setting. For example, in an offer to sell perishable goods, the time the goods stay fresh is a key factor.

Once an offer is terminated, any attempted acceptance becomes a counteroffer, which the original offeror can either accept or reject.

Operation of law. Any one of several events occurring before acceptance can terminate an outstanding offer by operation of law. Operation of law automatically terminates the offer. "Operation of law" means that rules of law apply automatically to a situation without any act by the parties. For example, an offer is terminated if performing a contract becomes illegal after the offer is made. If a statute makes it unlawful to sell certain goods, then a preexisting offer to sell those goods would be automatically terminated by the enactment of the statute. Similarly, if the subject matter of an offer is destroyed before acceptance, the offer terminates at the time of destruction, even if the offeree does not know about the destruction.

Also, if an offeror or offeree dies or is formally declared insane before making or accepting the offer, the law automatically terminates the offer. Once a contract arises, death or insanity will not terminate it unless it involves the deceased or insane party's personal or professional service. A contract not involving personal or professional services is enforceable against the deceased party's estate.

Offeree's rejection. The offeree's rejection of the offer terminates it. A rejection occurs when the offeree notifies the offeror of an intention not to accept. An offeree may reject an offer either by expressly refusing to accept it or by making a new offer to the offeror, called a counteroffer. Like the offer, the offeree's rejection is not effective until communicated to the offeror. Once the rejection is communicated, the offeree cannot attempt to accept the offer. Any such attempt is considered a new offer.

Counteroffer
A proposal an offeree makes to an offeror that varies in some material way from the original offer, resulting in rejection of the original offer and constituting a new offer.

Counteroffers. A **counteroffer** is any proposal the offeree makes to the offeror that varies in some material way from the original offer. A counteroffer rejects the original offer and constitutes a new offer. A counteroffer is not the same as a request for more information, and a request for information is not a rejection of the offer. For example, if Gene offers to sell Pat a television set for $200 and Pat says, "I'll give you $150 for it," Pat's reply is a counteroffer. It automatically rejects Gene's original offer, and Pat cannot later accept the original $200 offer. If Pat had replied to Gene's offer by inquiring, "Will you accept $150?" Her question is not a counteroffer or a rejection; it is an inquiry. If Gene had responded to the inquiry that $150 was unsatisfactory, Pat could still accept the $200 offer.

Counteroffers do not terminate an offer that includes a statement that the offer will remain open beyond any counteroffers. Similarly, an offer remains open if the offeree makes it clear that the counteroffer does not reject the original offer.

Offeror's revocation. Generally, an offeror can revoke, or withdraw, an offer any time before acceptance. As in the case of the offer itself, the revocation is effective only when communicated, in this case to the offeree, and only when the offeree actually receives it. Similarly, if the offeror mails a revocation, but the offeree accepts the offer by telephone before receiving the mailed revocation, a contract exists.

Offerors must revoke offers to the general public through the same means of communication they used in making the original offers. For example, one who has offered a reward in an advertisement can revoke it only through another advertisement. The revocation, once advertised, is effective even if someone who has not seen the advertisement tries to accept the original offer.

The offeror's statement that the offer is irrevocable for a period of time is not usually sufficient to remove the right of revocation; generally, the offeror can revoke the offer anyway. However, some important qualifications, such as those concerning option contracts, apply to this rule.

An **option contract** is an agreement to keep an offer open for a stated period, supported by consideration (payment of some kind). Once consideration has been given, the offer cannot be revoked within the prescribed period. Option contracts are common in real estate transactions, such as when a buyer pays for a binding option to buy in which the offeror agrees to hold the offer to sell open for a specific period. The offeree can reject the offer but, while the option period remains open, can later accept it.

Option contract
An agreement to keep an offer open for a stated period, supported by consideration.

The UCC has specific rules concerning the revocability of merchants' offers to buy and sell goods. Any such firm offer, in writing, that contains a statement that the offer is irrevocable for a specified period (up to three months) cannot be revoked, even in the absence of consideration.[2]

If, in a unilateral contract offer, the offeree has partially performed the acts requested by the offer, most courts hold that the offer is irrevocable. For example, Marie promises to pay John $2,000 if John excavates Marie's property. John has completed one-third of the excavation when Marie attempts to revoke the offer. The revocation is ineffective. Most courts require a substantial performance, more than just preparation to make a revocation ineffective. Once a substantial start occurs, the offeree has reasonable time to perform the entire acceptance. Whether substantial performance has begun is a question of fact, not law, in a trial.

Acceptance

The first element of a valid contract, agreement, requires that the offer be accepted. An **acceptance** occurs when an offeree agrees to a proposal or does what the offeror proposed.

Acceptance
The second step of an agreement; occurring when an offeree agrees to a proposal or does what the offeror proposed.

To create an enforceable agreement, an acceptance must meet the following three requirements:

1. The acceptance must be made by the offeree.
2. The acceptance must be unconditional and unequivocal.
3. The offeree must communicate the acceptance to the offeror by appropriate word or act.

Acceptance by Offeree

The first requirement of an acceptance is that only the offeree can make the acceptance because the offeror has the right to choose with whom to contract. Therefore, if Dan dies after receiving an offer from Alan, the executor of Dan's estate cannot accept the offer. Alan had the right to choose Dan, and no one else, as the offeree.

An offer can be made to one person, to a group or class of people, or to the public. The offer's language and circumstances determine the identity of the offerees. For example, Janet promises to sell and deliver books to Lisa if Lisa's father promises to pay $100 for the books. Lisa's father is the offeree; therefore, only he can accept the offer by making the return promise.

When an offer is made to a particular group, any member of the group can accept it. For example, a form letter containing an offer to many may be accepted by any recipient. If an offer is made to the public, as in the case of a reward advertisement, any member of the public can accept it. Once someone accepts the offer, no one else can accept it.

An acceptance expresses the offeree's consent to the offer's terms as binding. Use of the term "accept" is not necessary to bind the offeree; any language showing that the offeree agrees to the proposal suffices as long as it meets all three requirements for a binding acceptance.

Unconditional and Unequivocal Acceptance

The second requirement of an acceptance is that it must be unconditional and unequivocal. If the acceptance deviates from the offer's terms, it becomes a counteroffer. An offeree must comply strictly with provisions in an offer relating to time, place, or manner of acceptance.

Acceptances sometimes contain wording that appears to be conditional but that is not. For example, a real estate buyer's acceptance that states, "Good title must be passed," is an unconditional acceptance. The law implies good title in real estate transactions. Good (legal ownership) title would pass regardless of whether the parties say so; therefore, good title is not an added condition. Some acceptances are made subject to wording such as "details will be worked out."

Whether such an acceptance is unconditional depends on the extent of the details. If the details are routine clerical matters, an unconditional acceptance results. If the details involve substantial matters, such as determining the boundaries of a piece of land, the acceptance is conditional, and therefore, not valid. Likewise, a reply made subject to "details that you and my lawyer will work out" is a valid acceptance if the details concern matters such as the form of the agreement or a title search on property.

In contrast, a reply that leaves essential terms open that a court cannot determine and therefore cannot deem implied by the acceptance under legal rules cannot be an acceptance. For example, an offer to build a house and a reply that accepts the offer "subject to details to be worked out" does not create a binding agreement because too many essential elements are missing.

In addition to being unconditional, an acceptance must be unequivocal. An equivocal response is not an acceptance, a counteroffer, or an outright rejection. For example, a response that an offer "will receive our immediate attention" does not express a clear intent to enter a contract. Similarly, an expression of hope, such as "I hope to have the cash for you next Friday morning," is so vague as to preclude an acceptance, and it falls short of a counteroffer or a rejection.

The UCC takes a different approach to offers that involve the sale of goods. In the UCC, a variation between the acceptance and the offer cannot preclude contract formation. A definite, reasonable expression of acceptance, or a written confirmation from the offeree within a reasonable time, is a valid acceptance, even if it states terms additional to, or different from, those originally offered or agreed upon. If the additional or different terms are expressly conditional, they do not comprise a valid acceptance, but are instead proposals for additions to the contract. Such terms, if between merchants, become part of the contract. The UCC makes three exceptions to this rule. Additional or different terms in an acceptance do not become part of the contract if any of the following are true[3]:

- The offer expressly limits acceptance to the offer's terms.
- Additional terms materially alter the contract.
- The offeror objects to the terms within a reasonable time after receiving notice of them.

The UCC provides different rules when the offeror and offeree are not merchants. In such a case, additional terms do not become part of the contract unless the offeror and offeree mutually agree to them. Therefore, a response to an offer that proposes additional terms in sales contracts involving goods is neither a conditional acceptance nor a rejection of the offer. Instead, the terms are additional proposals to the contract. If the offeror fails to object to the proposed additions within a reasonable time, they become part of the contract. For example, if the buyer's acceptance states "inspection of goods will be allowed before their acceptance," the addition becomes part of the contract unless the original offeror objects to it. The other terms of the contract remain unchanged.

This UCC rule regarding nonmerchants applies unless an intended acceptance of an offer for the sale of goods states terms that vary the agreement materially. Then the response is a counteroffer and a rejection of the original offer, and the offeror need not notify the offeree of objection to the added terms. To make the added terms a part of the contract, the offeror must expressly accept the counteroffer. For example, if the proposed acceptance changes the quantity for delivery or the unit price, the change is a counteroffer as well as a rejection of the original offer. To avoid rejecting the offer when including proposals for material change in an acceptance, the offeree can take either of the following actions: ask whether the offeror would consider new terms, or state that the offeree's proposal to change the terms is not a rejection.

Offeree's Communication of Acceptance

The third requirement of an acceptance is the offeree's communication of the acceptance to the offeror by appropriate word or act. If an offer specifies certain means of acceptance, the acceptance must comply to form a contract. If no means of acceptance are specified, customary means of acceptance in similar transactions or those reasonable under the circumstances are permissible. If an offer specifies that an acceptance be in writing, an oral response does not create a contract.

Under the UCC, an offeree can accept in any commercially reasonable manner.[4] If an offer requires acceptance by return mail, an acceptance mailed the same business day of receipt of the offer is generally necessary. If no time for acceptance is specified, then acceptance must occur within a reasonable time.

Some situations do not require formal notice of acceptance. For example, if an offer to sell contains the words, "This proposal becomes a contract when an executive officer of the company accepts and approves it," the acceptance occurs when an executive officer indicates acceptance on the document by signing it. However, some courts still impose a duty on the offeree to inform the offeror of an acceptance within a reasonable time.

A complaint does not negate an acceptance. For example, a contract results even if an offeree replies to an offer by stating, "Your price is unfair. If I didn't urgently need the property, I would never accept at this price. Enclosed is my check for the unreasonable amount you demand." Despite the complaint, the acceptance is unequivocal.

An offeree's silence is not an acceptance. Language in an offer cannot circumvent this rule. For example, if Jack offers an item for sale to Jerry by stating in a letter, "If I do not hear from you within ten days, I will assume you accept my offer," no acceptance occurs if Jerry remains silent.

In some cases, the parties' prior dealings impose a duty to reject the current offer. For example, if the parties' customary way of dealing has been for the buyer to send goods and the seller to pay for them later, the buyer receiving an unrequested and unwanted additional shipment would have to reject it. Silence would indicate acceptance.

In the absence of a pattern of prior dealings, the party receiving unrequested goods has no duty to reply or to maintain the goods. For example, under the law of contracts a person receiving unordered merchandise has the right to use or dispose of it in any manner without returning or paying for it, and federal postal law explicitly confirms that right.

What the offeree must communicate depends on the contract offer. Most offers are bilateral in the sense that they contemplate a return promise to perform rather than performance itself. When it is unclear whether the parties intended a unilateral or a bilateral contract, courts usually find that the intent was for a bilateral contract.

For unilateral contracts, the offeror wants the offeree either to perform or not to perform an act. The legal term for agreed-to nonperformance of an act is **forbearance**, the act or promise to give up a legal right. When the offeree, with knowledge of the offer, performs, or forbears, the offeree is accepting the offer. The offeree does not have to communicate the agreed-to performance or forbearance because, presumably, the offeror will learn of it. In some cases, an offer specifies that the offeree must give notice of performance.

Forbearance
The act of giving up or the promise to give up a legal right.

Problems arise when the offeree begins to perform the act, and the offeror revokes the offer before the performance is completed. Most courts hold that an offeree's substantial performance suspends the offeror's right to revoke the offer. **Substantial performance** is performance of the primary, necessary terms of an agreement. A unilateral contract offer includes the understanding that, if substantial performance occurs, the offeree can complete performance within the prescribed time. No contract forms until the offeree completes all the work, but the offeror's right to withdraw the offer is suspended temporarily. What constitutes substantial performance sufficient to suspend the offeror's right of revocation is a question of fact, not law, in a court. Generally, preparations for performance are not substantial performance.

Substantial performance
The performance of the primary, necessary terms of an agreement.

For bilateral contracts, the acceptance is not complete until the offeree gives the offeror the appropriate return promise. The offeror can revoke the offer at any time until the offeree communicates the return promise to the offeror or to the offeror's authorized agent.

While the usual bargained-for response in a bilateral contract offer is a return promise, the offeree can choose to perform the act requested rather than to give a return promise. For example, Jill writes to Barry, "I'll pay you $1,000 if you'll promise to paint my garage by June 1." Barry does not reply to the letter but proceeds to paint Jill's garage, with her knowledge, and completes the work before June 1. The contract is valid. A court would likely conclude that Barry impliedly accepted Jill's offer and agreed to its terms; that Jill impliedly agreed to this form of acceptance; and that, therefore, a bilateral contract resulted.

An acceptance in a manner invited by an offer is effective as soon as it leaves the offeree's possession. The acceptance is effective even if it never reaches the offeror, so long as the offeree has intended it to go directly to the offeror. However, if the offeree simply tells a third person about accepting the offer, the acceptance is ineffective.

When acceptance by mail is an approved means of response to an offer, the acceptance is effective when the letter is mailed. Mailed acceptances create legally binding contracts when they leave the offeree's possession. This rule also applies to other communication services not under the offeree's control. A contract is created when an acceptance is delivered to a private messenger or faxed, for example. In all such cases, the offeree must accurately address the acceptance to the offeror. If an incorrectly addressed acceptance arrives at the wrong address, it is effective only when the offeror receives it. For example, if an offer is received on stationery with a business address and the offeree mails the acceptance to the offeror's home, only when the offeror receives the acceptance is the contract formed.

An offeror can expressly state that an offer is conditional upon the receipt of the acceptance. For example, Amy mails an offer to lease land to Victor, stating, "Send me a yes-or-no answer. If I do not hear from you by noon Wednesday, I will conclude that your answer is no." Victor mails an acceptance, but Amy does not receive the letter until after noon on Wednesday. Victor and Amy have not formed a contract because Amy did not receive the acceptance within the period she prescribed.

An offeree cannot withdraw or revoke an acceptance once made. That the offeree conceivably can reclaim a mailed acceptance from the post office does not prevent the acceptance from taking effect when sent.

Sometimes determining the exact time of a particular action is crucial to determining whether a contract has formed, as illustrated by the scenarios in the box.

Examples: Contract Acceptance

Situation One

May 3—Joel mails an offer to construct a building to Carl and requests an answer by mail.

May 4—Carl receives the offer at 11:00 AM.

May 4—Joel mails a revocation of his offer at 3:00 PM.

May 4—Carl mails an acceptance at 6:00 PM.

May 5—Carl receives the revocation at noon.

May 5—Joel receives the acceptance at 2:00 PM.

The acceptance is effective; the revocation is not. The contract became effective when Carl mailed the acceptance on May 4 at 6 PM. Joel's earlier revocation would not become effective until Carl received it, but by that time, Carl had already accepted it. The acceptance became effective before the revocation arrived. An acceptance is effective when the offeree sends it. A revocation is not effective until it is received.

Situation Two

May 7—Joel mails an offer to Carl to construct a building.

May 7—Carl receives the offer at 11:00 AM.

May 8—Carl mails a letter of rejection at noon.

May 9—Carl telegraphs an acceptance at 2:00 PM.

May 9—Joel receives the rejection letter at 3:00 PM.

May 9—Joel receives the acceptance telegram at 4:00 PM.

The parties do not have a contract because Joel received the rejection before receiving the acceptance. Acceptance is usually effective immediately upon leaving the offeree's control. However, in this case the offeree took the conflicting actions of first mailing a rejection and then following with an acceptance; the results depend on a race between the two communications. Technically, the first communication Joel receives—in this case the rejection letter—is binding. Most courts would agree, but some courts might treat the succeeding attempted acceptance as a counteroffer.[5] Similarly, if the offeree first mailed the acceptance and then telegraphed a rejection that the offeror received first, a contract technically would result because the acceptance was effective upon mailing. However, if the offeror substantially relies on the rejection while remaining unaware of the acceptance, the offeree may not enforce the contract.

SECOND ELEMENT OF AN ENFORCEABLE CONTRACT: CAPACITY TO CONTRACT

A valid offer and a valid acceptance form an agreement, but, to qualify as a contract, the parties must have legal capacity to contract. Capacity refers to one's ability to sue or be sued or to enter into an enforceable contract and it includes the ability to understand the consequences of one's actions. A party who lacks legal capacity to contract is incompetent under the law. A **competent party** is a party to a contract who has the basic or minimal ability to do something and the mental ability to understand problems and make decisions. An incompetent person who enters a contract can challenge its validity. The term that describes a successful challenge of a contract is "avoiding" the contract.

Parties who may lack capacity to contract include the following:

- Minors
- Insane persons
- Intoxicated persons (under the influence of alcohol or drugs)
- Artificial entities (such as insurers) that are restricted by law or corporate charter from entering into certain contracts

Competent party
A party to a contract who has the basic or minimal ability to do something and the mental ability to understand problems and make decisions.

Minors' Contracts

Each state has its own statute that sets the age of majority for contracts. The most common age of majority today is eighteen.

The law protecting minors from disposing of their property while they are underage reflects public policy. Generally, a minor always can assert minority as a defense against liability in contracts, except those involving the purchase of necessaries, discussed later in this section.

Minors' contracts can be an issue for insurers. For example, claim representatives should retain settlement files involving minors' claims until the minor reaches the age of majority, plus the statute of limitations period, in case the minor repudiates settlement. A statute of limitations defines the period within which a person can sue. If a minor has not avoided a contract within a reasonable time after coming of age, most courts hold that the minor has ratified the contract. What constitutes a "reasonable time" is a decision for the court. Although minors can avoid contracts during minority, they cannot confirm contracts during minority. A minor can avoid a contract by any expression of intent to renounce the agreement. Accordingly, any act inconsistent with the contract constitutes avoidance. For example, a minor who contracts to sell property to one person but sells it to another immediately after reaching the age of majority has effectively renounced the sale and avoided the original contract. A minor who elects to avoid a contract cannot affirm some parts of the contract and avoid others.

Courts limit minors' rights to avoid contracts for the sale of real estate. To protect a minor's interests, some courts give the minor, on reaching the age of majority, the right to repossess any real estate sold during minority. The person cannot challenge the real estate contract until reaching majority, and, if successful, can receive rents and profits for the period the buyer possessed the real estate.

Courts may consider whether a contract is executory (not fully performed by the parties) or executed (fully performed by the parties) when determining the minor's right of avoidance at majority. Courts may hold that an executed contract is binding unless the minor disaffirms it after reaching majority. Executory contracts are not binding unless ratified by the minor's conduct after reaching majority. In short, executed contracts are valid until rescinded (canceled), and executory contracts are invalid unless ratified.

Restitution
The act of making an injured party whole again.

Most courts require a minor to make restitution of any benefits received before avoiding a contract. **Restitution** is the act of making an injured party whole again. A minor cannot challenge a contract and at the same time retain contract benefits. A minor who has received something of value must return it upon rejecting the contract. A minor who has purchased an item and then trades it for something else must return the same or a comparable item available upon rejecting the contract.

In some cases restitution might not be possible. For example, if the minor has purchased an item and demolished it, most courts permit the minor to reject the contract by returning the wreckage to its original owner. Moreover, the minor can obtain a full refund of the purchase price upon rejection of the contract. Some courts consider this rule too harsh and allow the minor to receive only a refund for the depreciated value of the property. In the case of the demolished item, for example, these courts would order the minor to refund only its salvage value.

Even if a minor misrepresents age to induce another party to enter into a contract, the minor can avoid the contract. In this case, however, the other party can also avoid the contract, on the grounds of misrepresentation.

Unlike most contracts entered into by minors, a minor's contract to purchase necessaries is not voidable. Necessaries include anything related to a minor's health, education, and comfort appropriate to the minor's standard of living. This exception to the general rule is for a public policy reason: to protect minors. If contracts for necessaries were easily voidable, people would be discouraged from entering into them. Consequently, minors whose parents are unwilling or unable to provide for them would have difficulty obtaining what they need. The exception may not apply to minors whose parents supply the necessities of life; contracts those minors enter into for necessaries may be voidable. For example, minors whose parents do not provide clothing for them must pay for any clothing purchased.

Historically, courts have not viewed vehicles as necessaries. However, the increasing use of vehicles and the lack of public transportation in many areas have led courts to determine a minor's need for a car on a case-by-case basis.

The concept of necessaries usually does not apply to items used for business purposes. Courts have held minors not liable under contracts for fire and life insurance because insurance contracts are not for necessaries. However, when a vehicle is one of a minor's necessaries, mandatory auto insurance could arguably be necessary for that minor.

A minor is liable only for the reasonable value of necessaries actually received, for example, the reasonable value of necessary clothing purchased. However, if the contract was with the seller to make clothing for the minor, and the clothing had not been made or delivered, then such an executory agreement would not be enforceable against the minor. Only when the minor receives the necessaries and the contract is executed does an obligation to pay arise.

Contracts involving minors are nonvoidable in several other circumstances. For example, if a minor has married, enlisted in the armed services, assumed the obligation of a bail bond, or has the duty of child support, overriding public policy considerations require binding the minor to those commitments. Similarly, if a court has approved a contract for performance of services by a child, such as a child actor, the court will enforce the contract against the minor. In some jurisdictions, minors actively engaged in business pursuits are liable for contracts involving the conduct of those pursuits, for example, matters involving transferring stock, handling bank accounts, and obtaining loans for higher education.

A parent is generally not liable for a minor child's contracts. For a court to hold otherwise would permit indirect enforcement of a minor's agreement. For example, if a minor contracts to purchase a boat and a parent has not become a party to the agreement by signing or otherwise promising to assume the obligation, then the parent is not liable if the minor defaults. In contrast, a parent who *has* cosigned a minor child's contract is personally liable if the child fails to perform the contract obligations. The parent's liability is the same as that imposed on any other cosigner who assumes liability for another's default.

However, the law imposes liability on a parent for a minor child's contracts in several other situations. For example, the parent is liable if a child has acted in the parent's behalf in a transaction or if a parent has directed a child to sign a contract for the parent's benefit. Similarly, if a parent has neglected or refused to pay for necessaries for a child and the child contracts to purchase them, the contracting party can take legal action against the minor or the parent to recover the reasonable value of the necessaries.

An adult who contracts with a minor obtains only a voidable title to goods. Title means legal ownership. If the minor refuses to honor a contract and claims rightful ownership of goods, the adult must surrender the goods to the minor. Special problems arise when the adult has sold the goods to a third party, who has purchased the goods in good faith without knowledge of the minor's prior ownership or interest. At common law, the minor's rights would prevail, even against an innocent third party, and the minor could repossess goods in the third party's possession.

The UCC takes a different approach: A person with a voidable title, such as a party dealing with a minor, has the power to transfer a good title to a person who purchases in good faith for value.[6] In such cases, the purchaser is immune from a minor's later decision to reclaim title to those goods. The UCC applies only to the sale of personal property.

Insane Persons' Contracts

Any agreement entered by an insane person is void. For contractual liability, the law recognizes two classes of insane people:

1.   Those adjudged insane
2.   Those who claim insanity or mental incompetence

A person can be adjudged, or formally declared, insane by a court. A court's adjudication is conclusive and makes any contract that person has entered into while insane void, whether or not anyone challenges it.

Some people attempt to avoid liability under their contracts by claiming that they were insane or otherwise mentally incompetent at the time they entered into the contracts. Contracts of people who claim insanity, but whom courts have not adjudicated insane, are voidable; they remain in full force and effect until avoided by the parties claiming insanity.

To avoid a contract, a person claiming insanity but not adjudged insane must prove one of the following conditions:

- The person did not know that a contract was forming.
- The person did not understand the legal consequences of acts purporting to form the contract.

That a party suffers from delusions, has insane intervals, or is eccentric does not affect a contract in the absence of one of those two conditions. It is not necessary to show that a person is permanently insane, only that the individual was insane at the time of contract formation. Contracts made by mentally ill people during lucid intervals are binding. A person confined to or receiving treatment in a mental institution could be competent to contract, if neither judged insane nor meeting one of the two conditions.

As in the case of minors' contracts, only the incompetent or insane party has the power to avoid a contract. If the insane person has a guardian, then the guardian can avoid the contract. An insane party who has regained competency can affirm a previously made contract. An insane party who has avoided a contract must make full restitution if the other party acted in good faith and was unaware of the insanity.

Insane persons' liability for contracts for necessaries is the same kind of liability as that for minors. To determine what are necessaries, courts examine the individual's station in life, including the need for nursing and medical attention. For example, if the person is institutionalized, legal services to obtain release from custody can be necessary.

The public policy protecting insane people also protects their families and personal estates. The insane person is obligated for necessaries provided to a spouse and family and for items needed to preserve the person's estate. Necessaries are not limited to things required for the individual's personal maintenance, as is the case for minors. For example, repairs to the insane person's home might be deemed necessaries.

If an agreement benefits an insane person and the other party is ignorant of the infirmity, the insane person cannot avoid the contract. The party to a contract with an insane person can enforce the contract by proving the following:

- The sane party lacked knowledge of the insanity.
- The contract benefits the insane person.

For example, an insane person contracts to have her house painted. The other party, who does not know about the insanity, paints the house. The painter has a right to compensation for those services, and the insane person cannot disaffirm the contract. However, if the contracting party knew or should have known of the person's insanity at the time the parties created the contract, the insane person is not liable if the contract is not yet performed (executory). A court will try in such a case to achieve fairness for both parties.

Intoxicated Persons' Contracts

Generally, a person who was intoxicated, by use of either alcohol or drugs, when entering a contract, cannot avoid the contract. The law usually does not protect people from their own follies. Case law has tempered this rule, however, and exceptions have developed making contracts voidable if the previous judgment was impaired, using the same conditions applied to cases of insanity:

- The person did not know that a contract was forming.
- The person did not understand the legal consequences of acts purporting to form the contract.

Contracts made by people under the influence of alcohol or drugs but not meeting one of the two conditions are valid.

If a party to a contract has purposely caused the other party to become intoxicated to obtain an unfair advantage, the innocent party can avoid the contract. In most states, courts can adjudge people as habitual drunkards, just as they can adjudge them insane. Adjudication is a matter of public record and serves as notice to the public that contracts such a person makes are void. In such cases, the other party to the transaction cannot claim lack of knowledge of the party's condition. Conversely, if a contracting party has no knowledge of the other party's intoxication, the contract may be enforceable.

For example, Dolly, who was extremely intoxicated, signed and mailed a written offer to sell a business to John, who had no reason to know of the intoxication. He accepted the offer. Under these circumstances, Dolly cannot avoid the transaction.

A person who was intoxicated when entering into a contract can either avoid or ratify the contract upon becoming sober. The intoxicated party is the only one with the right of avoidance. However, the other party can claim lack of knowledge of the person's condition to avoid the contract. The party who avoids a contract cannot later retract the avoidance and must return any things of value received.

Artificial Entities' Contracts

Corporations, as artificial creations of the state, are people in the eyes of the law. They can hold property, sue and be sued, commit crimes and torts, and enter into contracts. The extent of a corporation's competence to enter into contracts depends on the scope of the power its charter grants.

Most states permit corporations to engage in any lawful business and do not restrict the types of contracts they can make. However, specially licensed and controlled corporations, such as those in, insurance, banking, and transportation, have different restrictions.

Traditionally, an attempted contract that was not within corporate powers was voidable as an *ultra vires* contract, meaning a contract "beyond its power." Either party could avoid such a contract while it was fully executory (still unperformed). If either party had performed its part of the contract, however, the other party must perform. As for a fully executed contract, neither party could avoid the agreement even though an *ultra vires* act was involved. Most states have abolished the defense of *ultra vires*, but courts often use the term when discussing corporate concepts in written decisions.

Insurance Contracts

Beyond issues of competence of parties entering into contracts, other capacity issues can arise regarding insurance contracts. Such issues relate to insurers, insurance producers, and insureds.

Insurer's Capacity

Insurers receive their legal capacity to do business from the state in which they are incorporated. They also must obtain licenses to conduct business in each state in which they operate. Each state's regulatory authorities and statutes establish the following:

- The financial requirements for insurers to incorporate in that state
- The requirements for out-of-state insurers to obtain licenses to write insurance in the state

The states stipulate conditions on the right to conduct insurance business, the types of contracts insurers can enter into, and contract language. A state can refuse to grant a license or can withdraw it if an insurer does not meet all of the legal requirements. Insurers must consult state statutes and insurance department regulations to determine the qualifications necessary for each state in which they intend to do business.

Insurance policies are contracts. The state statutes and regulations influence the nature and scope of insurance policies and usually require policy language to be approved by regulatory authorities before insurance policies are sold. An insurance policy that exceeds or differs from the authority granted the insurer nevertheless can bind that insurer. Regulatory authorities can revoke the insurer's license, but the insured can enforce the policy as written. The insurer cannot assert its own wrongdoing as a defense.

Similarly, the policies of insurers not licensed to do business in a state are enforceable against them. For example, if Insurance Company X is licensed to write health insurance in State A and also solicits applications by mail from State B residents, the policies are enforceable in either state. These policies also must conform to the law of the state in which the insurer issues them.

While courts can offer relief, regulatory authorities have difficulty with non-admitted insurers because the state has no power to withdraw nonadmitted insurers' licenses. These regulatory authorities communicate with regulatory authorities in the insurer's state of domicile, the state of the insurer's incorporation, to achieve compliance with state law.

Insurance Producer's Capacity

State statutes and regulations control individuals' capacity to act as insurance producers. Each state administers tests to prospective insurance producers before issuing licenses to ensure competence. A license grants a producer the privilege of writing a certain type of insurance for a designated company. A producer can have licenses to write business for more than one company.

Because the licensing procedure is designed to ensure that all producers are competent, cases about producers' legal competency to contract are rare. Because courts consider a producer's act the insurer's act, the agent need not have contractual capacity. Consequently, an insurer cannot avoid a policy issued by a producer who is a minor or an incompetent because of mental disability as long as the producer can complete instructions. It is the insurer's responsibility to appoint a competent representative to complete the insurer's business.

Insured's Capacity

Insureds are subject to the same general rules of contract law that apply to others. Unless incompetent because of insanity, minority, or intoxication, insureds cannot avoid insurance policies. In the few cases that have arisen concerning insureds' capacity, those who were incompetent for any reason when they entered the insurance contract could obtain return of the full amount of the paid premiums after avoiding the insurance policy because of incompetence.

In practice, any insured can avoid an insurance policy by ceasing to pay premiums. The insurer then cancels the policy, making an adjustment, in the case of life insurance, for paying any existing cash values due under the policy.

In several jurisdictions, people as young as fifteen can obtain life insurance policies on themselves. A minor in those states has no right to avoid a life insurance contract and no right to obtain a refund of all premiums paid on reaching the age of majority.

SUMMARY

Contracts are categorized in several different ways, including the following:

1. As either bilateral or unilateral
2. As either executed or executory
3. As either express or implied
4. Voidable contracts and void contracts

The four elements of an enforceable contract are as follows:

1. Agreement
2. Capacity to contract
3. Consideration
4. Legal purpose

This chapter examines the first two elements, the agreement and competent parties. The agreement includes an offer and an acceptance. The following are the three elements of an offer:

1. Intent to contract
2. Definite terms
3. Communication to the offeree

The law applies objective tests, including the "reasonable person" test, to determine intent to contract. Definite terms must convey reasonable certainty about the offer and cannot consist of illusory promises. Issues related to communication to the offeree involve adequacy of communication and the offeree's initiation of performance before learning of the offer. Offers raising specific issues include general statements of intention, invitations, bids, social invitations, predictions, and offers made in excitement or jest. Other issues relating to offers include the duration of an offer; and termination of the offer by lapse of time, operation of law, the offeree's rejection or counteroffer, or the offeror's revocation. Some of these issues arise in requirements and options contracts.

An acceptance must include the following three elements:

1. The acceptance must be by the offeree.
2. The acceptance must be unconditional and unequivocal acceptance.
3. The offeree must communicate the acceptance to the offeror by appropriate word or act.

Issues concerning acceptances include conditional and equivocal responses; the manner of acceptance, such as acceptances accompanied by complaints, silent acceptances, and acceptances by mail; and withdrawal or revocation of acceptance.

The second element of an enforceable contract is capacity to contract. Capacity is the ability to make legally binding agreements. Capacity issues in insurance relate to insurers, insurance producers, and insureds. Only competent parties, or those with capacity to contract, can create a contract. Competence issues often relate to contracts involving minors, insane people, intoxicated people, and artificial entities such as corporations.

Chapter 3 examines the final two elements of enforceable contracts: consideration and legal purpose.

CHAPTER NOTES

1. UCC, §§ 2-204(3), 2-305. The Uniform Commercial Code (UCC), a statute that most states have adopted, sets forth these rules in some detail. The UCC embodies the common-law rules relating to sales of goods.

2. UCC, § 2-205.

3. UCC, § 2-207(1).

4. UCC, § 2-206(1)(a).

5. Restatement (Second) of Contracts, § 39. Restatements of the law are a series of books from the American Law Institute (ALI) that generally describe American law in specific areas, such as contracts, torts, and agency. They also tell how the law is changing and explain changes in the law. Because the books are written by ALI, which is not a government entity, the restatements are not themselves the law. They are, however, highly regarded by lawyers, judges, and legal educators and commentators.

6. UCC, § 2-403.

Chapter 3

Direct Your Learning

Contracts: Consideration and Legal Purpose; Genuine Assent

After learning the content of this chapter and completing the corresponding course guide assignment, you should be able to:

- Given a case, apply the legal principles governing the types of consideration, the exceptions to the consideration requirement of contract formation, and the adequacy of consideration.

- Apply legal principles involving contracts that are illegal, narrowly interpreted, or partially enforced.

- Given a case, apply the elements of fraud to contract formation.

- Explain how the legal principles of mistake apply to contract formation.

- Describe the legal principles of each of the following to contract formation:
  - Duress
  - Undue influence
  - Innocent misrepresentation

- Define or describe each of the Key Words and Phrases for this chapter.

Develop Your Perspective

What are the main topics covered in the chapter?

The previous chapter introduced the basics of contract formation, then addressed the first two elements for legally enforceable contracts: agreement and capacity to contract. This chapter continues the discussion of the elements of contract formation with the final two, consideration and legal purpose, and also discusses the concept of genuine assent.

Describe key aspects of consideration, legal purpose, and genuine assent in contract formation.

- What constitutes an adequate consideration and when are exceptions made to the need for consideration?

- How do duress, undue influence, and misrepresentation contradict genuine assent?

Why is it important to learn about these topics?

Insurance professionals must be familiar with basic contract law because insurance is based almost entirely on contracts, in the form of insurance policies, between insurers and insureds. The contractual relationships between insurers and insureds, between insurers and producers, and between producers and insureds give rise to most legal disputes involving insurance issues.

Consider the kinds of contracts your organization might have with others and the kinds of issues that could result in lawsuits.

- What kinds of consideration might be involved in contracts between your organization and the following other parties: other organizations, employees, employee benefits providers, real estate owners, and suppliers?

- What are examples of illegal purposes that insurance policies might involve?

How can you use what you will learn?

Analyze contracts you have entered into and work with to determine the consideration and mutual assent.

- What is the consideration in each kind of contract to which you might be a party in your personal life?

- How can insurance producers determine if mutual assent is present in contracts with different insureds?

Chapter 3
Contracts: Consideration and Legal Purpose; Genuine Assent

The previous chapter covered the first two elements of a legally enforceable contract, the parties' agreement and capacity to contract. This chapter discusses the final two elements: consideration and legal purpose.

A contract that includes all four elements might still be unenforceable if one of the parties did not give genuine assent. Fraud, mistake, duress, and undue influence can negate a party's genuine assent and therefore void a contract. Therefore, this chapter concludes with an examination of these issues.

THIRD ELEMENT OF AN ENFORCEABLE CONTRACT: CONSIDERATION

The third element of an enforceable contract, in addition to an agreement (offer and acceptance) and capacity to contract, is consideration: The legal benefit or value each party exchanges in the contract. For the element of consideration to create a valid contract, the promisor must receive a legal benefit, such as money, or the promisee must suffer a legal detriment, which is inconvenience, loss, or relinquishment of something of value. The consideration necessary to make a promise enforceable can be one of the following:

- A return promise
- An act performed
- A forbearance from acting

Consideration makes a promise a contract. A promise to make a gift or to do something without receiving consideration in return is not enforceable. For example, saying, "I'm going to give you this ring," involves a promise to make a gift but does not bind the promisor. Once the gift is made, however, the promisor cannot take it back for lack of consideration.

Types of Consideration

Not all kinds of consideration are sufficient to form a binding contract. Types of consideration that are sufficient for forming an enforceable contract include the following:

- Valuable consideration
- Forbearance
- Present consideration
- Future consideration
- Binding promises

Types of consideration that are insufficient for forming a binding contract include the following:

- Past consideration
- Promises to perform existing obligations
- Compromise and release of claims

Each type of consideration has its own set of legal rules.

Valuable Consideration

Valuable consideration
The consideration necessary and sufficient to support a valid contract.

Good consideration
Consideration based on natural love or affection, or on moral duty, that is not sufficient to support a contract.

Gratuitous promise
A promise not supported by valuable consideration and, therefore, not binding.

The law distinguishes between good consideration and valuable consideration. The consideration necessary and sufficient to support a valid contract is a **valuable consideration** (one that has inherent value). **Good consideration**, which is based on natural love or affection or on moral duty, is not sufficient to support a contract. For example, a father signs this written promise: "For and in consideration of the love and affection I have for my daughter, I will transfer my property to her on November 1." This expression of love and affection is good consideration but not valuable consideration that can create an enforceable contract. The father's promise is a **gratuitous promise**, a promise not supported by valuable consideration, and is therefore not binding.

If the father actually transfers the property to his daughter, then he has executed the transaction, and the contract does not lack consideration. If the father decides not to transfer the property to his daughter, she cannot legally enforce the promise because the consideration is not sufficient to create a contract. An unperformed transaction is unenforceable for lack of consideration.

Forbearance

Forbearance, the giving up or the promise to give up a legal right, is sufficient to support a contract. Forbearance is commonly the consideration in cases of compromise. For example, a person injured in an automobile accident may have a right to sue for damages. A promise to refrain from suing in return for the other party's promise to pay a sum of money constitutes valuable consideration. If, however, the claim has no basis either in fact or in law (the injured person has no cause of action), then a promise to forbear from suing is not valid consideration because it surrenders no right. In another example, an agreement by the seller of a business not to compete with the buyer involves forbearance. Mutual promises to forbear are valuable consideration.

Forbearance can be valuable consideration even if it benefits the party asked to make the promise. For example, an uncle promised $5,000 to his sixteen-year-old nephew if the nephew would refrain from smoking, drinking, or gambling until age twenty-one. The court held that this forbearance was sufficient to enforce the promise.[1]

Present, Past, and Future Consideration

To be valuable consideration, an act or a promise must involve a present or a future commitment sufficient to support a contract. Past consideration is insufficient to support a contract.

For example, if a person mows a lawn without the property owner's knowledge, the owner's subsequent promise to pay for the work is not enforceable. The owner made no demand for the performance; therefore, the performance cannot later become the bargained-for exchange. Similarly, if one finds a wallet and returns it to its owner, who then promises to pay a reward, the consideration for the owner's promise (the return of the lost wallet) represents a past consideration and is not sufficient to support the promise.

Many state courts and legislatures have created exceptions to the rule concerning past consideration. Most jurisdictions enforce a new promise to pay a debt that has become unenforceable for one of the following three reasons:

1. One of the parties is a minor.
2. The promisor is bankrupt.
3. The time for payment has ended.

Although no new consideration supports the new promise to pay the obligation, some courts hold that the new promise couples itself to the preexisting debt, and that, therefore, valuable consideration supports the promise. Other courts find renewal promises enforceable because of a preexisting moral obligation sufficient to support the new promise.

To illustrate, when she was seventeen, Francine promised to buy a car from Joy for $200. Francine's promise was unenforceable because she was a minor. Upon reaching eighteen, the age of majority, and having paid none of the purchase price, Francine promises to pay $100 for the car. Although Joy could have disaffirmed the contract entirely and therefore owed no duty of performance (delivery of the car), Francine's new promise to pay $100 is enforceable. However, Joy cannot legally collect the price Francine promised initially.

A new promise to pay a debt barred by bankruptcy is enforceable without any additional consideration. The promisor must clearly express the promise to pay, and some states require renewal promises to be in writing. A mere acknowledgment of the debt or partial payment, without an express promise to pay all or part of the preexisting obligation, is not sufficient to create a binding renewal promise to pay. A new promise to pay a debt barred by a statute of limitations is also enforceable.

Binding Promise

To be valid consideration and sufficient to support a contract, a promise must be binding. Therefore, one party's promise to make certain payments for work requested of another party is not binding because the promisor might ask for no work. A promisor who requests work can be bound to pay for it, but the promisee cannot claim that the promisor is legally obligated to request any work.

Courts generally use a different approach for requirements or output contracts. For example, a promisor's agreement to buy from the promisee all the coal required during a period is a binding promise. Similarly, a company's promise to sell all the coal it produces, or outputs, to a particular promisee is a binding promise. In each case, however, the question is whether any requirements or outputs are involved. If some level of previous output or expected requirement exists, then the promise to continue meeting those requirements, or providing the output, is sufficient consideration. If the promisor does not anticipate any need for coal, then the promise is illusory and is not consideration.

Promise to Perform an Existing Obligation

A promise to perform an act that the promisor is already legally required to perform is not consideration. For example, a police officer's promise to the public to arrest a criminal is not enforceable because the arrest is the officer's job. However, if someone offers a firefighter a reward to enter a burning building to retrieve property at great risk, and beyond the firefighter's duty, that performance supports a claim for the reward.

In another example, a contractor refuses to complete construction under an existing agreement unless the project owner makes an additional payment. The project owner's promise to pay the additional amount is not enforceable. The contractor has made a one-sided modification to an existing contract with no new consideration required. However, if the contractor promises to do additional work in exchange for a promise to pay more, the promises are enforceable.

The rule just discussed has two exceptions. First, if extraordinary circumstances cause entirely unforeseen difficulties in construction, a promise of additional compensation could be enforceable. For example, if the contractor had no reason to expect that quicksand lay under a construction site, then the project owner's promise to pay additional compensation for completion of the building as in the original contract could be valid. The law finds an implied condition in the contract that the facts will be as the parties expected when they entered the contract.

The second exception to the rule about one-sided modifications applies under the Uniform Commercial Code (UCC) to contracts for the sale of goods. No consideration is required for such modifications. For example, Jean has agreed to manufacture and sell goods to Frank for $1,000. Subsequently, market conditions make it impossible for Jean to sell the goods without suffering a loss. Frank agrees to pay an additional $500 for the goods but later refuses to pay more than the original $1,000. At common law, Frank's promise to pay the additional $500 would not be enforceable for lack of consideration because Jean had a preexisting duty to deliver the goods. The UCC, however, overrides the common law and requires no new consideration.[2] Therefore, Frank must pay the additional $500.

Compromise and Release of Claims

Generally, partial payment of money owed is insufficient consideration to discharge an original obligation. When a debtor owes $100 and promises to pay $50 if the creditor will accept that amount as full payment, the promise is not binding. However, for some situations, such as the following, a promise to accept less than the original debt amount can be binding:

- *Bona fide disputes.* In bona fide, or good faith, disputes about the amounts of money owed, the parties believe that their claims are just. Many such claims involve damage to property or injury to people. Each party's promise to surrender a claim for the amount in question is sufficient consideration for the return promise. In another example, when the parties to a construction contract disagree in good faith about price, any compromise agreement about the price is binding on both parties.

- *Payment before debt is due.* A debtor may pay an amount less than a debt's total before the debt is due. If the creditor has led the debtor to believe that an early payment would discharge the entire obligation, then the promise to accept the lesser amount is binding on the creditor. In this situation, the debtor's modification of performance by early payment is sufficient consideration to support the creditor's promise to accept a lesser amount. Both parties have agreed to a different performance with legal detriment to each: the debtor pays earlier, and the creditor receives less money. Similarly, an offer to pay the debt at a different place from that specified in the original agreement may be binding if the creditor agrees.

- *Accord and satisfaction.* If the debtor makes partial payment and also offers additional consideration in some form other than money, the creditor's agreement to accept is binding. For example, if the original debt involves a $100 obligation, and the debtor promises to repay $50 plus a book, the creditor's assent to such agreement is binding, notwithstanding the value of the book. **Accord and satisfaction** is an agreement (accord) to substitute performance other than that required in a contract and the carrying out of that agreement (satisfaction). In the example, the agreement to substitute a different performance for the one in the contract is the accord, and the performance of that substitute agreement is the satisfaction.

Accord and satisfaction
An agreement (accord) to substitute performance other than that required in a contract and the carrying out of that agreement (satisfaction).

- *Composition of creditors.* A composition of creditors forms when several creditors join and each agrees to take a certain percentage of the original obligation owed. The resulting composition agreement is binding on the assenting creditors and completely extinguishes the original debt. Each creditor's agreement to accept a percentage of the full debt is sufficient consideration for the other creditors' same promise. If, following such an agreement, a debtor promises to pay one of the creditors 100 percent of the original obligation, the promise would not be binding. This situation differs from bankruptcy, in which a debtor's promise to pay debt discharged by bankruptcy is binding without additional consideration. Composition agreements extinguish debts, but bankruptcy bars only the right to sue.

Adequacy of Consideration

Courts generally do not inquire into the adequacy of consideration. Attempts to weigh the fairness of the numerous bargains in business would result in excessive litigation. Courts are not concerned if people are willing to pay $50 for a $20 item.

Courts do review the value of consideration in some situations. For example, a court could find an agreement unconscionable if a large seller charged an excessively high price to a small buyer who had no alternative but to deal with the seller.

Example: Adequacy of Consideration

Mike has written a book and has given it to Bridget to read. Bridget, thinking the book is publishable, offers Mike $10,000 for the manuscript. Mike accepts the offer. Before paying Mike, Bridget attempts unsuccessfully to find a publisher. Mike sues for the $10,000, and Bridget defends on the basis that she received no consideration because the manuscript was not worth $10,000. A court would rule Bridget's defense invalid because adequacy of the consideration is not an issue. The manuscript was sufficient consideration; that it proved unpublishable is immaterial. Bridget must pay the $10,000.

Exceptions to Consideration Requirement

In some cases, contracts are enforceable despite the lack of consideration. These promises are enforceable for equitable or public policy reasons, or because laws make specific exceptions. For example, contracts without consideration are enforceable when one of the following concepts or exceptions applies:

- Promissory estoppel
- Charitable subscriptions
- Specific exceptions under the UCC provisions
- State statutory exceptions

Promissory Estoppel

Promises to make gifts, called gratuitous promises, do not involve payment and are therefore generally unenforceable. Inequities resulting from application of this rule led courts to develop the concept of promissory estoppel. **Promissory estoppel** is the legal principle that a promise made without consideration is nonetheless enforceable to prevent injustice. The principle applies when the following three elements are proven:

1. A party has made a promise expecting another party to act, or to forbear from acting, in reliance on that promise.
2. The other party has justifiably relied on the promise to his or her detriment and acts or forbears from acting.
3. Only enforcement of the promise would achieve justice.

For example, Nancy promised to employ Barry for an indefinite term. Barry, who lived a thousand miles away, incurred considerable expense to move closer to Nancy's company because of her promise. When Barry arrived at Nancy's office to accept the job, Nancy reneged on her promise. Barry can sue Nancy for damages even though he provided no valuable consideration in exchange for Nancy's promise.

In another example, Nathan says to his granddaughter Gail, "None of my other grandchildren has to work in a factory like you do. I'm going to give you my promissory note for $50,000 so that you do not have to do factory work if you choose not to." Gail quits her job, relying on her grandfather's offer. Promissory estoppel requires Nathan to keep his promise because it induced Gail to quit her job and because it is likely that the only way to avoid injustice is to enforce the promise. Nathan's gratuitous promise was not a bargain in exchange for Gail's quitting her job. It was an unconditional promise made *in the event* that she left her job. Gail reasonably relied on the promise to her detriment. On the other hand, if Nathan had said to Gail, "If you quit your job, I'll give you $50,000," then Gail's act of quitting would have involved real consideration in the form of her detriment.

Promissory estoppel involves questions of fact to be determined by a judge or jury. Generally, evidence of substantial economic damage is necessary for a court to enforce the promise. Under the doctrine of promissory estoppel, a court seeks to grant whatever remedy is necessary to prevent injustice.

Charitable Subscriptions

When a person makes a subscription or otherwise pledges money to a charitable organization that depends on voluntary contributions, the obligation involves more than a gratuitous promise to make a gift. The commitment is as fully binding on the pledging party as if consideration had supported it. In this situation, some courts apply the doctrine of promissory

Promissory estoppel
A legal principle that permits enforcement of a promise made without consideration in order to prevent injustice.

estoppel on the basis that the organization has relied on the pledge to its detriment by undertaking projects the pledge would support and that injustice would result if the promise was not enforced. However, in practice, many pledge solicitations include statements that the pledge is not legally binding.

Exceptions Under the UCC

In regard to contracts for the sale of goods, the UCC specifies that consideration is not necessary to make the following types of promises enforceable:

- A written waiver or discharge of a claim involving an alleged breach of a commercial contract[3]
- An agreement that modifies a contract for the sale of goods[4]
- A merchant's firm written offer for goods that includes a statement that the offer is irrevocable for a fixed time, not to exceed three months[5]

The UCC supports the need for certainty of result in commercial contracts involving the sale of goods. In some situations, commercial paper can be enforceable even without consideration.

State Statutory Exceptions

Many states have adopted the Model Written Obligations Act or similar acts. In those states, a person who has indicated in writing an intention to be legally bound by a promise cannot later assert the lack of consideration defense.

Consideration in Insurance Contracts

The insurance contract (policy), like any other contract, requires valuable consideration. The insurer's consideration is its promise to indemnify an insured for loss resulting from a covered occurrence. The insured's consideration is the premium payment or the promise of premium payment. An insured's obligation to pay a property-casualty insurance premium differs from the obligation to pay a life insurance premium.

In property-casualty insurance, prepaying the premium is not a condition necessary to make the contract valid. Courts readily find an implied promise to pay a premium. Therefore, if an insured suffers a loss before paying a premium at the outset of a policy period, an insurer cannot refuse to pay damages based on failure of consideration.

The property-casualty insurance contract usually applies to the entire period of the contract coverage. Payment of the entire premium becomes an obligation as soon as the coverage begins. However, parties can agree that the insured will pay the premium for a three-year policy on a year-to-year basis. Even so, the consideration is generally due and payable at the beginning of the agreed-on period. Any premium owed becomes the insured's debt, and it must be paid to the extent that policy coverage for a period is actually in force. Canceling the policy during the coverage period requires an appropriate adjustment for a premium refund, or unearned premium, depending on whether the insurer or insured instituted the cancellation.

In life insurance, the application or the policy itself usually provides that the insurance will not take effect until the purchaser pays the first full premium. The policyholder has no duty to pay premiums after payment of the first premium, but nonpayment of premiums can result in forfeiture of policy rights. The insurer may have the right to avoid the life policy. If the policyholder has paid premiums for a number of years, the insurer might have to return any accumulated cash values to the insured at policy termination.

FOURTH ELEMENT OF AN ENFORCEABLE CONTRACT: LEGAL PURPOSE

An agreement between competent parties, supported by consideration, requires a final element to be an enforceable contract: It must have a legal purpose. A contract is illegal when either its formation or its performance is a crime or another wrongful act (tort). Ordinarily, an illegal contract is void, and neither party can sue under the contract.

Consequently, the parties to an illegal contract can neither recover damages for breach of contract nor seek recovery for the value of any partial performance they have made. Although this rule can result in a wrongdoer's unjust enrichment, it deters parties from entering illegal contracts.

Types of Illegal Contracts

Contracts may be illegal either because they are contrary to constitutional, statutory, or case law or because they are against public policy. A contract that is illegal at the outset does not become enforceable by a subsequent change in the law that makes similar contracts legal. Conversely, if a contract is legal at the outset but later becomes illegal as the result of a statute or court decision, the parties need not perform further. In this situation (supervening illegality) the parties could recover the value of performance while the contract was still legal. No recovery is available for acts the party performs after the declaration of illegality.

Contracts to Commit Crimes or Torts

Any agreement between parties under which one agrees to commit a crime or another wrongful act (tort) is illegal and void. For example, contracts to cause another's injury or death, to induce a breach of contract, or to violate a patent right or copyright are illegal and unenforceable agreements.

Contracts Harmful to the Public Interest

Courts have found agreements illegal because they harm public interest. An example is an agreement to buy or sell a public office. Similarly, agreements to procure government contracts illegally, agreements to contribute amounts exceeding legal limits to political campaigns, and illegal lobbying agreements are contrary to public policy and are therefore void.

Agreements to interfere with or obstruct legal processes are also illegal. For example, agreements to bribe witnesses or to suppress evidence impede the administration of justice and are against the public interest. Likewise, agreements that stir up unnecessary litigation are illegal and unenforceable.

Usury Contracts

Usury
The charging of an illegally high rate of interest on a loan.

Usury is charging an illegally high rate of interest on a loan. Each state's law limits the amount of interest that lenders charge for loans. Any contract allowing a lender more than the maximum legal interest is a usury contract and is therefore illegal. In most states, a lender who has charged an illegal rate is barred from collecting interest on the loan but can still obtain the principal amount loaned. Other states permit recovering interest up to the maximum legal rate.

Usury statutes treat different types of loans differently. The following are the three types of loans:

1. *Loans to corporations and to individuals who borrow large sums to conduct business or to secure large mortgages.* These loans are not subject to usury statutes because, presumably, these borrowers are financially sophisticated enough to bargain effectively.
2. *Loans by lending institutions, such as banks and insurance companies, and private loans based on personal credit or security.* These loans are subject to varying state-imposed maximum interest rates.
3. *Small consumer loans and retail credit transactions.* Many different institutions provide these loans; for example, licensed small loan companies, credit unions, credit card companies, banks, retailers, and pawnshops. These loans are subject to many state and federal laws.

Wagering Contracts

Wagering (gambling) contracts are contracts entirely for sport, and their performance depends on the occurrence of an uncertain event. Most states have statutes making wagering contracts illegal. A bet placed on the outcome of a sporting event is an example of a wager.

Insurance contracts are distinct from wagering contracts because the insurance contract provides protection against the potential financial consequences of a loss. To obtain coverage, an applicant must have an insurable interest in the property or life to be insured. Only if the insured would suffer a financial loss as the result of destruction of property or loss of the other's life does an insurable interest exist.

Determining whether a contract involves wagering is difficult in some situations. Futures contracts in the commodity markets are an example. Under these contracts, a seller promises to sell goods, usually agricultural products, that he or she does not currently own. Futures contracts generally include hedging transactions, making simultaneous contracts to purchase and sell particular commodities at a future date. The intention is that a gain on one transaction will offset a loss on another transaction. These contracts protect against market price fluctuation and are not considered wagering contracts because they protect legitimate business profits.

Contracts With Unlicensed Practitioners

State statutes require people engaged in particular trades or occupations to have licenses. Licensees must meet minimum levels of competence established by the state. Such laws are designed to protect the public against unqualified and incompetent people performing specialized services. Lawyers, doctors, dentists, pharmacists, barbers, insurance producers, and architects are required to have licenses in most states.

If a person engages in an occupation without a required license, the recipients of the services can refuse to pay for them because the contract was illegal. Licensing laws apply in the state in which services are performed. For example, a surveyor licensed in one state cannot sue for a fee for work performed under contract in another state because the license does not extend to other states.

Practicing law without a license raises special issues. People who give legal advice without a license to practice law are not entitled to a fee for their services and are subject to criminal prosecution. Specialists such as insurance producers, real estate salespeople, bankers, and accountants should be aware that giving legal advice and preparing legal documents may expose them not only to lost compensation but also to criminal sanctions. They should be aware of the applicable laws in their state defining what constitutes the practice of law. One state might permit a real estate broker to draft a deed or lease in a transaction. Another state might require that all deeds and leases be drafted by lawyers. Still another state might permit the broker to complete a printed form drafted by a lawyer.

States also require licenses for those dealing in certain articles of commerce, such as liquor, firearms, poisons, and other potentially harmful goods. Selling goods in violation of these licensing requirements is illegal, and courts will not enforce sales contracts for such transactions.

Some statutes requiring licenses are primarily to raise revenue rather than to protect the public. Contracts violating such statutes might be enforceable. For example, a builder who has failed to obtain a building permit under an ordinance designed primarily to provide revenue could collect damages for breach of a construction contract. Similarly, a business that has failed to pay a license tax for selling a product could collect damages for breach of contract.

Contracts Violating Sunday Laws

During the first 200 years of United States history, colonies and states enacted statutes prohibiting certain business operations on Sundays. Most of these laws, referred to as "blue laws," have been repealed. However, where they still exist, some types of contracts formed on Sundays, or contracts that require performance of work on Sundays, are illegal and void. When parties negotiate a prohibited contract on Sunday, but actual acceptance does not occur until another day, a court may consider the contract to have been formed on the day of acceptance and therefore will enforce it. Nearly all the Sunday laws contain an exception for works of necessity and charity. Therefore, contracts relating to acts necessary to preserve life, health, or property can still be enforceable even though the acts are performed on Sunday. If property is in danger, work performed to protect or save it can form the basis of a valid contract.

Contracts to Transfer Liability for Negligence

Another type of illegal contract involves the attempt to transfer one's negligence liability. Negligence is the failure to exercise the standard of care that a reasonable person would exercise in a similar situation. A contractual provision purporting to excuse a party from liability resulting from a negligent or an otherwise wrongful act is an **exculpatory clause**. Courts interpret such clauses narrowly against the parties attempting to limit their own liability. Courts often declare exculpatory clauses illegal as contrary to public policy, especially when the other party is at a bargaining disadvantage. An example of an exculpatory clause is a term in a residential lease excusing the owner from liability if the building burns down because of the owner's negligence. In most situations, courts would not enforce such a clause.

Exculpatory clause
A contractual provision purporting to excuse a party from liability resulting from negligent or an otherwise wrongful act.

Bailees' attempts to disclaim liability for negligence also raise illegal contract issues. When the owner of personal property (bailor) temporarily gives its control to another person (bailee), the transaction is a bailment. Examples are a customer (bailor) who entrusts car keys to a parking attendant (bailee) or a coat to a checkroom attendant (bailee). The bailee of the goods generally has a duty to exercise reasonable care under all circumstances. Many bailees attempt to limit their liability for negligence in such places as parking lots or coat checkrooms by placing on the receipts for the goods notices disclaiming liability for lost or damaged property. Some courts hold these clauses to be illegal because the limitations could encourage all bailees to attempt to restrict liability, a result contrary to public policy.

Common carriers, such as trains, airplanes, and buses, attempt to restrict their liability for negligence, as do certain public utilities and other monopolies. Such limits are prohibited unless permitted by statute, administrative agency ruling, or international agreement. The lack of equality of bargaining power between a large and powerful entity and the relatively powerless consumer is an important consideration in determining the legality of limits to liability.

Contracts in Restraint of Marriage

Contracts restraining the freedom to marry, such as the following examples, are contrary to public policy and therefore illegal:

- Contracts between two persons to bring about or prevent the marriage of a third person
- Marriage brokerage contracts restraining the freedom of choice in entering into marriage

Restraints on marriage incidental to another legitimate purpose might not prevent recovery in a lawsuit. For example, violating a promise not to marry while employed can be a legitimate basis for discharge from employment. People who promise not to marry until age twenty-one can enforce such contracts against parties who have promised to pay them to delay marriage. However, contracts not to marry that have no time limits are unenforceable. Contracts that seek to dissolve marriage are also questionable on social and public policy grounds. A promise by one spouse to pay the other for a divorce is illegal.

Contracts in Restraint of Trade

Under statutory and common law, contracts that unreasonably restrain trade or stifle competition are illegal and void. Restraint of trade issues often arise in the sale of businesses and in employment contracts. Reasonable limits on trade or competition in contracts are legal if they impose no undue hardship on the restricted party and only if they are necessary to protect the parties.

A common provision in contracts involving the sale of a business requires the seller to refrain from opening a new business to compete with the buyer within a certain distance and time. For example, a person buying an insurance agency would have a legitimate interest in preventing the seller from setting up a new agency nearby and retaining the customers of the agency sold.

Whether such a restriction is legal depends on its extent. If the restriction bars the seller from ever again competing in the same business or in a particular area, the restriction is unreasonable and invalid. If the restriction prohibits the seller from competing with the buyer for one year and within two miles from the business sold, the restriction is probably enforceable.

An employer can restrict an employee from competing in the same business for a reasonable time after terminating employment. If the restriction is necessary to protect the employer and is reasonable regarding the time and distance constraints on the employee, courts will enforce it. For example, an employment contract requiring an insurance producer to promise, on termination of employment with an insurer, not to compete for one year and within a radius of ten miles probably is reasonable and enforceable. If the producer violates the contract, the insurer could bring a court action to restrain the producer from competing.

Courts may void contracts not to compete. Courts generally look more favorably on contracts not to compete that are related to the sale of a business than on those that apply to employment contracts. Businesses generally have greater equality of bargaining power in contracts than do individuals in employment situations.

Unconscionable Bargains

At common law, courts of equity would not enforce contracts containing provisions so harsh and unfair that they cause undue suffering to the party resisting performance. The UCC incorporates this common-law approach for sales contracts, permitting courts to refuse to enforce or to limit the application of a contract or clause found to be unconscionable when created.[6] The court can revise such sales contracts to include more reasonable terms.

Illegality in Insurance Contracts

Like all contracts, insurance contracts must involve legal subject matter. In addition, courts refuse to enforce any insurance contract that is contrary to public policy. For example, an insurance contract purporting to pay fines for traffic violations is invalid because it might encourage insureds to disregard the law. Some states prohibit insurance coverage for punitive damages, which are damages intended to punish a defendant for acting with recklessness, malice, or deceit and to deter wrongful conduct by others.

Coverage of Contraband

Insurance coverage of illegally owned or possessed goods is invalid. For example, an insurance policy covering illegal drugs or illegal weapons is void and unenforceable. However, if the insurance is only incidental to an illegal purpose, then the contract is enforceable. For example, a property insurance policy on a building housing illegal gambling or prostitution is still enforceable, notwithstanding the illegal activity, because the coverage is on the building, not the activity. However, business interruption insurance on an illegal gambling activity or a house of prostitution would be void and unenforceable.

Lack of Insurable Interest

As previously discussed, public policy requires that the insured have an insurable interest in any property or life to be covered by the policy. Policies not covering an insurable interest are illegal and void because they are considered wagering contracts, gambling on others' lives or property. Such contracts increase the likelihood of intentional harm or destruction.

A person has an insurable interest in property if its destruction would cause that person direct monetary loss. The insurable interest must exist at the time the loss occurs. People can purchase life insurance on their own lives. They have an insurable interest in another's life only if they receive economic benefit from the relationship with the covered person. Relationship by blood or marriage is generally sufficient. The insurable interest in a life must exist at the time the applicant obtains insurance coverage.

Contracts That Allow an Insured to Profit From Wrong

A legal insurance contract can become unenforceable because of the insured's wrongful conduct. For example, when an insured has intentionally burned down his or her house, the insurance policy on the property does not permit recovery. The insured's illegal act precludes any right to insurance proceeds. If the insured sues for payment, the insurer must establish by a preponderance of evidence that the insured committed arson. A criminal conviction of arson, which requires proof beyond a reasonable doubt, a stricter standard of proof than that required in a civil case, is not necessary. In fact, an acquittal on the criminal charges does not preclude a civil lawsuit based on intentional damage for insurance proceeds. Although the insured who caused the damage could not recover, a majority of states allow an innocent insured spouse to receive a fair share of the insurance proceeds.

Similar issues apply in life insurance. When the beneficiary has caused the insured's death, courts in many states limit the conditions under which the beneficiary can recover policy proceeds. Generally, a beneficiary who has willfully caused or contributed to the death cannot recover, and any proceeds go to the deceased insured's estate or to a secondary beneficiary. In most states, a beneficiary who has accidentally caused an insured's death does not forfeit life insurance proceeds. A beneficiary who has killed an insured in self-defense or when insane also can recover benefits.

If a beneficiary has obtained a life insurance policy intending to kill the insured for the proceeds and does in fact kill the insured, the insurer can avoid payment. Both the beneficiary's illegal intent and fraudulent concealment are bases for avoidance of the contract, and the policy is entirely void with no benefits payable to anyone.

Qualifications to Illegal Contract Rules

A contract that might be illegal can still be totally or partially enforceable under the following conditions, each involving overriding considerations of equity or public policy:

- *Protective laws.* When a specific group is protected by law, an illegal contract might be enforceable. For example, when a corporation issues a type of stock that it is prohibited by law from issuing, the purchaser of the stock can sue to recover money paid under the illegal transaction. Similarly, an insurer that issues an illegal policy cannot use its own wrongdoing to defend itself in an insured's lawsuit to collect policy proceeds. The policy's illegal nature does not prevent someone from asserting the right to protection under the policy.

In pari delicto agreement
An illegal transaction in which both parties are equally at fault.

- *In pari delicto agreements.* **In pari delicto agreements** are illegal transactions in which both parties are at fault. If both parties are equally at fault, the contract is not enforceable. But if the degree of the parties' faults is significantly unequal, an illegal contract might be enforceable against the party at greater fault. Courts apply the concept of *in pari delicto* only in cases involving a clear disparity of guilt between the contracting parties.

Severable contract
A contract that includes two or more promises, each of which a court can enforce separately.

- *Severable contracts.* A **severable contract** includes two or more promises, each of which a court can enforce separately. Failure to perform one promise does not necessarily put the promisor in breach of the entire contract. When contracts contain some provisions that are legal and others that are illegal, courts can enforce the legal parts. Enforcement is at the court's discretion and occurs only in cases in which the legal and illegal parts are readily separable. If the illegal provisions have tainted the entire transaction, a court can void the contract entirely. To illustrate, a contract to deliver goods to a sporting goods store, including separate provisions for sale of camping equipment, bows, arrows, and guns, does not become illegal and void if the weapons subsequently become illegal for sale. The court can enforce the contract for the sale of camping equipment, bows, and arrows but not the sale of the guns.

Although courts will not enforce illegal contracts, they do not aid a party who has knowingly entered an illegal contract to recover any loss. However, some courts permit a party to repent before the completion of an illegal contract and to obtain return of whatever consideration the party paid. For example, for a racing wager in which two parties have placed $500 each in a stakeholder's hands, either of the parties can repudiate the contract before the race and get the $500 back. A person electing to repent an illegal act before consummating it can recover any money or goods transferred under the contract. However, once a contract is performed, courts do not assist the repentant party.

As previously discussed, when a contract is incidental to an illegal transaction, courts do not preclude the enforcement of the contract. The contract itself is legal. Therefore, an owner can recover for fire damage for an insured building even if the business conducted in the building was illegal. However, if the insurance covered illegal goods, such as contraband weapons, it would be void because its purpose would be illegal.

Genuine assent
Contracting parties' actual assent to form a contract or their indication of intent to contract by their actions and words.

GENUINE ASSENT

An apparently valid contract with all four elements (agreement, contractual capacity, consideration, and legal purpose) can be still unenforceable if either party has not given genuine assent. **Genuine assent** in a contract means that the parties have actually intended to form a contract or that they have indicated their intention to contract by their actions and words. An innocent party who has not given genuine assent can avoid the contract. Genuine assent may be lacking if a party was induced to enter a contract by any of the following five factors:

1. Fraud
2. Mistake
3. Duress
4. Undue influence
5. Innocent misrepresentation

In these five situations, courts do not uphold the contracts and sometimes award money damages to aggrieved parties.

Fraud

Fraud by a party to a contract can result in a lack of genuine assent from the other party. **Fraud** is intentional misrepresentation resulting in harm to a person or an organization. It is a tort, and it can be a crime. When one party to a contract has committed fraud, the contract is voidable if the innocent party chooses to repudiate it.

Fraud
An intentional misrepresentation resulting in harm to a person or an organization.

In a lawsuit alleging fraud, the plaintiff must prove six elements. Courts will generally rescind a contract if the first five elements of fraud are proven. In a suit for damages, the plaintiff must prove a sixth element, detriment. The definition of fraud is divided into six elements.

Fraud is:

1. a false representation
2. of a material fact
3. knowingly made
4. with intent to deceive
5. on which the other party has placed justifiable reliance
6. to his or her detriment.

False Representation

The first element of fraud is false representation of a fact. The fact must be a past fact or an existing fact, such as a business's profit for a previous year or the identity of an artist who created a painting. A false statement of opinion is not in itself fraudulent, but it can create the basis for a possible fraud action. If a person states an opinion knowing it to be contrary to the truth, courts have found fraud. For example, if the seller in a transaction to sell an apartment building, describes the current tenant as "very desirable," knowing that the tenant consistently fails to pay rent, the statement may be fraudulent.

A layperson's opinions about a property's value are not statements of fact, but a false opinion about value by one who is or claims to be an expert in the subject matter can be the basis for fraud. For example, a layperson's statement about the value of an artistic work would be an opinion. An art expert's similar statement, falsely made, could be fraudulent. Similarly, a layperson's interpretation of the law would be opinion, whereas a lawyer's interpretation of a law, if false, could be the basis of fraud. Whether a statement is fact or opinion is a matter for a court to resolve.

A statement can be oral or written, or it can be conduct, such as a gesture. A misleading statement that is partially true can be as fraudulent as an entirely false statement. In most business transactions, silence, or the withholding of information, is not fraud. The law does not impose a duty to speak on parties who deal at arm's length, in the marketplace, and in a purely businesslike manner. However, in some situations, a duty to speak the truth exists, and failure to reveal information is the basis for fraud. Four such situations are the following:

1. *When the parties are in a fiduciary relationship, which entails special duties of trust and confidence.* For example, a partner who sells property to the partnership without revealing material facts about the property's condition can be as culpable of fraud as if the partner had made false representations.

2. *When property with latent defects, that is, defects that a reasonable inspection would not reveal, is sold.* For example, a person who sells a house knowing that it is infested with termites must reveal that information to a prospective buyer. For withholding of such information to be fraudulent, the seller must have actual knowledge of the condition; a mere reason to know of the termite infestation is not sufficient to hold the seller liable.

3. *When the parties have made representations during previous negotiation and, subsequently, the facts change before the contract is formed.*

4. *When contracts require utmost good faith between parties, as insurance policies do.* The parties to the insurance policy owe a duty to reveal all material facts relating to the contract. For example, an insured's withholding of the fact that a building under a fire insurance policy has an unworkable sprinkler system could be fraudulent.

Of a Material Fact

Proving fraud requires proving a second element: that the misleading statement involves a material fact. A material fact is one that a party would consider important in deciding on a course of action. Courts use the reasonable person standard to determine whether a fact is material: whether a reasonable person would attach importance to the fact's existence or nonexistence in making a decision. Some courts may rule a fact material if the maker of the representation had reason to know that the recipient regarded, or was likely to regard, the matter as important in making the decision, whether or not a reasonable person would. For example, a car's mileage is a material fact in a contract for sale of the car. When the gas tank was last filled is probably not a material fact.

Knowingly Made

A third element of fraud is that the maker of the statement either knew that the statement was false or was indifferent to whether the statement was true or false. An innocent misrepresentation is not fraud. Knowledge implies competence to make such a statement; people who are mentally incompetent, who are chemically impaired, or who are minors may in some cases be deemed not competent to have the requisite knowledge.

With Intent to Deceive

As a fourth element of fraud, a party must have intended to make the other party take action in reliance on the statement. Surrounding circumstances establish intent. The previously discussed element of fraud, knowledge of falsity of or indifference to the truth, is often sufficient to establish intent. For example, a seller of a car says the mileage is 50,000 without knowing the mileage or making an attempt to verify it. If the mileage significantly exceeds 50,000, the statement may be fraudulent. A buyer who purchases the car believing the seller's statement can challenge the contract on the basis of fraud implied by the seller's indifference to the truth.

On Which the Other Party Has Placed Justifiable Reliance

The fifth element of fraud is justifiable reliance. A misrepresentation is fraud if it induces a person to enter a contract and if the person would not have entered the contract without that inducement. Courts have ruled that a party's reliance on the false statement need not be the sole inducement of the party's decision to enter the contract. The reliance, however, must be justifiable. For example, a car buyer's reliance on a statement of mileage would not be justifiable when a look at the odometer would reveal the true mileage. If the party knows a statement is not true and enters a contract anyway, fraud has not occurred, because the party did not rely on the false statement.

For example, Sam, when offering to sell a horse to Barbara, has told her falsely that Carol bred the horse. Carol is not a renowned horse breeder, and Carol's horses do not bring premium prices. Barbara would not be induced to purchase a horse in reliance on this information, so she could not claim the contract was fraudulent based on Sam's statement. Suppose, however, that Sam, intending to deceive Barbara, told her that Carol was a renowned horse breeder. Barbara may well be induced to buy the horse in reliance on that representation. Barbara, however, would have to prove that her reliance was justifiable. In a court case, Sam might use Barbara's failure to investigate his statement as a defense.

To His or Her Detriment

A final element of fraud, which the plaintiff must prove if seeking damages, is detriment, which is damage, injury, or loss. For example, the plaintiff might have received property of less value than that contracted for.

Remedies for Fraud

If fraud is proved, the plaintiff can seek one of the following two remedies:

1. **Rescission**, the complete unmaking of a contract (rescind is the verb form of rescission), is the usual remedy. If the court rescinds a contract, the plaintiff has no further duties under the contract and is entitled to reimbursement of all payments made to the defendant. The plaintiff also must return anything of value received under the contract. With rescission, courts attempt to put the parties in the condition they were in before they entered the contract. Proof of monetary damages is not required.

2. Damages may be awarded in some cases. If rescission would not make the plaintiff whole, the plaintiff can sue for damages in a tort action, usually called an action in deceit. The plaintiff must prove detriment in addition to the five elements of fraud necessary for rescission. The plaintiff can seek compensatory damages for actual quantifiable harm and punitive damages to punish the defendant and deter future, similar fraudulent actions. When seeking damages, the plaintiff must prove the extent of the loss or detriment.

Fraud in Insurance Contracts

A person fraudulently induced to make or sign an insurance application can sue to cancel or rescind the insurance policy. If an insurance producer has fraudulently misrepresented the nature of the document an applicant has signed or the coverage the applicant has purchased, the applicant can rescind the contract and recover any premium paid.

The insurer also has the right to cancel an insurance policy because of fraud by the insured. Any fraudulent action or statement the insured has made in procuring the policy, if material to the policy, permits the insurer to avoid it. For example, if an applicant for a health insurance policy has misrepresented the fact that she was receiving treatments for a serious condition, the insurer can avoid the policy.

If a sick applicant for life, accident, or health insurance has a healthy person take a medical examination in his place, he has committed fraud. In cases of fraudulent impersonation, courts uniformly hold the insurance contract void. Proof that misrepresentation was material, such as that the named applicant was uninsurable, is not necessary, nor is proof that the named applicant participated in the fraud. A finding that the applicant's signature was forged or that a fraudulent misrepresentation as to the nature of the document induced the applicant to sign it so taints the transaction that it voids the policy from inception.

Collusion is an agreement by two or more people to defraud another. For example, if the applicant for health insurance and an insurance agent have colluded to withhold adverse information about the applicant's medical history from the insurer, the insurer can avoid the policy. However, if the applicant has instead informed the agent about bad health and the agent has failed to record it, no collusion has occurred. Consequently, the insured can recover damages under the policy.

In insurance, the technical term for misrepresentation by silence is **concealment**. The concealment defense is very important in both property and life insurance. Unlike typical business contracts, in which the parties deal at arm's length, insurance contracts require utmost good faith. For the promise of a relatively large sum of money, payable when an uncertain event occurs, the insured pays a much smaller sum, the premium. The insured owes a duty to the insurer to share any knowledge about the loss exposure. The insurer relies on the applicant's full disclosure about the exposure to determine appropriate coverage and premium. An insured who withholds material facts about an exposure does not deal in utmost good faith. For example, a homeowner who finds fire damage in his home and immediately purchases insurance coverage effective before the damage occurred has concealed a material fact, and the insurer can avoid the policy.

Concealment
A misrepresentation by silence.

Fraudulent concealment is generally a question of fact to be determined by a jury. To assert the concealment rule defense, the insurer must prove the following:

- The insured knew that the fact concealed was material.
- The insured concealed the fact with the intent to defraud.

If the insurer suspects concealment but does not ask the insured questions to elicit the material information, the insured's silence is not a ground for the insurer to avoid the insurance policy, absent intent to defraud. If no questions were asked, the insured could have assumed that the insurer was satisfied with the information made available.

To constitute a defense, concealment must involve information material to the transaction. In insurance, a fact is material if its disclosure would have influenced the insurer's decision to accept the application. Materiality is primarily a question of fact to be decided by a judge or jury.

Courts agree that any fact that is the subject of a specific inquiry is material. Standard applications for life insurance ask questions about drug use, scuba diving, auto racing, parachute jumping, aviation, speed contests, body-contact sports, and other risky activities; therefore, facts relating to these activities are material. Courts find intent to defraud only when the facts are clearly and obviously material, particularly if life or accident insurance is involved. Examples of obviously material facts are an applicant's skydiving hobby and an applicant's plans to embark on a hazardous venture. In such cases, the insurer could refuse to pay even for injuries not related to skydiving or to the hazardous venture. Similarly, in life insurance, if an applicant falsely denies drug use in response to an application question and later dies of a nondrug-related accident, the insurer can avoid the contract.

Insurance application questions can concern a possibility of loss not covered by the policy applied for. For example, a life insurance application form, containing a specific exclusion for death that results from aviation, could ask questions about participation in aviation activities. Most courts would find that the facts unrelated to policy coverages provided are not material. Therefore, failing to answer or incorrectly answering a question about participating in aviation activities would not be material to the contract, and a court would permit recovery of proceeds for death resulting from a covered cause.

When the insured is aware of an unusual loss exposure not addressed in the application, the test of materiality is the same: whether the information would influence the insurer's decision to enter into the contract. In an application for a life policy or an accident policy, the applicant's plan to embark on a dangerous trip probably is material, even if the application does not ask about such plans. A trier of fact would probably conclude that an insurer, knowing of the trip, would likely have denied the application (or might have charged a higher premium to cover the risk). Courts use the reasonable person standard to determine materiality.

Example: Material Fact in Insurance Contract

Brian purchased credit life insurance, which protects a creditor when a debtor dies, on his wife. She died of cancer six weeks after Brian purchased a boat in their joint names, financing $5,000 of the price with the credit life policy. The insurer refuses to pay, charging that Brian concealed the material fact of his wife's cancer. A court would examine the conflicting interests involved. Denial of the concealment defense might encourage spouses of terminally ill persons to shift the payment of debts to policyholders generally. However, credit life policies do not make health inquiries or require medical examinations. A court might conclude that a reasonable person would not expect an insurer, knowing of the wife's terminal illness, to write a credit life policy. The illness would be considered a material fact, and the insurer could avoid the policy.

Example: Immaterial Fact in Insurance Contract

Rosa loses her jewels on a cruise. She has received insurance payments for items she has lost on several occasions in the past. The insurer rejects her claim on the ground that, in applying for the policy, she should have disclosed her history of similar losses as well as her history of financial difficulties. The jury holds for the insured, finding no fraudulent intent to conceal information. In the absence of the insurer's inquiry before issuing the policy, the insured properly assumed that concealment of prior losses of similar articles was not material, the jury concludes.

Courts have also considered whether previous losses or claims must be disclosed in the absence of a specific question about loss history on an insurance application. Courts generally consider such information immaterial.

Often cases have dealt with the question of whether applicants for life or health insurance must reveal intimate and embarrassing facts in the absence of a specific question. Courts have found that such information is not material and have affirmed insurance policies, even when insureds have failed to reveal the following:

- Excessive use of intoxicants when applying for a life insurance policy
- A previous insanity commitment
- Pregnancy when applying for a life insurance policy
- Impending job loss

In each of these cases, the application made no specific reference to the fact in question.

Some courts have ruled that failure to reveal a previous history of a socially transmitted disease on a life insurance application is fraudulent.

Examples: Nondisclosure Issues in Insurance Contracts

- The applicant conceals a prior conviction for conspiring with others to submit a false proof of claim under an insurance policy. A court could find concealment. Fraudulent concealment is generally a question of fact that a jury determines.

- A court found that the insured concealed a material fact even though he told the truth. Joseph DeBellis applied for a $5,000 life insurance policy. Five months later, his body was found, stabbed to death, under a railroad bridge. The death certificate named the deceased as Joseph DeLuca, the first notice to the insurer that the insured had an alias. The insurer denied the claim on the ground that the insured had concealed a material fact from the company by not revealing his alias and introduced evidence showing that Joseph DeLuca had an extensive criminal record. The court found in the insurer's favor, holding that the insured should have told the insurer of the alias even though the insurer had not inquired about aliases. The insurance contract requires good faith, and the insured's concealment of his alias breached the obligation of good faith.[7]

- A life insurance applicant indicated that he had been employed as a plasterer for the past fourteen years. In fact, for almost half that period, he had been in a penitentiary serving a sentence for robbery. He later died in a gun battle. The court held that the policy was voidable by the insurer because of the insured's intentional concealment of his past.[8]

Most courts agree that an insurance applicant must be reasonably diligent in notifying the insurer of material facts that come to the applicant's knowledge after applying and up to the time the contract becomes effective. The insured owes no duty to disclose facts learned after the contract becomes effective even though the contract has not yet been delivered. The effective date of policy inception, therefore, is crucial.

To illustrate, suppose Bert has applied for health insurance to become effective when Insurance Company's home office approves it. After submitting the application but before the home office has approved it, Bert discovers that he suffers from an ulcer. Under these conditions, Bert owes a duty to disclose the new condition.

> ### Example: Nondisclosure in Insurance Application
>
> On June 22, at 5:00 PM at the Iberra Insurance Agency (Iberra), Mimms completed an application to Adams Mutual Insurance Company (Adams) for automobile liability insurance. Coverage was to start at 12:01 AM on June 22. The agency mailed the application to Adams that day. Van Gundy, Adams' vice president and underwriting manager, reviewed the application on June 25.
>
> Mimms had stated on the application that he had no prior accidents. Iberra had no authority from Adams to issue a binder for auto liability insurance to Mimms. On June 25, Adams processed and approved the application and on June 26 mailed Iberra the policy, bearing an effective date of June 22 at 12:01 AM. Mimms was in an accident on June 22 at 10:00 PM. Later, Adams recovered the policy from Iberra, and it never appeared on the insurer's books. Mimms had not paid a premium on the policy.
>
> The company's acceptance had not been conditional on either policy delivery or premium payment. The issue was whether the applicant's uninsured motorists coverage was in force. The court held that the company was not liable under the policy, stating that the applicant had a duty while the application was pending to notify the insurer of any changed condition, such as an accident, materially affecting the loss exposure. Not having done so, the applicant did not satisfy the good faith requirement. The insurer had relied on his previous statement that he had experienced no accidents. Consequently, the uninsured motorists coverage was not in force.[9]

Most courts impose a duty on the insured to reveal material facts to the insurer. Words or actions constituting concealment are not required. The insured's silence or failure to advise the insurer of material facts can constitute concealment. An applicant who knows that the property is subject to an unusual hazard must reveal that information to the insurer. Failure to do so could constitute concealment and avoid the policy.

Mistake

Mistake
A perception that does not agree with the facts.

Unilateral mistake
A perception by one party to a contract that does not agree with the facts.

Bilateral mistake
A perception by both parties to a contract that does not agree with the facts.

Like fraud, a mistake in a contract can also result in lack of genuine assent. A **mistake** is a perception that does not agree with the facts. People can make mistakes regarding the facts of a transaction or the law affecting an agreement. Mistakes can involve errors in typing, in arithmetic, or in the value of property in question. While some mistakes do not affect the parties' rights, others make the agreement voidable or unenforceable. A common way of classifying mistakes is to determine whether one or both parties to a transaction were mistaken. If only one party was mistaken, a **unilateral mistake** occurred. If both parties were mistaken, there was a **bilateral mistake**.

Unilateral Mistake

A unilateral mistake ordinarily does not affect a contract. For example, if an offeree accepts an offer that was mistakenly transmitted, a contract is formed because only the offeror was mistaken. Courts do not permit one party to knowingly exploit another's mistake. For example, if a contract bid is so low that it is obvious that a clerical or mathematical mistake has occurred, the offeree cannot take advantage of the error by accepting the offer.

In certain situations, parties can avoid a contract in construction bids because of a unilateral mistake of fact. For example, a contractor who has made a material mistake in a bid on a public works project can retract the bid if both of the following occur:

- The contractor makes the retraction promptly after discovery.
- The governmental agency involved has done nothing more in reliance on the bid than accept it.

Ordinarily, however, one party's mistake of fact does not affect the parties' rights. To illustrate, Larry contracts with Jenny to buy an expensive ring on credit. Jenny believes she is selling the ring to another, wealthier man also named Larry, because she knows he will be able to pay for the ring. Larry, the buyer, unaware of Jenny's mistake, acts in good faith. Jenny's unilateral mistake is immaterial, and the contract is enforceable against her.

Bilateral Mistake

Bilateral mistakes occur when both parties to a contract make the same mistake of fact. Agreements under such conditions are generally voidable. Because both parties have acted on inaccurate information, neither has given genuine assent to the contract; therefore, no contract forms. The mutual mistake must relate to a material fact. Mistakes about collateral considerations, which the parties did not perceive as crucial to their contract, are not grounds for avoidance.

Bilateral mistakes about the subject matter's value do not make a contract voidable. For example, if parties contract for the sale of a jewel, neither knowing the jewel's true value nor making value a condition of their contract, they cannot avoid the contract if the jewel has a different value than either or both parties anticipated. Courts do not remake such bargains. However, if the mistake is about the jewel's identity, the parties can rescind the contract. For example, parties might mistake a relatively inexpensive cubic zirconium for a diamond.

Parties often make contracts with awareness that they do not know all the facts. For example, neither the buyer nor the seller of a used car can know the extent of wear on each part of the car. This lack of knowledge does not constitute a mistake. In another example, if an insurance company issues a "lost or not lost" policy on a ship, it takes the chance that the ship could already be lost, even though both parties think the ship is safe. Finally, in agreements to settle disputes, both parties give up their rights to sue even though facts discovered later might provide a basis for a suit.

Mistakes in Insurance Contracts

Of the thousands of insurance policies issued each year, a considerable number contain mistakes. The correction of mistakes over one party's protest can create difficult legal problems. The law does not correct mistakes in judgment or relieve a party of the consequences of an act just because that party did not foresee or desire the consequences. However, under some circumstances, courts do correct errors in expression by interpreting ambiguous policy language or reforming the contract. Court interpretation and reformation are two remedies for mistakenly worded insurance policies.

When interpreting an ambiguity or incorrect description in an insurance policy, courts seek to arrive at language that conforms to the parties' intent when entering the contract. The court's ability to interpret the policy is limited to some extent by the restrictions of the parol evidence rule, which prohibits the use of parol (oral) evidence to show that the contract terms were different from those in the written policy. However, several exceptions apply to the parol evidence rule. For example, if an insurance policy contains the incorrect address for an insured property, a court will interpret the policy to cover the property the parties intended. Similarly, if an insured designates "my brother-in-law, Charles Jones," as the beneficiary of a life insurance policy, and two brothers-in-law have that name, the court will permit the introduction of parol evidence to determine which brother-in-law the insured intended to benefit.

Reformation
An equitable remedy by which a court rewrites, or reforms, a contract to reflect the parties' intentions.

Courts grant the remedy of reformation only on proof of mutual mistake or of unilateral mistake of which one side was aware. **Reformation** is an equitable remedy by which the court rewrites, or reforms, a contract to reflect the parties' intentions. For example, if both the applicant and the insurance producer understood when entering a contract that particular coverage applies but that coverage is not included in the policy, the court can reform the policy in keeping with the contract.

Mistakes of law, whether unilateral or bilateral, do not affect the binding nature of a contract, particularly when the law is not clear. Court decisions can change the law after parties form a contract. For example, both parties to an insurance contract mistakenly believe that property insurance obtained in an individual partner's name protects the partnership's interest in the property. After a loss occurrence, the court could correct the policy to cover the partnership's interest, even though the belief was a mistake of law.

Duress

Duress
The use of restraint, violence, or threats of violence to compel a party to act contrary to his or her wishes or interests.

A party who enters a contract under duress may not have given genuine assent. **Duress** is the use of restraint, violence, or threats of violence to compel a party to act contrary to his or her wishes or interests. The question for a fact finder is whether the wrongdoer deprived the plaintiff of free will in entering the agreement. In weighing this decision, a court considers the victim's physical health, mentality, experience, education, and intelligence.

Threats to do bodily harm to someone or to his or her close relatives constitute sufficient duress to justify contract avoidance. Similarly, a threat to burn down a person's home or to destroy other valuable property belonging to a person constitutes duress.

A threat to prosecute someone for a crime also constitutes duress. For example, Danielle confronts George with an allegation that George's son embezzled funds from George's business. Danielle threatens to report the embezzlement to the police unless George agrees to give her stock in the company. If George agrees to meet Danielle's demands, he later may avoid the stock agreement on the ground of duress.

Generally, the threat of economic loss or the threat of a civil lawsuit is not sufficient to deprive a reasonable person of free will. However, a court might find duress if one party would suffer irreparable loss under the contract. A contract formed under threat of eviction or of damage to one's credit standing could constitute duress.

Conversely, the threat to cease doing business with a person does not constitute duress sufficient to avoid a contract. Likewise, a threat to withhold payment for work already done unless additional work is performed free of charge is not duress. In such cases, the fear of force imposed on the person is not sufficient to avoid the contract.

Undue Influence

Undue influence, the improper use of power or trust to deprive a person of free will and substitute another's objective, can also result in lack of genuine assent to a contract. Undue influence arises in confidential relationships in which one party exercises some control and influence over the other. Such relationships include parent and child, nurse and invalid, attorney and client, doctor and patient, and guardian and ward. In contracts between such individuals, the law will assist the victim of undue influence.

Undue influence
The improper use of power or trust to deprive a person of free will and substitute another's objective, resulting in lack of genuine assent to a contract.

In a challenge to a contract alleging undue influence, the dominating party must prove that the contract was free of undue influence. Mere persuasion and argument or nagging are not by themselves undue influence. Undue influence is sometimes a catch-all defense for matters not embraced in other elements affecting genuineness of assent, such as fraud or duress.

Mental infirmity can be the basis for an undue influence allegation. Even when no fiduciary relationship exists between parties, a person with a mental infirmity that seriously impairs judgment may claim undue influence. This is so even though the infirmity is insufficient to constitute mental incompetence and even though the mentally infirm person knows the subject matter of the contract. If the motive for entering into the contract was the result of seriously impaired judgment, the contract can be avoided.

Most cases of undue influence concern gifts and wills made by people, often recently bereaved spouses who may be temporarily infirm or elderly persons suffering from physical ailments or dementia, who may have been dominated by others.

Innocent Misrepresentation

A person who has reasonably relied on an innocently misrepresented material fact can later avoid a resulting contract because of lack of genuine assent. Even when no intent to defraud exists, the materiality and reasonable reliance elements of fraud also apply to misrepresentation. Misrepresentation is easier to prove than fraud because the plaintiff need not prove intent to deceive.

The victim of an innocent misrepresentation asks a court to rescind the contract. Courts do not award money damages for innocent misrepresentation.

SUMMARY

The final two requirements necessary for an enforceable contract are consideration and legal purpose. Types of consideration sufficient to support a contract include the following:

- Valuable consideration
- Forbearance
- Present consideration
- Future consideration
- Binding promises

Types of consideration insufficient for forming a valid contract include the following:

- Past consideration
- Promise to perform existing obligations
- Compromise and release of claims

Adequacy of consideration can be an issue in determining whether a contract is valid. Courts do not usually inquire into the adequacy of consideration unless an agreement is unconscionable.

Exceptions to the consideration requirement include the following:

- Promissory estoppel, which a court may apply when a party has justifiably relied on another's promise and has suffered detriment
- Charitable subscriptions, which are in some cases considered legally binding
- Exceptions under the UCC, which apply to certain types of promises relating to contracts for the sale of goods
- State statutory exceptions

Like other contracts, property-casualty and life insurance contracts require consideration.

An enforceable contract also must have a legal purpose. Types of contracts that do not have legal purposes and that are therefore unenforceable include the following:

- Contracts to commit crimes or torts
- Contracts harmful to the public interest
- Usury contracts
- Wagering contracts
- Contracts with unlicensed practitioners
- Contracts in violation of Sunday laws
- Contracts attempting to transfer liability for negligence
- Contracts in restraint of marriage
- Contracts in restraint of trade
- Unconscionable bargains

Under certain circumstances, illegal contracts are enforceable. Qualifications to the rule requiring legal purpose are as follows:

- Contracts covered by laws that protect specific groups
- Illegal contracts in which both parties are at fault (*in pari delicto*) but are unequally at fault, that is, one party's fault is much greater than the other's
- Severable contracts (of which only the illegal parts are unenforceable)

Some courts permit a party to an illegal contract to repent before the contract is executed and to obtain return of consideration paid. Courts also may enforce contracts in which illegality is only incidental.

Types of illegal insurance contracts include the following contracts:

- Contracts involving contraband
- Policies for property or a life in which an insured has no insurable interest
- Contracts that make it possible for insureds to profit from their wrongs

Even if a contract contains all the elements necessary to make it valid, it might not be enforceable if genuine assent is lacking because of one of the following:

- Fraud
- Mistake
- Duress
- Undue influence
- Innocent misrepresentation

To constitute fraud, a situation must involve six elements.

Fraud is:

1. false representation
2. of a material fact
3. knowingly made
4. with intent to deceive
5. on which another party has placed justifiable reliance
6. resulting in the other party's detriment.

Fraud in insurance policies usually involves impersonation of an applicant, collusion, or concealment. A mistake can be either unilateral or bilateral. Mistakes in insurance policies often require court interpretation, and a common remedy is reformation of the contract.

In relation to contracts, duress is wrongful force to obtain assent to a contract, and undue influence is duress by a party in a position of dominance over another party. An innocent misrepresentation of a material fact makes a contract unenforceable only if the other party proves detrimental reliance. A victim of innocent misrepresentation can ask a court to rescind the contract and need not prove intent to deceive.

CHAPTER NOTES

1. *Hamer v. Sidway*, 124 N.Y. 538 (1891).
2. UCC, § 2-209-1. Example drawn from *Uniform Commercial Code in a Nutshell*, Stone, West Publishing Co., 1989, pp. 26–27.
3. UCC, § 1-107.
4. UCC, § 2-209(1).
5. UCC, § 2-205.
6. UCC, § 2-302.
7. *DeBellis v. United Benefit Life Ins. Co.*, 93 A.2d 429 (Pa. 1953).
8. *DePee v. National Life & Accident Ins. Co.*, 62 P.2d 923 (Kan. 1936).
9. Restatement (Second) Contracts, § 502, illus. 4 (1973).

Chapter 4

Direct Your Learning

Contracts: Form, Interpretation, and Obligations

After learning the content of this chapter and completing the corresponding course guide assignment, you should be able to:

- ■ Explain whether the statute of frauds would apply in a case.

- ■ Explain whether the parol evidence rule would apply in a case.

- ■ Apply contractual rules of interpretation in a case.

- ■ Describe the types of rights that are assignable and the rights of the respective parties in an assignment.

- ■ Describe the rights of third-party beneficiaries in a case.

- ■ Explain whether discharge of contract by performance, new agreement, or impossibility has occurred in a case.

- ■ Explain how the three types of contractual conditions apply in a case.

- ■ Describe breach of contract and types of remedies available for breach in a case.

- ■ Define or describe each of the Key Words and Phrases for this chapter.

Develop Your Perspective

What are the main topics covered in the chapter?

This chapter describes contract form, interpretation, and obligations. Although oral contracts are generally enforceable, the statute of frauds requires that six kinds of contracts be in writing, including some insurance contracts. Courts apply rules of interpretation to contracts, and third parties can have defined rights in contracts. Parties can discharge contracts by performance, agreement, impossibility, and fulfillment of conditions. They also can breach contracts, and they have remedies at law and equity for breach.

Identify the types of contract form, interpretation, and discharge that apply to insurance contracts.

- Why must insurance contracts be in writing?
- How might a policyholder breach an insurance contact, and what would be the remedy for such a breach?

Why is it important to learn about these topics?

Insurance professionals must be familiar with basic contract law because insurance policies are contracts between insurers and insureds. The contractual relationships between insurers and insureds, between insurers and producers, and between producers and insureds give rise to most legal disputes involving insurance issues.

Consider how the legal rules governing the elements of enforceable contracts laid the foundation for insurance contracts.

- Why might courts interpret insurance contracts differently than intended by the policy developers?
- What third-party rights arise from contracts?

How can you use what you will learn?

Analyze the contractual formation of your own insurance policies for your home or automobile.

- Did you and your agent create a binding insurance contract orally before you received a written policy?
- Under what circumstances might third parties have rights under your insurance policies?

Chapter 4
Contracts: Form, Interpretation, and Obligations

Forms of contracts, as well as rules for interpretation, breach, and discharge of contracts, are determined by the common law, state or federal statutes, court interpretations, and the Uniform Commercial Code (UCC). Most states have adopted the UCC, which applies to the sale of goods. When appropriate this chapter compares UCC provisions with the common law when the UCC restates, enhances, or differs from the common law.

Statutes of frauds also have significant effects on contracts. These laws require written contracts in certain situations but allow oral contracts in others, and also may permit parol (oral) evidence in some cases, if needed, to interpret a written contract. A variety of other rules have evolved in the courts for interpretation of contracts or determination of the meaning of contradictory or ambiguous terms.

STATUTE OF FRAUDS

Early common law enforced oral contracts. All contracts were valid and enforceable so long as the parties could establish their terms in a court of law. Even today, most contracts are oral and, if provable, are enforceable contracts in courts of law. The statutes of frauds changed common law by requiring certain types of contracts to be in writing. A **statute of frauds** is a law to prevent fraud and perjury by requiring that certain contracts be in writing and be signed by the party responsible for performing the contract. All states have enacted statutes of frauds, designed to provide certainty with respect to an obligation by requiring written proof of intentions and to reduce the possibility of fraud. The usual statute of frauds provision states that "no action shall be brought unless the agreement, or some memorandum or note thereof, shall be in writing, and signed by the party to be charged therewith...."

Statute of frauds
A law to prevent fraud and perjury by requiring that certain contracts be in writing and be signed by the party responsible for performing the contract.

Contracts Requiring Writing

While state statutes of frauds sometimes include additional provisions, most of them name the following six situations for which contracts must be written to guarantee enforceability:

1. Contracts for the sale of land or any interest in land
2. Contracts that cannot be performed within one year
3. Contracts to pay another's debt
4. Contracts in consideration of marriage
5. Contracts by executors of decedents' estates to pay estate debts from executors' own funds
6. Contracts for the sale of personal property for $500 or more

Some contracts fall into more than one of these categories.

Contracts for the Sale of Land

The first kind of contract requiring a writing under the statute of frauds relates to the sale of real property or legal interests in real property. Real property is land and attachments to land, such as buildings. Legal interests in real property can be complete, such as actual ownership, or partial, such as a renter's interest. Oral contracts for the sale of these interests are unenforceable under the statute of frauds.

The writing requirement extends to all interests in land, including mortgages, easements, and leases. A life estate, that is, a transfer of an interest in land for a party's life, must be in writing. For example, Sarah has given her nephew John a life estate in her farm, meaning that he can use and enjoy the farm during his life as if he owns it. However, he cannot sell the farm, and his interest terminates completely upon his death. This life estate is unenforceable unless it is in writing.

While it is usually not difficult to determine whether a transfer of an interest in real property is involved, problems of interpretation can arise in sales of minerals, timber, and growing crops. Are these items real property or personal property (all property that is not real property)? Generally, if formal ownership, or title, to the property passes along with the real property itself, no dispute arises. For example, a field of ripening corn would be real property. However, if the owner harvests the corn and sells a small amount of it to a neighbor, the contract involves personal property and need not be in writing unless its selling price is $500 or more. The UCC provides that a contract for the sale of such items as timber and minerals is a contract for the sale of goods if the seller severs them from the property.[1] If the buyer severs them, the contract involves land and is subject to the statute of frauds provision requiring a writing.

Courts have qualified some statute of frauds requirements relating to real estate contracts. For example, when the purchaser of real property has taken possession of the property and made substantial improvements in reliance on an oral contract to sell, most courts enforce the oral contract in the interest of fairness. Under these conditions, the case is "outside the statute of frauds," and the contract may be enforceable, notwithstanding the absence of a writing. The trier of fact, whether judge or jury, must decide what constitutes substantial improvements. If a buyer takes possession of real property but does not make substantial improvements, performance is not sufficient to avoid application of the statute of frauds. Neither does payment of the purchase price alone satisfy the statute if the contract is not in writing.

The statute of frauds does not allow rescission of a contract but only serves as a defense to a suit for breach of an executory, or incomplete, contract. It does not apply to executed contracts (those already carried out). A party who has purchased or sold land under an oral contract, therefore, cannot obtain a refund of money or a return of the deed to land.

Oral contracts not complying with the statute of frauds are not void, but are merely voidable. Either party may use lack of compliance with the statute as a procedural defense in a lawsuit to enforce the contract, but if neither party raises that defense, the contract can be carried through to completion. Third parties who are not participants in an oral contract cannot raise the defense of lack of compliance with the statute of frauds.

Contracts That Cannot Be Performed Within One Year

Disputes over the terms of long-term oral contracts arise frequently. For this reason, statutes of frauds usually require written evidence of contracts that cannot be performed within one year from the date of their formation.

Courts have not favored the one-year requirement and generally hold the provision inapplicable if there is any possibility that the contract can be performed within one year. For example, a promise to perform an act "upon John's death" does not have to be in writing, even though it may be years before John dies. John could die within a year, making performance within a year possible. Similarly, a fire insurance contract covering a three-year period need not be in writing to be enforceable because the contract could be performed if a fire occurs within a one-year period. The *possibility* of performance controls the one-year provision's applicability.

A contract for personal services calling for performance of services extending beyond one year must be in writing. To illustrate, an oral contract under which Annie agreed to work for Bob for a period of two years would not be enforceable. Similarly, an oral contract involving the sale of a business in which the seller has agreed not to compete for three years would not be enforceable because the period exceeds one year.

The one-year provision of the statute of frauds applies only to mutual promises to perform, or bilateral contracts. Unilateral contracts, those fully performed by one party, made orally and not capable of being performed within a year, are enforceable. For example, if Jim sells and delivers a car to Kelly for $400, and Kelly promises orally to pay for the car eighteen months after its delivery, the contract is enforceable. Jim has completely performed his side of the contract, and his performance made Kelly's promise unilateral. Therefore, Jim can recover the $400 from Kelly based on the oral promise.

Courts disagree about the enforceability of an oral contract that extends for more than a year but that also permits cancellation by one or both parties within a year. Some courts hold that the oral contract is not enforceable because it may continue beyond a year. Most courts hold that the oral contract is enforceable because there is a possibility of discharge, by cancellation, within one year.

Contracts to Pay Another's Debt

Statutes of frauds require a writing for a party's promise to another person to pay the debt of a third person. If Bob owes Carol money and Annie promises Carol that she will pay Bob's debt if he fails to do so, Annie's promise must be in writing to be enforceable. Annie's obligation is secondary to Bob's. She has promised to pay Carol only if Bob defaults on his obligation to Carol. Annie has made her promise to the creditor, Carol, and not to the debtor, Bob. To fall under the statute of frauds, the promise must involve the discharge of an obligation owed by someone other than the promisor, Annie. If the debt is either directly or indirectly that of the promisor, then the statute does not apply, and no writing is necessary.

When the promisor's main purpose in making the promise is not to answer for another's debt or default but to protect the promisor's own interests, then the case does not fall under the statute of frauds, and no writing is necessary. In each case, two obligations must exist for the statute to apply: a party must have assumed a primary obligation, and a new promisor must have agreed to pay the debt if the primary obligation is in default. The primary contract need not be in writing, but the secondary contract must be in writing if it is to be enforceable.

If Jean promises to pay Patty for clothing that Burt might obtain from Patty, the promise need not be in writing. In this case, Burt has no obligation to pay for the clothing and no debt. The only obligation in this case is Jean's obligation to pay for clothes that Burt obtains from Patty. Jean has assumed primary liability and cannot assert the lack of a writing as a defense.

Similarly, assume George is a prime contractor, Ellen is a subcontractor, and Sadie is a supplier of materials to Ellen. George orally promises Sadie that he will pay her if Ellen does not pay for the supplies. The oral promise is enforceable. In this case, the promise to pay Ellen's debt is primarily for George's benefit, because he wants the work to continue. Because George's objective is to accomplish his own business purpose, the case is not within the statute of frauds, and no writing is necessary.

Contracts in Consideration of Marriage

Another area subject to fraud and abuse at common law involved promises made in consideration of marriage. The statute of frauds requires that promises to pay money or property if someone marries or promises to marry a person must be in writing to be enforceable.

While the statute of frauds does not apply to mutual promises to marry, it does apply to a promise by one party to pay another to marry either the promisor or a third party. For example, Will orally promises $5,000 to Bea if she will marry Carl, and Bea accepts the offer by marrying Carl. Bea cannot recover the $5,000 unless the contract is in writing. Marriage is not sufficient substantial performance to take the case outside the requirements of the statute of frauds under this provision.

In another example, two provisions of the statute of frauds apply: Bea promises orally to transfer title to a house to Carl if he will marry her. Carl marries Bea in reliance on Bea's promise. The promise is not enforceable. Both the provision of the statute of frauds relating to transfer of real property and the provision relating to promises in consideration of marriage would prevent enforcement of the oral contract.

Contracts to Pay Estate Debts From Executor's Funds

Oral promises to pay debts against a decedent's estate are enforceable. Such promises may be made by **executors**, who manage estates left by a will, and **administrators**, who manage estates of deceased persons who have not written a will. Most contracts an executor or administrator makes in settling an estate do not require writings. However, any promise made by an executor or administrator to pay an estate debt from his or her personal funds must be in writing to be enforceable. This rule applies only to promises to pay debts against the estate that arose during the decedent's life. Generally, an executor or administrator would have no legal obligation to pay the decedent's debts out of personal funds. Therefore, a writing is the only way to make such a binding commitment.

Executor
The person who manages an estate left by a will.

Administrator
The person who manages an estate of a deceased person who has not written a will.

For example, Paul upon his death owed Peter $2,000. Susan, executor of Paul's estate, orally promises to pay Peter the $2,000 from her funds. If Susan does not pay Peter, he cannot collect from her because such a promise must be in writing to be enforceable.

In another illustration, Paul left Peter $1,000 in his will, to be paid after all of Paul's debts and estate expenses are paid out of the estate. Susan, the executor of Paul's estate, makes an oral promise after Paul's death to personally pay Peter the $1,000 if the estate runs out of money before payment can be made. Assume that, after Susan meets all Paul's estate expenses, no money remains to pay the $1,000 to Peter. He then sues Susan under the oral promise to pay. Susan's oral promise does not fall under this provision of the statute of frauds because the statute applies only to debts the deceased incurred during his lifetime, and Paul did not owe the $1,000 in his lifetime. Based only on the statute of frauds, Susan's promise could be enforceable. However, the enforceability of Susan's contract depends on ordinary rules of contract law; and, in this case consideration is lacking.

Contracts for Sale of Personal Property for $500 or More

The UCC provides that a contract for the sale of goods for the price of $500 or more is not enforceable unless it is in writing. The $500 limit applies to the total price of all the goods the contract purports to sell. If several items, each with a value under $500 but totaling more than $500, are the subject of one contract, then the contract must be in writing. If the parties intend the items to fall under several contracts, no writing is necessary as long as the price or value of the goods does not exceed $500 in any one of the contracts.

Today in most states, the UCC provides that a required contract writing need not set forth all the material terms of the contract. Terms can be omitted or incorrectly stated. The only necessary term is that relating to the quantity of goods for sale. Even if that term is not accurate, the contract is enforceable up to the quantity in the written contract. The plaintiff need not have signed the contract—only the defendant must have signed.

The UCC has special provisions for merchants who deal in goods of a particular kind. In the interests of furthering trade and of providing certainty in obligations between merchants, the UCC provides that one merchant can satisfy the requirement of a writing by sending a written confirmation of a transaction to another merchant within a reasonable time following an oral contract. Unless the merchant receiving the communication responds within ten days with a written notice of objection, the confirmation satisfies the requirements for a writing.[2]

The UCC provides that oral contracts for the sale of goods are enforceable in the following situations:

- The buyer accepts and receives part of the goods.
- The buyer makes part or full payment for the goods.

Each of these conditions reflects the parties' acknowledgment that a contract does exist. Therefore, written evidence of a contract is not necessary. Part performance, either by acceptance of goods or payment of a portion of the price, is effective to bind the parties only to the extent to which the buyer has actually accepted or paid for the goods.[3]

Still another situation in which an oral contract for the sale of goods can be enforceable involves goods manufactured specifically for the buyer. Under the UCC, an oral contract is enforceable in the following two situations[4]:

1. The goods are not suitable for resale to others in the ordinary course of business.
2. The seller either has made a substantial beginning in manufacturing the goods or has made commitments to procure them.

The seller, of course, must establish the contract's terms as part of the proof of claim.

Some UCC provisions relate to intangible personal property, property that is not physical but the right to which is created by law. Examples of intangible property rights are claims arising out of contracts or out of ownership of bonds or rights to patents or copyrights.

Tangible property can be physically possessed. Intangible property rights can be enforced only by a legal action. A promissory note, for instance, is not the underlying debt but merely evidence of a debt. The destruction of the note does not destroy the debt; however, a claimant must prove the existence of the debt by other legally acceptable means.

The UCC requires writings for the enforceability of all sales of investment securities, such as stocks and bonds.[5] It also requires writings in credit sales or secured loans that provide special protection for sellers or lenders.[6] Oral contracts in both cases are not enforceable, regardless of amount. Therefore, a contract to sell a share of stock for $10 must be in a writing to be enforceable under the UCC.

A special UCC section covers other types of obligations. Sales of contract or royalty rights, notes, insurance policies, and similar intangibles exceeding $5,000 are not enforceable unless written evidence of a sales contract exists.[7] Although oral assignments of such contracts are enforceable if the amount is below $5,000, the difficulties of proof make a written contract, signed by the party against whom enforcement is sought, desirable.

Form Required

The writing required as evidence of a contract under the statute of frauds may be a simple note or memorandum. No formal written contract is necessary. The writing can be in any form and can consist of several communications, so long as it provides evidence of the contract's existence.

A written memorandum created by the parties sometime after the original negotiations can be sufficient to satisfy the statute's requirement, even if the writing appears to avoid the original contract. For example, Millie agrees orally to sell her condo to Tina but later writes a letter to Tina stating, "I don't want to honor my contract to sell the condo to you for $250,000," signed "Millie." The letter makes the original oral contract enforceable against Millie because it reflects the essential elements of the contract, including the parties, subject matter, and price, a sufficient writing to satisfy the requirements of the statute of frauds.

The statute of frauds requires that the writings be signed by parties against whom contracts are to be enforced. Signings can consist of signatures, initials, typewritten names, electronic signatures, or any marks that appropriately identify the parties acknowledging the memorandum or communication as their writings. Similarly, signatures, in any of those forms, of representatives who have authority to execute such contracts for others will satisfy the statute's requirement of signed writings. An example would be a producer with authority to sign on an insurance agency's behalf.

Insurance Contracts

Oral insurance policies are valid and enforceable. The customary statute of frauds provisions do not apply to insurance policies. While it is desirable that insurance policies be in writing, the hardship of enforcing this requirement would fall upon insureds, and courts therefore do not require written contracts.

A few states have specific laws requiring that fire or life insurance policies must be in writing, but most jurisdictions hold oral insurance contracts valid and enforceable. Oral contracts are common in fire and casualty insurance. For example, Joe calls his insurance agent requesting homeowners insurance for his new home. The agent responds, "Fine. You're covered." Joe has coverage immediately, even without a written policy. In life and health insurance, oral contracts are not common, but temporary written receipts provide evidence of interim coverage. An agent cannot initiate life insurance coverage orally. In virtually all insurance policies, the contract eventually becomes a written policy, which generally stands by itself as the best evidence of the contract between insurer and insured.

An assignment is a transfer of rights or property. To the extent the law permits, any assignment to another person of an insurance policy or of rights under the policy for an amount over $5,000 must be in writing and must bear the signature of the party obligated on the policy.

Of the six situations to which the statute of frauds applies, courts have considered applying only the following two situations to insurance contracts:

1. Policies that are contracts that cannot be performed within one year
2. Policies that are promises to answer for another's debt

Performance Within a Year

Courts have held generally that the statute of frauds provision requiring a writing for contracts that cannot be performed within a year is never applicable to insurance contracts. An oral contract of fire insurance for a three-year term would be enforceable because the contractual performance can occur at any time an insured suffers a loss. Courts interpret this provision of the statute of frauds strictly, and the possibility of performance within one year takes such policies outside the statute of frauds.

When an insurance broker enters into an agreement with a property owner to procure yearly renewals of insurance on property for a definite future period beyond one year, a contract to procure insurance exists. Such an agreement would not be enforceable unless it is in writing because the agreement cannot be performed within a year and because it involves an agreement to procure insurance rather than an agreement to insure. Some courts hold in this situation that an oral agreement in which the insured has reserved the right to terminate the agreement with the broker would be enforceable. In the view of some courts, the insured's option to terminate would take the agreement outside the one-year provision.

Another's Debt

The statute of frauds provision requiring a written memorandum of an agreement by one party to answer for another party's debt does not apply to insurance contracts. Such an agreement is a three-party relationship in which one party guarantees payment of another's debt to a third party. For example, Joe promises Lois to pay for Dan's debt if Dan does not pay his own debt. The reason a writing is necessary is to protect Joe from fraud by someone falsely asserting Joe's obligation to pay and from enforcement to pay an obligation he did not assume.

In the past, private sureties guaranteed payment and performance to third parties on behalf of others, playing roles similar to Joe's in the example. When professional surety companies replaced private sureties, the legal assumption was that the statute of frauds might apply to their contracts. Today, however, courts view these agreements not as contracts to perform an original debtor's obligation, but as contracts to indemnify a creditor against loss or damage as the result of a debtor's default or nonperformance. Therefore, oral surety contracts are not subject to the statute of frauds provision requiring written evidence of a contract to pay another's debt.

PAROL EVIDENCE RULE

The **parol evidence rule** limits the terms of a contract to those expressed in writing. The rule is based on the assumption that all prior negotiations, conversations, and agreements were merged into the final, written contract, which then becomes the complete statement of the parties' agreement. Once the parties have reduced any agreement to writing, no oral evidence may be admitted to contradict its terms. Words spoken by the parties before or at the time of contracting, and letters or memoranda they might have prepared before the drafting of the final contract, cannot alter the written words of the contract. The written contract is the only admissible evidence of the agreement.

Parol evidence rule
A rule of evidence that limits the terms of a contract to those expressed in writing.

The parol evidence rule applies to all written documents. In addition to ordinary contracts, it applies to such writings as deeds, wills, leases, insurance policies, releases, and similar legal instruments. The three purposes of the rule are as follows:

1. To carry out the parties' presumed intention
2. To achieve certainty and finality as to the parties' rights and duties
3. To exclude fraudulent and perjured claims

For example, Roy sells a car to Steve and orally warrants during their dealings that the car will develop no mechanical defects within six months of the sale date. The parties then sign a written agreement of sale, but the writing contains no warranty. Steve may not introduce evidence later to prove the oral warranty. A court would assume that the parties have merged all negotiations into the written contract and would exclude evidence of the oral warranty under the parol evidence rule.

In another example, Roy sells a boat to Steve. The bill of sale indicates the boat's price, make, model, and year. Steve later claims in a lawsuit that Roy had promised to include other items, such as communications equipment, in the sale. Steve attempts to support his claim in court with a letter Roy wrote and signed before the date of the final bill of sale, in which he promised to include the claimed items. Under the parol evidence rule the contract will not admit the letter into evidence because its terms were not part of the final contract, the bill of sale.

A contract can consist of a series of letters or other documents. The possibility that several documents can constitute a contract can give rise to uncertainty concerning the contractual terms. Parties to a contract can avoid such uncertainty by including the entire agreement in the final contract and not relying on other documents or conversations.

The parol evidence rule applies only to prior or contemporaneous statements and not to oral or written agreements the parties make subsequent to the written contract. Evidence of subsequent agreements is admissible to show that, after entering into the written agreement, the parties agreed to modify or cancel their written contract.

Exceptions to the Parol Evidence Rule

Oral evidence is always admissible to help interpret or explain a written agreement, but not to alter its terms. The parol evidence rule prohibits oral evidence only when it is for the purpose of altering the terms of an agreement. Legal decisions have established a number of exceptions to the parol evidence rule. They permit the admission of oral evidence of prior or contemporaneous agreements in the following situations:

- To prove terms of incomplete contracts
- To clarify ambiguity in a contract
- To support an allegation of fraud, accident, illegality or mistake relating to a contract
- To prove the failure of a condition precedent to a contract

The UCC also makes exceptions to the parol evidence rule.

Incomplete Contracts

When an essential contract term is missing, parol evidence is admissible in court to prove that term. For example, Sharon has orally agreed to sell her city condominium and her beach house to Tom for $350,000 each, and they agree that they will execute a written agreement to that effect. Sharon prepares the agreement of sale for $700,000, which she and Tom both sign, but which does not refer to the beach house. In an action to reform the contract, Tom can show that the contract was incomplete by introducing evidence of their oral agreement regarding both the condominium and the beach house.

Ambiguity

If the written contract contains ambiguous language, oral evidence is admissible to clarify the parties' intent. For example, when Isabel provides in her will for payment of money "to my nephew, Bill," and Isabel has two nephews named Bill, after Isabel's death parol evidence can be admitted to determine which nephew Isabel intended to receive the money. The testimony does not change Isabel's wording or intent but establishes her true intent.

When an insurance policy is ambiguous, such as when the policy says it covers "property of the Smith sisters," parol evidence can establish whether the parties' intention was to cover property the sisters' owned as partners, property the sisters owned individually, or both.

Fraud, Accident, Illegality, or Mistake

When fraud or illegality taints a transaction, oral evidence can be admitted to support an allegation of wrongdoing. If, for example, one of the parties intentionally substituted the wrong document for the other party's signature, oral testimony is allowed to prove fraudulent conduct. Similarly, if a sale of guns occurs under illegal circumstances, oral testimony can prove the illegality even though the writing itself does not reflect it. If, by accident or mistake, a copy of a contract is not a true copy, the parties can show the mistake using oral evidence. The parties' oral testimony also can show mistakes resulting from the writing process, such as typographical errors.

Condition Precedent

Parol evidence is admissible to show that a written document that appears to be a contract never became a contract because of failure of some condition precedent to the agreement. A condition precedent is an event that must occur before a duty of performance arises. For example, if delivery is a condition required before performance, oral evidence can be used to show that delivery did not occur. When one party has delivered the contract to the other with the understanding that it is not to take effect until certain conditions have been met, parol evidence can prove the conditions did not occur. As with other exceptions to the parol evidence rule, the oral evidence does not vary the parties' written agreement. The objective is to show the parties' true intent.

To illustrate further, a writing provides for completion of a building by December 1. The written contract does not include the time at which work is to begin. Oral evidence can show that work was not to begin until official recording of the new owner's mortgage in the appropriate local government office. The oral evidence does not prove the agreed-on time of performance but relates to the question of whether the parties complied with a condition precedent to performance. The evidence does not vary or contradict the terms of the writing and does not violate the parol evidence rule. Oral evidence can affect a written promise when pertinent facts do not appear in the writing, and oral evidence is admissible to prove the condition.

Parol Evidence and UCC

The UCC specifically recognizes the parol evidence rule, providing that

> "Terms…set forth in a writing intended by the parties as a final expression of their agreement…may not be contradicted by evidence of any prior agreement or of a contemporaneous oral agreement…"[8]

The UCC also permits oral evidence of the following three facts to explain or supplement a written contract[9]:

1. A prior course of dealings between the parties
2. Usage of the trade
3. The course of performance

The UCC allows introduction of oral evidence of consistent additional terms unless the court finds that the parties intended the writing as a complete and exclusive statement of the terms of the agreement.[10] Again, these provisions help in ascertaining the parties' true intent. The assumption is that the parties took prior dealings and usages of the trade for granted when they formed the contract.

CONTRACT INTERPRETATION

Just as courts interpret legislative enactments and constitutions, they also interpret contracts to determine the intentions of the parties who draft them. If contract language is clear and unambiguous, it is easy to apply the parties' intent.

When the language of a contract is ambiguous or obscure, courts apply established maxims of construction to ascertain the parties' intent. Maxims of construction are not strict legal rules but are well-accepted guidelines for interpretation. They do not make a new contract or rewrite an old one. Courts apply them only to resolve doubts and ambiguities in a contract.

Application of the maxims of construction is more an art than a science. They do not point with unerring accuracy to particular interpretations. They are instead courts' customary way of attempting to interpret contracts by bringing out alternative interpretations of contractual terms.

The general standard of contract interpretation is to apply the meaning that a reasonable person familiar with the circumstances would understand the words to mean. Courts use this objective standard rather than a subjective standard based on specific parties' interpretations of contract language.

Plain Meaning

A fundamental standard of contract interpretation is that words are to be understood in their plain and usual meaning. This standard applies even though the parties who agreed to the wording might not have anticipated the consequences. A court looks at contract language within the context of the contract's subject matter, nature, objectives, and purposes.

For technical language, courts apply technical meanings, and legal terms are given their established legal meaning. In interpreting the words and conduct of the parties to a contract, a court seeks to put itself in the positions of the parties at the time they made the contract. The law of the place in which the contract was made controls the formation of the contract. For example, New Mexico law applies to a contract made in that state.

In every case, the circumstances under which the parties entered into the contract are relevant, whether the contract was oral or written. The circumstances of the agreement, the subject matter, the parties' relationship, and the subject of the agreement all can be considered in determining the meaning of the agreement and in giving effect to the parties' intent.

Although the plain meaning standard can help ascertain the intention of both parties to a contract, it might not apply when only one party's intention is unclear. For example, a life insurance applicant names his beneficiary as "my wife." At the time the insured obtained the policy, he was living with a woman who was not his legal wife because he had gone through a ceremony of marriage with her without divorcing his first wife. The plain meaning of the term "my wife" clearly conflicts with the insured's actual intention, and a court can ignore the plain meaning and apply the insured's intention.

Effectuation of Intent

A fundamental principle of contract construction is that courts apply an interpretation that best carries out (effects) the parties' intentions. To ascertain those intentions, a court reads the contract as a whole. If several writings relate to the transaction, a court considers all of them together.

Courts interpret individual clauses and specific words in relation to the main purpose of the contract. The intention expressed in the contract applies, not the subjective intention of one of the parties. If the intention appears clear from the words used, courts have no need to go further.

Courts do not attempt, under the pretext of interpretation, to make new contracts for the parties. Neither do they change written contracts to make them express intentions different from those the parties expressed in the contractual language. Courts generally take people to mean what they say. Courts do not make agreements for the parties, but they ascertain what their agreements were.

Entire and Divisible Contracts

In an entire contract, one party must complete performance to be entitled to the other party's performance. For instance, unless a contract provides other- wise, delivery of goods is necessary before payment. In contrast, in a divisible contract, the performance of a portion of the contract entitles the performing party to immediate payment.

A contract providing for the delivery of goods in installments usually states the price for each installment upon delivery, and payment for each installment is due upon delivery. Similarly, in most employment contracts courts permit an employee to sue for compensation for the period of service rendered on the theory that these contracts are divisible. Therefore, employees who sign contracts are entitled to payment before the end of the contract.

A contract is divisible if each party's performance can be divided into two or more parts and if it appears that the parties to the contract contemplated separate compensation for each installment of the performance. Failure to perform one installment is not failure to perform the entire agreement. If, however, the division of the contract into parts is only to provide periodic payments applicable toward the amount due upon contract completion, the contract is entire and not divisible.

Courts prefer to interpret contracts as divisible when possible to avoid hardships that can result from delaying payments under the contract until full performance is completed.

The UCC provides that a sales contract is entire unless the parties have agreed otherwise. Therefore, all of the goods a contract calls for must arrive in a single delivery, and payment in full is due upon that delivery.[11] If the contract permits installment deliveries, the seller can demand a proportionate share of the price as each delivery occurs, provided the price can be apportioned, as when goods cost a certain price per item. If a substantial default occurs on an installment, such as delivery of nonconforming goods, the buyer can reject the installment.[12]

When a seller cannot cure an installment breach, or if the seller will not give adequate assurance that the breach will be cured, the buyer can rescind the entire contract. If the buyer accepts a nonconforming installment without giving notice of cancellation or without demanding that the seller deliver conforming goods, the breach cannot be a basis for rescission, and the contract stands.[13]

Clerical Errors and Omissions

Courts correct obvious clerical errors or mistakes in writing and grammar in contracts. They may transpose, reject, or supply words, if necessary, to clarify language to reflect the parties' intent, unless the error or omission makes it impossible to determine the parties' intent.

Courts consider some contractual terms implied if needed to carry out the parties' intent. The unexpressed or implied obligations in these instances are those the court believes to be inherent in the transaction. The parties must abide not only by what they expressly intended, but also by intentions the court presumes the parties would have had if they had given more thought to the matter. For example, courts generally presume that payment under a contract is not to be in foreign currency or in some substitute for money. In service contracts, courts find the implication that the parties will render the service with reasonable care and skill. If the parties have not specified the time of performance, it must occur within a reasonable time. If it is customary in the trade to extend credit, a court will read that trade practice into the contract. Therefore, the parties need not have set forth every contractual provision.

The UCC restates and expands the rule of what must be included in binding contracts for the sale of goods. The UCC provides that, "even though one or more terms are left open a contract for sale does not fail for indefiniteness if the parties have intended to make a contract and there is a reasonably certain basis for giving an appropriate remedy."[14] Therefore, in contracts for the sale of goods, if the parties fail to state a price for the goods, a court will assume that the contract implies a reasonable price.[15] If the parties do not mention a time for performance, it is to occur within a reasonable time.[16] In both of these cases, a reasonably certain basis for affording a remedy exists.

If the parties have failed to specify the quantity of goods, the courts are reluctant to speak for the parties concerning the amount intended. A court probably will find such a contract invalid because of indefiniteness. If a buyer has agreed to purchase all the goods the buyer requires from the seller in a requirements contract, or to sell all output to the other party in an output contract, the UCC considers these provisions to imply "such actual output or requirements as may occur in good faith…."[17] In interpreting those types of contracts a court determines whether the output tendered or requirements demanded were in good faith or whether they were "unreasonably disproportionate to any stated estimate or…to any normal or…comparable prior output or requirements…."[18] Strictly speaking, output and requirements contracts do not have indefinite duration. They are indefinite only as to quantity at the time the parties agree, but actual events make the quantities definite as output or requirements become known.

Contradictory Terms

If clauses in a contract conflict but can be interpreted in a way that makes them effective, a court will adopt that interpretation. When the parties have made typewritten or handwritten changes in a printed contract form, the courts apply the following system of priorities:

- Handwriting prevails over typewriting.
- Typewriting prevails over printing.
- Words prevail over figures.

This is a common-sense approach because parties usually make handwritten changes last. If a writing is printed, it is safe to assume that any typing on the document occurred later. Words written on a check, for example, prevail over figures.

In interpreting conflicting language, the courts give preference to acts that require greater attention to detail and effort. The result presumably reflects the party's intent most accurately.

Ambiguity

Ambiguity is the capability of being understood in two or more ways, or the uncertainty of meaning. In contract law, ambiguity appears in the following two different forms:

1. A contractual provision can be reasonably interpreted in more than one way.
2. The meaning of a provision cannot be determined even by application of all the tools of interpretation.

If a provision can have more than one reasonable meaning, the courts adopt the interpretation least favorable to the party who put the provision into the contract and most favorable for the party who assented to it. For example, a court interprets an insurance policy against the insurer that created it. Similarly, courts interpret words in offers against the offerors and words in acceptances against the acceptors. They interpret words in loan instruments against the lenders and words in property sales against the sellers. The principle for this rule is that people are responsible for ambiguities in their own expressions. If they initiate expressions and have the power to phrase them as they please, they cannot expect courts to interpret ambiguities in their favor.

If a provision is so ambiguous that its meaning cannot be determined with the usual tools of interpretation, the court can admit evidence from outside the contract. For example, a court will permit evidence of prior or contemporaneous agreements to shed light on the meaning of the ambiguous language.

The parol evidence rule does not apply to the introduction of evidence to explain ambiguities. The purpose of this evidence is to clarify what the parties intended the final contract to mean. Evidence to clarify ambiguities explains but does not contradict. Therefore, evidence of the course of performance under the contract, of the parties' prior course of dealings, or of the usages of trade, is all admissible to assist the court in determining contractual meaning.

Parties' Own Interpretation

The interpretation that the parties have placed on their contract, as shown by their subsequent conduct, has great weight for determining the meaning of doubtful terms. The parties know best what they meant by their words, and their actions under the agreement are some of the best indications of what they meant.

A contract for the sale of goods may involve repeated occasions for a party's performance along with the other party's knowledge of the nature of the performance and opportunity to object to it. The second party's acceptance or acquiescence concerning the performance can help determine the contract's meaning.[19] The UCC thus recognizes that the parties' actions are strong evidence of their intentions.

However, if a court finds no ambiguity in the contract, and the meaning of its terms is clear, the parties' subsequent conduct placing an unreasonable and erroneous interpretation upon the contract does not prevent a court from enforcing it according to the contractual terms. A court will not remake the contract for parties that have acted contrary to its provisions.

Legal and Fair Interpretations

If both a legal and an illegal contractual interpretation are possible, the courts assume that the parties intended the legal interpretation. If the court has a choice, it will interpret a contract as reasonable and fair rather than unreasonable and harsh to one of the parties. Under that approach, courts adopt interpretations that avoid forfeitures of property when possible. If the terms of the contract itself leave its meaning in doubt, courts attribute to the parties the intent to enter into a fair agreement and therefore interpret the contract equitably.

The UCC "unconscionable contract or clause" section enunciates this approach. That section, applying to the sale of goods, provides that a court may find all or any part of a contract "unconscionable" and either can refuse to enforce it at all or can apply it in a way that avoids "any unconscionable result."[20] This approach transcends and ignores interpretation and means that a harsh and one-sided sale of goods contract is not enforceable. The parties' intention is not material. Courts are incorporating this approach gradually into areas of law other than the sales of goods.

Trade Usage, Course of Dealings, and Performance

As discussed, courts in interpreting contract language give common words their ordinary meanings and technical terms their technical meanings; and they consider local, cultural, and trade usage meanings. In attempting to establish the parties' intent, courts also consider their prior course of dealings and their course of performance under the contract. The UCC, recognizing that these considerations can make interpretation difficult, attempts to define and distinguish "trade usage," "course of dealings," and "course of performance" and establishes an order of priority among the three concepts to resolve conflicts among them.

The UCC defines "trade usage" as "…any practice or method of dealing having such regularity of observance in a place, vocation or trade as to justify an expectation that it will be observed with respect to the transaction in question."[21] Mercantile law has used this standard for centuries, and it differs from the common-law "custom" applied in nonmercantile cases, which generally required universal observance from the beginning.

A course of dealings relates to similar transactions between the parties before the contract in question. Course of performance involves the actual performance of the contract that has occurred without either party's objection.

The UCC has established the following priorities to use when these four considerations are in conflict:[22]

1. Express terms of the contract
2. Course of performance
3. Course of dealings
4. Trade usage

If a court seeks to determine the parties' intent not clearly expressed in the terms of the agreement, the parties' prior course of dealings has preference over usage of the trade to establish the meaning of the contract. Courts admit evidence on these questions.

THIRD-PARTY RIGHTS

The general rule of contract law is that only the parties to a contract have rights under that contract. Although a third party might expect to benefit under another's contract, the third party ordinarily does not have any rights. However, in the following two situations, third parties do have rights enforceable under contracts others have made:

1. An assignment of a contract, by which one party transfers rights arising under a contract to a third party
2. Third-party beneficiary contracts, in which one party contracts with another party to confer a benefit on a third party

Contract Assignments

Assignment
The transfer of rights or property.

An **assignment** is the transfer of rights or property. Assignment of contracts is common. Contractual assignments involve transfers of contractual performance rights to other people. Creditors often assign the right to receive money from debtors to third parties, such as banks. The party to the contract who makes the assignment is the **assignor**, and the party to whom the assignment is made is the **assignee**. If the nonassigning party does not honor the assignment, the assignee may sue the nonassigning party just as though the assignee were a party to the original contract.

Assignor
The party to a contract who makes an assignment.

Assignee
The party to a contract to whom an assignment is made.

Rights Assignable

Most contract rights are assignable. Therefore, a seller can assign the right to receive payment for the sale of goods to a third person (the assignee). The party owing the obligation to pay for the goods, the obligor, then must pay the assignee. Ordinarily, any right to collect a debt is assignable because it is usually no more difficult for a debtor (obligor), to pay the assignee the amount owed than it would have been to pay the original creditor (assignor).

Rights Not Assignable

Notwithstanding the general rule that contract rights are assignable, certain contractual rights are not assignable without the obligor's consent. The following are the most common situations in which contract rights are not assignable:

- *Legal restrictions.* A statute may prohibit assignment of specified contract rights. Laws restrict prior assignment of such rights as veterans' disability benefits, government pensions, wages, inheritances, and workers' compensation benefits.

- *Contract restrictions.* The parties to an agreement might specify that they cannot, under the contract, assign the rights. These agreements are valid and enforceable. Therefore, the standard fire insurance policy prohibits insureds from assigning it to new owners of the insured property without the insurer's consent. The insurer would have no obligation to a new owner of the property in the event of loss, even if the seller had attempted to assign the policy to the buyer.

- *Personal contracts.* Personal rights and personal duties are not assignable. For example, a lawyer who promises to provide services, such as representation in court, cannot validly delegate those personal duties to another. Personal service contracts require actual performance by the person who contracted. Courts do not enforce attempts to shift that performance to a third party unless the original parties to the contract have agreed to the change.

- *Alteration of performance.* When the assignment materially alters or varies the obligor's performance, a court usually will not uphold it. For example, if Bob contracts to deliver oil to Nancy's house, Nancy cannot assign the right to receive oil delivery to Dan, who lives in a distant location. The assignment would materially alter Bob's performance.

- *Personal satisfaction contracts.* When the contract provides that the goods or services are to be satisfactory to the purchaser, the purchaser's judgment is a requirement of the contract. The buyer cannot substitute a third-party assignee's judgment.

- *Damages for personal injury.* When a judgment is pending in a personal injury case, the general rule is that the injured person cannot assign a claim against another for damages resulting from the injury. A final judgment, however, is assignable. The right to sue for damages for property loss or damage is assignable. For example, a property owner receives an insurance payment to cover the damage to property caused by vandals. The owner can assign the right to sue the vandals to the insurer that paid for the damage. These assignments involve the right of subrogation, which enables the insurer to "stand in the shoes" of the insured to obtain damages.

Assignment and the UCC

The UCC permits either party to a sale of goods contract to delegate contract duties (1) unless the parties have agreed otherwise or (2) when the nondelegating party has a substantial interest in having the "original promisor perform or control the acts required by the contract."[23] Therefore, a seller usually can delegate the duty to perform obligations under the contract to someone else.

The UCC also prohibits assignment of rights "where the assignment would materially change the duty of the other (nonassigning) party, or increase materially the burden or risk imposed on him by his contract, or impair materially the chance of obtaining a return performance."[24] Under the UCC, "unless the circumstances indicate the contrary," a contract provision prohibiting assignment restricts only the delegation of duties and does not prohibit the assignment of rights.[25]

Forms of Assignment

To be effective, an assignment needs neither formality nor writing. Any words or conduct that indicate the assignor's intention to transfer contractual rights effects a valid assignment. Assignments are transfers and need not be contracts. Therefore, assignments made as gifts are nevertheless enforceable against the obligor.

However, an assignment involving subject matter covered by a statute of frauds, such as an assignment of rights under a land sale contract, must be in writing to be enforceable. Statutes of frauds in all states require that transfers of interests in land be in writing.

Consideration

Although an assignment is a transfer and not a contract, a *promise* to make an assignment is enforceable only if it is a valid contract. Therefore, if Al (assignor) promises to assign a contract right to Bob (assignee), all of the elements of a valid contract, including consideration, must be present for Bob to enforce Al's promise.

If Al makes the assignment as a gift, Bob can enforce the assigned contract right against a party to the contract who has a contractual obligation even though Bob has given no consideration to Al for the assignment. This result is consistent with the general law of gifts, which does not require consideration. A promise to give a gift is not enforceable; but, once the gift is delivered, it is legally effective and irreversible. An assignor who has not received consideration for a gift from an assignee can rescind the assignment at any time before the obligor has performed the contract without liability to the assignee. In the example just discussed, Al can rescind his assignment of contract rights to Bob at any time until the contract is performed.

Assignee's Rights

As a general rule, the assignee's rights do not exceed the assignor's. The legal principle applicable here is that the assignee's rights can rise no higher than the assignor's. If, for example, a party assigns contract rights to an assignee, but a third party to the contract has a defense against the assignor, the third party can assert that same defense against the assignee. For example, if the assignor obtained the original contract through fraud or duress, this defense can be valid against the assignee. To illustrate, Cathy defrauded Anne in forming a contract for Anne's consulting services. Cathy (assignor) assigns her contract rights for Anne's services to Laura (assignee). If Laura attempts to enforce the contract against Anne for her consulting services, Anne can refuse to perform for Laura, basing her defense on Cathy's fraud.

Many consumer sales contracts provide that, if the seller assigns the contract, usually to a finance company or bank, the buyer agrees not to assert any defenses against the assignee that might be valid against the seller-assignor. Adding such provisions to a sales contract makes the contract more marketable because it places the assignee in a favored position. For the most part, however, people who receive assignments of sales contracts accept them subject to any defenses good against the assignor.

Assignee's Duties

Although the assignee usually obtains rights under an assignment, the assignment also may impose duties. The assignor who undertook performance is not relieved of those duties simply by delegating them to the assignee. A primary obligation to perform usually remains with the assignor. If the assignee fails to perform according to the original contractual terms, the assignor must perform. The assignor has a right to sue the assignee for failure to perform. Whether the assignee is also liable to the nonassigning party for the faulty performance is a question that a court can determine only by examination of the entire transaction.

In general, if a party assigns rights and delegates obligations to the assignee, the third party can enforce against either the assignee or the assignor, but not against both of them. For example, in construction contracts, the prime contractor typically delegates performance of all or a portion of the construction to subcontractors. Delegation of such duties is usually routine, and the other parties to the contract expect that subcontractors will be involved. If a subcontractor fails to perform properly, either the assignor or the third party (obligee) can sue the assignee (subcontractor). If, however, there was an attempt to assign a nondelegable duty, as in personal service contracts, the assignor alone remains liable for faulty or improper performance unless the other party (obligee) has agreed to accept the assignee's performance.

Under the UCC, an assignment general in its terms, such as "all my rights under the contract," is both an assignment of rights and a delegation of obligations under the agreement. The assumption is, absent an indication to the contrary, that the assignee promised to perform the contract obligations. Either the assignor or the nonassigning party can enforce the promise.[26]

Notice of Assignment

A valid assignment is effective immediately, even though the assignor has not yet advised the obligor of the assignment. The assignee should nevertheless notify the obligor of the assignment to ensure that the obligor pays the assignee rather than the assignor, thus defeating the original assignor's right to demand the obligor's payment or performance. In such a case, the assignee might have a right to sue the assignor for refusal to, in turn, pay the assignee.

An assignee's notice of assignment to the obligor on the contract also protects additional parties who might take subsequent assignments from the assignors. An assignor would not have the right to make a second assignment but would have the power or ability to do so, and the original obligor might pay the second assignee. To illustrate, John (assignor) assigns his contractual rights with George (obligor) to Dennis (assignee). Subsequently, John assigns the same contractual rights to Howard (a second assignee). If Dennis has not given George notice of his own (first) assignment, George has no reason to know about it and might pay Howard (second assignee) instead. Therefore, it would have been to Dennis's benefit to have let George know of the first assignment at the outset.

Which of the two assignees has superior rights against the obligor depends on which of the following three principles is applied:

1. At common law, once rights had been assigned, a second assignment was impossible because the assignor had nothing left to assign. The second assignee merely had a cause of action against the assignor.
2. Some courts hold that the first assignee to notify the obligor of the assignment has superior rights, and the tardy assignee merely has rights against the assignor.
3. Other courts hold that the first assignee has superior rights regardless of notice unless the second assignee receives payment from or a judgment against the obligor and has no knowledge or notice of the prior assignment.

If the obligor has received notice from both assignees or notice from one assignee and a demand for payment from the other, the obligor should sue both assignees as defendants, pay the money into court, and have the court determine which assignee has a right to payment. Otherwise, if the obligor pays one or the other assignee, it is still possible that the wrong party is receiving payment. To illustrate, Jim owns a building extensively damaged by fire and hires a general contractor to repair the building. G.C., the general contractor, assigns his right to Jim's payment to the drywall contractor. G.C. also assigns his right to Jim's payment to the roofing contractor, without telling the roofer that he has already assigned the same rights to the drywall contractor. When payment time comes, Jim's insurer receives payment demands from both the drywall and the roofing contractors. Lacking enough money in the settlement to satisfy both contractors, the insurer would ask the court to distribute the available funds as fairly as possible.

Third-Party Beneficiaries

At common law, only the parties to a contract could enforce it. Those parties were those who gave or received consideration or those who were in privity, the direct contractual relationship. Today, third parties that benefit from contracts may have enforceable rights under those contracts.

Types of Beneficiaries

Third-party beneficiary contracts are contracts between two parties that benefit third parties, either directly or indirectly. Third-party beneficiaries include the following types:

- Creditor beneficiaries
- Donee beneficiaries
- Incidental beneficiaries

Donee and creditor beneficiaries have enforceable rights against the original promisor, but an incidental beneficiary has no enforceable rights.

A **creditor beneficiary** is a third-party beneficiary owed a debt that is to be satisfied by performance of the contract. For example, Henry owes Chuck $500. Henry sells his car to Jeremy for $1,000. Henry receives $500 in cash and Jeremy's promise to pay $500 to Chuck to discharge Henry's debt to Chuck. If Chuck does not receive payment, he has two possible remedies:

1. To proceed as a creditor beneficiary against Jeremy
2. To proceed against Henry under the original $500 debt

If Henry's intent in obtaining the promise from Jeremy was to discharge his obligation to Chuck, the third party (Chuck) is a creditor beneficiary. It is the promisee's intent as the party obtaining the promise that governs these situations. The promisor's or the third-party beneficiary's intent is not the decisive factor.

A **donee beneficiary** is a third party beneficiary who receives the benefit of the contract's performance as a gift from the promisee, with the intent of the contracting parties. To illustrate, Henry wishes to make a $500 gift to Chuck. Henry sells his car to Jeremy for $500 and obtains Jeremy's promise to pay Chuck the $500 price for the car. Chuck is a donee beneficiary of Jeremy's promise for $500, and Chuck can sue Jeremy for $500.

An **incidental beneficiary** has no contractual rights but benefits from a contract even though that is not the intent of the parties to the contract. For example, Middletown contracts with Water Company to maintain sufficient water pressure at Middletown's hydrants for fire protection. A Middletown citizen's house burns down because of insufficient water pressure. The citizen is an incidental beneficiary and has no enforceable rights under the contract. Any duty to the citizen is, at best, indirect.

The legal distinction between creditor and donee beneficiary contracts is becoming less important. They are often treated as one class, **intended beneficiaries**, who are third-party beneficiaries to whom a benefit was

Third-party beneficiary contract
A contract between two parties that benefits a third party.

Creditor beneficiary
A third-party beneficiary owed a debt that is to be satisfied by performance of a contract.

Donee beneficiary
A third-party beneficiary who receives the benefit of a contract's performance as a gift from the promisee, with the intent of the contracting parties.

Incidental beneficiary
A third-party beneficiary who has no contractual rights but benefits from a contract even though that is not the intent of the parties to the contract.

Intended beneficiary
A third-party beneficiary to whom a benefit was intended by the contracting parties.

intended by the contracting parties. For instance, Chuck contracts to purchase land from Jeremy, breaches the contract, and forfeits a deposit to Jeremy. Helen wants to buy the land, but finds out about Chuck's forfeited deposit. She does not know Chuck but believes that Jeremy should not keep Chuck's deposit. She agrees to purchase the land only if Jeremy promises to repay Chuck's deposit. Jeremy agrees. Helen intended to benefit Chuck, and, regardless of her motive, Chuck is an intended beneficiary with a right to obtain the forfeited deposit from Jeremy in some jurisdictions.

When a person claims beneficiary status, the court must decide whether the contracting parties intended to confer a benefit upon that person. Unless the claimant can show a direct interest in the performance of the contract about which the contracting parties are aware, the third party is an incidental beneficiary only.

Characteristics of Beneficiary Contracts

Exhibit 4-1 shows the relationship between the parties to a beneficiary contract. The rules applicable to a third-party beneficiary contract are as follows:

- A binding contract must exist between the promisor and promisee.

- The parties to the contract must intend that the third party receive benefits and acquire rights under the contract. If the intent is to discharge an existing obligation, the contract is a creditor beneficiary contract. If the promisee's intent is to make a gift to a third party, the contract is a donee beneficiary contract. Some courts have held that the promisee must have the intention only to benefit the third party.

- The parties must take care in each case to clarify to whom the performance is due. If the parties owe performance to a third party, the third party can sue to enforce it. If, however, performance is due to the promisee only, only the promisee can sue and a third party has no rights against the promisor.

- The beneficiary is always subject to defenses the promisor might have against the promisee, including the usual defenses in contract actions, such as lack of consideration, illegality, and fraud.

Beneficiaries' Rights

In general, a beneficiary under a contract, whether creditor, donee, or intended (but not incidental), can enforce the contract. Suppose, however, that the original parties—the promisor and the promisee—agree to annul or change the contract and to eliminate or reduce the beneficiary's rights.

Parties may agree in a contract either to retain or not to retain the right to eliminate or modify the promisor's duty to the third-party beneficiary. The modern legal trend is to permit the original parties in all cases to cut off the beneficiaries' rights unless the beneficiaries can prove that their positions have changed materially in reasonable reliance on the contracts.

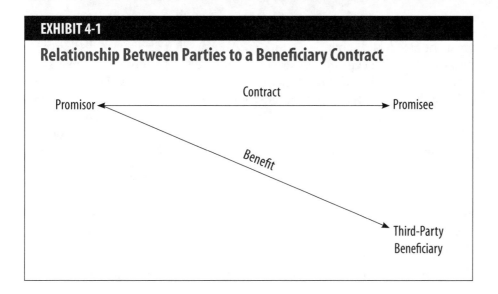

EXHIBIT 4-1

Relationship Between Parties to a Beneficiary Contract

DISCHARGE OF CONTRACTS

The end of contract obligations discharges a contract, terminating the parties' contractual duties. Parties can discharge their contractual obligations in many ways, including the following:

- Complete performance of contractual obligations
- Agreement of the parties
- Substitution of a new contract, by waiver, novation, accord and satisfaction, or other agreements
- Impossibility of performance, such as the destruction of the contractual subject matter
- Operation of law, as by bankruptcy or a change in the law that makes performance illegal

Performance

Performance discharges most contracts. When each party fulfills all promises, no obligations remain and the contract ceases to exist. Performance under a contract can occur in a number of ways, such as the following:

- Payment
- Tender of performance
- Substantial performance
- Personal satisfaction
- Agreed time

Payment

Payment of a debt discharges a contract. An issue that arises with discharge by payment is, if a person owes several separate debts to another and makes a part payment, which debt is discharged? Generally, the debtor can specify the debt discharged, and the creditor must apply the payment as directed. If the debtor does not indicate the specific debt, the creditor can use discretion in applying the payment. The creditor might even apply the payment to a debt barred by the statute of limitations.

Tender of Performance

Tender
An offer to perform one's duties under a contract.

A **tender** is an offer to perform one's duties under a contract. Tenders fall into two categories: offers to perform a promise to perform an act and offers to perform a promise to pay.

Depending on whether a party tenders an act or a payment, the other party's rejection of that tender has different results. Rejection of a tender to perform an act discharges that obligation. Rejection of a tender of payment of a debt does not discharge the debt.

To illustrate, in a contract for the sale of goods, if the seller attempts to deliver the goods and the other party refuses delivery, the refusal discharges the seller from performance. However, refusal to accept permits the tendering party to sue for breach of contract and to defend a later action for that breach. Moreover, if the performance due is the payment of money, an offer to pay the money and a refusal to accept will not discharge the debt. A valid tender, however, stops any interest from accruing on the debt, and the most the creditor can collect is the amount due on the date of the tender. For the tender to be valid, it must include the entire amount of the debt.

Substantial Performance

Many contractual obligations are difficult to perform entirely. For example, deviations of performance can occur in a major construction contract because of weather, lack of materials, or some other difficulty as the building progresses. Rather than permit the promisee to escape liability completely on the ground of nonperformance—by refusing to pay for services, for example—courts consider whether the performance actually given was substantial performance and whether the party performed in good faith. If so, a court will permit a plaintiff to recover notwithstanding a minor deviation from contract specifications.

Courts carefully compare the nature of expected performance with actual performance and determine whether any deviation was willful. Failure to perform substantially or intentional deviations in performance probably will result in a court determination that the contractual obligations have not been discharged. If a court finds substantial performance, the party receiving performance must pay the contract price, with possible allowance for variance in the value of the performance. The important result is that the party that has substantially performed can receive the contract price minus damages for nonperformance, rather than nothing at all for failure to perform.

Personal Satisfaction

If a contract provides that the promisee must be personally satisfied, or that satisfaction is guaranteed, the promisor must satisfy the promisee's taste or personal judgment. The promisee's good faith decision controls because that was the parties' agreement.

Unless the promisor can show bad faith on the promisee's part, performance in a personal satisfaction contract is not adequate unless the promisee experiences personal and subjective satisfaction. For example, Jane, an artist, is to paint Mark's portrait to his satisfaction, Mark's good faith rejection of the portrait precludes Jane's recovery for payment. Only if Jane could show that Mark rejected the painting in bad faith could she recover payment.

Courts apply an objective standard to determine personal satisfaction relating to utility, fitness, or value. For example, if the promise is that a vehicle is to be fit for operation, fitness is determined according to what a reasonably prudent person would expect under the circumstances. If a reasonable person would be satisfied, the performance is adequate.

Agreed Time

Many contracts fail to provide the time of performance. In general, each party has a reasonable time to perform. Whether performance occurs within a reasonable time is a question for the trier of fact.

Additional problems arise when parties specify a time for performance but fail to perform by that date. For example, a contract requires delivery by November 1, but delivery occurs on November 5. Must the promisee accept the late delivery? Does the date set in the contract establish a condition that creates obligations under the contract? If it is clear that late delivery has decreased or negated the recipient's benefit, the stated delivery time is a necessary condition and the promisee need not accept delivery. If the contract expressly provides that time is of the essence, then a court will enforce that provision. Delivery on the due date is a necessary condition to recovery unless enforcement would result in an undue hardship or penalty on the promisor. If time is not of the essence, either in actuality or according to the contract terms, the promisor must complete performance within a reasonable time after the time stated. In general, failure to deliver within either a specific time or a reasonable time is a breach of contract.

Agreement of the Parties

The parties to a contract can agree in advance that a certain event will discharge their obligations to one another. For example, Arthur agrees to paint Don's house unless Don sells the house by June 1. If Don sells the house before June 1, Arthur is discharged from the obligation. The occurrence of that contractual condition, sale of the house, relieves the parties of performance.

Just as the parties can agree to form a contract, they also can agree to rescind it. Unless the original contract requires that any modification or rescission be in writing, the rescission can be oral. Even if the contract requires written rescission, an attempted oral rescission can be effective as a waiver of the writing requirement. The effectiveness of such a waiver can depend on whether the contract is for the sale of goods or for the sale of land.

In a contract for the sale of goods, a party who attempts to waive a writing requirement for rescission can retract that waiver by letting the other party know that strict contractual performance is necessary. This retraction is not effective, however, if the other party has changed position materially in reliance on the waiver.[27]

A rescission of a contract for the sale of land, on the other hand, usually must be in writing because the original sale agreement resulted in a transfer of the equitable ownership of the land to the buyer. An equitable (or beneficial) owner is a person (e.g., land buyer) recognized in equity as the owner of something because use and less-than-legal title belong to that person, while legal title still belongs to someone else (e.g., land seller). To retransfer that equitable interest in the land to the seller, the statute of frauds requires a new writing.

Rescission is not a remedy for breach of a contract. The nonbreaching party has a right to sue for damages, but the breach has discharged the contract. A court can rescind only rights and duties the parties have not executed. The party entitled to sue, however, can waive or renounce the right to sue; in general, such a waiver or renunciation requires consideration or, in some states, a seal to be legally binding. However, in transactions covered by UCC, "Any claim or right arising out of an alleged breach can be discharged in whole or in part without consideration by a written waiver or renunciation signed and delivered by the aggrieved party."[28]

Substitution

Just as the parties can agree to rescind a contract, they can agree to substitute a new contract for a previous one. The decision to replace an old contract with a new one is subject to the same rules that apply to rescission of agreements. In addition, the UCC provides that, in sales of goods, a modification of a written contract must be in writing if the original contract is required to be in writing.[29]

Novation
An agreement to replace an original party to a contract with a new party.

A **novation** is an agreement to replace an original party to a contract with a new party. For the substitution to be effective, all parties must agree to it. The remaining party must agree to accept the new party and must release the withdrawing party. The latter must consent to withdraw and to permit substitution of the new party. The presence of these essentials discharges the withdrawing party from the contract.

To illustrate, Harvey contracts to perform cleaning services for Eileen. Later, Eileen and Harvey agree that Toby will perform Harvey's obligations, and Eileen expressly releases Harvey from the original contract. Toby's agreement to replace Harvey discharges Harvey from the contract. If Eileen does not expressly release Harvey, no novation occurs. Harvey has merely delegated performance to Toby and remains liable under the contract.

An accord and satisfaction, the substitution of a different performance for the performance required in a contract, can discharge a debt. An accord is an agreement between contracting parties that one of them is to substitute a different performance for the performance required in the contract. Completion of performance is the satisfaction. For example, if Bill owes John $200, and they agree that Bill will paint John's home in satisfaction of the debt, an accord exists. Bill's painting the home is the satisfaction that discharges the obligation because the accord and satisfaction are complete.

If Joe owes Betty $500, Betty's agreement to accept less than $500 in full payment is not binding unless Betty receives consideration for the promise to discharge Joe. However, Betty can agree to discharge the debt for a lesser sum in return for payment before the due date or in return for a lesser sum plus an item of value. The value of the additional item may or may not equal the amount of the unpaid debt. The parties have agreed to performance other than that required by the contract (accord), and performance has occurred (satisfaction).

Problems arise when a creditor accepts an early partial payment without having agreed that the early payment is consideration for discharging the entire debt. Therefore, to avoid the argument that an accord and satisfaction has occurred, parties may choose not to accept payment for less than the original debt.

Impossibility

A promisor's duty to perform is discharged if, after the contract has formed, performance becomes objectively impossible. If the objectively impossible performance was the major undertaking of the contract, both parties are discharged from all contractual duties. For example, an insurance producer has promised an applicant to place a homeowners insurance policy only with a specific insurer, but that insurer becomes insolvent. Performance is impossible, and the producer is not liable to the applicant.

The following discussion summarizes three similar terms that are often confusing—frustration, impracticability, and impossibility:

1. Frustration is the prevention or hindering of the attainment of a goal, such as contractual performance. Commercial frustration arising from some unforeseeable and uncontrollable circumstance that causes a fundamental change, at neither party's fault, can excuse a party's nonperformance.
2. Impracticability is an excuse for nonperformance of an act, especially a contractual duty the performance of which, though possible, would be extremely or unreasonably difficult.

3. Impossibility is the condition of not being able to occur, exist, or be done, excusing performance.

Impossibility may be either objective or subjective. Objective impossibility means that a promisor cannot conceivably perform. An example would be a one-of-a-kind antique that is destroyed by fire after a contract for its sale is entered. Subjective impossibility means that the promisor will not perform even though performance is conceivable. An example would be depletion of a contracted-for item that the seller could conceivably obtain elsewhere. Most courts hold that only objective impossibility excuses the promisor's performance. Subjective impossibility does not discharge the obligation, because the promisor has assumed the chance of personal inability to perform.

Causes of Impossibility

Changes in circumstances affecting contract parties and subject matter can lead to impossibility of performance. The following are several circumstances that may make performance of a contract impossible:

-   *Change in law.* If performance of a contract becomes illegal after the contractual formation because of a change in the law, or through some other governmental act, the promisor's performance is excused. To illustrate, changes in zoning ordinances or building codes can discharge a builder's duty to construct because building specifications have become illegal. Similarly, governmental embargoes on certain exports discharge contracts for exporting the goods.

-   *Death or incapacity.* The death or incapacitating illness of a specific person necessary to performance of a personal service discharges the duty to perform. For example, Bill has promised to build John's house, Bill's death or illness discharges the contract. John's death or illness has the same effect. Ordinary contracts of production and sale of property are not personal, and the death or illness of one or both parties does not affect them. The deceased's personal representatives must perform the contract.

-   *Destruction of subject matter.* If the specific subject matter of the contract is destroyed or becomes nonexistent after contract formation without the promisor's fault, impossibility of performance discharges the promisor's duty. Exhaustion of an oil well, for example, discharges a contract to furnish oil. Similarly, the destruction of an auditorium discharges a contract to use it for entertainment. In contracts for the sale of goods, discharge by impossibility occurs only if specific, identified goods are the subject matter of the agreement and if those goods are destroyed. In the absence of specific identification, the promisor is obligated to deliver identical goods from another source. Therefore, failure of a crop on a particular parcel of land discharges a contract to sell so many bushels of wheat grown on that land. However, if a contract does not identify specific land or wheat, the promisor's duty to supply wheat is not discharged even if the intent was to fill the contract from the failed crop.

- *Other party's act.* If the other party's act prevents the performance of a contract, a court will excuse performance because of impossibility. For example, if a contract requires the promisor to perform certain services on the promisee's land, and the promisee prevents entry to the land, the promisor cannot perform and a court will discharge the contract. Whether a promisor can demand the right to perform after removal of the disability depends on whether the late performance has materially affected the party who prevented the performance. If late performance is material, a court will discharge the contract.

Temporary and Partial Impossibility and Partial Performance

Impossibility may affect less than the entire performance of a contract. It may be temporary or partial, or it may arise after the contract has been partially performed. Temporary impossibility suspends, but does not discharge, the promisor's duty. After the impossibility has ended, the duty to perform renews. To illustrate, when a promisor's illness or entry into the armed services prevents performance of a service contract, the obligation of performance can arise again when the promisor has recovered or has been discharged from military service.

If performance is only partially impossible, a court will excuse the duty to perform only to the extent that it is impossible. The promisor must perform the balance of the duty regardless of added expense or difficulty. For example, Bill contracts to build a house and to use a certain kind of pipe for the plumbing. That this kind of pipe is no longer available discharges only the use of that pipe and not the entire contract. Bill must build the house and substitute pipe of similar quality.

Impossibility of performance often becomes apparent only after partial performance. The performing party is entitled to payment for reasonable value of all the work performed and other expenses. For example, a painter who has put one of two coats of paint on a house that is then destroyed by fire may recover the reasonable value of the service.

A mere additional burden does not constitute legal impossibility. The destruction of a partially completed building, for example, does not make performance impossible. Performance still is possible by starting construction anew, although the cost is greater than anticipated, and the owner must bear the additional cost.

Frustration of Purpose

Frustration of purpose can discharge a contract that is possible to perform, when a supervening event destroys the purpose or value of the contract. To illustrate, Richard's house is on a street where a parade is to pass. Richard rents a room to Ashley for the day so that she can view the parade. The parade route does not pass Richard's house, and the frustration of purpose excuses Ashley's performance of the contract.

Commercial Impracticability

The UCC has several provisions relating to commercial impracticability. The standards for impracticability are commercial, compared with actual, impossibility. For instance, impossibility to perform a contract because of a wartime shipping stoppage is a hazard a shipper assumes because the parties made the contract on the eve of a war at a time when a shipping stoppage was foreseeable.[30] On the other hand, a drastic increase in shipping costs might make shipment impracticable but not impossible. The question of impracticability, therefore, is a factual issue to be decided in each case.

The UCC excuses both delay in delivery and failure to deliver goods "…if performance as agreed has been made impracticable by the occurrence of a contingency, the nonoccurrence of which was a basic assumption on which the contract was made, or by compliance in good faith with any applicable foreign or domestic governmental regulation or order whether or not it later proves to be invalid."[31] However, the seller must allocate production and delivery of available quantities among the buyers and must give the buyer reasonable notice of the problem and information on how much, if any, of the goods the seller can deliver.[32]

The UCC expressly provides that increased cost does not constitute commercial impracticability, but that commercial impracticability can arise because of "a severe shortage of raw materials or of supplies due to a contingency such as war, embargo, local crop failure, unforeseen shutdown of major sources of supply or the like, which either causes a marked increase in cost or altogether prevents the seller from securing supplies necessary to his performance."[33] Even in these cases, however, the seller must take commercially reasonable precautions to protect the source of supply.

To refute an old rule that shipment must originate from the place and by the transportation mode the contract specifies, the UCC allows a seller to substitute the origin of shipment or the transportation mode if the contract requirements become commercially impracticable and if a "commercially reasonable substitute is available."[34]

Statutes of Limitations

Statutes of limitations prescribe time limits within which a lawsuit can be filed after a cause of action arises. If a plaintiff brings suit after the prescribed time expires, the defendant can raise that issue as a defense. A plaintiff can lose a case entirely for failure to file within the statute of limitations period. A defendant who does not assert a statute of limitations defense loses the right to use it at any future time.

The times within which actions must be initiated vary among states and types of contract. In some states, claimants may have two years to file suits on oral contracts and six years on written contracts. Another state can prescribe periods of four years for oral contracts and fifteen years for written agreements.

Fraudulent Alteration

If a party to the contract intentionally makes a material alteration to the contract, the contract is discharged. To illustrate, if the payee on a check fraudulently increases the amount payable, the material alteration discharges the liability of the check's maker to the payee.

CONDITIONS

Failure to fulfill a contract condition may alter, limit, or discharge contractual obligations. For example, if a party does not deliver goods on the specific day required by the contract, the buyer can treat the nondelivery as a breach of condition that extends the duty to pay to a later date.

Contracts contain the following three types of conditions:

1. *Condition precedent.* A **condition precedent** is an event that must occur before a duty of performance arises. Nonfulfillment of a condition precedent can discharge a contractual obligation. For example, filing a notice of loss under an insurance policy is a condition precedent to claim payment. Although it is not a promise, until the insured files a claim, the insurer has no duty to perform its contractual obligation.

2. *Condition concurrent.* A **condition concurrent** must occur or be performed at the same time as another condition. If a contract expressly or impliedly provides that both parties are to perform at the same time, the conditions are concurrent. To illustrate, a sale of goods contract includes a condition for cash payment upon delivery, a concurrent condition. If the goods are delivered and the buyer cannot pay, the seller can retain the goods because the buyer cannot perform under the contract. This condition is a promise, and the seller can sue for breach.

3. *Condition subsequent.* A **condition subsequent** is an event that, if it occurs, discharges a duty of performance. A condition subsequent is a future event that may occur after the contract becomes legally enforceable. Occurrence of a condition subsequent terminates contractual rights. For example, a store lease (the contract) in a mall provides that the mall owner is to receive a certain rent plus a percentage of the store's gross sales. If the store's sales drop below a set dollar amount per month (condition subsequent), the lease terminates at the mall's option. If the sales do not reach a set dollar amount per month within a year (condition subsequent), the lease terminates at the mall's option. If either of the conditions subsequent occur, the mall can terminate all lease rights and duties. Neither condition is a promise.

Many contracts contain several conditions that can affect the parties' rights. To determine the legal consequences of the conditions, it is important to know whether they exist as conditions precedent, concurrent, or subsequent. The insurance policy is an example of a contract containing multiple conditions, and it is not always easy to determine whether the parties to the policy

Condition precedent
An event that must occur before a duty of performance arises in a contract.

Condition concurrent
An event that must occur at the same time as another condition in a contract.

Condition subsequent
An event that, if it occurs, discharges a duty of performance in a contract.

intended a condition to be precedent or subsequent to liability. The following are examples of insurance policy conditions:

- The premium payment is a condition precedent to liability under a policy.
- A loss is a condition precedent to an insurer's liability under a policy.
- A condition that an insured must sue within one year from the date of a loss is a condition subsequent.
- The requirement that an insured submit a notice of loss within sixty days of the loss is either a condition precedent to an insurer's liability or, depending on the wording of the condition, a condition subsequent to the insured's loss. For example, a policy can state, "The insurer's obligation will be discharged if no notice of loss is given within sixty days."

Determination of the intent and legal effect of a condition in an insurance policy often requires careful scrutiny by a court.

BREACH OF CONTRACT

A breach of contract is a party's unjustifiable failure to perform all or part of a contractual duty. A breach can be total or partial and may occur when a party fails to perform acts promised, hinders or prevents performance, or otherwise indicates an intention to repudiate the contract. The nonbreaching party has legal remedies against a breaching party.

Types of Breach

The remedy for breach may depend on its timing in relation to performance and on its effect on complete performance. Types of breach include those made in repudiation or anticipation, and material and minor breaches.

Repudiation

Repudiation
A party's refusal to meet obligations under a contract.

A **repudiation** of a contract is the refusal to meet obligations under the contract. Repudiation must be positive and unequivocal to constitute a breach. A statement of inability to perform in the future is not a repudiation. For example, Bill and John formed a contract requiring performance on November 1. If, on October 15, Bill says to John, "I doubt that I can perform the contract—and, the way prices are going up, I don't think I want to anyway," Bill has not repudiated the contract and John may not sue for breach. John cannot sue successfully for breach until the time for performance has arrived and Bill has failed to perform. A party must give a positive repudiation by words as well as by conduct. If, on November 1, Bill says "I cannot perform," he has repudiated the contract.

Anticipatory Breach

Anticipatory breach
A party's unequivocal indication before contract performance is due that he or she will not perform when performance is due.

Anticipatory breach is a party's unequivocal indication before a contract's performance is due that he or she will not perform when performance is due.

The concept of anticipatory breach developed to avoid "enforced idleness" on the part of an aggrieved party, who must wait until the time of performance to sue for breach, and to make it unnecessary for that party to tender performance at the time stated in the contract to prove the other party's breach.

The concept gives the nonbreaching party the option of not waiting until the actual date of performance to determine whether the other party will breach the contract. The aggrieved party can treat the repudiation as a present total breach and can sue immediately if both of the following anticipatory breach requirements are present:

1. A clear expression of the promisor's intention not to perform
2. An executory, bilateral contract entailing mutual and dependent conditions

For example, Millie promises to sell her land, and Tina promises to buy it, for $150,000 on December 1. On November 15, Tina says to Millie, "I cannot and will not go through with our contract." Tina's statement is a breach of contract by anticipatory repudiation. Millie need not wait until December, but may sue immediately for damages for breach of contract.

Anticipatory breach does not apply to a unilateral contract because the promisee has the option to perform an act and to become entitled to compensation. If the promisee does not perform the act, the promisor has no basis to sue.

Material Breach

Many courts distinguish between material breaches and minor ones. The materiality of the breach is a question of fact. Several circumstances affect the materiality of a breach, including the following:

*   The extent to which the breaching party has performed
*   Willfulness of the breach
*   The extent to which the nonbreaching party has obtained benefits and can receive adequate compensation

One party's material breach excuses the other party's performance and immediately gives rise to remedies for breach of contract. In contrast, a minor breach causes only slight delay in performance or a slight deviation in quantity or quality. A minor breach has the following effects:

*   It temporarily suspends any duty of performance by the nonbreaching party that would have arisen on proper performance.
*   It gives the aggrieved party a basis to sue for damages for the breach—usually an offset to the agreed price—but not for remedies for breach of the entire contract.

Remedies for Breach

If a contract is breached, the injured party can seek a legal remedy by suing to collect money damages. An injured party in a breach of contract for the sale of goods can sue either for money damages or for the price of the goods. Alternatively, an injured party can ask a court for one of the following two equitable remedies to correct the situation: specific performance of the contract or injunction.

Damages

Damages in breach of contract lawsuits fall into the following categories:

- Compensatory
- Consequential
- Punitive
- Extracontractual
- Liquidated

Compensatory damages
A payment awarded by a court to indemnify a victim for actual harm.

The most frequent remedy for breach of contract is money damages. **Compensatory damages** indemnify the victim for the actual harm caused by the breach. Such damages are to give the injured party the "benefit of the bargain," that is, return the injured party to approximately the position he or she would be in if the breaching party had performed the contract. Compensatory damages comprise the difference between the value of the promised performance and the plaintiff's cost of obtaining that performance elsewhere. They include losses caused by the breach and gains the breach prevented.

In the case of breach of a contract for the sale of goods, the UCC provides that the measure of damages is the difference between the contract price and the market price at the time of breach.[35] The objective is not to punish breaching parties, but to put them in as good a position as they would have been in if the breaching parties had performed fully.

Consequential damages
A payment awarded by a court to indemnify an injured party for losses that result indirectly from a wrong, such as a breach of contract or a tort.

In addition to the standard measure of compensatory contract damages, a breaching party is also liable for any **consequential damages**, losses that do not flow directly and immediately from the breach but that result indirectly from it. Recoverable losses are those resulting from the breach that the defendant, as a reasonable person, should have foreseen at the time of contract formation. A plaintiff can recover consequential damages only when the defendant was aware of the probable occurrence of the damages.

To illustrate, a manufacturer orders a supply of raw materials for delivery on a certain date. The seller does not deliver until after that date, and the manufacturer cannot obtain the materials anywhere else and must shut down the plant. The manufacturer then demands as part of the damages the loss incurred because of the plant shutdown. Although that loss flowed directly from the breach, the manufacturer cannot successfully sue for these damages because manufacturers usually order raw materials for delivery in advance of actual need. Additionally, raw materials are usually available from substitute sources. The seller, therefore, has no reason to believe that delayed shipment will cause a shutdown. However, if the manufacturer had informed the seller of the critical need and the seller, with that knowledge, promised to deliver on the given day, delayed delivery would make the seller liable for the foreseeable loss arising from the shutdown.

Punitive, or **exemplary damages** punish a defendant for a reckless, malicious, or deceitful act and need not bear any relationship to a party's actual damages. Courts more commonly award them in tort actions, such as for an unprovoked and malicious assault and battery. One purpose of punitive damages is to deter such conduct.

Punitive damages are not appropriate in most contract cases because the purpose of contract damages is to give the plaintiff the benefit of the bargain. If a seller of personal property has committed fraud or misrepresentation, however, punitive damages can be appropriate, based on the fraud rather than on breach of contract. An insurer that has unreasonably delayed a claim payment or contested a claim without reasonable grounds can, by statute, be liable for the insured's attorney's fees as a penalty.

In an insurance case, a court can award **extracontractual damages**, which are damages exceeding the usual contract damages for the insurer's breach of contract. Other terms referring to these damages in insurance cases are excess damages and excess-liability damages. The grounds for assessing extracontractual damages are as follows:

- Breach of the insurer's duty of good faith and fair dealing in insurance contracts
- Intentional infliction of emotional distress on the insured by the insurer's extreme and outrageous conduct

Extracontractual damages for either of these causes can include both consequential and punitive damages. Consequential damages can include compensation for physical and mental suffering and distress, loss of assets, and attorney fees. In most cases extracontractual damages far exceed contract damages resulting from the breach.

The nonbreaching party to a contract owes a duty of **mitigation of damages**, which means that, upon learning of a breach, the injured party must take reasonable action to minimize the loss. When the buyer breaches a contract for the sale of goods, the seller must dispose of the goods elsewhere at the best price possible. If a seller delivers a defective product and the buyer knows that the product is dangerous and could cause injury, the buyer must not permit its use.

If a dismissed employee does not try to mitigate damages by getting another position, a suit for damages for breach of contract may fail because the employee cannot prove damages. However, if the employee locates a position for a lower salary, the maximum recovery would be the difference between the salary for the new job and the salary under the breached contract. If a seller breaches a contract for the sale and delivery of goods, and the purchaser does not buy the goods elsewhere, damages are appropriate for the difference between the price a buyer could have paid for the goods and the price under the breached contract.

Punitive, or **exemplary damages**
A payment awarded by a court to punish a defendant for a reckless, malicious, or deceitful act or to deter similar conduct; need not bear any relationship to a party's actual damages.

Extracontractual damages
A payment awarded by a court that exceeds the usual contract damages for a breach of contract.

Mitigation of damages
A duty owed by an injured party to a lawsuit to take reasonable action, upon learning of a breach, to minimize a loss.

Liquidated damages
A reasonable estimation of actual damages, agreed to by contracting parties and included in the contract, to be paid in the event of a breach or for negligence.

The parties can agree in the contract on an amount of damages they will pay if a breach occurs. These **liquidated damages** are a reasonable estimation of actual damages in the event of breach or for negligence. To be a valid liquidated damages clause, the clause must specify a sum determined by the parties' good faith effort to estimate actual damages that probably would result from a breach. A court will not enforce a liquidated damages provision if it finds the damages to be a penalty. In that case, the injured party then must prove actual damages. A court considers in each case whether the contract involved subject matter that would make damages difficult to ascertain and whether the amount the parties agreed on represented a reasonable estimate of the damages that might actually result from breach.

Action for Price

In a contract for the sale of goods, the seller has the following two remedies for breach:

1. Damages
2. Contract price

The first remedy, damages, is available if the seller appropriately resells the goods and receives less than the contract price. The difference between the contract price and the price on resale is the damages. If the seller receives more than the agreed price, the excess need not go to the buyer and belongs to the seller.

In some cases, a seller will sue for the agreed price, but only in the following circumstances[36]:

- When the buyer has received and kept the goods
- When the goods are destroyed or damaged after the buyer has assumed the risk of loss
- When the buyer has wrongfully rejected delivery and the goods cannot be sold after reasonable effort to sell them at a reasonable price

A material breach allows the nonbreaching party to sue the breaching party in court for damages.

Equitable Remedies

A suit for damages is not always an effective remedy for the nonbreaching party. In some cases, only equitable remedies can make that party whole. The burden of loss passes to the buyer in the following situations, which often give rise only to equitable remedies[37]:

- When the buyer has accepted the goods
- When a carrier has tendered the goods to the buyer if the contract requires the seller to ship them to the buyer
- When the seller has delivered the goods to the carrier if the contract provides only for delivery to the carrier and not to the destination

- When a third party holds the goods for delivery without moving them
- When the buyer has received a document indicating the buyer's right to the goods
- When the third party acknowledges the buyer's right to possession

When dollar damages are not an adequate remedy for an injured party, a court might order the breaching party to perform the contract by performing the promise. **Specific performance** is a court-ordered equitable remedy requiring precise fulfillment of a legal or contractual obligation when money damages are inappropriate or inadequate. To determine whether money damages are adequate, courts consider the following:

- The difficulty of valuing the subject matter of the contract
- The existence of sentimental and aesthetic qualities of the subject matter that make it unique
- The difficulty or impossibility of obtaining a duplicate or substantial equivalent of the subject matter

Lawsuits requesting specific performance of a contract occur most frequently in contracts for the sale of real estate, which is unique. A court will order a seller to perform a contract and transfer title to an injured party.

Specific performance is an appropriate remedy for damages from breach of a contract to sell personal property only if the item is in some way unique, such as an antique or painting. Courts do not direct specific performance of personal service contracts, which would require them to supervise the performance to assure that it is adequate. Courts do not order specific performance of contracts requiring supervision, such as building contracts.

Although a court will not order specific performance of a personal service contract, if the personal services are truly unique, a court can issue an injunction to prevent the promisor from performing elsewhere during the term of the contract. An **injunction** is a court-ordered equitable remedy requiring a party to act or refrain from acting. When a court grants an injunction, it is "enjoining"—ordering or preventing—an action. A court probably would not grant an injunction against a singer in an opera chorus who broke a contract to refrain from singing elsewhere, because such a performance would not cause loss to the other party, but probably would grant such an injunction against an important soloist.

Commercial contracts containing negative agreements are enforceable by injunction. If an owner sells a business and promises not to compete with the buyer in a given area for a certain time, the restriction is legal. If the seller breaches the provision and starts to compete, the buyer can request an order enjoining the seller from competing.

In both of these cases, money damages would be inadequate. A court has no way to assess the money value of the soloist's performance, and a series of lawsuits for damages from the illegal competition would be too burdensome on the buyer. Therefore, an injunction is appropriate.

Specific performance
A court-ordered equitable remedy requiring precise fulfillment of a legal or contractual obligation when money damages are inappropriate or inadequate.

Injunction
A court-ordered equitable remedy requiring a party to act or refrain from acting.

Reformation
An equitable remedy by which a court modifies a written contract to reflect the parties' actual intent.

Another contract remedy, but not necessarily involving breach, is a request for reformation of a contract. **Reformation**, an equitable remedy by which a court modifies a written contract to reflect the parties' actual intent, is appropriate when the parties made a mistake in reducing their oral agreement to writing, or in contract cases in which one party made a mistake that the other party induced. The court reforms, or changes, the contract to conform to the parties' intention.

Courts require that the evidence of the mistake be clear and convincing before ordering reformation. To illustrate, if an insurer issues a policy that does not contain the coverage the parties orally agreed upon, a reformation action can change the contract to conform to the parties' true intent.

SUMMARY

Oral contracts usually are valid, even for most insurance policies. However, the statute of frauds requires written contracts in the following six situations:

1. Contracts involving the sale of land or any interest in land
2. Contracts that cannot be performed within one year
3. Promises to answer for another's debt
4. Promises in consideration of marriage
5. Promises by executors of decedents' estates to pay estate debts from executors' own funds
6. Contracts involving sale of personal property for $500 or more

The parol evidence rule limits contractual terms to those terms the parties chose to commit to writing. Parol, or oral, evidence is not admissible to alter the terms of a contract. Parol evidence is admissible only for the following purposes:

- To prove terms of an incomplete contract
- To clarify ambiguity in a contract
- To support an allegation of fraud, accident, illegality, or mistake relating to a contract
- To prove the failure of a condition precedent to a contract

Courts interpret contracts by using several rules or maxims to enforce the parties' intent. They give words their plain and ordinary meaning, examine parties' prior courses of dealings, and apply trade usage of terms where necessary. Courts decide in some cases whether contracts are entire or divisible. They correct clerical errors and omissions and may find implied terms in addition to those terms the parties have expressed. Courts often must reconcile contradictory terms and ambiguities. In the end, a court must determine what is legal and fair in each situation.

Third parties obtain rights under contracts either by assignment or by their status as third-party beneficiaries. Some contract rights are assignable and some are not. The UCC permits assignment of rights in contracts to sell goods, but not if the parties have agreed otherwise, if the nondelegating party has a substantial interest in preventing delegation, or if the assignment would materially change the duties or risks of the nonassigning party. Third-party beneficiaries include creditor, donee, and incidental beneficiaries. Each has different rights under contracts.

Discharge of contract can occur by the parties' performance or agreement. Performance can come about legally through payment, tender of performance, or substantial performance. Parties can agree to rescind a contract, or they can substitute new agreements, create novations, or discharge a contract by accord and satisfaction.

Contract performance can become impossible because of unanticipated events. Impossibility of performance may be objective or subjective. Impossibility can result from changes in law, a party's death or incapacity, destruction of the subject matter of a contract, the other party's acts, temporary or partial impossibility, partial performance, frustration of purpose, commercial impracticability, statutes of limitations, and fraudulent alterations. The UCC also applies to impossibility of performance in specific situations.

Contracts may contain conditions that affect contract performance. In any given contract they can be either precedent, concurrent, or subsequent conditions, or any combination of the three.

Breach of contract can occur by repudiation or anticipatory breach and can be either material or minor. The remedies for breach of contract include compensatory, punitive, extracontractual, and liquidated damages. Equitable remedies include specific performance, injunction, and reformation.

CHAPTER NOTES

1. UCC, § 2-107.
2. UCC, § 2-201(2).
3. UCC, § 2-201(3c).
4. UCC, § 2-201(3a).
5. UCC, § 8-319.
6. UCC, § 9-203.
7. UCC, § 1-206.
8. UCC, § 2-202.
9. UCC, § 2-202-a.
10. UCC, § 2-202-b.
11. UCC, § 2-307.
12. UCC, § 2-612(2).
13. UCC, § 2-612(2)(3).

14. UCC, § 2-204(3).

15. UCC, § 2-305(1).

16. UCC, § 2-309(1).

17. UCC, § 2-306(1).

18. UCC, § 2-306(1).

19. UCC, § 2-208.

20. UCC, § 2-302.

21. UCC, § 1-205(2).

22. UCC, § 1-205(4) and 2-208(2).

23. UCC, § 2-210(1).

24. UCC, § 2-210(2).

25. UCC, § 2-210(3).

26. UCC, § 2-210(4).

27. UCC, § 2-209(5).

28. UCC, § 1-107.

29. UCC, § 2-209(2).

30. *Madeirence Do Brasil, S.A. v. Stulman-Emrick Lumber Co.*, 147 F.2d 399 (2d Cir. 1945), cited in UCC, §615, comment 8.

31. UCC, § 2-615(1).

32. UCC, § 2-615(2)(3).

33. UCC, § 2-615, comment 4.

34. UCC, § 2-614(1).

35. UCC, § 2-708 and 2-713.

36. UCC, § 2-207.

37. UCC, § 2-509. See also UCC, § 2-510.

Direct Your Learning

Insurance Contract Law

After learning the content of this chapter and completing the corresponding course guide assignment, you should be able to:

■ Describe the following characteristics of insurance contracts:

- A conditional contract

- A contract involving fortuitous events and the exchange of unequal amounts

- A contract of utmost good faith

- A contract of adhesion

- A contract of indemnity

- A nontransferable contract

■ Given a case, determine whether an insurance contract has formed based on the elements of insurance contracts.

■ Given a case involving third-party interests, determine how an insurance policy can provide coverage.

■ Evaluate a representation in an insurance application to determine whether a misrepresentation has occurred.

■ Explain the effects of warranties in an insurance contract case.

■ Explain how insurers can waive their rights or face estoppel from asserting their rights against their insureds.

■ Explain how reservation of rights letters and nonwaiver agreements affect insurers' and insureds' rights.

■ Define or describe each of the Key Words and Phrases for this chapter.

Develop Your Perspective

What are the main topics covered in the chapter?

This chapter applies contract principles from the preceding three chapters to insurance contracts. Insurance contracts have distinct features as contracts of adhesion indemnifying insureds for losses from fortuitous events. They are also contracts in the public interest subject to the principles of utmost good faith. Insurance agreements, while requiring all contractual elements, also have distinct rules governing oral contracts and policy delivery. Insurance contracts often benefit third parties and include representations and warranties. The rules and concepts of waiver, estoppel, and election qualify the insurers' and insureds' rights in litigation.

Contrast the principles of contract law with those of insurance contracts.

- How are the offer and acceptance of an insurance contract affected by binders and conditional receipts?
- How are third-party beneficiaries covered by liability insurance contracts?
- How might an insurer's actions create waiver of its right to later deny liability coverage?

Why is it important to learn about these topics?

Insurance professionals, after learning the basics of contract law, must know how contract law applies to insurance contracts because the entire insurance relationship is based on contract law.

Consider why insurance professionals must understand contract basics.

- What rules must insurers and insureds follow regarding contract formation and formality?
- How might courts interpret insurance contracts?
- What rights do third parties have arising from insurance contracts?

How can you use what you will learn?

Examine the events that occurred when you obtained coverage for your own house, apartment contents, or car.

- What actions defined the offer and acceptance?
- What was the exchange of consideration between you and the insurer?

Chapter 5
Insurance Contract Law

Insurance contracts must contain all the necessary elements of a legally enforceable contract and are in many ways similar to other contracts. However, insurance contracts have distinctive features and their own body of law.

An insurer and insured form an insurance contract, by which the insurer provides protection if the insured suffers specified losses. When the insurance contract becomes a formal written document, it is an **insurance policy**. Conditions, limitations, and exceptions become part of the insurance contract because they define and limit the losses it covers. Creating an understandable contract that defines covered losses, as well as numerous and often complex exclusions and conditions, is a challenge that has troubled both insurers and insureds since the inception of written policies. State regulatory efforts to require "plain English" policies have resulted in clearer insurance policies, but the policies' necessary complexity often makes the goal of understandable policies difficult.

Insurers attempt to write their policies today in more simplified language as part of a movement toward plain language in insurance policies and other consumer contracts generally. Any new language in insurance contracts, however, can require new court interpretation when an insured sues for denial of coverage.

Insurance policy
A formal written contract by which an insurer provides protection if an insured suffers specified losses.

The Insurance Policy: "A Mere Flood of Darkness and Confusion"

In reviewing the language of a homeowners insurance policy in 1873, a judge made the following comments:

"Whether [people] ought to be what they are, or not, the fact is, that in the present condition of society, men in general cannot read and understand these insurance documents. . . . Forms of applications and policies, of a most complicated and elaborate structure, were prepared, and filled with covenants, exceptions, stipulations, provisos, rules, regulations, and conditions, rendering the policy void in a great number of contingencies . . . The compound, if read by [an insured], would, unless he were an extraordinary man, be an inexplicable riddle, a mere flood of darkness and confusion. . . . [I]t was printed in such small type, and in lines so long and so crowded, that the perusal of it was made physically difficult, painful, and injurious. Seldom has the art of typography been so successfully diverted from the diffusion of knowledge to the suppression of it. There was ground for the premium payer to argue that the print alone was evidence, competent to be submitted to a jury, of a fraudulent plot. . . ."[1]

Continued on next page.

In another court case, in 1975, the court refused to bind the insureds of the policy in question to its terms because its printing was of "a size type that would drive an eagle to a microscope." The court added the following:

"It cannot be reasonably assumed that the insured having average sight of a human being would be aware of the content of the questioned clause, at least in the absence of special optical equipment....It should not be necessary for the insured to provide himself with a microscope in order to inspect the small print contained within his insurance policy. Neither should it be necessary for an insured to provide himself with an insurance policy to protect himself against the provision to be found within such small print of his insurance policy."[2]

SPECIAL CHARACTERISTICS OF INSURANCE CONTRACTS

In addition to having the four essential elements of all contracts, insurance contracts have certain special characteristics. An insurance policy is all of the following:

- A conditional contract
- A contract involving fortuitous events and the exchange of unequal amounts
- A contract of utmost good faith
- A contract of adhesion
- A contract of indemnity
- A nontransferable contract

Conditional Contract

Conditional contract
A contract that one or more parties must perform only under certain conditions.

An insurance policy is a **conditional contract** because the parties have to perform only under certain conditions. Whether the insurer pays a claim depends on whether a covered loss has occurred. In addition, the insured must fulfill certain duties before a claim is paid, such as giving prompt notice to the insurer after a loss has occurred.

A covered loss might not occur during a particular policy period, but that fact does not mean the insurance policy for that period has been worthless. In buying an insurance policy, the insured acquires a valuable promise—the promise of the insurer to make payments if a covered loss occurs. The promise exists, even if the insurer's performance is not required during the policy period.

Contract Involving Fortuitous Events and the Exchange of Unequal Amounts

While noninsurance contracts involve an exchange of money for a certain event, such as the provision of goods or services, insurance contracts involve an exchange of money for protection upon the occurrence of uncertain, or fortuitous, events. Insurance contracts involve an exchange of unequal amounts. Often, there are few or no losses, and the premium paid by the insured for a particular policy is more than the amount paid by the insurer to, or on behalf of, the insured. If a large loss occurs, however, the insurer's claim payment might be much more than the premium paid by the insured. It is the possibility that the insurer's obligation might be much greater than the insured's that makes the insurance transaction a fair trade.

For example, suppose an insurer charges a $1,000 annual premium to provide auto physical damage coverage on a car valued at $20,000. The following three situations may occur:

1. If the car is not damaged while the policy is in force, the insurer pays nothing.
2. If the car is partially damaged, the insurer pays the cost of repairs, after subtracting a deductible.
3. If the car is a total loss, the insurer pays $20,000 (minus any deductible).

Unless, by chance, the insurer's obligations in a minor accident come to exactly $1,000, unequal amounts are involved in all three of these cases. However, it does not follow that insureds who have no losses—or only very minor losses—do not get their money's worth or that insureds involved in major accidents profit from the insurance.

The premium for a particular policy should reflect the insured's share of estimated losses that the insurer must pay. Many insureds have no losses, but some have very large losses. The policy premium reflects the insured's proportionate share of the total amount the insurer expects to pay to honor its agreements with all insureds having similar policies.

Contract of Utmost Good Faith

Because insurance involves a promise, it requires complete honesty and disclosure of all relevant facts from both parties. For this reason, insurance contracts are considered contracts of **utmost good faith**. Both parties to an insurance contract—the insurer and the insured—are expected to be ethical in their dealings with each other.

Utmost good faith
An obligation to act in complete honesty and to disclose all relevant facts.

The insured has a right to rely on the insurer to fulfill its promises. Therefore, the insurer is expected to treat the insured with utmost good faith. An insurer that acts in bad faith, such as denying coverage for a claim that is clearly covered, could face serious penalties under the law.

The insurer also has a right to expect that the insured will act in good faith. An insurance buyer who intentionally conceals certain information or misrepresents certain facts does not act in good faith. Because an insurance contract requires utmost good faith from both parties, an insurer could be released from a contract because of concealment or misrepresentation by the insured.

Concealment

Concealment is an intentional failure to disclose a material fact. Courts have held that the insurer must prove two things to establish that concealment has occurred. First, it must establish that the failure to disclose information was intentional, which is often difficult. The insurer must usually show that the insured knew that the information should have been given and then intentionally withheld it.

Material fact
In insurance, a fact that would affect the insurer's decision to provide or maintain insurance or to settle a claim.

Second, the insurer must establish that the information withheld was a **material fact**—information that would affect an insurer's decision to provide or maintain insurance or to settle a claim. In the case of an auto insurance applicant, for example, material facts include how the applicant's autos are used, who drives them, and the ages and driving records of the drivers. If an insured intentionally conceals the material fact that her sixteen-year-old son lives in the household and is the principal driver of one of her cars, that concealment could void the policy.

Insurers carefully design applications for insurance to include questions regarding facts material to the underwriting process. The application includes questions on specific subjects to which the applicant must respond. These questions are designed to encourage the applicant to reveal all pertinent information.

Misrepresentation

In normal usage, a misrepresentation is a false statement. As used in insurance, a **misrepresentation** is a false statement of a material fact on which the insurer relies. The insurer does not have to prove that the misrepresentation is intentional.

Misrepresentation
A false statement of a material fact on which a party relies.

For example, assume an applicant for auto insurance has had two speeding tickets during the eighteen months immediately before he submitted his application for insurance. When asked if any driving violations have occurred within the past three years (a question found on most auto insurance application forms), an applicant giving either of the following answers would be making a misrepresentation:

- "I remember having one speeding ticket about two years ago."
- "I've never been cited for a moving violation—only a few parking tickets."

The first response provides incorrect information, and this false statement may or may not be intentional. The false statement made in the second response is probably intentional. The direct question posed in the application requires a full and honest response from the applicant because the insurer relies on the information. Anything less is a misrepresentation, whether intentional or not.

As with a concealment, if a material fact is misrepresented, the insurer could choose to void the policy because of the violation of utmost good faith.

Contract of Adhesion

The wording in insurance contracts is usually drafted by the insurer (or an insurance advisory organization), enabling the insurer to use preprinted forms for many different insureds. Because the insurer determines the exact wording of the policy, the insured has little choice but to "take it or leave it." That is, the insured must adhere to the contract drafted by the insurer. Therefore, insurance policies are considered to be **contracts of adhesion**, which means one party (the insured) must adhere to the contract as written by the other party (the insurer). This characteristic significantly influences the enforcement of insurance policies.

Contract of adhesion
A contract to which one party must adhere as written by the other party.

If a dispute arises between the insurer and the insured about the meaning of certain words or phrases in the policy, the insured and the insurer are not on an equal basis. The insurer either drafted the policy or used standard forms of its own choice; in contrast, the insured did not have any say in the policy wording. For that reason, if the policy wording is ambiguous, a court will generally apply the interpretation that favors the insured.

Contract of Indemnity

The purpose of insurance is to provide indemnification—that is, to indemnify an insured who suffers a loss. To indemnify is to restore a party who has had a loss to the same financial position that party held before the loss occurred. Most property and liability insurance policies are contracts of indemnity. With a **contract of indemnity**, the insurer agrees, in the event of a covered loss, to pay an amount directly related to the amount of the loss.

Contract of indemnity
A contract in which the insurer agrees, in the event of a covered loss, to pay an amount directly related to the amount of the loss.

Property insurance generally pays the amount of money necessary to repair covered property that has been damaged or to replace it with similar property. The policy specifies the method for determining the amount of the loss. For example, most auto policies, both personal and commercial, specify that vehicles are to be valued at their actual cash value (ACV) at the time of a loss. If a covered accident occurs that causes a covered vehicle to be a total loss, the insurer will normally pay the ACV of the vehicle, less any applicable deductible.

Liability insurance generally pays to a third-party claimant, on behalf of the insured, any amounts (up to the policy limit) that the insured becomes legally obligated to pay as damages due to a covered liability claim, as well as the legal costs associated with that claim. For example, if an insured with a liability limit of $300,000 is ordered by a court to pay $100,000 for bodily injury incurred by the claimant in a covered accident, the insurer will pay $100,000 to the claimant and will also pay the cost to defend the insured in court.

A contract of indemnity does not necessarily pay the full amount necessary to restore an insured who has suffered a covered loss to the same financial position. However, the amount the insurer pays is directly related to the amount of the insured's loss. Most policies contain a policy limit that specifies the maximum amount the insurer will pay for a single claim. Many policies also contain limitations and other provisions that could reduce the amount of recovery. For example, a homeowners policy is not designed to cover large amounts of cash. Therefore, most homeowners policies contain a special limit, such as $200, for any covered loss to money owned by the insured. If a covered fire destroys $1,000 in cash belonging to the insured, the homeowners insurer will pay only $200 for the money that was destroyed.

Principle of indemnity
The principle that insurance policies should compensate the insured only for the value of a loss but should not provide a benefit greater than the loss.

According to the **principle of indemnity**, insurance should provide a benefit no greater than the loss suffered by an insured. That is, the insured should not be better off financially after the loss than before. Insurance policies usually include certain provisions that reinforce the principle of indemnity. For example, policies generally contain another insurance provision to prevent an insured from receiving full payment from two different insurance policies for the same claim. Insurance contracts usually protect the insurer's subrogation rights, as discussed earlier. Other insurance provisions and subrogation provisions clarify that the insured cannot collect more than the amount of the loss. For example, following an auto accident in which the insurer compensates its insured when the other driver is at fault, the subrogation provision stipulates that the insured's right to recover damages from the responsible party is transferred (subrogated) to the insurer. The insured cannot collect from both the insurer and the responsible party.

Another factor enforcing the principle of indemnity is that a person usually cannot buy insurance unless that person is in a position to suffer a financial loss. In other words, the insured must have an insurable interest in the subject of the insurance. For example, property insurance contracts cover losses only to the extent of the insured's insurable interest in the property. This restriction prevents an insured from collecting more from the insurance than the amount of the loss he or she suffered. A person cannot buy life insurance on the life of a stranger, hoping to gain if the stranger dies. Insurers normally sell life insurance when there is a reasonable expectation of a financial loss from the death of the insured person, such as the loss of an insured's future income that the insured's dependents would face. Insurable interest is not an issue in liability insurance because a liability claim against an insured results in a financial loss if the insured is legally responsible. Even if the insured is not responsible, the insured could incur defense costs.

Valued policy
A policy in which the insurer pays a stated amount in the event of a specified loss (usually a total loss) regardless of the actual value of the loss.

Some insurance contracts are not contracts of indemnity but valued policies. When a specified loss occurs, a **valued policy** pays a stated amount, regardless of the actual value of the loss. For example, a fine arts policy might specify that it will pay $250,000 for loss of a particular painting or sculpture. The actual market value of the painting or sculpture may be much smaller or much greater than $250,000, but the policy will pay $250,000 in either case. In most valued policies, the insurer and the insured agree on a limit that approximates the current market value of the insured property.

Nontransferable Contract

The identities of the persons or organizations insured are extremely relevant to the insurer, which has the right to select those applicants with whom it is willing to enter into contractual agreements. After an insurance policy is in effect, an insured may not freely transfer, or assign, the policy to some other party. If such a transfer were allowed to take place, the insurer would be legally bound to a contract with a party it might not wish to insure. Most insurance policies contain a provision that requires the insurer's written permission before an insured can transfer a policy to another party.

Traditionally, insurance textbooks used the language that "insurance is a personal contract" to indicate its nontransferable nature and have cited clauses in property policies to illustrate the principle. The policy language does differ between typical property and liability policies, but in both types, the intention is to prohibit the insured from transferring the policy to another party without the insurer's consent.

INSURANCE CONTRACT ELEMENTS

To be enforceable, an insurance contract, like any other contract, must have the following four elements:

1. An agreement consisting of a legally binding offer and an acceptance
2. Capacity to contract
3. Legally sufficient consideration
4. Lawful purpose

The parties must have given genuine assent, but an insurance contract need not be in writing. This chapter discusses the insurance policy as an agreement, issues related to the effective date of the policy, and the effects of silence or delay on acceptance of an insurance contract.

Agreement

Insurance sales are almost always handled by insurance producers. Producers who represent insurers are agents, and producers who represent insureds are brokers. Insurers rely on agents to solicit business, take applications, and sometimes issue policies. Agents can create contract liability for insurers even though the insurer may not have intended to be bound. Under the law of agency, insurance agents' commitments can be binding on insurers.

Offer and Acceptance

When a producer contacts a prospective insured to sell an insurance policy, is the producer making an offer to contract or merely soliciting offers? Generally, the producer's selling efforts are merely a solicitation of offers that the insurer might not accept and are not offers themselves. The insurance application, signed by the applicant and sent to the insurer through the producer, is the offer. The insurance policy issued later is the acceptance. If the policy issued does not conform to the application—the initial offer—the policy is a counteroffer requiring the applicant's specific acceptance.

Often the insurance applicant does not make an offer but merely invites the insurer to make an offer. For example, if an applicant has not decided to take the insurance but submits an application to determine whether the insurer will accept the risk, the application is not an offer. In that case, when the insurer issues the policy and the insured accepts it by paying the premium, they have concluded an offer and acceptance. Similarly, if the policy as issued does not comply with the coverage or rates the applicant requested, the policy is a new offer that the applicant can then accept or reject.

When a policy issued is merely an offer, the named insured does not have to accept it. To help avoid lawsuits in these cases, the agent should not deliver the policy to the proposed insured until receipt of a premium. Insureds do not always pay their premiums immediately on receiving a policy; in fact, a considerable time can elapse. During that time, the status of the contract is questionable. Although no contract exists until the premium is paid, disputes over validity of the contract and alleged promises to pay the premium can be grounds for a lawsuit.

As with contracts in general, the communication of the offer to the offeree is essential in an insurance agreement. Only the person to whom an offer is addressed, or that person's agent, can accept an offer. For example, if a proposed insured has died before taking action to accept a policy, the widowed spouse cannot accept the offer.

The mailing of an acceptance binds an insurance contract at the time of mailing, whether or not the other party receives it. Thus, if the insurer's issuance of a policy is the offer, the insured's mailing the premium in response to that offer is the binding acceptance.

Oral insurance contracts are as binding as written ones, except for life insurance contracts. When the insurance producer has authority to enter into oral agreements to bind coverage, the parties' words and conduct govern the offer and acceptance just as with any other contract. Generally, acts or words of intent to offer and accept establish a binding insurance contract. For example, Mary calls her insurance agent asking to increase the limits on her policy, and the agent tells her, "Done! We'll send you the new policy in the mail." Before Mary receives the policy, she suffers a loss that exceeds the old limits of her policy. The agent's oral promise is binding. In the field of property-casualty insurance, oral applications and contracts are common.

The accelerated pace of the modern business environment has necessitated immediate insurance coverage in many situations. For example, a person who contracts to purchase property may assume the risk of loss or destruction of the property and may, therefore, require immediate insurance coverage. In property-casualty insurance, producers usually have authority to bind insurance companies immediately. For example, Judy telephones agent Kathy and asks for "immediate homeowners insurance coverage on my home in the amount of $200,000." Kathy replies, "You're covered." The homeowners insurer Kathy represents must provide insurance protection under this oral agreement.

When an agreement between a producer and a prospective insured for a property-casualty insurance policy does not specify immediate coverage, examination of the parties' conversations, as well as the producer's authority, is necessary to determine when the policy became effective. Without the immediate coverage requirement, the application is an offer that the insurer can accept by issuing a policy conforming with the offer.

Unless the parties have agreed otherwise, when an acceptance is made in the manner requested, the agreement is completed.

The life insurance contract differs from the property insurance contract in several important ways. A life insurance policy has the following characteristics:

• A potentially long period of coverage: the insured's life

• A large coverage amount

• Specialized underwriting considerations regarding such factors as medical history and life expectancy

These considerations have made insurers cautious in extending authority to insurance producers to enter into life insurance contracts. In the life insurance contract, the prospective insured offers to contract by submitting an application. Acceptance of the offer and formation of the contract are not effective under most life insurance policies until actual delivery of the policy to the insured and payment of the first premium. If the insurer does not accept the original application with the coverage and rate offered, the insurer may be making a counterproposal, or counteroffer, for the prospective insured to accept or reject.

In the absence of a specific policy provision or an agreement to the contrary, the life insurance contract is effective under the usual contract rules of offer and acceptance. For example, Judy applies to Insurance Company for a life insurance policy and pays the first premium with the understanding that the insurance must be approved at Insurance Company's home office. Insurance Company's notification of approval is effective as an acceptance upon mailing, without regard to whether Judy has actually received the acceptance.

In contrast, when Judy applies in writing for life insurance to the Insurance Company, pays the first premium, and receives a receipt stating, "This insurance shall take effect on the date of approval of the application," subsequent approval at the home office is an acceptance of Judy's offer even though Insurance Company does not notify her of the approval. The parties have agreed that acceptance will occur upon approval, and actual notification to Judy is not essential.

The rules are similar for offer and acceptance of health, accident, and disability insurance policies. The application for coverage requires examination and approval in the insurer's home or regional office. There, an underwriter considers the special risk factors in the applicant's employment and health history before making any final decision to accept. As in the case of most life insurance policies, the coverage becomes effective upon delivery of the policy to the insured and upon the insured's payment of the first premium.

For example, many travelers obtain air terminal insurance through machines in airports. The forms provided are the insurer's offer. The prospective insured accepts the offer by completing the forms and mailing the application. A contract is created when the application is mailed, even if the insurer never receives it.

In group insurance coverages, the insurer issues the policy to a group policyholder, which can be an employer, a labor union, or another association. The agreement is binding when the insurer accepts the group policyholder's application. These agreements usually provide that the group policy is effective on a specified date, provided that a certain percentage of eligible group members agree to accept the coverage and to become certificate holders under the policy. Once the group policy is effective, individual certificate holders can obtain coverage automatically by applying to the plan (that is, the employer), subject to the group policyholder's approval. If the plan requires individual underwriting of certificate holders, coverage must await underwriting approval for each insured.

Effective Date

Determination of the exact moment insurance contract coverage begins and ends can be crucial in some cases when a loss occurs. Unless a loss occurs within the policy coverage period, no benefits are payable.

The general rules of contract law concerning the time at which acceptance becomes effective also apply to the insurance contract. Frequently the policy itself specifies the effective date and time of the contract. Binders and conditional receipts have both aided and complicated the law with respect to the effective dates of insurance contracts. Binders frequently apply to property-casualty insurance, and conditional receipts apply to life insurance.

Binder
An oral or written agreement to provide temporary insurance coverage until a formal written policy is issued.

A **binder** is an insurer's oral or written agreement giving the insured temporary coverage until a formal written policy is issued. The binding slip, or binder receipt, although temporary in nature, provides evidence of insurance and interim coverage until the policy is issued. Binders are informal written contracts summarizing the basic coverages and terms of the insurance agreement. They frequently provide extension of coverage for thirty days, pending issuance of the policy.

Even though a binder is usually evidence of an insurance contract, the insurer can produce evidence to prove that the parties orally agreed that the insurance was not to take effect until a specific condition was met. For instance, the parties might have agreed that temporary coverage was not to be effective until another insurer assumed part of the risk.

Absent such conditions, all policy provisions are effective the moment the binder is created. The binder is effective until actual notice of cancellation or until a policy is issued. An insurer's cancellation of a binder must conform to the methods the policy prescribes.

In property-casualty insurance, binders provide immediate coverage when issued by authorized agents. Most insurers have written policies that control the binder's actual coverage. Although brief, the binder must contain the basic information needed for an agreement and must indicate types of coverage.

The binder should identify the insurer and the insured. If an object such as a car is insured, the binder should describe the car briefly and indicate the amounts of coverage clearly enough to establish policy limits. With agreement on these basic points, the more detailed policy provisions can be determined by reference to the policy the insurer will issue.

Most disputes about temporary insurance contracts concern life, health, and accident insurance. The long periods of policy coverage, the potentially large amounts of coverage involved, and the need for highly specialized underwriting regarding health history cause insurers to be cautious in binding these types of insurance, even temporarily.

These insurers do not use binders. Instead, they use **conditional receipts**, which, they emphasize, are not binders and are not intended to provide immediate coverage. Conditional receipts may provide coverage back to the date of receipt under certain conditions. To avoid being bound before learning whether the applicant is insurable, insurers attempt to phrase the premium receipt in life insurance so that it avoids immediate coverage to the applicant. Many legal disputes have arisen over the question of whether these receipts, despite insurers' intent, are binding, and courts have reached different decisions in these cases.

Conditional receipt
A premium receipt used by life insurers and accident and health insurers that is not intended to provide immediate coverage but that may provide coverage back to the date of receipt under certain conditions.

The life insurance conditional receipt has at least the following three major forms:

1. A **binding receipt** provides coverage on the date of receipt until a specified time or until the insurer disapproves the application. A few life insurers use binding receipts in much the same way that property insurers use them.

2. An **approval receipt** reflects the insurer's intention not to be bound by a receipt until it actually gives approval. The approval is a condition precedent to coverage. Most courts have upheld the condition when it is clear. Other courts have interpreted approval receipts as affording insurance coverage as of the date of the receipt but subject to later determination of insurability. These courts conclude that the insurers are collecting premiums while giving little more coverage than if they had received no premium. These interpretations have led to the more extensive use of a third type of conditional receipt, the insurability receipt.

Binding receipt
A conditional receipt that provides coverage on the date of receipt until a specified time or until the insurer disapproves the application.

Approval receipt
A conditional receipt that reflects the insurer's intention not to be bound by the receipt until the application is approved.

Insurability receipt
A life insurance or accident and health insurance conditional receipt that stipulates that the insurance is effective on the date of the receipt or on the date of the medical examination, provided the applicant is insurable on that date.

3. An **insurability receipt** is the most frequently used life, accident, and health receipt. The typical language of insurability receipts stipulates that the insurance is effective on the date of the receipt or on the date of the medical examination, provided the applicant is insurable on that date. Under these receipts the insurance is not effective unless the applicant is insurable, but the insurer can determine, even after the applicant's death, whether the applicant was insurable on a specific date. If the applicant dies after the receipt is issued and the insurer finds, by applying its objective underwriting standards, that the applicant would have been insurable on the date of the receipt, the coverage applies. Exhibit 5-1 is a typical example of an insurability receipt in life, accident, and health insurance.

The variety of conditional receipts and the complexity of their language have led some courts to find them ambiguous and to interpret any doubts against insurers by holding that the conditional receipt provides immediate interim coverage. Most courts, however, find no life insurance in force until determination of an applicant's insurability.

When an insurer determines an applicant insurable, the insurance effective date is retroactive to the receipt date. An insurer that has not determined insurability at the time of an applicant's death must then determine if the applicant would have been insurable. The evaluation must be in good faith, using the insurer's usual underwriting standards. If the insurer's decision is appealed, a judge or jury must decide what insurability finding the company should reasonably have made.

Silence or Delay

Contract law requires unequivocal manifestation of both parties' mutual assent, by either words or conduct. At common law, courts consider either a party's silence or a party's delay as equivocal and insufficient acceptance to form a contract. This rule was subject to the qualification that, if a prior course of dealings indicated that silence was acceptance, those prior dealings would control.

For example, Gina, a producer, has for years handled insurance on Mike's property under annual policies. At the expiration of a policy, and consistent with prior dealings, Gina sends Mike a renewal policy and a bill for the premium. This year, Mike holds the policy for two months, remaining silent, and then refuses to pay the premium on demand. Mike is liable for the premium that accrued before his rejection. The course of prior dealings between the parties gave Gina, the offeror producer, a reasonable basis for concluding that silence would constitute acceptance.

Assume instead that Gina directs a letter to Mike indicating, "Your homeowners insurance policy will be renewed for another three years unless I hear from you to the contrary." Mike does not reply. Because there was no prior course of dealings indicating that Gina could infer acceptance by silence, continued coverage does not result automatically. Mike's silence is not an unequivocal promise to accept Gina's promise to renew and is not sufficient to infer acceptance.

Another reason for the contract rule that mere silence is not an acceptance of an offer involves unsolicited offers. If silence were always acceptance of an offer, salespeople could flood consumer mail with offers that would bind recipients to buy unless they expressly rejected the offer. The law prohibits

---

EXHIBIT 5-1

Conditional First Life Premium Receipt

This receipt must not be detached unless settlement of the first full premium has been made by the Applicant at the time of application and such premium amount meets the Company's minimum Premium rules.

CONDITIONAL FIRST LIFE PREMIUM RECEIPT: NO INSURANCE WILL BECOME EFFECTIVE PRIOR TO POLICY DELIVERY UNLESS THE ACTS REQUIRED BY THIS RECEIPT ARE COMPLETED. NO AGENT OF THE COMPANY IS AUTHORIZED TO CHANGE ANY ACT REQUIRED.

Received from _____ this _____ day of _____ ,20___, the sum of _____ Dollars ($ _____) in connection with an application for Life Insurance in Insurance Company which application bears the same date and printed number as this receipt.

If the sum indicated above equals the first full premium on the premium payment basis selected in the application for the insurance applied for and if the following acts are completed: (a) receipt by the Company of a fully completed application and amendments thereto, if any, which includes fully completed medical examinations if required by published underwriting rules because of the age of the Proposed Insured, the amount of insurance applied for or because of the Proposed Insured's past medical history or current condition and (b) completion of all investigation by the Company and the Company is satisfied that the Proposed Insured and (without prejudice to the Proposed Insured) each person proposed for coverage under the Family Rider or the Children's Rider (whichever is applicable and if applied for) is insurable and qualified under the Company's established rules, limits and standards on the plan and for the amount applied for and at the premium specified herein, the said insurance shall take effect and be in force subject to the provisions of the policy applied for from the date of the application or the last medical examination, whichever is later, or if no medical examination is required, the insurance shall take effect on the application date. Unless all acts required are completed, no insurance shall take effect nor be in force under the application or this receipt unless and until a policy has been manually delivered to and received and accepted by the Applicant and the full first premium specified in the policy has actually been paid to and accepted by the Company during the continued insurability of the Proposed Insured and (without prejudice to the Proposed Insured) during the continued insurability of each person proposed for coverage under the Family Rider or the Children's Rider (whichever is applicable and if applied for). Insurance under the Family Rider or the Children's Rider (whichever is applicable and if applied for) shall take effect at the same time and under the same conditions as the insurance on the Proposed Insured.

In any event, the amount of insurance becoming effective under the terms of this receipt is hereby limited to the extent that in the event of the death of the Proposed Insured the total liability of the Company shall not exceed $150,000, said amount to include any life insurance then in force with the Company and any benefits payable by the Company as a result of accidental death.

If the application is declined, the amount evidenced by this receipt shall be refunded.

(Agent must sign here) _____ Agent

NOTICE: This receipt is not valid for any premium for the insurance applied for except the first full premium thereon which in no event shall exceed one annual premium for such insurance together with the premium for interim term insurance, if any.

sellers from forcing prospective buyers to reject or return offered goods or services. The enterprising insurance agent who mails policies to everyone in the area advising, "Unless I hear from you in a week, I will assume that you accept this coverage," imposes no duty to respond on the recipients of the offers. Similarly, if a merchant mails an unsolicited item to a person's home, the recipient has no duty either to respond or to return the item.

Similarly, when an applicant submits an application for coverage to an insurer and the insurer fails to act within a reasonable time, the insurer's silence or delay is not acceptance. An insurer, however, can be liable under its contract if it delays action on an application beyond a reasonable time. Courts apply the rationale in this situation that insurance is a business affected with a public interest. Because insurers have generally solicited these offers, and because applicants frequently pay premiums in advance, the insurer must act promptly in accepting or rejecting the offer.

The nature of the insurance business imposes a duty to act on the insurer when considering applications for insurance. Some courts consider the obligation an implied contract, while others assert that, after the lapse of a reasonable time, the insurance company should be estopped, or prevented, from claiming that the application was not accepted. Most courts, however, base recovery on the theory that the insurer has been negligent, having breached its duty to act on the application without unreasonable delay. If the applicant suffers a loss as a result, then the insurer can be held liable. The court bases recovery on the tort of negligence instead of on contract law. What constitutes unreasonable delay is a question of fact, not law. The following are some important facts a court will consider:

- The distance of the insurer's office from the agent's office at which the applicant submitted the application
- Special difficulties in underwriting the risk
- The insurer's seasonal or other workload problems
- The type of coverage involved

Some state statutes prescribe the time limits within which an insurer must act on an application. The issue of unreasonable delay can arise despite the immediate coverage provided by property and casualty binders or life insurance conditional receipts. Property insurance binders often stipulate coverage for "thirty days only." Life insurance conditional receipts can be conditional and might not provide any interim coverage. In either case, an unreasonable delay in acting on the application could result in the insurer's liability for coverage.

Insurance Policy Content

The insurance contract is usually a result of negotiations. A frequent question concerns which papers and conversations form the ultimate contract. Once an insurer writes the policy, courts consider all prior negotiations or agreements, written or oral, as merged into the writing. Every contractual term in the policy at the time of delivery, as well as those written in afterwards as policy riders or endorsements with both parties' consent, are part of the written policy. The policy must refer to conditions, endorsements, applications, and other papers if they are to be part of the policy.

Insurers' advertising materials and circulars are not part of a policy unless the contract expressly states that they are. If these materials contain false representations, an insured can sue the insurer for fraud, but courts do not usually allow the wording of advertising materials to change actual policy terms.

In the insurance business, it is often necessary to add a new term to a policy or to modify or waive an existing term. For these purposes, insurers issue policy riders or endorsements, which state the terms in writing, and which can be binding on the parties as though they were in the original policy. Courts require evidence that insurers have communicated the addition of riders or endorsements to insureds.

Written Versus Oral and Informal Written Contracts

Even though oral insurance contracts are valid, written policies are preferable. Oral agreements often give rise to lawsuits, usually involving the insurer's word against the insured's, with a court making final judgment. An insured who does not have a written policy may be unable to recall an oral conversation with sufficient accuracy to persuade a jury of its content.

Oral Insurance Contracts

Oral contracts to write property-casualty insurance are common, particularly when the applicant completes the application process and binder by telephone. Oral contracts are not as frequent in life insurance and in accident and health insurance. In the life and health fields, conditional receipts frequently provide evidence of interim coverage. In all oral insurance contracts, as well as in the case of informal written contracts, such as preliminary binders and conditional receipts, the final contract is the policy form itself. The crucial question is what contract language is in force from the time of the original oral agreement or informal written contract until the insurer writes the insurance contract into a policy.

Necessary Terms

To be effective, an agreement to insure, whether oral or written, must have the following components:

- *The types of coverage sought.* The risks or events covered must be specific, such as fire, accident, liability, or life.
- *The object or premises, if any, to be insured.* If liability insurance in connection with ownership of property is involved, for example, the address of the premises must be clear. If the policy says only "my residence" and the

proposed insured has several residences, the identification is ambiguous and can result in no coverage.

- *The amount of insurance.* This establishes policy limits and the insurer's liability.
- *The insured's name.* Establishment of the insurer's identity at the moment of the agreement is not necessary (as when a producer acts for an insurer).
- *The duration of coverage.* In some cases, duration of coverage might be implied from the parties' past dealings.

Implied Terms

If the parties have agreed to these basic elements, then they and the courts can turn to several other sources, including previous dealings between the parties, customary usage of terms, and legal requirements, to establish the terms from the oral or informal written agreement.

Previous dealings between the parties provide the most accurate bases for determining implied terms of an insurance contract. If an insured has requested that an producer "renew my fire policy," the renewed policy implies all the terms of the previous policy, including the coverage and premium amounts. Provisions of renewal contracts by implication are the same as those of an existing policy. An insurer's customary usage of terms provides another important source for establishing terms the parties have not mentioned explicitly, such as the type of policy an insurer usually issues in a given situation or the type of policy most insurers usually issue.

The policy language and conditions set forth in the insurer's other policies are a good source for supplying implied terms. If the insurer does not usually provide a certain coverage, the policy in question impliedly contains the provisions of policies the insurer customarily issues for the unclear coverage. When the parties have not specified the premium amount and the insurer and insured have had no previous dealings, a court will conclude that the contract implies the rate the insurer has filed with the insurance regulatory authorities or the rate the insurer usually charges others for the same type of risk.

Finally, courts consider the insured's coverage needs and practices by comparing them with those of others engaged in similar endeavors. Even so, while these needs and practices can bear on the implied terms, an insured's unique situation might not necessarily result in implied insurance provisions.

In many lines of coverage, statutory and administrative requirements have prescribed policy language. When an oral contract or a binding receipt for homeowners insurance is involved, statutory provisions usually contain all applicable language. State law prescribes many provisions, such as definitions of terms, the right to convert group life insurance to other types of coverage, and life insurance coverage in the event of suicide.

Insurance Company Designation

A producer representing two or more insurers can agree to provide coverage to an applicant without designating the insurer's identity at the outset. If a loss occurs before an insurer issues a policy, a question can arise as to which insurer the producer intended to bind to coverage.

If a producer has placed previous business or oral renewals for an insured with a particular insurer, that producer's acceptance of another oral agreement usually binds the same insurer. The parties' previous dealings imply that insurer's liability. When, however, the parties have had no previous dealings, or when the producer has changed insurers several times for renewals, more difficult problems arise.

If the producer has made a note or memorandum indicating that an insurer will write the coverage, the note is sufficient to bind that insurer. The producer must have made some outward indication of intent. For instance, a calendar notation might be a sufficient record. The producer's mere mental resolve to place business with "Insurer A tomorrow" is not sufficient to bind Insurer A if the loss occurs before the producer makes an actual notation.

To illustrate, an insurance applicant asks an insurance producer to place builders' risk insurance on two properties the applicant owns, one property on Oak Street and another on Elm Street. The agreement is oral, and the producer makes an ambiguous note to place the coverage with Tree Insurance Company. The producer later submits an insurance application for coverage on the Elm Street property, but not for the Oak Street property.

A tornado damages the Oak Street property before Tree Insurance issues the actual policy, and Tree denies the claim. A court might find that the oral binder obligated Tree to provide the requested coverage. While the oral binder might have been sufficient to bind coverage, the producer must designate a company to assume the coverage. Here the producer clearly indicated a choice (Tree Insurance), although, through inadvertence, it omitted the Oak Street property from the actual application.

The needs of modern business require and justify reliance on insurance producers' oral agreements formed while acting within their apparent authority. Courts reason that producers have considerable latitude in granting oral binders, and in this case the obvious intent was to bind Tree Insurance, which was responsible for the tornado damage.

Therefore, if the producer selects the insurer, the insured may never have heard of the insurer that has issued the policy. A producer who has designated an insurer is no longer liable even though the insurer received no notification. The producer may have violated his or her duty to the insurer in disregarding instructions, but the responsibility to the insured remains the same.

Delivery of Insurance Policies

Delivery is placing an insurance policy in the insured's control. Key legal issues concerning delivery involve whether the parties have intended a contract to become effective before delivery of the final contract. General contract law does not require delivery of a contract for it to be enforceable.

In most bilateral contracts involving the exchange of promises, delivery is not essential to contract formation. In unilateral contracts involving an offeree's performance of an act, delivery of goods or services may be necessary as acceptance.

In the case of insurance contracts, no common law or statutory enactment requires delivery of an insurance policy to complete its formation. Still, in cases in which no oral agreement, binder, or other written memorandum exists, the contract usually does not bind the insurer until delivery of the policy and the first premium payment. Delivery provides evidence of contract formation and communication of the insurer's acceptance of the insured's offer. The insurance policy is binding only upon delivery.

In property-casualty insurance, delivery is rarely in dispute. The wide use of preliminary oral agreements and written binders gives rise to effective dates of coverage that seldom involve the question of policy delivery. However, policy delivery has been the subject of litigation in life insurance. Customarily, life insurers provide that coverage is not effective until two conditions precedent occur: delivery of the policy and of premium payment. Delivery of the life insurance policy is clear evidence of the insurer's intent to be bound. However, courts have interpreted the term "delivery" broadly.

Constructive Delivery

In some cases, courts find constructive delivery, which is an intended but not an actual delivery, as equivalent to physical delivery. For example, Insurance Company mails a life insurance policy to its agent with a letter stating, "This policy is effective when you physically deliver it to Mike." Insurance Company also writes a letter to the applicant, Mike, stating, "We have mailed your policy to the agent, and it will be effective when the agent hands the policy to you." Mike dies in an accident after the letters and policy are mailed, but before actual receipt. Under these circumstances, Mike's beneficiary can recover the life insurance proceeds, notwithstanding Insurance Company's expressed intention requiring actual physical delivery. When no other decision or act remains to be performed other than the mere physical delivery of a policy, a court will decide that a constructive delivery has occurred.

On the other hand, required delivery of a life insurance policy may be subject to a condition before it becomes an acceptance. For example, Insurance Company mails a life insurance policy to Mike with a letter stating, "This policy will become effective when you pay $100 to the agent." Mike dies in an accident after receiving the letter and policy but before paying the $100. Insurance Company is not liable under the policy. Delivery of the policy was

Insurance Contract Law   5.21

subject to a condition that has not been met. Evidence can show that Mike possessed the policy, subject to the condition of premium payment.

Conditional Receipts

Although life insurance conditional receipts can provide interim coverage, the policy delivery requirement is still important. A court will view actual delivery of the policy as communicating the insurer's acceptance of the insured's application. If the conditional receipt gives the insurer the right to refuse to deliver a permanent policy, actual delivery or the insured's declination of delivery is key in determining whether the policy has taken effect.

Clauses relating to delivery of life insurance policies, inserted in both policies and applications, are valid and enforceable. The increased use of conditional receipts has reduced the significance of delivery, and some courts have applied the concept of constructive delivery so broadly as to decrease the importance of the delivery requirement. Still, the delivery requirement continues to be important for most life policies and continues to be the subject of litigation when death occurs before actual policy delivery.

First Premium Payment

A property-casualty insurance producer usually collects one of the following at the time the applicant completes the application and the producer provides the binder:

- A down payment on the premium
- Complete payment of the premium
- A promise of payment by means of a payment plan or a premium financing arrangement

As in the case of policy delivery, the insurance contract parties can stipulate that the policy is not effective until the first premium payment. In the absence of a clear and express agreement, generally the first premium payment is not necessary to the validity of an oral preliminary contract, but payment will occur upon policy delivery.

Even in the absence of an express promise to pay a premium, an implied promise to pay a reasonable premium is sufficient consideration to support an insurance contract. However, if the parties clearly intend that no contract is to form until the first premium payment, then that intent is the determining factor.

INSURANCE AS THIRD-PARTY BENEFICIARY CONTRACT

Insurance contracts provide many examples of third-party beneficiary agreements. The life insurance policy is one of the best-known examples because the contract between the insured and the insurer is for the benefit of a third person, the beneficiary, who seldom gives consideration for this benefit and is usually a donee beneficiary. During their life, insureds usually can alter or eliminate beneficiaries' rights under life insurance policies if permissible under the policy provisions. Property insurance also can provide benefits to third parties in some circumstances, particularly when property interests are being transferred or when interests in real estate are limited or shared.

Third-Party Interests in Liability Insurance

Liability insurance protects against loss resulting from the insured's causing injury or damage, usually by negligence, to a third person. Although a named insured obtains the policy, the protection can extend to others, such as additional drivers of an insured's car.

Direct-action statute
A law that permits a negligence victim to sue an insurer directly or to sue both the insurer and wrongdoer jointly.

The victims of an insured's negligence also benefit from liability coverage. In recent years some states have adopted **direct-action statutes** permitting negligence victims to sue the wrongdoers' insurers directly, or at least to sue both the insurer and the wrongdoer jointly as plaintiffs in the same lawsuit. In most jurisdictions, however, the purpose of liability insurance is to indemnify only insureds for their losses in paying damages to the victims. In these situations the third-party victims cannot sue under the liability policies until courts have ordered judgments against the insureds. If an insurer denies claim payments after a judgment, then a third party can sue an insurer directly.

Real Estate Sellers and Buyers

Real estate sellers have loss exposures, even though they may be unaware of them. A real estate buyer obtains an equitable interest in the property as soon as both parties sign the agreement of sale. The real estate is the buyer's, subject to the payment of the purchase price, under the doctrine of equitable conversion. One result of this equitable ownership is that the buyer bears the risk of loss. If the property is destroyed before it is legally transferred, the buyer must still pay the full purchase price.

The buyer can avoid bearing the risk of loss by including in the contract a provision that places the burden of any loss on the seller until actual title transfer. After transfer, of course, the loss exposure goes to the buyer, and the seller's risk terminates.

The loss exposure can be on the buyer in the following three situations:

1. *Only the seller has property insurance*. This arrangement is most common in residential sales. If fire damages or destroys the property, the sale still goes through. Which party receives the insurance proceeds depends on the sales contract terms.
2. *The seller and buyer each have property insurance to protect their respective interests*. This arrangement is typical in commercial transactions and in some residential sales. It is good for the buyer, who then controls the type and amount of coverage and the selection of insurer. Both seller and buyer can recover to the extent of their respective losses.

3. *The seller and buyer purchase a policy together.* This arrangement is the most sophisticated. If the seller and buyer together have purchased homeowners insurance covering their respective interests in the property, insurance proceeds go to make each party whole. For example, the seller collects policy proceeds to the extent of the unpaid purchase price, and the buyer collects proceeds to the extent of the deposit.

Mortgagor's and Mortgagee's Interests

Both the mortgagor and mortgagee have separate and distinct insurable interests in mortgaged property. The mortgagor is the property buyer who gets a mortgage, and the mortgagee is the lender who provides the mortgage. It is customary for the parties to agree in the mortgage on who will obtain insurance on the property. If such a provision is not included on the mortgage, one of the following three situations can occur:

1. The mortgagor can obtain separate insurance on the property, solely for the mortgagor's benefit.
2. The mortgagee can obtain separate insurance on the property. If so, money the insurer pays in the event of loss does not accrue to the mortgagor's benefit and therefore is not payable to the mortgagor.
3. The mortgagor can obtain insurance for the mortgagee's benefit either by assigning the policy to the mortgagee or including on the policy a standard mortgage clause making any proceeds under the policy payable to the mortgagee "as the mortgagee's interest may appear."

Limited Interests in Realty

Legal issues often arise with respect to limited interests in real property. Limited interests are any interests in real property short of legal ownership, such as lease interests or life estates.

Lease Interests

Courts are divided with respect to the lessor's and the lessee's rights to recover under property insurance policies. The lessor is the owner of the leased property, and the lessee is the tenant or renter.

Until relatively recently, lessors' fire insurers did not make subrogation claims against lessees for the lessees' liability in causing fire damage to insured property. Protection can now take the following forms:

- The insurer waives its subrogation rights against the lessee by endorsement to the lessor's fire policy.
- A lease provision placing "all-risks" loss on the lessor is included on the policy.
- The lessee is included as an additional insured on the lessor's policy.

- The lessee purchases an insurance policy protecting against liability for causing damage to the lessor's property.
- The lessee purchases a separate fire policy covering the leased premises.

Life Estates

A life estate is an interest in real property for the duration of a person's life. The person having that interest is a life tenant, and the person who has an interest in the property after the life tenant's death has a remainder interest.

The general rule is that, if a building has been insured before the creation of a life tenancy and is destroyed afterward, the interests in the property are converted to interests in personal property, and the life tenant has a life estate in the insurance contract proceeds. In other words, the life tenant's interest is no longer in the building or land, but only in its monetary worth. This arrangement is not satisfactory from the life tenant's or the remainderperson's standpoint, and both would be better off if specific arrangements were made in advance for insurance coverage to apply toward repairs.

Assume a life tenant holds a policy in his own name and does not designate the remainderperson as an additional insured. If the property is destroyed, the life tenant can recover the entire value of the property, even if it exceeds the cash value of the life estate. Insurers often choose to overlook this deviation from the principle of indemnity. Otherwise, they would be asserting a position inconsistent with having collected the premium corresponding to the full value of the property. Furthermore, the amount saved by resisting the life tenant's claim might not be worth the defense cost in expense and loss of goodwill. In addition, the life tenant could be the named insured on the policy, possessing a representative insurable interest in part on behalf of the remainderperson. In this case, if a loss occurs, some of the proceeds would go to the remainderperson's benefit.

Generally, in the absence of specific provisions to the contrary, the life tenant is not required to insure the premises for the remainderperson's benefit and is not required to repair accidental damage to the property not resulting from his or her actions.

Sellers and Buyers of Goods

The doctrine of equitable conversion applies only to real estate and not to sales of goods. Even after full payment of the purchase price, a seller who keeps possession of goods until the buyer comes to get them assumes the chance of loss until the buyer either receives the goods or refuses to accept them.[3] The seller, having control of the goods, must take care of them and, to protect against possible casualty or theft loss, should insure them.

REPRESENTATIONS AND WARRANTIES IN INSURANCE

Statements on an insurance application are declarations, which fall into the following two categories:

1. Representations
2. Warranties

Representations

Representations are oral or written statements that are made by an insurance applicant concerning the loss exposure and that induce an insurer to enter into the insurance contract. Representations precede and accompany the contract and are not matters about which the parties contract. For example, to induce an insurer to issue an auto policy, a prospective insured might represent on an application that she has no history of traffic violations or accidents. The representation, however, is not the subject matter of the contract.

False representation, or misrepresentation, makes an insurance contract voidable. Misrepresentations are misstatements of past or present facts. The following are the three elements required for a plaintiff insurer to establish false representation:

1. A statement is made that is false or misleading.
2. The statement relates to a material fact.
3. The insurer relies on the false or misleading statement in issuing the policy.

These elements are the same as those for fraud, except that intent is not a necessary element of false representation but is necessary for fraud. An insurer's detriment is presumed in cases of false representation because the insurer has issued a policy in reliance on the false information.

The lack of intent to deceive or reckless disregard for the truth distinguishes misrepresentation from fraud. Even an innocent misrepresentation, if material and if the insurer has relied on it, makes the contract voidable. Statutory language sometimes specifies that the misrepresentation must be willful or intentional.

Representations and misrepresentations refer only to those conditions existing at the time the parties form the contract. Promises or statements about conditions that will exist after the contract completion do not involve representations. An applicant can withdraw representations found untrue at any time before the completion of the contract, but not afterwards.

False or Misleading Statement

While an insurer might easily verify some facts, such as the kind of building construction, the make of a car, or the location of property, other facts are not so easily verifiable and depend on the applicant's word.

Most of the confusion in law regarding misrepresentation has arisen in automobile insurance cases. For example, in completing an application for auto insurance, the applicant must answer the following questions:

- Where is the car principally garaged?
- Have you had an accident within the past five years?

The insured answers that the car is garaged in a suburb, when it is really in a large city that is a higher risk area. Because the insurer might not have issued the policy had it had the correct information, the representation is material. However, if the applicant has answered in good faith, mistakenly believing the car is in the suburbs, the insurer cannot avoid the policy. In another example, however, a statement regarding prior medical consultation is a representation of fact. If the insured falsely denies having had a medical consultation, even without fraudulent intent, the insurer could avoid the policy. Even innocent misrepresentations of material facts permit avoidance of an insurance policy.

Some expressions of opinion raise issues regarding misrepresentation. Statements of opinion and belief involve matters of judgment, possible inaccuracy, and personal viewpoint, rather than objective fact. Because an insurer should recognize subjectivity, courts frequently require evidence of fraudulent intent before they permit avoidance of the policy. In insurance law, therefore, it is important to determine whether the misrepresentation was of fact or of opinion.

Statements of opinion are false only if the person does not hold the opinion stated. Thus, the insured's intent is important, and the insurer must establish that the insured spoke fraudulently. For example, a person owns a building with an actual value of $150,000, carrying a mortgage of $75,000. In applying to insure the building, the owner represents that the building is worth $175,000, with an outstanding mortgage of $50,000. The representation of the building's value is an opinion and, although the amount estimated is far from accurate, that fact alone does not justify the insurer's avoidance of the policy. The insurer must show that the applicant actually did not hold this opinion but fraudulently misrepresented its value.

Mere silence on the insured's part is not a representation. A representation requires an active statement or conduct, such as shaking one's head. Mere silence can, however, give rise to the defense of concealment. A duty to speak exists in cases involving concealment, but no such duty applies to misrepresentation. Concealment requires fraudulent intent.

Material Fact

The second element required to prove misrepresentation is that the false statement relates to a material fact. The test for materiality is whether the insurer was influenced or induced to enter into the contract in reliance on the representation.

For example, that a homeowners insurance application represents a house to be brick when the house actually is wood involves misrepresentation of a material fact. The insurer assumes a much different loss exposure than the applicant represented. The insurer could avoid the policy, assuming that its reliance on the representation was reasonable. If, however, the applicant says the house is white when it is blue, the statement involves a false representation but does not relate to a material fact.

A court can determine materiality on the following two different bases:

1. Using the objective reasonable insurer standard, the court asks, essentially, "What would a reasonable insurer have done with knowledge of the true facts?" The court would examine what most insurers would have done in a similar situation.

2. Using the subjective individual insurer standard, the court asks, essentially, "What should this insurer have done with knowledge of the facts misrepresented?"

Reliance on False or Misleading Statements

Proof of misrepresentation also requires a showing that the insurer relied on the statement. If investigation discloses facts that place the duty of further inquiry on the insurer, then it is difficult for the insurer to show reasonable reliance. An insurer that discovers the falsity of the representations before issuing a policy cannot then claim reliance on them.

For example, suppose Mary received notice of revocation of her driver's license four days after she applied for an automobile policy. The insurer knew Mary had been previously insured with an insurer specializing in high-risk automobile insurance business. Mary's application reported two tickets for traffic violations in an eight-month period before the application. The insurer hired an independent investigative agency to look into Mary's background but did not check on her motor vehicle records. Because the application itself revealed facts that placed a duty on the insurer to investigate further, the insurer had no right to rely on Mary's representations. An insurer cannot avoid a policy because of misrepresentation if its reliance on the representation is not justified.

Statutory Approaches to Misrepresentation

State statutes limiting an insurer's misrepresentation defense may require that the misrepresentation be intentional or material, or both. The New York Standard Fire Policy of 1943, adopted as the standard fire policy in nearly every state, provides as follows:

> This entire policy shall be void if, whether before or after a loss, the insured has willfully concealed or misrepresented any material fact or circumstance concerning this insurance or the subject thereof....[4]

Therefore, insurers cannot avoid the homeowners insurance policy or similar policies because of innocent misrepresentation. Many states have similar provisions for life insurance and set forth alternative requirements that the misrepresentation must have either been made with the "intent to deceive" or affected or materially increased the likelihood of loss. Under such statutes, a statement of fact is material if it might have influenced the insurer's appraisal of the risk or influenced the premium rate.

Many states have enacted statutes to permit a materiality defense on the basis of the effect of an alleged misrepresentation. These statutes basically fall into the following two groups, requiring proof of either an increase of the insurer's risk or of contribution to the insurer's loss to prove materiality:

1. Increase-of-risk statutes are more common and can set either an objective or a subjective standard for determining materiality. Under such a statute, an insured's representation that, contrary to fact, no driver under twenty-five years of age lives in the household would be misrepresentation of a material fact. Automobile insurers customarily charge higher premiums to younger insureds because they increase the risk of loss.

2. The less common contribute-to-loss statutes modify the law more radically. The rule under most of these statutes is that, regardless of materiality, a misrepresentation does not allow an insurer to avoid the contract if, from its very nature, it could not contribute to the destruction of the property. On this theory, a court could find, for example, that a contribute-to-loss statute prohibits an insurer from avoiding a homeowners insurance policy if the misrepresentation relates to a statement that the insured had never been refused other insurance or to the fact that an insured had other, concurrent, or additional insurance in violation of the policy.

Construction of Representations

Misrepresentation of facts, ideas, and circumstances can assume many forms. The problem of when a representation becomes a misrepresentation sufficient to justify avoidance of an insurance policy can be complex. Courts often interpret representations in favor of insureds. Even when a representation is not literally true, it is not a misrepresentation if it is substantially true, that is, more true than false.

To illustrate, an application for an accident and health policy asks whether the adult insured has ever experienced a "serious injury." In a lawsuit based on the policy, the insurer shows that the applicant had fallen forty feet from a tree as a child. Whether that injury was serious is for the jury to determine. If an insurance applicant's failure to mention all injuries sustained in life can form the basis for an insurer's policy avoidance, many policies would be unenforceable.

Whether an inaccurate objective fact is substantially true depends on its materiality to the agreement. The test of materiality, in turn, is whether the contract would have formed had the applicant told the truth.

Warranties

In contract law, a warranty is a written or oral statement that a certain fact is true. In insurance contract law, warranties are statements or promises in a policy that, if untrue, would render the policy voidable, whether or not they are material. In the past, strict application of this common-law definition too often resulted in insurers' attempting to escape liability for reasons not material to the person or property involved. In response, courts, whenever possible, have interpreted statements as representations rather than as warranties. For a promise to be a warranty, the following two requirements must be present:

1. The parties must have clearly and unmistakably intended it to be a warranty.
2. The statement must form a part of the contract itself.

Absent either of these requirements, the stated fact or promise is a representation, rather than a warranty.

An insurer can require an applicant to agree to a policy provision that statements of fact or promises in the application are warranties. Therefore, if the facts the applicant stated are wrong in any respect, the insurer can avoid the policy. Examples are a warranty of seaworthiness or a jewelers block policy in which the application becomes part of the policy and the statements made in the application are warranties.

Distinguished From Representation

The different legal requirements and consequences of warranties and representations make it important to distinguish them clearly. Exhibits 5-2 and 5-3 clarify the following distinctions:

- Warranties are part of the final insurance contract. Representations are merely collateral, or indirect, inducements to the contract.
- The law presumes warranties to be material, and their breach makes the contract voidable. To constitute a valid defense, representations must be proven to be material.
- Insurers either write warranties in the policy or incorporate them by reference. Representations can be oral, written in the policy, or written on another paper and need not be incorporated by reference expressly.
- Warranties require strict compliance, but representations require substantial truth only.

Incontestable Clause

In insurance, it is customary for the parties to agree that they will not contest the validity of the contract after a certain period. This agreement in an insurance contract, the **incontestable clause**, is required by all states in life, accident and health, and group life insurance policies.

Incontestable clause
An agreement included in an insurance policy that the insurer will not contest the policy after it has been in force for a specified period.

Unique to insurance, the incontestable clause is contrary to one of the basic maxims in contract law: that "fraud vitiates [negates] consent." Genuine assent cannot be based on fraud. In life insurance and accident and health insurance, the maxim is that "fraud vitiates consent, except in an insurance contract after the contestable period has expired." Therefore, an insurer cannot assert material misrepresentation, concealment, or fraud in connection with life insurance applications when the policy has been in force longer than the contestable period, usually two years, during the insured's life. The **contestable period** is a period during which an insurer can challenge the validity of a life insurance policy. The insurer agrees to waive these defenses after this period. Incontestable clauses are considered valid because the insurer has reasonable opportunity to investigate an applicant's statements during the contestable period.

Contestable period
A period during which an insurer can challenge the validity of a life insurance policy.

The incontestable clause assures policyholders that their beneficiaries will receive payment. In the past, policies that had been in force many years could be challenged upon insureds' deaths, creating serious problems for beneficiaries and insurers. People were reluctant to purchase policies that might be deemed invalid after their death.

EXHIBIT 5-2

Insured's Statements Pertaining to Risk in Application for Insurance

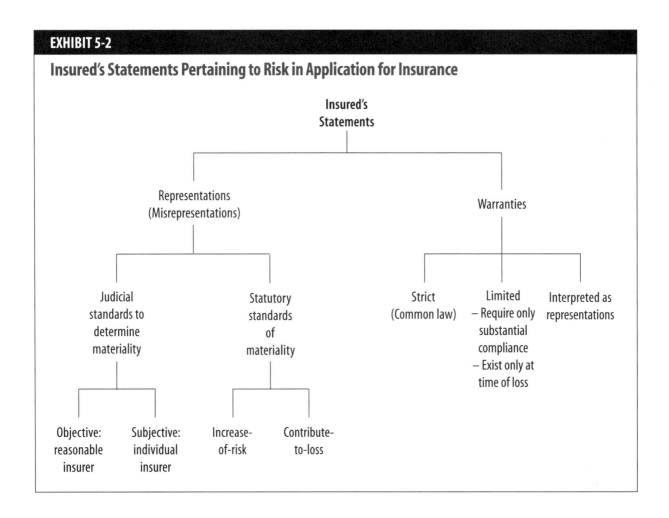

EXHIBIT 5-3

Insurer's Defenses Arising Out of the Description of the Risk

Defenses

Warranty	Misrepresentation	Concealment
Part of the final contract.	Inducement to contract.	Nonmarine insurance:
Contained in policy or incorporated by reference.	Need not be included or incorporated.	• Proof of materiality and insured's intent required.
No proof of materiality needed.	Proof of materiality required.	• No duty to reveal prior losses voluntarily.
	If material, good faith mistake is no defense.	• Applies to material facts learned between application and effective date of policy.
	Insurer must prove reliance on misrepresentation; reliance may be negated if insurer failed to investigate reasonably.	Marine insurance:
	Must be substantially false.	• Only proof of materiality and of insured's actual knowledge.
		• Required to avoid policy.

To contest a life insurance policy before the incontestable period expires, the insurer must institute a "contest," that is, a formal court action, such as a lawsuit, to cancel the policy. An insurer's mere denial of liability is not a contest. The date of issue of the policy or the date the coverage became effective, whichever is earlier, controls the period within which an insurer must commence the contest. The usual incontestable clause requires that the policy must have been in effect for two years during the insured's lifetime. Thus, an insurer can contest a policy if the insured dies during the two-year contestable period.

The incontestable clause does not extend coverage. If a policy excludes death resulting from flying an airplane, the policy will not cover death from flying an airplane even though two years have elapsed. Nor does the incontestable clause preclude showing that the person who purchased the policy had no insurable interest in the insured party's life. The strong public policy requiring insurable interest when a person buys a life insurance policy and against wagering on human life prevails over the public policy favoring the incontestable clause.

Although the incontestable clause applies to fraud, if the fraud is particularly vicious, a court can permit proof of fraud even after the contestable period has expired and can find the policy was invalid at the outset. For example, when one purchases a life insurance policy to profit from the murder of the insured, or when another person takes the insured's medical examination, the incontestable clause will not prevent the insurer from legally refusing to pay insurance proceeds. The public policy against these flagrant wrongs outweighs the reasons for the incontestable clause.

Classification

Warranty
A written or oral statement in a contract that certain facts are true.

A **warranty** is a written or oral statement in a contract that certain facts are true. Warranties can take any one of the following three forms:

1. Affirmative
2. Continuing (promissory)
3. Implied

Affirmative warranty
A guarantee that specific facts exist at the time a contract forms.

An **affirmative warranty** states that specific facts exist at the time the contract forms. A **continuing**, or **promissory**, **warranty** states that the parties will do certain things or that certain conditions will continue to exist during the policy term.

Continuing, or **promissory**, **warranty**
A guarantee that parties to a contract will do certain things or that certain conditions will continue to exist during the term of a contract.

Because they relate only to conditions that existed at the time of the contract, affirmative warranties are less strict than continuing warranties, and courts prefer to interpret warranties as affirmative. This approach is consistent with the general rule that if an insurance policy has two interpretations, a court will apply the interpretation favorable to the insured. If an insurer wants a continuing warranty, the policy language must state clearly that the warranty is to apply to future and continued use.

For example, a homeowners insurance application asks, "Who sleeps in the store?" The applicant writes, "A guard on premises at night." This statement is an affirmative warranty of conditions at the time of contract formation. If a guard slept on the premises at the application time, but not later, the insured has not breached the affirmative warranty. If the insurer wants a guard on the premises at night during the policy term, the policy language must say so clearly. Language referring to the future (continuing), such as that a guard "will be on the premises at night," is necessary.

Implied warranty
An obligation that the courts impose on a seller to warrant certain facts about a product even though not expressly stated by the seller.

An **implied warranty** is an obligation that the courts impose on a seller to warrant certain facts about a product even though not expressly stated by the seller. They are considered to exist in order to render transactions reasonable and fair, particularly in sales of goods transactions. For example, safety is generally an implied warranty for all products. All warranties in insurance law, however, are generally expressed in the policies or incorporated by reference.

Lessening Warranty Effects

Insurers prefer that courts interpret their statements as warranties rather than as representations because a representation must be material to be grounds for an insurer's avoidance of a policy. Insurers also prefer that warranties be continuing and that they therefore extend through the policy period.

State laws usually require that insureds' life insurance statements be considered representations. Although the principle that insureds' statements are usually warranties applies, courts have reduced the harsh effects this doctrine can cause by interpreting statements as factual representations and not as warranties whenever possible. They also prefer to interpret warranties as affirmative rather than as continuing.

When possible, courts also interpret policies as severable. If one policy provision is invalid, it need not invalidate the entire policy but can be severed, or separated, from other provisions. Therefore, noncompliance with a warranty concerning one type of covered property will not defeat coverage for another type of property to which the warranty does not relate.

The parties' intention determines whether a policy statement is a warranty or a representation. A court interprets a policy as a whole, including the hazards insured, the language used, and the parties' situations. A court does not consider the use of the word "warranty" or "representation" as conclusive. For instance, a declaration that factual statements are warranties might have no effect if no other provisions or circumstances indicate this characterization as the parties' intention. A statement is a representation rather than a warranty unless the language unequivocally states that it is a warranty. When any doubt exists, the statement is not a warranty.

Some state statutes make a breach of warranty no more burdensome for the insured or beneficiary than a material false representation. A typical statute provides that no oral or written misrepresentation or warranty by the insured will be material or defeat or avoid a policy unless an actual intent to deceive is apparent, or unless the misrepresentation or breach of warranty increases the risk of loss. Some states use a contribute-to-loss statute to eliminate the distinction between representations and warranties.

Some state statutes prevent insurers from specifying that representations have the same effect as warranties. Other statutes relate to the strict compliance aspect of warranties and specify that only substantial compliance is necessary. Still other statutes relate to the time in which the breach of warranty existed and prevent avoidance of the policy unless it existed at the time of the loss.

WAIVER, ESTOPPEL, AND ELECTION

In insurance, the issues of waiver, estoppel, and election usually arise when an insured sues for payment of damages under the policy and the insurer asserts a defense, such as fraud, misrepresentation, concealment, mistake, or breach of a condition. In turn, the insured argues that the insurer has forfeited or is prevented from asserting the defense by one of the following:

- Waiver of the defense
- Estoppel from asserting the defense
- Election not to take advantage of the defense

Insurance law uses the doctrines of waiver, estoppel, and election more frequently than any other field of the law. The terms are often confused or appear incorrectly as if they were synonyms—they are not. In essence, however, they have the same result: they legally prevent an insurer from reviving a defense it has forfeited earlier. The three doctrines apply to almost every ground on which an insurer can successfully deny liability.

Waiver

Waiver
The intentional relinquishment of a known right.

Waiver is the intentional relinquishment of a known right. A waiver can be express or implied, depending on the circumstances. In insurance, waiver means that an insurer's conduct has the legal effect of giving up a defense to a lawsuit. It applies to defenses based either on the insured's noncompliance with a condition or on misrepresentation.

For example, a homeowner makes a claim for water damage to the contents of his basement. The adjuster instructs the homeowner to make a list of the damaged items, then to throw the items out. Under these circumstances, the adjuster's instructions resulted in a knowing waiver of the insurer's right to inspect the contents, which are no longer available. The insurer cannot later deny the claim on the basis that the insured failed to make the contents available for inspection.

Use of Waivers

A party can waive almost any contractual right or privilege. An insurer can waive any policy provision (providing it involves a right), even standard policy language, and even a policy provision that specifically prohibits waivers. Producers, for example, can waive the following:

*   Notice of loss or proof of loss requirements
*   Property inspection or medical examination requirements
*   Policy suspension for premium nonpayment
*   Occupancy requirements for insured property

Insurers cannot waive some matters, including privileges that further public policy, such as the requirement that an insured have an insurable interest in the insured property or life. Insurers also cannot waive actual facts.

For waiver to occur, an insurance policy must exist. A statement made before an insurance contract comes into existence is not a waiver of a known right, but an attempted waiver of a future right. For example, Carmen applies for an inland marine insurance policy that allows the insurer to declare the policy void if the insured fails to maintain the security system at the insured premises. In the application, Carmen expresses the intent to disconnect the system later, and the producer tells her that the insurer does not intend to enforce the security system clause. The producer is attempting to waive a future request in a policy that does not yet exist. The producer's attempted waiver of the clause is also ineffective because the parol evidence rule would exclude evidence of the conversation; therefore, the policy itself would represent the entire contract.

A waiver of a condition differs from an exclusion. For example, if an insurer waives a policy condition that gives the insurer the right to cancel under certain conditions, the policy remains in force. An insurance contract might contain a written exclusion of a cause of loss, such as earthquake damage. By definition, an exclusion of a cause of loss cannot be waived. Waiver applies only to the relinquishment of a *right*. An exclusion represents not the insurer's *right* not to cover a cause of loss but a *duty* the insurer has chosen not to assume. For example, if an insurance policy excludes coverage for earthquake damage, the insurer has expressly chosen not to assume the duty of paying an earthquake loss under the policy. It cannot then waive the exclusion and assume the duty. The only way to cover a cause of loss excluded by a policy is to change the policy to delete the exclusion. That requires additional consideration in the form of an increased premium.

A producer's representation that a policy covers something that it does not cover, does not constitute a waiver. For example, a producer tells an insured that the policy applies when the insured is driving an employer's car. In reality, the policy contains a nonowned automobile clause excluding such coverage. The producer might be liable for the misrepresentation, but the insurer would not be liable.

Consideration

In general contract law, voluntary waivers are not binding, and a binding waiver requires consideration. In insurance law, some waivers are binding without consideration. For example, an insurer pays for a loss after the policy period for filing proof of loss has elapsed and without having received proof of loss. The insurer has waived its right to proof of loss and has received no consideration from the insured in exchange for the waiver.

Some waivers in insurance policies arguably have consideration in the form of the insured's reliance on a promised waiver. An example is an insurer's promise not to enforce the required occupancy clause of a fire insurance policy, followed by the insured's extensive absence from the premises in reliance on the insurer's promise.

Knowledge Requirement

An insurer must know of a breach of condition under the policy before it can waive that condition. Once it has knowledge of a breach, the insurer must act immediately to avoid a waiver. Whether the insurer has waived a right depends on the facts of each case. For example, a policy has a clause requiring that, after denial of a claim, the insured has twelve months to file suit. Fourteen months after denying the claim, the insurer requests information regarding the loss on which the claim was based. This inquiry is not a waiver of the time limit. But if an insurer denies liability and refuses to pay a claim for which the insured has furnished no proof of loss, the refusal can be a waiver of the proof of loss requirement in the policy.

Only pertinent knowledge can form the basis for a waiver. For example, a producer knows that an insured is constructing an addition to an insured building that has a sprinkler system to control the spread of fire. The producer, however, does not know that the building contractor will shut off the sprinkler system temporarily during construction. The producer's failure to act is not a waiver of the automatic sprinkler clause. But if the producer learns that the sprinkler system has been turned off and fails to inform the insured that coverage will be affected, the producer has waived the clause.

Policy Provisions

Courts generally do not enforce policy provisions requiring all waivers to be in writing, even though waiver is based on the contract principle that courts will enforce valid contractual provisions. Permitting insurers to negate the defense of waiver simply by inserting provisions in the policies would defeat the law of waivers entirely. Even if a nonwaiver clause is enforceable, however, there can be loopholes. For example, if a producer who has the authority to make written and oral changes in a policy makes an oral change that results in a waiver, the producer's authority may negate the waiver provision.

To illustrate, an insurance producer offers Ed an auto insurance policy containing the condition that the policy will not take effect unless the insured pays the first premium in cash. The policy also provides that any waivers must be in writing. Ed, who has no money, offers a ninety-day note, which the producer accepts. The producer's acceptance is a waiver, even though it appears to contradict one of the contractual terms, because the producer has the authority to make such a decision.

Acts Constituting Waiver

Any words that express, or acts that imply, an insurer's intention to give up the right to assert a known defense can constitute a waiver. As previously discussed, the insurer must know of the breach in a policy condition before it can waive it. With knowledge of the breach, the insurer has the option of declaring the policy void. If the insurer does not do so, a waiver occurs. Insurers' acts that can show an intent to continue a contract in force, therefore constituting waivers, include the following:

- Receipt of a premium with knowledge of a breach of policy conditions.
- Demand for appointment of appraisers or submission of a dispute to arbitration according to policy provisions, or any other demand the insurer is entitled to only if the policy is in force.
- Waiver in open court during court proceedings.
- Request for proof of loss after knowledge of a breach in a contract without a nonwaiver agreement.

- Silence beyond a reasonable time after learning of a breach. For example, when a proof of loss is defective, the insurer's silence concerning the defect beyond a reasonable time constitutes a waiver.
- Delivery of a policy to the insured with full knowledge of facts that would permit avoidance of the policy, such as the falsity of the insured's representations in the application. For example, an insurer who knows at the time of delivery of a health insurance policy that the insured suffers from asthma cannot later claim the insured was not in good health, as required by the policy, at the time of delivery.

Parol Evidence Rule

Waivers are subject to the parol evidence rule. As discussed, the parol evidence rule prohibits the introduction into evidence at trial of any oral agreements made before, or contemporaneous with, the formation of a written contract. The law assumes that final written insurance policies contain all waiver agreements that have arisen from words or acts before or during the writing of the policy. Thus, oral evidence of agreements preceding or accompanying a written insurance policy cannot be used to prove a waiver. An agent's oral promise to waive future breaches before or during the finalizing of a policy is ineffective as a waiver because of the parol evidence rule and is not admissible as evidence. On the other hand, parol evidence is admissible to prove waiver agreements made after the policy has been written and properly authorized.

Estoppel

Estoppel is a legal principle that prohibits a party from asserting a claim or right that is inconsistent with that party's past statement or conduct on which another party has detrimentally relied. For example, Kim makes a statement to Carlos. Carlos relies on the statement and takes action as a result of the reliance. Kim refuses to abide by the statement. Carlos suffers injury or detriment because of having relied on the statement.

Carlos, in a lawsuit, might assert that Kim is estopped from acting in contradiction to the original statement. Parol evidence is admissible to prove estoppel, and it is immaterial whether the words or acts occurred before or after the making of the written contract.

Insurance Law and Estoppel

Estoppel arises in insurance law from the following sequence of events:

1. False representation of a material fact
2. Reasonable reliance on the representation
3. Resulting injury or detriment to the insured

Estoppel
A legal principle that prohibits a party from asserting a claim or right that is inconsistent with that party's past statement or conduct on which another party has detrimentally relied.

For example, an insurer issues a fire insurance policy covering a building on leased land, a fact the insured disclosed on the application. The producer delivers the policy to the insured, saying, "Here is the policy, and it fully covers your building." The policy expressly provides that it is void if the building insured is located on leased land. The insured accepts the policy without reading it and puts it with other valuable papers. When the building later burns, the insurer denies the claim.

All the elements leading to estoppel are present in this case. The insurer, through its producer, made a false representation by stating that the policy covered the building. The insured reasonably relied on the representation by accepting the policy and not purchasing other insurance. The insured's failure to read the policy does not mean reliance is unreasonable. For the insurer to defend its actions based on the policy would harm the insured, who would have no insurance coverage. The insurer is prevented, or estopped, from denying that coverage exists. The producer's statement was not a waiver, because the insurer did not intend to give up any right under the policy.

Distinguishing Estoppel From Waiver

In insurance law the distinction between waiver and estoppel is often blurred. Although the legal effect of the two defenses is the same, they are different in the following ways:

- Waiver is contractual in nature and rests upon agreement between parties. Estoppel is equitable in nature and arises from a false representation.
- Waiver gives effect to the waiving party's intention. Estoppel defeats the inequitable intent of the estopped party.
- The parol evidence rule applies to waiver and does not apply to estoppel.

Factors Establishing Estoppel

When an insurer knows that an insured has breached a policy condition, any of the insurer's words or acts that the insured can reasonably interpret as representations that the contract is valid will prevent the insurer from avoiding the contract. The insured asserting estoppel, however, must come to court with "clean hands," that is, must not have committed fraud or have acted in bad faith.

The insured also must show that he or she acted in good faith and in reasonable reliance on the insurer's representation. In one case, an insurance applicant told an insurer that he was not interested in life insurance unless he could obtain $50,000 in coverage. The insurer advised him that he was eligible for only $30,000 in coverage. After negotiations, the insurer agreed to issue a $50,000 policy. The insured died accidentally, and his widow submitted a claim. The insurer discovered that the insured had been eligible, under established underwriting criteria, for only $30,000 in life coverage. The insurer paid $30,000 and refunded the premium for the $20,000 over that coverage. The court held that all the elements from which estoppel arises were present: A false representation of a material fact (that the insured was covered for $50,000), reasonable reliance, and resulting injury or detriment. The insurer had to pay the additional $20,000.[5]

Estoppel applies when an insurer's producer misinterprets questions or falsifies answers in an application and the insurer issues a policy based on the misleading information. Because the producer made the misrepresentation, the insurer cannot deny (is estopped from denying) the truth of the statements.

For example, a woman purchases life insurance for her son, who plays high school football and works during vacations as a salesperson. The producer describes the son on the insurance application as a salesperson but says nothing about football. Had the insurer known that the son played football, it would have charged a higher premium. The son later dies from a football injury. The insurer attempts to avoid the policy obligation on the ground of false representation, proving in court that the premium would have been higher had the insurer known that the son played football. In this case, the insurer cannot dispute the truthfulness of the answers on the application. Unless the insurer introduces evidence at trial of wrongful collusion between the insured and the producer, the insurer is estopped from claiming misrepresentation and avoiding payment. The policy covers this loss.

Similarly, if an insurer's producer states that agreed-on acts, such as including a certain policy endorsement, have occurred when they have not, that representation, on legal challenge, might be subject to estoppel. For example, if a producer states that an endorsement will be added to a policy to permit a building to be unoccupied for certain periods, and the policy issues without that endorsement, the insurer cannot deny the validity of the intended endorsement. That the insured failed to check the policy does not negate the element of reasonable reliance. Oral evidence is admissible in court to prove the facts.

In all of the cases just discussed, the insurer might have a right to sue the producer for wrongful acts, but the law protects the innocent insured.

Following is a further illustration of how waiver and estoppel operate:

One of an insured's duties is to report a loss promptly. This notice should include how, when, and where the loss happened and also should include any injured parties' and witnesses' names and addresses. The insured's failure to meet this obligation could result in a denial of coverage.

An insurer accepts a notification that the insured experienced a loss. This notice could come from anyone, not necessarily the insured, and is usually sufficient for the claim department to create a file and begin an investigation. If the insurer does so without issuing a reservation of rights letter to the insured, the insurer has waived its right to deny coverage on the basis of the insured's failure to fulfill the obligation to report the loss fully.

In this case, estoppel also applies. The insurer has accepted whatever notice was given and begins an investigation without a reservation of rights letter. Relying on the belief that the insurer will fulfill its contractual obligation to indemnify and defend, the insured takes no further action, neither investigating the loss further or preserving the evidence. The insurer, then, cannot use the defense of insufficient notice to deny its duty to indemnify and defend. Denial would put the insured in a detrimental position, and the insurer would be estopped from denying coverage.

Election

Election
The voluntary act of choosing between two alternative rights or privileges.

Election is the voluntary act of choosing between two alternative rights or privileges. A choice of one available right can imply a relinquishment of the right not chosen. For example, an insurer that treats a contract as valid for the purpose of collecting premiums cannot treat it as invalid for the purpose of covering a loss. The thrust of the election doctrine is that an insurer or insured cannot adopt a "heads I win, tails you lose" position.

Application

Waiver, estoppel, and election are not interchangeable doctrines. Application of the doctrine of election limits a party's range of choices. Election requires proof of neither the waiver requirement of voluntary relinquishment of a known right nor the estoppel requirement of detrimental reliance.

Examples of election are evident whenever a party chooses between alternatives. Frequently an insurer must decide between rejecting an insured's premium and providing the insured's coverage. An insurer that elects to accept a premium is bound by that choice and cannot later declare that no coverage exists.

Another example of election involves choosing between alternative rights under a fire policy, which usually gives an insurer the option to repair or rebuild instead of paying monetary compensation in case of loss. An insurer whose words or acts have led an insured to expect monetary compensation has elected that method of discharging its duty under the policy. The insurer has reserved the right to elect between two alternative duties and, having elected one (monetary compensation), has lost the right to choose the second alternative (repairing or rebuilding). Election applies even though the insurer has not voluntarily relinquished a known right, as would occur with a waiver, and no detrimental reliance applies that would lead to estoppel.

Insured's Election

The doctrine of election also applies to choices by the insured. In many instances the insured must choose between two inconsistent legal remedies. Having elected one course of action, the insured cannot pursue the other.

For example, an insurer cancels a life insurance policy including provisions for the payment of disability benefits. The insured elects to sue the insurer for fraudulent breach of the contract and receives damages, but not reinstatement of the policy. Later, the insured attempts to sue to recover disability benefits that would have accrued before the previous lawsuit had it not been for the insurer's cancellation of the policy.

In the first suit, the insured alleged a breach of contract and a right to damages. In the second suit, the insured demanded benefits that would have been payable absent a breach of contract. Election of the first remedy bars the insured's right to use the second remedy. The insured elected to treat the policy as canceled and demand damages in the first lawsuit and is therefore barred from pursuing the second remedy, disability benefits, on the assumption that the policy had not been canceled.

Choosing Among Waiver, Estoppel, and Election

While the doctrines of waiver, estoppel, and election are available to either party to the insurance contract, insureds are more likely to assert them. Insureds are usually most successful when they rely on the doctrine of estoppel in lawsuits, compared to the other two doctrines.

The central element giving rise to estoppel is that the insured has acted or refrained from action in reliance on the insurer's position and has consequently suffered detriment. Reliance and detriment are usually easier for the insured to prove, leading to estoppel, than the factors needed to establish waiver (that the insurer intentionally relinquished a known right) or to establish the election (that the insurer chose between two remedies). Exhibit 5-4 summarizes waiver, estoppel, and election.

Insurer's Protection Against Waiver, Estoppel, and Election

When a third party sues an insured for a questionable loss, the insurer has the following three alternatives (illustrated in Exhibit 5-5):

1. To refuse to defend the insured
2. To investigate or defend under a reservation of rights notice or nonwaiver agreement (or both)
3. To investigate or defend (or both) without any reservation of rights

Justified Refusal

The insurer's refusal to defend is justified if the policy does not cover the claim. Court opinions agree that an insurer that justifiably refuses to defend has not breached the policy and therefore has no obligation under the policy concerning any claim arising out of a noncovered loss.

EXHIBIT 5-4

Distinguishing Factors of Waiver, Estoppel, and Election

	Waiver	Estoppel	Election
Defined	Insurer's voluntary and intentional relinquishment or abandonment of a known right	Insurer's prohibition from enforcing certain conditions of a policy when insurer's representation, express or implied in words or conduct, caused insured to rely on the representation	Insurer's voluntary choice of inconsistent alternatives, which precludes subsequent selection of the other alternative
Relative advantages for insured	Requires no proof of insured's reliance and resulting detriment	Requires no proof of the insurer's voluntary relinquishment of a known right	Requires no proof of either voluntary relinquishment of a known right or detrimental reliance
Relative disadvantages for insured	Requires proof of the insurer's voluntary relinquishment of known right	Requires proof of detrimental reliance	Difficult to prove
Other distinguishing characteristics	Requires proof of insurer's act or conduct	Requires proof of act or conduct of both parties to the contract: • Insurer's representation of a fact • Insured's reliance on the representation and resulting detriment	Requires proof of insurer's act or conduct

Unjustified Refusal

An insurer that wrongfully refuses to defend an action against the insured is liable for breach of contract even if the refusal was an honest mistake. In such a case, the insurer is liable for the judgment against the insured or for a reasonable settlement with the insured. Judgment can exceed the policy limit, and reasonable expenses, such as court costs and attorney fees, are also recoverable.

If an insurer refuses to defend, the insured is released from a policy obligation to leave litigation management to the insurer. The insurer, then, cannot complain later about the conduct of the defense in the lawsuit. Similarly, a court will release the insured from other affirmative policy provisions, such as proof of loss; notice of suit; and provisions requiring cooperation, aid, and assistance. The insurer by unjustified refusal waives any possible defense based on such noncompliance.

EXHIBIT 5-5

Insurer's Post-Loss Alternatives When Coverage Is Questionable

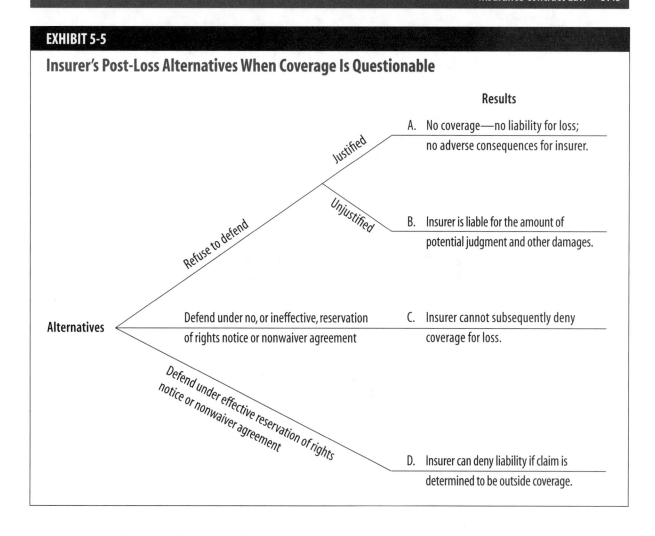

Results

A. No coverage—no liability for loss; no adverse consequences for insurer.

B. Insurer is liable for the amount of potential judgment and other damages.

C. Insurer cannot subsequently deny coverage for loss.

D. Insurer can deny liability if claim is determined to be outside coverage.

Alternatives

Justified

Unjustified

Refuse to defend

Defend under no, or ineffective, reservation of rights notice or nonwaiver agreement

Defend under effective reservation of rights notice or nonwaiver agreement

Reservation of Rights Notice or Nonwaiver Agreement

Insurers use reservation of rights notices and nonwaiver agreements to preserve certain defenses against liability that they might have under policy terms. Claim personnel frequently use them when loss investigation reveals the possibility that the insurer might deny coverage under the policy.

A **nonwaiver agreement** is a written contract in which the insured and the insurer agree that neither will waive any rights under the policy as a result of the investigation or defense of a lawsuit against the insured. The contract is bilateral in that both parties make promises. A **reservation of rights letter** is a notice sent by an insurer advising the insured that the insurer is proceeding with a claim investigation but that the insurer retains the right to deny coverage later. It differs from a nonwaiver agreement in that the notice is unilateral, usually in the form of a letter from the insurer to an insured. Both the reservation of rights notice and the nonwaiver agreement prevent subsequent claims not only of waiver, but also of estoppel, election, and any other theories of rights that vary with policy provisions. Exhibits 5-6 and 5-7 are illustrations of a reservation of rights notice and a nonwaiver agreement.

Nonwaiver agreement
A written contract in which the insured and the insurer agree that neither will waive any rights under the policy as a result of the investigation or defense of a lawsuit against the insured.

Reservation of rights letter
A notice sent by an insurer advising the insured that the insurer is proceeding with a claim investigation but that the insurer retains the right to deny coverage later.

EXHIBIT 5-6

Reservation of Rights Notice

To: (insured's name)

Subject: Accident or loss on (date) at or near (place)

Your letter reporting the above accident was received on (date). In view of the delay in reporting this matter and for other reasons which may become evident as a result of our investigation, this investigation is being made with full and complete reservation of all rights afforded to the (insurance company) under policy number _____ issued to you.

Signed (Insurance Company Representative)

EXHIBIT 5-7

Nonwaiver Agreement

It is hereby agreed by and between the (insurance company) and (insured) that no action heretofore or hereafter taken by the (insurance company) shall be interpreted as a waiver of any of its rights and defenses under a policy number issued to (insured) with respect to any claim or suit arising in connection with an accident or loss which occurred on or about (date) and at or near (place).

It is further understood and agreed that, by the execution of this agreement, (insured) does not waive any rights which he or she may have under the policy.

Signed (Insured)

Signed (Insurance Company Representative)

The possibility of denying coverage poses a dilemma for the insurer. If the insurer continues to investigate the loss on its merits without determining whether it can legitimately deny coverage, its rights might be prejudiced. Such actions can raise issues of waiver, estoppel, or election that could negate the insurer's lack of coverage defense. However, if the insurer does not investigate, it might forfeit all defenses, and the loss can increase.

Nonwaiver agreements and reservation of rights notices help solve the insurer's dilemma. They inform an insured that the insurer's activities regarding the loss are not the relinquishment of its right to stand on policy provisions. Such activities might establish that the insurer is not liable under the policy. The insurer can continue to investigate and evaluate the loss on its merits, an activity beneficial to both the insurer's and insured's interests. Simultaneously, the insurer can determine whether the insured has violated policy terms and whether the insurer will accept liability under the policy. When the insurer, knowing of grounds for forfeiture or noncoverage, manages the defense of a lawsuit against its insured without giving timely notice of its reservation of rights, it cannot refuse coverage on those grounds.

The insurer should attempt to enter into a nonwaiver agreement with the insured as soon as the potential coverage question surfaces. The nonwaiver agreement requires both the insurer's and insured's signatures. Occasionally the following practical difficulties arise in the attempt to secure the insured's consent and signature:

- The insured might refuse to sign a nonwaiver agreement, even after the claim representative has clearly explained its significance. This refusal can delay the investigation of the loss.

- The insured could challenge the nonwaiver agreement if the claim representative has not explained the importance of the agreement fully and fairly. The lack of adequate explanation can lead an insured to claim lack of contractual intent, misunderstanding, duress, or other defenses that can jeopardize the agreement's validity.

If the insured refuses to sign a nonwaiver agreement, the only way the insurer can protect itself against later claims of variance is to resort to the reservation of rights notice. This unilateral declaration gives notice to the insured that the insurer intends to safeguard its rights to dispute liability under the policy terms and that its conduct in investigating the loss should not be interpreted contradictorily in this respect.

Certain elements must be present for a reservation of rights notice or nonwaiver agreement to be effective. First, the insurer must communicate the reservation of rights notice to the insured, usually by letter. Oral notice is not advisable because it would be too difficult to prove oral notice. Second, the notice must be timely. A reservation of rights or nonwaiver agreement prevents estoppel because it gives the insured the option to hire a lawyer to take over the defense from the insurer. Because the notice must give the insured reasonable time to take over the defense, the insurer's safest course is to give notice as soon as it obtains knowledge of the policy defense.

The reservation of rights notice must inform the insured fairly of the insurer's position, citing the policy provisions on which the insurer relies and the facts that, if proven, would result in a denial of liability.

If the insurer has acted in good faith and used every reasonable method to contact the insured, the insurer can assert its policy defense. For example, a liability insurer who questions coverage under an automobile policy writes six letters to the insured informing her that it will defend an action against her but with express reservations of its rights to contest the policy. The insured contends that she never received the letters. Because the letters were addressed to her both at her residence and workplace, a presumption arises that she received the letters.

Example: Timeliness of Liability Disclaimer

The insured is involved in an automobile accident. The application and the policy provide that the insured's use of his car is for pleasure and business. The insurer investigates the claim under the policy provisions. Seven months after the accident the insurer discovers that, at the time of the accident, the insured used the car to carry passengers for hire, a use excluded from coverage. Upon learning of this use, the insurer denies liability. The insurer is not estopped from raising the policy defense in spite of the seven months that have elapsed between the accident and denial because of the following:

- The insurer could have reasonably relied on the insured's accident report, which did not disclose that he was carrying passengers for hire at the time of the accident.

- The insurer denied liability as soon as it learned the facts.

- A year and a half elapsed before the case went to trial, so the insured had ample time to prepare his own defense.

SUMMARY

This chapter concluded the examination of contract law by focusing specifically on insurance contracts and discussing their distinctive features and formation.

Insurance contracts have special characteristics as distinguished from other contracts. An insurance policy is all of the following:

- A conditional contract
- A contract involving fortuitous events and the exchange of unequal amounts
- A contract of utmost good faith
- A contract of adhesion
- A contract of indemnity
- A nontransferable contract

Like all contracts, an insurance contract requires an agreement consisting of an offer and an acceptance as well as competent parties, consideration, and a legal purpose. Issues relating to offer and acceptance may be specific to insurance and can depend on whether a policy is for property-casualty insurance or for life insurance.

The effective date of insurance contracts can depend either on binders for property-casualty insurance or on conditional receipts for life insurance. Conditional receipts include binding, approval, and insurability receipts.

Oral insurance contracts can be binding. However, some terms must be in writing, but others can be implied, such as those drawn from previous dealings, customary usages, or statutory requirements. Courts frequently do not require that insureds read their policies because of their complexity.

Insurance contracts also provide many situations involving third-party beneficiary arrangements.

Third parties may be the beneficiaries of life insurance policies, persons other than the named insured who are covered by the policy under certain circumstances, or persons injured through the insured's negligence. Third-party issues also arise in the sale of real estate and in mortgagor-morgagee relationships. Statements on an insurance application are usually either representations or warranties. Warranties are statements or promises in an application that, if untrue, would render the policy voidable, whether or not they are material. A misrepresentation can make an insurance contract voidable. The three elements of false representation are as follows:

1. A statement is made that is false or misleading.
2. The statement relates to a material fact.
3. The insurer relies on the false or misleading statement in issuing the policy.

Some state statutes modify the common law in these situations with either increase-of-risk or contribute-to-loss statutes.

An insurer might not have the defenses of fraud, concealment, mistake, misrepresentation, or breach of a condition because the insurer has done one of the following:

- Waived the defense
- Become estopped from asserting the defense
- Elected not to take advantage of the defense

A waiver is the intentional relinquishment of a known right, requiring knowledge of the facts and relinquishment of a right based on knowledge of those facts. In insurance law, estoppel is one party's representation of fact that the other party relies upon so that it would be unfair to allow the first party to refuse to be bound by the representation. Estoppel arises in insurance from the following sequence of events:

1. False representation of a material fact
2. Reasonable reliance on the representation
3. Resulting injury or prejudice to the insured

Election is voluntarily choosing between alternative rights or privileges. An insurer's or insured's choice between available rights can imply a relinquishment of the right not chosen.

Either party to the insurance contract can use the doctrines of waiver, estoppel, and election. In most cases, however, insureds use them. Parties are usually more successful when they rely on the doctrine of estoppel in lawsuits instead of waiver and election.

Insurers use reservation of rights notices and nonwaiver agreements to protect certain defenses against liability that they might have under the policy terms from insureds' assertions of waiver, estoppel, or election. These notices and agreements allow insurers to advise insureds that the insurers' activities regarding losses do not waive their rights to stand on policy provisions. An insurer can continue to investigate and evaluate losses on their merits.

CHAPTER NOTES

1. *Delancy v. Insurance Company*, 52 N.H. 581 (1873).
2. *Drake v. Globe American Casualty Company*, Ohio 10th Circuit Court of Appeals, unreported case No. 74AP-472, March 11, 1975.
3. UCC, § 2-509(3), and comment 3.
4. New York Standard Fire Policy of 1943, lines 1–5.
5. *Clauson v. Prudential*, 195 F.Supp. 72 (D.Mass. 1961).

Chapter 6

![Direct]

Direct Your Learning

Commercial Law

After learning the content of this chapter and completing the corresponding course guide assignment, you should be able to:

■ Regarding sales contracts, describe the following:

- Rules of contract law applying to the sale of goods

- Warranties made in sales of goods

- Types of sales contracts

- Delivery terms

■ Given a case, explain what risk of loss each party to a sales transaction bears.

■ Given a case, explain whether and why a breach of sales agreement occurs and what remedies buyers and sellers have.

■ Explain what legal principles apply to the following:

- Commercial paper

- Elements of negotiability

- Transfer and negotiation

- Holders in due course

- Checks

- Security interests

■ Explain how provisions relating to the following apply in a case:

- Fair trade laws

- Consumer warranty laws

- Consumer credit laws

- Bankruptcy

■ Define or describe each of the Key Words and Phrases for this chapter.

Develop Your Perspective

What are the main topics covered in the chapter?

Many laws govern commercial transactions. Fair trade laws include the Federal Trade Commission Act (FTC Act), state unfair trade practice acts, and state and federal consumer warranty laws. Insurance fair trade practice acts prevent unfair and deceptive activities in the insurance business. Consumer credit laws include the Truth in Lending Act, the Fair Credit Reporting Act, the Fair Debt Collection Practices Act, and the Equal Credit Opportunity Act. The federal Bankruptcy Act governs all bankruptcies except those involving insurance companies, which are subject to state regulation.

Identify the laws that affect insurance transactions and operations.

- How do those laws restrict insurance commerce?

Why is it important to learn about these topics?

Commercial law affects individuals and business entities. Commercial relationships give rise to many legal disputes involving both insureds and insurers.

Consider the kinds of commercial transactions your employer might encounter on a daily basis.

- How are the sales contracts or negotiable instruments your employer enters into affected by commercial laws that govern those transactions?

How can you use what you will learn?

Evaluate the importance of commercial law in your daily transactions.

- How might consumer laws protect your personal credit information?
- How has commercial law protected you in sales contracts?

Chapter 6
Commercial Law

This chapter provides an overview of the following five areas involving commercial law:

1. Sales contracts
2. Negotiable instruments
3. Secured transactions
4. Consumer law
5   Bankruptcy

The Uniform Commercial Code (UCC) governs sales contracts, negotiable instruments, and secured transactions. Most states have adopted the UCC to regulate commercial transactions. Federal and state statutes regulate consumer matters, and the federal Bankruptcy Act regulates most bankruptcy matters.

Each of these topics is addressed in a simplified overview format because these subjects involve a complex web of terminology, definitions, and statutory law. Law schools generally treat these subjects in four or five individual courses.

SALES CONTRACTS (UCC ARTICLE 2)

Under the UCC, a sales contract is a legally enforceable agreement by which a seller and a buyer transfer, or agree to transfer, ownership of property for a fixed sum. Article 2 of the UCC governs the law of sales of goods. General contractual terms and concepts also apply to these sales. In general, goods refers to property that is tangible and movable, other than money. Growing crops and timber, for example, are goods. Things that are part of or emanate from land, such as minerals, oil and gas, structures, or parts of structures, are goods if a sales contract provides that they are to be severed from land.

One unique characteristic of the law of sales is its many special rules for merchants. A merchant is a person who deals in goods, or a professional, including an agent, who purports to have special knowledge or skill concerning those goods.

General Contract Law Application

General contract rules apply to contracts for the sale of goods, except that a sales contract need not state the price of the goods to be enforceable. If a contract leaves the price open or provides a method of fixing the price, the price is the reasonable price at delivery time. Statutes of frauds apply to sales contracts under the same rules applicable to other contracts, such as requiring a written contract for sales of goods exceeding $500 and written contracts that cannot be performed in one year.

The general rules of fraud, mistake, duress, and undue influence apply to contracts for the sale of goods. In addition, the UCC provides that a contract that was unconscionable at its inception is unenforceable.

Offer and Acceptance

A contract requires an agreement, which, in turn, requires an offer and an acceptance. The general contract principles of offer and acceptance apply to contracts for the sale of goods. However, unlike general contract law, the law of sales does not always require a formal acceptance. In transactions between merchants, it is common for an offer to require a shipment of goods as the acceptance.

Article 2 of the UCC, which governs the law of sales, defines conforming and nonconforming goods. Conforming goods are goods stipulated in the contract or those that fall within trade usage or the parties' prior course of dealing.[1] All other goods are nonconforming goods. Generally the shipment of nonconforming goods is a breach of contract, but Article 2 provides the following two exceptions to that rule:

1. A shipment of nonconforming goods is not an acceptance or a breach of contract if the seller notifies the buyer that the shipment is only an accommodation to the buyer.
2. If a buyer rejects goods as nonconforming, the seller can notify the buyer of its intention to "cure" the nonconformity of the shipment by delivering conforming goods. This notification must be made before the time for contractual performance has expired. If the performance time has expired, and if the seller had reasonable grounds to believe that the goods conformed to the contract, the seller still has a reasonable time to substitute conforming goods. An example of reasonable grounds would be the buyer's acceptance of the same kind or condition of goods as conforming in prior transactions.

An offer of any bilateral contract can be accepted by either a promise to perform or a tender (an offer) of performance or by completed performance within the time allowed for accepting the offer. Similarly, an offeree (seller) can accept an offer to buy goods for prompt shipment either by a prompt promise to ship or by prompt shipment. An acceptance of an offer by a promise to ship the goods can be made in any reasonable manner unless the offer clearly indicates that only one method is acceptable.

If a definite expression of acceptance of an offer to buy or sell goods contains additional or different terms, it is still an acceptance of the original offer unless it is expressly conditioned on the offeror's consent to the new terms. Whether the new terms become a part of the contract depends on the following two variables:

1. If one of the parties is a nonmerchant, the new terms become part of the contract only if the offeror expressly agrees to them.

2. If both parties are merchants, the new terms become part of the contract unless they would materially alter the contract or unless the offeror objects within a reasonable time.

Whether the parties are merchants or nonmerchants, any proposal that would materially alter a contract does not become part of the contract unless the offeror expressly agrees to the alteration. A proposal would materially alter a contract if its inclusion in the contract would result in hardship for the other party. For example, a proposal to negate certain standard warranties would alter a contract materially, but a proposal to limit the time for complaints would not.

Consideration

Consideration is essential to sales contracts. However, contrary to general contract law, the parties' agreement to modify a contract for the sale of goods is binding even without new consideration.

Warranties

A warranty is a promise that something is true. Contracts for sales of goods can contain statutory warranties, as well as the sellers' warranties, which can be express or implied. A seller's overt words or actions can create an express warranty. The law infers the existence of an implied warranty because of the circumstances of the sale.

Express Warranties

If a statement forms the basis of the sale, it is an express warranty. The following are three kinds of express warranties:

1. An affirmation of fact about the goods, such as the seller's promise that the goods conform to a certain standard, is a warranty. For example, a statement about a car's gas mileage is a warranty even without the words "warranty" or "guarantee."

2. Any description of goods in a contract is a warranty that the goods conform to the description. For example, a contract to sell a new hay baler is an express warranty that the hay baler is new.

3. A contract based on a sample or model is a warranty that the goods will conform to the sample or model.

Implied Warranties

Implied warranties in sales of goods fall into the following two categories:

1. Implied warranty of merchantability
2. Implied warranty of fitness for a particular purpose

An implied warranty of merchantability applies only to transactions in which the seller is a merchant. It requires that any goods sold by a merchant meet the following five qualifications:

1. The goods must pass without objection in the trade under the contract description.
2. Fungible goods, such as grain, must be indistinguishable and interchangeable and must be of average quality for the kind of goods sold. (Land, for example, is not fungible.)
3. The goods must be fit for the ordinary purpose for which they will be used.
4. All goods in a lot must be of approximately like kind and quality.
5. The goods must conform to the specifications, if any, on the container or label.

In addition, implied warranties can arise from the parties' course of dealings or from the usages of a particular trade.

Implied warranty of fitness for a particular purpose
An implied warranty that applies when the buyer relies on the seller's expertise in selecting a particular product for a particular purpose.

When a buyer relies on the seller's expertise in selecting a particular product for a particular purpose, an **implied warranty of fitness for a particular purpose** arises. This implied warranty applies to both merchants and nonmerchants. For example, suppose that John has never been deep-sea fishing but wants to fish for marlin. He asks a sporting goods dealer to recommend suitable equipment. The dealer recommends certain equipment as suitable, and John buys it. Without negligence on John's part, the equipment breaks while he is using it for marlin fishing. John relied on the dealer's expertise to select the appropriate equipment for deep-sea marlin fishing. The seller has apparently breached a warranty of fitness for a particular purpose.

A seller can orally exclude or modify a warranty of merchantability only if the contract itself is oral and if the seller uses the word "merchantability" in a disclaimer. A seller can exclude any implied warranty by describing the goods as "as-is" or "with all faults" or by using similar language.

Implied warranty of title
An implied promise in a contract for the sale of goods that the seller has legal ownership of goods and has no knowledge of any security interest or other lien on the goods other than those disclosed to the buyer.

A common type of implied warranty in contracts for the sale of goods is an **implied warranty of title**, a promise that the seller has legal ownership of the goods. The seller also warrants having no knowledge of any security interest or other lien on the goods other than those disclosed to the buyer.

A contract may exclude the warranty of title if the buyer has reason to know that the seller does not have full title. For example, agents sell goods as representatives of owners. The agent relationship alerts the buyer that the agent does not have title. Another example of a warranty is a promise by a merchant that the sale of a piece of equipment does not violate the right of the person who invented it.

If the buyer inspects, or refuses the opportunity to inspect, the goods at the time of forming the contract, no implied warranty applies to nonlatent defects that the buyer's inspection would have revealed. If, however, the seller has made statements about the goods that cause the buyer to fail to inspect, the law might deem the seller's statement an express warranty.

Past practice between the parties, or trade usages, can also result in the exclusion of implied warranties, just as they can result in the creation of implied warranties. If a contract contains one or more express warranties and a general exclusion of "all warranties, express or implied," the express warranty prevails.

Third-Party Beneficiaries of Warranties

Products liability involves the noncontractual (tort) liability of a contractor, manufacturer, or vendor for injury to a third party. Article 2 of the UCC deals with sellers' contractual liability arising from express or implied warranties to third parties who are not the immediate buyers of goods.

Article 2 provides that a seller's warranty extends to any person in the buyer's family or household, or any guest in the buyer's home, who suffers injury resulting from breach of the warranty, if it is reasonable to believe that the person would either use or be affected by the goods. An express or implied warranty about a ladder, for example, would extend to the buyer's child or to a houseguest.

Types of Sales Contracts

The specialized categories of sales contracts include the following:

- Sale on approval—sale to a consumer who wants to try the goods before buying them. A buyer who is not satisfied with the goods can return them at the seller's risk. Title and risk of loss remain with the seller until acceptance. The seller should insure the goods.

- Sale or return—sale to a person who intends to resell the goods but who has the right to return them if they do not sell. The seller retains title until payment or resale. However, the buyer's creditors can attach the goods, that is, seize them under legal authority, if the creditors are not on notice of the seller's interest in the goods. For example, if the creditor knows that the buyer is in the business of selling other people's goods, the creditor cannot seize them. Return of the goods is at the buyer's risk.

- Auction sales—public offering in which the highest bid is the acceptance of an offer. For some auction sales, the auctioneer sets a minimum bid for the goods, and if all bids are under the minimum, withdraws the goods from bidding. Auction sales of goods without a set minimum bid must be advertised as "without reserve," and the highest bidder must get the article.

FOB (free on board) place of shipment
A shipping condition under which the seller delivers goods to the carrier at the seller's risk and expense and the ownership then shifts to the buyer.

FOB (free on board) place of destination
A shipping condition under which ownership passes from the seller to the buyer when the carrier delivers the goods to the buyer's premises.

FAS (free alongside) vessel
A shipping condition under which ownership passes from the seller to the buyer when the seller delivers the goods alongside a vessel for loading onto that vessel.

FOB (free on board) vessel
A shipping condition under which goods are loaded on board the vessel at the seller's risk and expense and then ownership passes to the buyer.

CIF (cost-insurance-freight)
A shipping condition under which the seller is obligated to pay for the insurance and freight charges for delivery to the buyer.

CAF (cost and freight)
A shipping condition under which the seller is obligated to pay for the freight charges but not for the insurance for delivery to the buyer.

COD (collect on delivery)
A shipping condition under which the buyer pays when the goods are delivered and has no right to inspect the goods as a condition to acceptance and payment.

In any type of auction sale, however, the bidder can retract the bid at any time before the auctioneer announces completion of the sale. The bidder's retraction does not revive any prior bid. Instead, bidding begins again.

Delivery Terms, Inspection, and Time

Buyers and sellers have several options as to where goods will be delivered and which party bears the risk and expense of delivery. The following are common delivery and shipping terms in sales contracts, many of which are used in marine insurance:

- **FOB (free on board) place of shipment**. The seller delivers goods to the carrier at the seller's risk and expense and the ownership then shifts to the buyer.
- **FOB (free on board) place of destination**. Ownership passes from the seller to the buyer when the carrier delivers the goods to the buyer's premises.
- **FAS (free alongside) vessel**. Ownership passes from the seller to the buyer when the seller delivers the goods alongside a vessel for loading onto that vessel.
- **FOB (free on board) vessel**. Goods are loaded on board the vessel at the seller's risk and expense and then ownership passes to the buyer.
- **CIF (cost-insurance-freight)**. The seller is obligated to pay for the insurance and freight charges for delivery to the buyer.
- **CAF (cost and freight)**. The seller is obligated to pay for the freight charges but not for the insurance for delivery to the buyer.

Inspection

Upon delivery, the buyer generally has the right to inspect the goods as a condition to acceptance and payment. The inspection can include reasonable testing at the buyer's expense. If a buyer rejects the goods for failure to conform, the buyer can recover the testing cost from the seller.

Buyers have no right to inspect in the following two situations:

1. When the carrier delivers the goods **COD (collect on delivery)**, the buyer pays when the goods are delivered and has no right to inspect the goods as a condition to acceptance and payment.
2. When a contract requires the buyer to pay at the time of delivery of the document of title (unless the contract also requires payment only after the goods are available for inspection)

Time for Delivery

If the time for delivery is not set in or cannot be implied from the contract or the parties' past practices, delivery must occur within a reasonable time. Unless a seller assumes a greater obligation, such as by agreeing in the contract that time is of the essence, delay in delivery or nondelivery is not a breach of contract if performance becomes impracticable because of an occurrence unforeseen by both parties.

Title and Risk of Loss

As a practical matter, under the UCC, the potential financial consequence of loss (liability) follows title except when identified goods are at the seller's residence or place of business and the buyer is to pick them up. If the seller is a merchant, liability does not pass to the buyer until the buyer receives the goods. If the seller is not a merchant, liability passes to the buyer when the seller completes delivery.

When a buyer rejects delivered goods because they do not conform to the contract, the liability remains with the seller until the seller remedies the deficiency or until the buyer accepts the goods.

The parties can agree that the liability will pass at some other time than the UCC specifies, and the parties' prior practice, trade usage, or circumstances of the case also can change the time that liability passes.

Legally, one can transfer only such title as one has. For example, a person who unwittingly holds stolen goods has no legal title and can transfer no title, even to a good-faith purchaser. The UCC has established the following two exceptions to this rule:

1. *A person who holds a voidable title can transfer good title.* For example, Karl holds title to property. The title is voidable because the seller from whom Karl purchased the property misrepresented a material fact relating to the property. Karl transfers the title to Ellen. Ellen has full title to the property. Her title is not voidable, as was Karl's—unless the contract between Ellen and Karl is voidable for other reasons under contract law. For example, if Karl made the same misrepresentations to Ellen that the original seller made to Karl, Ellen could void the contract.

2. *A person to whom goods have been entrusted can transfer valid title even absent legal title to the goods.* **Entrusting** is the transfer of possession of goods to a merchant who deals in goods of that type and who may, in turn, transfer the goods and all rights to them to a purchaser in the ordinary course of business. Such a merchant can transfer whatever title the entruster has to a buyer in the ordinary course of the merchant's business. For example, Mary takes a watch to a jeweler who repairs and sells new and used watches. The jeweler sells the watch to John, who is unaware of Mary's interest in it. John will get the full title that Mary had. Mary's recourse is to sue the jeweler.

Breach of Sales Contracts

If goods do not conform to a contract, the buyer can accept or reject all or part of them. To sue for breach of contract, the buyer must first give reasonable notice of rejection to the seller, stating the particular defect.

This notice gives the seller an opportunity to cure the defect. Between merchants, the seller may also make a written request for a written statement of the defects claimed by the buyer.

If the seller has no agent or place of business in the buyer's market area, the buyer must follow the seller's instructions for what to do with the rejected goods. The buyer can demand indemnity for necessary expenses incurred in holding or shipping the goods. If the goods are perishable, the buyer can sell them on the seller's behalf. If the goods are not perishable, and the buyer does not receive instructions within a reasonable time, the buyer can sell them, store them, or reship them to the seller. In these cases, the buyer's acceptance of nonconforming goods does not waive or forfeit any right to sue for the breach. To sue for breach, however, the buyer must have notified the seller of the nonconformity within a reasonable time and must prove that the goods were nonconforming.

Revocation of Acceptance

A buyer can revoke an acceptance of goods under the following circumstances:

*   The buyer reasonably assumed that the seller would cure the defect but the seller did not do so.
*   The buyer accepted the goods before discovering the nonconformity.
*   The buyer accepted the goods in the first place because it would have been difficult to discover the defect and because the seller gave assurances about the quality of the goods.

In each of these situations the buyer has reasonably relied on the seller's delivery of acceptable goods and should not bear the liability.

Excuses for Nonperformance

The following circumstances provide excuses for nonperformance of a sales contract:

1. *Loss of identified goods.* If specific and identified goods are destroyed before the liability passes to the buyer, and if neither party was at fault, the contract is void. If the loss is partial, the parties may avoid the contract. The buyer can accept damaged goods with an allowance in the price for the deficiency. In neither case, however, can the buyer sue the seller.
2. *Unavailability of agreed-on shipping.* If the agreed-on carrier or berthing, loading, or unloading facilities become unavailable, at either party's fault, the buyer must accept any offer by the seller to use a commercially reasonable substitute.
3. *Failure of a presupposed condition.* A seller of goods need not complete the sale if that performance becomes commercially impracticable or if a domestic or foreign governmental regulation stops performance. The impracticability must be caused by an unexpected contingency affecting

a condition that both parties assumed would continue undisturbed. The outbreak of war, for example, might make shipping impossible between two points. If, however, the outbreak of war was foreseeable, the parties might have expected the contingency; therefore nonperformance is not excusable. A severe shortage of materials caused by an embargo or by a natural disaster can also cause commercial impracticability.

Seller's Remedies

The seller's remedies for breach of contract depend on whether the breach occurs before or after delivery of the goods. If the buyer declares an intent not to perform the contract before delivery—an anticipatory breach—the seller can resort immediately to any remedy for breach. Alternatively, the seller can wait for performance for a reasonable time or can simultaneously pursue a remedy for the buyer's breach. If the buyer revokes the acceptance, repudiates the agreement, or fails to make a required payment, the seller can withhold delivery of the goods.

If a seller discovers before delivery that the buyer is insolvent, the seller can refuse to deliver the goods. If the goods are en route, the seller can stop delivery unless the buyer has already received a document of title for the goods, or unless a carrier or warehouse operator has notified the buyer that it is holding the goods for the buyer.

If the seller discovers that the buyer has received the goods on credit while insolvent, the seller can demand their return within a reasonable time period. When a buyer wrongfully repudiates the contract, fails to make a payment due before delivery, or wrongfully rejects the goods, the seller can sue. If the lawsuit is successful, the seller can recover the difference between the contract and the market price at the time and place of delivery plus lost profits, if any.

If the goods still are being manufactured at the time of breach, the seller can complete their manufacture and sell them to another party or stop their manufacture and sell them as they are or for scrap value.

If the buyer fails to pay for goods after accepting them or after the liability passes to the buyer, the seller can sue for the goods' contract price even if the seller still possesses them, but only if the seller cannot sell them to another party at a reasonable price.

Buyer's Remedies

If the seller fails to deliver the goods or repudiates the contract, the buyer is entitled to the difference, if any, between the contract price at the time the buyer learned of the breach and the market price. Alternatively, if the undelivered goods are unique or if the buyer cannot obtain them from another source, the buyer is entitled to specific performance (delivery of goods). Specific performance is also the remedy if a buyer cannot obtain substitute goods to replace the undelivered goods.

Because buyers often need goods immediately, they might purchase substitute goods within a reasonable time after learning of a breach and then recover from the seller any difference between the cost and the contract price. A buyer who rightfully rejects delivery or revokes acceptance and who possesses the goods has all the rights that a seller has when the buyer breaches before delivery. The buyer can hold the goods for the seller's instructions or sell them.

A buyer who accepts nonconforming goods and informs the seller of the nonconformity is entitled to the difference, if any, between the value of the goods accepted and the value they would have had, at the time and place of acceptance, if they were as the seller warranted. In addition, the buyer can recover any loss resulting from the nonconformity that the seller had reason to know might follow from a breach and the buyer could not have prevented.

NEGOTIABLE INSTRUMENTS (UCC ARTICLE 3)

Negotiable instruments are the written documents that allow parties to pay at a distance or at a future time. In face-to-face trade or commerce, a buyer strikes a bargain with the seller, takes possession of the goods, and gives something in exchange. However, when parties conduct commerce at a distance or over time, written legal documents ensure payment. To be negotiable, an instrument must be in writing and must meet the following four requirements under UCC Article 3:

1. It must be signed by the maker, or drawer.
2. It must contain an unconditional promise or order to pay a certain sum in money and contain no other promise, order, obligation, or power on the part of the drawer or maker except as otherwise provided by Article 3.
3. It must be payable on demand or at a definite time.
4. It must be payable to order or to bearer.

Article 3 of the UCC governs negotiable instruments payable to order (to a designated payee) or to bearer (to the holder of the paper). (Order refers to order paper, an instrument payable to a specific payee or to any person the payee designates. Bearer refers to anyone who possesses the paper.)

Types of Commercial Paper

Commercial paper is any written or printed document or instrument, including a negotiable instrument, evidencing a debt. Article 3 covers the following types of commercial paper, the two most common of which are the draft (check) and the promissory note:

Draft, or **check**
A type of commercial paper containing an unconditional order by the drawer (person making out the draft), requiring the drawee, usually a bank, to pay a certain sum to the payee or to the bearer.

*   **Draft**, or **check**—A paper containing an unconditional order by the drawer (the person making out the draft), requiring the drawee, usually a bank, to pay a certain sum ("sum certain") in money to the payee or to bearer

- **Certificate of deposit (CD)**—A document issued by a financial institution acknowledging receipt of money and promising to repay it, with interest, at a specific time
- **Promissory note**—A written promise to pay money on demand or at a definite future time
- **Trade acceptance**—A two-party draft used when a seller wants cash immediately but when the buyer cannot provide it until the goods are resold

Exhibit 6-1 shows a draft, and Exhibit 6-2 shows a promissory note. A basic requirement of commercial paper is that it be negotiable—readily salable, so that the seller does not have to wait for payment. To get immediate payment, the seller can sell the negotiable paper. If the paper is nonnegotiable, a buyer of the instrument would take the following two steps before purchasing it:

1. Check the credit rating of the payer
2. Determine whether the payer has any defenses against a seller who sues, such as that full or partial payment was already made

Certificate of deposit (CD)
A type of commercial paper issued by a financial institution acknowledging receipt of money and promising to repay it, with interest, at a specific time.

Promissory note
A type of commercial paper containing a written promise to pay money on demand or at a definite future time.

Trade acceptance
A type of commercial paper that is a two-party draft, used when a seller wants cash immediately but when the buyer cannot provide it until the goods are resold.

EXHIBIT 6-1

Draft (in the form of a check)

	(Date) June 1, 20XX
Pay to the order of _____ (Payee)	$10.00
Ten and _____	⁰⁰/₁₀₀ Dollars
Bank/Drawee	
	_____ (Drawer)

EXHIBIT 6-2

Promissory Note

$10,000   Anytown, June 1, 20XX

One year after this date I promise to pay to the order of Peter Finch Ten Thousand Dollars ($10,000).

Due June 1, 20XY   (Signed) Mary Chen

A negotiable instrument avoids these time-consuming steps. The buyer of a negotiable instrument also buys the seller's personal liability and therefore needs to know only the seller's credit rating. In addition, the purchaser of the instrument can sometimes be free and clear of virtually all defenses that the drawer or maker might have against the payee, such as poor quality of delivered goods. These advantages can expedite the transaction. The instrument becomes freely transferable, almost like cash.

Transfer and Negotiation

Transfer of a negotiable instrument gives the new holder the same right to enforce payment as the original holder had. For example, Allen buys goods from Bob and gives Bob a promissory note as payment. Bob gives the promissory note to Catherine in payment of a debt he owes her. Allen fails to pay on the promissory note. Catherine has the same right as Bob would have had, had he kept the promisory note, to sue Allen for payment.

If the original payer has a defense against payment, the new holder is subject to that defense. In the example just given, assume Bob delivered defective goods and Allen refused to accept them. If Catherine, holding the promissory note, sues Allen for payment, Allen can use the same defense he would have used against Bob: that the goods were defective.

Primary and Secondary Liability

Primary liability
The absolute obligation to pay a negotiable instrument according to its terms.

A person who is absolutely required to pay the instrument according to its terms has **primary liability**. A person who becomes liable on the instrument only if someone else refuses to pay or to accept the instrument has **secondary liability**. Therefore, the maker of a note is primarily liable. For a draft, the acceptor is primarily liable; the drawer is not primarily liable because a drawer's liability arises only when the drawee refuses to accept or pay the draft. One who endorses a negotiable instrument assumes secondary liability only when the maker or drawee rejects (dishonors) the instrument.

Secondary liability
The obligation to pay a negotiable instrument only if someone else refuses to pay or to accept the instrument.

Endorsements

An endorsement is a signature or the equivalent of a signature that legally transfers a negotiable instrument. An endorsement must appear in some form of writing, even a rubber stamp, on the instrument, usually on the back, and must transfer the entire sum. (The term "endorsement" here is not the same as an endorsement to an insurance policy.) As long as a document contains a signature, other words do not affect the endorsement. For example, the words "I hereby assign my interest in this note to Lindsey—signed Mark" are an effective endorsement. If the payee's or transferee's name is not correct, that person can do one of the following:

- Endorse the instrument in the name in which it was made out
- Endorse it with the correct name
- Endorse it in both names

Special endorsement
A signature or the equivalent of a signature that specifies the person to whom a negotiable instrument is payable.

A **special endorsement** specifies the person to whom the instrument is payable. For example, the payee of a check can negotiate it to another person by writing "Pay to the order of Richard Roe," or "Pay to Richard Roe," above his or her signature on the back of the check.

A **blank**, or **general endorsement** names no specific payee, making the instrument payable to the bearer. A **restrictive**, or **collection endorsement** includes language placing additional limits on further negotiation, such as "pay Jill Doe only if she appears on June 23," or "for deposit only."

A **qualified endorsement** passes title to the instrument but limits the endorser's liability to later holders if the instrument is later dishonored. A qualified endorsement usually is made by writing "without recourse" over the signature. **Unqualified endorsements** are more common; they place no limits on the endorser's liability on the paper.

Holders in Due Course

Although assignees of negotiable instruments are generally subject to any defenses the original payer may have, some holders can possess negotiable instruments free of all defenses. A **holder in due course** is one to whom a negotiable instrument has been issued or endorsed and who possesses it under the following three conditions:

1. For value
2. In good faith
3. Without notice that it may not be valid, can be claimed by another, is overdue, or was previously dishonored

A party often must establish qualifications as a holder in due course to attain maximum rights on the instrument. Such proof is important only if the original holder has a legal defense to the instrument, for example, a defense for nonpayment.

One who obtains an instrument in one of the following ways does not become a holder in due course:

*   Purchasing the instrument at a judicial sale or taking it under legal process
*   Acquiring it in taking over an estate
*   Purchasing it as part of a bulk transaction (such as the purchase of all the assets of a business), not in the regular course of the transferor's business

Holder in due course status can be sold and transferred with a negotiable instrument. The status does not apply to a transferee who was a party to any fraud or illegality affecting the instrument or who, as a prior transferee, had notice of a defense against or claim to the instrument.

A holder in due course is free of **personal defenses**, which are all claims to the instrument by any person and any defenses that would be effective in a simple contract transaction, such as lack or failure of consideration, misrepresentation, or fraud. **Real defenses** go to the very existence of the

Blank, or **general endorsement**
A signature or the equivalent of a signature on a negotiable instrument that names no specific payee, making the instrument payable to the bearer.

Restrictive, or **collection endorsement**
A signature or the equivalent of a signature that includes language placing additional limits on further negotiation of a negotiable instrument.

Qualified endorsement
A signature or the equivalent of a signature that passes title to a negotiable instrument but limits the endorser's liability to later holders if the instrument is later dishonored.

Unqualified endorsement
A signature or the equivalent of a signature that places no limits on the endorser's liability on the paper.

Holder in due course
The person to whom a negotiable instrument has been issued or endorsed and who possesses it for value, in good faith and without notice that it may not be valid, can be claimed by another, is overdue, or was previously dishonored.

Personal defense
A claim to an instrument by any person and any defense that would be effective in a simple contract transaction.

Real defense
A defense of an obligor of a negotiable instrument that may be asserted even against a holder in due course.

obligation and can be asserted even against a holder in due course. Examples of real defenses are the incapacity of the maker, drawee, or drawer; duress; illegality; and discharge in bankruptcy. For example, the maker's insanity might negate the existence of the obligation in the first place.

Checks

Checks are the most familiar negotiable instruments. A bank depositor is a bank's creditor to the extent of the balance in the bank account. The bank is the depositor's agent in making disbursements from that account. The following summarizes common check transactions:

- Failure to honor checks—A bank is liable for all damages caused by its failure to honor a check when the depositor's account contains sufficient funds.

- Overdrafts—A bank can honor a check not covered by the depositor's balance, thus creating an overdraft and making the depositor the bank's debtor.

- Altered checks—A bank can charge an altered check to the depositor's account only to the extent of the check's original terms. For example if a wrongdoer changes $10 on a check to $100 by adding a zero, the bank can charge only $10 to the depositor's account.

- Stale checks—A bank need not pay an uncertified check presented more than six months after its date. However, the bank has the right to do so and to charge the customer's account.

- Stop-payment orders—An oral stop-payment order is effective for only fourteen days. A written stop-payment order is effective for only six months, unless renewed in writing.

- Certified and cashier's checks—Certification equals acceptance. A **certified check** is a check guaranteed by a bank to be covered by sufficient funds on deposit. A **cashier's check** is a check drawn by a bank on its own funds. The purchaser of either such check is secondarily liable on it only if the check is payable to the purchaser and the purchaser endorses it.

- Drawer's death or incompetence—When a drawer dies or becomes legally incompetent, the bank can pay outstanding checks until it knows or should know of the death or incompetence. Even with such knowledge, a bank can pay or certify a check drawn by the deceased for ten days after the date of death.

- Forged signatures—A bank cannot permanently charge a check against the customer's account if the check has a forged drawer's signature, a forged signature of a necessary endorser, or a materially altered check for more than its original amount. The customer must use reasonable care and promptness to notify the bank of such defects, so that the bank can avoid payment on future frauds by the same parties.

Certified check
A check guaranteed by a bank to be covered by sufficient funds on deposit.

Cashier's check
A check drawn by a bank on its own funds.

SECURED TRANSACTIONS (UCC ARTICLE 9)

Buyers pay for goods with their own cash, with borrowed cash, or on open credit granted by the seller. The seller or a third-party lender can require the buyer to give the seller or lender a **security interest** in the goods sold, creating a **secured transaction**, which is a business arrangement in which a buyer or borrower gives collateral to the seller or lender to guarantee payment of an obligation. A security interest authorizes the seller or lender to take the goods or otherwise prevent the buyer from disposing of them if the buyer defaults on payments. The seller or lender is the **secured party**. The goods sold, covered by the security interest, are **collateral**. The security device affects only recovery of the goods. Even if a security device is ineffective, contract common law still provides relief in the form of damages.

Security devices in the sale of goods include pledges and suretyship, described as follows:

- A **pledge** is a device by which a borrower guarantees payment by delivering collateral to the lender to hold as security for the debt. If the borrower does not repay the money, the lender can retain the article. For example, Kathy borrows money from Nancy and gives Nancy her diamond ring as security for the loan.

- A **surety** agrees to be responsible for the performance of another person's contract to repay money borrowed or to perform a certain duty. The party whose performance is required and is guaranteed by the surety is the **principal**. A surety joins the principal in making the promise, and both are primarily liable to the third party, the **obligee**. A surety promises to perform only if the principal does not perform and has secondary liability. The surety who performs is entitled to reimbursement from the principal.

Perfecting a Security Interest

The following are the three methods to perfect a security interest, that is, to make it valid, depending on the type of collateral:

1. *Filing a financing statement.* A financing statement is the instrument filed in a public records office that gives the public notice of a security interest in the collateral. It bears the name and address of the debtor and the secured party and a description of the collateral. Filing a financing statement is the most common method of perfecting a security interest.

   The security interest is perfected when two events have occurred: (1) The security interest has attached; that is, the goods have been sold and the security agreement has been executed, and (2) the financing statement has been filed. If the seller delays filing the financing statement until after delivery of the goods to the buyer, the security interest is unperfected, and another security interest might attach to the property in the meantime.

   When a debtor has met all obligations under the security agreement, a termination statement should be filed so that the secured party can no

Security interest
An interest in property that exists by contract as security for payment or performance of an obligation.

Secured transaction
A business arrangement in which a buyer or borrower gives collateral to the seller or lender to guarantee payment of an obligation.

Secured party
The seller or lender in a secured transaction who has a security interest in property or goods sold.

Collateral
The goods covered by a security interest in a secured transaction.

Pledge
A security device by which a borrower guarantees payment by delivering collateral to the lender to hold as security for the debt.

Surety
The party in a secured transaction who agrees to be responsible for the performance of another party's contract to repay money borrowed or to perform a certain duty.

Principal (in a surety)
The party in a surety relationship whose performance is required and is guaranteed by the surety.

Obligee
The party in a surety to whom the surety and principal are liable.

longer claim a security interest under the financing statement. If more than one perfected security interest applies to the same collateral, they rank in priority according to time of filing or perfection.

2. *Transferring collateral*. Actual possession of the collateral is transferred from the debtor to the secured party.

3. *Attaching goods*. Attachment (physical seizure) of consumer goods is a way to gain priority over conflicting security interests. Attachment does not require filing a financing statement. Perfection occurs when a legal interest attaches to the goods.

The method of perfection used depends on the nature of the collateral. For example, transferring actual possession is the only method of perfecting a security interest in a negotiable instrument because delivery transfers ownership. Possession, however, is not practical for perfecting a security interest in equipment, consumer goods, and farm products that the buyer wants to use.

Rights of Perfected Security Interests

A perfected security interest is superior to a later perfected security interest and to most subsequent lien creditors, with limited exceptions, such as the following:

• A holder in due course takes a negotiable instrument free of any perfected security interest in that instrument.

• An artisan's lien for services or materials with respect to the collateral takes priority over a perfected security interest in that collateral.

Rights of Unperfected Security Interests

Even if a security interest is not perfected, it is still good between the parties and against a third party who buys the goods from a person who deals in them. However, the secured party's rights are subordinate to the following parties' rights:

• One who obtains a perfected security interest

• A lien creditor, assignee, bankruptcy trustee, or receiver

• One who buys the property from a person who does not deal in that type of goods, if the buyer does not know about the unperfected security interest

Default

Nonpayment is the most obvious form of default, but a security agreement defines other events as defaults, such as failure to insure the collateral, the debtor's bankruptcy, loss or destruction of the collateral, or removal of the collateral to another place. The following are the secured party's rights in the event of default:

- *Right to sue on the underlying debt.* The secured party can proceed as though no security agreement existed and can sue the debtor.

- *Right to foreclose.* The secured party can foreclose the debtor's interest in the collateral by retaining the collateral in full satisfaction of the debt or by selling or leasing it and applying the proceeds to satisfy the claim.

- *Right to regain possession.* The secured party has the right to regain possession of collateral through the courts or by other legal means, such as lawful repossession.

- *Right to retain or sell the collateral.* The secured party can choose either to keep or to sell the property in full satisfaction of the obligation.

- *Right to dispose of the collateral as desired.* The secured party may sell or lease the collateral at a public or private sale with notification to the debtor. The purchaser at such a sale takes the goods free of the security interest and any subordinate security interests or liens.

The debtor or any other person subject to a security interest in the collateral can redeem the collateral at any time before its sale by tendering full performance of the contract.

CONSUMER LAW

Consumer law includes federal and state legislation intended to ensure fair treatment of consumers in dealings with suppliers of goods and services. Consumers have the protection of both fair trade and consumer credit laws.

Fair Trade Laws

Fair trade laws include the following:

- The Federal Trade Commission Act
- State unfair trade practice acts
- State and federal consumer warranty laws

Federal Trade Commission Act

The Federal Trade Commission (FTC) Act of 1914[2] prohibits unfair methods of competition and unfair or deceptive acts or practices that affect interstate commerce. The act does not apply to the insurance industry.

Federal antitrust laws, notably the Sherman Act,[3] protect commerce from unlawful restraints, price discrimination, price fixing, and unlawful monopolies. Under the McCarran-Ferguson Act, the federal government generally does not regulate the business of insurance because it is subject to state regulation, and states usually apply their own antitrust laws to insurance. However, if a state does not have antitrust legislation applicable to insurance, federal antitrust laws apply. Additionally, even if states do regulate insurance antitrust matters, federal antitrust laws can apply in cases of insurance practices involving boycott, coercion, or intimidation.

The FTC Act is not strictly an antitrust act, although it overlaps with the Sherman Act. The FTC Act is broader, prohibiting unfair or deceptive acts that have no relationship to competition. For example, restraint of trade is a violation of the Sherman Act and also an unfair method of competition. However, misrepresentation is not usually a violation of the Sherman Act but is an unfair act affecting commerce within the meaning of the FTC Act.

The five-member Federal Trade Commission takes action against unfair or deceptive practices in commerce in the following three ways:

1. *Cease-and-desist orders.* Following a hearing, the commission may issue a cease-and-desist order to violating parties.
2. *Trade practice conferences.* A trade practice conference deals with a subject, such as false and misleading advertising in a given industry, by devising a set of trade practice rules. In effect, a trade industry has the opportunity to help write its own regulatory rules, which can deal with unfair methods of competition or with anticompetitive or unfair business practices.
3. *Informal settlements and consent orders.* The accused party, for settlement purposes, executes a stipulation agreeing to stop the challenged practice, a remedy usually employed when the violation was unintentional. The consent order is used when a complaint and call for a formal hearing have been issued. In effect, it is similar to a pretrial settlement in a lawsuit.

State Unfair Trade Practices Acts

In addition to federal laws, states have their own deceptive trade practices acts, insurance fair trade practices acts, and unfair claim settlement practices acts.

Every state now has a Deceptive Trade Practices Act (DTPA). State laws vary, but they generally prohibit one or more of the following practices:

- Unfair acts (oppressive or bad faith conduct)
- Deceptive acts (fraud, deceit, and misrepresentation)
- Unfair methods of competition (including antitrust violations such as price fixing and group boycotts)

State laws are designed to compensate for perceived inadequacies in the FTC Act. For example, some acts extend rights to sue that the FTC Act does not provide. Many of the state acts apply to insurance, unlike the FTC Act.

Many states also have unfair trade practices acts specific to insurance, which generally follow the National Association of Insurance Commissioners (NAIC) model Insurance Fair Trade Practices Act. These acts generally prohibit anyone in insurance from engaging in any unfair methods of competition or unfair and deceptive acts or practices, defined as follows:

- Misrepresentation and false advertising of policies
- Defamation of competitors
- Boycott, coercion, and intimidation

- Creation of false financial statements
- Unfair discrimination
- Use of rebates
- Use of stock operations and advisory board contracts

In reference to the last practice, the model act prohibits insurers from issuing capital stock, certificates, or securities or using advisory board or similar contracts that promise returns or profits as an inducement to purchase insurance, a sophisticated form of rebate.

Under the model act, a state commissioner who believes an act is unfair or deceptive under the law can call a hearing and may order the person or organization to cease the act.

Consumer Warranties: Magnuson-Moss

The principal laws governing consumer warranties for many years were the UCC provisions relating to express and implied warranties. These provisions codified implied warranties of merchantability and fitness for a particular purpose and described the creation of express warranties. The problems with these warranties were that only a consumer could enforce them and that a consumer also could unwittingly waive them. Inadequate controls led to increasing deception in product warranties and resulted in the passage of the Magnuson-Moss Act in 1975,[4] which supplements the FTC Act and the antitrust laws. The FTC enforces Magnuson-Moss. Some states have also passed warranty laws, such as "lemon" laws applicable to cars.

Under Magnuson-Moss, a producer of goods need not give a warranty at all; but, if the producer does provide a written warranty, it must conform to certain standards. The law applies to consumer products, defined as tangible personal property for personal, family, or household use, including fixtures.

The regulations require a written warranty to disclose the following:

- What it will and will not cover
- When it expires
- To whom it applies
- What the warrantor will do if a malfunction occurs
- What service and parts are free
- How to obtain redress under the warranty

If the product costs are within certain dollar limits, full and complete disclosure of the terms of the warranty must be provided. If the product costs more than the stated dollar limits, the warranty must be either "full" or "limited."

A **limited warranty** must contain the elements just discussed, but it limits the consumer's rights in some other respects, such as by setting a time for separation of the implied warranty of merchantability.

Limited warranty
A warranty that limits the consumer's rights in some respects.

Full warranty

A warranty that promises to remedy a product defect within a reasonable time and without charge and to refund the purchase price or to replace the product if the repairs fail ("lemon provision").

A **full warranty** has two important provisions:

1. The warrantor must remedy the product defect within a reasonable time and without charge.
2. The warranty must have a "lemon" provision.

The lemon provision takes its name from slang describing a product that never seems to be right, no matter how often it is repaired. A lemon law applies only to full warranties and is general in nature, thus limiting its application. If repeated efforts to repair the product fail, lemon provisions require that consumers of such products must have a choice of a full refund or a replacement without charge. To avoid the lemon provision requirement, some manufacturers call their warranties limited even though they probably otherwise constitute full warranties. For example, a car manufacturer might redesignate a "twelve-month unlimited mileage" warranty as a limited warranty to eliminate the possibility it might have to replace "lemons." Many states have adopted their own lemon laws.

The UCC provides for implied warranties of merchantability and fitness for a particular purpose but permits sellers to disclaim them. Magnuson-Moss does not permit disclaimers of implied warranties but allows a limited warranty to restrict implied warranties to the same length of time as the express warranty. Under a full warranty, implied warranties cannot be limited in any way.

Consumer Credit Laws

Consumer credit laws include the federal Truth in Lending, Fair Credit Reporting, Fair Debt Collection Practices, and Equal Credit Opportunity Acts.

Truth in Lending Act

As credit transactions increased rapidly following World War II, many consumers overextended themselves and often did not know of their credit terms or interest rates. In an effort to correct this situation, Congress passed the Consumer Credit Protection Act of 1968, or the Truth in Lending Act.[5] This act does not replace or preempt state credit disclosure acts unless they are clearly inconsistent with the act, and then does so only to the extent of the inconsistency.

The Truth in Lending Act applies only to individuals' credit and only to credit transactions for personal and real property purchased for personal, family, household, or agricultural purposes. It does not apply to business or commercial transactions.

The act applies to all persons or organizations that regularly extend credit or make finance charges in connection with installment purchases. It also applies to situations in which the purchaser can pay for the item in more than four installments, whether or not there is credit or a finance charge. It is not applicable to the usual insurance installment payment plan under which credit is not actually extended, but it does apply to a premium financing plan under which the insured pays a creditor for premium charges plus a finance charge and to any plan under which the premium is payable in more than four installments, regardless of charges.

The act does not control the terms of a credit transaction. Its purpose is to ensure that the consumer knows what those terms are. Creditors must disclose finance charges. Costs incidental to real estate transactions, such as the cost of title examination and title insurance, attorney's fees, escrow payments, appraisal fees, and credit report charges, are not finance charges. When in connection with the sale of personal property or with a consumer loan, however, loan fees, finders' fees, charges for credit reports, and service or carrying charges are finance charges. In all cases, interest or time-price differentials are finance charges.

Premiums for credit life or accident and health insurance are finance charges unless the creditor informs the debtor in writing that the insurance is not a condition for obtaining credit and the debtor buys it voluntarily. In the same situations, premiums for required property or casualty insurance are also finance charges, unless the insurer informs the insured debtor in writing of the cost and the insured debtor is given the option to purchase it from a third party.

In the ordinary credit transaction for the sale of goods, the seller must disclose all the finance charges, the cash price, the down payment (including any trade-in), other charges that are not part of the finance charge, and the annual percentage rate of interest charged. The seller must state the terms of payment clearly, including any charge for delinquent payments, and must give a description of any security interest in the goods sold.

In a consumer loan with a definite amount and definite time of payment (a close-end loan), the creditor must provide the same information. In a "revolving" or continuous credit plan (an open-end plan, the usual department-store charge card) the seller must state the conditions of making a charge, the method of calculating the balance due, the method of determining the amount of the finance charge, and any different rates for different balances. The seller also must disclose the conditions under which it might make other charges and under which the creditor retains a security interest. The debtor can request the average effective annual rate or a projected rate of return.

After opening the open-end plan account, the creditor must furnish the following:

- Complete periodic statements that show the amount due at the beginning of the statement period
- The amount and date of each additional extension of credit
- The debtor's payment during the period
- The finance charges added
- The interest rate for the period

- The annual percentage rate
- The outstanding balance at the end of the statement period
- The method of determination

Congress amended the Truth in Lending Act in 1970 to cover the issuance of credit cards and the liability of credit card holders. The amendment prohibits companies from issuing credit cards to people who do not request or apply for them. One who holds a requested credit card is liable only for its authorized use. If a card is lost or stolen and used without authority, the holder's liability does not exceed $50. The buyer also has the right to withhold payment without incurring a finance charge until the settlement of disputes over the price or quality of goods purchased.

Under the Fair Credit Billing Act,[6] a person who is dissatisfied with property or services purchased with a credit card has the right not to pay the remaining amount due if he or she first tries in good faith to return the property or give the merchant a chance to correct the problem. The credit card holder's bank usually charges the bill back to the bank servicing the merchant, who in turn charges the merchant, who must make good or sue for the bill.

Electronic funds transfer (EFT) system

A system that moves funds from one institution to another by means of electronic signals rather than the physical exchange of money or checks.

Different rules apply to **electronic funds transfer (EFT) systems**, which move funds electronically rather than by physical exchange. EFT system cards, commonly known as debit, or ATM, cards, have the following two features:

1. Using the card at point of purchase, the seller instantly transfers the sales amount to the seller's account from the buyer's account.
2. People can use most debit cards to make deposits and withdraw cash at automated teller machines (ATMs). The Electronic Funds Transfer Act of 1978[7] and Regulation E of the Federal Reserve Board define the parties' rights and responsibilities. Valid cards can issue only in response to specific requests. Liability in general is limited to $50 if the owner of the card reports the loss within two business days.

The Fair Debt Collection Practices Act,[8] an amendment to the Truth in Lending Act, prohibits unfair and oppressive collection practices by agencies specializing in debt collecting for creditors. The act prohibits collection practices such as using violent or criminal acts, using profane language, publishing lists of debtors, calling debtors repeatedly or in the middle of the night, threatening legal action with no intent to follow through, and contacting the debtor at work or at any unusual time or place except with the debtor's consent. The act also prohibits contacting the debtor's employer, neighbors, or friends, except for the limited purpose of locating the debtor, and even then, no information can be revealed concerning the agent's role in the collection process. The collection agency can send a written notice to the debtor. A debtor who wants to prevent any further communications by the collection agency may indicate in writing the desire to stop all further contacts, in which case the collector can choose to sue.

Fair Credit Reporting Act

The Fair Credit Reporting Act[9] attempts to ensure that consumer-reporting agencies exercise their responsibilities with fairness, impartiality, and a respect for consumers' rights. Improper use of consumer credit reports can result in both criminal and civil liability. The act applies only to consumer reporting agencies, defined as any entity that, for money, or on a cooperative nonprofit basis, regularly assembles or evaluates consumer credit information or other information on consumers to furnish consumer reports to third parties.

A consumer report is a consumer-reporting agency's communication on the consumer's creditworthiness, credit standing, and capacity, general reputation, personal character, or mode of living, used in whole or in part in establishing the consumer's eligibility for the following:

- Credit or insurance primarily for personal, family, or household purposes
- Employment
- A business transaction, with a legitimate need, involving the consumer for personal, family, or household purposes

The agency can furnish a credit report only under the following three circumstances:

1. In response to a court order
2. Under written instructions of the subject of the report
3. To a person who, it has reason to believe, intends to use the information
   - In connection with a credit transaction
   - For employment purposes
   - In connection with insurance underwriting
   - To determine eligibility for a business license if the applicant's financial status is relevant
   - For a legitimate business need for the information in connection with a business transaction

The law requires that the consumer receive notice of denial of credit or insurance for personal, family, or household purposes or employment. The consumer also must receive notice of the consumer-reporting agency's name and address.

The consumer has the right to obtain the information in the reporting agency's file, but not directly from the person who used the report. The consumer must also receive the identity of any other people who have obtained consumer reports on him or her within the past six months and can question any information in the report. The agency must then reinvestigate and change its report if warranted. The agency cannot issue any report containing adverse information that antedates the report by more than seven years, except that bankruptcies remain on credit reports for a fourteen-year period.

An investigative report is a report in which a consumer-reporting agency obtains information on a consumer's character, reputation, characteristics, or mode of living through personal interviews with neighbors, friends, or associates. The subject of an investigative report receives notice within three days of the order for such a report.

Equal Credit Opportunity Act

The Equal Credit Opportunity Act[10] prohibits credit discrimination based on age, race, color, religion, national origin, or receipt of welfare benefits. It also prohibits treating married applicants more favorably than unmarried applicants, such as by failing to consider alimony payments as income.

A lender who rejects an application or withholds credit must either give the applicant specific reasons or advise the applicant of the right to obtain specific reasons for rejection. Married people can have separate credit histories so that they can develop credit histories and references under their own names, which is valuable if they become divorced, separated, or widowed.

BANKRUPTCY

Bankruptcy law
The body of federal law that allows debtors who are unable to pay their creditors to divide their assets among their creditors to discharge the debts.

Bankruptcy law allows debtors who are unable to pay their creditors to divide their assets among their creditors to discharge the debts. Bankruptcy provides the following two avenues for relief:

1. Liquidation of the debtor's assets and distribution of the proceeds to the creditors
2. Reorganization of the debtor's affairs, free of creditors' claims during that process, and partial or full repayment of the debts

The federal Bankruptcy Act[11] and federal bankruptcy courts control bankruptcy in the U.S. States do not govern bankruptcy matters. Insurance companies, however, are unique in that they are not subject to federal bankruptcy law and are governed by state laws when they become insolvent.

The Bankruptcy Act does not provide for relief of domestic or foreign insurers, or for banks, savings and loan associations, or other financial institutions, which are covered by other state and federal legislation. The act provides for reorganization, but not for liquidation, of municipalities and railroads. Liquidation and reorganization are available to individuals, married couples, corporations, and partnerships.

Chapter 7
The last resort chapter of the federal Bankruptcy Act under which the bankrupt organization's nonexempt assets are distributed to its various creditors, and the balance of the debtor's obligations are forgiven or discharged.

Bankruptcy Act

The following chapters of the Bankruptcy Act are the most relevant to this discussion:

• **Chapter 7** is the last resort chapter of the federal Bankruptcy Act. Under a successful Chapter 7 bankruptcy, the bankrupt organization's nonexempt assets are distributed to its various creditors, and the balance of the debtor's obligations are forgiven or discharged.

- **Chapter 11** is the general reorganization chapter of the federal Bankruptcy Act. Under Chapter 11, a partnership or corporation can continue doing business but must set up a plan for paying a portion, or possibly all, of the creditors of the ongoing business. This chapter permits the bankrupt's attempt to reorganize without the threat of creditors' lawsuits, which can involve multiple judgments and attachments of property or executions on property. If the reorganization is unsuccessful, a Chapter 11 bankruptcy can turn into a Chapter 7 liquidation.

- **Chapter 12** gives farm operations, other than large corporate farms, the same reorganization opportunities available to corporations and partnerships under Chapter 11.

- **Chapter 13** gives small business operators or wage earners the same reorganization opportunities available to corporations and partnerships under Chapter 11.

Any person or entity can apply voluntarily for Bankruptcy Act relief. Any creditors who believe that a bankrupt person or organization favors other creditors or who continues to dispute the remaining assets of a bankrupt estate can petition the federal bankruptcy court for involuntary bankruptcy under any of the chapters just discussed. The alleged bankrupt party can contest an involuntary bankruptcy proceeding. The bankruptcy court, after a hearing, determines whether to allow the bankruptcy action to proceed or to dismiss it. If the action is dismissed in the debtor's favor, the debtor is also entitled to costs and expenses arising out of the court proceedings.

The parties to a federal bankruptcy proceeding include the following:

- The debtor
- The creditors (both secured and unsecured)
- A trustee
- A referee
- A bankruptcy judge
- Attorneys for any or all of the parties

Creditors, which might be numerous, can be represented by creditors' committees and can have more than one committee for each type or class of creditor. Usually, secured creditors have priority interests in secured property up to the value of the security interest in that property. If the debt exceeds the security, then the secured creditor is unsecured to that extent.

The trustee must inventory the bankrupt's assets and, depending on the type of bankruptcy proceedings, either conserve them or dispose of them economically. The referee's job is to sort out the various creditor and trustee claims and to suggest the equitable payments under the law for the bankruptcy judge's approval. All parties have a right to legal representation.

Federal law exempts a limited number of the debtors' assets from the bankruptcy estate. Exempt assets are the bankrupt's property that cannot be

Chapter 11
The general reorganization chapter of the federal Bankruptcy Act under which a bankrupt partnership or corporation can continue doing business but must set up a plan for paying a portion, or possibly all, of the creditors of the ongoing business.

Chapter 12
A chapter of the federal Bankruptcy Act giving farm operations, other than large corporate farms, the same reorganization opportunities available to corporations and partnerships under Chapter 11.

Chapter 13
A chapter of the federal Bankruptcy Act giving small business operators or wage earners the same reorganization opportunities available to corporations and partnerships under Chapter 11.

sold or dissipated in the bankruptcy proceedings. Examples are tools of the bankrupt's trade, a limited homestead exemption for the bankrupt's home, and life insurance.

The bankruptcy system requires the debtor's good faith. If the debtor shows preference by paying a disproportionate share of assets to a creditor immediately before filing for bankruptcy, the court can avoid the preferred payment. The creditor must then repay the sum to the trustee. If the debtor hides assets, the bankruptcy court can rescind a bankrupt's discharge from debts.

Liquidation Proceedings

Liquidation

A bankruptcy proceeding in which a bankrupt organization does not have enough assets to pay all creditors, and the creditors are prioritized and paid according to the types of their claims.

In a **liquidation** proceeding, the bankrupt organization usually does not have enough assets to pay all the creditors. Therefore, those creditors are prioritized according to the following six types of claims they have:

1. Administrative expenses of the bankruptcy proceeding
2. Unsecured business debts
3. A limited amount of wage claims
4. Contributions to employee benefits plans
5. Claims of unsecured individuals
6. Unsecured claims of governmental units

The goal of bankruptcy is to eventually discharge the debtor from all debts that arose before the date of the court's order for relief and to give the bankrupt a fresh start. A corporation or a partnership is not eligible for discharge because the corporation will not continue in business and therefore has no need for a fresh start. In reorganization, full performance of the plan discharges the debtor. In liquidation, the court discharges an individual.

Bankruptcy does not discharge some debts, including the following:

- Certain tax claims
- Money, property, or services obtained by fraud
- Claims for willful and malicious injury to people or property
- Alimony or support
- Educational loans
- Debts incurred in court actions arising from drunk driving

Discharge is not automatic. In general, a debtor who illegally and unjustifiably does not cooperate in a proceeding may not obtain discharge. The act sets penalties for debtors who intentionally hinder, defraud, or delay creditors; who unjustifiably conceal, destroy, mutilate, falsify, or fail to keep or preserve records; or who knowingly and fraudulently make false oaths.

Prior bankruptcy within the previous six years will usually result in the denial of a discharge. A court can revoke a discharge in a later proceeding if the debtor obtained it by fraud or concealed property from the trustee.

SUMMARY

Article 2 of the UCC, the law of sales contracts, applies only to sales of goods. Although general contract law rules apply to these sales, neither a stated price nor a formal acceptance is necessary in a sales contract. Consideration, however, is essential to sales contracts; and the general rules of fraud, mistake, duress, and undue influence are applicable to sales contracts.

Article 3 of the UCC governs negotiable instruments, best exemplified by checks and promissory notes. To be negotiable, an instrument must meet the following four requirements:

1. It must be signed by the maker or the drawer.
2. It must contain an unconditional promise or order to pay a certain sum of money.
3. It must be payable on demand or at a definite time.
4. It must be payable to order or bearer.

A holder in due course possesses a negotiable instrument and must have taken the instrument under the following three circumstances:

1. For value
2. In good faith
3. Without notice that it is overdue or has been dishonored or notice of any defense against it or claim to it

UCC Article 9 treats all security interests in personal property as secured transactions. When a buyer agrees to give a seller or lender a security interest in an article sold, the seller or lender (secured party) can take the goods (collateral) or otherwise prevent the buyer from disposing of them. A perfected security interest is superior to a later perfected security interest and to most subsequent lien creditors. The three methods of perfecting a security interest are the following:

1. Filing a financing statement
2. Transferring actual possession
3. Perfecting by attachment

Fair trade and consumer credit laws protect consumers in commercial transactions. Fair trade laws include the following:

- The Federal Trade Commission Act (FTC Act)
- State unfair trade practice acts
- State and federal consumer warranty laws

The FTC Act prevents unfair competition and unfair or deceptive acts or practices affecting interstate commerce. State unfair trade practice acts also prevent such activities.

Insurance fair trade practice acts prevent unfair and deceptive activities in the insurance business. The Magnuson-Moss Act supplements the FTC Act and antitrust laws and applies to consumer products, regulating written warranty provisions by defining full and limited warranties.

Consumer credit laws include the following:

- The Truth in Lending Act
- The Fair Credit Reporting Act
- The Fair Debt Collection Practices Act
- The Equal Credit Opportunity Act

The Truth in Lending Act applies only to individual credit for personal and real property purchased for personal or agricultural purposes and does not control the terms of a credit transaction but ensures that consumers have information about those terms. The Fair Credit Reporting Act requires that consumer reporting agencies exercise their responsibilities fairly by controlling reporting and investigation practices.

The Fair Debt Collection Practices Act prohibits unfair and oppressive collection practices by agencies specializing in debt collecting. The Equal Credit Opportunity Act prohibits credit discrimination on several grounds, such as sex, race, and national origin.

The federal Bankruptcy Act governs all bankruptcies, except those involving insurance companies, which are subject to state regulation, and contains the following chapters:

- Chapter 7—Last resort chapter by which bankrupt's nonexempt assets are distributed to creditors and the balance discharged
- Chapter 11—General reorganization chapter under which most individuals and corporations attempt to continue doing business and set up payment plans for paying creditors
- Chapter 12—Section dealing with farmers' special problems
- Chapter 13—Reorganization of individual bankrupts who are small business operators or wage earners

CHAPTER NOTES

1. UCC, § 2-106 (2).
2. 15 U.S.C., § 45.
3. 15 U.S.C., §§ 1–8.
4. 15 U.S.C., § 2312.
5. 15 U.S.C., § 1601.
6. 15 U.S.C., § 1681.
7. 15 U.S.C., § 1693.
8. 15 U.S.C., § 1692.
9. 15 U.S.C., § 1681.
10. 15 U.S.C., § 1691.
11. 11 U.S.C., § 101.

Chapter 7

Direct Your Learning

Property Law

After learning the content of this chapter and completing the corresponding course guide assignment, you should be able to:

■ Given a case involving personal property:

- Describe what interests in personal property exist.

- Describe what interests in intellectual property exist.

- Describe the respective rights and duties under a bailment.

- Describe the required elements of the transfer of property as a gift.

■ Given a case involving real property:

- Describe what interests in real property exist.

- Describe the requisites for contracts of sales and deeds.

- Determine the nature and creation of any security interests and liens.

- Describe what incidental real property rights exist.

- Describe what land use restrictions affect the use of real property.

- Compare the rights and duties of landlords and tenants.

■ Define or describe each of the Key Words and Phrases for this chapter.

Develop Your Perspective

What are the main topics covered in the chapter?

This chapter introduces the legal concept of property, both personal and real. Issues relating to personal property include ownership and possession. Real property issues include estates, sales, recording, security interests, liens, incidental rights, and land use restrictions. The chapter concludes with a discussion of landlord and tenant law and all the rights, duties, and liabilities of the landlord-tenant relationship.

Identify the property rights that are basic to personal and real property ownership.

- What rights guarantee uninterrupted enjoyment of property?
- What rights guarantee compensation to the builder of real property?
- What rights protect a tenant against unconscionable actions by a landlord?

Why is it important to learn about these topics?

Most property-casualty insurance professionals' work, of whatever nature, involves losses relating to property rights in some way.

Examine the provisions of insurance policies that protect personal and real property.

- Whose rights do policies protect?
- Under what circumstances do the policies protect those rights?

How can you use what you will learn?

Analyze the kinds of property you own or lease and your own property.

- How do land use restrictions affect your neighborhood?
- What kinds of personal property rights might affect you in your everyday life?
- How might the property law provide a remedy for you personally or for your organization?

Chapter 7
Property Law

Property is the real estate, buildings, objects or articles, intangible assets, or rights with exchangeable value of which someone may claim legal ownership. Ownership is the unrestricted and exclusive right to something. In the United States, the law views property as a bundle of legal rights (interests), which are generally insurable, and protects them. In some societies, the concept of private property ownership is either nonexistent or more limited than in the U.S.

Property falls into the following two categories:

1. **Real property**, or **realty**—Land, including structures or rights attached to the land. Real property includes rights to water, minerals, and things attached to land, such as buildings, trees, and fixtures that have become part of the realty. It also includes rights closely related to land, such as the right to pass over another person's land.

2. **Personal property**—All property that is not real property. Some property, such as goods one possesses physically, is tangible. Other property, such as patents and insurance policies, is intangible.

Although the law of real property and that of personal property differs in many respects, many rules apply to both types of property. The methods of transferring property and the requirements of inheritance are examples of areas in which the bundle of legal rights a person has in property differs depending on the nature of the property. The first part of this chapter discusses personal property, and the second part discusses real property.

Ownership is a relationship between the owner and the rest of society that includes the following three features:

1. The right to exclude all others from use and enjoyment of the property owned
2. The right to pass valid ("good") title to the property
3. The obligations of ownership, such as the obligation to pay taxes and to use property so as not to interfere with others' rights

Another term for legal ownership of property is **title**. Title is the highest right to property that a person can acquire.

Possession is the exercise of custody or control over property and is not, of itself, ownership. A person can possess property without owning it. When a person possesses property the law generally protects that possession against everyone except the owner. When the owner grants possession, the possessor's

Property
The real estate, buildings, objects or articles, intangible assets, or rights with exchangeable value of which someone may claim legal ownership.

Real property, or realty
Any land, including structures or rights attached to the land.

Personal property
All property that is not real property.

Ownership
The singular rights of a property owner to exclude others from the property and to pass a valid title to the property; the obligations associated with the property.

Title
The legal ownership of property; the highest right to property that a person can acquire.

Possession
The exercise of custody or control over property.

rights to custody and control can be superior in some situations to the owner's, at least during the period for which possession is granted.

PERSONAL PROPERTY

Owners and possessors of personal property have legally protected rights. Protection of those rights varies by the circumstances of the property's creation and the type of property ownership. This section focuses on the law of tangible personal property and discusses how one comes into possession and ownership of personal property; how one can hold, use, and enjoy personal property; how one can give it away or transfer it; and the rights and duties of a person who holds property for someone else.

A person can acquire possession of personal property in several ways, including by creating the property. A person can also obtain personal property through accession, confusion, bailments, or gifts.

Intellectual Property

One can create property from one's own endeavors, such as writing a book or a song, inventing a device, or developing a process. The results of the creative process are both of the following:

1. The intellectual property, that is, the expressed form of the idea or intangible subject matter.
2. **Intellectual property rights**, that is, the legal entitlement to the intellectual property. Such rights include copyrights, trademarks, trade secrets, and patents.

Intellectual property rights
The legal entitlement attached to the expressed form of an idea or of other intangible subject matter.

Intellectual property rights protect the creations of a person's mind and talents and are insurable property rights. For most purposes, federal, not state, law governs all intellectual property rights, although the states have limited common-law intellectual property rights.

Copyrights

Copyright
The legal right for a period of years to exclusively use and control an original written document, piece of music, software, or other form of expression.

A **copyright** is the legal right for a period of years to exclusively use and control an original written document, piece of music, software, or other form of expression. A copyright grants the exclusive right to copy or otherwise reproduce the copyrighted material and to create additional, or derivative, works from the original. The federal Copyright Act of 1978[1] permits the **fair use** of copyrighted material in a reasonable manner without the owner's consent. Thus, people other than the copyright owner can use copyrighted material, for certain purposes such as teaching, research, criticism, or comment. What constitutes fair use is not always easy to determine. Courts consider the following in determining fair use:

Fair use
The right to use copyrighted material in a reasonable manner without the copyright owner's consent.

- Purpose of the use
- Nature of the work

- Amount and substantiality of the portion used
- Effect of the use on the work's value
- Extent to which the use might deprive the copyright owner of economic advantage

Under the Copyright Act, an individual creator's copyright extends for the life of the creator plus fifty years. If the copyright owner is a corporation or an association, the copyright extends for 100 years from the date of creation of the work or 75 years from the date of copyright, whichever expires first. Under prior law, if a creator published a work without obtaining a copyright, the publication was considered a dedication to the public, and anyone could copy or publish it. A later attempt to obtain a copyright was not possible. Under current law, a creator who publishes a work without obtaining a copyright can copyright a later printing. Copyrights apply to written works, such as books and music, and also to computer software programs.

Patents

The federal government grants a patent to a person who has given physical expression to an idea. A **patent** gives an inventor or applicant the right for a limited period to exclusively use and control a new, useful, and nonobvious invention. For example, an inventor conceives of an invention, then physically creates it. The person obtaining the patent has the exclusive right to make, use, and sell the invention for seventeen years.

A patent is not renewable, and, once the period has elapsed, others can use the idea. To be patentable, an invention can be a new and useful device or machine or a combination of known elements to perform an additional or different purpose. Over-the-counter and prescription drugs are examples of patentable items.

Patent
An intellectual property right granted to an inventor or applicant for a limited period to exclusively use and control a new, useful, and nonobvious invention.

Accession

Accession is an increase or addition to property. Accession can be by natural accretion, as when an animal produces offspring. It can result from a union of one thing with another, as a coat of paint applied to a house; or it can result from transformation of raw materials into a finished product, such as wooden barrels. The owner of an animal that gives birth also owns the offspring. Therefore, the owner of a cow owns each calf born to the cow.

Questions of ownership arise when one person adds value to another's personal property, knowingly without the owner's consent. The owner is not required to pay for the added value. Additionally, a person who wrongly takes another's property and then improves it does not acquire title to the finished product and is not entitled to payment for the improvements.

However, if the property is taken innocently, as when one mistakenly cuts trees on another's land and transforms them into lumber, a relative value test may be applied. Under this test, if the value of the finished product is greatly

Accession
An increase or addition to property.

disproportionate to the value of the original goods, the innocent trespasser would retain title to the finished goods after reimbursing the owner for the reasonable value of the goods before improvement. The relative value test is applied to restore innocent parties as nearly to their original status as possible.

Confusion

Confusion

In property law, the intermingling of goods belonging to different owners.

Confusion is the intermingling of goods belonging to different owners. Fungible goods are goods that are commercially interchangeable with other property of the same kind. Confusion usually arises when fungible goods, such as wheat, belonging to different owners, are mixed so that identification and separation of the goods are impossible.

Courts consider whether the confusion resulted from willful misconduct or from an innocent act. If the intermixture of goods was willful or fraudulent, the wrongdoer loses title to the goods, and the original owner has title. When the confusion is innocent or accidental, the parties jointly own the entire mass in proportion to their respective interests. If the parties can determine the original numbers or amounts they own, they will each own a proportionate interest in the mass. If determination of the original amounts contributed is impossible, the loss falls on the party who caused the intermixture. For example, Bill and George own sheep in adjoining pastures. A storm breaks down a fence between the pastures, and the sheep intermingle. They are unidentifiable. Although Bill and George each know the number of sheep they had, they now jointly own the sheep. Each has an interest in the mass of sheep in proportion to the original number owned. However, any loss would fall on a negligent party who causes the fence to break.

Bailments

Bailment

The transfer of possession of personal property from one person to another for a specified purpose and the return of the property when the purpose has been fulfilled.

Bailor

A person or an entity who delivers property to another (the bailee) under a bailment contract.

Bailee

A person or an entity who receives property from another (the bailor) under a bailment contract.

Everyone is a bailor or bailee at some time. A **bailment** is the transfer of possession of personal property from one person (the bailor) to another (the bailee) for a specified purpose and the return of the property when the purpose has been fulfilled. The person who delivers personal property to another is a **bailor**, for example, a person who takes clothes to a cleaner or a car to a garage for repair, or who lends a lawnmower to a neighbor. One who rents some tools, borrows a car, or undertakes to care for someone else's personal property becomes a **bailee**, the person who receives personal property from another.

A bailment has the following three elements:

1. *The transfer of possession of personal property without the transfer of title.* The transfer of possession is something more than mere custody. In other words, when a shopkeeper hands an article to a customer to examine, the customer has custody, not possession, and therefore is not a bailee. Similarly, an employee such as a milk-delivery person is not a bailee of the company's milk; the employee merely has custody of the milk for delivery.

2. *The bailee's acceptance of the bailed property.* For example, a restaurant customer who hangs her coat in an unattended cloakroom in the restaurant does not create a bailment, because no delivery to the restaurant owner has occurred. A bailment does arise, however, if the customer leaves the coat with a cloakroom attendant. A car owner who parks his car in a commercial parking lot and takes the keys does not create a bailment but merely rents space. However, an attendant who parks a car and assumes control over it creates a bailment with a duty of care.

3. *The bailee's express or implied agreement to redeliver the property to the bailor or to a designated third person.* If the person receiving the goods has the option to return other property in exchange for the goods, or to pay for the goods, no bailment exists.

Bailee's Rights and Duties

A bailee has possession only and cannot transfer title to a third party. If the bailee attempts to sell the bailed goods, the bailor can recover them from the third party unless the bailor has represented the bailee as the owner of the goods. The bailee must surrender the goods to the bailor on request unless the bailment is for a term, such as a car rental, in which case the bailee can retain possession for that period. The bailee's possession is superior to any claims by third persons, and the bailee can sue third parties for damage to the bailed property.

A **lien** is a creditor's legal right or interest in another's property, usually lasting until satisfaction of the debt or duty that the lien secures. A **possessory lien** is the bailee's right to retain possession of a bailor's property as security for the payment of a debt or performance of some other act. It is not an interest in the property itself, but only in possession of that property. A lien can be nonpossessory, such as a mortgage on real estate. Most possessory liens arise from bailments of personal property. For example, an auto repair shop can keep a car until the owner pays the repair bill.

The lienholder is entitled to exclusive possession of the property until receipt of money owed. A property owner who wrongfully regains possession is liable to the lienholder. For example, a car owner disputes an auto repair bill, grabs the car keys from the auto repair shop owner, and drives the car away without paying the bill. The car owner is liable to the shop for the repair bill.

Recovery is limited to the amount of money that the lien secures. The lienholder has the same right as any other bailee to hold third persons liable for damages to the property while it is in the lienholder's possession. The lienholder, as a bailee, must take reasonable care of the property, including making repairs and expenditures reasonably necessary to protect and preserve the property.

The extent of the bailee's right to use the bailed property varies depending on whom the bailment is intended to benefit: the bailee, the bailor, or both.

Lien
A creditor's legal right or interest in another's property, usually lasting until satisfaction of the specific debt or duty that the lien secures.

Possessory lien
A bailee's right to retain possession of a bailor's property as security for the payment of a debt or performance of some other act.

In a bailment for the bailee's sole benefit, as when a bailee borrows a bailor's car for personal use, the right to use the property is limited to the use the bailor contemplated. If the purpose is to travel between two points, any deviation from the route reasonably contemplated by the bailor can make the bailee liable for any loss that occurs during the deviation.

In a bailment for the bailor's sole benefit, the bailee may use or handle the property only to the extent necessary to preserve and protect it. For example, a bailee who accepts a fur coat for safekeeping should not wear it.

In bailments for mutual benefit, the bailee can use the property as specified within the agreement or contract. A person who leases a car can use it only according to the lease agreement's terms. On the other hand, if a person bails a car for the purpose of storage or parking, the bailee can only store or park the vehicle and cannot use it for other reasons.

Some bailment contracts require compensation. For those that do not, courts assume that the bailor intended to pay a reasonable value for the bailee's services if a reasonable person would have realized the services require payment. A bailment for the bailee's sole benefit does not imply a charge for services because it is not reasonable to assume charges. When expressed or implied compensation is not paid, the bailee can assert a lien.

A bailee can assert a lien only for charges due for the current transaction. If Roger, a bailee, repairs Amy's car, releases it to Amy (the bailor), and subsequently regains possession, Roger cannot assert a lien against the car for the price of the original repairs. Although he still has a right to compensation for the work, Roger lost the original right to assert a lien when he surrendered the car to Amy.

In addition to rights, a bailee also has duties. The bailee must take reasonable care of the bailed goods. If the bailee exercises due care, any loss or damage to the bailed property falls on the bailor because the bailor has title to it. Each type of bailment requires a different degree of care described as follows:

- When the bailment is for the bailor's benefit, the bailee is gratuitously in charge of the goods and only slight care is required. For example, if a bailor asks the bailee to care for his car, the bailee is liable for damage to the vehicle only if damage was foreseeable and the bailee could have prevented it without substantial trouble or expense.

- When the bailment is for the bailee's sole benefit, the bailee must exercise an extraordinary degree of care. For example, a bailee who borrows the bailor's car must exercise great care.

- When the bailment is for the bailor's and bailee's mutual benefit, the bailee must exercise reasonable care under the circumstances. For example, a bailee who rents a tent for a lawn party must exercise reasonable care.

A bailee can extend or limit liability for the bailed goods in the bailment contract. For example, household goods movers and airlines restrict liability for goods and baggage, often to a certain amount of money per pound. The right to limit liability extends only to liability for ordinary negligence, not to willful or wanton misconduct.

Because of the bailee's legal duty to care for the goods and to return them to the bailor, the bailee has an insurable interest in the goods and can obtain insurance to protect that interest. In the absence of a statute or specific contract requirement, however, the bailee has no duty to obtain insurance on the bailed goods. The bailee must hold insurance proceeds paid for the bailed property's damage in trust for the bailor, except for that amount representing the bailee's interest under the bailment agreement.

Bailor's Rights and Duties

In mutual benefit bailments and in bailments for the bailee's benefit, the bailor has a right to compensation according to the agreement. However, in bailments for the bailor's sole benefit, the bailor is not entitled to compensation.

A bailor can sue a bailee who does not return the bailed property at the end of the bailment term. If the goods have been damaged, either negligently or willfully, the bailor can sue either the bailee or a third person responsible for the damage.

In mutual benefit bailments, the bailor owes a duty to supply goods that are reasonably fit for the purpose the parties envision. The bailor must make a reasonable inspection of the goods to determine any defects. In fact, the bailor makes an implied warranty that the goods are in proper condition and is responsible for any damage the bailee suffers because of unknown defects. In a bailment for the bailee's sole benefit, as when the bailor lends the goods to the bailee, the bailor must notify the bailee of known defects.

A bailor is not usually liable for a bailee's negligent use of bailed property. For example, if Carol borrows Mark's car and operates it negligently, injuring another person, Mark cannot be held liable for negligence. Automobile liability insurance policies also cover permitted users of the insured car. Because car bailees ordinarily have insurance protection, an injured third party has that source for recovery.

However, a bailor who negligently entrusts property to an incompetent bailee can be held liable for resulting injuries to third persons. Negligent entrustment is leaving a dangerous article, such as a gun or car, with a person who the lender knows, or should know, is likely to use it in an unreasonably risky manner. For example, a car owner who permits an unlicensed minor to operate the car on the highway can be liable to a third party who is injured in an accident caused by the minor.

A bailor who knows that the bailed property is in a dangerous condition can be liable for injury to a third party if the bailee is not aware of the danger.

In some cases, a bailor has a duty to reimburse the bailee. The cost of repairs ordinary and incidental to the use of bailed goods under a rental contract is usually the bailee's responsibility. However, the bailor must pay the cost of extensive repairs to the property. For example, a bailee must pay for repair of a flat tire but need not pay for a new tire. If a bailee makes repairs that the bailor should have made, such as installation of a new transmission in a car, the bailor must reimburse the bailee.

A bailment for a specified period entitles the bailee to possession only for that period. If the bailment has no set period, the bailor can terminate at any time and end the bailee's right to possession. The bailee must redeliver the goods within a reasonable time after the bailment period ends. A bailee's attempt to sell the bailed goods, or to cause extensive damage to the goods, automatically terminates the bailment and entitles the bailor to immediately recover the goods, as well as any repair or replacement costs.

Special Bailments

In some situations, bailees have unique obligations because they owe special duties of care to bailors. Special bailments include the following:

Common carrier
A transportation provider that offers its services to the public and that is licensed by federal or state agencies.

Shipper
A party that owns or orders the shipment of goods.

Factor
A bailee entrusted with possession of another's goods for sale on commission.

- *Common carriers.* A **common carrier** is a transportation provider that offers its services to the public and that is licensed by federal or state agencies. Examples are public transit systems and airlines. Federal and state governments regulate common carriers' routes and rates. Carriage of goods is a mutual benefit bailment, but, because of the public interest involved, common carriers have a very high standard of care. Common carriers can limit their liability to shippers by contract if they comply with laws and regulations for doing so. A **shipper** is the party that owns or orders shipment of the goods. The common carrier's liability arises at the time it receives goods and terminates either at delivery of the goods to a freight terminal or when the recipient has had reasonable time to inspect and remove the goods from the carrier or terminal, depending on the situation. Public policy does not permit a common carrier to relieve itself entirely of liability for negligence.

- *Hotelkeepers.* Like common carriers, hotelkeepers, those who offer lodging accommodations to transients, are responsible for the safety of their guests' personal belongings and goods. As a mutual benefit bailment, the hotelkeeper is liable only for failure to exercise reasonable care in protecting the property of guests. A hotelkeeper can further limit liability by providing a safe for storing guests' valuables.

- *Warehouse operators.* Public warehouses store goods for the public. Warehouse operators can specify the type of goods they will accept for storage. The warehouse bailment is a bailment for mutual benefit, requiring a duty of reasonable care under the circumstances. The warehouse operator does not insure the stored goods and can limit liability in the receipt issued for goods received.

- *Factors.* A **factor** is a bailee entrusted with possession of another's goods for sale on commission. Factors treat goods as though they own them, and, unlike an ordinary bailee, who must return goods to a bailor, can sell them. The factoring relationship is a bailment for mutual benefit, and the factor must take reasonable care of the goods and return them in good condition if there is no sale.

Gifts

A **gift** is the voluntary and gratuitous transfer of property without consideration. The giver is the **donor** and the recipient is the **donee**. A gift requires the following three elements:

1. *Donative intent.* The donor must intend to make a present gift in the present. A promise to make a future gift is not enforceable. Although the donor's subjective intent determines donative intent, objective manifestations, such as the donor's comments and statements, can help prove intent. Subjective intent is what the donor believes is being done, and objective manifestations are what others might interpret as the donor's intent.

2. *Delivery.* Delivery of a gift can be by actual physical transfer or by constructive delivery, which is implied by law. In either case, the donor must give up all control over and possession of (dominion over) the property, and the donee must assume dominion over the article. If the donee already has the property, the donor need not repossess it and then return it to the donee. A donor handing car keys to a donee, for example, can establish constructive delivery of a car. When the tangible property is so extensive as to be incapable of physical delivery, a symbolic act is sufficient to accomplish delivery. A written document can prove delivery of an intangible item, such as a bank account.

3. *Acceptance.* Parties rarely dispute acceptance. However, when a donee does not want the burdens of ownership, such as having to pay taxes, acceptance becomes important. One cannot force a gift on a donee. The donee must agree to accept the goods.

Gift
The voluntary and gratuitous transfer of property without consideration.

Donor
The giver of a gift.

Donee
The recipient of a gift.

REAL PROPERTY

Real property is land and interests closely associated with land. The laws governing such matters as sales, mortgages, and transfers at death differ significantly according to whether property is real or personal.

Real property includes the surface of land and everything that is in, on, or above it, including oil, water, minerals, and gravel under the surface, as well as trees, shrubs, and plants on the surface. Real property includes buildings permanently affixed to the land, as well as **fixtures**, which are personal property affixed to real property in such a way as to become part of the real property.

Fixture
Any personal property affixed to real property in such a way as to become part of the real property.

Real Property Estates

Real property estate
Any of a variety of ownership interests in real property.

Real property estates are various types of ownership interest in land. An **interest** is a right, claim, or legal share of property. The total interest in real property consists of the following two elements, which define the quality and the duration of the interest:

1. Complete, outright, and full ownership (the quality of ownership)
2. Unlimited time (the duration of ownership)

Interest
A right, claim, or legal share of property.

A **fee simple estate** is a full ownership interest in property with the unconditional right to dispose of it. The owner can leave the property to heirs and can sell, lease, or use it. A person who says he owns land usually means that he has a fee simple estate.

Fee simple estate
A full ownership interest in property with the unconditional right to dispose of it.

Property owners can carve out part of a total interest to create lesser interests either for the quality of the ownership or for the length of time ownership exists. A life estate is one type of lesser property interest. The **life tenant** is entitled to exclusive possession of the real property and all income the land produces for the duration of that person's or another person's life. A life estate lasts only until the life estate holder or another named person dies. For example, David grants land to Mary for the period of her life. Alternatively, David grants land to Mary for the period of Betty's life. In each case, Mary is the life tenant. On Mary's death, or Betty's, title to the property reverts to David or to David's estate. The life tenant is entitled to exclusive possession of the land and to all income the land produces. If the life tenant sells the land, the buyer's interest lasts only as long as the life tenant lives. Therefore, a prospective buyer must be concerned with the life tenant's life expectancy.

Life tenant
A person entitled to exclusive possession of real property and to all income the land produces for the duration of that person's or someone else's life.

Concurrent Estates

Two or more persons, particularly husband and wife, often own property concurrently. This concurrent estate ownership can be any of the following forms:

*   Joint tenancy
*   Tenancy by the entirety
*   Tenancy in common
*   Community property

Tenancy
A right to possession or ownership, or both, of property.

In each of these situations, the property owners can have interests they can insure even though they share the property with at least one other person. A **tenancy** is a right to either possession or ownership, or to both.

Joint tenancy
A concurrently owned and undivided interest in an estate that transfers to a surviving joint tenant upon the death of the other.

Joint tenancy is a concurrently owned and undivided interest in an estate that transfers to a surviving joint tenant upon the death of the other. It is probably the oldest form of concurrent ownership and usually occurs today among members of the same family. The distinguishing feature of joint tenancy is that, on one joint tenant's death, the estate goes entirely to the other joint tenant. If David, Mary, and Betty are joint tenants and David dies, his interest goes

Common-Law Marital Rights

The common law provides a solution to a widow's need for support (dower). At common law, a widow received a one-third interest for life in all real estate her husband had owned at any time during the marriage. The husband could not cut off the wife's right to dower without her consent. Dower rights took effect only when the husband died. Even today, a husband generally cannot disinherit a wife. If a husband's will gives a wife less than her dower portion, she can elect to receive the dower portion.

An important remnant of the common law is that a married man cannot transfer clear title to his real property without his wife's consent. If her husband attempts to sell real property without her consent and he dies before she does, she can sue a purchaser for the value of her interest. A real estate buyer, when obtaining a deed from a married man, must ensure that his wife signs the deed. A divorce bars the ex-wife's dower rights, but a separation does not. This consent requirement does not apply to personal property (nor does it apply to some very specific real property situations).

The husband has an equivalent common-law right, called curtesy. At common law, curtesy was an interest in all the wife's real property owned during the marriage, for the husband's life, provided that a child was born of the marriage, even if the child died. State statutes have altered this right to grant the husband a certain minimum from his wife's property. When the wife sells her individually owned real estate, a buyer must obtain the husband's signature.

Both dower and curtesy differ according to state law. Some state laws adhere much more closely to the common law than others, and parties to real estate transactions must always consult state law.

equally to Mary and Betty. If Mary then dies, the whole estate goes to Betty. If David is married, his wife has no dower interest in the property.

The parties create joint tenancy at one time, from one grantor, in equal shares. With two joint tenants, each must hold a one-half share, and so on. One of the joint tenants cannot be subject to a condition that does not apply to the others. The same deed must name them all as owners.

A **tenancy by the entirety** is a joint tenancy created only between husband and wife. The usual form of deed is "to Husband and Wife, as tenants by the entirety." If the deed does not state "tenants by the entirety" explicitly, the law considers that phrase implied. Half of an estate may be taken as tenants by the entirety, and the other half by another person, as "to Husband and Wife, and Third Person." For example, Doris and Rick own half of a farm as tenants by the entirety, and Cheryl owns the other half.

Tenancy by the entirety
A joint tenancy between husband and wife.

A tenancy by the entirety is similar to a joint tenancy because the survivor takes the entire property. It differs from a joint tenancy in the following ways:

- A sale or contract to sell does not sever the tenancy.

- Individual creditors of either the husband or the wife cannot subject the property to a claim.

- Neither party individually owns a portion that can be mortgaged.

Divorce ordinarily severs a tenancy by the entirety, and both spouses can terminate it by joining in a transfer of the property or by transferring one spouse's interest to the other.

Tenancy in common differs from joint tenancy and tenancy by the entirety in the following ways:

- It involves no survivorship.
- The parties can own unequal shares.
- The parties need not derive their interests in the same deed from the same grantor.

A will or deed can create a tenancy in common expressly, as when a deed is "to David and Mary, as tenants in common." More commonly, operation of law creates a tenancy in common. For example, if David dies intestate (without a will) and has three heirs, they inherit David's real property as tenants in common.

A few southern and western states follow the Spanish civil law concept of **community property**, that a husband and wife should equally share all property acquired during marriage by their communal efforts. Under this concept, two types of property can belong to a spouse—separate property and community property. The separate property of either spouse is that which the spouse owned at the time of marriage as well as any property that the spouse acquires individually after marriage by gift or inheritance. Separate property is the respective spouse's sole property because communal effort did not produce it, and it is free from the other spouse's interest or control.

Under the community property concept, a husband and wife share equally in all community property, and the amount of their individual contribution to the joint effort does not change the equal interest. A gift to both spouses becomes community property. On a spouse's death, unless a will states otherwise, the property is divided in half. One-half goes to the surviving spouse; the other half goes to the deceased spouse's heirs, if any. A spouse cannot, by will, dispose of more than one-half of community property, and neither dower nor curtesy right apply to community property.

Cooperative Ownership

Cooperative ownership, is similar to concurrent ownership. However, it does not involve unity of possession or an equal right to occupy the entire premises with all other tenants. Cooperative ownership is a common method of owning real property, usually apartments.

In **cooperative ownership**, a corporation holds title to the property. The cooperative owner purchases stock in the corporation and receives a long-term proprietary lease for a certain apartment. The lease sets forth the parties' rights and liabilities, including provisions for monthly payments. The number of shares in the corporation that each tenant owns can be equal or can vary according to the values of the apartments. For example, ten people form a

Tenancy in common
A concurrent ownership of property, in equal or unequal shares, by two or more joint tenants who lack survivorship rights.

Community property
Property owned or acquired by both spouses during a marriage by their communal efforts.

Cooperative ownership
Ownership, usually of real property such as an apartment building, by a corporation, the stockholders of which receive long-term proprietary leases to a portion of the property and a proportional vote in its affairs based on the number of shares owned.

cooperative venture to construct ten apartments at a cost of $1 million. The five apartments on the ground floor are each valued at $120,000, the five on the second floor at $80,000 each. The corporation issues one hundred shares of $10,000 stock. Those desiring ground floor apartments purchase twelve shares, and those wanting the second floor purchase eight shares each.

The corporation ordinarily obtains a mortgage, constructs the building, and then operates it. Each tenant, as a shareholder in the corporation, has a proportional vote in its affairs based on the number of shares owned. The corporation levies monthly assessments to pay mortgage principal and interest, taxes, cost of operations, insurance on the structure in the name of the corporation, and other items.

Cooperative ownership provides for operation and maintenance by someone other than the tenant, while guaranteeing a right of occupancy for as long as desired. A disadvantage is the owner's limited control over external conditions, which can lead to a deterioration of the investment. Finding a purchaser for the premises can be difficult, particularly if it is beginning to deteriorate. Additionally, if other tenants do not keep up their payments, and as a result the mortgage payments lapse, the mortgagee can foreclose on the property. In that case, all tenants can lose any equity they have built up in the property.

Condominium Ownership

A **condominium** is a single unit in a building or complex for which the unit owner has a separate title and exclusive ownership as well as the joint ownership of the common areas and facilities. Condominium ownership, like a cooperative, is similar to concurrent ownership. However, it is closer to a true concurrent ownership than the cooperative and has the following two legal elements:

1. Individual ownership of a "unit," or separate, defined area
2. An undivided interest in common or public areas (common elements) that serve all individual units

Unless both elements exist, no condominium interest exists, and the two elements cannot be separated. A unit owner cannot retain title to a unit and sell the undivided interest in the common element. Condominiums are usually multi-unit buildings, but sometimes groups of single-unit buildings qualify in this category.

The common element is essentially the land and the building, together with attached or outside areas, such as parking and storage areas, and heating and cooling systems. The unit an individual owns often is described as just a "box of air."

A written declaration that details the number of units and the percentage interest that each unit has in the common elements creates a condominium. Bylaws usually govern day-to-day operations through an association established

Condominium
A single unit in a building or complex for which the unit owner has a separate title and exclusive ownership as well as the joint ownership of the common areas and facilities.

to run the common elements. All unit owners have interests as tenants in common in the common elements that can be, but usually are not, equal.

In contrast to cooperative ownership, the condominium owner, as a tenant in common, has a direct property interest in the land and buildings, rather than a secondary interest as a shareholder of a corporation. The individual can sell, transfer, mortgage, or leave to heirs his or her condominium interest.

Real Property Sales

Contracts of sale and deeds establish most real property sales. The contract of sale is the agreement between the buyer and seller; the deed transfers title.

Contracts of Sale

A contract of sale usually precedes a transfer of real property. The contract need not be complex or lengthy, but it must contain certain elements to be binding, and the parties must be competent to enter into a contract.

Vendor and **vendee** are the terms that apply, respectively, to the real property seller and purchaser. After they execute the deed, they become the **grantor** and **grantee**, respectively. Even if title is in the vendor's name only, if the vendor is married, the spouse should sign the contract of sale. The spouse's signature is necessary to eliminate later claims for dower or curtesy, community property rights, or other rights.

A contract of sale for real property requires the following three elements:

1. *Writing.* Under the statute of frauds, any agreement to transfer an interest in real property must be in writing and signed by the persons to be bound. If the vendor attempts to enforce the contract against the vendee, the vendee must have signed it, and vice versa. The parties, however, can orally rescind a contract of sale because the rescission does not transfer an interest in real property. Any modification of the contract must be in writing.

2. *Essential terms.* The contract must describe the premises to be sold and the price. The description need not be precise but must be sufficient to identify the property. Thus, a reference to "1000 Park Avenue, to be sold for $100,000," would be sufficient.

3. *Nonessential terms.* Certain terms are not essential but are usually covered in a complete contract of sale. For example, the time of closing, if not stated, is to be within a reasonable time, and payment usually occurs at closing.

Deeds

The written instrument that actually transfers title to land is a **deed**. There are three principal types of deeds, described as follows:

1. The **quit-claim deed** transfers only the title or interest, if any, the grantor has in the land at the time of transfer. It contains no warranties, and, if

---

Vendor
The seller of real property.

Vendee
The purchaser of real property.

Grantor
The seller of real property after execution of the deed.

Grantee
The buyer of real property after execution of the deed.

Deed
A written instrument that transfers interest in real property.

Quit-claim deed
A deed that transfers only the title or interest, if any, the grantor has in land at the time of transfer.

mortgages or liens encumber the land, or any other claimants assert rights to the land, the grantee acquires those problems.

2. The warranty deed can be of two types: general warranty and special warranty. A **general warranty deed**, in addition to transferring whatever title the grantor has, contains the grantor's warranty that the title is free of all encumbrances (prior claims on the property), that the grantor has the title being transferred, and that no one else has a better title. In the event of breach of any of these warranties, also called covenants, the grantee can sue the grantor. The deed states whether an encumbrance, such as a mortgage on the property, exists. A **special warranty deed** contains warranties against only those encumbrances and defects in title that might have been created since the grantor took title. A title insurance policy is particularly important for a special warranty deed because otherwise the grantee has no protection against earlier defects.

3. The **bargain-and-sale deed** transfers real property to a buyer for valuable consideration but lacks any guarantee from the seller about the validity of the title.

A deed must be absolutely accurate, more so than the contract of sale, because, if the two conflict, the deed prevails. The basic requirements of deeds are as follows:

- Under the statute of frauds, the deed must be in writing.
- The grantor must be legally competent; the grantor's name must be in the deed; and the grantor must sign the deed.
- The deed must name the grantee.
- The deed must state the consideration.
- The deed must contain words that specifically state that a transfer of the property is occurring.
- The deed must contain a description of the property conveyed.
- The deed must be dated.
- The deed usually contains a paragraph reciting who transferred the property to the grantor, date of transfer, and the location of the recorded copy of the deed.
- Some states require the grantor's signature under seal.
- Several states require witnesses to the grantor's signature.
- The deed must be delivered to effect a transfer.
- Most states require an acknowledgment, which is a formal, written statement by a public official, usually a notary public, that the grantor has appeared before the official and has transferred the property voluntarily.

Recording and Priorities

To record a deed, the buyer takes it to a local government office, usually known as the office of the recorder or register of deeds, and files it. The purpose of recording is to give notice to the world that the transfer of real property has occurred.

General warranty deed
A deed that contains the grantor's warranty that the title is free of all encumbrances, that the grantor has the title being transferred, and that no one else has a better title.

Special warranty deed
A deed that contains warranties against only those encumbrances and defects in title that might have been created since the grantor took title.

Bargain-and-sale deed
A deed that transfers real property to a buyer for valuable consideration but that lacks any guarantee from the seller about the validity of the title.

All states have recording acts under which any deed, mortgage, or other instrument affecting land is not valid against a subsequent purchaser for value who had no notice or knowledge of the previous sale unless the instrument has been recorded. For example, if David sold land to Mary in 2000 and later sells the same land to Betty in 2005, Mary would prevail if she had recorded the deed, even though Betty knew nothing about the prior transaction. However, if Mary does not record the deed, and if Betty, unaware of the sale to Mary, purchases the land from David and records the deed, Betty's ownership takes priority over Mary's.

An unrecorded document affecting property rights is effective between the immediate parties and persons who are not purchasers, such as donees and heirs, but not against subsequent purchasers for value without notice or knowledge.

Real Estate Security Interests

Real estate is commonly used as collateral for loans, often to secure the funds to purchase the same real estate. Three principal types of contractual security devices apply to real property as security: (1) mortgages, (2) trust deeds, and (3) land contracts.

Mortgages

The mortgage used in most states today is in the form of a deed or transfer of land by the borrower to the lender, with a statement of the debt and a provision that the mortgage will be void at full payment of the debt. The **mortgagor** is a borrower who pledges real property as security for the money to purchase the property. The **mortgagee** is the lender, such as a bank or other financing institution.

Mortgagor
A borrower who pledges real property as security for the money to purchase the property.

Mortgagee
A lender in a mortgage arrangement, such as a bank or another financing institution.

A real estate mortgage transfers an interest in real property and must be in writing and signed in the same manner as a deed. If not properly executed, it may not be eligible for recording in a local government office, which gives notice to the public of the transaction. Between the parties, a mortgage's validity does not depend on compliance with other formal requirements. Thus, if the parties intended the transaction as a loan and security type of transaction, it is a mortgage, regardless of the form of the contract. However, an unrecorded mortgage is not valid against good-faith purchasers, subsequent mortgagees without knowledge, or creditors with liens on the property.

The mortgagor has the specific rights to sell, lease, or even put another mortgage on property. The mortgagor is effectively the property owner as far as everyone else except the mortgagee is concerned. However, transactions after recording of a mortgage do not affect the mortgagee's rights. For example, assume that David mortgages land to Mary to secure a loan of $70,000 and records the mortgage properly. David then conveys the land to Betty. The sale is appropriate, but if David or Betty does not pay the loan when it falls due, Mary has a right to foreclose the mortgage. Betty can lose her interest because it is subject to Mary's mortgage rights. If the proceeds of the sale are insufficient to satisfy the debt to Mary, she has the right to obtain a deficiency judgment against David as the original mortgagor, and possibly against Betty, the subsequent buyer, for the amount of the deficiency. If the sale yields excess money, it goes to David as mortgagor or to Betty, the subsequent buyer.

A purchaser's rights and liabilities depend on the wording in the deed. A purchaser who takes property subject to an existing, properly recorded mortgage, on which the mortgagor later defaults, can be liable to the mortgagee for a deficiency in payments. However, if the deed states that the buyer takes the property "subject to" the mortgage, the buyer is not liable for any deficiency in mortgage payments. If the deed states that the buyer "assumes and agrees to pay the mortgage debt," the buyer also becomes liable for any deficiency.

The original mortgagor who sells a property remains liable on the original agreement to pay the debt and cannot be relieved of this liability without the mortgagee's consent. In most states, the original mortgagor is a surety, or guarantor, for a buyer who assumes the debt. Therefore, if that buyer defaults in paying the mortgage and a deficiency in payments occurs, the mortgagee can proceed against either the original mortgagor or the purchaser. However, an original mortgagor who pays when the buyer defaults can recover the amount paid from the buyer, if the buyer is solvent.

The mortgagee's interest in the property is assignable at any time, and the assignment must include the debt. If a note, or series of notes, evidences the debt, assignment is accomplished by negotiating the notes and making an outright assignment of the mortgage paper to the assignee. In most states, negotiation of the notes carries with it the right to the security, and their holder receives the benefits of the mortgage.

Mortgage **foreclosure**, a legal proceeding to terminate a mortgagor's interest in property, is the mortgagee's remedy when the mortgagor defaults on mortgage payments. Foreclosure through public sale is the most common method. To foreclose, the mortgagee sues the mortgagor. Following trial, the court enters a judgment for the amount owed and orders the property's sale. The proceeds of the sale first pay the judgment to the mortgagee. The surplus, if any, goes to the mortgagor. Generally, the mortgagor, or any other party claiming an interest in the property that a foreclosure might cut off, can redeem the property after default and before expiration of a redemption period, usually six months or one year.

Foreclosure
A legal proceeding to terminate a mortgagor's interest in property; the mortgagee's remedy when the mortgagor defaults on payments.

Trust Deeds

A regular mortgage has only two parties, the borrower (mortgagor) and the lender (mortgagee). The **trust deed**, also known as a **deed of trust** or **trust indenture**, has the following three parties: (1) the borrower (trustor) who transfers the land; (2) the trustee, to whom the land is transferred; and (3) the beneficiaries, for whose benefit the transfer is made. The trust deed is common in some Midwestern states and in California and is useful when large loans

Trust deed, or **deed of trust**, or **trust indenture**
A secured interest in real property that is held by a trustee to protect the lender (beneficiary) until the loan is repaid by the borrower (trustor).

are involved. The trustee is in many respects a mortgagee, and the standard mortgage clause in an insurance policy usually refers not only to a mortgagee but also to a trustee.

Trust deeds have the following three important advantages:

1. In several states, the trust deed can be foreclosed by a trustee's sale without any court proceedings, although some states treat it exactly like a mortgage and require court foreclosure.

2. The trust deed facilitates borrowing large amounts of money. For example, a company borrows a large sum from a bank and executes a trust deed on its property to the bank as trustee. The bank, in turn, sells a large number of notes or bonds authorized by the trust deed to investors who are secured by the trust deed, simplifying what might have been a very complicated mortgage procedure of separate notes and separate mortgages for each investor.

3. The holder of a bond secured by a trust deed can sell the bond with a minimum of expense and trouble. Sale of a note secured by a mortgage requires an assignment of the mortgage, a complex arrangement.

The principal disadvantage of trust deeds arises when the number of beneficiaries or bondholders is large. When the borrower pays off the trust deed, the trustee must be certain that all bondholders are paid. If not, the trustee is personally liable. Additionally, in a sale resulting from foreclosure, the trustee cannot purchase the property at a foreclosure sale in most states, and a committee of bondholders must consummate the purchase.

Land Contracts

Land contract
A secured interest in real property based on a stipulation that the seller will not transfer title to the property until payment of a certain percentage of the price.

Under a **land contract**, the parties enter into an agreement of sale of property with a stipulation that the seller will not transfer title to the property until payment of a certain percentage of the price, frequently 100 percent. The percentage can be less than 100 percent, with the option to enter into a standard mortgage arrangement for the balance.

Land contracts are frequently used when buyers have poor or inadequate credit ratings or do not have enough money for down payments. The buyer takes possession of the land, pays all the taxes and assessments, insures the property, repairs it, and assumes all the obligations of an owner. In fact, the law treats the buyer as the owner, and the seller has only the legal title. If the buyer defaults, the seller can declare the contract breached and repossess the property, treating the buyer as an ordinary tenant.

Mechanics' Liens on Real Property

As discussed, a lien is a right that certain creditors have to obtain payment of debts secured by a debtor's real property. The creditors' recourse is usually to seek sale of the property. Mechanics and material suppliers furnish labor and material for the construction of improvements on land. Because those improvements become part of the real property, mechanics and material suppliers have statutorily created security interests in the property to ensure that they receive payment.

A **mechanic's lien** is a lien granted by law to anyone who repairs a specific piece of property, that secures payment for the repairs. A mechanic's lien may cover labor or materials supplied in improving, repairing, or maintaining real or personal property, such as a building or a car. Usually the work or material for real property must become a permanent part of the property.

In some states, a lien claimant must show that the owner hired the claimant to furnish work or material. In other states, a lien claimant can show that the owner consented to the work, even though another person, such as a tenant, ordered it. Frequently, the owner cannot prevent a person from putting improvements on property. For example, a buyer of land under a long-term contract orders the construction of improvements. The owner cannot object, but it would not be fair for a lien to attach automatically. In these cases, the owner's actual consent is necessary to bind the owner on a mechanic's lien.

A general contractor who seeks to assert a lien usually must show the following:

- Substantial performance of the contract
- Improvement of a specific piece of property under the contract
- Specific mention in the contract of the property to be improved

State statutes usually require filing a notice of lien in a public office, such as the county clerk's office, within a specified period after completion of the work. Generally, the notice must state the following:

- Amount claimed
- Claimant's name and address
- Type of improvement
- Description of the land
- Owner's name

A mechanic's lien is usually operative for a specified time, and the lienholder must take steps to enforce or foreclose it within that time.

Priorities for Mechanics' Liens

The following are four rules that states use to determine when a mechanic's lien attaches to property to create priority over other secured interests:

1. In most states, mechanics' liens relate to the day the work started. A mortgage recorded on the following day is subordinate to the lien of a subcontractor who was not hired until later because that lien relates back to the start of the work. Lienholders have no priorities.
2. In some states, the lien attaches when the mechanic starts work. The lien cannot have priority over a mortgage recorded earlier.

Mechanic's lien
A lien, granted by law to anyone who repairs a specific piece of property, that secures payment for the repairs.

3. The lien attaches on the date the mechanic makes the contract for improvement. Such a lien is a "secret lien" because improvement contracts are usually not recorded, and even an inspection of the property would not disclose that work is starting later. Nevertheless, a mortgage recorded after the date of the improvement contract is subordinate to the mechanic's lien.

4. The lien attaches on the notice filing. A previously recorded mortgage, therefore, has priority.

Foreclosure

Foreclosing a mechanic's lien resembles foreclosing a mortgage. In some states, the lien attaches only to the building but not to the land, and in some places only to the additions or improvements themselves. Usually, removal of the materials furnished would damage the property. Therefore, courts frequently order sale of the property and give the mechanic's lienholder a share of the proceeds.

Waiver of Lien

Parties can waive the right to a mechanic's lien in a contract for improvements. In some states, such a provision is not valid unless the contract is filed. In some states, the waiver is valid against everyone, including subcontractors, but in other states it is valid only against the general contractor.

Another method of waiver is to obtain a partial waiver from the mechanic as work progresses and when the mechanic receives partial payments. The waiver usually recites that the mechanic waives all liens "for work and materials furnished" up to the date of the waiver. A property owner can pay off a lien, then clear the public records by filing a release of mechanic's lien form in the office where the lienholder filed the lien.

Incidental Real Property Rights

Ownership of real property can result from possession. Ownership can also include more than the real property itself. This section discusses the following five important rights that are incidental, that is, that arise from either possession or ownership of land:

1. Adverse possession
2. Rights under, above, and on the land's surface
3. Rights to lateral and subjacent support
4. Water rights
5. Ownership of fixtures

Adverse Possession

Conflict can arise when a person who possesses land claims ownership, and another who does not possess it also claims ownership. For example, Elliott lives on a lot for which Dianne has had legal title for over thirty years. During that thirty-year period, Dianne knew of Elliott's residence and did not object. Finally, Dianne asserts that she owns the land and wants Elliott to leave. Dianne, the person who is not in possession but who claims legal ownership, can sue the person in possession, Elliott. Elliot may claim he owns the land by **adverse possession**, which has the following four elements:

1. The adverse party must have exclusive possession of the property and occupy it in the usual way, such as living in a residence.
2. Possession must be open and obvious.
3. Possession must be adverse, or hostile, and without the owner's permission.
4. Possession must be continuous for a statutory period, usually a lengthy period, such as twenty years or more.

Adverse possession
The claim of ownership of land by possession that is exclusive, open, hostile, unpermitted, and continuous for a statutory period.

Rights Under, Above, and on the Land's Surface

Ownership of land includes the incidental rights to whatever is under, above, and on the surface. Ownership of land below the surface includes such things as minerals, clay, stone, gravel, and sand. A transfer of land also transfers these materials; however, a seller can reserve mineral rights in the deed. Oil and gas, on the other hand, flow freely under the surface, and no person owns them without possessing the land. Ownership of land carries with it limited rights over the air space above the land. An owner can halt unauthorized intrusion into this air space, such as projections from an adjoining building or utility lines stretched across the air space. Generally, planes can fly over land as long as they do not interfere unreasonably with the owner's use and enjoyment of the land. The property owner also has rights to products of the soil. Annual products, such as crops, are personal property. Perennial products, such as timber, can be real property.

Rights to Lateral and Subjacent Support

A landowner also has the right to lateral and subjacent support systems that might not be on the landowner's property.

Lateral support is support of land by adjacent land. The right of lateral support applies to land in its natural condition only. For example, David and Mary own adjoining vacant lots, and David excavates his land close to the property line, causing a part of Mary's land to fall into the excavation. David is liable to Mary for the damage to her land. However, if Mary's lot has a building on it, David is not liable for damage to the building because the duty to provide lateral support extends only to land in its natural state. The support of the land need not be natural; for example, David can avoid liability by building a retaining wall to support Mary's land.

Lateral support
A property owner's right to have land supported by the land adjacent to it.

If a building stands on Mary's land, David must give her reasonable notice of his intent to excavate so that she can take steps to support the building. David must also excavate with reasonable care. If David fails to give notice and fails to excavate with reasonable care, he might be liable to Mary for damages should Mary's building collapse.

Subjacent support
A property owner's right to have land supported by the earth below it.

Subjacent support is the right to have one's land supported by the earth that lies underneath it. Two parties can have rights in one piece of land: One party owns the land, and the other owns the rights to minerals under that land. For example, Bob sells mineral rights to Fred but retains a natural right of subjacent support from the underlying mineral area. If Fred removes minerals, withdrawing subjacent support for Bob's land, and the surface subsides, Bob can recover damages without proving any negligence on Fred's part. Additionally, as with lateral support, a subjacent owner can furnish artificial supports, such as columns or braces, to prevent damage to the surface land.

Water Rights

Another incidental land ownership right is water rights. Property owners have rights to both underground and surface waters.

An owner can remove underground waters that percolate through the soil and follow no defined course. The owner can remove any quantity of the water, even if it deprives adjacent owners of water, so long as the owner uses it on the land and does not sell it at a distance, to the adjoining landowners' detriment. When water is scarce, an owner can use only a reasonable amount.

Discharging surface water from one's land onto another's land is not a basis for a suit as long as the water is not collected by artificial means and discharged on the adjoining land in new or concentrated channels, causing damage.

Riparian owner
An owner of land that contains or borders on a naturally flowing waterway.

Streams can be property boundaries or can pass through property. Owners with naturally flowing waterways on, or adjoining, their properties are **riparian owners**. A riparian owner can use as much water from the waterway as needed for domestic purposes but must use only a reasonable amount for industrial purposes and must consider downstream owners' needs. Riparian owners have a right to a pollution-free stream, and polluters may be liable to them for resulting damages. Water beneath the surface and flowing in a well-defined course, such as an underground river, is subject to the same rules as those applicable to surface streams.

Ownership of Fixtures

Fixtures are property installed on, attached to, or used with land or buildings in such a way as to become real property themselves. Thus, if a tenant installs fixtures that were originally personal property, they become part of the real property and at installation belong to the owner of the real property. For example, a tenant installs a cabinet purchased as personal property at a home improvement store. Installation can make the cabinet part of the real property. A seller of land transfers personal property that has become a fixture, without specific reference, along with the sale of land. The following three tests help in determining whether an item is a fixture:

1. If an article cannot be removed without substantial injury to the realty, it is a fixture, even though damage can be repaired. For example, a fireplace is a fixture even though the wall from which it is removed can be rebuilt.

2. If an article is specially constructed or fitted for use in a building, or if the article is installed in the building to enable people to use the building, the article is a fixture. A heater and a door in a house are examples.

3. If the party who attached an item intended it to become part of the land or building, that item is a fixture. The relationship of the parties often controls what becomes a fixture. For instance, a landlord who hangs a mirror that cannot then be removed from the wall without substantial damage to the premises might intend it to stay there permanently. However, a tenant who attaches a similar mirror might intend to remove it at the end of the lease term.

When a tenant rents a building for business, the test of intention regarding fixtures usually applies in the tenant's favor. Between a landlord and tenant, the law considers all **trade fixtures**, which are items attached to real property solely for trade purposes during a tenancy, as removable, including such articles as bakery ovens, cabinetry, and steam boilers. An article is a trade fixture if the tenant can remove it without permanent injury to the land or building and if the tenant installed it solely for trade purposes.

Trade fixture
An item attached to real property solely for trade purposes, which is removable without permanent injury to the land or building.

For insurance purposes, **improvements and betterments** are alterations to premises made by a tenant that make it more useful for the tenant's purpose and become part of the leased structure. For example, painting and wallpapering as a part of a general plan of altering the premises for a tenant's initial occupancy is an improvement, not a repair and not a fixture.

Improvements and betterments
Alterations to premises made by a tenant that make it more useful for the tenant's purpose and become part of the leased structure.

Land Use Restrictions

In addition to rights incidental to possession and ownership, landownership can involve restrictions that benefit either private parties or the public. They include the following: (1) incorporeal interests, (2) licenses, and (3) government controls.

Incorporeal Interests

The law recognizes four major **incorporeal interests**, which are nonmaterial interests, in real property. This section discusses three of those interests. Lease situations, which include rentals, are discussed in a later section.

Incorporeal interest
A nonmaterial interest in real property.

1. *Easements.* An **easement** is the nonpossessory right to use another person's real property for a particular purpose. It can be created by express words, by implication, or by prescription (adverse possession). Parties can expressly create an easement by reserving it when the land to which it is to attach is sold. For example, David owns a piece of land fronting on a road. He subdivides the property into two lots. Lot 1 is on the back of the property with no access to the road. Lot 2 is in front with all the road frontage, and it blocks access to Lot 1. David's house is on Lot 1. David sells Lot 2 but expressly reserves a right of access to the road across Lot 2 to his Lot 1. Parties also can create an easement by implication. In the previous example, if David sells Lot 2 without expressly reserving an easement, the easement might be implied by law to give David access to the road.

Easement
A nonpossessory right to use another person's real property for a particular purpose.

Profits *à prendre*
A right or privilege to enter another's land and take away something of value from its soil or from the products of its soil.

2. *Profits à prendre.* A **profit *à prendre*** ("to take" in French) is a right or privilege to enter another's land and take away something of value from its soil or from the products of its soil (as by mining, logging, or hunting). The usual easement must benefit adjacent land and be next to that land. Profits *à prendre* can be next to the land, but they are independent of the ownership of any other land. The rights to mine coal, remove sand and gravel, and cut down trees are examples of profits *à prendre* rights. Rights to water or oil are not profits *à prendre* because the term applies only to a part of the land that is subject to ownership. Liquids are not the subject of ownership until removed and reduced to possession because they flow freely on or under the land and are not in a fixed position. The profits *à prendre* right includes the right to do anything reasonably necessary to obtain the materials, including entering the land and digging holes to get to the substances.

3. *Seller's restrictions on land use.* In selling real property, an owner can restrict its use to preserve or enhance the value of any land retained by the seller or to benefit the public. Examples of legally valid restrictions are contracts prescribing the minimum cost of homes to be built on land, the minimum size of buildings, and the types of construction. On the other hand, discriminatory agreements prohibiting sale to certain racial or ethnic groups are unenforceable. Some states expressly limit restrictions on land use to a statutory period of, for example, thirty or forty years. Changed conditions, such as economic conditions in the area, can make restrictions unenforceable.

Licenses

License
The permission to use real property for a particular purpose.

A **license**, as distinguished from an easement, is permission to use real property for a particular purpose. Without that permission the use would be a trespass (illegal entry) or another illegal act. Permission to hunt or fish on another's land, a ticket for a theater seat, and renting a hotel room are typical licenses. The license gives no interest in the land. A license can be oral, written, or implied. For example, by implication the public has a license to use the public halls in an office building.

Government Controls

Government has certain powers over the use of land on the public's behalf. The government cannot, under the guise of protecting the public, interfere arbitrarily with lawful land use or impose unreasonable and unnecessary restrictions on it. An example of the lawful exercise of government's power is the regulation of the number of oil and gas wells allowed on property and the flow of oil and gas from those wells. The government can protect the public as well as adjoining landowners against waste from wells. The condemnation and requirement to destroy diseased trees or plants is another example of valid government control of land use. The most common methods governments employ to restrict land use are the following: (1) zoning, (2) building codes, and (3) eminent domain.

Zoning is government's regulation of building construction and occupancy and of land use according to a comprehensive plan. A zoning ordinance must provide a comprehensive general plan for the entire community and must be uniform for each class or kind of occupancy or use of land within a given district. Requirements can vary by district. However, within limits, all property in like circumstances must be treated the same. Matters affected by zoning laws include, for example, lot size, minimum building size, number of families that may reside in the buildings, maximum height of each building, and parking areas.

A zoning ordinance cannot allow **spot zoning**, that is, assign a different use for a small area of land than that of the surrounding area, when the result would benefit the owner of the area to the neighbors' detriment. Zoning restricting land use either by prohibiting additional building or by requiring high standards, such as five-acre lots or single-family dwellings, is **exclusionary zoning**. Two ways to relieve a property from compliance with a zoning ordinance are special exceptions and variances.

A **special exception** is a use explicitly permitted by the zoning ordinance but subject to certain limitations. Exceptions are special uses considered desirable for the general welfare, but only when controlled, such as the building of a school or a church in a residential zone. An ordinance can permit the use, but only if the governing body approves it.

A **variance** is relief from the strict application of an ordinance to permit a use that is not permitted otherwise. The following are the two types of variances:

1. A **hardship variance** applies to lots that, because of size, topography, or other physical limitations, do not conform to the ordinance requirements for the zone. If strict application of the requirements would result in peculiar and exceptional difficulties or undue hardship on the owner, the governing body can grant a variance.
2. In particular cases and for special reasons, the government can grant a **use variance** to permit an otherwise prohibited use within the zone. An example of a special reason is a use that would benefit the general welfare.

A **nonconforming use** is a use that is impermissible under current zoning restrictions but that is allowed because the use existed lawfully before the restrictions took effect. To avoid the constitutional prohibition against taking property without due process, any nonconforming use existing at the time an ordinance passes can continue. The use cannot be enlarged and can be terminated by total destruction of the structure, by abandonment of the use, or by a change in use.

Many cities and states have adopted local ordinances or state statutes that regulate construction of buildings, called **building codes**, which sometimes overlap zoning ordinances. However, they address the more technical construction details, such as electrical wiring and heating. An owner must submit building plans to a government regulator to determine whether construction conforms to the building code. If it does, a building permit issues.

Zoning
A government's regulation of building construction and occupancy and of land use according to a comprehensive plan.

Spot zoning
A provision in a general zoning plan that assigns a different use for a small area of land than that of the surrounding area.

Exclusionary zoning
The act of restricting land use either by prohibiting additional building or by requiring high standards.

Special exception
A land use explicitly permitted by a zoning ordinance but subject to certain limitations.

Variance
An exception to the strict application of a zoning ordinance to permit a use that is not permitted otherwise.

Hardship variance
An exception to the application of a zoning ordinance for lots that, because of size, topography, or other physical limitations, do not conform to the ordinance requirements for the zone.

Use variance
An exception to the application of a zoning ordinance to permit an otherwise prohibited use within the zone.

Nonconforming use
A land use that is impermissible under current zoning restrictions but that is allowed because the use was lawful before the restrictions took effect.

Building codes
The local ordinances or state statutes that regulate construction of buildings.

Eminent domain
The right of a government to seize private property for public use.

Condemnation proceeding
A legal procedure by which a government body seeks a court's permission to seize private property by eminent domain.

After the structure's completion, an inspector from the regulatory agency inspects the structure before anyone can occupy it and, if approved, issues a certificate of occupancy.

Another method by which government controls the use of private property is the exercise of **eminent domain**, the right of a government to seize property for public use. Eminent domain usually requires a **condemnation proceeding**, by which a government body files a petition in court seeking permission to seize private property by eminent domain. The petition states the exact property desired and the public use involved and seeks a court's permission to seize property. The following are the two conditions for granting the petition:

1. The land must be taken for public use.
2. Just compensation must be paid to the owner. Just compensation is the fair market value at the time of the taking.

Landlord and Tenant

Tenancy at will
A landlord-tenant estate in which the tenant has permission to occupy a premises as a landlord desires.

Estate for years
A landlord-tenant estate created for a definite period.

Periodic tenancy
A landlord-tenant estate with no fixed termination date and automatic renewal until one of the parties gives notice of intent to terminate.

Landlord (lessor) and tenant (lessee) law governs lease interests in real property, which are property interests of limited duration. State and local laws vary significantly regarding landlord-tenant law. The three types of landlord-tenant estates are as follows:

1. **Tenancy at will** is permission to occupy a premises as the landlord desires. Under a tenancy at will, the landlord can require the tenant to leave at any time without advance notice.
2. An **estate for years** is created for a definite period, such as three months or twenty years.
3. **Periodic tenancy** is a variation of tenancy for years. It does not have a fixed termination date but runs for a period, such as one year, and renewal for each period is automatic until one of the parties gives notice of intent to terminate.

Holdover tenant
A tenant who has a lease for a number of years and, at the expiration of the lease, continues to occupy the premises.

Tenant at sufferance
A tenant who has a lease for a number of years and, at the expiration of the lease, continues to occupy the premises, without the agreement of the landlord.

A landlord and tenant can create a periodic tenancy by an express agreement, usually called a "tenancy from year-to-year" or "from month-to-month." The parties also can create a periodic tenancy by implication. For example, a lease states no expiration date but states that the rental is $10,000 per year, payable one-twelfth each month. This implies a tenancy from year to year, based on the periodic rent payments.

A periodic tenancy also can arise by implication of law. This result occurs when a tenant is a **holdover tenant**, who has had a lease for a number of years and, at the expiration of that lease, continues to occupy the premises. If the landlord expressly approves the occupancy or accepts rent, then a periodic tenancy is implied. If the landlord does not agree to the occupancy, the tenant becomes a **tenant at sufferance** and can be ejected by the landlord.

The periodic tenancy can be from month-to-month or year-to-year, depending on the terms of the prior tenancy. By statute in some states, it is a month-to-month tenancy unless the parties have agreed otherwise. The other terms of the prior lease continue to apply. The notice of lease termination period is usually one entire lease period. However, if the period is a year or longer, most states require three-to-six months' notice.

Landlords' Rights and Duties

The landlord's primary duty is to deliver possession of the premises to the tenant on the lease's inception date. The landlord's primary rights are to receive the rent when due and to recover the premises at the end of the lease in the same condition in which they were leased, except for reasonable wear and tear.

If the tenant defaults, the landlord has no duty to lessen the financial loss by trying to find another tenant. If a tenant abandons the property, the landlord can treat abandonment as an anticipatory breach and receive as damages the amount of the remaining rent payments. In these cases, the landlord must mitigate, or lessen, the loss. Many long-term leases provide that, in event of default, the landlord can accelerate the payments, reenter the premises, act as the tenant's agent to sublet, and sue the tenant for any resulting losses.

Many landlords require tenants to pay a **security deposit** at the inception of leases, which is either a percentage of the rent or equivalent to a specified period of rent. The lease usually provides that, in case of default, the security deposit represents damages that the landlord can retain. Some statutes provide that the security deposit is the tenant's property, that the landlord must keep it in a bank escrow account, and that the landlord must return it to the tenant after lease termination.

Security deposit
A payment required by a landlord from a tenant at the inception of a lease that the landlord can retain for default in payment or damage to the property.

Landlords' Remedies

When a tenant remains in possession at lease termination, or if the tenant owes rent or has breached the lease, the landlord can evict the tenant with or without court assistance. In a "self-help" eviction, the landlord can remove the tenant's possessions from the premises and bar the tenant from reentering by changing door locks or by other peaceful means. The landlord must first demand rent from the tenant, or correction of other breaches, to make the tenant a tenant at sufferance. If the landlord uses force or threat of force, the eviction is unlawful, and the tenant is entitled not only to reenter but also to recover damages.

The landlord can also apply to a court for help. Many states provide for summary eviction proceedings when the lease is terminated and the tenant refuses to move, or during the lease term if the tenant defaults on the rent. The landlord must send the tenant a written notice terminating the tenancy and demanding possession. After a period of time, the landlord serves a summons and complaint, and a hearing is held. If the landlord establishes a right to possession, the court enters an order of repossession followed by a warrant of removal. The tenant has only two defenses: that the tenant has paid the rent, or that the rent is not legally due.

Eviction can be either actual or constructive. Actual eviction from the whole or even a part of the premises ends the obligation to pay rent. **Constructive eviction** occurs when actions or inactions of a landlord prevent the tenant from enjoying a substantial or integral part of the premises. Examples include the landlord's allowing inadequate heat or hot water, leaky plumbing, serious disturbances by other tenants, and pest infestation. If a landlord seeks a court eviction for nonpayment of rent, the tenant may assert a defense of constructive eviction.

When the tenant defaults on rent, the landlord can seize possession of the tenant's property and hold it for the rent, a right called **distraint**. The landlord must seize the goods peacefully and sell them at a public sale. Distraint and self-help are similar, particularly if the landlord removes the tenant's property from the premises in the self-help proceedings.

In addition to distraint, a landlord also has a nonpossessory lien on the tenant's property for rent due. This lien applies frequently to commercial leases, when a tenant becomes insolvent. The lien attaches merely by the landlord's declaring that the goods on the premises are subject to the lien and notifying the defaulting tenant of the lien. Any purchaser of the goods, or creditor of the tenant, who takes the goods with notice of the lien can be liable for damages.

Constructive eviction
Actions or inactions of a landlord that create conditions that prevent the tenant from enjoying a substantial or integral part of the premises.

Distraint
A landlord's right to seize possession of a tenant's property and hold it for rent when the tenant has defaulted on the rent.

Tenants' Rights and Duties

The tenant's rights and duties complement the landlord's. For example, the tenant must pay rent and leave the premises in the same condition they were in at the lease inception, except for reasonable wear and tear. The tenant has a right to occupy the premises; and, on eviction, the obligation to pay rent can end.

When a defective condition in the property exists, the tenant need not pay rent when the following three conditions have occurred sequentially:

1. The tenant has demanded that the landlord correct the situation.
2. The landlord has not done so within a reasonable time.
3. The tenant has left the premises at the end of that reasonable time.

The tenant's remaining on the premises can constitute a waiver of the right to withhold rent. The tenant has a right to vacate the premises and escape liability for rent but does not have an action for damages. However, if an express agreement in the lease requires the landlord to make repairs, the tenant might have a right to sue for damages, if any, for breach of contract.

Liability of Parties

As a general rule, landlords are liable to third parties for injuries sustained on the premises to the same extent they are liable to tenants. Liability is restricted to a landlord's negligent acts or latent defects on the premises.

In many states, the landlord can escape liability to the tenant by including an exculpatory clause in the lease in which the tenant agrees to relieve, or excuse, the landlord of any liability, either to the tenant, to third parties, or both. However, such a clause usually does not affect the landlord's liability to third persons. If property becomes defective after the inception of the lease and the lease does not require the landlord to repair the premises, the landlord is usually not liable even to third parties, although the tenants can be liable. However, if the condition still exists at the time of lease renewal, the landlord may become liable to the tenant and the third party because of a continuing problem of which the landlord had notice at time of renewal. For example, a landlord has no duty to make repairs under a lease with a tenant shopkeeper. After the inception of the lease term, a step into the tenant's shop develops a defect on which customers can trip on their way into the shop. The tenant does not repair the step, and the landlord renews the lease without repairing it. If a customer coming into the shop trips or falls because of the defective step after the lease renewal, the landlord might be liable to the injured customer.

The tenant is liable to third parties for injuries caused by the tenant's acts or negligence when the tenant has sole possession of the premises and when the landlord has no obligation to repair. The tenant is also liable to the landlord for any damages to the premises exceeding ordinary wear and tear. Here again, a clause exculpating the tenant from liability could be included in the lease.

SUMMARY

Real property is land, including structures or rights attached to the land. Personal property is all property that is not real property. Personal property can be obtained through creation, accession, confusion, bailments, or gifts. One can also create property rights in intellectual property and therefore have a copyright or a patent right. Property rights can be increased by accession, an addition to property through natural accretion, a union of one thing with another, or transformation of raw materials. Confusion, the intermingling of goods of different owners, can give both owners property rights that vary with the circumstances.

In bailments, a bailor leaves personal property with a bailee for safekeeping or repair. A bailment has the following three elements:

1. The transfer of possession without transfer of title

2. The bailee's acceptance of possession

3. An express or implied agreement to redeliver the property to the bailor or to a third person whom the bailor designates

A bailee has possession only and cannot transfer title to the property but may have a right to use the property. Special bailments involve common carriers, hotelkeepers, warehouse operators, and factors. Each type of bailment requires a different degree of care. A bailee may also have a possessory lien, the right to retain possession of a bailor's property as security for the payment of a debt or performance of an act. Such a lien is not an interest in property.

A property interest can be acquired through a gift. A gift of personal property is the donor's voluntary transfer of property to a donee without consideration. A gift has the following three elements:

1. Donative intent
2. Delivery
3. Donee's acceptance

Interests in real property can also be total or partial. Total interest in real property has the following two elements:

1. Complete, outright, and full ownership (quality)
2. Unlimited time (duration)

A fee simple estate is complete ownership of real property. Parts of this total interest can be carved out to create lesser interests, either as to the quality of the ownership or the length of time it exists. Examples are life estates and dower and curtesy rights.

Concurrent estates include the following:

*   Joint tenancy, an undivided interest that transfers to a surviving joint tenant on the death of the other
*   Tenancy by the entirety, a joint tenancy between husband and wife
*   Tenancy in common, equal or unequal shares with no survivorship rights
*   Community property, acquired by both spouses during a marriage
*   Cooperative ownership, held by a corporation and stockholders who hold a long-term proprietary interest
*   Condominium ownership, individual ownership of a unit of a building and an undivided interest in the common elements.

A real property sale involves a contract of sale and a deed, both of which, under the statute of frauds, must be in writing. Recording of real estate transfer documents protects buyers against subsequent purchasers. Security interests in real property include mortgages, trust deeds, and land contracts. Liens give certain creditors rights to have their debts paid out of debtors' property, usually by sale. Mechanics' liens give those who repair property a right to retain the property to secure payment.

Incidental real property rights include adverse possession claims; rights under, above, and on the land's surface; the right to lateral and subjacent support; water rights; and the ownership of fixtures. Land use restrictions include easements, profits à prendre, restrictions on land use, rents, licenses, zoning, building codes, and eminent domain.

Landlord-tenant law governs lease interests in real property, which are limited interests of limited duration. A landlord's primary duty is to deliver possession of the premises to the tenant at the inception of the lease. The tenant must pay rent and leave the premises in the condition in which they were received, except for reasonable wear and tear. The landlord has the same liability to third parties for injuries sustained on the premises as does the tenant, and the tenant is liable to third parties for injuries caused by any of the tenant's acts.

CHAPTER NOTE

1.   17 U.S.C., § 101.

Chapter 8

Direct Your Learning

Tort Law—Negligence

After learning the content of this chapter and completing the corresponding course guide assignment, you should be able to:

■ Given a case, explain which classification of tort law and state law applies.

■ Given a case, determine whether the elements of negligence are present.

   • Describe the elements required to prove negligence.

   • Describe the various proofs of negligence and of imputed negligence.

■ Given a case, explain whether any of the following defenses would affect a plaintiff's right to recovery:

   • Contributory negligence

   • Comparative negligence

   • Last clear chance

   • Assumption of risk

   • Release of liability

   • Immunity

■ Explain how a person can assume vicarious liability by hiring independent contractors.

■ Explain how the following agreements affect contractual liability:

   • Liquidated damages agreement

   • Hold-harmless agreement

   • Exculpatory agreement

■ Given a case, evaluate the liability of landowners or occupiers for negligence relating to natural or artificial conditions.

■ Define or describe each of the Key Words and Phrases for this chapter.

Develop Your Perspective

What are the main topics covered in the chapter?

Torts fall into many classifications, but negligence is the basis of most property and casualty insurance claims. Understanding negligence law requires comprehending the elements and proof of negligence, imputed negligence, and defenses to negligence allegations. The chapter concludes by examining the liability of landowners and land occupiers for negligence, including liability for natural and artificial conditions on land and liability to those who enter the land.

Describe the elements that must be present for a negligence claim.

- In what ways can a legal duty be created?

- How is the required standard of care determined?

- How might a proximate cause be interrupted?

Why is it important to learn about these topics?

Insurance liability (casualty) coverages focus almost entirely on negligence, a form of tort. Torts are civil wrongs between people or entities, and negligence is the most common tort.

Consider the kinds of torts your employer might experience.

- What act of negligence might cause harm to someone else and result in a lawsuit?

- What is an example of vicarious liability your employer might have in a negligence lawsuit?

How can you use what you will learn?

Evaluate the protection your insurance policies provide for negligent acts you might inadvertently cause.

- What insurance policies do you have, if any, covering your negligence?

- What exceptions are included in those policies for your negligent acts?

Chapter 8
Tort Law—Negligence

Tort law applies to most civil wrongs between people other than breaches of contract. Torts can involve actions directed toward people or their property. Generally, torts are either unintentional or intentional. Negligence is the broad term used for unintentional torts, and all other torts are intentional. Although torts fall into many classifications, negligence is the most important tort classification for insurance professionals to understand because it is the basis of most property and casualty insurance claims.

Subsequent chapters continue the tort discussion by examining various intentional torts, such as defamation and "torts of outrage;" and by examining strict liability, products liability, toxic torts, environmental law, and torts involving property.

DEFINITION AND CLASSIFICATION OF TORTS

A **tort** is a wrongful act or omission, other than a crime or a breach of contract, for which the remedy is usually monetary damages. Torts are civil wrongs, or private wrongs, as distinguished from crimes, which are public wrongs. A tort results from a breach of duty, resulting in an injury or loss. Some torts are simultaneously private wrongs and crimes that violate the public at large.

A tort is a legal wrong as distinguished from a moral wrong. The law does not judge an act by moral standards. For example, if Connie sees Alvin starting to cross the street in front of an oncoming car, she generally has no legal duty to warn him. Failure to warn in such a situation ordinarily does not constitute a legal basis for a lawsuit even though some people would think a moral duty exists.

The same act can be both a tort and a breach of contract. For example, suppose that a train passenger is injured through the train crew's negligence. The passenger might have an action in tort for negligence but might also have an action for breach of a contract for safe transportation. In the typical medical malpractice situation, the injured person usually has a right to sue for the cost of medical services in tort or for breach of a contract.

Tort
A wrongful act or omission, other than a crime or a breach of contract, for which the remedy is usually monetary damages.

Separating torts into precise categories is almost impossible without overlaps, but the following are examples of broad classifications of torts:

Intentional tort
A tort committed with intent to cause harm or with intent to do the act that causes harm.

Tortfeasor
One who commits a tort.

- *Intentional torts.* As its name implies, an **intentional tort** requires intent to cause harm or intent to do the act that causes harm. One who commits a tort is a **tortfeasor**. Intent differs from motive. For example, one person could shoot at another with the intent to kill but with the motive of self-defense, jealousy, or rage.

  Generally, intent and motive have no relationship, and at early common law, doing an otherwise legal act with a malicious motive would not provide grounds to sue. For example, if a person says something malicious to another, those words do not by themselves give the other person a right to sue. However, motive can influence recoverable damages. For instance, an act done in self-defense might justify lower damages than an act done in rage. A tortfeasor's malice might warrant high, or even punitive, damages.

- *Unintentional torts.* Many acts are legal wrongs even if they are not intentional. Unintentional torts are termed negligence. For example, a driver who is in a hurry fails to see a stop sign and drives through it, causing an accident. The driver did not intend to cause the accident but failed in her duty to drive carefully and is therefore negligent.

- *Physical torts.* Sometimes torts are classified by whether they involve physical acts on another's person or property, as distinguished from nonphysical acts that might invade a legal right. Assault is a physical tort that a person commits when threatening another with physical harm, but without physical touching. Battery is a physical act of harming a person by actual touching. Other examples of physical torts are false imprisonment and false arrest.

- *Nonphysical torts.* Nonphysical torts do not involve physical acts or contacts. Examples of nonphysical torts are defamation (libel and slander), which involves only written or spoken words; outrage; malicious prosecution; and fraud.

APPLICABLE LAW

Courts must often decide what law to apply to cases before they ever consider factual issues. For example, in a case involving pollution, a court might have to decide whether state environmental or common law applies, or whether federal statutory law preempts state law. In a case in which a citizen of Kansas sues a citizen of Oregon for slander, the court must decide whether Kansas or Oregon law is applicable. Deciding which law to apply is often a complex issue.

Where one can sue for tort depends on whether the cause of action is local or transitory. A cause of action is a factual situation that entitles a person to sue. A local cause of action can occur only in one place. A transitory cause of action can occur anywhere. For example, a person can sue for a tort involving real property only where the real property is located.

Therefore, it is a local action. Conversely the tort of negligence can happen anywhere and is therefore transitory.

Determining which law to apply in a transitory tort case depends on the forum and the situs. A **forum** is the jurisdiction, or place in which a party sues. In relation to a tort case, the **situs** is the place at which the wrong occurred. When a plaintiff sues in a forum that is not the place where the wrong occurred (situs), the court must decide whether the law of the forum state or of the situs state governs. State laws vary regarding damages and many other tort law matters, so the choice of law to apply is often of great significance to the parties. In resolving this matter, the courts divide the law as follows:

- *Lex loci*—the law of the place where the wrong occurred
- *Lex fori*—the law of the place in which the plaintiff sues

The general rule in tort actions is that the *lex loci* governs any substantive matter having to do with the lawsuit, such as the parties' rights, the validity of defenses, or the measure of damages. The *lex fori* governs procedure, such as application of evidentiary rules.

Some states apply the doctrine of *lex loci* rigidly. However, many courts have developed a different rule based on a theory of interest analysis. Under the **rule of significant contacts**, in a case involving parties from different states with conflicting laws, a court selects the law of the state that has a greater interest in protecting its citizens by applying its law to the specific case. If both states have equally legitimate interests, then a court must choose the rule of law with higher authority. Under the rule of significant contacts, the law of the forum state is irrelevant except when neither state has a legitimate interest or when the court prefers the forum state rule.

As an example of significant contact rule application, Al and Bob, citizens of State Y, travel together to State Z. While in Z, Al negligently injures Bob, who dies there. Bob's legal representative sues in State Y, Al's and Bob's native state. The court might find that, because both Al and Bob lived in State Y, they had such significant contacts there that the court should apply State Y substantive law. If State Z, the place of Bob's injury, had a statutory limit of $100,000 for wrongful death and State Y had no limit, the choice of law could have a very significant effect because application of State Y's law could result in a substantially higher damage award.

Courts apply various types of interest doctrines, examining the policies behind certain laws, as well as legal rules and procedures. While some states apply the most significant contacts test, others apply a comparative impairment test. For this test, the court determines which state's policy, as reflected by its laws, might suffer more adverse effects if the court did not apply its law. For example, in a child custody case, application of one state's law might have more significance for all children in that state than would application of the other state's law.

Forum
The jurisdiction or place in which a party sues.

Situs
In a tort case, the place at which a wrong occurs.

Rule of significant contacts
A court rule, applied in cases involving parties from different states with conflicting laws, that favors the law of the state that has a greater interest.

NEGLIGENCE

Negligence, an unintentional tort, is the failure to exercise the degree of care that a reasonable person in a similar situation would exercise to avoid harming others. Negligence is a constantly expanding area of tort law. In many cases, insurance liability coverage pays the damages awarded in negligence cases.

Elements of Negligence

A plaintiff in a negligence claim must establish each of the following four elements of negligence:

1. The defendant owed a legal duty of care to the plaintiff.
2. The defendant breached the duty of care owed to the plaintiff.
3. The defendant's negligent act was the proximate cause of the plaintiff's injury or damage.
4. The plaintiff suffered actual injury or damage.

Legal Duty

The first element of negligence is legal duty owed to the plaintiff. **Legal duty** has no precise definition, but it exists when the parties are in such a relationship that the law imposes on one party a responsibility for the exercise of care toward the other party. In establishing the existence of a legal duty, the courts ask whether the plaintiff's interests are entitled to legal protection against the defendant's conduct.

The defendant's duty to the plaintiff to use due care must be a legal duty and not just a moral obligation. Thus, if Manuel sees Sheila drowning and fails to go to Sheila's rescue, Manuel has no liability for Sheila's death because he owed her no legal duty even though he might have had a strong moral duty to save her.

A person who voluntarily undertakes a moral duty has a legal duty to exercise reasonable care in carrying it out. When one volunteers to undertake an act or to perform a service necessary to another's safety, and that person suffers harm in reasonable reliance on the volunteer's performance, the volunteer is liable. Once a volunteer has undertaken a task, the volunteer must act as an ordinary, reasonable person would act in performing it.

A volunteer's negligent performance is called misfeasance. Nonperformance, or nonfeasance, does not create liability in a moral duty situation. The one exception involves failing to perform a promise—even a gratuitous promise (one given for no consideration). For example, Manuel on learning that Sheila is ill, promises her that he will call a doctor. Sheila, relying on the promise, does not call a doctor herself. Manuel fails to call the doctor, and as a result Sheila dies. Although Manuel's promise was gratuitous, his failure to perform nevertheless has created liability.

Statutes and contracts also create legal duties. For example, hit-and-run laws impose a duty on drivers involved in accidents to stop and give assistance to injured persons. Failure to do so generally constitutes negligence, and the violator is liable for any damages directly caused by failing to give assistance.

Failure to perform a contract or performing a contract improperly can violate a legal duty. For example, a surgeon's contract to perform an operation imposes a legal duty on the surgeon to perform it properly. If the duty is breached, the patient can sue for negligence rather than for breach of contract.

Finally, the common law, or case law, has created by far the greatest number of legal duties. Plaintiffs in lawsuits argue for an increasing number of legal duties that they claim defendants have violated. In response, the courts may develop new rules that form a compromise between the conflicting positions of plaintiffs demanding protection and defendants claiming they should have no legal duties.

Statutes and the common law recognize the following six duties arising out of certain familiar relationships:

1. *Employers*. Statutes govern employers' duties to employees. An employer owes a duty to aid an employee who becomes ill on the job. Employers also have duties to third parties injured by employees. The law also restricts employers' right to terminate employees' jobs.

2. *Common carriers*. Common carriers are required by law to convey passengers or freight without refusal if the fare or charge is paid. Common carriers owe a duty to provide safe passage for goods and passengers, including preventing personal attacks on passengers and theft of their property. Common carriers also have the duty to aid passengers in distress. In most jurisdictions, common carriers cannot waive this duty by contract.

3. *Hotel operators*. Hotel operators, or innkeepers, have a duty to provide safe and secure premises for guests, including preventing personal attacks on them and theft of their property, and to aid guests who become ill. The duty to provide safe premises also extends to a failure to take reasonable steps to reduce the likelihood of personal injury or property damage by fire or other causes.

4. *Parents and children*. Generally, parents are not liable for their children's torts unless they condone the torts, except for certain exceptional situations. A parent has a duty to exercise reasonable care to control a child who is known to be dangerous or to have vicious propensities that might cause harm to others.

5. *Landlords*. At common law, a landlord did not owe a duty to tenants or others to keep premises in repair but did owe a duty to make repairs with due care and to eliminate any undisclosed concealed dangers on the premises. At common law, a landlord had no duty to protect tenants from intruders, but many courts now impose that duty.

6. *Landowners*. Landowners' duties extend to trespassers, licensees, and invitees. A **trespasser** is a person who enters onto the property of another without the owner's or occupant's permission or any legal right to do so.

Trespasser
A person who intentionally enters onto the property of another without permission or any legal right to do so.

Licensee
A person who has permission to enter onto another's property for his or her own purposes.

Invitee
A person who enters onto another's property upon invitation for the benefit of the owner or for their mutual benefit.

A landowner owes no duty to keep premises safe for trespassers but does have a duty to use reasonable care for a trespasser's safety after becoming aware of the person's presence on the land. A landowner cannot set a trap for a trespasser. A **licensee** has the owner's express or implied permission to enter onto the land for the licensee's own purpose. A landowner owes no duty to make or keep the premises safe for a licensee but cannot injure a licensee willfully or wantonly. Examples of licensees are social visitors and people soliciting money door-to-door for charity. An **invitee**, or business visitor, enters onto land by the owner's invitation, for the owner's benefit, or for the invitee's and owner's mutual benefit. An example is a customer in a store. A landowner owes an active duty to exercise ordinary care for an invitee's safety.

For a negligence lawsuit to be successful, the defendant must have owed a duty to the plaintiff. A general duty owed to everyone cannot become the foundation for a tort suit. However, the duty need not be owed to a specific person. That the defendant could foresee that harm would occur to someone because of the negligent act or omission is sufficient. Duty extends to all persons and property within the zone of hazard, or area of danger. For example, the duty might extend to an unforeseen plaintiff, such as a guest of the purchaser of a defective product.

Breach of Duty

Reasonable person test
A standard for the degree of care exercised in a situation that is measured by what a reasonably cautious person would or would not do under similar circumstances.

The second element of negligence is the breach of duty; that is, the failure to conform to the standard of care required in the situation. The courts usually apply a **reasonable person test** to determine the standard of care, asking what a reasonably cautious person would or would not do under similar circumstances. Stated another way, the question is whether the person's conduct would be the conduct of a reasonable person under the circumstances.

The reasonable person test is an external, objective test under which the defendant's individual or personal judgment or that of other parties involved (subjective factors) are not considered. The test is not based on how jury members would have acted under like circumstances, but only on how the jury perceives that a reasonable person would have acted.

The reasonable person test is further qualified by the circumstances. For example, if applied to a person with disabilities, the general legal rule would be to consider how a reasonable person with a disability would act under the circumstances. However, the rule varies according to incapacity. Courts hold insane people to the same standards as reasonable, sane people and hold intoxicated people to the same standards as sober people.

At common law, courts generally presume minors less than seven years of age incapable of negligence. Children between seven and fourteen are also presumed to be incapable of negligence, but a plaintiff can challenge that presumption in court. The presumption grows weaker with each year until the minor reaches the fourteenth year, after which capability of negligence is presumed.

Courts in many jurisdictions now apply a reasonable person standard that takes age into consideration: that measure of care that other minors of like age, experience, capacity, and development would ordinarily exercise under similar circumstances. However, when a minor engages in an activity usually undertaken only by adults and for which adult qualifications are required, such as operating a car, motorboat, or airplane, the minor is held to the same standard of care as an adult.

Courts usually hold defendants to a standard of care based on the normal experience of their communities. Based on that standard, ignorance that a certain condition will cause harm may or may not be an excuse.

Courts assume that all adults, no matter what their backgrounds, have certain knowledge, such as that certain substances can ignite and that tires with no treads can be dangerous on slippery roads. For other conditions, people may have a duty to find out about the potential for harm. For example, a person may not know that placing a gas stove in a confined space can create a dangerous level of carbon monoxide, but that person may have a duty to inquire about it.

A person in a situation not usually encountered by one with a similar background, such as an urban dweller in a rural area, would be judged on the basis of a reasonable person with an urban background, not a farm background.

The standard applied in cases of negligence of professionals is the skill and knowledge of average members of that profession applied with reasonable care. Professionals are not liable for mere errors in judgment, provided that they have used reasonable care in reaching a judgment. This standard applies to persons in practically all professions and skilled trades, such as lawyers, engineers, accountants, and airline pilots.

The legal standard applied to professionals is usually the standard of professionals in the local community. For example, a rural doctor may not be expected to know about sophisticated diagnostic machines used only in metropolitan teaching hospitals. The duty is not based on the particular community in which the tort occurred, but on that general type of community in the same geographic area. Doctors coming to the aid of an injured person in a volunteer, or "good Samaritan," situation are subjected to the standard of care for the doctors in their own community.

The general legal rule is that a defendant who has followed the customs, standards, or practices of his or her particular trade, business, or industry can use that as evidence of having met the required standard of care, or reasonable person test. However, such evidence is not conclusive on the issue of due care, and it can be challenged by the plaintiff. For example, a physician defendant can introduce evidence of having adhered to standard practice in a complicated medical situation. However, many courts are reluctant to permit a profession to set its own standards for what is appropriate. Juries frequently consider whether certain medical practices that might be standard still are negligent, such as a standard practice to delegate to nurses the responsibility to remove sponges or forceps from incisions.

The reasonable person standard also applies to cases involving emergencies. In an emergency, a person might have little or no time to weigh alternate courses of action and may have to make a quick decision based largely on instinct and impulse. This situation, however, does not totally absolve the defendant of negligence. In such cases, the defendant must still act as a reasonable person would act in like circumstances.

The standard or degree of care varies with the nature of the activity. Therefore, the care required of a reasonable person varies according to the possibility of harm involved. As the possibility of harm increases, the party must exercise greater caution, that commensurate with the risk. Many courts have established different degrees of care, such as ordinary care or a high degree of care.

A high degree of care is legally necessary in the following two situations:

1. Common carriers, those who operate buses, trains, and taxicabs, for example, must exercise the utmost caution characteristic of a very careful person, which is the highest possible care commensurate with the risk or nature of the undertaking.

2. People who handle or store dangerous materials, such as explosives, must exercise care commensurate with the risk associated with the materials' dangerous character.

Similarly, courts attempt to classify care by degrees of negligence, based on the concept that conduct causing harm can extend from a totally innocent act all the way to intentional misconduct with an unintended result. The following are the five common classifications of degrees of negligence:

1. Slight negligence (failure to use great care)
2. Negligence (failure to use ordinary care)
3. Gross negligence (failure to use slight care)
4. Willful, wanton, or reckless misconduct
5. Intentional misconduct with an unintended result

Some legal commentators say that no degrees of care—or degrees of negligence—apply as such, but only that the reasonable care required in specific situations is greater than in others. The test is still the same: what a reasonable person would do under the circumstances. As a practical matter, the use of degrees of care and degrees of negligence is probably helpful to juries and serves a beneficial purpose even if not theoretically correct.

Reckless misconduct
A deliberate performance or nonperformance of an act with knowledge or reason to know that harm to another will probably result.

Although courts' use of the five degrees of negligence has become less common, they still apply the concept of willful, wanton, or reckless misconduct. **Reckless misconduct** is a deliberate performance or nonperformance of an act with knowledge or reason to know that harm to another person will probably result. To establish reckless misconduct, a plaintiff must show the defendant's total disregard for consequences.

Reckless misconduct differs from ordinary negligence in the following ways:

- The defense that the plaintiff was also negligent might not be a sufficient defense.

- Courts may award punitive damages—damages in excess of actual damages intended to punish the defendant and deter such behavior.

- Many courts impose liability on a landowner for injury to a trespasser only when the landowner's willful misconduct can be proven.

- Most automobile guest statutes do not permit recovery for ordinary negligence but only for "aggravated misconduct," which courts describe in such terms as gross negligence; reckless misconduct; or willful, wanton, or reckless misconduct.

Proximate Cause

The third element of negligence is proximate cause. Proof of a wrongful act and harm are not sufficient to prove negligence. The wrongful act must also have been the proximate cause, or direct cause, of the harm. **Proximate cause** is the event that sets in motion an uninterrupted chain of events leading to a loss.

Proximate cause
The event that sets in motion an uninterrupted chain of events leading to a loss.

For example, a guest in a hotel is severely injured in a fire and sues the hotelkeeper. At the trial, the plaintiff proves that the hotel did not have sprinklers and that sprinklers were required by the law. This violation of law is not enough to create liability on the hotelkeeper's part. The plaintiff also must prove that the absence of the sprinklers was the proximate cause of the injuries. To illustrate further, the plaintiff might have been at the other end of the hotel with an easy escape route that the plaintiff failed to use.

In determining tort liability, courts have always attempted to place the burden of loss on the person responsible, at the same time recognizing that some limit of liability should exist when the act was so remote as not to be chargeable to the actor. An early case, *Scott v. Shepherd*, known as the lighted squib case, illustrates this concept.[1]

In the lighted squib case, the defendant, Shepherd, threw a lighted squib, a type of firecracker, into a crowd. It fell near Y, who picked it up and threw it near Z, who in turn threw it near Scott, where it exploded, injuring Scott. The question was whether the injury was the result of Shepherd's original act of throwing the squib into the crowd or whether Y or Z, who actually threw the squib near Scott, caused the injury. The court held that Shepherd had set the cause of loss, the squib, in motion and was liable for the resulting injury.

The question in the case was whether, if the squib had been thrown successively by, say, five persons, or had landed in a powder keg rather than near a person in a crowd, Shepherd still would be liable. The controlling doctrine is that one who commits a wrongful act is responsible for the ordinary consequences that can foreseeably flow from the act. The person is not liable for results that could not have been reasonably foreseen, or if an independent intervening cause breaks the chain of causation. Some courts deem proximate cause as a substantial, direct cause, one that would have caused all or at least a substantial part of the injury on its own.

Distance between the act and the injury is not in itself sufficient to make the cause remote. Remoteness is a matter of degree, as the Squib case indicates. Likewise, passage of time does not necessarily create remoteness. For example, when a fire damaged a building and a wall of the building collapsed thirty-eight days later, the fire was still considered the proximate cause of the collapse.

Many courts apply proximate cause differently to tort and contract situations, particularly insurance contracts. The doctrine as applied to torts is broader and goes back to both the harm and the physical cause to fix the blame on the one who created the situation in which the physical laws of nature operated. The happening of the event does not, in itself, establish the liability. The question in tort law is always why the harm occurred.

In adapting proximate cause to contract or insurance cases, many courts focus more on the nature of the harm and how it came about. In contract cases, these courts base damages on the losses contemplated by the parties when they made the contract as evidenced by the wording of the contract and the conduct of the parties.

In tort law, the following rules have evolved to determine proximate cause:

- *"But for" rule.* Under the **"but for" rule**, the defendant's act was the proximate cause of the harm to the plaintiff because the harm could not have occurred but for the defendant's act. Thus, if Al drove his car onto a sidewalk and injured Bob, it is readily apparent that, but for Al's action, Bob would not have been injured. The act is the proximate cause of Bob's injury.

- *Substantial factor rule.* Sometimes two parties' acts coincide to cause a loss, and the "but for" rule does not produce a satisfactory result. In these situations the substantial factor rule applies. Assume that cars driven by Al and Bob collide at an intersection, and Al's car then swerves onto a sidewalk, injuring Carol. Evidence shows that both Al and Bob are at fault in the collision. If the "but for" test is applied, the loss would not have occurred "but for" both drivers' negligence, and neither could be held liable. To avoid this unsatisfactory result, the courts have developed the **substantial factor rule**, under which, if a person's act is a substantial factor causing an injury, it is a proximate cause.

- *Proof of defendant's responsibility.* An injured person cannot succeed in a lawsuit merely by proving that harm resulted from another person's act. The plaintiff still must prove by a preponderance of the evidence that the defendant caused the harm. When the evidence is clear that it is at least as probable that the act was as much the responsibility of a third person as it was the defendant's responsibility, the plaintiff has failed to win the case.

- *Foreseeability rule.* Under the **foreseeability rule**, the plaintiff's harm must be the natural and probable consequence of the defendant's wrongful act and such that an ordinarily reasonable person would

"But for" rule
A rule used to determine if a defendant's act was the proximate cause of a plaintiff's harm based on the determination that the plaintiff's harm could not have occurred but for the defendant's act.

Substantial factor rule
A rule used to determine proximate cause when two parties' acts coincide to cause a loss by determining which act is the substantial factor in causing the harm.

Foreseeability rule
A rule used to determine proximate cause when a plaintiff's harm is the natural and probable consequence of the defendant's wrongful act and when an ordinarily reasonable person would have foreseen the harm.

have foreseen it. However, the defendant need not have foreseen the particular result that followed.

The defendant is not liable if the harm is caused by an independent, intervening agency, or **intervening act**, that breaks the chain of causation and sets a new chain of events in motion. The intervening agency, rather than the original cause, then becomes the proximate cause. The intervening agency must be independent of the original act and not readily foreseeable as one that would arise from the original act.

Concurrent causation arises when two or more independent causes combine to cause harm. The tort rule is that, when separate, independent causes combine to produce a single harm, each defendant is liable for the entire harm even though the act of either would not have produced the harm. For example, on a cold, icy day, Jane and Martha, each driving cars at excessive speeds, slide on the ice, collide, go up on the sidewalk, and injure Kelly. In this case, both Jane and Martha are liable. Their individual acts combined to produce Kelly's injury.

Actual Injury or Damage

The fourth element of negligence is actual injury or damage. For a person to sue successfully for negligence, the negligent act must result in actual injury or damage, or quantifiable harm for which the plaintiff seeks damages. The harm could be bodily injury, or financial loss of some type, such as property loss. Damages for harm are an essential remedy in a negligence action.

Proof of Negligence

In a negligence lawsuit, the plaintiff has the burden to prove all the elements of negligence, and the defendant has the burden of proving any defense. The defendant is presumed at the outset of a lawsuit to have used due care until the plaintiff proves otherwise. In some kinds of cases, presumptions favor the plaintiff. For example, a bailee who returns the plaintiff's property in a damaged condition is presumed to be negligent and has the burden of proving otherwise.

If the facts are undisputed and point to only one presumption, the court must decide whether, as a matter of law, negligence occurred. If the facts are in dispute or uncertain, or if they are undisputed but are such that fair-minded people might reasonably reach different conclusions, then the court must make findings of fact and may also have to make findings of law to determine whether negligence occurred.

Negligence per Se

The law treats certain actions as **negligence per se**, conduct that no reasonable person would follow, and that are therefore inherently negligent as a matter of law. A court can determine negligence per se without submitting the question to the jury.

Intervening act
An act, independent of an original act and not readily foreseeable, that breaks the chain of causation and sets a new chain of events in motion that cause harm.

Concurrent causation
The proximate cause resulting when two or more independent causes combine to produce harm.

Negligence per se
An act that is considered inherently negligent as a matter of law.

Often failure to comply with a statutory standard is negligence per se, and proof that the defendant violated the statute is sufficient to establish liability. However, not all statutes create standards of care for negligence suits. For example, a victim is killed when his vehicle collides with a disabled truck parked in the fast lane of a divided interstate highway. The truck's location violates traffic regulations requiring that disabled vehicles (1) move immediately from the traveled portion of the highway and (2) provide adequate warning devices to other motorists. Proof that the truck driver neither moved the truck nor provided the warning devices might be sufficient to establish negligence per se.

Res Ipsa Loquitur

Res ipsa loquitur
A legal doctrine that provides that, in some circumstances, negligence is inferred simply by an accident's having occurred.

Res ipsa loquitur, Latin for "the thing speaks for itself," is a legal doctrine that provides that, in some circumstances, negligence is inferred simply by an accident's having occurred. The doctrine permits an inference of negligence if the action or event causing injury was under the defendant's exclusive control and the accident ordinarily would not have happened if the defendant had exercised appropriate care. The doctrine is based on the conclusion that, in the absence of the defendant's better explanation, such an accident would likely arise from lack of due care. Although negligence is not actually presumed, the circumstances provide evidence from which a jury might presume negligence.

The *res ipsa loquitur* doctrine involves the following two factors:

1. The probability that, under the given circumstances, the defendant was negligent
2. The defendant's duty to explain otherwise as the party who had exclusive control of, and who therefore had superior knowledge of, the causative circumstances

Exclusive control
The control of only one person or entity; in tort law the control by the defendant alone of an instrument that caused harm.

Exclusive control, which means a defendant was the only one in control of an instrument that caused harm, is a flexible concept that the courts have adapted to modern manufacturing, packing, shipping, and marketing practices. For example, a plaintiff injured by an exploding soda bottle can use the doctrine of *res ipsa loquitur* against the bottler even though the bottle was not in the bottler's physical possession. The bottler could challenge application of the doctrine with evidence that either the plaintiff had mishandled the bottle or that other parties did so after, the bottle left the bottler's control. *Res ipsa loquitur* can also apply to airplane crashes because the airlines have control over the equipment and airplane operation.

Courts frequently apply *res ipsa loquitur* in lawsuits by passengers against common carriers. The doctrine also can apply in instances such as bricks that have fallen off buildings, poisonous drugs sold as harmless medicine, and sponges or surgical instruments left inside a patient during an operation.

Res ipsa loquitur does not apply merely because an unexplained injury has occurred. For example, that a person is found dead near a railroad track would not justify use of *res ipsa loquitur* in a suit against the railroad. Similarly, a plaintiff cannot use *res ipsa loquitur* in a lawsuit against a driver whose car skidded into the plaintiff's car. In both cases, several explanations are conceivable other than that the defendant failed to act with due care.

Imputed Negligence

The general rule in negligence cases is that a defendant cannot avoid liability by showing that a third person's negligence occurred simultaneously with the defendant's negligence to cause the plaintiff's injury. However, a court may hold a third party responsible for another person's negligence by virtue of the relationship between the two parties; in such a case, the third party is liable by **imputed negligence**. Imputed negligence occurs in two circumstances, involving either imputed contributory negligence or vicarious liability.

Imputed Contributory Negligence

Practically nonexistent today, the concept of **imputed contributory negligence**, imputing the defendant's negligence to the plaintiff, was important at early common law in several circumstances. For example, a driver's negligence was imputed to the passenger because the passenger was assumed to be aware of the driver's skills or lack of them. Therefore, if a collision occurred in which both drivers were negligent, and if a passenger in one of the cars was injured, under imputed contributory negligence, the injured party would not prevail in a lawsuit against the driver of the other car. The driver of the passenger's car was considered to have contributed to the accident through negligence, and that negligence was imputed to the passenger. Today, however, a passenger who reasonably believed a driver to be competent is not deemed to have contributed to his or her injuries by making a negligent decision to be a passenger.

In community property states, each spouse's individual property is treated as community property, as an entity, with each spouse having an undivided one-half interest. A wife's lawsuit against another party for personal injury becomes a property right of the "community," of which her husband has an equal share. Therefore, if the husband is found to have contributed to the wife's injury through negligence, that negligence is imputed to the wife, barring her recovery. The reasoning behind this result is that, if the wife could recover damages, which then become the property of the husband—as community property—the husband would benefit from his own negligence.

Vicarious Liability

The second situation involving imputed negligence is **vicarious liability**, holding one person liable for another's negligence by virtue of the relationship between the parties. Although imputed negligence was more prevalent at early common law, vicarious liability is a common legal concept today.

Imputed negligence
A concept holding one party responsible for another's negligence by virtue of the relationship between the two parties.

Imputed contributory negligence
At common law, the plaintiff's imputed responsibility for the defendant's negligence.

Vicarious liability
A legal responsibility that occurs when one party is held liable for the actions of a subordinate or an associate because of the relationship between the two parties.

Vicarious liability applies to torts other than negligence, but it applies to negligence in two specific situations, negligent entrustment and negligent supervision.

Negligent entrustment is the act of leaving a dangerous article (such as a gun or car) with a person who the lender knows, or should know, is likely to use it in an unreasonably risky manner.

Negligent entrustment is a variation of the **dangerous instrumentality doctrine**, whereby a parent is liable for negligently permitting a child to obtain or use a dangerous instrumentality that injures a third person. Such a situation is, arguably, not true vicarious liability because it involves an independent act of negligence on the parent's part rather than substitute liability for the child's act—or the situation might involve both the personal liability of the parent and vicarious liability for negligence. That is, the parent is vicariously liable for the child's act and is also liable for his or her own negligence in not adequately supervising the child. A common negligent entrustment situation involves a parent who permits a child to use a car, resulting in the child's negligent injury of a third person. Negligent entrustment also applies to a case in which a person in charge of a minor negligently entrusts the minor to an intoxicated driver.

Some insureds use negligent entrustment to attempt to overcome the motor vehicle exclusion of the homeowners policy. The theory is that the independent tort of a parent's negligent entrustment is separate from the negligent act of driving the motor vehicle and that only the negligent driving is subject to the homeowners exclusion. However, proof of negligent entrustment requires proof that the entrustment is the proximate cause of the harm. As a separate tort, then, the entrustment clearly comes within the automobile exclusion, and coverage does not apply. This result is logical because the mere negligent entrustment, without more, does not produce an injury. The injury results from the further negligent operation of the car, which the policy excludes. The entruster still might be liable for the tort, but homeowners insurance does not cover it.

Negligent supervision and negligent entrustment are similar and are frequently confused. **Negligent supervision** is a parent's liability for failing to exercise reasonable control and supervision over his or her child. An example illustrates the difference. Assume parents buy a motorized bicycle for their twelve-year-old daughter, who then operates it negligently and injures a third person. The injured person can allege negligent entrustment: that the parents were negligent in giving the bicycle to their daughter when they should have known that it would create an unreasonable risk of harm to a third person. The injured person can also allege that the parents are liable because of negligent supervision: failing to exercise reasonable control and supervision over their daughter in her operation of the bicycle. Negligent supervision also can arise when a younger child is crossing a street and the parents did not properly supervise the crossing.

Negligent entrustment
The act of leaving a dangerous article with a person who the lender knows, or should know, is likely to use it in an unreasonably risky manner.

Dangerous instrumentality doctrine
A legal doctrine in which a parent is liable for negligently permitting a child to obtain or use a dangerous instrumentality that harms a third party.

Negligent supervision
A parent's liability for failing to exercise reasonable control and supervision over his or her child.

Defenses to Negligence Actions

A defendant has several available defenses to a negligence action. Some defenses can bar recovery, even though the defendant might have been negligent; other defenses can reduce the amount of potential recovery. The burden is on a defendant to prove a defense.

Contributory Negligence

A defense of contributory negligence asserts that the plaintiff's negligence contributed to the plaintiff's injury. **Contributory negligence** is a common law principle that prevents a harmed party from recovering damages if that person contributed in any way to his or her own harm. Contributory negligence occurs when a plaintiff's conduct falls below the standard required for his or her own protection. The defense is based on the principle that people should not recover for injuries resulting from their own fault.

Between two wrongdoers, the law leaves the parties where it finds them and does not help one against the other. Therefore, even though the defendant's negligence has caused the plaintiff's injury, a plaintiff who was also at fault cannot prevail in a lawsuit.

To use contributory negligence as a successful defense, the defendant must show that the plaintiff contributed to the occurrence itself and that a causal connection existed between the plaintiff's acts or omissions and the plaintiff's injuries. A plaintiff's behavior that merely increases the injury does not fulfill this requirement even though it might affect the amount of damages.

For example, a person not using a seat belt is injured in an automobile accident. The defendant claims that the plaintiff's failure to use the seat belt was contributory negligence. Most courts would hold that the plaintiff's failure to use the seat belt had nothing to do with the occurrence of the accident; it was neither a proximate cause nor a substantial factor in producing the accident. However, if the plaintiff's injuries were much more serious because the seatbelt was not used, damages might be decreased. A few courts hold that failure to use a seat belt can be contributory negligence when using the seat belt would have eliminated or substantially decreased the damages.

Contributory negligence, as a successful defense, must be one of the contributing causes of the accident but need not be the sole proximate cause.

Comparative Negligence

Comparative negligence is an apportioning of damages in proportion to the degree of fault of the respective parties when both the plaintiff and the defendant are at fault. Both the contributory and comparative negligence theories recognize that, when a plaintiff's negligence helps cause the injuries, the plaintiff's damages should diminish.

Contributory negligence completely prevents a plaintiff from winning a lawsuit, while comparative negligence prevents a plaintiff from recovering any damages

Contributory negligence
A common-law defense that prevents a person who has been harmed from recovering damages if that person contributed in any way to his or her own harm.

Comparative negligence
A defense to negligence that apportions damages to the respective degree of fault when both the plaintiff and the defendant are at fault.

for which he or she was responsible. Today, practically all states have abandoned contributory negligence in favor of a comparative negligence approach.

The specific rules for the application of comparative negligence vary by state but fall into the following four variations:

1. Pure comparative negligence rule
2. 50 percent rule
3. 49 percent rule
4. Slight versus gross rule

Pure comparative negligence rule
A comparative negligence rule that allows the plaintiff to recover damages diminished by his or her proportion of fault, however substantial that fault might be.

The **pure comparative negligence rule** is the maximum departure from the contributory negligence rule. It provides simply that a party can recover damages diminished by his or her proportion of the total negligence. Under the pure rule, a plaintiff who is 99 percent at fault can still recover 1 percent of his or her damages.

A principal objection to the pure rule is that it does not base recovery on apportionment of fault but on the relative amount of loss. It allows a party whose negligence was a major factor in the incident to recover damages from a party who was less at fault. It can permit the most negligent party with the greatest amount of loss to recover damages for some of those losses up to the point at which the other party is solely at fault. The pure rule focuses only on the amount of damages and not on the degree of fault.

50 percent comparative negligence rule
A comparative negligence rule that permits a plaintiff to recover reduced damages so long as the plaintiff's negligence is not greater than 50 percent of the total negligence leading to harm.

The **50 percent comparative negligence rule** permits a plaintiff to recover reduced damages so long as his or her negligence is not greater than that of the other party. The plaintiff recovers damages reduced by his or her proportion of the total negligence up to the point at which the plaintiff's negligence constitutes not more than 50 percent of the total in a two-party situation.

If the plaintiff's negligence is greater (51 percent or more) than the other party's negligence, the plaintiff can recover none of the damages requested. Thus, if the plaintiff is 30 percent at fault and the damages were $100,000, a court would reduce damages to $70,000. If the plaintiff is 49 percent at fault, a court would reduce the damages in the example to $51,000. If the plaintiff is 50 percent at fault, a court would reduce the damages to $50,000. A plaintiff 51 percent at fault could not recover.

49 percent comparative negligence rule
A comparative negligence rule that permits a plaintiff to recover reduced damages so long as the plaintiff's negligence is less than the other party's negligence.

The **49 percent comparative negligence rule** permits a plaintiff to recover reduced damages so long as his or her negligence is less than the other party's. The plaintiff recovers damages reduced by his or her proportion of the total negligence up to the point at which he or she is equally, or greater, at fault (50 percent or more). Under this rule, the recoveries in the previous example would be the same except that there would be no recovery when the plaintiff is 50 percent or more at fault, rather than 51 percent.

Slight versus gross rule
A rule of comparative negligence that permits the plaintiff to recover only when the plaintiff's negligence is slight in comparison with the other party's gross negligence.

Under the **slight versus gross rule** of negligence, the plaintiff can recover only when his or her negligence is slight in comparison with the other party's

Example: Multiple-Parties' Degrees of Fault

Al, Barry, and Connie were all negligent in causing an accident, but not equally so. They contributed to the accident in the following degrees:

Party	Degree of Fault
Al (plaintiff)	30 percent
Barry	30 percent
Connie	40 percent

If Al is the plaintiff, and if the court follows the 50 percent rule, Al would recover against both Barry and Connie because his negligence is not greater than that of either Barry or Connie. Under the 49 percent rule, Al would not recover against Barry because his negligence is not less than Barry's. However, he could recover against Connie, who would have to pay 70 percent of the total.

Party	Degree of Fault
Al	30 percent
Barry	30 percent
Connie (plaintiff)	40 percent

Assume that Connie is the plaintiff in this case. Under the straight application of either modified rule, Connie could recover nothing, although her negligence is less than half the total. To deal with this situation, many states have modified the rule to provide that the comparison of negligence must be against the combined fault of those against whom recovery is sought.

gross negligence. A court then reduces the plaintiff's damages by an amount proportional to his or her contribution.

Last Clear Chance

Strictly speaking, the concept of last clear chance is not a defense to a negligence action but is another attempt by courts to alleviate the harsh results of contributory negligence. The **last clear chance doctrine** is that the one who has the last clear chance to avoid harm, and fails to do so, is solely responsible for the harm, because his or her negligence is the proximate cause of harm.

In a typical situation, the plaintiff's person or property is put in a potentially harmful situation because of the plaintiff's own negligent act. The defendant discovers the plaintiff's negligent act and, if using reasonable care, would be able to prevent injury. A defendant who fails to use such care is liable for the injury and cannot rely on the plaintiff's original negligence as a defense. According to this approach, the defendant had the last clear chance to avoid the accident and negligently failed to do so.

Last clear chance doctrine
A defense to negligence that holds the party who has the last clear chance to avoid harm and fails to do so solely responsible for the harm.

For the doctrine to apply, the plaintiff's negligence must have ceased before the harm and in time to permit the defendant to act to avoid the harm. Otherwise, the plaintiff's negligence is the sole cause of the harm and bars recovery. In some cases, the doctrine applies only when the defendant knows or has reason to know that the plaintiff is inattentive to danger or is unable to escape it and nevertheless fails to take reasonable steps to avoid harming the plaintiff.

The last clear chance doctrine frequently applies to traffic intersection accidents. For example, Joyce negligently drives through a stop light. Sheila, who is driving beyond the speed limit, approaches the intersecting street, and has ample time to stop or swerve to avoid Joyce but instead continues straight ahead and hits Manuel. For Manuel to prevail in suit against Sheila, he must establish that she had ample time to stop or that the circumstances were such that she could have swerved to avoid the accident, even though Joyce was the one who was originally negligent. Sheila was also negligent and had the last clear chance to avoid the accident.

Assumption of Risk

Assumption-of-risk defense
A defense to negligence that bars a plaintiff's recovery for harm caused by the defendant's negligence if the plaintiff voluntarily incurred the risk of harm.

Under the **assumption-of-risk defense**, a plaintiff cannot recover for harm caused by the defendant's negligence if the plaintiff voluntarily incurred the risk of harm as a result of the defendant's negligence. The doctrine is based on a legal principle that a person cannot commit a legal wrong to a person who consents. States that have adopted comparative negligence generally do not apply the assumption of risk defense.

For assumption of risk to be a valid defense, the defendant must show that the plaintiff had full knowledge of the risk and, having an opportunity to elect to avoid it, voluntarily chose to incur it. Either actual or implied knowledge of the risk is the essential element of the defense. Furthermore, the plaintiff must have voluntarily assumed the risk, a choice that would not occur if no alternatives were available. For example, if the only way a plaintiff can escape a burning building is through an unlit hallway that the defendant building owner has negligently failed to maintain, a plaintiff hurt in the hallway has not voluntarily assumed the risk.

Although sometimes confused, the defenses of contributory negligence and of assumption of risk differ. Assumption of risk requires knowledge and deliberate choice, while contributory negligence involves lack of care and, therefore, the absence of deliberate choice. For example, Jason knows that the sidewalk on one side of the street is in poor repair, but he leaves the safe sidewalk and deliberately walks on the faulty sidewalk. Jason has assumed the risk of injury even though he might be using due care while walking on the faulty sidewalk. In the same case Jason would be contributorily negligent only if he failed to use due care in walking on the faulty sidewalk.

The defense of assumption of risk formerly applied only to an employee's actions against an employer for injuries in the course of employment caused by the employer's negligence. However, it now applies to many other areas, such as when a spectator is injured by an errant ball at a sporting event. Generally, the person knowingly assumed the risks of the event. The doctrine also applies when a person is injured after voluntarily accepting a ride from a known reckless or intoxicated driver.

Release of Liability

A written general release of liability, agreed to by both parties, can prevent a tort lawsuit. Although a mutual mistake voids a release, a misconception of the extent of the injuries the plaintiff suffered is not a mutual mistake that voids a release. To void a release, the mutual mistake must relate to a past or present fact and not to an opinion about a future condition based on a present fact. The release also can work conversely against a defendant who pays out a substantial sum for a supposedly serious injury that later turns out to be minor.

Immunity From Liability

Primarily for reasons of public policy, the common law granted immunity from liability for torts to certain classes of people under certain conditions. Court decisions and legislatures have followed a steady trend towards restricting or eliminating these immunities. The trend varies by state and also by the type of immunity involved.

Defendants in negligence suits have four possible major classes of immunities to invoke as defenses.

Immunity Defenses in Negligence Lawsuits

1. Sovereign, or governmental, immunity
2. Public official immunity
3. Charitable immunity
4. Intrafamilial immunity

---

1. *Sovereign, or governmental, immunity.* Under the doctrine of **sovereign**, or **governmental, immunity**, the states and the federal government cannot be sued in tort without their consent. This doctrine derived its name from the English system in which the sovereign rulers exercised all powers of government and theoretically could do no wrong. In addition, rulers were not accountable to their subjects and were, therefore, immune from suit unless they consented. Because royal edicts established local governments, they inherited the same immunity as alter egos of their national rulers. The English rule eventually came to the United States and extended to all types of governmental units.

    Municipal corporations occupy a peculiar status with regard to sovereign immunity. They are political subdivisions of the state and, therefore, should enjoy the same immunity as the state. On the other hand, they perform many functions that private enterprise also performs. From this

Sovereign, or **governmental, immunity**
A defense to negligence that protects the states and the federal government against lawsuits for tort without their consent.

Proprietary function
A local government's act that could be performed by a private enterprise.

Governmental function
An act that can be performed only by government.

situation came the common-law application of sovereign immunity to municipal bodies only when functioning in a governmental capacity, that is, performing a function that only government can perform.

Today governments frequently engage in ordinary business pursuits that any private enterprise could perform. A city might supply gas or electricity or maintain a swimming pool or a theater. These functions, when performed by a local government, are termed **proprietary functions**, as contrasted to **governmental functions**, acts that can be performed only by government. A political body performing proprietary functions is subject to suit just as any private entity is. The state, however, can by statute confer immunity on certain of these proprietary activities, such as those performed by a municipal transit authority.

In many cases, it is difficult to decide whether a given function is governmental or proprietary. For example, traffic regulation, as such, is a governmental function and not usually performed by a private party. However, if a municipality's installation and maintenance of traffic lights is something a private entity could do, it is proprietary in nature. Therefore, the municipality has no immunity from liability for negligence for such a function.

Local governments are not immune from suit under civil rights laws for discriminatory acts that arise out of an official policy or action and not out of the doctrine of *respondeat superior* (under which an employer is held liable for an employee's wrongful acts committed within the scope of the employment). Local governments still have a qualified (limited) immunity in that they can avoid liability if their actions meet the **objective reasonableness standard**, meaning that, when viewed objectively, the action taken was reasonable under the circumstances.

Objective reasonableness standard
A local government's qualified immunity from negligence lawsuits for actions that were reasonable under the circumstances.

Courts created the doctrine of governmental immunity, and some state courts have held that they have the power to change or eliminate it. Several state courts, in fact, have eliminated state governments' immunity from tort liability. Other courts have held that the immunity is so firmly embedded in the law that only legislation can change it. In fact, some state laws virtually remove tort immunity, and others impose liability on cities for governmental functions such as controlling riots or other violence, street and sidewalk repair, and removal of ice and snow.

The Federal Tort Claims Act (FTCA) of 1946[2] provides a limited waiver of sovereign immunity for claims against the federal government. This law provides the only means for suing for damages and collecting them from the U.S. government in any cause in which the government, if it were a private person, would be liable. Many states have enacted similar tort claim acts.

2. *Public official immunity.* The second class of immunity, public official immunity, also extends to state and municipal officials. Judges and legislators have absolute immunity for acts done in their official capacity. Other officials have only a qualified immunity.

The extent of the immunity depends on whether the acts are administrative or ministerial. An **administrative**, or **discretionary, act** is one that the official has discretion to perform or not to perform. For example, a district attorney has discretion to decide whether to prosecute an alleged criminal. Public officials generally have full immunity in carrying out discretionary acts, as long as those acts are within the scope of their authority and performed with no malice or bad faith.

A **ministerial act** is one directed by law or other authority, and the official has no discretion about whether or how to perform it. An official is liable for damages for ministerial acts performed improperly, even if performed in good faith and without malice. Most tort claim acts grant immunity to public officials while they are acting within the scope of their duties, to the same extent as they would grant immunity to a governmental body. However, these laws frequently do not grant immunity for certain acts, such as operation of cars, assault and battery, and malicious or fraudulent acts.

3. *Charitable immunity.* At common law, all charitable organizations enjoyed immunity from suit in tort on two theories: (1) the quasi-governmental theory and (2) the trust fund theory. Under the **quasi-governmental theory**, charities (often hospitals and similar organizations) were considered to have assumed some governmental responsibilities and, therefore, were entitled to some of the immunities. Under the **trust fund theory**, the legal reasoning was that people made gifts to charity on the condition that the charities would devote the money to a charitable purpose. Therefore, the charity held the funds in trust to be expended only for charitable purposes. As the charity had no other source of funds, it would be a breach of trust for the charity to use donated funds for other purposes, such as to pay tort claims. A majority of states have rejected the doctrine of charitable immunity, particularly as applied to hospitals, and treat such cases under the general rules of negligence, specifically vicarious liability.

4. *Intrafamilial immunity.* As the name suggests, this is the immunity among various members of a family. Under this doctrine, one family member cannot sue another in tort. This doctrine includes not only torts committed during the family relationship, but also premarital torts, in the case of spouses. Thus, if man assaults the woman whom he subsequently marries, the wife cannot sue the husband for the tort.

The reasons given for the immunity are varied, including the belief that such suits would disrupt family peace and harmony, deplete family financial resources, and lead to collusion and fraud, particularly when insurance is involved. These immunities can be divided into two principal categories: (1) inter-spousal immunity and (2) other family relationship immunities.

All states have abolished, in whole or in part, **interspousal immunity,** the immunity of one spouse from the other spouse's lawsuits for torts committed before, during, and after the marriage. The concept originated in feudal times when the married woman had no separate identity at law. Only the husband had property rights. From this, the rule developed that the husband was immune from suits brought by his wife, including tort

---

Administrative, or **discretionary, act**
An act that an official has discretion to perform or not to perform.

Ministerial act
An act that is directed by law or other authority and that requires no individual judgment or discretion about whether or how to perform it.

Quasi-governmental theory
A theory that extends governmental immunity from lawsuits to charities that have assumed some governmental responsibilities.

Trust fund theory
A theory that extends immunity from lawsuits to charities because they hold donated funds in trust to spend for charitable purposes, not to pay tort claims.

Interspousal immunity
A defense to negligence that grants immunity to one spouse from the other spouse's lawsuit for torts committed before, during, and after the marriage.

actions for torts committed before, during, and after the marriage. Passage of the Married Women's Acts in the middle 1800s established a separate legal identity for the wife, but most courts held that these acts did not abolish the immunity doctrine.

Parent-child immunity
A defense to negligence that grants immunity to parents from their children's lawsuits for torts.

English common law did not recognize **parent-child immunity**, parents' immunity from their children's lawsuits for torts. It developed early in the nineteenth century in the United States. Many jurisdictions extend parent-child immunity in lawsuits involving personal injury, while others permit lawsuits between parent and child for property torts.

Parent-child immunity was not based on the same theory as inter-spousal immunity; but the reasons given, such as family peace and preservation of family resources, are equally applicable. Also implicit in the parent-child relationship is the necessity to maintain parental authority. Most states have abolished parent-child immunity wholly or in part.

If a child has been released from parental control (emancipated), or if a statute imposes liability, the parent-child immunity rule does not apply, and a child can recover if injured in a parent's business activity. The parent-child immunity rule has never extended to other family relationships. For example, siblings cannot claim immunity against each other.

The abolition of parent-child immunity has created a problem in insurance coverages. Many insurers now insert an intrafamilial exclusion in liability policies and sometimes property insurance policies. Courts vary as to whether such an exclusion is void because it violates public policy requiring coverage.

Independent Contractors

Although employers can have many reasons to hire independent contractors, such as economic practicality and contractor expertise, to some extent an employer can also avoid vicarious liability for an independent contractor's torts, particularly negligence.

An independent contractor differs from an employee or agent, primarily regarding control. Independent contractors are free to complete assigned jobs on their own time and in their own way, subject to no other person's direction or control. If the employer retains any control or right of control, other than directing the order in which the work is to be done, or retains the right to forbid work to be done in a dangerous manner, then the person is not an independent contractor and the employer is vicariously liable for the person's negligent acts.

The general rule is that the employer of an independent contractor is not liable for the independent contractor's torts. This prevailing rule is subject to several exceptions, grouped as follows:

- *Employer's negligence.* An employer who is negligent in selecting an independent contractor, in giving directions, or in failing to stop any unnecessarily dangerous practices that come to his or her attention is liable for such negligence directly, not vicariously.

- *Nondelegable duties.* An employer cannot delegate performance of nondelegable duties to another person. Such duties are created by statute, contract, or the common law. The law does not precisely define the types of duties that are nondelegable, but they include a common carrier's duty to carry passengers safely, a landlord's duty to maintain safe premises for a tenant, and a landowner's duty to maintain lateral support for adjacent property.

- *Inherently dangerous work.* One who employs an independent contractor to do work that is inherently dangerous to others is liable for bodily harm caused by the act. Inherently dangerous activities include acts such as blasting, excavating in or near a public highway, and similar acts that involve a special and unusual risk of harm to others.

Contractual Liability

Another defense to a negligence action is contractual liability, which, as used in this section, is essentially a type of vicarious liability arising out of an agreement rather than from an implication of law. Contractual liability is one party's assumption by contract of another's tort liability. There are two parties to such a contract—the indemnitor who assumes the obligation and the indemnitee whose liability the indemnitor assumes. Many contracts contain these agreements, including the following:

1. Leases of real or personal property
2. Easements
3. Elevator and other service and maintenance contracts
4. Construction contracts
5. Demolition contracts
6. Architectural and engineering design contracts
7. Particular store occupancies, such as liquor stores
8. Purchase orders

This section reviews the following three most common forms of contracts affecting liability:

1. Liquidated damages agreements
2. Hold-harmless agreements
3. Exculpatory agreements

A liquidated damages agreement is an agreement in a contract that specifies the damages that a party will pay for any negligence or breach of contract. Courts usually favor such agreements when actual damages are uncertain, difficult to prove, or purely speculative.

A **hold-harmless agreement**, or an **indemnity agreement**, is a contractual provision obligating one party to assume another party's legal liability in the event of a specified loss. Hold-harmless agreements are probably the most common type of contract affecting liability. Such an agreement might merely reaffirm an indemnitor's liability for negligence (giving some protection to

Hold-harmless, or indemnity, agreement
A contractual provision obligating one party to assume another party's legal liability in the event of a specified loss.

an indemnitee, who can be vicariously liable), or it can involve a complete assumption of liability for all loss and an agreement to hold the indemnitee totally harmless.

Hold-harmless agreements are typically used in construction contracts. Consider for example, a contract between Lyle, a contractor, and Tim, the owner. Lyle agrees to indemnify and hold Tim harmless for any liability that Tim might incur because of injuries to third persons arising out of Lyle's construction work. An injured party can sue Tim, the owner, or Lyle, the contractor, or both. By virtue of the hold-harmless agreement, Lyle, the contractor, ultimately bears the loss.

Hold-harmless agreements conflict with the underlying principle of tort law that every person should be responsible for his or her own acts. Therefore, the courts examine them very closely, particularly when the relative bargaining power of the parties is unequal. Some state laws prohibit hold-harmless agreements in certain situations, particularly consumer-type contracts such as the sale or lease of a dwelling.

Finally, parties frequently use exculpatory agreements, or exculpatory clauses, in contracts to avoid liability for negligence. For example, under an exculpatory clause, Lyle agrees not to sue Tim for any injuries that Lyle might sustain as a result of Tim's negligence. The exculpatory clause merely relieves a person of any liability, while a hold-harmless clause results in actual indemnification for liability. Courts view exculpatory agreements with even less favor than hold-harmless agreements.

To make exculpatory agreements more legally acceptable, parties sometimes set them up as liquidated damages provisions. If liquidated damages in a contract are so minuscule as to be nominal, a court will probably find that the liquidated damages clause is actually an exculpatory clause. A court will uphold an exculpatory clause under the following circumstances:

- The exculpatory clause is not adverse to a public interest and not against public policy. Therefore, an exculpatory clause in a contract involving the use of dangerous instrumentalities, such as explosives, or in a contract for the sale or lease of residential premises, is void.

- The party excused from liability is not under a duty to perform, such as a public utility or common carrier is.

- The contract does not grow out of the parties' unequal bargaining power or is not otherwise unconscionable.

Exculpatory agreements can excuse or limit liability expressly for negligent contract performance, including gross negligence, but they are void if they exclude willful or wanton misconduct. Some state legislatures have enacted laws that limit or prohibit the use of exculpatory clauses in a variety of situations.

LIABILITY OF LANDOWNERS AND OCCUPIERS FOR NEGLIGENCE

The landowner or occupier owes certain duties to the public and to adjoining landowners. A breach of these duties gives rise to a lawsuit in tort for damages. Usually a plaintiff sues the party in possession, who may or may not be the owner. However, sometimes ownership rather than possession determines liability. Therefore, often both the owner and occupier are defendants in a lawsuit. The nature of the duty can also vary depending on the injured party's status.

Natural Conditions

In general, a landowner is not liable for natural conditions on the land that cause injury either on or off the land. For example, if a rock falls down a hillside and injures someone on a highway below, the landowner is not liable. However, if a defendant's sloping land contains part of a landslide, which slides onto neighboring property, the landowner can be liable for negligent failure to correct or control the landslide condition.

The natural conditions rule is modified for trees. When a tree falls and causes damage on an adjacent premises or a highway, the landowner might be liable for negligence if he or she knew that the tree might fall and failed to take reasonable steps to remove it. In rural areas, the rule usually is that is the landowner or occupier has no affirmative duty to inspect trees to discover whether they are prone to collapse or dropping branches. However, the owner or occupier of land with trees in urban areas has a duty to use reasonable care to inspect the trees.

A landowner is not liable for the normal flow of natural waters that may go from the land onto adjoining land or public ways. Similarly, a landowner has no common-law liability for failure to remove snow or ice that has collected naturally on the land or adjoining ways. Ordinances requiring snow removal usually do not create a duty to individuals but only to the municipality and therefore do not create grounds for private lawsuits.

The possessor of land is under no duty to correct natural conditions on the land even though they may create a danger to a trespasser. For example, a trespasser sleds on a hillside. The owner of the hillside has no duty to warn the trespasser of dangerous rocks on the hillside hidden by the snow.

Artificial Conditions

An owner who alters land in any manner can be liable either for negligence or for creating a **nuisance**, the unreasonable, unwarranted, or unlawful use

Nuisance
The unreasonable, unwarranted, or unlawful use of property that interferes with another's enjoyment of, or right to, his or her property.

of property that interferes with another's enjoyment of or rights to his or her property. Alterations that create a nuisance include the following:

- Concentrating the flow of water discharges on adjoining land
- Permitting artificial devices, such as downspouts, to discharge over public ways
- Creating any other artificial condition that discharges water or snow on adjoining premises or roads

Hidden Dangers

A landowner who creates an artificial condition on land that could cause severe injury or death has a duty to warn of the hazard if a trespasser probably would not discover it without warning. Posting signs, for instance, could provide adequate warning. Thus, in the previous example about sledding, an owner who had strung a potentially dangerous wire one or two feet off the ground across the hill where sledding occurred would have a duty to warn.

Attractive Nuisance

Attractive nuisance doctrine
A doctrine treating a child as a licensee, or guest, rather than a trespasser on land containing an artificial and harmful condition that is certain to attract children.

Most states have special rules regarding trespassing children. While in general the same rules apply to children as to adults, an exception is the **attractive nuisance doctrine**, which treats the child as a licensee, or guest, rather than as a trespasser under certain conditions. Under the attractive nuisance doctrine, if the possessor of land has something artificial on the land that is certain to attract children, it is an implied invitation for the child to enter on the land. The possessor must keep the premises in a suitable and safe condition and use ordinary care to protect trespassing children from harm.

The attractive nuisance doctrine originated in cases concerning children who entered railroad property to play on unlocked engine turntables and suffered injuries. Gradually, the doctrine extended to other potentially dangerous situations that attract children.

Sidewalks and Streets

An occupier of land abutting a sidewalk or street has a duty to avoid placing an unguarded excavation or ditch on the land that might endanger a traveler using the facility. The distance from the sidewalk or street to the excavation is not crucial, but is relevant to whether the owner could foresee that a traveler might be injured. This duty extends only to travelers and is not applicable to trespassers.

In most states, landowners are not liable for defects in adjoining sidewalks or streets. However, some states impose a duty on landlords and tenants of commercial properties to keep adjoining sidewalks and streets in repair because they benefit from these thoroughfares.

Licenses

The permission to use or enter another's land is called a license. The party who receives the permission is either a licensee or an invitee, and the duty the occupier owes to each is different.

An **express license** is the oral or written permission to enter onto another's land to do a certain act but does not grant any interest in the land itself. An **implied license** arises out of a relationship between the parties, such as a customer who has an implied license to enter a store to make a purchase. The person granted the license must conform to the conditions on which it was granted or risk becoming a trespasser. For example, entering a store and then going into a stockroom not open to the public without permission is a trespass.

An express or implied license is revocable at any time, even if the licensee gave consideration for it. The remedy for a wrongful revocation of license is a breach of contract action. Any act of the landowner showing an intention to revoke the license terminates it.

Express license
The oral or written permission to enter onto another's land to do a certain act, but not the granting of any interest in the land itself.

Implied license
The permission to enter onto another's land arising out of a relationship between the party who enters the land and the owner.

Licensee

The person granted a license is generally a licensee. A social guest, even though on the premises at the landowner's express invitation, is usually considered a licensee. A volunteer helper is also a licensee, as is a lodge member visiting another's house on lodge business. Firefighters and police officers are licensees when they enter property to perform their duties.

A licensee takes the property in the condition in which it exists. The only affirmative duty a landowner owes to an adult licensee is to refrain from willfully or wantonly injuring the person or acting in a way that would increase that person's peril. The landowner does have a duty to warn of hidden defects. Usually, the occupier is also not liable for the acts of third persons on the premises.

Invitee

An invitee is a special type of licensee. An invitee may be either a **public invitee** or a business invitee. A public invitee is a person invited to enter onto land as a member of the general public for a purpose for which the land is open to the public. For example, attendees at public meetings, visitors to national parks, and people entering amusement parks on free passes are all public invitees.

A **business invitee** is a person invited to enter onto land for a purpose connected with the business conducted on the premises. The business benefit necessary to convert a licensee to an invitee is ordinarily economic. A shopper, a restaurant guest, and a theater patron are examples of business invitees.

For invitees, the land occupier owes a duty to exercise reasonable care to keep the premises reasonably safe and to warn of concealed dangerous conditions. The occupier need not warn of dangers of which the invitee is aware.

Public invitee
A person invited to enter onto land as a member of the general public for a purpose for which the land is open to the public.

Business invitee
A person invited to enter onto land for a purpose connected with the business conducted on the premises.

Hotel Operators

At common law, hotel operators or innkeepers had to furnish lodgings to anyone who could pay for them, provided prospective guests were not objectionable for some valid reason, such as intoxication. If the innkeeper improperly refused lodgings, the person could sue the innkeeper. This common-law rule did not apply to those furnishing services at other public places, such as restaurants and theaters, although later anti-discrimination laws developed that applied similar statutory rules.

Landlords

At common law, the property owner who leased the property to another was not liable for injuries resulting from the disrepair of the property or from other dangerous conditions, whether the condition resulted in injury to the tenant or to a third person. Today the owner, or lessor, is liable when injury results from negligently made repairs or from a concealed danger on the premises that the lessor knows about but that the tenant cannot know or easily discover by the use of ordinary care.

At common law, the lessor was under no duty to protect tenants from intruders. However, this area of the law is changing. Many courts now impose a duty on lessors, hotel operators, and public entities to take reasonable precautions to secure their premises against foreseeable risks of harm by intruders. Failure to do so can result in liability.

What is reasonable involves an analysis of several factors, including prevailing practices in the type of occupancy, such as motels, the extent of crime in the area, and the kinds of security that it is reasonable to provide under the circumstances. For example, a hotel that fails to provide proper security measures can be liable to a guest who is a victim of an intruder's actions. Likewise, a lessor can be liable to a tenant for injuries received during an attack in an unlighted parking lot. This concept also applies to public parking garages, college campuses, condominium associations, and automated teller machine (ATM) premises.

SUMMARY

This chapter introduced the law of torts, which are wrongful acts or omissions, other than breaches of contract or crimes, between people. The major classifications of torts are the following;

- Intentional and unintentional torts
- Physical and nonphysical torts

A court's decision about which law applies to a tort case can be as complex as the ultimate determination of rights in the case.

Negligence is an unintentional tort and is the most important tort for insurance professionals to understand because insurance liability coverage pays court-awarded damages in many negligence cases. A plaintiff in a negligence lawsuit must establish the following four elements:

1. The defendant owed a legal duty of due care to the plaintiff.
2. The defendant breached the duty of care owed to the plaintiff.
3. The defendant's negligent act was the proximate cause of the plaintiff's injury or damage.
4. The plaintiff suffered actual injury or damage.

Some legal duties of care arise from relationships, such as the following:

- Employers and employees
- Common carriers and passengers
- Hotel operators and guests
- Parents and children
- Landlords and tenants
- Landowners and people on their land

Although the duties arising from some of these relationships require a very high standard of care, courts use the reasonable person test to determine the required standard in most other cases.

Degrees of negligence range from slight negligence to intentional, willful, wanton, or reckless misconduct. Even if a plaintiff proves all other elements of negligence, however, a court cannot hold a defendant liable for negligence merely with proof of a duty, wrongful act, and an injury. The wrongful act also must have been the proximate, or direct, cause of the injury.

Rules for determining proximate cause include the "but for," substantial factor, and foreseeability rules. The plaintiff has the burden of proving all elements of negligence, and the defendant has the burden of proving any defense.

Defenses to negligence actions include the following:

- Contributory negligence
- Comparative negligence
- Last clear chance
- Assumption of risk
- Release of liability
- Immunity from liability
- Independent contractors
- Contractual liability

Courts no longer widely recognize the contributory negligence defense because of its often harsh results. Comparative negligence falls under either a pure, 50 percent, 49 percent, or slight-versus-gross rule. Multiple-party litigation presents even more complex questions.

Immunities are either sovereign (governmental), public official, charitable, or intrafamilial. Use of an independent contractor can insulate an employer from liability in some cases.

Finally, contractual liability as a defense can involve liquidated damages, hold-harmless agreements, or exculpatory clauses.

CHAPTER NOTES

1. *Scott v. Shepherd*, 96 Eng. Rep. 525 (1773).
2. 28 U.S.C., §§ 2671–2680.

Chapter 9

Direct Your Learning

Tort Law—Intentional Torts

After learning the content of this chapter and completing the corresponding course guide assignment, you should be able to:

- Describe each of the following physical torts, the circumstances under which it can occur, and any defenses to it:
  - Battery
  - Assault
  - False imprisonment and false arrest
  - Intentional infliction of emotional distress

- Describe each of the following types of defamation, the circumstances under which it can occur, and any defenses to it:
  - Libel
  - Slander

- Describe each of the following types of intentional torts, the circumstances under which it can occur, and any defenses to it:
  - Invasion of the right of privacy
  - Fraud
  - Bad faith, or outrage
  - Interference with the relationships between others
  - Misuse of legal process

- Describe each of the following types of intentional torts, the circumstances under which it can occur, and any defenses to it:
  - Trespass
  - Conversion
  - Nuisance

- Define or describe each of the Key Words and Phrases for this chapter.

Develop Your Perspective

What are the main topics covered in the chapter?

Intentional torts include physical torts against a person: battery, assault, false imprisonment and false arrest, and infliction of emotional distress. Other intentional torts against people are defamation (slander and libel), invasion of the right of privacy, fraud, outrage (bad faith), interference with relationships between others, and misuse of legal process. Intentional torts also include torts against property and nuisance. A variety of defenses to torts are available.

Contrast what a plaintiff must prove to establish each of the intentional torts with the defenses a defendant might have.

- What kinds of harm must a plaintiff prove if the tort is not physical?

- For which intentional torts is consent a defense?

Why is it important to learn about these topics?

Although insurance policies generally exclude most intentional torts, insurance professionals must recognize and understand intentional torts that occur between people. Intentional torts give rise to many legal disputes involving both insureds and insurers.

Consider the kinds of intentional torts you as an individual, as well as your employer, might encounter.

- What kinds of intentional torts might affect you in your everyday life?

- What kinds of intentional torts might you encounter in your professional career?

How can you use what you will learn?

Analyze the insurance contracts you purchase or work with to determine the coverage provided for intentional torts.

- What kinds of insurance policies exclude intentional torts?

- What, if any, intentional torts might insurance policies cover and why?

Chapter 9
Tort Law—Intentional Torts

In addition to the unintentional tort of negligence, intentional torts are those committed with the intent to cause harm, or sometimes only with the intent to perform a specific act that causes harm. Whether the actual harm that results was intentional can create ambiguity relating to insurance coverage provided for the resulting loss.

The most common forms of intentional torts are the following:

- Intentional physical torts against persons
- Defamation
- Invasion of right of privacy
- Fraud
- Bad faith, or outrage
- Interference with relationships between others
- Misuse of legal process
- Intentional torts against property
- Nuisance

INTENTIONAL PHYSICAL TORTS AGAINST PERSONS

Intentional physical torts may be committed against persons or property. Intentional physical torts against persons may result in significant damages, even if a plaintiff has not been physically injured. Intentional physical torts against persons include battery; assault; false imprisonment and false arrest; and infliction of emotional distress.

Battery

A **battery** is intentional harmful or offensive physical contact with another person without legal justification. Battery can be a crime as well as a tort. For battery to occur, some bodily contact, no matter how slight, must occur. Throwing a stone that hits another person, snatching a paper from another person's hand, or making contact with another person's clothing—each can be a battery. Fear of bodily harm is not required. In fact, the person need not be conscious of the contact. For example, a doctor can commit a battery on a person under anesthesia by performing an act the patient has not agreed to beforehand.

Battery
Intentional harmful or offensive physical contact with another person without legal justification.

To be a tort, the act must be intentional and hostile or offensive. Merely blocking passage by standing in front of a person is not a battery, nor is lightly touching a person to gain attention. The naturally occurring and inevitable touching in a crowd of people is not battery.

Intent can be transferred, as when Al intends to shoot Bob but actually shoots Carol. In this case Carol can sue for battery. Using excessive force in performing a lawful act can also be a battery, for example excessive force by a police officer making an arrest.

A person sued for battery may have one of several defenses, including consent, self-defense or defense of others, and physical discipline, described as follows:

- *Consent.* Consent to an act is permitting it. Consent can be actual or implied. For example, participation in a contact sport such as football can be implied consent to be touched. Consent also can be implied in an emergency, such as when an accident renders a person unconscious and an operation is necessary. Mere silence is not consent. Incompetents, such as insane persons, minors, or intoxicated persons, usually cannot give consent. Additionally, even when consent has been given, battery can occur if it goes beyond the person's consent. For instance, consent to a fistfight is not consent to a knife fight. If the act differs substantially from that agreed to, no consent exists. However, a defendant who has made a fraudulent misrepresentation that deceives the plaintiff cannot later claim the plaintiff's consent as a defense.

- *Self-defense or defense of others.* One can use reasonable force to repel an attack on one's own self or on another person. What is reasonable force depends on the circumstances. Usually deadly force, such as shooting a gun, can be used only when one is in fear of one's life. The common law required a person who was being attacked to attempt to retreat from danger to a safe place before using force. Most courts today accept the use of deadly force to repel an attack. All jurisdictions permit the use of deadly force as protection from bodily harm in one's home without attempting to retreat to a safe place.

- *Physical discipline.* Physical discipline as a defense involves the parent-child relationship or contact with persons who have legal authority such as police officers or military officers. The defense is successful only if the force used is reasonable, and the use of force must be in good faith.

Assault

Assault is the intentional threat of force against another person that creates a well-founded apprehension of immediate bodily contact. The apprehension does not have to be fear. Unlike battery, no actual physical contact is required, but the other person must anticipate, or expect, contact. For example, a person may point a knife at another or swing a fist close to another person's face. Mere words without the apparent intent or without ability to carry out the act usually do not constitute an assault. A statement such as "if you weren't so old, I would hit you" is not assault. However, a threat such as "your money or your life" is an assault. An assault can also be a crime.

Courts assume that any assault results in damages, but they are usually very low, or nominal. Therefore, few people sue for assault. The defenses to assault are similar to those for battery, including consent, self-defense or defense of others, and physical discipline.

Defenses to Battery and Assault

Plaintiff consented to the touching. The following rules apply to consent as a defense:

- Consent can be implied.
- Silence is not consent.
- Touching must stay within the limits of the consent given.

Defendant acted in self-defense or in defense of others. The following rules apply to self-defense:

- Reasonable force is permitted to protect one's self or another.
- Deadly force is permitted to protect one's life.

Defendant was using physical discipline. The following rules apply to discipline as a defense:

- Force must be reasonable.
- Discipline must be used in good faith.

False Imprisonment and False Arrest

False imprisonment is the restraint or confinement of a person without consent or legal authority. Either a police officer or a private individual can commit false imprisonment. Blocking passage down a one-way street or blocking the only door out of a room can constitute imprisonment. Causing a person's unlawful confinement to a mental hospital is false imprisonment. The gist of the tort is unlawful nonphysical restraint, no matter how mild. Malice is not an essential element. In contrast, **false arrest** is the seizure or forcible restraint of a person without legal authority. False arrest resembles false imprisonment in most respects; however, for false arrest, the restraint must be physical. For false imprisonment, the restraint can be by either physical force or mere threats of force.

False imprisonment
The restraint or confinement of a person without consent or legal authority.

False arrest
The seizure or forcible restraint of a person without legal authority.

Defenses to false imprisonment and false arrest relate to whether the acts occurred in connection with a crime. Whether the arrest or imprisonment is illegal depends on the type of crime and the capacity of the individual involved. For situations involving felonies (serious crimes), a police officer has almost complete immunity from charges of false imprisonment or false arrest when making an arrest under a warrant issued by a competent judicial authority. Police officers can make arrests without warrants for felonies committed in their presence and for felonies committed outside their presence if they have reasonable grounds to believe that those arrested have committed felonies. Under these conditions, police officers have no liability even if no felonies have occurred or even if those arrested did not commit them.

Defenses to False Imprisonment and False Arrest

Imprisonment or arrest was performed in connection with a crime, either a felony or a misdemeanor.

Felonies

Law enforcement officers' defenses include the following:

- The arrest was made under a legally issued warrant.

- The arrest was made without a warrant, but the crime was committed in the officer's presence.

- The arrest was made without a warrant, but the officer had reasonable grounds to believe that a felony was committed by the person arrested.

A private citizen's defense is that the crime was committed in the presence of the arrester, and the person arrested actually committed the felony.

Misdemeanors

Law enforcement officers' defenses include the following:

- The arrest was made under a legally issued warrant.

- The arrest was made without a warrant, but the misdemeanor was committed in the presence of the officer (usually applies to forcible breach of the peace).

- The arrest was made without a warrant, but the officer had reasonable grounds to believe that the person committed a misdemeanor (usually applies to forcible breach of the peace).

A private citizen's defenses include the following:

- The misdemeanor was committed in the citizen's presence.

- If not, the person arrested actually committed the misdemeanor. Reasonable belief that the person committed the misdemeanor is not a sufficient defense.

Private citizens generally do not make arrests under warrants. Citizens who make arrests without warrants to prevent commission of felonies in their presence usually can defend successfully against charges of false imprisonment or false arrest. Like police officers, citizens can make arrests for felonies committed out of their presence, provided they have reasonable grounds to believe that those arrested did commit felonies. However, private citizens can be liable if the particular felonies have not been committed, or if no reasonable grounds existed for believing that those arrested committed the felonies.

Different standards apply to defenses to false imprisonment or false arrest committed in connection with a misdemeanor (minor crime). As with felonies, a police officer's arrest under a valid warrant for a misdemeanor is usually a complete defense. Officers can make arrests without warrants for such misdemeanors as forcible breaches of the peace, like riots or civil commotions, and also for peace-disturbing activities such as vagrancy and public drunkenness.

Mere impudence or argument does not constitute a breach of the peace that would justify arrest. Misdemeanors, unlike felonies, must be committed in the presence of the officer and by the person arrested to render the warrantless arrest justifiable. An officer cannot arrest a person for a misdemeanor committed elsewhere, or for a past misdemeanor, without a warrant. As a general rule, private citizens cannot make arrests for misdemeanors except when they constitute breaches of the peace.

People detained by store personnel on suspicion of shoplifting have sued for false imprisonment. Many state laws now permit detention for a reasonable time so that stores can investigate suspected shoplifting without facing unreasonable litigation. A reasonable time usually is relatively short, such as an hour or less.

Infliction of Emotional Distress

The tort **intentional infliction of emotional distress** is an extreme and deliberate act causing mental anguish that results in physical injury. An example would be name calling that causes a person to feel mental distress, such as shame, and physical symptoms, such as vomiting. Plaintiffs can also allege **negligent infliction of emotional distress**, an unintentional act that causes mental anguish and physical injury.

At common law, it was necessary to prove physical injury resulting from emotional distress. A plaintiff could not recover for emotional distress alone, such as fear, anxiety, or sorrow. For example, a mother who saw a car hit her child and who suffered only emotional distress had no right to sue the driver for infliction of emotional distress unless she also suffered physical harm. This rule is no longer prevalent.

In the late 1800s, a trend developed to allow claims for negligent infliction of emotional distress in connection with traumatic events. Generally, this tort complaint was attached to other claims when the defendant was alleged to have acted intentionally or recklessly. Such torts were usually assigned in bystander cases, in which the plaintiff incurred severe emotional distress from observing an accident but did not suffer physical injury.

Both intentional and negligent infliction of emotional distress have gained prominence as separate torts on their own merits and in many situations other than bystander cases. Plaintiffs allege these torts as part of other tort actions and also frequently include them as separate causes of damages, similar to bodily injury or property damage.

Initially, the courts rejected this approach because of the following two concerns:

1. Possibility of fraudulent and unfounded claims
2. Potential for unlimited liability

These concerns led courts to impose the following two conditions, either one sufficient for recovery:

1. Actual physical injury
2. Actual impact

Intentional infliction of emotional distress
An intentional act causing mental anguish that results in physical injury.

Negligent infliction of emotional distress
An unintentional act causing mental anguish that results in physical injury.

Damages, then, would be awarded to a plaintiff only if either an actual physical injury or a physical impact (manifestation) of the emotional distress results from it. Courts reasoned that such conclusions were provable and that modern medicine can determine the legitimacy of mental injuries as well as the causal connection between emotional distress and physical injury or symptoms.

Some courts now interpret the term "physical injury" to mean any condition or illness capable of objective determination. A few courts have eliminated the physical injury requirement and permit a suit for pure emotional injury on the grounds that emotional injury alone can be as severe as physical harm.

Applying the impact (manifestation) rule in emotional distress cases, courts permit recovery only if a plaintiff proves that the emotional distress caused actual physical impact. Several courts permit recovery in bystander cases, even absent impact, if the defendant's conduct was not just negligent, but willful or intentional.

A defense for *intentional* infliction of emotional distress is that no intent was involved. For *negligent* infliction of emotional distress, the defense would be that negligence was lacking. Additionally, a defendant might defend on the basis that no actual physical injury or manifestation occurred, except in states where pure emotional injury is sufficient ground for a plaintiff's recovery. Obviously, state law varies as to available defenses.

DEFAMATION

Defamation

A false written or oral statement that harms another's reputation.

Defamation, another intentional tort, includes slander and libel. **Defamation** is the making of false written or oral statements that harm another person's reputation. To be defamatory, a statement must concern the complaining party personally. For example, one spouse cannot sue for defamatory statements made about the other spouse.

The law recognizes a difference between written and spoken defamatory words and treats them differently. Spoken defamatory words are slander, and written defamatory words are libel. In recent years, constitutional concepts of the right to free speech have modified the common-law concept of defamation.

Slander

Slander

A false oral statement that harms a person's reputation.

Slander is the making of false oral statements that harm another person's reputation. Because such statements are oral, they usually are heard only once. Unless spoken statements are repeated, the chance that a large audience will hear them is remote. Therefore, the law requires substantial proof of injury to a plaintiff's reputation.

Publication

In tort law, the communication of a defamatory statement to another person.

For a statement to be slanderous, a publication to a third person other than the party slandered must occur. **Publication** is communication to another person but, for slander, it is only oral—neither written nor recorded in any other way. If Al accuses Sarah of committing murder when the two are alone, no publication and no harm to Sarah's reputation have occurred. If, however, Al tells Carol that Sarah committed murder, Al's communication to Carol is publication.

Every new publication is a separate slander. If Al makes the statement about Sarah separately to Carol, Doug, and Evelyn, Al has made three separate slanderous statements, unless all three were together, in which case it would be a single slander. Also, if Carol told Doug, who in turn told Evelyn, both Carol and Doug would be liable for slander. That a person merely has repeated another person's statement is no defense to a slander suit.

Courts recognize certain classes of words as slanderous per se. **Slander per se** is slander that raises a presumption of malice and that, therefore, requires no proof of injury or damage. Because of the nature of the words, the court presumes that they caused injury. The plaintiff has to prove neither the words' slanderous nature nor the damage.

The following are the four traditional categories of slander per se:

1. Words imputing that the party is guilty of an indictable offense—a crime and not a petty offense such as illegal parking.

2. Words imputing that the party has a loathsome disease, such as, historically, leprosy or syphilis.

3. Words imputing general incompetence in business or profession. Stating that a chef cheats at poker is not slander, but saying the chef uses discarded animal byproducts in his recipes is slander per se. Similarly, a statement that a car dealer does not pay debts could be slanderous per se.

4. Words accusing a woman of unchastity: This category includes statements that the woman is involved in prostitution, adultery, or fornication.

That a person merely repeats something that another person has stated is no defense to a charge of slander per se. However, just as in other slander suits, the plaintiff must prove either financial loss or loss of status as a result of the repetition.

The defenses to a charge of slander are essentially the same as those for libel, discussed next.

Libel

Libel is a false written or printed statement that harms another person's reputation. Libel has wider circulation and is more permanent than slander; therefore the potential for damage to a person's reputation by libel is much greater than that of slander.

As with slander, publication of the libelous statement to a third person or persons is necessary for a successful lawsuit. If a person receives a letter containing false statements about him or her and reads it and destroys it, the letter is not libelous.

Slander per se
Slander that raises a presumption of malice and that, therefore, requires no proof of harm.

Libel
A false written or printed statement that harms a person's reputation.

Every new publication constitutes a separate libel, just as with slander. However, the rule is different for certain types of secondary distribution of libel. If the republication of defamatory material was innocent, such as a library's lending a book with libelous matter, or a newspaper vendor selling a newspaper containing libel, the distributor is not liable. The distributor must have had no knowledge of the libelous matter, and nothing in the publication should put the distributors on notice that it contained libelous material.

At common law, a plaintiff need not prove either actual malice or harmful intent. The law presumes malice from the defendant's having made a statement damaging the plaintiff's reputation. However, for news media, courts have found exceptions to that rule on constitutional grounds.

Libel per Se

Libel per se
A false written or printed statement that tends to degrade or disgrace a person and that requires no proof of harm.

A statement is **libel per se** if it is obviously defamatory on its face, meaning that it must tend to degrade or disgrace the person or expose the person to ridicule or contempt. The plaintiff need show only that the defendant made the defamatory statement. Except in cases involving news media, the plaintiff does not have to prove that the defendant understood the words to be libelous or that any special damages, such as job loss or marital breakup, resulted.

News Media

News media have a special status in defamation law. Until 1964, the same common-law principles that apply to all other persons applied to the media. However, in the landmark case *Sullivan v. New York Times*,[1] the United States Supreme Court held that public officials suing news media for libel must prove that the statement was false and, further, that the defendant made it with knowledge of its falsity or with reckless disregard for its truth or falsity.

Reckless disregard means a high degree of certainty of a statement's probable falsity, approaching the level of a knowing, calculated falsehood. The *Sullivan* decision balanced the importance of public, open debate as embodied in the First Amendment against the individual's right of privacy. Later, the rule expanded to include statements made about public figures, that is, people who have voluntarily assumed positions that place them in the public eye, such as politicians, entertainers, and sports figures.

Frequently, articles about public figures, if made about ordinary people, would be libelous. However, the law holds that accepting this form of communication is part of the price public figures pay for being famous. Therefore, a public figure must prove actual malice to recover damages in a libel suit, and malice can be very difficult to prove.

Individuals do not automatically become public figures merely by being involved or associated with an event that attracts public attention. For example, that one is merely the subject of a news article does not, in and of itself, render one a public figure. Courts protect the media only for matters involving people who have voluntarily placed themselves in the public eye, such as political leaders and other celebrities.

An ordinary person suing for libel by the media has to prove less than public figures do. A plaintiff must show that the item was reported carelessly and that the defendant acted negligently in failing to ascertain the statement's falsity. As in other libel cases, plaintiffs also must prove that the statements were false and that they damaged their reputations.

Essentially the same rules that apply to print media apply to radio and television broadcasts and Internet communications. In the case of television, a picture can make a lasting impression. Jurisdictions have been divided about whether television broadcasts constitute libel or slander. One legal authority, in discussing broadcaster liability, states, "One who broadcasts defamatory material by radio or TV is subject to the same liability as the original publication even though he has no reason to know of its defamatory character."[2] Many states have statutes excepting broadcasting companies from liability for libel unless negligence or actual malice is present.

Defenses

The defenses for slander and libel are essentially the same, as follows:

- Truth
- Retraction
- Absolute privilege
- Conditional or qualified privilege

Truth is a complete, or absolute, defense to defamation. This defense is valid regardless of the motive that prompted the statement, even if the defendant published it for no good reason, and even if the defendant did not believe the statement when publishing it. In sum, if the statement is true, the plaintiff has no case.

The defendant has the burden to prove the statement's truth. While a defendant need not prove the literal truth of the precise statement made—slight variations from truth are tolerated—the defamatory charge must be substantially true.

Defenses for Libel and Slander

- The statement was the truth.

- Defendant made or printed a retraction—not a complete defense, but it can reduce damages.

- The statement had absolute privilege—applies to statements made in judicial and legislative proceedings, executive officers' communications, spousal communications, and consent given by the injured party.

- The statement had conditional or qualified privilege—applies to statements made without malice as a matter of public interest, in petitions concerning appointments, in common interest communications, as fair comment on matters of public concern, and by credit reporting agencies.

The defense of truth by the news media requires more than a showing that the statement was an accurate report of words spoken by a third person. The media must go further and prove that the third person's words were true. The use of words such as "reportedly" or "allegedly" does not protect the media. If these words were a defense, the media could publish almost anything of a defamatory nature with impunity. When members of the media only quote others' statements and do not conduct their own investigative reporting about the truth of the statements, they can be liable.

A retraction printed after a defamatory statement has been made is not a complete defense. However, a court can consider a retraction that is fully, promptly, and adequately made when determining damages. A retraction can show lack of malice, thereby reducing or eliminating any award for punitive damages. A retraction may also minimize the damage to the plaintiff's reputation, therefore lowering a compensatory damages award.

Another defense to libel or slander is the defendant's absolute privilege. In some situations, the public's interest in open discussion so far outweighs the potential injury to the individual that the law grants absolute privilege to parties who have made defamatory statements. Absolute privilege means that the law protects the person making the statement completely, even if the statement is malicious. A plaintiff cannot defeat an absolute privilege in court and win a case. Absolute privilege applies to the following five areas:

1. *Judicial proceedings.* All parts of a judicial, or court, proceeding are subject to an absolute privilege. The privilege extends to statements made by the judge, counsel, witnesses, and jurors and to all legal papers in the proceeding, such as pleadings. The privilege also applies to quasi-judicial proceedings, such as administrative hearings.

2. *Legislative proceedings.* Legislative proceedings, such as Congressional sessions and hearings, are also subject to absolute privilege. This privilege also extends to comments published in the Congressional Record, which contains congressional proceedings and documents. Some state jurisdictions hold that the privilege does not extend to city councils and similar minor legislative bodies.

3. *Executive officers' communication.* Communications made by high executive officers of federal, state, and local governments, made as part of the performance of official duties, are subject to absolute privilege.

4. *Spousal communications.* Statements one spouse makes to the other, including statements involving libel and slander, are privileged for most purposes.

5. *Injured party's consent.* If an injured party consents to publication of defamatory material, absolute privilege applies. The consent is confined to the particular statement authorized, and the publication must be within the scope of the consent.

Conditional or qualified privilege is also a defense to libel or slander. Conditional privilege applies in instances in which the public has a great interest in the free flow of information, but not to the extent recognized in instances of absolute privilege. Conditional privilege is not an absolute defense, but is rebuttable by the plaintiff's showing that the defendant made the publication with express malice. Conditional privilege is no defense to a publication made with intent to injure, with knowledge that the statements were false, or were made with malice. The comments must be fair. The plaintiff must show not only malice but actual damage.

The following are the five areas to which conditional privilege applies:

1. *Public interest.* Conditional privilege applies to matters of public interest, such as reports of proceedings of legislative bodies, as well as to communications between the executive officers of a political subdivision and its legislative body.

2. *Petitions concerning appointments.* Petitions addressed to the executive or appointing person either in favor of or against appointment of a person to a position are subject to conditional privilege. The privilege also applies to petitions, applications, and complaints of all kinds addressed by citizens to an officer or governing body.

3. *Common interest communications.* Matters of common interest, such as communications to members of churches, lodges, and other voluntary societies, are subject to conditional privilege.

4. *Fair comment.* Conditional privilege applies to communications to the public at large. This privilege of "fair comment" on matters of public concern applies particularly to newspapers, magazines, and other publications. As its name implies, the comment must be fair and without malice. Several states have enacted shield laws, which protect the media from having to disclose confidential sources or confidential information.

5. *Credit agencies.* Statutes generally govern conditional privilege extended to commercial credit agencies. The privilege extends only to publication to persons who have a legitimate interest in receiving the information, and the burden is on the credit agency to ensure that publication is restricted to these persons.

Commercial Speech

A body of law has developed concerning commercial speech as a form of communication that can involve libel. Commercial speech is solely in the speaker's individual interest and concerns the speaker's specific business activity. These statements have much less constitutional protection than speech concerning public issues. Such speech might involve injurious falsehoods that are not personally defamatory. The major types of commercial speech that might be defamatory are comparative advertising and product disparagement.

Comparative advertising involves situations in which a party marketing Product A makes a direct comparison with Product B by name. Advertisers used to avoid direct comparison, but they now use it frequently. If the comparison is truthful and fair, advertisers are not liable for defamation.

Generally, the usual defamation rules apply to comparative advertising. To be actionable by a plaintiff, the claims of Product A's superiority over Product B must be specific and not just general "puffing" that the product is better or superior. The defendant must have made specific claims about product performance or must have described objective tests. Comparisons that are false, misleading, or incomplete can be libelous.

Product disparagement, or **trade libel** involves intentionally false or misleading statements about the quality of the plaintiff's product, resulting in financial damage to the plaintiff. Examples of product disparagement are false statements denying the plaintiff's title to property, the quality of the plaintiff's property, or the plaintiff's conduct of business.

The plaintiff must prove that the publication played a material part in loss of customers or prospective customers. The statement can be either intentional or negligent, and truth is a complete defense.

Product disparagement, or **trade libel**
An intentional false or misleading statement about the quality of a plaintiff's product, resulting in financial damage to the plaintiff.

INVASION OF RIGHT OF PRIVACY

Invasion of the right of privacy, or invasion of privacy
Interference with a person's right to be free from unwarranted public intrusion.

Invasion of the right of privacy, or **invasion of privacy**, another major kind of intentional tort, is the interference with a person's right to be free from unwarranted public intrusion. The tort of invasion of the right of privacy includes several different common-law torts, plus invasion of rights created by state and federal statutes. The right of privacy was first legally recognized in the late 1800s. Among federal statutes are the federal Privacy Act of 1974.[3]

The common-law tort invasion of privacy is based on an individual's right to be left alone and to be protected from unauthorized publicity in essentially private matters. A corporation, partnership, or unincorporated association has no personal right to privacy and thus has no right to sue on the basis of this tort. Acts that constitute invasion of the right of privacy include intrusion on solitude or seclusion; physical invasion; and torts that involve use or disclosure of information. The information used or disclosed must be by printed matter, writing, pictures, or other permanent records, not merely word of mouth.

Intrusion on Solitude or Seclusion

Intrusion on a plaintiff's physical or mental solitude or seclusion is an invasion of something personal, secluded, or private pertaining to the plaintiff. This intrusion is not confined to a physical invasion of the person or premises. Placing a hidden microphone, eavesdropping, tapping of telephone lines, using telephoto lenses, and using similar types of surveillance can be an unlawful invasion if the intrusion is highly offensive to a reasonable person.

The intrusion must be one that would outrage or cause mental suffering or humiliation to a person of ordinary sensibilities and must apply only when the defendant intrudes into a private place when the plaintiff believes that he or she is secure in person and affairs.

Invasion of privacy is a purely private action. The right to sue for this reason does not survive the party's death but dies with the party whose privacy was invaded.

Physical Invasion

Physical invasion is a separate version of the tort of invasion of privacy. Thus, searching a shopping bag in a store or the unauthorized taking of a blood sample can create a right to sue. Ordinarily, a defendant has no liability for taking photographs in a public place. However, photographs of a person in a compromising or embarrassing position can give rise to suit.

Torts Involving Use or Disclosure of Information

Several torts involving invasion of privacy relate to the use or disclosure of information. Unlike the similar torts of libel and slander, which are based on the falsity of the information, these torts are based on interference with privacy. These torts are the following:

- *Public disclosure of private facts.* This tort usually involves gossip columns or similar disseminations of stories about a plaintiff's private life. To a certain extent, a right to sue depends on the plaintiff's public prominence. An entertainer or politician, for example, is not entitled to privacy to the same degree as an ordinary citizen. Examples of grounds for suit are public disclosures revealing intimate details of the plaintiff's private life or disclosing personal facts, such as telling the plaintiff's employees that the plaintiff is deeply in debt.

- *Publicity placing plaintiff in a false light.* This tort is similar to the tort of public disclosure of private facts. It usually involves using a statement that has been taken out of context or is based on information that is not true. The defendant has presented the publicity in such a way that the plaintiff has good cause to be offended, even if the plaintiff's reputation is not damaged.

- *Unauthorized release of confidential information.* Sometimes courts treat unauthorized release of confidential information as a tort separate from invasion of the right of privacy, although it contains many of the same elements. People must give confidential information to other parties for particular purposes, such as to doctors for health matters, to hospitals for admission, to financial institutions for financial matters, and to consumer reporting agencies for credit reports. In each case, the confidential information has a specific purpose. In some cases, a person has a right to sue in tort if confidential information is disclosed by a third party without express or implied permission. The disclosing party might be able to use the defense that the information was released to a party with a legitimate business interest in it or that there was a justifiable private or public interest in the disclosure.

- *Appropriation of plaintiff's name or likeness.* The tort is based on one's rights to one's own name and likeness. Anyone who makes unauthorized use of another's name or likeness for publicity or commercial gain may be liable, but most courts base the tort on the defendant's commercial benefit. This tort includes the unauthorized use of a person's photograph to advertise or promote a product. Some courts recognize a right of action for appropriation for noncommercial purposes. A defendant is not liable for use of a name that is the same as the plaintiff's unless it is an obvious attempt to benefit from the plaintiff's name.

Defenses

In an action for any form of invasion of the right of privacy, one or several of the following defenses may apply.

- In disclosure of information cases, a plaintiff who previously published the information, consented to its publication, or authorized the release, in the case of confidential information, has no right to sue. Some organizations that regularly obtain confidential information, request or require express permission to disclose or require a release in advance. Additionally, consent can be implied from the circumstances surrounding the giving of the information. For example, a person gives information to a consumer reporting agency with the knowledge that the agency will share the information for the purpose for which the agency collected it. Therefore, the agency has implied consent to release the information to those with a business interest in the person's credit history.

- If the plaintiff is a public figure or if information disclosed is public knowledge, no right to privacy applies. If the plaintiff has become so prominent that, in effect, his or her life has been dedicated to the public, this prominence is a waiver of any right to privacy. No privacy right applies in activities that are already public or known. If facts disclosed are a matter of public knowledge, no liability applies. Examples include the amount paid for a house, reported in a publicly recorded deed and often in local newspapers, or a photograph of the plaintiff's house taken from a public street available to anyone.

- No right of privacy applies to news events, for example, events in the life of a person in whom the public has a rightful interest or newsworthy information that is of public benefit, such as facts about a person running for public office.

- Under the ordinary sensibility test, if publication of the plaintiff's name, likeness, or reputation would not offend an individual of "ordinary sensibility," the plaintiff has suffered no damages and no actionable invasion of privacy.

- No right of privacy applies in matters disclosed in judicial proceedings. This rule is analogous to the absolute privilege for such information in connection with libel and slander.

- When the public interest is involved, statutes have granted immunity for the disclosure of certain facts in such cases, and the disclosing party is immune from suit. For example, statutory immunity for giving information in connection with arson activities or other types of loss situations is not uncommon in the insurance field. In this connection, right-to-know laws permit a person to obtain many types of information in governmental records. Most of these laws contain exceptions for disclosure of trade secrets.

Defenses to Invasion of the Right to Privacy

- The plaintiff previously published the information.
- The plaintiff consented to publication.
- The plaintiff is a public figure or the information is public knowledge.
- The information was part of a news event.
- The publication would not offend an individual of ordinary sensibility.
- Matters were disclosed in judicial proceedings.
- The information is of public interest, such as the public's right to know.

FRAUD

The terms fraud, deceit, and misrepresentation are often interchangeable, but fraud is the generic term. As discussed in previous chapters, the issue of fraud often arises in contract disputes. The tort of fraud is an intentional misrepresentation resulting in harm to a person or an organization.

As discussed previously in relation to contracts, proof of fraud requires proof of six elements. Each element is subject to specific defenses, and a successful defense to any one element can defeat a fraud case. The six elements are as follows:

1. A *false representation*. A true representation made maliciously is not fraudulent.

2. *Material fact.* The misrepresentation must be material (important) and must concern a past or an existing fact. Trivial misstatements are not misrepresentations. A plaintiff who knows that a statement is false cannot sue for fraud. An expression of opinion is not fraudulent unless the person making the representation occupies a position of trust such that another party relies on that person's judgment in the matter as if it were fact. An opinion, or even a positive statement, about a future event generally cannot constitute fraud.

3. *Knowingly made.* The defendant must know that the representation is false, or must make it in reckless disregard of the truth or without knowing or caring whether it is true or false.

4. *Intent to influence or deceive.* The defendant must make the misrepresentation with intent to influence the other party's actions.

5. *Reasonable reliance.* The misrepresentation must be a reasonable inducement to the other party to act. If the party would act regardless of the representation, no fraud occurs. The reliance must be justified. Relying on a layperson for a medical opinion, for example, would not be justified.

6. *Detriment.* The complaining party must suffer a detriment, or actual damage. If a party buys land on a representation that it contains silver ore when, in fact, it contains more valuable gold ore, the buyer would find it difficult to show a detriment. If the misrepresentation is not the proximate cause of the plaintiff's detriment, the plaintiff has no action for fraud or deceit.

Defenses to Fraud

*   The statement was not false.

*   The statement did not relate to a material fact.

*   The defendant did not know the statement was false.

*   The defendant did not intend to deceive.

*   The plaintiff did not rely on the statement.

*   The plaintiff suffered no harm or loss because of relying on the statement.

BAD FAITH, OR OUTRAGE

Bad faith, or **outrage**
An intentional or reckless act, extreme or outrageous in nature, causing severe emotional distress that results in physical injury; generally applied in suits for breach of insurance contracts.

The recognition of outrage (bad faith) as an independent tort is a recent development in the law created in response to the principle that, for every wrong, there should be a remedy. **Bad faith**, or **outrage** is an intentional or reckless act, extreme or outrageous in nature, causing severe emotional distress that results in physical injury, and is generally applied in suits for breach of insurance contracts. It is a tort of intentionally or recklessly causing another person severe emotional distress through one's extreme or outrageous acts.

Bad faith is similar to intentional infliction of emotional distress but has principally been a separate cause of action in suits for breach of insurance contracts. It is based on the theory that, in certain cases, the plaintiff is entitled to additional damages above those typically awarded for breach of contract. These cases involve alleged outrageous or extreme conduct, or the defendant's breach of an implied duty of good faith and fair dealings. The tort involves conduct so outrageous in character and extreme in degree that it goes beyond all possible bounds of decency and is regarded as atrocious and utterly intolerable in a civilized community. Bad faith applies to several situations, including breach of employment contracts involving wrongful discharge or discrimination.

Damages

Traditionally, courts award only contractual damages for breach of contract. Contract damages do not include damages for mental anguish, compensatory damages arising out of the breach, or punitive damages. On the other hand, courts have long awarded these kinds of damages in tort actions.

A person can recover additional, punitive damages in a breach of contract action when a tort also has occurred with the breach, involving malice, fraud, or utter disregard for the insured's rights and resulting in an additional injury. Many jurisdictions recognize the independent tort of bad faith or outrage to provide the injured party with an additional recovery in breach of contract actions.

Insurance Cases

In insurance cases, the tort bad faith is based on an insurer's implied duty to act fairly and in good faith in discharging its duties under an insurance contract. Usually, insureds allege negligent or intentional denial of a claim or failure to process or to pay a claim without reasonable cause. Such allegations might include failure or delay in pursuing claim investigation and settlement or the delay of claim payment to coerce insureds into settling for less than the full amount due.

Most states hold that, if the defendant has a reasonable cause for payment delay, no bad faith has occurred. In addition to claim practices, courts also have recognized causes of action for retaliatory cancellations and unfair increases in premiums after filing of claims.

Practically all courts recognize that, for liability policies for third-party coverage, an insurer owes a duty to its insureds to act in good faith and without negligence because the insured has relinquished the valuable right to settle or defend the action. Some courts hold that failure to protect the insured's right makes the insurer liable for the full amount of the loss, even if the loss exceeds the policy limit.

Not all courts recognize the tort of bad faith or outrage in connection with breach of contract suits. Further, many states now have laws imposing various penalties for failure to settle insurance claims properly. Many states also have adopted unfair claim settlement practice acts or unfair trade practice acts, which can preempt any private lawsuits for bad faith.

Defenses

A defendant might counter a plaintiff's lawsuit for outrage or bad faith by claiming that no intent or recklessness was involved, nor any outrageous or extreme conduct. The defendant might also prove that he or she did not breach any implied duty of good faith and fair dealings. Because contract damages are involved, the defendant would defend on contract principles, such as lack of any contractual duty to the plaintiff. In an insurance case, a defendant might assert that a valid insurance contract never existed, therefore there was no duty to act fairly and in good faith under an insurance contract.

Defenses to Bad Faith or Outrage

Defendant acted without intent to commit the tort, without reckless disregard for the truth, and without outrageous conduct.

Defendant did not breach duty of good faith or fair dealing (in insurance cases).

Defendant can use any applicable defenses challenging the validity of the contract.

INTERFERENCE WITH RELATIONSHIPS BETWEEN OTHERS

Another category of intentional tort relates to interference with relationships between others. Many torts involve interference with either personal or business relationships of other parties. These torts are not mutually exclusive in that one court might recognize an act as a violation of one right, and another might recognize the same act as a violation of another right.

Torts involving interference with relationships between others include the following:

- Injurious falsehood
- Malicious interference with prospective economic advantage
- Unfair competition
- Interference with employment
- Interference with copyright, patent, or trademark
- Interference with right to use one's own name in business
- Interference with family relationships

Injurious Falsehood

Any kind of legally protected right in property that can suffer harm by disparagement can be grouped under torts constituting **injurious falsehood**. These rights include almost any intangible property right, such as an interest in a title, lease, or trademark.

Injurious falsehood
A group of torts involving disparagement that causes harm to any kind of legally protected intangible property right.

Injurious falsehood can include disparaging statements referring to the quality of merchandise or the validity of a person's title to property. The tort is similar to defamation, and both torts apply in some cases. Injurious falsehood differs from defamation primarily in that the plaintiff must prove both the falsity of the statement and the actual damage or loss, while defamation might not result in actual damages.

The essence of the tort of injurious falsehood is interference with an economically advantageous relationship resulting in monetary loss. Therefore, it primarily concerns damage to a property right, while basic defamation usually involves damage to a person's reputation. Examples are allegations of improper business conduct or poor quality of goods. Defenses to this tort are essentially the same as those for defamation.

The following are the five elements of injurious falsehood:

1. A false statement.
2. The intent to cause pecuniary harm to the plaintiff.
3. Publication to a third party.
4. Malice in making the publication. (A court will infer malice if the defendant knew the statement was false or acted in reckless disregard of its truth or falsity.)
5. Injury or loss incurred by the plaintiff resulting from the statement, which can include loss of profits, loss of reputation, and legal defense fees, among others.

Malicious Interference With Prospective Economic Advantage

Malicious interference with prospective economic advantage is intentional interference with another's business, or with another's expected economic advantage. The first recorded case involving this very old tort was an action for damages in which the defendant allegedly kept customers away from the plaintiff's market by threats of violence.[4] Most cases still involve interference with commercial dealings, such as interfering with one's obtaining a job or purchasing property. However, the concept has expanded to cases involving interference with an expected gift or legacy under a will and expectations of economic advantage other than those arising out of business.

Malicious interference with prospective economic advantage
A tort involving intentional interference with another's business, or with another's expected economic advantage.

Common-Law Principles

The tort of malicious interference conflicts with two other basic philosophies of the law. The first philosophy is that freedom of competition promotes public welfare. Therefore, courts treated any injury a person suffered because of competition, such as lost business or a decline in value of property, as a harm without a remedy. A party had no right to sue if a competitor sold at less than cost or joined with other competitors to drive that person out of business. Because such actions were legal, courts would not examine motives behind the acts.

The tort of malicious interference and its counterpart, unfair competition, developed as the courts recognized, over time, that unrestrained competition in business led to many unfair results. Currently, the tort applies if the acts were fraudulent or if they involved intimidation or circulation of false reports about a person's honesty or solvency.

Defense

The usual defense in a suit for malicious interference with prospective economic advantage is that the defendant was making a lawful effort to promote his or her own welfare and not to injure the plaintiff maliciously. The plaintiff then must demonstrate that the act involved express malice and the intent to injure the plaintiff and not to benefit the defendant. **Malice** as used here means intentionally doing a wrongful act without justification or excuse.

Malice
The intent to do a wrongful act without justification or excuse.

Unfair Competition

A counterpart of malicious interference with prospective economic advantage is **unfair competition**, or the use of wrongful or fraudulent practices by a business to gain an unfair advantage over competitors. The common law prohibited people or organizations from pretending that their goods were competitors' goods by using similar trademarks, labels, or wrappers. If such an action deprived the competitor of the value of the goodwill in the business, the competitor could sue for unfair competition.

Unfair competition
Use of wrongful or fraudulent practices by a business to gain an unfair advantage over competitors.

No unfair competition exists without competition. Conversely, no injury results unless the two parties are competing directly in the same product or service. However, one party cannot legally make or label goods in any manner that leads the public to believe they are the product of a manufacturer in another field, thereby obtaining the benefit of the other party's goodwill and reputation. It does not matter that the two parties are not in direct competition.

The essence of unfair competition is deception, and it starts when the imitation deceives the public into buying one party's product in the mistaken belief that it is another party's product. Unfair competition applies to literary and artistic properties as well as to merchandise. To illustrate, reproducing photographs or copying paintings and passing them off as the works of another photographer or artist creates a right to sue.

A defense to a lawsuit for unfair competition might include the assertion that the defendant did not do one or more of the following:

* Compete
* Compete directly
* Cause harm to the plaintiff
* Mislead the public
* Deceive anyone

Interference With Employment

Interference with employment
An unjustified intentional act that interferes with another's valid or expected business relationship.

The tort of **interference with employment** is an unjustified intentional act that interferes with another's valid or expected business relationship. It can take many forms and in certain instances overlaps with other torts involving interference with relationships. An example of this tort is spreading negative information about a person applying for a job. The same act also can be defamation, either libel or slander, depending on the means of publication, if the information is false.

Procuring Employee's Discharge

A discharged employee has a common-law right of action against a third party that has procured his or her discharge by an employer under any of the following circumstances:

- The third party ordered the employer to breach the employment contract.
- The act furthered an unlawful purpose of the third party.
- The third party used unlawful means to procure the discharge.

Preventing Employment

At common law, every person had an inherent right to seek lawful employment under the terms of an agreement with an employer. Interference with that right can be a tort.

The plaintiff must prove the defendant's motive was to prevent the plaintiff's employment and that the means were unfair means (such as false statements, threats, or coercion). Generally, if a defendant can show that the actions were legal, such as to obtain the job, and the means were fair, the actions fails. This tort can arise when a prospective employer contacts a former employer with inquiries about a job applicant. Any false statement by the former employer or any other act of fraud or deceit that contributes to the failure to hire the job applicant can create a right to sue. If, however, the answers are honest and complete, the defendant might have no liability. Truth is a complete defense. Today employers often give only dates of employment to prospective employers for former employees seeking work.

At common law, an exchange between employers of a list of persons deemed unworthy of employment, or a blacklist, was legal. However, if an employer made any false statements in connection with blacklisting, the employer was liable. Statutes now prohibit keeping blacklists.

Violating Implied Contract Provisions

The common-law doctrine that a person's employment is in the sole discretion of the employer and that the person, therefore, can be fired for any or no reason is called the employment-at-will doctrine. Exceptions to the employment-at-will doctrine can be made by contract. In the absence of an employment contract, a discharged employee can sue on the basis of an implied contract. (These are not really tort actions but are discussed here because of their similarity to the torts). A lawsuit for discharge can have one of the following two bases:

1. *Breach of a contract implied in law.* This basis closely resembles the tort of outrage or bad faith, discussed previously. It is based on the concept that a duty of good faith and fair dealing is implied in every employment-at-will contract. A breach of this duty occurs when a discharge is arbitrary or in bad faith. It usually arises in cases involving sales representatives whose employers have discharged them to avoid paying them commissions or other compensation.

2. *Breach of a contract implied in fact.* This basis rests on the concept that the employer's conduct can create the implication of a contract. One implied provision is an employee's expectation of continued employment and termination only for good cause. An employer's statements in employee manuals or handbooks, or oral statements by job interviewers or supervisors, can create this expectation.

Defenses

A defense to a lawsuit for interference with employment might include the defendant's allegations that he or she did not do any of the following:

- Interfere with or prevent employment
- Induce a breach of contract
- Damage the plaintiff
- Act in furtherance of an unlawful object
- Use unlawful means to procure discharge
- Blacklist

Interference With Copyright, Patent, or Trademark

Copyright, patent, and trademark rights are property rights, and interference with any of these rights has historically been a tort. Today, federal legislation preempts the common law and governs most matters concerning these rights.

As defenses to a lawsuit for interference with copyright, patent, or trademark, the defendant might assert that he or she did not interfere with the copyright, patent, or trademark or that the plaintiff did not own the intellectual property in question.

Interference With Right to Use One's Own Name in Business

A person has a right to use his or her own name in business even though a similar business is conducted under the same or a similar name. This right applies both to individuals and to corporations. In the case of corporations, businesses must register names, and most states will not grant a charter if a name is too similar to a name already registered.

Courts give the original user of a personal name some protection, and they require a notice that no connection exists with the original. For example,

John Doe Co. might be required to put a notice on its products reading "Not connected with the Jack Doe Co." to distinguish its products from Jack Doe's.

Interference With Family Relationships

The family has no collective rights. However, members of a family, because of the family relationship, do have rights. At common law, neither spouse could sue a third party for personal injury against the other spouse. Most states have abandoned this rule. Also, in most states, a spouse can now sue for assault and battery or false imprisonment. Many of the spousal rights discussed here were only for the husband's benefit at common law. Today, laws favoring husbands over wives either have been eliminated totally or apply equally to wives.

Spouses' rights against third persons fall into the following three general categories:

1. *Alienation of affection.* A third party's interference with the husband-wife relationship is commonly called alienation of affection. A spouse has a right to sue a person who persuades the other spouse to leave the marriage. This right extends to all types of wrongful interference by which the spouse is induced to leave, including enticement. A spouse has a right to sue another person who commits adultery with his or her spouse. The adulterous spouse's consent to the adultery does not bar the action. Some states, either by statute or court decision, have eliminated alienation of affection actions.

2. *Personal injury.* A spouse, or both spouses together, can sue a third person for causing personal physical injury to one spouse. In addition the spouse of an injured person can also sue for loss of consortium, discussed next.

3. *Loss of consortium.* Loss of the husband-wife relationship is commonly called loss of consortium and involves loss of services, companionship, and comfort. The amount of damages is based on the spouses' existing relationship.

Parents also have family relationship rights. At common law, parents could sue third persons for injury to children based on loss of services because children helped families economically. On farms, for example, children performed essential duties. Under modern law, it is not necessary to show an actual loss of services, even though that loss remains the underlying theory of the suit. Enticing a child away or kidnapping, negligently injuring, or seducing a child can give rise to a right to sue regardless of economic deprivation.

At common law, children had no right to sue their parents for injuries, including failure to support the children. Children also had no right of action against third persons who injured their parents and deprived them of their source of support. Today, a child can recover for injuries that third persons cause to parents. Also, although at common law, a child had no right to sue parents for cruel or abusive treatment, children now have that right through state laws.

Other torts relating to family relationships—wrongful life and wrongful pregnancy—are of recent origin and are not frequent bases for lawsuits.

Wrongful-life action
A lawsuit by or on behalf of a child with birth defects, alleging that, but for the doctor-defendant's negligent advice, the parents would not have conceived the child or would have terminated the pregnancy so as to avoid the pain and suffering resulting from the child's defects.

A **wrongful-life action** is a lawsuit by or on behalf of a child with birth defects, alleging that, but for the doctor-defendant's negligent advice, the parents would not have conceived the child or would have terminated the pregnancy so as to avoid the pain and suffering resulting from the child's defects. Most jurisdictions have rejected these claims. A child born with a physical disability can be the plaintiff in a suit for wrongful life, based on an allegation that the defendant, usually a doctor, negligently failed to diagnose or warn of the probability that the child would be born with the disability, thus depriving the parents of the ability to make an informed judgment about whether to carry the child to term. Recovery in such cases is limited to special damages and does not include pain and suffering or other general damages.

Wrongful-pregnancy action, or **wrongful-conception action**
A lawsuit by a parent for damages resulting from a pregnancy following a failed sterilization.

The companion tort to wrongful life, a **wrongful-pregnancy action**, involves a lawsuit by a parent for damages resulting from a pregnancy following a failed sterilization. In some jurisdictions, the action is called a **wrongful-conception action**. This claim is frequently alleged in wrongful life cases and can arise in the following two situations:

1. When an unplanned birth of a healthy baby follows a failed sterilization
2. When parents give birth to a child with disabilities after a doctor misdiagnosed or failed to detect a condition

In these cases, the parents can recover the extraordinary expenses involved in taking care of the child. Some courts limit recovery to the period before the child reaches majority; others impose no such limit. Courts in many states recognize the wrongful death cause of action, including those in several states that have rejected the wrongful life cause of action.

MISUSE OF LEGAL PROCESS

Another intentional tort, misuse of legal process, can result from using the legal process for an improper purpose. The tort takes two forms: malicious prosecution and malicious abuse of process. Courts do not encourage lawsuits alleging these torts because of public policy, which favors use of the courts to resolve disputes. However, misuse of legal process can sometimes be appropriate grounds for suit.

Malicious Prosecution

Malicious prosecution
The improper institution of legal proceedings against another.

Malicious prosecution is the improper institution of criminal or civil proceedings against another. Historically, malicious prosecution related only to criminal cases. For example, Al files a groundless criminal complaint against Bob to harass him. Bob is acquitted as defendant in the criminal action. Bob, as plaintiff in a civil action, can sue Al for malicious prosecution.

Today some jurisdictions apply malicious prosecution to certain civil proceedings, such as bankruptcy and actions to have a person declared incompetent. To establish a case, the plaintiff in the malicious prosecution case (referred to as Person A in the discussion), either civil or criminal, must prove the following four elements:

1. *Initiation of a suit or proceeding.* Person B prosecutes a lawsuit against Person A in either a court of law or a quasi-judicial proceeding, such as a license revocation hearing.

2. *Termination of that action in the plaintiff's favor.* Examples of a favorable termination for the plaintiff (Person A) would be acquittal of criminal charges, discharge on preliminary examination, quashing of an indictment, a grand jury's refusal to indict, or the defendant's (Person B's) voluntary withdrawal of the lawsuit. A plaintiff who is convicted is prevented from suing for malicious prosecution.

3. *No probable cause.* There must have been no probable cause for bringing the action. **Probable cause** consists of grounds that would lead a reasonable person to believe that the plaintiff committed the act for which the defendant is suing. Probable cause is lacking if the defendant believes the plaintiff is guilty but has no factual basis to support the belief.

Probable cause
The grounds that would lead a reasonable person to believe that the plaintiff committed the act for which the defendant is suing.

4. *Malice.* Lack of probable cause implies legal malice. A person with malice has a purpose other than fairly adjudicating the claim that is the basis of the proceedings. If probable cause for the suit exists, it does not matter that the defendant had malice. The plaintiff must prove both lack of probable cause and malice.

The requirement for proof of those four elements is called the American rule. Some states follow the English rule, which requires proof of a fifth element: special injury. Under the English rule, those damages and expenses reasonably flowing from civil litigation are not special injury. Therefore, allegations of lost business, lost profits, or legal fees for defense of the prior suit are not special injury. Special injury includes arrest, seizure of property resulting from the defendant's filing the original suit, or a court order against a company that prevents it from operating.

Defenses

The plaintiff's inability to prove any of the elements of the tort is a defense. In addition, the following acts can also bar the lawsuit for malicious prosecution:

- *Defendant's action on advice of counsel.* Lack of probable cause is an essential element of this tort. Showing that the defendant fully disclosed all facts to an impartial attorney and, with a genuine belief in the plaintiff's guilt, acted on the attorney's advice, strongly indicates the presence of probable cause.

- *Plaintiff's guilt of the crime.* If the defendant proves the plaintiff was guilty, and the plaintiff is convicted, no cause of action remains. The plaintiff's acquittal, however, is not conclusive evidence of lack of probable cause. Acquittal does not prove conclusively that a person is innocent but merely indicates that a jury was not convinced beyond a reasonable doubt of the defendant's guilt (in a criminal case).

- *Probable cause.* Proof of probable cause completely prevents a malicious prosecution action.

Malicious Abuse of Process

Malicious abuse of process is the use of civil or criminal procedures for a purpose for which they were not designed. Distinguished from malicious prosecution—maliciously *causing* process to issue—abuse of process relates to improper use of process *after* it has issued. This tort has the following two essential elements:

Malicious abuse of process
The use of civil or criminal procedures for a purpose for which they were not designed.

1. An improper, illegal, or perverted use of process
2. An ulterior motive, that is, an intent to use the process for a purpose for which it was not intended

An example of malicious abuse of process is bringing a person into a jurisdiction, supposedly as a party or witness in one action, but in reality to serve process in the form of a complaint in connection with another action. The plaintiff must prove malice, but the ulterior motive, service of process, generally infers malice.

The plaintiff's inability to prove an ulterior motive is the usual defense to a claim of malicious abuse of process. Therefore, if the defendant can show that the use of the process was regular and legitimate, even though the process was initiated with a bad intention, it is not a malicious abuse of process.

Additionally, because the essence of malicious abuse of process is improper use of legal procedures, a plaintiff need not show that any applicable lawsuit terminated in the plaintiff's favor or that there was no probable cause.

Coercion, such as starting a criminal case to compel a person to pay a debt, is frequently a basis for malicious abuse of process. Owing a debt is not a crime, so if a person files a criminal complaint against another because of a debt, it is tantamount to blackmail. Another example is obtaining execution on a judgment after satisfaction of a debt, which is nothing more than harassment.

INTENTIONAL TORTS AGAINST PROPERTY

Torts include intentional civil wrongs against property, as well as intentional civil wrongs against people. This section examines the torts of trespass to real and personal property and conversion.

Trespass

A **trespass** can be against either real or personal property, and the elements are essentially the same within both. Real property is land and buildings on land. Personal property is everything else a person can own.

Trespass is an act against possession and not against ownership. That is, the plaintiff must actually possess the property. An owner not in possession has no right to sue. A tenant in possession can sue only for injury to his or her interest. Entry upon another's land is justified if the owner or occupant either expressly or impliedly permits it.

Trespass to Real Property

Any unauthorized entry upon another person's land is a trespass. The law presumes at least nominal damages merely because an entry occurred. The defendant is liable even if the entry is accidental.

To sue successfully, a plaintiff need not prove either damage or intent to trespass. Actual damage and intent are material, however, to the amount of damages that a court might award. For example, a court might award significant damages if the defendant intended to trespass even though actual damage was insignificant. On the other hand, if the defendant's conduct was not intentional and caused no damage, the court might award only nominal damages. The magnitude of the entry is not important. Merely walking on the property is sufficient to claim trespass. In fact, actual entry is not required—throwing physical substances onto another's land is a trespass. For example, throwing debris onto a neighbor's land or cutting a tree that falls on another's land are both trespasses.

Under common law, land ownership extends from the core of the earth to the sky, and any invasion of that space is a trespass. Therefore, tunneling under another's land is a trespass, as is constructing a building so that a part of it overhangs adjacent land.

The flight of an aircraft over land is a technical trespass, but the courts balance the equities between the right to be secure in one's property and the public need for the right to fly over private property. For that reason, courts usually will not find a trespass for violation of air rights unless an airplane drops an object or creates actual damage.

Trespass to Personal Property

Trespass to personal property is the forcible interference with another's possession of the property. Any type of property, including animals, can be the subject of a trespass. Thus, if a person unjustifiably kills another person's dog, the killing would be a trespass to personal property.

The same elements apply to trespass to real property as to personal property. A plaintiff need not show intent, and the degree of force and the amount of damage are immaterial. For example, if Anne has a motorboat tied up to one side of a pier and George unties it and moves it to the other side, George's act is a trespass to personal property.

As with real property, trespass to personal property is an act against possession, and the plaintiff must prove possession.

A defendant can defend against trespass to real or personal property by alleging that the plaintiff never had ownership or possession of the property, or that the defendant did not enter onto or take control of the property.

Conversion

Conversion
The unlawful exercise of control over another person's personal property to the detriment of the owner.

Chattel
Tangible, movable personal property.

Conversion is the unlawful exercise of dominion or control over another person's personal property to the detriment of the owner. It applies to tangible, movable personal property, usually called **chattel**, and does not apply to land. The party must be deprived of possession of chattel by a wrongful taking, wrongful disposal, wrongful detention, or severe damage or destruction.

The interference with possession must be major and not just temporary or fleeting. Conversion is founded on the legal wrong of deprivation of one's right to property. Any person with a legal right to possession, including a finder or bailee, can sue for conversion.

The interference itself need not be an intentional or conscious act, but an intention or purpose to convert the goods or to exercise dominion over them, thus preventing the owner from getting or keeping possession, is necessary. For example, Anna takes the wrong coat in a restaurant. If she discovers the error immediately and returns the coat, no conversion has occurred. However, if Anna keeps the coat for three months before returning it, a conversion has occurred. A few of the many ways in which conversion can occur are discussed next.

Acquisition of Possession

If acquisition is without legal justification and with an intent to exercise dominion or control over chattel, conversion occurs. Acquiring property by fraud or theft is conversion. Likewise, a person who purchases property from another without being certain of the seller's title takes the purchase at his or her peril. The true owner may sue the buyer as a converter. However, under the Uniform Commercial Code[5] a good faith purchaser for value (that is, one who pays a valuable price) can acquire good title from any persons who did not have good title to convey.

Unauthorized Transfer of Chattel (Personal Property)

A person in legal possession of property can commit conversion by making an unauthorized transfer of the property to a third person. A common example is when a person contracts with an owner to store chattel (personal property) at 10 Main Street and then subcontracts with another to store it at

25 High Street. Moving the chattel to 25 High Street would be a conversion. Erroneous delivery of property to the wrong party is also a conversion, even if the person thought the delivery was to the appropriate party.

Not every unauthorized transfer is a conversion. Commercial necessity has required the relaxation of the rule in some circumstances for certain intermediaries. Intermediaries are generally not converters unless they know they are withholding the property from the owner or if they continue to hold it after gaining that knowledge.

Unreasonable Withholding of Chattel

The unreasonable withholding or possession of chattel usually involves a bailment, in which the bailor, who owns the property, leaves that property with another person, the bailee, for safekeeping. For example, a bailor leaves a coat with a coat-check person (bailee) in a restaurant. A bailor leaves a car with a parking attendant (bailee) in a parking lot.

If the bailor is refused possession, then a conversion occurs. If Cathy rents a lawnmower to Paul for ten days and demands it back in five days, no conversion occurs if Paul refuses to return it because Paul has a ten-day rental.

To put the other party in default, the owner must demand the return. The party holding the property then must make an unqualified refusal without legal reason. Rightful refusal includes, for example, retaining possession for a reasonable time to determine ownership or to collect reasonable storage charges. A holder's returning the property after originally refusing to return it is not a defense but might reduce damages.

Damaging, Altering, or Misusing Chattel

If a person possessing chattel seriously damages it or unlawfully and substantially alters it, a conversion occurs. For example, Al gives Bob a car to store in his garage. If Bob seriously damages the car or does major unauthorized work on it, a conversion occurs.

Misusing chattel consists of using the chattel in a manner inconsistent with the purpose for which the party has possession. In the previous example above, if Bob took the car, which he had only for storage, and drove it 100 miles on an errand, a conversion occurs. A casual or harmless use involving no defiance of the owner's right of dominion (control or possession) is not a conversion. If, however, the chattel is damaged, the holder can be liable for the damages.

A party can be liable for conversion caused by acts of the party's agents or employees. Thus, a corporation acting through an officer or employee can cause a conversion.

A significant feature of conversion is that, in some cases, the plaintiff need not accept the chattel if the defendant offers it back after a conversion has occurred. The plaintiff can recover the full value of the chattel, including loss of profits at the time and place of the conversion.

Defenses

Good faith is not a defense against conversion. However, the following are good defenses:

- A plaintiff's failure to establish the right to possession of the property or
- A plaintiff's refusal to demand return, followed by the defendant's consequent refusal to deliver

A bailee can defend by showing that the property is not in his or her possession because it was lost or destroyed without the bailee's fault, such as by an act of nature.

NUISANCE

The final intentional tort discussed here is nuisance, with all its variations. The tort of nuisance is, broadly, anything interfering with another's enjoyment or rights. A court will decide what constitutes a nuisance by considering the discomfort it inflicts on a normal person under normal conditions and not its effect on persons who are too sensitive or who are ill, either physically or mentally. Nuisance torts fall into the following four categories:

Private nuisance
An unreasonable and unlawful interference with another's use or enjoyment of his or her real property.

- *Private nuisance.* A **private nuisance** is an unreasonable and unlawful interference with another's use or enjoyment of his or her real property. The interference must be substantial enough to be unreasonable and can take almost any form, such as producing undue noise, causing dust to fall on adjoining property, blasting, or interfering in any other material way with the enjoyment of property. Private nuisance is based on an old common-law concept that all people should be able to use their property while not interfering with others' enjoyment of their own property.

Intentional nuisance
Purposeful interference with another party's enjoyment of his or her property.

- *Intentional nuisance.* The invasion of others' rights can be either intentional or unintentional. Defendants are liable for unintentional nuisances when their conduct is negligent, reckless, or ultrahazardous. An **intentional nuisance** (sometimes called an absolute nuisance) occurs when one purposely interferes with another's enjoyment of property or knows that such an interference is substantially certain to arise from the nuisance act. Examples of intentional nuisances are (1) a fence that one neighbor has intentionally erected high enough to interfere with an adjoining landowner's enjoyment of property and (2) a person's continuing to spray chemicals with the knowledge that they are damaging a neighbor's land.

Nuisance per se
An act, occupation, or structure that is a nuisance at all times and under any conditions, regardless of location or surroundings.

- *Nuisance per se.* **Nuisance per se** is an act, occupation, or structure that is a nuisance at all times and under any conditions, regardless of location or surroundings. A lawful enterprise generally cannot be a nuisance per se. However, a leaky hazardous-waste storage facility is a nuisance per se.

Public nuisance
An act, occupation, or structure that affects the public at large or a substantial segment of the public, interfering with public enjoyment or rights regarding property.

- *Public nuisance.* A **public nuisance**, as contrasted with a private nuisance, affects the public at large, or a substantial segment of the public. For example, a person who operates a plant that pollutes a river with poisonous waste commits a public nuisance. Only a person who has suffered personal damage can recover damages for injury resulting from a public nuisance. The injury must be particular to the individual plaintiff. The remedies for public nuisance include a civil tort suit for damages and criminal charges and usually include a court order demanding curtailment of the nuisance.

The defense to a nuisance claim depends to a large extent on the type of nuisance alleged. A common defense to a nuisance lawsuit is that the act complained of was a reasonable and legal use of the property by the defendant. Historically, people have been entitled to use their property in any way as long as the uses do not interfere unreasonably with others' enjoyment of their own property.

Nuisance does not include every discomfort that one might impose on another. What is reasonable depends on the circumstances of each case. If Alan erects a building or other structure on his land, his neighbor, Carol, could object that it has devalued her property or cut off light or air. Despite her objection, she cannot sue Alan successfully. However, if the structure projects over the lot line in any manner, it can become a nuisance.

SUMMARY

Intentional torts occur both against people and against property. Intentional torts against people include assault and battery, false imprisonment and arrest, and intentional infliction of emotional distress, all of which injure people directly and physically. Infliction of emotional distress can be either intentional or negligent but traditionally must be accompanied by physical as well as emotional harm, such as illness resulting from distress.

Defamation is making false statements injurious to another person's reputation, either by oral slander or by written (or otherwise recorded) libel. Truth is an absolute defense in a defamation case. Invasion of the right of privacy includes several different situations and is based on the individual's right to be let alone and to be protected from unauthorized publicity in private matters.

A plaintiff alleging fraud must prove the following six elements:

1. False representation
2. Knowingly made
3. Intent to influence or deceive
4. Material fact
5. Reasonable reliance
6. Detriment

The tort of bad faith, or outrage, is a relatively recent legal development and has principally been a separate cause of action in suits for breach of insurance contracts. The plaintiff is entitled to additional damages above those usually awarded for breach of contract, and the cases involve alleged outrageous or extreme conduct. Effective defenses require proving that the defendant acted without intent to commit the tort or did not breach a duty of good faith, or that the insurance contract in question was not valid.

Torts involving interference with relationships between others include the following:

- Injurious falsehood
- Malicious interference with prospective economic advantage
- Unfair competition
- Interference with employment
- Interference with copyright, patent, or trademark
- Right to use one's own name in business
- Interference with family relationships

A defendant might prove that the tort action of interference did not occur. A variety of additional defenses is available for the individual interference torts.

Using the legal process for an improper purpose can result in a tort claim for misuse of legal process, which takes the following two forms:

1. Malicious prosecution
2. Malicious abuse of process

Although malicious prosecution began as the improper institution of criminal proceedings without probable cause, with malice, and with an outcome favorable to the defendant, today it often applies to civil proceedings as well. Malicious abuse of process is use of the legal process for a purpose for which it was not designed and includes two essential elements:

1. An improper, illegal, or perverted use of process
2. The existence of an ulterior motive to use the process for a purpose for which it was not intended

Defenses are possible when the action was on the advice of legal counsel, the plaintiff was guilty of a crime or loses the civil proceeding, or the defendant has probable cause to believe the process was legitimate.

Torts include intentional wrongs against property, as well as against people. Intentional wrongs against property include trespass, conversion, and nuisance. A trespass can occur to either real or personal property, and the elements of both types of trespass are essentially the same. Trespass is an act against possession and not against ownership. Defenses against trespass involve the rightful ownership of the property and the defendant's actions.

Conversion is the intentional and unlawful exercise of dominion or control over tangible personal property to the detriment of the person who is entitled to control it. If a plaintiff did not own the property or demand its return, a defendant may successfully defend against the allegation of conversion.

Nuisance is anything interfering with another's enjoyment of rights. It falls into more specific categories, such as private nuisance, intentional nuisance, nuisance per se, and public nuisance. The invasion of another's right can be either intentional or unintentional. A person is liable for an unintentional nuisance when his or her conduct is negligent, reckless, or ultrahazardous. Defense to nuisance is possible if the defendants' actions involve the reasonable and legal use of their property.

CHAPTER NOTES

1. *Sullivan v. New York Times*, 376 U.S. 254 (1964).
2. Restatement (Second) of Torts, § 581(2).
3. 5 U.S.C., § 552 (a).
4. *The School-Master Case*, Y.B. 11 Hen. 4, f47, pl. 21 (1410).
5. UCC, § 2-403.

Chapter 10

Direct Your Learning

Tort Law—Special Liability and Litigation Concepts

After learning the content of this chapter and completing the corresponding course guide assignment, you should be able to:

■ Describe the conditions for strict liability.

■ Given a products liability case, explain how liability is established for any of the following causes of action:

  • Misrepresentation

  • Breach of warranty

  • Strict liability and negligence

■ Given a products liability case based on strict liability or negligence, explain what parties are potentially liable, what a defendant must prove to establish a defense, and what damages a plaintiff can recover.

■ Describe the legal bases for toxic tort and environmental damage claims and the coverage the CGL policy provides for such liability.

■ Given a tort case, describe the kinds of damages a court might award a plaintiff.

■ Given tort cases, explain whether any of the following concepts relating to litigation would apply:

  • Joint tortfeasor's liability

  • Expanded liability concepts

  • Tortfeasor's capacity

  • Vicarious liability

  • Good Samaritan issues

  • Class actions and mass tort litigation

  • Statutes of limitations and statutes of repose

■ Define or describe each of the Key Words and Phrases for this chapter.

Develop Your Perspective

What are the main topics covered in the chapter?

This chapter concludes the discussion of tort law, describing its application to products liability, toxic/environmental torts, and strict liability. Aspects of tort litigation, including damages, liability concepts, and statutes of limitation and repose, apply universally to cases brought in tort law.

Contrast what a plaintiff must prove to establish products liability with the defenses a defendant might have.

- Why would a plaintiff's attorney prefer to establish that strict liability exists instead of negligence?

- What warranties could a plaintiff's attorney attempt to prove if no written product warranty exists?

- What arguments could a defense attorney make about a plaintiff's assumption of risk in using a product?

Why is it important to learn about these topics?

Insurance professionals are likely to encounter issues in the ever-expanding areas of products liability, toxic torts, and environmental law. They must not only understand the substantive law but also have working familiarity with litigation rules and issues.

Consider the kinds of products and toxic tort liability, as well as environmental claims, you as an individual and your employer might encounter.

- What kinds of products liability and toxic torts or environmental issues might affect you in your everyday life?

- What kinds of products liability and toxic torts or environmental issues do you see frequently?

How can you use what you will learn?

Evaluate the insurance policies you work with regularly.

- What kinds of insurance policies and what policy provisions cover products liability and toxic torts, as well as environmental claims?

- What kinds of insurance policies and what policy provisions exclude products liability and toxic torts, as well as environmental claims?

Chapter 10
Tort Law—Special Liability and Litigation Concepts

Tort law includes the substantive areas of products liability and of toxic torts and environmental law. These areas are unique and are addressed separately because the proof of liability for and the defenses to these torts are different from those of the torts discussed in the previous chapter. Strict liability, another unique doctrine for establishing liability, applies to many kinds of torts and is an important concept in the area of products liability.

Tort litigation matters, such as damages, liability concepts, and time concerns affecting litigation are the vehicle for bringing a liability case to its conclusion. Many of the concepts are procedural in nature and apply to all tort cases.

Products liability, a rapidly expanding area of tort law, is a manufacturer's or seller's tort liability for harm suffered by a buyer, user, or bystander as a result of a defective product. Several common-law principles continue to apply to products liability.

> **Products liability**
> A manufacturer's or seller's tort liability for harm suffered by a buyer, user, or bystander as a result of a defective product.

At common law, contractors, manufacturers, and sellers of products were not liable for negligence to third parties with whom they had no contractual relationships. However, the following well-established exceptions to this rule evolved over time:

- One who marketed an inherently dangerous product that was also defective was liable to anyone injured because of the defect. For example, selling dangerously defective fireworks might create a liability with no defense.

- A manufacturer who made, assembled, or sold a product not inherently dangerous, but that could be inherently dangerous if defective, was liable, to any person injured while using the product in a reasonable manner, even though no contractual relationship existed. The plaintiff had to prove negligence. For example, a knife is not inherently dangerous, but a knife with a defective handle that could snap during use could be inherently dangerous.

- A manufacturer who was not only negligent in manufacturing a product but who also knowingly concealed the defect, could be liable for both negligence and fraud. For example, a manufacturer who painted a stepladder to conceal a defect in the ladder would be liable with no defense for any injury that resulted from the defect.

These exceptions to the contract rule applied only to the manufacturer's liability. In addition, a dealer could be liable for injury to a person other than the immediate purchaser when the injury resulted from a defect the dealer should have detected in the exercise of ordinary care.

For many years, the courts disagreed about whether to consider an automobile an inherently dangerous product. In the landmark case, *MacPherson v. Buick Motor Car Co.*,[1] the United States Supreme Court held that, while an automobile is not an inherently dangerous product, it could become inherently dangerous if negligently constructed. If so, the manufacturer becomes liable without defense for ensuing injuries. Proof that a defective part came from another manufacturer is not sufficient to relieve the manufacturer of liability if the defect could have been discovered by a reasonable inspection. The *MacPherson* case involved an injury caused by a defective wheel that the manufacturer had obtained from another vendor. The manufacturer did not inspect the wheel, and a reasonable inspection would have revealed the defect.

MacPherson doctrine

A court ruling extending a manufacturer's liability beyond the immediate purchaser of an article to any user and to those who would likely be affected by the article's use and who suffered harm from its use.

The **MacPherson doctrine** extended a manufacturer's liability beyond the immediate purchaser of an article to any user as well as to those who would likely be affected by the use of the article and who suffered harm from its use. For example, a pedestrian struck by a defective wheel coming off a vehicle, even though not a user, could sue the manufacturer. Courts refined this doctrine over the years to develop current law in the area.

Case law evolving from the MacPherson case eventually resulted in the doctrines of implied warranty and strict liability in tort used today. The MacPherson doctrine was expanded to include one who negligently repairs an article, as well as the manufacturer.

STRICT LIABILITY

In addition to liability based on intention or on negligence, sometimes tort liability is imposed even when a defendant has acted reasonably and is therefore not at fault. A person who commits certain acts is liable for injury to another regardless of whether the act was willful or negligent. This is the result of the doctrine of **strict liability**, the liability that arises from inherently dangerous activities, resulting in harm to another, regardless of the degree of care taken. Strict liability is also called **absolute liability**. At early common law, the scope of strict liability was extensive, and it continues to apply in products liability law and in situations involving hazardous activities. It also applies in situations involving animals.

Strict liability, or **absolute liability**

Liability that arises from inherently dangerous activities resulting in harm to another, regardless of the degree of care taken.

Hazardous Activities

Generally, people can use their property in any way they see fit as long as the use does not harm neighbors. In the landmark case of *Rylands v. Fletcher*,[2] the court extended the doctrine of strict liability to certain activities on real property. The court held that people who bring anything onto their land that, if it escapes, is likely to result in injury, are strictly liable for all damages that are the natural consequence of the escape.

The *Rylands v. Fletcher* case arose from the defendant's construction of a water reservoir. The defendant was unaware of abandoned mineshafts under the reservoir site. When the reservoir began to fill, the water broke through the mineshafts and flooded the mines on the plaintiff's property. The court held the defendant strictly liable for the injury. The decision applies only to things artificially brought onto the land and not to natural things such as trees and weeds. It also does not apply when the cause is natural, such as an unprecedented rainfall that causes a reservoir to overflow.

The justification for imposing strict liability on those who carry on ultrahazardous activities is that they have, for their own purposes, created an unusual risk in the community. If the activity causes an injury or damage, then another person's or animal's unexpected action, or a force of nature, is immaterial to the defendant's liability.

The storage and transportation of explosive substances is an ultrahazardous activity. Aviation is also an ultrahazardous activity, although many states take the position that it is now so commonplace as to present no unusual danger. Automobile use is common and therefore is not ultrahazardous.

The occupiers of adjacent property are not required to refrain from using their property as they please merely because of an ultrahazardous activity nearby. For example, even though blasting occurs, adjacent property owners are under no compulsion to vacate their premises, construct explosion-proof shelters, or take other protective steps. Similarly, a passerby who is injured does not forfeit a right to recover damages caused by a blast merely because that person knew explosives were stored on the property.

Animals

For liability for animals, the law differentiates between domestic and wild animals, based on local custom. At common law, an owner was strictly liable for damages caused by the trespass of any domestic animal. If, for example, a cow broke out of a fenced field onto a neighbor's land and caused damage, strict liability applied, and proof of negligence was not necessary.

Even though dogs and cats are domestic animals, because they seldom cause serious damage, the rule of strict liability did not apply to them unless the owner knew of the animal's vicious propensity to cause injury. In most jurisdictions, an owner who knows of a dog's propensity to be vicious is liable.

Owners of wild animals are absolutely liable for all acts of and damage caused by the animals. Wild animals are animals that, by local custom, are not devoted to people's use. Courts have held monkeys and elephants, for example, to be wild animals. The law distinguishes between wild animals native to the area and those that are not. Possessors are liable for acts of native animals as long as they are in the owners' possession. However, liability ends if an animal escapes because the exposure is then no greater than it was before capture of the animal. For wild animals that are not native to an area, a possessor is liable for acts both on and off the premises.

PRODUCTS LIABILITY

Today, most products liability suits are based on one or more of the following principles of law:

- Misrepresentation
- Breach of warranty
- Strict liability and negligence

The following discussion treats negligence and strict liability together. Although they are dissimilar in many respects, considering them together helps to compare how each applies in products liability cases.

Misrepresentation

Manufacturers make representations to the public through advertisements, brochures, labels on the goods, and instructions for use. These representations often go beyond mere sales promotion, providing information concerning safety that consumers rely on. For example, an automobile manufacturer's brochure described the windshield glass as shatterproof. The owner, injured when a pebble struck and shattered the glass, recovered damages from the manufacturer. The usual basis for a lawsuit based on a representation is that it is an express warranty. However, as in the windshield case, the court determined the liability on the basis of innocent misrepresentation, a form of deceit.

Breach of Warranty

A plaintiff can file a suit for breach of either an express warranty or an implied warranty. In a landmark case relating to warranty, *Henningsen v. Bloomfield Motors, Inc.*,[3] the wife of a new car buyer sustained injury while driving the allegedly defective car. In the contract of sale, the manufacturer had attempted to disclaim any liability relating to the quality or condition of the car. The court held, however, that the automobile was subject to a nonwaivable **implied warranty of merchantability** representing to the buyer that it was reasonably fit for the general purpose for which it was manufactured and sold. No privity (contractual relationship) was required, and the warranty ran to any person who might reasonably be expected to use the product.

The concept of implied warranty applies to such situations as an employee's lawsuit for injury caused by a defective machine sold to the employer and to a tenant's lawsuit against a faucet manufacturer for burns suffered by his child caused by exceedingly hot water from a bathroom faucet with no mixer valve.

Implied warranty of merchantability
A warranty representing to the buyer that merchandise is reasonably fit for the general purpose for which it was manufactured and sold.

Originally, the warranty principle applied only to bodily injury cases, primarily because liability was based on the likelihood that the defect would cause severe injury, an essential element of earlier cases. Later, the warranty principle expanded to cover property damage arising out of defects in product design.

The Uniform Commercial Code (UCC) applies the implied warranty of merchantability,[4] to a merchant-seller's sales of goods. Generally, the merchant-seller warrants that the goods meet the standards of the trade, are fit for the ordinary purposes for which such goods are used, and conform to representations made on the container or label, if any. The seller concept now includes suppliers, those who supply products for value (consideration).

Strict Liability and Negligence

Products liability cases can be based on negligence, on strict liability, or on both. Products liability lawsuits may involve both liability for harm caused by the product and liability for harm resulting from a service or process. Generally, if only a service or process is involved, the suit must be based on negligence. If the suit concerns a product, or a combination of product and service or process, then the suit can be based on either negligence or strict liability. Courts define products to include advertising materials, labels, computer software, instruction manuals, and aircraft instrument landing charts.

In a negligence case, the plaintiff must prove that the manufacturer failed to use reasonable care in designing or manufacturing the product that caused the injury. Negligence focuses on the reasonableness of the manufacturer's conduct.

As previously discussed, strict liability is the breach of an absolute duty to make something safe, and it applies most often to ultrahazardous activities or products. Proof of either negligence or an intent to harm is not required. The manufacturer's conduct is irrelevant, and the focus is on the product itself. In a products liability lawsuit based on strict liability, the plaintiff must prove the following five elements:

1. The seller was in the business of selling products.
2. The product had a defect that made it unreasonably dangerous, meaning dangerous to an extent beyond that which would be contemplated by the ordinary user who has common knowledge about the product. (Not all courts require this element.)
3. The product was dangerously defective when it left the manufacturer's or seller's custody or control.
4. The defect was the proximate cause of the plaintiff's injury.
5. The product was expected to and did reach the consumer without substantial change in condition.

The manufacturer could have used the utmost care in making the product. However, if, in fact, the product was unsafe, liability exists under the doctrine of strict liability.

As in negligence cases, proximate cause is a necessary element of a products liability suit. A plaintiff must establish not only that the defective product caused the injury, but also that it was the defect itself that caused the injury. A product containing a defect might injure a person even though the defect itself had no part in the injury. For example, a chain saw might have a defective guard, but if the defendant drops a nonoperating saw on the plaintiff's foot, the defect does not cause the injury. Here, the plaintiff may sue based on negligence but not on strict liability.

Proximate cause is also important when independent, intervening causes may have occurred between the time the product left the defendant's possession and the time of the injury. Thus, a manufacturer who has placed a defective product on the market is not liable for damage if something occurred after the product left the manufacturer that actually caused the plaintiff's injury. For example, if a machine-shop owner puts a defective machine back in operation with no changes after the manufacturer has reported that a safety device is available to remedy the defect, then the machine-shop owner has performed an independent, intervening act that insulates the manufacturer from liability.

Therefore, the time of the existence of the defect relates to proximate cause. The seller's liability arises at the time of the product's sale. A manufacturer is not liable for injury from a defect that occurred after the product has left the manufacturer's possession.

Types of Product Defects

Generally speaking, the following three major types of product defect can lead to liability suits:

1. *Defect in manufacture or assembly.* The product does not correspond to the original design.
2. *Defect in design.* The product corresponds to the design, and the manufacturer built the product exactly as intended, but the design itself is faulty, and that produces injury. The defendant is liable because of a design fault incorporated into all products of the same kind and not just because of one particular item that injured the plaintiff.
3. *Failure to warn.* The product is defective in neither design nor manufacture, but it has some inherent danger about which the manufacturer has failed to give proper warning.

Defect in manufacture or assembly usually involves the use of faulty materials or errors in putting a product together. Defect in manufacture is the simplest type of strict liability to prove because improper manufacture or assembly of the product, in itself, is a defect. Whether the product is unreasonably dangerous is not an issue, because the fact that it has caused injury demonstrates that it was dangerous or defective.

In some cases, the product is manufactured correctly according to the design, but the design is defective. Courts vary considerably in decisions about faulty design cases. Generally, a seller is liable for injuries caused by a product if, at the time of sale, it is not fit and safe for its intended or reasonably foreseeable use and is unreasonably dangerous. If the defect is not latent or hidden, but is open and obvious, the product is not unreasonably dangerous and strict liability does not apply.

Several states have eliminated the unreasonably dangerous requirement and replaced it with one of the following:

- A product is defective if it does not meet the consumer's reasonable expectations.
- A product is defective if it lacks any element that would make it safe.

A manufacturer must consider a product's safety within the constraints of cost, efficiency, weight, and style. Thus, a lawnmower could be so safe that it could not cut grass adequately, or an auto could be fully crash-resistant but thirty feet long or extremely heavy. Many courts now compare the practicality of selling a product with a certain level of safety features against the magnitude of the risk associated with that level of safety features.

Many design defect cases arise out of defective safety devices or failure to install safety devices. The manufacturer is strictly liable only if the failure made the product unreasonably dangerous in normal use. Common defects include lack of guards or defective guards on machines such as punch presses, metal shears, or pizza dough rollers. The manufacturer cannot escape the duty to install guards by alleging that the equipment user should have installed them.

Another area of design defect suits is automobile design. For example, the placement of the gasoline tank, the steering wheel, and other components can cause injury following collisions. Originally, courts held that a collision was not a normal use of a car, and manufacturers did not have to design their products in anticipation of an abnormal use. However, many courts later held that because collisions are common and foreseeable, manufacturers should take reasonable steps to avoid injury to occupants in the case of a collision.

Even if a product is defective in neither assembly nor design, it can still be the basis for liability if the manufacturer has failed to warn of the danger of the product. A manufacturer has a duty to warn when it would be unreasonably dangerous to market a product without a warning. A manufacturer should consider the following three factors in this regard:

1. Degree of the danger
2. Knowledge of the danger
3. Foreseeability of dangerous use

The degree of danger varies with products. A gun, for example, has a higher degree of danger than an automobile.

In failure-to-warn cases, the standard for manufacturers' liability is the same under both negligence and strict liability. Warnings must be given about all dangers associated with the product about which the manufacturer knows, or should know; that is, all foreseeable dangers. To hold a manufacturer liable for the unknown, unforeseeable potential for danger of a product would amount to absolute liability, leaving the manufacturer with no defenses in a suit.

The necessity for a warning creates a host of collateral problems, including the adequacy of the warning and advice about possible side effects. The adequacy of a printed warning can depend on its size, shape, place, color, and use of pictographs or words. The duty to warn extends to all foreseeable users. Therefore, picture symbols in place of words might be necessary if the ultimate user could be illiterate or unfamiliar with the language.

A warning is required when a product has a potential for danger not generally known to the public or, if known, is one that the user would not readily expect to find in the product. The seller must have actual knowledge of the danger or should reasonably know of the danger. Failure to give adequate warning under such conditions renders the product defective for strict liability. A seller who gives a warning can reasonably assume that the user will follow it, and a product bearing an adequate warning is not defective or unreasonably dangerous.

The duty to warn is particularly applicable to drugs. The test for drugs is whether the danger was foreseeable by a person using ordinary care, considering the number of persons who might use the product. Thus, an allergic reaction to drugs frequently falls outside the strict liability area when it is not foreseeable by the manufacturer.

Manufacturers have been liable for failure to warn that a certain type of hammer is likely to become brittle with use and thus be more susceptible to chipping, or that a car tire is likely to fail if more than six passengers ride in a nine-passenger station wagon.

Potentially Liable Parties

Just as major types of product defects lead to liability suits, major types of entities are subject to strict liability suits for products. Strict liability generally applies to entities that engage in the business of selling products. This includes the manufacturer. Most courts also include distributors, wholesalers, and retailers, but not those who make an occasional sale of a product outside the regular course of business. For example, a hardware store might offer holiday decorations and candies for sale, but those are not regular items of a hardware business.

Many courts have expanded the strict liability in sales to include bailors and lessors. For example, the lessor of a car with defective brakes may be strictly liable. Most jurisdictions accepting this expansion recognize a distinction between a lessor or bailor engaged in a regular leasing business, such as a rental car agency, and those who lease less frequently. This is consistent with the application of strict liability to those who make an occasional sale of a product outside the regular course of business. At least one state has extended strict liability to those using products in a service business, such as a beauty salon.

One significant extension of strict liability in many jurisdictions has been to builders and contractors. Courts have reasoned that the rationale for strict liability for defective product manufacturers is equally applicable to builders and contractors. For example, courts have held contractors strictly liable for installing a faulty hot water heater that caused a fire; for installing a defective heating system that required replacement; and even for failing to compact dirt in a filled lot on which a builder constructed a house, which later caused building damage.

Parties Protected

Strict liability for products protects certain types of people. Originally, strict liability permitted the injured buyer of a defective article to recover from the manufacturer without having to prove negligence. Alternatively, that buyer could circumvent contractual liability defenses, such as lack of a contractual relationship (privity), warranty disclaimer, or failure to notify the manufacturer promptly of a breach of warranty. The courts had little trouble eliminating the privity requirement because, as a result of changes in distribution methods, few manufacturers sell directly to the ultimate buyer. Protection can extend to the ultimate user or consumer, which can include the ultimate buyer, but the ultimate buyer might be different than the ultimate user or consumer. The ultimate user or consumer may include a person who has received the product as a gift or a buyer's family member, for example. However, the application of strict liability varies regarding nonusers, such as bystanders or other strangers the defective product might injure.

Today, most courts hold that, at least regarding suits against sellers, any nonuser, such as a bystander, may assert strict liability. For example, a person injured by the explosion of a companion's defective shotgun can assert strict liability. A special situation arises when a vehicle with a defect is struck by a second vehicle, injuring a passenger in the first vehicle. If the accident was the result of a defect in the first vehicle, most courts allow the injured party to assert strict liability against the manufacturer of the first vehicle. However, a few courts do not allow the application of strict liability.

In determining who can sue, either in negligence or in strict liability, most courts use the traditional foreseeability test. Anyone who could foreseeably have been injured by the product can sue. Because a plaintiff must allege specific injuries, courts generally do not permit class action suits in products liability cases.

Further restriction is placed on strict liability when plaintiffs are large corporations. The public policy supporting strict liability is to protect the individual consumer and to allocate the loss to the party best able to bear the loss. When the plaintiff is a large corporation, such protection is not necessary. Therefore, the plaintiffs can sue for negligence only.

Defenses

Several defenses are available for both negligence and strict liability for products. Some are complete defenses, meaning that they totally defeat plaintiffs' claims, while others merely reduce damages. Some of the defenses are as follows:

State of the art
The highest level of pertinent product scientific knowability, development, and technical knowledge existing at the time of a product's manufacture.

Scientific knowability
The technological feasibility of producing a safer product based on existing scientific knowledge.

- *State of the art defense.* The defendant claims that its product was safe according to the state of the art at the time the product was made. **State of the art** is the highest level of pertinent product scientific knowability, development, and technical knowledge existing at the time of a product's manufacture. This standard is more concise than the standard of a product's conformity with traditional industry customs and practices. **Scientific knowability** means the technological feasibility of producing a safer product based on existing scientific knowledge. If no indication of danger or no technique for obtaining knowledge of such danger exists, the manufacturer has no reason to prevent manufacture of the product. The state-of-the-art defense is not a complete defense. Additional evidence must be introduced to justify placing the product on the market.

- *Compliance with statutes and regulations defense.* Compliance with statutes and regulations (such as industrial safety codes) is not a conclusive defense against negligence or product defect. Evidence can show that a reasonable manufacturer could have taken additional precautions.

- *Compliance with product specifications defense.* Manufacturers frequently make products to conform to specifications established by buyers or others. In negligence suits, a manufacturer is generally not liable for products built to someone else's specifications unless the defect is sufficiently obvious to alert the manufacturer to the potential for harm. Third parties in such cases should sue the one who prepared the specifications.

- *Open and obvious danger defense.* A manufacturer has no duty to warn or take other precautions regarding a common, open, and obvious propensity of the product. Hazards connected with knives, guns, and gasoline, for example, are well known so that warnings would be superfluous.

- *Plaintiff's knowledge defense.* If the person who uses the product has knowledge of the product that is equal to the manufacturer's knowledge, the manufacturer has no duty to warn.

Passive negligence
A plaintiff's failure to discover a product defect or to guard against a possible defect.

Active negligence, or assumption of risk
A plaintiff's voluntary use of a defective product with knowledge of the potential danger resulting from the defect.

- *Assumption of risk defense.* As in general negligence cases, assumption of risk is a defense to a strict liability suit. The defendant asserts that the person using the product has taken on the risk of loss, injury, or damage. In considering this defense, most courts distinguish between active and passive negligence. **Passive negligence** is the plaintiff's failure to discover a product defect or to guard against a possible defect. Most courts hold that passive negligence does not bar recovery. **Active negligence**, or **assumption of risk**, applies when a person knows of the potential danger resulting from a product defect but voluntarily and unreasonably proceeds to use the product. For example, a worker who knows that a substance can burn skin but does not use protective gloves cannot sue successfully. The defendant has the burden of proving that the plaintiff knew of the defect or danger. Many states allow a comparative negligence defense in strict liability suits.

- *Misuse of product defense.* Closely akin to active negligence is product misuse or abnormal use. For example, failing to follow directions on the container or attempting to open a glass container by tapping it against a sink constitutes sufficient misuse or abnormal use to deny recovery for any resulting injury. In these cases, the plaintiff must negate misuse or abnormal use because the defendant's liability is based on the product's being defective. The plaintiff must therefore prove that the product was used in an appropriate and foreseeable manner to establish the defect.

- *Alteration of product defense.* The manufacturer is usually not liable for post-sale modifications for two reasons: (1) by definition, liability arises only for conditions as of time of sale, and (2) such modifications can be independent, intervening acts, thus breaking the chain of causation. Therefore, most courts hold that third-party alterations, no matter how foreseeable, do not create liability.

- *Post-accident remedial measures defense.* A federal court rule prohibits a plaintiff from introducing evidence of measures taken after an event that, if taken before the event, would have made it less likely to happen. Such measures include product recalls, warning letters, design changes, and changes in warnings. One reason for this rule is that use of such evidence to prove negligence would discourage manufacturers from making improvements while suits are pending. Many state courts follow the federal rule. Some apply it only in negligence suits and not in strict liability suits and some do not apply it at all. Courts also have admitted such evidence for other purposes, such as to show that the defect occurred while the product was still in the manufacturer's possession.

- *Written disclaimer defense.* Manufacturers sometimes attempt to use written disclaimers accompanying products in defense of strict liability suits, sometimes in UCC breach of warranty situations. However, in strict liability suits, the courts, almost without exception, have rejected the validity of disclaimers.

Damages

A plaintiff can recover damages for bodily injury via strict liability, and several jurisdictions permit strict liability in a wrongful death suit. A plaintiff can also recover punitive damages in a strict liability suit.

Most jurisdictions also permit strict liability recovery for property damage in cases of strict liability for physical damage to property from such causes as fires or explosions arising out of product defects. An example is recovery for fire damage to a dwelling caused by a defective television set.

A defect that results only in loss of the product's use, or loss of profits, produces consequential commercial loss, for which a plaintiff may or may not be able to recover. Most jurisdictions deny recovery for pure consequential economic loss in strict liability suits. Economic losses are those resulting from the inability of a product to perform its intended function because of defects. Economic losses usually arise from commercial transactions rather than from tort injuries. For example, if Martha buys a truck but cannot use it in her business because of a defect, she cannot sue for economic loss under strict liability. Similarly, a party using an ineffective crop chemical cannot sue under strict liability to recover for losses resulting from crop failure.

TOXIC TORTS AND ENVIRONMENTAL DAMAGE CLAIMS

Toxic tort
A civil wrong arising from exposure to a toxic substance.

The related concepts of toxic torts and environmental law represent a rapidly expanding and changing area of the law. A **toxic tort** is a civil wrong arising from exposure to a toxic substance, such as asbestos, radiation, or hazardous waste. Toxic torts are similar in many respects to products liability suits. The name "toxic tort" does not refer to a specific tort, but to several types of tort suits that can arise from the use of toxic substances.

The additional factor present in toxic torts is that, in many instances, liability is established by statute rather than by common law. Further, in many of these lawsuits, a governmental agency is a party and a private-party plaintiff may be involved.

Environmental law
The body of law that deals with the environment's maintenance and protection.

Environmental law deals with the maintenance and protection of the environment and includes measures to prevent environmental damage, such as requirements for environmental-impact statements, and measures to assign liability and provide cleanup for incidents resulting in environmental damage. Because most environmental suits involve governmental agencies as enforcers, environmental law is intertwined with administrative law.

Toxic tort lawsuits seek compensation for damages to individuals caused by toxic substances. As in all tort cases, a plaintiff in a toxic tort case must prove that the defendant breached a duty, that the breach caused injury or loss to the plaintiff, and that the loss resulted in actual damages.

Environmental suits arise from laws to protect the general public, for example a suit brought to clean up a waste site. In these suits, an administrative agency first determines whether a party is liable for damages, such as cleanup costs under a statutory regulation. Findings in those lawsuits relate more to whether the defendant violated a law than to whether the defendant actually has caused damage to someone. Both administrative agencies and courts may at times equate violation of regulatory statutes with proof of failure to discharge a duty of care that is the basis of tort liability.

Statutes and Common Law

Myriad federal and state statutes and regulations seek to prevent an unreasonable risk of bodily injury and environmental damage. Some environmental laws specifically aim to clean up current polluted sites, while others attempt to prevent pollution. Although the statutes vary in subject matter, they share some qualities. For instance, most of the environmental statutes have adopted the common-law concept of strict liability that a party may be held liable without evidence or proof of negligence or fault.[5]

The statute most often involved in environmental litigation, either directly or indirectly, is the Comprehensive Environmental Response, Compensation, and Liability Act (CERCLA). CERCLA's primary purpose is the cleanup of hazardous waste disposal sites. CERCLA established a **Superfund** to study and remediate hazardous waste sites listed on the National Priority List (NPL). This fund subsequently increased in dollar amounts under the Superfund Amendments and Reauthorization Act of 1986 (SARA). The NPL usually contains over 1,000 sites.

CERCLA imposes liability on the following four types of entities:

1.   Current owners and operators of hazardous waste facilities

2.   Past owners or operators of hazardous waste facilities

3.   Generators of hazardous waste

4.   Transporters of hazardous waste

Under CERCLA, the Environmental Protection Agency (EPA), the federal agency responsible for administering Superfund cleanup, can take action upon a release or threatened release of hazardous substances or other pollutants or contaminants into the environment. The EPA can order the cleanup of a site or can undertake the cleanup work itself and file a suit to recover the costs. In addition to the costs of removal or remedial action, the EPA can recover other necessary costs of response and damages for injury to or destruction of natural resources.

Once it has determined that cleanup of a site is necessary, or sometimes after it has started cleanup, the EPA sends out letters to all **potentially responsible parties (PRPs)**, or those parties the law defines as having potential liability and the duty to clean up the site. Such a letter is typically the first notice that a PRP receives of responsibility for site cleanup.

Other important federal environmental statutes are the following:

*   The Federal Insecticide, Fungicide, and Rodenticide Act (FIFRA), which regulates pesticides[6]

*   The Clean Air Act, which sets national emission standards for hazardous air pollutants[7]

Superfund
A program established by the Comprehensive Environmental Response, Compensation, and Liability Act (CERCLA) to study and remediate hazardous waste sites listed on the National Priority List (NPL).

Potentially responsible parties (PRPs)
Those parties CERCLA defines as having potential liability and the duty to clean up a Superfund site.

- The Federal Water Pollution Control Act (Clean Water Act), which regulates discharges into the waters of the United States[8]
- The Toxic Substances Control Act (TSCA), which regulates the testing, manufacturing, and distribution of toxic substances[9]
- The Resource Conservation and Recovery Act (RCRA), which regulates treating, handling, storing, and disposing of hazardous wastes and creates a "cradle-to-grave" system for hazardous wastes[10]

Most states have enacted statutes similar to the federal ones. In some cases the state statutes are stricter than their federal counterparts, and state authorities are generally stricter and more aggressive in their enforcement efforts. In New Jersey, for instance, the Environmental Clean-Up Responsibilities Act (ECRA),[11] prohibits "industrial establishments" from selling, transferring, or closing industrial property until the New Jersey Department of Environmental Protection is satisfied that it has been cleaned up.

Private plaintiffs who alleged personal injury or property damage as a result of exposure to hazardous substances have several common-law causes of action, such as nuisance, trespass, negligence, and strict liability. In addition, many federal and state statutes contain citizen suit provisions, which allow private plaintiffs to sue under those statutes.

Insurance Coverage

Because of potentially staggering pollution cleanup costs and personal injury judgments, insureds examine both current and expired insurance policies for coverage for toxic tort damages. Often, insurance is the only source of funds for cleanup. Therefore, some courts have interpreted insurance policies as providing coverage when insurers did not intend it. Most environmental liability coverage disputes generate claims under a commercial general liability (CGL) policy, although some other policies potentially provide coverage for environmental liabilities. A **commercial general liability (CGL) policy** is insurance that covers many of the common liability loss exposures faced by an organization, including its premises, operations, and products liability loss exposures.

Commercial general liability (CGL) policy
Insurance that covers many of the common liability loss exposures faced by an organization, including its premises, operations, and products liability loss exposures.

Environmental coverage issues commonly arise in several ways, as the following example illustrates. Various state laws govern insurance policies and are critical to determining these complex issues. Policy language is also an important factor.

Coverage Applications

Occurrence-based policy
Insurance policy that provides coverage for occurrences that happen within the policy period even though the policy may have expired.

Most CGL policies involved in environmental litigation are **occurrence-based policies**, which provide coverage for occurrences happening within the policy period even though the policy might have expired and the events creating claims occurred many years previously. The following are typical issues regarding coverage applicability:

Example: Environmental Coverage Issue

A company generated hazardous waste and paid a transporter to dispose of the waste at a local landfill. For thirty years, the waste migrated through the ground, contaminating the local water supply and neighboring properties. Several nearby residents got cancer from drinking the contaminated water. Various insurance policies covered the landfill owner, the company that deposited the waste in the landfill, and the hazardous waste transporter during a forty-year period.

In response to neighbors' complaints, the government closed the landfill and started a cleanup. The government then informed the landfill owner, the company that deposited the waste in the landfill, and the hazardous waste transporter that they were all liable for the cleanup costs. The neighboring landowners sued all three of these parties for damage to their property, and local residents also sued for personal injuries from drinking the contaminated water. The three defendant organizations, in turn, sued all insurers that had insured them during the thirty years, seeking a court determination that coverage applied to all the claims.

These facts raise important issues, including the following:

- Whether coverage applies for the property damage and the bodily injury

- Whether the government's claims for cleanup costs constitute "property damage" within the meaning of the applicable policies

- Whether any policy conditions or exclusions bar coverage

- *Whether the occurrence took place during the policy period.* A major issue in environmental insurance coverage lawsuits is whether bodily injury or property damage occurred during the policy period. Manifestation of damage might not occur for many years, even decades, after exposure to a harmful substance. Additionally, several insurance policies might have covered an insured during the applicable time periods.

- *Whether the occurrence was expected or intended.* The CGL policy covers only bodily injury or property damage the insured neither expected nor intended. Some courts apply a subjective standard under which the insured must have expected or intended the specific bodily injury or property damage giving rise to the claim for the exclusion to apply. Most courts, however, apply an objective standard under which the exclusion would apply if a reasonable person would have expected or intended that the bodily injury or property damage occur.

- *Whether the insured must pay cleanup costs.* A CGL policy covers those sums that the insured is legally required to pay as damages, but policies generally do not define the term "damages." The majority of courts hold that cleanup costs are not damages.

Policy Exclusions

Several common insurance policy conditions and exclusions, such as the owned property and pollution provisions, have been important in environmental insurance coverage disputes. Under owned property provisions, a liability policy protects an insured against liability to a third party and usually excludes coverage for bodily injury to the insured or damage to the insured's property. Insurers rely on this exclusion to deny coverage for the cost of cleaning up the insured's own property. Some courts have agreed; others have not. Courts may find that the exclusion does not bar coverage in cases involving an immediate or imminent threat of off-site contamination or a demonstration of a present injury.

Many CGL pollution exclusions preclude coverage except for discharge of contaminants or pollutants that are "sudden and accidental," a phrase interpreted in numerous lawsuits. Insurers usually claim that "sudden" connotes time and that the pollution must occur quickly or abruptly, as well as accidentally. Insureds typically argue that "sudden and accidental" means unexpected and unintended and that, even if the pollution occurred over a period of years, it does not fall within the exclusion if the damage was unexpected and unintended.

In response to litigation, most insurers have amended their CGL policies to contain an absolute pollution exclusion, applicable regardless of whether the insured's actions were accidental or intentional. Most courts have upheld this clause.

TORT LITIGATION

Several important concepts apply to most tort litigation. Among the concepts are the following:

- Damages
- Liability concepts
- Statutes of limitations and repose

Damages

To bring a tort suit, a plaintiff must prove resulting injury or loss sufficient for a court to impose damages. When a tort is proved, the law presumes that the plaintiff suffered damages. The purpose of awarding damages in a tort suit is to recompense the injured party and not to punish the tortfeasor. Punitive damages are an exception to this rule.

Nominal damages
A small sum awarded by a court to acknowledge that the plaintiff has suffered a legal wrong, but that the harm does not warrant substantial monetary relief.

In many instances, the law infers damage merely from the occurrence of the act, and a court awards nominal damages only to establish a right. **Nominal damages** are a small sum a court awards when the plaintiff has suffered a legal wrong with no substantial harm to justify compensation. To illustrate, when one person trespasses on another's property, the law presumes damages. As a practical matter, however, the amount of actual damage to the property might be very small or nonexistent, hence the term "nominal." Nevertheless, the plaintiff is entitled to nominal damages, which can be as small as one dollar, to justify the tort claim.

Types of Damages

Damages are usually monetary. Juries determine the amount of damages based on the facts of the case. In the usual suit, the plaintiff is entitled to those damages proximately caused by the injury, that is, that naturally result from the injury, whether or not the defendant could reasonably have foreseen the damage. In this respect, they differ from damages in a contract suit, which are limited to those that the parties would reasonably foresee.

In the usual tort suit, the award is for compensatory damages, discussed in a previous chapter. Compensatory damages, as the term implies, are the amount required to compensate the plaintiff for the bodily injury or property damage. These damages include both special and general damages.

Special damages (sometimes called particular damages) are for actual losses that a plaintiff claims resulted from a defendant's wrongful act. For damaged property, special damages include the amount expended to restore the property. For bodily injury, they include hospital and doctor bills and related expenses. **Loss of wages and earnings** includes any loss of income directly related to the tort.

General damages (also called direct damages or necessary damages) are compensatory damages that do not have an economic value and that are presumed to follow from the type of wrong claimed by the plaintiff. A plaintiff need not specifically claim or prove them. General damages may include compensation for pain and suffering; disfigurement; and loss of a limb, sight, or hearing, as well as emotional distress. **Pain and suffering** usually means physical pain, including that not connected to a physical injury. Many physical injuries leave some permanent effect such as scar tissue, torn muscles, and limited use of limbs. The injured person is entitled to have any future effect of permanent injuries considered in evaluating damages.

General damages also include damages for **emotional distress**, which compensate for a highly unpleasant mental reaction resulting from another person's conduct. Courts originally awarded them as an element of damages for another, underlying tort.

Damages for bad faith, another type of general damages, are similar to damages for emotional distress. Courts originally awarded **bad-faith damages** as an element of damages in suits for other, underlying torts. Bad faith, and bad-faith damages, arise when the defendant is liable for unreasonable conduct engaged in either with knowledge that it was unreasonable or with complete disregard of the fact that it was. Bad-faith damages also arise in connection with the independent tort of outrage. Bad faith can also result in punitive damages.

Special damages
Compensatory damages for actual losses that the plaintiff claims resulted from the defendant's wrongful act.

Loss of wages and earnings
The compensatory damages to compensate a plaintiff for any loss of income directly related to a tort.

General damages
Compensatory damages that do not have an economic value and that are presumed to follow from the type of wrong claimed by the plaintiff.

Pain and suffering
Physical pain, including that not connected to a physical injury.

Emotional distress
A highly unpleasant mental reaction resulting from another person's conduct for which a court can award damages.

Bad-faith damages
The damages awarded by a court when the defendant has engaged in unreasonable conduct either with knowledge that it is unreasonable or with complete disregard of the fact that it is unreasonable.

Usually the plaintiff in a tort suit is entitled to only compensatory damages. However, just as in contract law, in certain cases, courts may assess punitive damages, or exemplary damages. These damages punish and make an example of the defendant, thereby deterring the defendant and others from committing similar acts. The law does not intend these damages as compensation to the plaintiff.

Ordinary negligence or bad faith does not support a claim for punitive damages. A court can award punitive damages only in the following situations:

• The defendant actually intended to cause harm.
• The defendant acted oppressively, maliciously, or fraudulently.

These situations collectively fall under the term "outrageous conduct." Outrageous conduct can consist of fraud, malice, gross negligence, or oppression. A court can find it when a defendant commits a wrongful act with a motive to harm or so recklessly as to imply a disregard for social obligations; or if the defendant shows such willful misconduct or lack of care as to raise a presumption of the defendant's conscious indifference to the consequences.

Some courts do not require actual proof of malice or intent to cause harm but accept evidence of reckless disregard of the plaintiff's rights or interests as being sufficient. Although actual fraud is frequently difficult to prove, many courts accept a showing of deceit, which requires proof only that the defendant never intended to fulfill its obligation. A plaintiff can use this concept in breach of warranty suits or similar suits in tort founded on a contractual relationship.

To assess punitive damages, courts usually consider the following three factors:

1. Nature of the defendant's actions
2. Size of the defendant's assets
3. Purpose of punitive damages

The wealthier the defendant, the larger the punitive damages award, producing an incongruous result from the plaintiff's standpoint. If a wealthy defendant injures one plaintiff, but a less wealthy defendant injures another plaintiff, and both plaintiffs sustain the same compensatory damages, the one injured by the wealthier defendant can receive far more compensation in a judgment than the other. However, even in the same state, courts are not consistent in their approaches to punitive damages.

Generally, employers, or principals, are liable for punitive damages if they directed or ratified acts of employees or agents with knowledge of the malice, fraud, or oppression. A few courts have not held principals liable if they have not given direction to or ratified the acts in question.

Another type of damages is awarded in cases of wrongful death. Wrongful death is in a different category from the ordinary claim for bodily injury, and damages can vary depending on the relationship of the deceased to the claimant. Damages can compensate for lost earnings or for mental anguish, or they can be punitive. At common law, when an injured person died, any right to sue had died with the person. For example, a person might live for several months after sustaining an injury, incurring large expenses and suffering much pain from the injury, but at death the right to sue terminates. Likewise, if the tortfeasor died, the right to sue also ended. This inequity led to the enactment of survival statutes, under which a cause of action for an injury can survive after the injured person's death.

A typical survival statute might read as follows: "All causes of action or proceedings, real or personal, except suits for slander or libel, shall survive the death of one or more joint plaintiffs or defendants."

Survival statutes preserve the right of a person's estate to recover damages that person sustained between the time of injury and death. They permit recovery of compensatory damages, including general damages. They do not include any damages for shortening the person's life.

Survival statute
A statute that preserves the right of a person's estate to recover damages that person sustained between the time of injury and death.

If death is instantaneous, then a court will not award survival damages. However, if the person lives even a second or a minute after an injury, the estate can allege sufficient pain and suffering to support the suit. Any damages recovered pass into the person's estate.

In recent years, jury awards for general damages have grown so large that legislatures have made a concentrated effort to limit them, usually by placing a dollar limit, or cap, on some types of general damages. Many state statutes limiting damages apply only to medical malpractice, but several now apply more broadly.

Liability Concepts

To obtain a relief from a court, an injured person must not only be ready to prove damage suffered, but must also choose whom to sue and develop a theory of liability to present to the court. This section discusses the following with regard to tort liability concepts:

- Joint tortfeasors
- Expanded liability concepts
- Tortfeasor's capacity
- Vicarious liability
- Good Samaritan issues
- Class actions and mass tort litigation

Joint Tortfeasors

When an injury or loss results from negligence involving more than one person, issues of joint liability arise. Generally, all people participating in the act of committing a tort are jointly (together) and severally (individually) liable. Participation occurs by being an active contributor, either in person or through an agent or employee; by acting; by ratifying or permitting the act; or by advising about the act.

When two or more persons owe a common duty to a third party and, by a common act of neglect of this duty, cause injury to the third party, a joint tort has occurred. Additionally, when the separate negligent acts of two or more people come together to produce a single indivisible injury, a joint tort has occurred. For example, the drivers of two cars racing on a highway, then colliding and injuring a third person, results in a joint tort.

Tortious acts that are sequential or that involve some aspect of vicarious liability can complicate determination of liability. Also, certain relationships can create a joint tort. For example, employers are liable for the torts of their employees committed while in the scope of their employment; the employee is also liable. Similarly, each partner is jointly liable for the torts of all other partners.

Joint tortfeasors
Two or more parties who are jointly responsible for committing a tort.

Two or more parties who are jointly responsible for committing a tort are called **joint tortfeasors**. Under common law, joint tortfeasors were jointly and severally liable for the full amount of the damages. Therefore, the plaintiff could proceed against all tortfeasors jointly or against any number of them. If a plaintiff sued only one tortfeasor, that defendant could not use as a defense the fact that the plaintiff did not include the others in the suit. Each tortfeasor was responsible for the whole tort regardless of degree of participation in the tort. About half the states have abolished this rule and today do not hold a joint tortfeasor automatically liable for all of a plaintiff's damages. This change came in response to increased litigation against "deep-pocket" defendants who often had little role in causing plaintiffs' injuries but had to pay entire damage awards.

Traditionally, in earlier common law, a lone defendant in a suit could not compel a plaintiff to include other tortfeasors jointly in the suit. The plaintiff was entitled to bring individual suits against each tortfeasor, and the only limitation was a right to only one recovery for damages. In the case of successive suits, any defendant could show that the plaintiff had received the full amount of the loss from prior suits.

At common law, a release of one joint tortfeasor released all joint tortfeasors, even if the release specifically prohibited release of the other tortfeasors. Although this rule still applies in several states, it has fallen into disfavor. Most states, either by court decision or legislation, have provided that, when a plaintiff settles with one joint tortfeasor, a pro rata credit goes to the other joint tortfeasor if the intent of the agreement was to release only one tortfeasor and not to operate as a full release.

Many states have adopted the Uniform Contribution Among Joint Tort Feasors Act (UCAJTFA). UCAJTFA provides that, when two or more persons become jointly or severally liable in tort for the same injury or damage, or for the same wrongful death, they have a right of contribution among them even though the plaintiff has not recovered judgment against all or any of them. **Contribution** is the right of a tortfeasor who has paid more than his or her proportionate share of damages to collect from other tortfeasors responsible for the same tort. The act creates rights in favor of tortfeasors who have paid more than their pro rata share of their joint liability up to the amount of the excess. It provides that, in assessing pro rata liability, the relative degree of fault is not a consideration.

Under the UCAJTFA, the plaintiff can release one or more defendants without releasing the others, if it is a good-faith release, indicating an intent only to release part, not all, of the liability and that the payment is in full compensation. What constitutes good faith, particularly if the released defendant's payment appears nominal, is a matter of frequent dispute in these cases.

The harshness of the UCAJTFA has led to legal maneuvers to mitigate its effects. In some states that have not adopted the UCAJTFA, courts are creating a doctrine of primary and secondary liability, whereby the entire loss can shift from the tortfeasor compelled to pay the loss to the tortfeasor who should rightfully pay it. Courts apply this doctrine in so-called active-passive negligence situations, when the person whose negligence was passive can recover from another joint tortfeasor whose negligence was active. Thus, when one person is obviously the primary tortfeasor, but another is held liable for the damages, the courts have found a contract (either express or implied) of indemnification and have permitted the tortfeasor who is secondarily liable to recover.

The same doctrine applies in strict liability situations in which a retailer who has had to pay full damages can recover indemnity from the manufacturer. This places the burden on the manufacturer to avoid putting a defective product into the stream of commerce.

The concepts of active-passive negligence and many of the expanded liability concepts involve recovery under the doctrine of indemnification rather than under the doctrine of contribution. Indemnification involves shifting the entire burden of the damages from one tortfeasor to another. If a court allows indemnification, the tortfeasor who paid can recover the full amount of the judgment.

On the other hand, tortfeasors' contribution to indemnification in active-passive negligence suits is based on the common, although not necessarily equal, liability of two or more tortfeasors for the same injury or damage. It requires each tortfeasor to pay a proportionate share of the damages. A tortfeasor who has paid the entire judgment can recover only a portion of the judgment from the other tortfeasors because that person must still bear a share of the judgment.

As discussed, the UCAJTFA provides that, in assessing liability, the relative degree of fault cannot be a factor. This provision is counter to the concept of comparative negligence, as illustrated by the following example. (Comparative negligence allocates liability proportionate to a tortfeasor's portion of negligence, while contribution is a tortfeasor's right to collect damages he or she has

Contribution
The right of a tortfeasor who has paid more than his or her proportionate share of the damages to collect from other tortfeasors responsible for the same tort.

paid from other tortfeasors according to their proportionate obligations resulting from their negligence.)

Several states have abolished the concept of joint liability entirely and have adopted several liability only. Other states have adopted modifications, such as providing that joint liability applies only when the plaintiff's fault is less than the respective defendant's, or only when the defendant is at least a certain percent at fault, for example, 25 percent or 50 percent at fault. Several of these laws still retain the concept of joint liability for certain areas, such as product liability, toxic torts, or auto liability.

Example: Multiple-Party Degrees of Fault

Assume a court finds three parties partially at fault for an intersection accident as follows:

Party	Degree of Fault
Jane (plaintiff)	20 percent
Cathy (other driver)	70 percent
Bill (municipality)	10 percent

At the end of trial, the court awards a judgment for $100,000 and finds that Cathy is bankrupt. Under the UCAJTFA, however, Bill, though less negligent than the plaintiff, would be liable for 80 percent of the judgment.

Next, alter the facts slightly and assume that Cathy, rather than being bankrupt, makes a separate settlement with Jane for $10,000. Bill, although only 10 percent at fault, then becomes liable for the remaining $70,000 of the judgment. A combination of the concepts of joint liability and comparative negligence creates these anomalies. Because they produce such obviously inequitable results, efforts to limit joint and several liability have ensued.

Expanded Liability Concepts

A basic tort law principle is that the plaintiff not only must prove injury but also that a specific defendant caused the injury. For example, a person hit by an unidentifiable object from the sky cannot sue all the airlines that have flown in the area because one of them probably caused the injury. The injured person must prove which airline dropped the object. Because of mass production, many goods are not traceable to specific producers, and the problem is even more acute because it is usually impossible to identify which manufacturer produced the product that harmed an individual.

To help injured parties sue successfully, some courts have adopted expanded liability concepts. While these concepts have generally applied to products liability situations, they also can apply to other situations. Types of expanded liability concepts include the following:

- **Enterprise liability**, or **industry-wide liability**, is liability imposed on each member of an industry responsible for manufacturing a harmful or defective product. It is allotted by each manufacturer's market share of the industry. It was probably the first expanded liability concept. Under this concept, a limited number of entities engage in like businesses or enterprises, and they follow industry-wide standards promulgated by a trade association. If those standards result in a defective product that causes an injury or damage, a court can treat these entities as a single enterprise for proving causation. Therefore, an entire industry can be liable for a plaintiff's injury or damage. This concept usually applies only to industries with a limited number of potential defendants. For example, if several steel producers have manufactured defective steel under industry-wide standards promulgated by a trade association, and the defective steel has caused damage or injuries, each of the steel producers might be liable based on its market share of the steel industry.

  > **Enterprise liability**, or **industry-wide liability**
  > An expanded liability concept requiring each member of an industry responsible for manufacturing a harmful or defective product to share liability, when a manufacturer at fault cannot be identified.

- **Alternative liability** involves shifting the burden of proof to each of several defendants in a tort case when there is uncertainty regarding which defendant's action was the proximate cause of the harm.[12] If it is uncertain which one caused the injury, the defendants have the burden of proof of causation. Each must prove either that he or she did not cause the harm or that someone else did. Under this concept, a plaintiff can sue one or more defendants, but not necessarily all of them.

  > **Alternative liability**
  > An expanded liability concept that shifts the burden of proof to each of several defendants in a tort case when there is uncertainty regarding which defendant's action was the proximate cause of the harm.

- **Market-share liability** applies when a product that has harmed a consumer cannot be traced to a single manufacturer; all manufacturers responsible for a substantial share of the market are named in the lawsuit and are liable for their proportional share of the judgment. Market share liability strongly resembles the alternative liability concept. Alternative liability can potentially create a situation in which one defendant is liable for the burden of the entire industry. In market-share liability, the courts have added the additional requirement that the plaintiff must sue all manufacturers responsible for a substantial share of the market. Therefore, unsuccessful defendants are not liable individually for the entire amount but are liable only for their pro rata share of the judgment based on their respective shares of the market. They are liable unless they can prove that they could not have made the product involved.

  > **Market-share liability**
  > An expanded liability concept that applies when a product that has harmed a consumer cannot be traced to a single manufacturer; all manufacturers responsible for a substantial share of the market are named in the lawsuit and are liable for their proportional share of the judgment.

- **Concert of action** is probably the most commonly recognized expanded liability concept.[13] "Concerted action" means that the parties accused of wrongdoing acted together or cooperatively. Under the concert-of-action concept, a plaintiff must prove either of the following:

  > **Concert of action**
  > An expanded liability concept that applies when all defendants acted together or cooperatively.

  1. That the defendants consciously parallel each other as the result of an actual agreement or an implied understanding to do or not to do a given act.

  2. That, even though the defendants acted independently of each other in committing the wrongful act, the effect of their independent acts was to encourage or assist others' wrongful conduct.

Under this concept, a plaintiff need not sue all potential defendants. For example, several tire manufacturers, following industry standards, might have manufactured defective tires independently, but their close connections in the industry might have encouraged each of them to manufacture defective tires.

Conspiracy
An expanded liability concept that applies when two or more parties worked together to commit an unlawful act.

- **Conspiracy** is a group of two or more parties working together to commit an unlawful act. To establish the responsibility of defendants involved in a conspiracy, a plaintiff must prove an agreement among them either to commit a wrongful act or to carry out a legal act by illegal means, resulting in the plaintiff's harm.

- A joint venture is a group of people or entities working together toward a common goal. To establish a joint venture to prove causation, a plaintiff must prove the following: (1) an agreement by the parties to associate for a business activity; (2) profits and losses shared by each party; (3) joint control of the venture by the parties; and (4) contribution to the venture's assets by each party.

Tortfeasor's Capacity

All people are liable for their tortious act regardless of mental capacity. This rules applies to acts of minors and of insane or intoxicated persons. If the tort requires intent, the defendant can establish lack of capacity to form intent as a defense. At common law, minors were generally liable for torts if they were over the age of seven.

Vicarious Liability

A person can become liable for others' tortious acts under the concept of vicarious liability. This liability can result from contractual relationships and from partnerships. Vicarious liability also can arise out of the following three types of relationships:

1. *Principal and agent.* The term "agency" describes the relationship in which one person, the principal, authorizes another, the agent, to act on that person's behalf. Principals are vicariously liable for the torts their agents commit in the course of the agents' employment and within the scope of their actual or apparent authority. This liability applies even though the act directly contravened the principal's orders. The agent is also individually liable for the same act.

2. *Employer and employee.* Employers are vicariously liable for torts their employees commit while acting within the scope of their employment. Courts use several methods to determine the scope of employment, and determination of liability must meet certain criteria.

3. *Parent and child.* Generally, a parent is not liable for a minor child's torts merely because of the family relationship. However, several well-established exceptions exist. For example, if the child is acting as the parent's agent or employee at the time the tort occurs, the parent is liable just as any other principal or employer would be liable.

The parent is also liable for a child's torts when the tort involves a dangerous instrumentality, such as a gun or even a vehicle, that the parent has given to the child under such circumstances that the parent should expect the child to cause harm. Providing a potentially dangerous instrument to a child is negligent entrustment. A parent is also directly liable if negligent in failing to suppress or control a child, knowing the child's violent or dangerous habits or propensities. This failure to suppress or control is negligent supervision.

Some states have adopted the **family purpose doctrine**, which applies only to torts caused by a family-owned automobile. Under this doctrine, a parent who keeps an automobile for the entire family's use is liable for the torts a family member commits while using the automobile.

Finally, several states make parents liable for certain specific torts of their children under statutes. These statutes generally apply to theft or vandalism, and states adopted them to control and reduce acts children commit on certain properties such as schools. The statutes frequently limit parental liability to stated dollar amounts. Under parental responsibility statutes, a parent can be liable without proof of negligence.

Family purpose doctrine
A liability concept that holds the owner of an automobile kept for the family's use vicariously liable for damages incurred by a family member while using the automobile.

Good Samaritan Issues

Historically, helping a person one has no duty to help has been called a Good Samaritan situation. If a person owes no duty to another person, the refusal to act does not create grounds for a suit. For example, Al becomes ill in Bob's presence. If Bob owes no duty to Al, Bob can let Al become worse, or even die, and incur no liability. If, however, Bob voluntarily undertakes to save Al by some act and performs the act negligently, Bob can incur liability.

A common example of a Good Samaritan is a physician who stops to give first aid to an accident victim. If the victim later claims the physician was negligent, the victim may be able to sue the physician successfully.

The result of the previous two examples demonstrates an inequity: A person who does not volunteer to help another has no liability, even if the other dies but a person who does help can be liable for negligence. In response to this inequity, all states have adopted Good Samaritan laws. Most states protect any person who gives emergency assistance, but some states protect only medical personnel. Generally, state laws apply to gratuitous emergency services performed at the scene of an emergency and exempt one who provides such services from liability for ordinary negligence based on a standard of good faith.

Class Actions and Mass Tort Litigation

A single tort may have many victims. In such situations, a legal procedure called a class action permits one person, or a small group of people, to file suit on behalf of all of the harmed members of a group. In cases in which all of the injured parties have nearly identical injuries or damages and the same cause of action against the wrongdoer, a single suit filed on behalf of all the plaintiffs against the wrongdoer can be more efficient than suits that each party files individually.

With just a few plaintiffs, one lawyer might represent all of them, but this representation may not work for hundreds, thousands, or even millions of different claimants. To illustrate, hundreds of stockholders sue a company for fraud, or thousands of insureds sue a property-casualty insurer for systematically overcharging them.

Courts have allowed class actions when cases present common questions of law or fact that can be tried in one suit, reducing burdensome multiple litigation. Class actions historically involved claims in which the amount of damages in each claim was so small that it did not warrant individual suits.

Traditionally, class actions have seldom involved torts because each of the people harmed in tort claims has different injuries, damages, or liability issues. However, courts have recently begun to accept for litigation (certify) dissimilar tort victim members of a group. A class-action suit based on tort law, rather than contract law, is called **mass tort litigation**.

Mass tort litigation
A class-action suit based on tort law rather than on contract law.

Mass tort litigation has involved claims related to such products as tobacco, asbestos, birth control pills and devices, prescription drugs, and pollutants. In insurance, consumers have lodged class-action suits, for example, against insurers for their use of aftermarket auto parts in auto repairs and for the misuse of managed-care techniques. Today, a court can hear a case involving numerous plaintiffs presenting identical liability questions as a class action, with each party submitting a separate proof of damages.

Class action suits provide access to the courts for a large group of people who are interested in a single issue or suit. One or more of them can sue or be sued as a representative of the class. To illustrate, a driver drives through a red light and strikes a vehicle that, in turn, strikes two more vehicles, injuring the three drivers and several passengers. Can the injured individuals form a class and file a suit collectively against the first driver? Generally, if a court must decide separate substantial questions before determining whether a person is a member of a class, a class action is not appropriate. The type of claim just described would not be appropriate for a class action because the parties would likely have different injuries and damages and possibly different liability allegations against the driver. In addition, too few parties are attempting to combine claims.

Plaintiffs file class actions under Federal Rule of Civil Procedure 23 for federal courts, as well as in most state courts. The trial court must then certify the suit as a class action, considering the following four features:

1. *Numerosity.* People constituting a class must be so numerous that it would be impractical to bring all of them separately into court.

2. *Commonality.* An ascertainable class with a well-defined common interest in the questions of law and fact affecting the parties is necessary for class-action certification.

3. *Typicality.* The claims or defenses of the representative parties must be typical of all the class members.

4. *Adequacy of representation.* The named parties must fairly and adequately protect the interests of unnamed class members.

Courts also consider the following factors:

*   The extent to which individual class members would have interests in controlling the prosecution of their claims in a separate suit
*   The extent and nature of any litigation already started
*   The desirability of concentrating the litigation in one forum
*   The difficulties of managing a class proceeding

The court need not know the identity of all potential members to permit a class action to proceed. If proof of membership is simple and obvious, then not knowing a member's identity should not prevent certification of a class action.

Statutes of Limitations and Repose

Statutes of limitations fix the time period within which a plaintiff can file a suit, starting from the time the cause of action accrued, that is, when all the elements of a cause of action exist. The cause of action is the basis for the right to sue, for example, for tort or a breach of contract. An injured party who does not file a suit within time set by a statute of limitations may be barred from suing. **Statutes of repose** also limit the time periods within which plaintiffs can file suits, starting from some stated event. The time limit of a statute of repose might expire before a cause of action has even accrued.

Statute of limitations
A statute limiting the time for filing suit, starting from the time the cause of action accrued.

Statute of repose
A statute that requires a plaintiff to file a lawsuit within a specific time after a specific event.

For example, a state has a two-year statute of limitations that begins to run when the cause of action accrues. The state also has a six-year statute of repose that begins to run when a merchant first sells a product. Carla purchases the product seven years after the initial sale and sustains an injury from the product six months after purchase. She has no legal recourse. The statute of limitations has not run because the cause of action accrued within the two years (six months after purchase), but the statute of repose bars her from suing because she was injured seven and a half years after the original sale—a year and a half beyond the statute of repose period.

Time Cause of Action Accrued

At common law, courts strictly enforced statutes of limitations. However, today, courts are more liberal so as not to deny a plaintiff a day in court. The time periods vary by state and also within the same state for different torts.

In most states, the statute begins to run from the time the cause of action accrues. A major problem is establishing when all elements of the cause of action exist so as to start the statute running.

In many cases, such as an automobile accident, fixing the time of the accident and the time the cause of action accrued is simple. In some torts, the right to sue is complete upon the commission of the wrongful act, regardless of consequences, such as injury or damage. For example, the right to sue for trespass begins when the trespass occurs; damages are implied, and a plaintiff need not prove them. In such a case, the cause of action accrues and the statute begins to run when the wrongful act is committed.

In other torts, the right to sue is not complete unless harm results. In these cases, the cause of action accrues and the statute begins to run from the date the plaintiff sustains injury or damage. For example, the defendant negligently installs lightning rods on the plaintiff's house. Six years later lightning hits the house and destroys it. Did the cause of action accrue when the defendant negligently installed the lightning rods or when the house burned? Many courts would say it accrued at the time of installation, but others at the time the house burned.

Types of Suits

Tort statutes of limitations that apply to bodily injury suits range from one to six years, with two years the most common. In the case of injury to reputation, such as libel or slander, the time is usually one year. Many statutes of limitations for suits for invasion of privacy run for six years.

Tort statutes of limitations, unless otherwise indicated, also apply to products liability and medical malpractice suits. Because of the peculiar problems these suits present, most states have enacted special statutes of limitations for medical malpractice, usually ranging from one to three years. Many states also have a statute of repose for medical malpractice, usually ranging from three to ten years.

A few states have enacted special statutes of limitations applicable to products liability, usually ranging from one to four years. Either as part of their tort statute or as a special statute, many states also have statutes of repose for products liability, usually ranging from five to twelve years starting to run from a stated event.

Property Suits

The statutes of limitations for damage to real or personal property are usually longer, and can run up to ten years. Suits for breach of warranty usually fall under the statute applying to contracts, and the applicable statutes of limitations can range from four to six years. Thus, an injured party could lose the right to file a suit in tort by the running of the statute and still be able to recover under a breach of warranty suit. Many states have statutes of repose for architects and builders, limiting suits to four to fifteen years after a building's completion, with the average length of time being about eight years.

Infants and Incompetents

The law does not penalize an infant or incompetent for failing to file suit while an infant or incompetent. For example, if a child suffers injury from a tort, the infant should not suffer from the parents' failure to file suit within the statutes of limitations period. For infants and incompetents, the time period of the statute of limitations begins to run from the date the infant or incompetent comes of age or the incompetency is removed (such as, by court order). This rule applies only if the incompetency existed before the statute began to run. Once the time period for the statute begins to run, it is not tolled (stopped) by the occurrence of a subsequent disability or other event.

When the plaintiff dies before the expiration of the time within which a suit must be filed, the plaintiff's personal representative usually has one year after the plaintiff's death within which to sue. If the defendant is not in the jurisdiction and the plaintiff cannot, therefore, serve a complaint on the defendant, the running of the statute is tolled until service of the complaint is possible.

SUMMARY

This concluding chapter on tort law focuses on current areas of concern, several involving insurance coverage issues. Products liability, toxic torts, and environmental claims are rapidly expanding areas of tort law that present increasingly complex issues.

Common law required a contractual relationship for products liability, but exceptions to this rule eliminated this requirement. Today, products liability suits are based on one of the following:

- Misrepresentation
- Breach of warranty
- Strict liability and negligence

Product defects include defects in manufacture or design and failure to give warning, creating potential liability for parties involved in the manufacture, sale, or distribution of the product. Defenses to products liability claims are as follows:

- State of the art
- Compliance with statutes and regulations
- Compliance with product specifications
- Open and obvious danger
- Plaintiff's knowledge
- Assumption of risk
- Misuse of product
- Alteration of product
- Post-accident remedial measures
- Written disclaimer

Toxic torts are similar to products liability suits. In toxic torts and environmental law, plaintiffs can file two types of suits: toxic tort suits and environmental suits.

Federal and state statutes address specific environmental problems. Common-law suits available to private plaintiffs include nuisance, trespass, negligence, and strict liability.

Generally, an environmental liability coverage dispute generates a claim under a commercial general liability (CGL) policy, which usually is occurrence-based and covers only damage the insured neither expected nor intended. Important policy exclusions are the owned property exclusion and the pollution exclusion except for sudden and accidental discharge of contaminants or pollutants.

Under the doctrine of absolute liability, a person who commits certain acts is liable for harm to another, regardless of willful wrongdoing or negligence. Strict liability has particular application in products liability cases, other cases involving inherently dangerous or ultrahazardous activity, and cases involving animals. Strict liability law distinguishes between domestic and wild animals, based on local custom.

The remedy for torts is damages. Tort damages can be either general or special compensatory damages, and sometimes a court may impose punitive damages as well. Factors that can increase the amount of damages include pain and suffering, emotional distress, and the bad faith of the defendant.

Generally, all people participating in the commission of a tort are jointly and severally liable. Many states have adopted the Uniform Contribution Among Joint Tort Feasors Act (UCAJTFA), which provides a right of contribution among joint tortfeasors.

Expanded liability concepts apply when more than one actor could have caused the damage injuries, but not all of them can be identified. These concepts include the following:

- Enterprise, or industry-wide, liability
- Alternative liability, involving shifting the burden of proof in a case
- Market-share liability, closely resembling alternative liability
- Concert of action, probably the most commonly recognized extension of liability
- Conspiracy
- Joint venture

In some cases a person can be held liable for the torts of another. Thus vicarious liability can apply to principal-agent, employer-employee, and parent-child relationships.

Statutes of limitations fix the period of time within which one can file a suit, with the time beginning to run from the time the cause of action accrued. Statutes of repose also preclude suits, but with the time beginning to run from some stated event and potentially expiring before a cause of action has accrued.

CHAPTER NOTES

1. *MacPherson v. Buick Motor Car Co.*, 217 N.Y. 382 (1932).

2. *Rylands v. Fletcher*, 1 Eng. Rul. Case 235 (1868).

3. *Henningsen v. Bloomfield Motor Inc.*, 32 N.J. 358 (1960).

4. UCC, § 2-314.

5. For example, see: *General Electric Co. v. Litton Indus. Automation Systems, Inc.*, 920 F.2d 1415, 1418 (8th Cir. 1990), *cert. denied*, 111 S. Ct. 1390 (1991); *United States v. Monsanto Co.*, 858 F.2d 160, 167 (4th Cir. 1988), *cert. denied*, 490 U.S. 1106 (1989).

6. 7 U.S.C., §§ 136–136y.

7. 42 U.S.C., §§ 7401–7626.

8. 33 U.S.C., §§ 1251–1387.

9. 15 U.S.C., §§ 2601–2671.

10. 42 U.S.C., §§ 6901–6992.

11. N.J.S.A., § 13:1K-6, et seq.

12. Restatement (Second) Torts, § 433B(3).

13. Restatement (Second) Torts, § 876.

Chapter 11

![Direct]

Direct Your Learning

Agency Law

After learning the content of this chapter and completing the corresponding course guide assignment, you should be able to:

■ Given a case, explain whether appointment, estoppel, or ratification created an agency.

■ Given a case, explain whether an agent has actual or apparent authority to act on a principal's behalf and how the principal can create agency relationships by actual or apparent authority.

■ Describe the following:

• Duties an agent owes to the principal

• Remedies a principal has for an agent's default or wrongdoing

• Duties a principal owes to the agent

• Remedies an agent has for a principal's default or wrongdoing

■ Describe the various means by which parties can terminate agency relationships.

■ Explain the following:

• Third-party rights and liabilities toward principals and agents

• A principal's rights against third parties

• An agent's rights against third parties

■ Describe the factors required for *respondeat superior* to apply and the torts that might make an employer liable for an employee's torts.

■ Given a case, explain whether workers are employees or independent contractors.

■ Given a case, explain whether an employer is liable for an employee's torts and what liability an employer may have for an employee's torts.

■ Define or describe each of the Key Words and Phrases for this chapter.

Develop Your Perspective

What are the main topics covered in the chapter?

The law of agency applies to many insurance relationships. This chapter introduces the law of agency, including agency creation, agents' authority, agents' and principals' duties and remedies, agency termination, and third-party contract and tort rights and liabilities regarding agents and principals. The next chapter relates agency principles to insurance relationships.

Consider how agencies are created.

- How might an agency be created inadvertently?

- What are a principal's recourses when an agent acts inappropriately?

Why is it important to learn about these topics?

Insurance is a business revolving around agency law, with some agents working for insurers and some for agencies. Insurance professionals must understand the rights of agents and principals, but particularly the ways in which agents can bind their principals and create liability for them.

Consider the kinds of agency relationships you might encounter.

- What kinds of roles do you play in your organization as an employee?

- How might you create liability to third parties for your employer as your principal in your daily work?

How can you use what you will learn?

Examine the ways that tort can be created for organizations through agency law.

- What kind of contractual liability might you create for your organization?

- What, if any, torts might someone in your position commit that would create liability for your organization?

Chapter 11
Agency Law

Agency describes the legal consensual relationship that exists when one party, an agent, acts on another party's, the principal's, behalf. The **principal** is the party that authorizes the **agent** to act on the principal's behalf. Agency is a fiduciary relationship created by express or implied contract or by law. To create an agency, both the principal and the agent must agree to the relationship. An agent can influence a principal's legal relationships and can bind the principal by words or actions. If, for example, an agent negotiates a contract on a principal's behalf, the principal is bound to the contract just as though the principal negotiated it personally. Some, but not all, employer-employee relationships are examples of agency relationships, as are the relationships between insurers and their insurance agents.

The law of agency and the law of partnership have much in common. A partnership is an association of two or more persons as co-owners of a business for profit. Partners are agents of the partnership. Because each partner is both an agent and a principal, the usual agency rules apply to all of their dealings.

Agency
A legal, consensual relationship that exists when one party, the agent, acts on behalf of another party, the principal.

Principal
The party in an agency relationship that authorizes the agent to act on that party's behalf.

Agent
In an agency relationship, the party that is authorized by the principal to act on the principal's behalf.

AGENCY CREATION

Ordinarily, a principal and an agent do not need a contract to create an agency. The relationship is consensual, not necessarily contractual, and no consideration is required. One can consent to be an agent without compensation. The consent of the parties can be written or oral, express or implied. However, statutes of frauds require that if agency contracts are to last beyond a year, then they must be in writing.

Agency by Appointment

The usual method of creating an agency is by express appointment. That is, A authorizes B to act in A's behalf, and B assents to the appointment. The agent must consent to the relationship because agency requires the agent to assume fiduciary duties, those involving trust.

As in contract formation, the principal's proposal can make a communicated acceptance unnecessary. If the principal asks another to act and indicates that no further communication is necessary, and the other person acts, the agency relationship arises. For example, Margaret writes to Joe, a real estate broker, and asks him to purchase a particular piece of real property for her in his name. Joe purchases the property in his own name and then refuses to convey it to Margaret. The circumstances indicate an implied agreement to form an agency relationship. Joe purchased the property on Margaret's behalf and must transfer it to her.

A principal can extend additional power to an agent through power of attorney. A **power of attorney** is a written document giving an agent the power to sign personal documents on the principal's behalf. If an agent contracts to sell a principal's real estate, the principal must sign the deed. Otherwise, unless the agent has a power of attorney, the agent's signature on a deed has no effect. A power of attorney can be specific, such as a power to sell real estate, or it can be general, giving the agent power over all the principal's property.

Power of attorney
A written document by which a principal gives an agent the power to sign personal documents on the principal's behalf.

Agency by Estoppel

If a principal's words or conduct cause a third person to reasonably believe that an agency exists and to rely on that representation in dealing with the supposed agent, the principal is estopped (prevented) from denying the agency, resulting in **agency by estoppel**. For example, if an insurer's owner allows a customer service representative to promise to find insurance coverage for applicants, the owner has created an agency by estoppel and cannot deny coverage placed by the employee. The reason for agency by estoppel is that one should be bound by one's words and conduct if another person materially relies on them.

Agency by estoppel
An agency relationship created by a principal's words or conduct that causes a third party to reasonably believe that an agency exists.

Because the principal has given the agent no actual authorization, an agency by estoppel is not a genuine agency. The practical legal effects, however, are the same to the third party as if the principal had appointed the agent. The acts of the apparent agent bind the principal.

No agency by estoppel forms if the person for whom the act is performed (who would be principal in an agency relationship) is not aware of the supposed agent's action. For example, Bob has created the appearance that he is Paul's agent by printing stationery that falsely implies an agency relationship. As long as Paul neither knows nor should know of Bob's deception, Paul can deny the agency. Anyone relying on the deceptive stationery relies on appearances that Bob, not Paul, created. Therefore, Paul would not be liable for Bob's actions as an alleged agent.

However, a person who knowingly permits another person to represent that an agency exists can be estopped from denying the agency. For instance, Paul owns a jewelry store and permits his friend, Anne, to display and sell her handcrafted jewelry in his store. Their businesses are separate, but customers could reasonably believe that Anne works for Paul. Although Paul and Anne are not principal and agent, any customer who deals with Anne and believes her to be Paul's agent can hold Paul liable as a principal if the customer has suffered loss in reasonable reliance on that belief.

What if Anne has falsely represented that Paul is her principal? Must Paul disavow the relationship? Can his silence create an agency by estoppel?

The answer is not certain. A court would consider Paul's silence in relation to what a reasonable person would do to disavow the relationship. Clearly, if Paul were to come face to face with a person who believes that Anne is Paul's agent, he must disavow the agency relationship. Suppose, however, that Anne advertises the purported agency in newspapers in a distant city where Paul does no business? Although the legal question concerns what a reasonable person would do, it is doubtful that a court would submit this question to a jury in the absence of unusual circumstances.

Agency by Ratification

If a person acts as agent to one who has given no actual consent or authority, the purported principal has the following two options:

1. Ratify or confirm the transaction
2. Refuse to approve the purported agent's unauthorized acts

Ratification of an agency relationship is a purported principal's affirmation of the relationship, with knowledge of all material facts. If the principal ratifies the agent's transaction, the agent's authority comes into existence, and a contract arises between the principal and the third party.

A ratification must meet the following four conditions to be effective:

1. The agent must have purported to act for the principal. If the agent failed to disclose a principal's existence, then ratification by the undisclosed person will not create an agency relationship. The purported agent need not identify the principal but must purport to act for someone.
2. The principal must ratify the entire transaction, not just favorable parts.
3. The principal must ratify the agreement before the third party elects to withdraw from the agreement. If the third party has withdrawn, died, or become incompetent to contract before the principal ratifies the agreement, the ratification is ineffective.
4. The principal must have all material facts available before the ratification is binding.

Ratification
An agency relationship created when a purported principal affirms the act of a party who acted as the principal's agent without prior authorization.

Ratification establishes the agency relationship. In contrast, an estoppel does not create an agency relationship but only prevents the third person from a loss that would result if the agency were denied. In both agency by estoppel and agency by ratification the legal effect to the third party is the same. The third party has an enforceable contract with the principal.

Rather than ratification, a purported principal may refuse to approve the acts of a person who has claimed to be an agent. The following set of facts illustrates both ratification and refusal. Steve is an agent for Movers Insurance Company, which has given him authority to bind coverage up to $200,000 for cargo policies. Steve issues a transit certificate to Planes, Inc., for $500,000 for the transportation of a shipment from Florida to California. The tractor-trailer hauling the cargo overturns, completely destroying the cargo. Planes, Inc., files a claim for the $500,000. Movers Insurance has a problem: Steve had authority to write a policy up to only $200,000, and he violated his agency authority in writing the $500,000 transit certificate. Movers can ratify Steve's actions by accepting the loss and paying the $500,000, or it can refuse to approve Steve's actions and deny the claim.

AGENT'S AUTHORITY

For a principal to be liable for an agent's transactions, an agency must have been created by appointment, estoppel, or ratification and the principal must have authorized the transaction. Even if the agency is valid, an agent must act within the source, scope, and limitations of the authority granted.

Scope of Authority

The scope of an agent's authority takes two forms, actual or apparent. Actual and apparent authority stem from different circumstances and can have different legal effects, depending on the particular situation. Actual authority can be express or implied. A court analyzing a question about an agent's authority should look first for actual authority. If no actual authority exists, the court should determine whether apparent authority exists.

Actual Authority

Actual authority is, as the name implies, authority the principal intentionally gives the agent. Actual authority can be express or implied. **Express authority** is anything the principal specifically instructs the agent to do, and it includes acts incidental to carrying out the specified instructions. The words used in granting the authority control its scope. To determine the scope of the express authority, courts examine the specific agency goals in light of all surrounding circumstances, such as the nature of the business. For example, the power to sell is generally authority to sell for cash and to make customary warranties. A sales agent who has no possession or indication of ownership has no authority to collect the purchase price. In most commerce situations, the agent has authority only to solicit orders or to produce a buyer with whom the principal can deal.

Implied authority is actual authority implicitly conferred by custom, usage, or a principal's conduct indicating intention to confer such authority. Custom is the most common source of implied authority. Agents can reasonably infer that their actions agree with prevailing custom unless the principal gives different instructions. Without different instructions, an agent's authority extends to, and is limited to, what a person in this agent's position usually does. To illustrate, for many years Paul delivered equipment to Anne, a dealer. Anne sold the equipment for the best price available. On Paul's current delivery of the equipment, and in the absence of different instructions, Anne has implied authority to sell and deliver the equipment at the best price.

Implied authority can also apply when an agent acts beyond the usual scope of authority in an emergency. If the agent needs to act to protect or preserve

Actual authority
The authority, both express and implied, that a principal intentionally gives to an agent.

Express authority
The actual authority conferred by a principal on an agent through specific instruction, including acts incidental to carrying out those instructions.

Implied authority
The actual authority implicitly conferred on an agent by custom, usage, or a principal's conduct indicating the intention to confer such authority.

the principal's property or rights but is unable to contact the principal, and if the agent reasonably believes that an emergency exists, he or she has authority to act beyond, or even contrary to, the principal's instructions to protect the principal's interests. To illustrate, while conducting Rob's business, Ken negligently injured a third person. Immediate communication with Rob was not possible, and Ken obtained the services of a physician to treat the injured party. The physician later can collect from Rob for the value of the services. Although Ken's authority usually does not include employment of a physician, he had emergency authority to hire a physician under the circumstances.

An agent who acts reasonably in an emergency has authority to act even though the agent is mistaken about the necessity for the actions or even though the agent is at fault in creating the emergency. The agent, however, can be liable to the principal for any expenses resulting from the agent's wrongful conduct.

Apparent Authority

Unlike actual authority, a principal does not give apparent authority to the agent. Nor does the agent ever create this authority. **Apparent authority** depends on a third party's reasonable belief, based on appearances the principal has created, that the agent has authority. Apparent authority includes all the authority that a reasonable person, acquainted with the customs and nature of the business, could reasonably assume the agent has. It generally arises in one of the following two overlapping circumstances:

Apparent authority
The authority that a reasonable person could believe that an agent has to act on a principal's behalf.

1. A principal grants less actual authority to the agent than agents in the same position in that business usually have.
2. The method of operation of the principal's business differs from the method of operation of other businesses of the same kind in the principal's area.

For example, principal Paul instructed agent Anne not to sell goods on credit if the total credit to a customer exceeds $200, an unusual restriction in Paul's business. Anne sold goods on credit to Lee for $250 with no actual authority to do so. Lee, however, neither knew nor had reason to know of the restriction. A third party could have reasonably believed that Anne had the usual authority in that situation. The authority was apparent, and Paul cannot deny it.

As a second example, Paul puts Anne in charge of a jewelry store and instructs her not to stock or sell watch batteries. All other jewelry stores in that area do stock and sell watch batteries. Anne contracts with Larry to purchase a supply of watch batteries. Anne has apparent authority to do this as long as Larry is unaware of the restriction on Anne's authority.

Duty to Ascertain Scope of Authority

A principal's representation to a third party determines the existence and the scope of an agent's apparent authority. A third person is not entitled to rely on an agent's statements about the scope of the agent's authority. Only the actual authority the principal has given, or the apparent authority the principal has manifested to the third party, controls the extent of the agent's authority.

If an agent acts in a way adverse to the principal's best interests, the third party has notice that the agent might be exceeding his or her authority. The third party must ascertain the scope of the agent's authority by a direct inquiry to the principal. If the third party fails to inquire, and the agent does not have authority, the transaction in question does not bind the principal.

Delegation of Authority

An agent cannot delegate the authority granted by a principal to another person. The principal selects the agent because of personal qualifications. For an agent to permit performance by someone else is unfair to the principal. The following three qualifications apply to the nondelegation rule:

Ministerial duties
The routine or mechanical tasks performed by agents.

1. *Ministerial duties.* Agents often perform routine or mechanical tasks, called **ministerial duties**. If certain tasks do not require judgment or discretion, an agent can delegate their performance.
2. *Customary appointments.* If custom and usage of a particular business involve the delegation of authority, the agent can delegate.
3. *Emergency appointments.* In an emergency that requires the appointment of another to protect the principal's interests, the agent can make an emergency appointment.

DUTIES AND REMEDIES

The principal and agent owe different obligations, or duties, to each other. The remedies available to them if duties are breached are also distinct and can take the form of damages or equitable relief.

Agent's Duties to Principal

An agent's implied fiduciary duties to a principal include the following:

*   Loyalty
*   Obedience
*   Reasonable care
*   Accounting
*   Information

Violation of any of these duties subjects the agent to discharge and to liability for any damages to the principal even if the agency contract does not expressly state the duties.

A subagent, who is the agent of an agent, owes the same duties to the principal that the original agent owes. An original agent is responsible to the principal for a subagent's violation of duty, even though the agent has exercised good faith in selecting the subagent. Further, a subagent owes the agent who did the hiring substantially the same duties.

If a subagent is employed without a principal's authority, no agency relationship arises between the principal and the subagent. The principal is not liable to third parties for an unauthorized subagent's acts. At the same time, the unauthorized subagent owes no duties to the principal.

Loyalty

One of the agent's most important duties is loyalty to the principal's interests. The agent must not undertake any business venture that competes with or interferes with the principal's business.

The principal can claim any profits the agent realizes in dealing with the principal's property. For example, any gift the agent receives from a third party while transacting the principal's business belongs to the principal.

The duty of loyalty, however, does not obligate the agent to shield a principal who is acting illegally or dishonestly. To illustrate, Jo learns that her principal, Pete, cheated Tom on various contracts that Jo had arranged between Pete and Tom. Jo can disclose Pete's actions to Tom. If Tom obtains a judgment against Pete for his improper dealings, Pete cannot recover from Jo for breach of the duty of loyalty. Jo's duty does not extend to concealing Pete's dishonest acts from persons those actions affect.

Obedience

An agent owes a duty to obey a principal's lawful instructions. If the agent disobeys a reasonable instruction, the principal can sue for any resulting damages and can also terminate the relationship. Generally, the agent cannot challenge the instruction, unless it calls for illegal or immoral acts.

The agent owes a duty to perform according to the principal's instructions, and the test is what a reasonable person would do under similar circumstances. If harm to the agent is possible, or if an emergency arises, the agent might be justified in disobeying the principal's instructions. If the principal has given ambiguous instructions, the agent owes the duty to exercise his or her best judgment in carrying them out.

Reasonable Care

An agent must exercise the degree of care and skill that a reasonable person would exercise under the same or similar circumstances. An agent with special skills or training is held to the standard of care of a reasonable person possessing those skills. Thus, a real estate broker employed to sell property must exercise the reasonable care of any real estate broker dealing with the property.

An agent's failure to act when action is reasonably required also constitutes a breach of this duty. An agency contract carries an implied promise that the agent will carry out the duties of the agency with reasonable care to avoid injury to the principal. To illustrate, Charles asks Marcie, an insurance broker, to obtain an automobile insurance policy with collision coverage for his car. Marcie obtains a policy and delivers it to Charles, but the policy does not include collision coverage. Charles has an accident and finds that no collision coverage is in force. Charles can sue Marcie for breach of the duty of reasonable care.

Reasonable care is required whether the agent is paid or not paid for the services. Unpaid agents cannot be compelled to perform duties, but once they begin performance, they are held to the standard of reasonable care under the circumstances. For example, real estate broker Betty gratuitously promises to act as Clark's agent in the sale of his real estate. Clark cannot sue Betty for her failure to try to sell the property. However, suppose Betty procured Tony as a buyer of Clark's property and failed to have Tony sign a binding sales agreement. If Tony later declined to proceed with the sale, Clark could sue Betty for negligence for her failure to exercise the degree of reasonable care.

An agent and a principal can agree that the agent is not to be liable to the principal for ordinary negligence. An agent, however, cannot evade liability for gross negligence. To limit the agent's liability would be against public policy.

Accounting

An agent must account to the principal for all the principal's property and money that come into the agent's possession. As part of this duty, the agent must keep the principal's property, including money, separate from the agent's. If the agent commingles the property or money, then the law assumes that it all belongs to the principal unless the agent clearly proves otherwise.

Money held by the agent should be deposited in a separate bank account in the principal's name. If the agent deposits it in his or her own name and the bank then fails, the agent is liable for any loss the principal sustains. The agent should account promptly for any of the principal's money held. Failure to do so makes the agent liable for interest payments to the principal.

Information

An agent owes a duty to keep the principal informed of all facts relating to the agency. Therefore, if a principal authorizes an agent to sell property for a specified amount and the agent later learns that the property's value has materially changed, then the agent must give the principal that information. Generally the agent owes a duty to make reasonable efforts to provide the principal with information relevant to the affairs entrusted to the agent. Failure to perform this duty makes the agent liable to the principal for any resulting loss.

The law imputes the knowledge an agent obtains during the course of performing a principal's business to the principal and therefore imposes on the agent the duty to give the information to the principal. Most courts do not impose a duty to communicate information that the agent obtains outside the scope of the agent's employment. Additionally, if an agent acts adversely to the principal's interest, by colluding with a third party to defraud the principal, for example, that knowledge will not be imputed to the principal.

Principal's Remedies

Depending on the offense, a principal can sue an agent for breach of the agency contract or in tort for harm done. Remedies include requiring the agent to transfer improperly held property or to pay the value of the benefit the agent received, or damages for negligence or tort.

If the agent is insolvent, the principal's best remedy is a suit to transfer the property. If the agent has personally profited from the transaction, then a suit for the value of the benefit the agent received represents the principal's best alternative. In other cases, a suit for breach of agency contract may be preferable to a suit in tort for the agent's harm because the statute of limitations for contract actions is generally longer for contract suits than for tort suits, such as those for products liability.

In still other cases, the principal can sue for an injunction prohibiting the agent from revealing trade secrets obtained during the course of employment or from competing with the principal after termination of employment in violation of an agreement not to compete.

Principal's Duties to Agent

The principal owes the following duties to the agent:

- Agreed-on period of employment
- Compensation
- Reimbursement for expenses
- Indemnity for losses

Agreed-on Period of Employment

Either party can terminate an employment contract at will unless the contract specifies a fixed period of employment. A contract to pay a salary by the month or year does not necessarily indicate that employment is guaranteed for the stated period.

A contract with a fixed period of employment makes the parties liable for any breach of their contract within that period. Because the agency relationship is consensual, the parties can refuse to continue the relationship during the contractual period, but they are subject to damages for breach of the contract.

When an employment contract provides for a specified period of employment and the principal's business terminates during the period, the agency also terminates because of changed conditions.

Compensation

The principal must pay the agent the agreed compensation for the services performed. If no compensation agreement exists, the agent is entitled to the reasonable value of the services rendered. If the contract does not mention compensation but an agent under similar circumstances would receive compensation for services, compensation is required for the reasonable value of the services. However, an agent who breaches agency duties is not entitled to compensation.

A principal is not responsible for a subagent's compensation if the agent was given no authority to hire subagents. Likewise, if the agent has the authority merely to delegate duties to a subagent, the agent, not the principal, is responsible for compensation.

Reimbursement for Expenses

A principal must reimburse an agent for any expenses necessarily incurred for the discharge of agency duties. For example, if the agent must incur travel and advertising expenses to accomplish agency purposes, the principal must reimburse these expenses. The agent must spend the money reasonably. If the agent's negligent conduct results in unnecessary expense, the agent bears the expense rather than the principal.

Indemnity for Losses

The principal owes a duty of indemnity, or reimbursement, for any losses or damages the agent has suffered arising because of the agency and incurred through no fault of the agent. If a principal directs an agent to commit a wrong against a third party, and the agent does not know that the act is wrongful, the agent is entitled to indemnity for the amount paid as a result of a lawsuit arising from the act. To illustrate, a principal directs an agent to cut down and sell trees on land that the principal incorrectly believes he owns. The landowner sues the agent to recover damages for loss of the trees. The agent is entitled to indemnity by the principal.

A principal must indemnify an agent for the expenses incurred in defending any lawsuits resulting from the agent's authorized acts. If the expense resulted from the agent's own intentional or negligent conduct, even though the principal directed the act, the agent is usually not entitled to indemnification. To illustrate, Paul promises to reimburse his sales representative, Anne, for money she pays out in illegal gratuities to purchasing agents to whom she sells goods. Anne is not entitled to indemnification from Paul for money she pays illegally.

An agent who makes payments or becomes subject to liability to third persons because of a subagent's authorized conduct has the same right to indemnity from the principal as if the conduct were the agent's. Because a subagent is both the agent's and the principal's agent, the subagent is entitled to indemnity from either of them.

Agent's Remedies

An agent can sue for compensation, indemnity, or reimbursement and can also obtain a court order requiring an accounting from the principal. An agent discharged by a principal during a specified employment period can sue for compensation for the remainder of the period.

An agent also can exercise a lien, or right to retain possession of the principal's goods, until the principal has paid amounts due. Some agents, such as attorneys, bankers, and stockbrokers, can enforce a **general lien** against the principal; that is, they can hold the principal's goods and papers until all accounts between the principal and agent are settled. The general lien is not limited to the immediate transaction between the parties but to all transactions between the agent and principal. Many other kinds of agents can assert only a **special lien**, which allows retention of the principal's property until the account for the immediate transaction between the principal and agent is settled.

AGENCY TERMINATION

Parties often find it more difficult to terminate an agency relationship than to enter into one. If the agency is "at will," either the principal or the agent has both the power and the right to terminate the agency at any time without legal liability. If, however, the agency is to continue for a certain time period or until accomplishment of a specific purpose, then both the principal and the agent have the power, but not the right, to terminate the agency.

Wrongful termination is a breach of contract, and the terminating party can be liable. The agency, as well as the principal, can terminate in the following seven ways:

1. Just cause
2. Lapse of time
3. Accomplishment of purpose
4. Revocation
5. Renunciation
6. Death or incapacity
7. Changed circumstances

Just Cause

An agency can be terminated for just cause. Examples of just cause are fraud, criminal activity, and flagrant violations of agency contracts. If an agency is at will, it can be terminated without cause.

General lien
A creditor's legal right or interest in a debtor's property until satisfaction of any debt; in an agency, the agent's right in a principal's goods and papers held by the agent until all accounts between the principal and agent are settled.

Special lien
A creditor's legal right or interest in specific property until satisfaction of a debt related to that property; in an agency, the agent's right to retain a principal's property until the account for the immediate transaction between the principal and agent is settled.

Lapse of Time

Lapse of time can also terminate an agency. Authority granted to an agent for a specified time period terminates at the expiration of that period. If the parties specify no time, a reasonable amount of time applies, depending on the circumstances. For example, if Margaret authorized Joe to sell property five years ago and they have not communicated since, the agency probably has terminated through lapse of time. If, however, Joe made occasional reports to Margaret about prospective buyers and Margaret gave no indication that the agency was terminated, Joe would continue to have authority to sell.

Accomplishment of Purpose

Many agencies are terminated through accomplishment of purpose. If the agent has the authority to accomplish a specific result, authority terminates upon its accomplishment—even if the performance is accomplished by another agent or by the principal. The agency usually continues until the agent has received notice that the agency's purpose has been accomplished. To illustrate, Paul has given authority to two separate agents, Anne and Betty, to lease or sell Paul's house. With Anne's knowledge, Betty leases the house to Terry. Anne's authority to lease or sell the house ends, as does Betty's.

Revocation

Another way to terminate an agency is through revocation. The principal can terminate an agency by revoking the agency. To revoke, the principal notifies the agent, by any word or act, that the agent no longer has authority. A contract provision requiring a specific manner for revocation does not always prevent agency termination through other means. The principal always has the power to terminate the agency, although the agent can sue for damages if the termination violates the agency contract.

If the principal appoints another agent to accomplish the authorized act, and if the new appointment is inconsistent with the first, the original agent's authority is terminated. For example, if a client engages a new attorney to try a case with the knowledge of the original attorney, the original attorney's agency ends because the two agency relationships conflict. However, the mere fact that a second agent has authority to sell the same property as the first agent is not of itself sufficient to terminate the original agency. Unless an agent has an exclusive right to sell property, the principal reserves the right to sell or to authorize another agent to sell. The appointments are consistent, and the first agent who sells gets the benefit.

Renunciation

Another way to terminate an agency is through renunciation. An agent's termination of the agency relationship is a "renunciation of authority." The renunciation is effective even if it breaches the contract that binds the agent to perform. For example, Lyle, an actor, hired Joan to represent him as his agent for two years. After one year, Joan resigned. Although Joan might be liable under the contract to Lyle for the cost of finding a replacement, Joan's renunciation (resignation) has terminated her authority as his agent and ended the agency relationship.

Death or Incapacity

The death or incapacity of either the principal or agent also terminates the agency relationship. Agency termination occurs upon a principal's death even though the agent or third party has no actual notice of death. Death is a matter of public record, so the law assumes that the public has notice of death. However, courts have found that the necessities of modern banking and commerce require relaxation of this rule. For example, until a bank receives actual notice of a depositor's death, the bank has authority to pay checks drawn on the depositor's account. Similarly, when a check holder deposits the check for a bank's collection, the bank can proceed with the collection even after the depositor's death until the bank receives notice.

A principal can also become incapacitated. Courts generally treat a principal's incapacity and death the same way. Because the agent acts in the principal's place and the principal cannot act, agency authority ends during incapacity. Incapacity that terminates agents' authority can occur when principals are declared legally incompetent, for example, when a principal is declared mentally incompetent because of the inability to understand the consequences of his or her actions.

Different rules apply to an agent's incapacity. Principals who permit legally incompetent agents to represent them can be bound. However, a court declaration of an agent's incompetence terminates the agency.

An agent does not need capacity to contract to be an agent. The principal's capacity is the determining factor, not the agent's. A mentally incompetent agent may represent a principal, and the agent's contract binds the principal unless a party involved in the contract knows of the incompetency. To illustrate, Paul authorizes Anne to sell his property. Anne contracts to sell the property to a buyer, who does not know that Anne is under the influence of drugs. Anne's contract binds Paul to sell the property to the buyer. The principal can terminate the agency upon learning of the agent's incompetency.

Changed Circumstances

Changed circumstances can terminate an agency. If, because of a substantial change in circumstances, the agent should reasonably infer that the principal would not want the agency to continue, authority to act terminates. For example, if Paul has authorized Anne to sell his land for $100,000, and Anne learns that discovery of oil on the land has increased the land's value to $5 million, Anne's authority to sell the land for $100,000 terminates. An agent can exercise authority only with a reasonable belief that the principal still wants that exercise of authority.

The principal's bankruptcy is a changed circumstance that usually terminates the agent's authority regarding all assets under a bankruptcy court's control. In bankruptcy, the principal's assets and the power to deal with those assets pass to a trustee in bankruptcy, even without notice to the agent. Ordinarily, the principal's mere inability to pay bills is not sufficient to terminate the agent's authority. If an agent's bankruptcy affects the agent's ability to perform the agency's purpose, or if the agent's bankruptcy affects the principal's business standing, the agency terminates.

THIRD-PARTY LIABILITIES AND RIGHTS

Agency law governs activities between agents and third parties and binds principals as though they had dealt personally with the third parties. These activities can result in legal questions regarding contract or tort.

In contract liability cases, the questions that must be answered to determine the parties' liabilities and rights include the following:

- Did an agency exist?
- What was the extent of the agent's authority?
- Was the principal disclosed?

In tort liability cases, the questions that courts must ask to determine the parties' liabilities and rights include the following:

- Did an employment relationship exist?
- Was the act committed within the scope of that employment?

Agency Contract Liability

Agency contract liability focuses on the following respective rights:

- A third party's rights against a principal
- A principal's rights against a third party
- An agent's liability to a third party
- An agent's rights against a third party

Disclosed principal
A principal whose existence and identity are known to the third party dealing with the agent.

Partially disclosed principal
A principal whose existence is known, but whose identity is not known, to the third party dealing with the agent.

Third Party's Rights Against a Principal

Third parties have rights against principals for agents' properly authorized and executed contracts, depending on the principal's status as one of the following:

- **Disclosed principal**—A principal whose existence and identity are known to the third party dealing with the agent
- **Partially disclosed principal**—A principal whose existence is known, but whose identity is not known, to the third party dealing with the agent

- **Undisclosed principal**—A principal whose existence is unknown to the third party dealing with the agent.

Undisclosed principal
A principal whose existence is unknown to the third party dealing with the agent.

The law relating to partially disclosed principals is much the same as that relating to undisclosed principals. The parties enter into agreements largely on the strength of the agent's credibility, and the agent is liable for agreements made until the third party elects to hold the principal liable. The third party, on learning of the principal's existence or identity, can elect to enforce the contract against the principal rather than against the agent.

The undisclosed principal is responsible for all contracts the agent enters into within the scope of the agent's actual authority, and the third party can sue the principal when the principal's existence becomes apparent. Being unknown to the third party, the principal could not have created any apparent authority. Therefore, liability is limited to the agent's actual authority.

The right to sue an undisclosed principal on a contract is subject to the following exceptions.

- *Principal's settlement with the agent.* If the principal has made a good faith settlement of the account with the agent regarding the contract, the third party cannot sue. For example, when an undisclosed principal has supplied an agent with money to purchase goods, but the agent purchases the goods on credit and keeps the money, a settlement has occurred. The principal is not liable to the creditor for a second payment. The settlement can occur before or after the contract formation, but it must occur before disclosure of the principal to the third person.

- *Third party's election to hold the agent, and not the principal, liable.* When the third party learns of the principal's existence and identity, an expression of intention to hold the agent liable for the contract is usually binding on the third party. Election of the agent discharges the principal. However, election does not apply if the principal is partially disclosed. The third party can obtain a judgment against either the agent or the partially disclosed principal without discharging the right against the other.

Principal's Rights Against a Third Party

If a contract binds a principal to a third party, it also binds the third party to the principal. It is immaterial that the third party knew nothing of the principal's existence and thought the contract formed was with the agent alone. Thus, in transactions between agents of disclosed or partially disclosed principals and third parties, the principals have rights against the third parties to the same extent as if the principal had conducted the transaction.

When undisclosed principals are involved, their rights against third parties can be limited in the following four situations:

1. *Fraudulent concealment of principal's identity.* If an agent has fraudulently represented to a third party that the contract is on the agent's behalf alone or that the agent represents someone other than the real principal,

the third party has the right to rescind the contract. If the agent or principal knows, or should know, that the other party is unwilling to deal with the principal, the principal's identity becomes a material fact. Representations that no principal exists, or that the principal is someone else, constitute fraud, and the third party can void the contract. If the agent does not actively misrepresent the principal's identity but knows that the third party would not enter into the contract knowing the facts, a duty of disclosure exists.

2. *Greater burden imposed.* An undisclosed principal also cannot enforce a contract against a third party if enforcement would impose a substantial additional burden on the third party. To illustrate, Sophie contracts to purchase from Katie "all of the oil that Sophie requires." If Katie did not know that Sophie in fact represents Will, whose oil requirements are substantially greater than Katie knows, Will cannot enforce the contract against Katie.

3. *Personal performance contracts.* An undisclosed principal cannot substitute his or her own personal performance for the agent's performance if the contract specifies the agent's personal performance. However, the principal can enforce the agent's contract. For example, assume that Peter is an undisclosed principal and that Danielle is Peter's agent. Danielle contracts to paint Kyle's portrait. Danielle must do the painting personally. If Danielle completes the painting, Peter can demand payment from Kyle under the contract.

4. *Judgment between third party and agent.* When a third party sues the agent on a contract that the agent entered into on an undisclosed principal's behalf, a judgment against the agent destroys the principal's right against the third party. Because the agent's actions could have destroyed the contract before the principal's identity becomes known, a judgment against the agent is equally effective to defeat the principal's rights. However, a judgment either for or against the agent obtained by the third party after the principal's identity becomes known does not necessarily diminish the rights of a principal who took no part in the suit.

Agent's Liability to a Third Party

Generally, an agent is not liable to a third party for a contract made on a disclosed principal's behalf. The principal alone is liable. The agent acts only on the principal's behalf and does not assume personal liability under the contract. Exceptions to that rule include the following six situations:

1. *Breach of warranty of authority.* An agent can attempt to act for a principal even with no actual authority to do so. An agent who acts on a principal's behalf by implication warrants that he or she has actual authority to represent the principal. If the agent is not authorized or exceeds the authority granted, the agent breaches the implied warranty of authority and is liable for the breach. The principal is not liable in the absence of ratification of the agreement or apparent authority. An agent who intentionally misrepresents the existence or extent of authority also might be liable for fraud. If the third party knows or has reason to suspect that the agent lacks

authority, the agent is not liable for breach of warranty. The agent can avoid liability for damages arising from lack of authority by making a full disclosure to the third party of all facts relating to the agent's authority.

If the principal ratifies the contract, the agent's liability for breach of warranty terminates. Ratification must occur before the third party withdraws from the contract. If the third party notifies the agent of contract termination because of the agent's lack of authority, or if the third party sues the agent for breach of warranty of authority, the principal's later attempt to ratify the contract is ineffective to discharge the agent from liability to the third party.

2. *Incompetent principal.* If an agent acts on a minor's behalf or a mentally incompetent person's behalf, the agent is personally liable for breach of warranty of authority if the third party was not aware of the incapacity. Part of the agent's implied warranty of authority is that the principal can be legally bound under the contract.

3. *Undisclosed and partially disclosed principals.* If a third party has intended to contract with the agent, and the agent purported to act personally and not for a principal, the agent must disclose both the existence and the identity of the principal to avoid personal liability on a contract with the third party. It is not sufficient that the third party knows facts that could disclose the principal's identity.

4. *Agent's personal liability.* The third party can ask the agent to agree to personally guarantee the contract. An agent who voluntarily assumes responsibility for performing the agreement is liable for the principal's nonperformance. The principal is liable on the contract, and the agent is liable on the guaranty.

5. *Agent's liability to account.* An agent owes a duty to the principal to account for any money or property received during the agency. No fiduciary relationship exists between the agent and the third party; therefore the agent owes no duty to account to the third party. If an agent can receive money from a third party and does not provide it to the principal, the principal can recover it in a suit against the agent. In contrast, if a third party pays money to an agent who has no authority to collect it and who does not turn it over to the principal, the third party can sue the agent for the money. For example, if a sales representative collects a payment on an open account without authority and fails to deliver the money to the principal, the third party can sue the agent to recover the payment. Similarly, a third party can recover payments made to an agent resulting from the agent's mistake or misconduct even though the agent has turned the funds over to the principal. An agent cannot avoid liability by subsequently paying wrongfully collected funds to a principal.

6. *Agent's liability for torts and crimes.* An agent is liable for fraudulent or malicious acts that harm a third party. That the agent was acting in good faith under the principal's direction is not a defense against personal tort or criminal liability. An agent who wrongfully injures a third party or is guilty of theft is personally liable.

Agent's Rights Against a Third Party

A third party is usually not liable to an agent for breach of a contract between the agent and the third person on a disclosed principal's behalf. However, just as an agent might be liable to the third party, the third party can be liable to the agent if the agent intended to be bound or the principal is undisclosed or partially disclosed.

An agent can sue a third party for breach of contract if both the agent and the third party have agreed that the contract obligates the agent. For example, if the principal's credit standing is not acceptable to the third party, the agent can become an actual party to the contract. The agent is therefore potentially liable but also has a right to sue the third party for breach of the contract.

An agent also can sue a third party for breach of contract entered into without the third party's knowledge of the principal's existence and identity. However, the principal can also sue, and the principal's right to sue the third party is superior to the agent's right.

In a suit by an agent in the agent's name, but for the principal's benefit, the third party can raise any substantive defense that could be raised in a suit by the principal. For example, a third party can raise the defense of nonperformance or misrepresentation, whether the principal or the agent sues.

An agent who falsely represents authority to act on a principal's behalf and who, therefore, fails to bind the principal to the contract cannot later sue under the contract. The agent cannot prove the existence of the alleged contract.

To illustrate, Alice tells Tim that she has authority to contract on Pete's behalf to sell Pete's goods to Tim. The contract indicates that Alice is acting for Pete. On the date of delivery of the goods, Alice admits that she had no authority from Pete and that Pete has not ratified the contract. Although Alice offers delivery of the goods, Tim can refuse to accept. If Alice sues Tim for refusal to accept, Tim can defend successfully based on Alice's misrepresentation.

In a suit by a third party against an agent concerning a contract entered into on a principal's behalf, the agent can set up personal defenses as though the agent were the sole contracting party. These defenses include the following:

- That the principal or agent performed the contract
- That a third party failed to perform the contract
- That requirements of the statute of frauds or statute of limitations were met

With the disclosed or partially disclosed principal's consent, the agent can assert the principal's defenses or counterclaims against the third party. The third party should not be in a better position by suing the agent than by suing the principal because defenses that are purely personal to the principal are not available to the agent. For example, defenses of the principal's personal incapacity or immunity, such as when the principal is a minor or is bankrupt, are not available to the agent.

Tort Liability—Employment

In agency law, the crucial question about a principal's possible tort liability for an agent's actions is whether the agent is the principal's employee. In this kind of agency, traditionally called the **master-servant relationship**, the employer (master) has vicarious, or substitute, liability for any harm the employee causes to third parties while acting within the scope of the employment. The employer is liable regardless of fault.

In the usual agency relationship, the principal is not liable for the physical harm caused by the agent. Only when the principal has retained the right to control the agent's physical conduct in the performance of agency duties does the employment relationship exist and, consequently, liability for the agent's physical conduct.

Master-servant relationship
A relationship in which an employer (master) has vicarious liability for any harm the employee (servant) causes to third parties while acting within the scope of the employment.

Respondeat Superior

Respondeat superior, or "let the master respond," is the legal principle that describes an employer's vicarious liability for employees' torts connected with their employment. Any third person injured by the employee's torts can proceed against both the employee and the employer. The employee is liable for his or her wrongful act because all people are responsible for their own wrongdoings. The employer's liability is vicarious.

Respondeat superior
The legal principle under which an employer is vicariously liable for the torts of an employee acting within the course and scope of employment.

For an employer to be vicariously liable for an employee's torts, the following three factors must be present:

1. The employee has committed a wrong for which he or she can be liable.
2. The employer has retained the right to control the employee's physical conduct.
3. The employee has committed the wrong within the scope of the employment.

The employer might also be liable for an employee's torts in either of the following situations:

- The employer has been negligent in the selecting or supervising of an employee.
- The employer has tried to delegate a nondelegable duty to an employee.

Employees and Independent Contractors

Courts have heard many cases on issues related to distinguishing between employees and independent contractors. Such issues are important and often complicated. An **employee** is a person who is hired to perform services for another under the direction and control of the employer.

Employee
A person who is hired to perform services for another under the direction and control of the employer.

The employer-employee relationship, like that of principal and agent, exists only if both parties agree to the agency. The contract can be oral but must be in writing under the relevant statute of frauds if the employment contract cannot be performed within one year. Any competent person can contract to employ another. Incompetent people cannot appoint employees or agents.

An employee performs an employer's services, with or without pay, and is subject to the employer's right or power of control regarding the physical aspects of service. The employment relationship creates the employer's potential for tort liability. Whether someone is an employee is a question of fact, and the answer can vary according to applicable law, whether federal or state. For example, someone might be an employee under a federal tax law but not under a state workers' compensation or federal or state occupational safety and health law. Who falls into the category of "employee" can also vary according to whether employers' liability law or unemployment compensation, social security, or other employment laws apply.

Someone who is employed to enter into contracts might be an employee. For example, a traveling sales representative, who solicits sales contracts with customers, can be an employee. Consequently, the employer can become liable for any negligence the employee commits while driving a car while on the employer's business. The important distinction is that the employee's performance and time while performing services for the employer are under the employer's control. In contrast, an independent contractor provides service under an agreement to accomplish results independently of the employer's control.

An employer who has the right to control the employee's physical performance can be vicariously liable for the employee's conduct. When the person engaged retains the right of control over the physical performance of a job, the principal is not vicariously liable. In determining whether a person's conduct is subject to an employer's control, courts consider the following:

- What extent of control the parties' agreement specifies
- Whether the worker is engaged in a distinct occupation
- What skill the occupation requires
- Who (the employer or worker) supplies the instrumentalities, tools, and the place of work for the worker
- What length of time the worker is employed
- What method of payment applies, whether according to time or job
- Whether the work is part of the employer's regular business

The term employee is not restricted to those who perform routine or manual labor. The president of a company, whose actions are subject to a board of directors' right of control in performing various duties, is an employee of that board. "Employee" indicates the closeness of the relationship between the one giving and the one receiving the service rather than the nature of the service or the status of the one giving it.

An apparent employer-employee relationship can be created despite a contractual arrangement. The employer in such a relationship may not be able to legally deny the existence of an employment if both the following two circumstances apply:

1. The employer has intentionally or negligently created an appearance that the worker is an employee.
2. A third party relies on the appearance of employment.

To illustrate, a store advertises that it employs a physician to perform cosmetic wrinkle-removal procedures. Relying on the advertisement, Mary has her wrinkles treated by the physician. If the physician's negligence results in injury to Mary, the store is liable for the physician's work as an employee, not as an independent contractor. The store created the appearance of employment, on which Mary reasonably relied.

An **independent contractor** is a person hired to undertake a specific project, but who is left free to do the work and choose the method for the project. In many cases, independent contractors are not agents because they have no responsibility to contract with third persons for their employers. Independent contractors are generally not employees because employers usually have no control over the details of independent contractors' job performance.

Independent contractor
An agent hired to undertake a specific project but left free to do the work and choose the method for the project.

If an independent contractor is negligent in the performance of the contract and thereby causes physical harm to a third person, the employer is not liable. To illustrate, Will contracts to build a fence for Rob at a cost of $2,000 and according to certain specifications, with no supervision. Will is an independent contractor. If Rob had instead engaged Will to assist him in building the fence under his supervision, an employer-employee relationship would have resulted.

The legal distinction between an employee and an independent contractor is easy to state but more difficult to apply in practice. Frequently, the extent of an employer's control over an independent contractor is unclear.

A general contractor who erects a building is usually an independent contractor, as is the subcontractor who promises to furnish materials and services for a particular part of the job. Each usually has its own organization and employees, and the property owner usually has no right of control over the manner used to accomplish the job.

Skilled professionals, such as lawyers, are independent contractors even though they might be employed on a retainer basis (with regular, periodic payments). Such professions involve considerable skill and learning, and professionals do not usually work under others' complete control. An exception is a physician employed by a hospital as a resident.

Many insurance producers are independent contractors because the insurers they represent seldom retain the right to control their job performance. However, an insurance agent who is in one insurer's employ, uses the insurer's car, and is closely supervised is probably an employee. Either as employee-agents or as independent contractors, insurance producers subject their principals to contractual and tort liability (such as for fraud or deceit), connected with any contracts they form. Before an insurer-principal can have vicarious liability for a producer's physical torts, however, the insurer must have the right to control the producer's agency's job performance.

However, well established exceptions have developed to the rule that an employer is not liable for an independent contractor's torts, and the following are the three most general categories:

1. *Employer's negligence.* The employer can be liable for his or her own negligence, such as in selecting an unqualified independent contractor or failing to give the independent contractor adequate directions.
2. *Nondelegable duty.* The employer can be liable if the employer delegated nondelegable duties to an independent contractor. For example, a landlord might not legally delegate the duty to keep common areas of rented property safe.
3. *Inherently dangerous activities.* Employers who use independent contractors to carry out inherently dangerous activities are strictly liable for any resulting harm. For example, an employer is liable for harm an independent contractor's blasting operations cause.

Scope of Employment

For an employer-principal to be liable for an employee's torts, the employee must have acted within the scope of the employment. The employee must have been engaged in work for the employer of the type that he or she is employed to perform. The employer is not liable when the employee has acted outside the scope of the employment to commit a tort to further his or her own interests.

The law provides no simple test to determine whether a tort has occurred within the scope of employment, but a court would ask the following questions:

- Did the employer authorize the act, or was the act incidental to an act the employer did authorize?
- Was the act one that such employees usually perform?
- When and where did the act occur, and what was its purpose?
- To what extent did the parties intend to advance the employer's interests by performing the act?
- To what extent did the parties intend to advance the employee's interests by performing the act?
- Did the employer furnish the instrumentality by which the employee committed the tort?
- Did the employer authorize the extent of departure from the usual method of accomplishing the act?
- Did the act involve the commission of a serious crime?

Few employers knowingly authorize torts. However, it is not necessary to show that the act causing the injury was permitted, as long as the act occurred in the scope of the employee's regular duties and employment. To illustrate, Mary employs Steve to deliver goods, using her truck. Steve uses his own car to make a delivery for Mary and negligently injures Ted in the process.

Because the injury occurred within the scope of Steve's duties, Mary is liable even though Steve used a personal car.

The employee must be employed at the time and place of the specific act. For instance, a person is usually not acting as an employee while commuting to and from the person's place of employment. However, an employee who is on the street most of the time while working might be within the scope of employment if he or she goes directly from home to a customer's place of business, if that is the usual procedure. A sales representative's making calls at businesses is an example of such a situation.

An employee instructed to go from one point to another might, for personal reasons, detour via another route. This detour can be slight or major. If slight, the employee might not have left the scope of employment. If major, the employee might be outside the scope of employment.

Also, for an employer to be liable, the act must be within the scope of the employment. Suppose that a gasoline station attendant smokes a cigarette while filling Tom's gas tank, causing an explosion. Modern court cases indicate that smoking is merely an unauthorized way of doing an authorized act and is therefore within the scope of employment. On the other hand, an employer probably wouldn't be liable for injuries resulting from an accident caused by an employee while running a personal errand during work hours.

The employer can be liable for an employee's acts even though the employer specifically forbade the act committed. To illustrate, Mary instructs her employee, Steve, that he should never permit customers to enter the supply room of Mary's store. Steve violates the instructions by allowing Ted to go into the supply room, and Ted is injured through Steve's negligence while there. Mary is liable for Steve's actions, notwithstanding his violation of her instructions.

An employer might be vicariously liable for an employee's negligence and intentional torts as long as they occur within the scope of employment. For intentional torts, the employer is liable whether or not the employee or agent intended to benefit the employer. For example, an insurer's authorized agent fraudulently misrepresents that the insured's commercial automobile insurance is effective and keeps the premium. Although the agent's act is a crime and the agent does not intend to benefit the insurer, the insurer is responsible for the agent's act. The insured has no reason to believe that the agent's statements were not true, and the agent acted within the apparent scope of employment.

If the employee's actions are not within the apparent scope of employment, the question of the employee's intention becomes material. The following three examples illustrate questions that arise in these cases:

1. Employee Ed drives his employer's truck and collides with Diane's car. Ed and Diane leave their vehicles, argue, and Ed assaults Diane.

2. Vic, a department store manager, accuses Kay, a customer, of shoplifting, and he detains and searches her. Vic learns that the accusation, although innocently made, was false.

3. Joe is employed to collect payment for goods Millie sells to third persons. He is specifically instructed not to attempt repossession of the goods, even peaceably, and is only to request payment. Joe nevertheless uses force in attempting to repossess goods from Jan. Jan resists the repossession, and Joe injures Jan.

Each of the employees' acts was intentional. Each employee would not have committed the acts in question except for the employment. The following two legal tests apply:

1. The employer should be liable when the employee's tort is within the scope of employment.
2. The employer should not be liable if the employee committed the tort solely for personal reasons.

Ed's employer employed him not to get into fights but to drive the truck. A court might characterize the argument with Diane as personal. Therefore, both the scope-of-employment and the intention tests suggest that the employer is not liable, although some courts might decide otherwise.

In the case of false imprisonment or false arrest, both the scope-of-employment and the intention tests appear to suggest the employer's liability to Kay. The department store manager is responsible for protecting the employer's property from theft. In addition, the employee thought the detention was in the employer's best interests, although it turned out otherwise.

The repossession was not within the employee's scope of employment, so under that test, the employer is not liable. However, in attempting to repossess the goods, Joe apparently was acting in the employer's interests, even though contrary to instructions. Some courts would find liability, while some would not.

An employer is subject to tort liability for any loss sustained by third parties resulting from misrepresentations an employee makes within the scope of employment. The tort of misrepresentation requires proof that a false statement concerning a material fact was made with an intent to deceive and that a third party reasonably relied on the statement to the third party's detriment. If these requirements are proved, and if the employee or agent is authorized to make representations, the employer is vicariously liable for the resulting harm even if the employee informs the third party of a lack of authority to make the representation.

For example, Gary authorizes Debbie to sell land but does not authorize her to make any representations about the land. Debbie tells Peg that the land is good "growing land," adding, "But of course, I have no authority to evaluate it." Peg buys the land, relying on Debbie's statement, only to learn that the soil is poor, and sues Gary to rescind the sale. Gary's defense is that he did not authorize Debbie to make the representation. Even though Debbie indicated she had no authority to make the statement, she did make it, and Peg relied on it. Gary is liable for Debbie's misrepresentation, and Peg can obtain rescission of the agreement.

An employer's vicarious liability may also extend to an employee's crimes, in some cases. Generally, no one is responsible for another person's crime. An employer, therefore, is not vicariously liable for an employee's crime. However, if the employer orders the employee to commit a crime, both are guilty. The employee cannot defend on the basis that the employer ordered the act, and the employer cannot defend on the basis that someone else committed the act.

An employer is liable if he or she has ratified the employee's criminal act. An employer would be criminally responsible if he or she should have been aware of repeated criminal activity. For example, an agent with authority to bind the principal contractually writes a letter containing fraudulent statements to a prospect. Relying on the fraudulent statements, the third party enters into a contract with the principal. If the crime of using the mail to defraud occurs only once, the principal is not criminally responsible. If, however, the agent makes a practice of writing fraudulent letters and has done so for a considerable time, a court might find that the principal either knew or should have known of this activity and is therefore criminally responsible.

Not all crimes require intention. If a statute provides a criminal penalty for performing an act, regardless of intention, the person who commits the act is criminally responsible. Automatic criminal responsibility often applies to business crimes such as selling alcoholic beverages to minors or intoxicated persons, or polluting waterways. Both the employee committing the criminal act and the employer are criminally responsible, regardless of intent.

Other crimes require intention, not necessarily intention to commit a crime but intention to commit the act that constitutes the crime. A person might be ignorant of a statute that makes a certain act a crime but might intentionally commit the criminal act.

SUMMARY

Agency is a relationship that exists when an agent acts on a principal's behalf. A person who performs a task for another can be an employee or an independent contractor. A person who affects another's legal relationships is an agent and also can be either an employee or independent contractor. Principals can be disclosed or undisclosed, and agents can be general or special.

An agency relationship can arise by appointment, estoppel, or ratification. An agent's authority can be actual or apparent. Actual authority can be express or implied, or it can be authority to act in an emergency. An agent generally cannot delegate authority to others, except for ministerial duties, customary appointments, and emergency appointments.

Principals and agents owe different obligations to each other. An agent's implied fiduciary duties to a principal include the following:

- Loyalty
- Obedience

- Reasonable care
- Accounting
- Information

The principal has the following four possible remedies for an agent's default or wrongdoing:

1. Suit to require the agent to transfer to the principal the property improperly held
2. Suit for the value of the benefit the agent received
3. Suit for breach of the agency contract
4. Suit in tort for harm done

A principal has the duty to provide the agent with the following:

- Agreed-on period of employment
- Compensation
- Reimbursement for expenses
- Indemnity for losses

Agency can terminate in the following ways:

- Just cause
- Lapse of time
- Accomplishment of purpose
- Revocation
- Renunciation
- Death or incapacity
- Changed circumstances

To determine third-party liabilities and rights in contract cases, courts must answer questions about the existence of the agency, the extent of the agent's authority, and disclosure of the principal. To determine third-party rights and liabilities in tort cases, courts must answer questions about whether any employment relationship existed and whether the act committed was within the scope of that employment.

Respondeat superior, or "let the master respond," is the legal phrase that describes an employer's vicarious, or substitute, liability for employees' torts connected with their employment. For an employer to be vicariously liable for an employee's torts, the following three factors must be present:

1. The employee must commit a wrong for which he or she can be liable.
2. The employer must retain the right to control the employee's physical conduct.
3. The employee must commit the wrong within the scope of the employment.

Chapter 12

Direct Your Learning

Agency Law: Insurance Applications

After learning the content of this chapter and completing the corresponding course guide assignment, you should be able to:

- Describe the duties of the following:
  - Producer
  - Agent (general, special, or soliciting)
  - Broker
- Explain how to create producers' authority.
- Describe the extent of producers' authority.
- Explain how producers' authority can be terminated.
- Describe producers' duties and liabilities to insurance customers, third parties, and insurers, as well as their claim settlement authority.
- Describe errors and omissions coverage and an insurer's liability for a producer's acts and omissions.
- Given a case, explain how to create a claim representative's authority, and justify your answer.
- Describe claim representatives' duties to insurance customers, third parties, and insurers.
- Define or describe each of the Key Words and Phrases for this chapter.

Develop Your Perspective

What are the main topics covered in the chapter?

This chapter further applies the principles of agency law discussed in the previous chapter directly to insurance relationships and personnel, including producers and claim representatives.

Contrast the duties of insurance agents and brokers in an agency relationship.

- To whom does an insurance agent have duties?

- How do a broker's duties differ?

Why is it important to learn about these topics?

An understanding of agency law is crucial for insurance professionals because insurance is a business revolving around agency law, with agents working for principals that are insurers and those that are insurance agencies. Insurance professionals must understand how agents can bind their principals and create liabilities for them.

Compare the duties and liabilities you can see in any professional or personal dealings you have with the following:

- Agents

- Brokers

- Claim representatives

How can you use what you will learn?

Evaluate the application of agency law in your organization.

- Identify the different kinds of producers in your organization or in organizations with which you deal.

- Does the law in this chapter apply to your own role? If so, in what ways?

Chapter 12
Agency Law: Insurance Applications

Like other businesses, insurers act through various representatives to accomplish their goals. Some of these representatives are insurer employees, and others are independent contractors who perform certain functions for the insurer. The acts of these persons on behalf of the insurer may legally bind the insurer.

Courts have ruled that all parties to an insurance contract are required to act with utmost good faith and to deal fairly and openly with one another. These requirements, and the high degree of importance of insurance to society, create duties of care and competence to which insurer representatives must adhere.

This chapter discusses insurer representatives' duties and authority. Because insurance producers and claim representatives interact directly with the public, their activities are the primary focus of this chapter. However, the general principles illustrated apply to all insurer representatives.

INSURANCE PRODUCER CLASSIFICATIONS

To understand producers' respective duties, including those of agents and brokers, an understanding of what these terms mean and how the roles interrelate is necessary.

Producer classifications have distinct legal significance, depending on whether they are general, special, or soliciting agents, or brokers. The authority, as well as potential liability, of each type of producer can vary significantly.

The insurance business uses the generic term **insurance producer** to denote the broad category of persons involved in arranging to place insurance business with insurers and who represent either insurers or insureds, or both. The person or group acting as intermediary between the insurer and insured in placing business with the insurer "produces" the business and, thus, is a producer. The term producer encompasses agents and brokers.

Insurance producer
Any of several kinds of insurance personnel who place insurance business with insurers and who represent either insurers or insureds, or both.

Agents

The term **insurance agent**, or agent, like the term producer, refers to intermediaries between insurers and prospective insureds to arrange contracts of insurance. More specifically, an insurance agent represents a specific insurer in an ongoing relationship. The prospective insured is the customer. Insurance

Insurance agent
A producer who represents one or more insurers.

agents can fall into the following three categories based on the degree of discretion they have in carrying out their functions: (1) general agent, (2) special agent, and (3) soliciting agent.

Historically, the general agent has been the primary means through which insurers have marketed their insurance products. The **general agent** has broad powers within underwriting guidelines to enter into insurance contracts. The agent is often in charge of an insurer's business in a defined area and acts under general instructions only. The general agent has the authority to do the following:

General agent
A producer who has broad powers within underwriting guidelines to enter into insurance contracts on behalf of one or more insurers.

- Solicit applications for insurance
- Receive premiums
- Issue and renew policies
- Appoint subagents
- Adjust losses, in some instances

Insurance marketing systems are changing and evolving. Recently, many insurers have reduced their marketing through general agents in favor of other marketing systems, including the use of special agents. Generally, the term **special agent** describes an insurer's agent whose authority is established and restricted by express agreement with the insurer. The agency contract with the insurer creates and expressly restricts the special agent's powers. The special agent typically has the authority to do the following:

Special agent
An insurance producer whose authority is established and restricted by express agreement with an insurer.

- To induce third parties to apply for insurance
- To forward the application to the insurer
- To deliver the policy to the insured on the receipt of the first premium

The agency contract might specify additional duties for the special agent, such as inspecting property, quoting rates, collecting premium payments, and assisting with changes in coverage.

Soliciting agent
An insurance producer whose authority is limited by contract with an insurer to soliciting applications for insurance and performing other acts directly incident to those activities.

A **soliciting agent** is a special agent with even narrower authority. Like the special agent, the soliciting agent derives all powers and duties directly from the agency contract. The soliciting agent is only to solicit applications for insurance, forward them to the insurer for consideration, and perform other acts directly incident to those activities. Ordinarily, the soliciting agent has no authority to bind the insurer to coverage.

Brokers

Broker
An independent producer who represents insurance customers.

While an insurance agent represents the insurer, the insurance **broker** represents the insurance customer. An insurance broker is independent, does not work for a particular insurer, and typically assists large insureds by using concentrated bargaining power to obtain the most favorable terms from competing insurers. The broker's focus is on the client's insurance needs rather than on obtaining business for an insurer.

Some insurance brokers have expanded their roles beyond finding available insurance coverage and coordinating the placement of their clients' insurance business. They have become insurance consultants, who evaluate client insurance needs and advise clients as to how to handle their loss exposures, whether that involves insurance or some other risk management technique.

Producers' Authority

Insurance producer authority arises in the same ways that agency relationships in other businesses arise, with each means of creating the principal/agent relationship having legal significance for duties and liabilities. Likewise the types of producer authority are the same as those for other agents, as follows:

1. Actual authority, which can be express or implied
2. Apparent authority

The insurer can bind itself to the unauthorized acts of an agent by its subsequent conduct to ratify the agent's acts. If an insurer ratifies an agent's unauthorized actions with full knowledge of the facts, then the insurer accepts the benefits of those actions. For example, an insurer accepts a premium and issues a policy on an application submitted by an unauthorized agent. The insurer has ratified the agent's acts and cannot disavow the agent's actions under the policy.

The insurer alone can decide whether to ratify the actions of an insurance agent who lacks the authority to bind the insurer. Insurers typically ratify such actions when they would benefit. For example, an insurer might choose to issue a policy to a customer represented by an agent not authorized to solicit and forward applications when the insurer believes both that the risk is favorable and that issuing the policy will not compromise the insurer's relationship with other agents.

However, an insurer must be careful in ratifying such agent actions. If the insurer develops a pattern or practice of ratifying this agent's actions, an agency relationship can arise by implication. The insurer must evaluate whether it should enter into a formal relationship through an agency contract or deny the relationship and refuse to ratify the agent's submissions.

Actual Authority

Actual authority is that which the principal (insurer) intentionally confers upon the agent or allows the agent to believe he or she possesses.

Typically, the insurance producer and the insurer establish the terms of the principal/agent relationship by a formal written contract that grants the producer express authority. This agency contract states the producer's powers and authority and specifies any restrictions on the producer's authority. If the contract does not state an authority, the producer does not have that express authority. An insurance producer who is an exclusive agent of one insurer might have one contract. A producer who is an independent agent representing multiple insurers might have several contracts.

Example: Agent's Authority

Jane is an insurance agent associated exclusively with MutualCo, a regional insurer. When MutualCo appointed Jane as an agent, they entered into a standard written agency contract that MutualCo uses for all agents. This agreement sets out, among other things, the following terms:

- The agent's commission arrangement with the insurer, financial assistance, and other support that MutualCo will provide to Jane's agency

- Jane's authority and methods allowed for binding coverage

- Types of insurance Jane can write

- Duration of the agency contract

- Termination methods for the agency contract

Jane has express authority to act within those terms.

The application for insurance and the insurance policy itself also can limit the extent of the producer's express authority. A producer has no express authority to act inconsistently with any such limitations. Unless the producer has some other basis for the authority, such an action does not bind the insurer. For example, a clear insurance application provision that the producer has no authority to bind coverage eliminates the producer's express power to do so.

Actual authority can be implied as well as express. Although express agreements create most insurance principal and agent relationships, the parties can agree to the relationship by less formal means. For example, an agent's submission of an insurance application can create an agency relationship if the producer has solicited and forwarded insurance applications to the insurer previously, and if the insurer has accepted them. The agent has the implied authority to bind the insurer in this manner. The insurer must voluntarily accept the applications from the agent and then voluntarily issue policies. Merely forwarding applications for insurance under an automobile assigned risk or other residual market automobile insurance plan does not create an implied authority for the agent.

To illustrate, Alice is an independent insurance agent who places her insurance customers' business with a variety of insurers with whom she has agency contracts. Alice does not have a contract with CoverageCo, a large national insurer. In a local professional meeting, Alice hears that CoverageCo is soliciting independent agents to send business to them. Alice sends business to CoverageCo on several occasions, and CoverageCo issues a policy and forwards its standard commission to Alice. CoverageCo then forwards to Alice its application forms for use in soliciting more insurance applicants along with rating material and manuals describing CoverageCo's products and procedures. Alice is CoverageCo's agent by implication, not by express authority. The parties did not create an agency contract, nor did CoverageCo give Alice any direct expression of authority to act on its behalf. CoverageCo's conduct in accepting applications submitted by Alice and forwarding to her applications and manuals, however, gives her implied authority in the agency relationship.

Apparent Authority

Even without actual authority, express or implied, an agent can have apparent authority. While the apparent authority (agency by estoppel) is similar to that of implied authority, the focus is different. In questions of implied authority, the insurer's and the agent's conduct toward one another helps determine the existence of implied authority, which then creates an agency relationship.

A producer may have apparent authority when no actual agency relationship exists. In such cases, to protect any third parties who may deal with the agent, the law holds that, legally, an agency relationship does exist. The focus is only on the insurer's conduct. Thus, an insurer might be barred from denying an agency relationship when others were misled into believing that an agency relationship existed. For example, if an insurer sends a broker numerous blank copies of an insurer's automobile policies and receives from the broker numerous copies of policies the broker has issued, the broker would be the insurer's agent by estoppel. By dealing with the broker, the insurer has granted apparent authority.

Third parties who see that an agent has the insurer's application forms, signs, and stationery, would reasonably assume that an agency relationship exists. The third party has legal protection should the insurer attempt to deny the agency relationship to the third party's detriment.

However, if a third party's assumptions about an agent's authority are unreasonable and are not supported by facts, the insurer can legally deny the existence of the agency relationship. Likewise, the purported agent's statements or actions are insufficient to create an agency by estoppel. The insurer's acts alone create the apparent authority. For example, an insurance agent cannot create an agency relationship with an insurer by stating falsely that he or she is its agent, by misappropriating its company logo, or by copying its applications without authorization. The insurer could deny the agency relationship because it did nothing to create this misunderstanding. However, if the insurer becomes aware of this situation and fails to act in a timely fashion to prevent the agent from improperly using its logo, an agency by estoppel can arise.

Extent of Producers' Authority

The extent of producers' authority depends on the following:

- Producers' status as general or special agents or as brokers
- Producers' notice and knowledge
- Producers' authority to bind coverage
- Appointment of subagents

Once an agency relationship between an insurer and a producer is established, the producer can act on the insurer's behalf. The producer's actions must be consistent with the authority granted within the agency relationship. An insurer, like any other principal, is liable for the acts performed or contracts made by one of its agents within the scope of that agent's actual (either express or implied) or apparent authority.

Examples: Producer's Authority

- Paul has an agency contract with InsurCo that calls him a general agent and that specifically grants him several powers, among them the power to renew policies. One of Paul's insurance customers' policies comes up for renewal. Without consulting InsurCo, Paul tells the customer that the policy is renewed and collects the renewal premium. Paul is acting pursuant to express authority, and his action binds InsurCo, whether or not InsurCo wanted to renew the policy.

- JoAnne has an agency contract with InsurCo that does not attach any description to the relationship created. The contract gives JoAnne several powers, among them the powers to bind the insurer to new business, to collect premiums, to issue policies, and to adjust small claims. JoAnne does not have the power to renew policies. Her office displays the company logo prominently in several places, and all of InsurCo's forms that JoAnne uses have her name on them and label her as InsurCo's agent. JoAnne places a substantial amount of insurance with InsurCo. One day, JoAnne decides to renew one of her best customers' insurance on her own, without consulting InsurCo, and collects the appropriate renewal premium. A covered loss occurs the next day. Despite JoAnne's lack of actual authority to renew the policy, she has bound InsurCo to cover the loss. JoAnne acted with apparent authority. Under these circumstances, JoAnne's customer reasonably believed that she had the authority to renew the policy on InsurCo's behalf. InsurCo has acted as though JoAnne is its general agent and is estopped from denying this relationship.

Producers' Status

The extent of producer authority varies depending on whether the producer is a general agent, special agent, or broker. The general agent has the broadest authority of all insurance agents and fully represents an insurer. The general agent can accept loss exposures, agree on and settle the terms of insurance, waive policy provisions, issue and renew policies, collect premiums, and adjust claims. Any actions the producer takes according to the agreed-on authority binds the insurer.

Clearly, if the contract with the insurer expressly empowers the producer to act as a general agent, the producer has all the broad powers discussed. Even if the contract does not confer them, the producer may have those powers by apparent authority.

If a contract between producer and insurer expressly limits the producer's power to soliciting business, the producer has no additional actual authority. Any actions of these agents beyond soliciting and forwarding prospective business to the insurer usually do not bind the insurer unless an insured can establish apparent authority.

The extent of producer authority for brokers is different than that of general and special agents. Brokers represent insureds. Thus, the broker's principal is the insurance customer, not the insurer. Accordingly, an insurance broker generally has no actual or, typically, no apparent authority to bind the insurer. Instead, the broker has the power to bind the insurance customer.

Among the duties brokers typically assume are the following:

- To procure insurance for the insurance customer-principal
- To select the insurer to provide the desired coverage
- To arrange for the payment of premiums
- To cancel and receive unearned premiums on a policy the broker has obtained
- To obtain a new policy upon cancellation of one previously obtained

A broker can be both an agent and an insured's representative in two instances. First, if the insurer, through its dealings, allows the broker to act in a manner leading a reasonable third party to believe that the broker is the insurer's agent, the broker is legally the insurer's agent. Apparent authority does not arise merely by the insurer's furnishing a broker with application forms that the broker routinely submits to the insurer. However, a broker who has a particular insurer's application forms, receives premiums ostensibly on that insurer's behalf, and issues material identifying the customer as presently covered by that insurer can be the insurer's agent.

Second, some state statutes provide that, for some specific purposes, a broker is the insurer's agent. Once a policy is issued, the broker acting on the insured's behalf is the insurer's agent regarding premium payments, and the broker's receipt of the payments is effectively the insurer's receipt. The reasoning behind such statutes is that, once a policy is issued, the broker who facilitated the placement of the customer's business with the insurer is indistinguishable from an insurance agent in many customers' eyes; therefore the laws provide some extra protection to insurance customers.

Producers' Notice and Knowledge

In agency law, a principal is considered to have any knowledge possessed by any of its agents, general or special. This general rule applies in the insurance context. The authorized agent's knowledge is imputed to the insurer. Whether the insurer actually receives the information the agent has is irrelevant.

Questions of imputed knowledge often arise when agents possess knowledge that would have caused the insurer to decline coverage, had the insurer had the information. In these circumstances, a court will hold that the insurer knew what the agent knew, and the court typically finds that coverage exists.

> ### Example: Imputed Knowledge
>
> John, the insurer's authorized agent, assisted a customer, Mary, in arranging automobile insurance for a car owned by Mary's son. John told Mary that the insurer's policy provided the coverage. Later, a loss occurs. The insurer denies coverage based on policy language conferring coverage only for a named insured's vehicles, and not for the insured's son's vehicle. The insurer cannot deny coverage, because it is held to know what its agent knew at the time the policy was issued.

Imputed knowledge also applies to a location to be insured. For example, a court might hold that a binder conferring coverage on an insured's business is effective over an insurer's objection that it would not have provided coverage if it had known about the location of the insured. In such a case, the insurer's authorized agent might have been aware of the location of the property to be insured and that the binder issued was broad enough to cover the location. The insurer's lack of actual knowledge would be irrelevant.

A court might not bind an insurer by a producer's knowledge in the following circumstances:

- When no actual agency relationship exists between the producer and insurer
- When the agent has supplied false information

An agent's knowledge is not imputed to an insurer if no agency relationship exists between them. Therefore a general agent's knowledge is imputed to the insurer, but under most circumstances, an insurance broker's knowledge is not imputed. The broker's agency relationship is with the insured, not the insurer.

Cases involving soliciting agents are less clear. Some courts hold that the limited nature of the soliciting agent's authority is such that the insurer is not chargeable with that agent's knowledge. Because the soliciting agent cannot bind coverage, these courts reason that the connection between principal and agent is too tenuous to bind the insurer by the producer's knowledge.

Other courts hold that a soliciting agent is a general agent under their state laws; therefore the soliciting agent's knowledge can be imputed to the insurer. Still other courts impute some of the soliciting agent's knowledge to the insurer if it is consistent with that agent's more limited authority to obtain and forward insurance applications.

Many courts refuse to bind an insurer by an agent's knowledge when the agent gives the insurer false information. Typically in these situations, if the insurer had known the facts, it would not have issued a policy.

If the agent is aware that information provided by an insured is false and still submits it to the insurer, courts permit the insurer to avoid liability under the policy because the agent's decision to act adversely to the insurer interests has broken the agency relationship that is the basis of the imputed knowledge rule. No hardship results to the insurer as an innocent third party because the insured was involved in the dishonest behavior. If an agent is unaware that information provided by an insurance customer is false, no knowledge is imputed to the insurer, and the insurer can avoid liability under the policy if it can prove fraud, misrepresentation, or some other defense.

The key issue in these cases concerns whether the insurance customer knew that the agent was providing false information. If the applicant has given correct answers to the agent, but the agent enters incorrect answers, the law will impute the agent's knowledge of the correct information to the insurer. Arguably, in these cases the producer's improper conduct should provide a basis on which a court should view the agency relationship as severed. If that were so, the agent's knowledge would not be imputed to the insurer and the insurer would be able to avoid coverage. However, courts generally rule otherwise because the insurance customer is an innocent party. Although the insurer is also innocent, courts protect the insurance customer. This rule encourages insurers to exercise greater care in their selection of authorized agents.

Examples: Imputed Knowledge and False Information

Agent's False Information

James visits Steve, a general insurance agent for InsurCo., to insure all of his family cars through Steve's agency. James tells Steve that a member of his household has been convicted of driving while intoxicated. Steve knows this information would disqualify James from coverage with InsurCo. Eager to receive the commission from the sale, Steve falsely enters on the application that no driving offenses have occurred in James's household. James signs the application without reading it, and a policy issues. Later James has a loss, and InsurCo discovers the conviction.

InsurCo must cover the loss. The knowledge of its agent, Steve, is imputed to InsurCo. Steve (thus, InsurCo) knew of the conviction, but a policy issued anyway. This knowledge estops InsurCo from denying coverage under the policy.

Insurer's False Information

The result changes if, instead, James falsely tells Steve that no driving offenses have occurred in the household. Steve is unaware of the truth and enters the information James has provided him on the application. James later has a loss, and InsurCo discovers the false information entered on the application and denies coverage on the basis of fraud or misrepresentation.

A final example involves the same factual situation, but Steve and James both know of the conviction and collude to enter false information on the application. InsurCo can deny coverage. Steve's lack of truthfulness to InsurCo breaks the agency relationship, and no countervailing argument of fairness in favor of protecting James applies because he participated in providing false information.

Producer's Authority to Bind Coverage

The need for immediate insurance coverage arises frequently. In many cases, people or organizations acquire property or assume duties suddenly and with little or no advance notice. Before issuing a policy on a given loss exposure, however, insurers usually must undertake an underwriting process that can take several weeks or longer to complete. Because this delay leaves applicants unprotected, many insurers authorize producers to issue temporary oral or written policies pending acceptance of the application.

In many cases, a producer can form an oral insurance contract with a customer. For example, an applicant can call an insurance producer from a car dealership, provide the details of the car to be purchased, and request immediate insurance on the car. By consenting to provide the coverage, the producer has created a valid insurance contract, which binds the insurer.

Courts generally have upheld the propriety of oral insurance contracts, although they are not valid in a few states. These contracts must contain sufficient agreement on essential terms, such as the following:

- Subject matter of the insurance
- Loss exposures insured
- Premium
- Insurance contract duration
- Coverage amount
- Identity of parties

The contract need not mention these terms specifically, but the parties must agree to them, even if implicitly. In many situations a party can prove essential contractual elements by evidence showing an understanding, express or implied, that the insurer's customary policy terms are to apply.

Sometimes, a writing, such as a binder, (binder receipt, or binding receipt), can provide a temporary insurance contract. A binder receipt contains a written temporary contract of insurance, sets out its essential terms and conditions, and proves the main elements of the temporary insurance contract. The contract remains in effect until cancellation occurs, the time period elapses, or the final insurance policy issues. The issuance of the insurance policy usually supersedes and replaces the temporary insurance contract.

The two legal issues encountered most often regarding oral and temporary insurance contracts are as follows:

1. A producer's lack of authority to form the contract
2. A producer's failure to designate which insurer was to be bound by the oral or temporary contract

If the producer has actual authority, the oral or temporary insurance contract is valid and binding on the insurer. The legal issue shifts to whether the producer had apparent authority. A third party could reasonably believe that a general agent had the power to bind coverage orally or in writing. If the producer is not a general agent, no apparent authority exists, and the producer's oral or temporary contract would not bind the insurer.

If a producer representing multiple insurers contracts with a customer and then fails to designate the insurer providing coverage before a loss occurs, the legal issue is which, if any, insurer is liable for the loss. Courts look for reliable evidence that the producer intended to bind a particular insurer to the contract, such as the following:

- The producer represents only one insurer that issues the coverage on the terms sought.

- In previous dealings, the producer has placed all the insured's business with one insurer.

- The producer issued a note or memorandum before the loss showing an intention to form the contract with a particular insurer. A mere mental note or a subsequent writing does not bind an insurer.

If the evidence does not reveal that the producer selected an insurer before the loss, the contract does not bind any insurer. The insured has no coverage but can sue the agent for errors and omissions and seek damages equivalent to the loss. Producers protect themselves from liability losses with an **errors and omissions (E&O) liability policy**, which covers the producer's mistakes (errors), as well as failure to act (omissions). If the producer does not have adequate insurance coverage for errors and omissions, the customer might suffer a severe hardship for lack of coverage. In cases of producer failure to designate, all insurers the producer represents who write the insurance the customer seeks might provide coverage for the loss on a proportionate basis. This alternative shifts the loss from the innocent insurance customer to all insurers that have authorized the producer to act on their behalf for a particular type of insurance.

Errors and omissions (E&O) liability policy
An insurance policy covering liability for the mistakes (errors) and failures to act (omissions) of professionals and businesspeople, including insurance producers.

Appointment of Subagents

The general rule is that an insurance producer cannot delegate duties to another when the duties involve the producer's individual care, skill, and judgment. In many instances, insurance producers employ people to assist them in various aspects of their duties. These persons are subagents because they are the producer's agents. Insurance producers also may have clerical employees who assist in administration of their agencies, and they may retain the services of others who assist in the sales or marketing of their insurance products.

The appointment of subagents is permissible because of the following three exceptions to a general rule against delegation to subagents:

1. Producers can appoint subagents to discharge their mechanical, clerical, and ministerial (nondiscretionary) duties, including tasks relating to the placement or renewal of insurance with the producer's principal insurance agency. These acts include soliciting insurance applications, countersigning insurance policies when discretion is not involved (if state law allows), delivering policies, and collecting premiums. An insurance producer retained to use skill and judgment can delegate any duties that do not involve this skill and judgment.

2. A subagent can discharge even discretionary duties and those involving skill and judgment when those acts are ratified by the insurance producer. For example, a producer could authorize a subagent to bind coverage for an insurer or could ratify the subagent's act. As long as the producer accepts full responsibility for the subagent's actions, a court will view those actions as the producer's actions.

3. Appointing subagents is authorized when discharging the producer's duties to the insurance principal would not be otherwise possible. To illustrate, a producer might need to appoint a subagent to conduct business in another state. If the insurer has authorized the producer to market its products in the state and state law allows such marketing only by residents of that state, the producer may appoint a resident subagent.

The doctrine of apparent authority also can apply to subagents. To the public, an insurance producer's subagents appear to have authorization to act for the insurer, even when they do not have such authority. In many such circumstances, these subagents' acts bind the insurer under the doctrine of apparent authority. One frequent example involves commitments by producers' office employees to extend coverage in various situations. Generally, the insurer is bound by these commitments even if the employee acted without actual authority.

Example: Subagent's Apparent Authority

Martha is an agent representing multiple insurers. Alice, Martha's office administrator, has varied job duties, including taking new applications for personal insurance and making changes to existing accounts at customers' requests. Paula insures her cars, home, and business through Martha's agency. Paula has changed her car and homeowners insurance by telephoning Alice. Paula visits the agency to add business interruption coverage to her commercial coverage. Alice tells Paula she can handle this addition, obtains the necessary information, and issues a thirty-day binder. In fact, Alice has no authority to issue the binder, and Martha would not have approved adding this coverage for Paula. A court would have to determine whether Alice's action has bound Martha's agency to provide Paula the additional coverage. Paula probably reasonably believed that Alice had the authority she purported to have. Alice assumed a large number of duties for Martha, and a customer probably would not distinguish between Alice's other duties and the issuance of a binder.

Termination of Producer Authority

Usually the circumstances for termination of the producer/insurer relationship are specified in the contract. For example, the contract might identify a period after which the relationship will terminate, or it might set out circumstances, such as failure to meet production standards or producer misconduct, that warrant termination of the relationship.

As with other agency relationships, if one of the parties no longer wants the relationship to continue, that party has the power, if not the right, to terminate the relationship. Thus, an insurer can revoke a producer's authority to act on the insurer's behalf even if a valid agency contract that would not support the termination exists between the parties. Under these circumstances the agency relationship terminates, but the producer has an action for wrongful termination against the insurer.

Example: Agent's Termination

Jane is an insurance agent associated with CoverageCo, a large commercial insurer. Under the agency contract, Jane has the right to market CoverageCo's insurance products indefinitely, unless she or CoverageCo terminates the contract. The contract allows CoverageCo to terminate only if Jane's sales fall below a specified level or if Jane violates insurer rules or procedures.

Jane's level of sales exceeds the standards specified in the agency contract, and she has violated no CoverageCo rules or procedures. However, CoverageCo terminates Jane's agency contract for no stated reason. The agency relationship between CoverageCo and Jane ends, and Jane has no actual authority to market any of CoverageCo's insurance products. However, she has a valid cause of action against CoverageCo for breach of contract.

The producer/insurer agency relationship is terminated by any act of one of the parties that the other party might reasonably construe to show the intent to terminate. Typically, termination occurs through a written or oral communication, which severs the producer's actual authority to bind the insurance principal. The principal must take appropriate action to inform third parties that the relationship has terminated to avoid the operation of apparent authority. After notification to third parties, the producer cannot bind the insurer in any way regarding that party. If a third party who has dealt with the producer does not receive notification, however, the producer's acts, purportedly on the insurer's behalf, might bind that insurer.

The producer can bind the insurer regarding third parties with whom he or she has not dealt previously if these parties had prior knowledge of the existence of the former agency relationship, but no notice of the termination. The safest way to avoid the possible adverse consequences of apparent authority is for the insurer to do the following:

- Notify all third parties known to have dealt with the producer of the termination
- Repossess from the producer any evidence of the agency relationship, such as application forms and insurer stationery

Although termination by the parties' contract or expression is most common, the agency relationship can terminate by other means, including operation of law, the producer's death or insanity, or the insurer's insolvency.

Example: Agency Termination

John is an independent insurance agent. One of the insurers with which John has an agency contract for ten years, MutualCo, decides to terminate its arrangement with him and instructs him to stop writing business. John still has MutualCo application forms, manuals, and rating information in his office and displays a MutualCo plaque on the wall. MutualCo remains listed in the local telephone directory as one of the insurers with which John is associated.

One month after John's agency termination with MutualCo, a new customer, Alex, consults with John about his personal insurance needs. John issues a thirty-day binder to Alex through MutualCo covering all of Alex's cars, then forwards Alex's application for a one-year car insurance policy to MutualCo.

John's actions in issuing the binder bind MutualCo to coverage for Alex. John's actual authority has ended, but the various indications that John is still a MutualCo agent (manuals, office plaque, application forms, telephone listing) have created apparent authority on John's part.

A second example assumes the same facts, except that at the time John's association with MutualCo terminates, MutualCo representatives repossess from John all application forms, rating materials, manuals, and other material displaying the MutualCo company logo. At the time Alex visits John, John possesses no indication that he ever represented MutualCo. John's only connection to MutualCo is his unsupported assertions that he represents the insurer.

Because John has never represented Alex as a MutualCo agent, John's attempt to bind coverage probably would not bind MutualCo. John, of course, has no actual authority because MutualCo expressly terminated it. John also probably has no apparent authority because he possesses nothing that would support a reasonable conclusion that he represents MutualCo. Unless other facts emerge that provide Alex with a reasonable basis to conclude that John represents MutualCo, John's issuance of the binder is not authorized and thus is not binding on MutualCo.

Producers' Duties and Liability

Insurance producers often act on behalf of persons who have little or no knowledge of insurance matters. Insurance purchasers expect their producers to assist them capably in obtaining appropriate insurance. The law recognizes the reasonableness of this expectation and accordingly has imposed various duties and responsibilities on insurance producers.

Insurance producers have a duty to exercise reasonable care and skill in performing their duties, to deal with their customers in good faith, and to exercise reasonable diligence on their customers' behalf. They also have a duty to have reasonable knowledge about the insurance policies they sell, the policy terms, and the coverages available in the areas for which their customers seek insurance protection. Insurance producers also have a duty to follow their customers' instructions. Producers who accept requests to insure must not exceed their authority or depart from the customers' instructions. The standard of care imposed on producers generally reflects the public's expectations that the producers be competent, diligent, loyal, and professional.

Duties and Liability to Insurance Customers

The general standard of care governing insurance producers applies to a variety of specific factual situations. This section examines five duties that producers owe their customers and explains the liability associated with failing to perform each duty.

Producer's Duties to Customers

1. Duty to follow instructions

2. Duty to procure insurance

3. Duty to maintain coverage

4. Duty to place insurance with a solvent insurer

5. Duty to advise

---

1. *Producer's duty to follow instructions.* The duty to follow instructions is clear and fundamental to the insurance producer and customer relationship. Stated simply, a producer must strictly follow the customer's instructions and is liable to the customer for any damages that result from not doing so. Therefore, a producer who fails to add an available coverage requested by an insured is liable for a subsequent loss that the policy would have covered had the producer followed instructions. Additionally, a producer who fails to add newly acquired property to the list of the insured's covered properties at the insured's request would be liable for the financial consequences resulting from any uninsured loss involving the property.

   The insurance customer, however, also has duties. The customer has the duty to provide clear instructions to the producer. If instructions are ambiguous, the producer is justified in acting in good faith on any reasonable interpretation of the instructions.

2. *Producer's duty to procure insurance.* The duty to procure insurance is similar to the duty to follow instructions. Although the latter duty generally might involve ministerial or nondiscretionary acts, the duty to procure insurance involves additional care, skill, effort, and diligence on the insurance producer's part.

   The producer cannot guarantee to the customer that the insurance can be obtained, because coverage might not be available for the customer's loss exposures, or at the price or limits the customer wants. However, the producer must make a good faith effort to procure the desired insurance and promptly inform the customer if this is not possible.

   Issues about this duty arise when the customer solicits an insurance broker's services to locate an insurer who will accept the customer's business on favorable terms. The broker, as the customer's agent, has the duty to exercise reasonable skill, care, and diligence in assisting the customer in obtaining insurance. A producer who undertakes to procure

Example: Producer's Duty to Follow Instructions

Paul is Jane's insurance producer for her personal and business insurance needs. Jane purchases two cars, a new Pontiac and an older Toyota. She instructs Paul to place liability coverage and physical damage coverage on the Pontiac and only liability coverage on the Toyota, because of its age, effective immediately. Paul erroneously reverses the coverages on the cars and places only liability coverage on the Pontiac and liability and physical damage coverages on the Toyota. The Pontiac then sustains physical damage.

Paul has breached his duty to follow the insured's instructions. Jane's instructions were clear and not subject to reasonable disagreement or interpretation.

As a second example, Alice is Joe's business insurance producer. Joe insures ten trucks through Alice's agency, all under separate business vehicle policies. Eight of the ten trucks are covered for liability and physical damage. The liability coverage limit is $500,000 per vehicle, aggregate. The physical damage coverages have $500 deductibles under each policy. The other two trucks in Joe's business are insured only for liability, with aggregate limits of $300,000 on each vehicle.

Joe contacts Alice just before he purchases two additional trucks and asks her to insure them. Joe then says, "Because these are new trucks, I'll need more than just the liability coverage. Go ahead and write them with the full coverage." Jane places the same coverages on the new vehicles as on eight of the others owned by Joe: $500,000 aggregate liability limits and physical damage coverage with $500 deductibles.

The next day, one of the new vehicles is involved in a serious accident resulting in substantial damage to the vehicle and serious injury to another driver. When Joe learns of the coverage on the vehicle, he claims that Alice failed to follow his instructions. He asserts that by "the full coverage" he meant the maximum liability limits written by his insurer on commercial vehicles, $5 million aggregate, and the lowest physical damage deductible offered, $100 per vehicle.

If Joe sues Alice, she would probably prevail. Her interpretation of Joe's meaning was probably at least one of several reasonable interpretations. Sound judgment on Alice's part, of course, would have dictated a thorough inquiry into what Joe meant by "the full coverage." Still, Alice is probably not liable to Joe for breaching the insurance producer duty to follow the customer's instructions.

insurance and through neglect and fault fails to do so is liable to the customer for any resultant damages.

To sue the producer, the customer must prove that the producer agreed or undertook to obtain insurance coverage. If, for example, the producer promised to contact only one insurer on the customer's behalf, did so, and then advised the customer of the insurer's decision, no ongoing agreement to procure insurance existed. The producer would have no liability in that case. On the other hand, a producer who assumes the obligation to procure insurance could be liable for not doing so. For example, a producer who agreed to locate an insurer and then waited several months before making any contacts on the customer's behalf, eventually making only one unsuccessful contact and failing to report to the customer, would be liable. In this set of circumstances, an insurance customer would reasonably believe that the producer has placed the insurance business promptly.

The duty to procure insurance also includes the duty to procure the appropriate coverage. A producer who succeeds in arranging the coverage the customer requests but who fails to advise the customer of exclusions for certain persons, property, or causes of loss for which the customer requested coverage, is liable for a subsequent uninsured loss falling within the exclusions. For example, a broker who promises to locate snowmobile coverage for all persons using a snowmobile, but who procures coverage only for the named insured and his family, would be liable to the customer for not obtaining the requested coverage.

The following questions are important in cases of alleged failure to procure insurance:

- Was there an agreement to procure insurance?

- Did the producer fail to discharge the duties under the agreement?

- Did the insurance customer reasonably believe that the producer would secure the requested coverage under the facts presented?

The customer who can answer these questions affirmatively can sue the producer for failure to procure insurance. The producer would be liable for any damages resulting from the failure to obtain coverage.

Example: Producer's Failure to Procure Insurance

Dave, a claim representative of Insurance Brokerage, agrees to procure a $1 million aggregate general liability policy for Sue's business. Despite his assurances, Dave does not procure Sue's insurance. During the time Dave was to have obtained general liability coverage for Sue's business, her firm sustains a major liability loss.

Assume that Sue can satisfy the test necessary to establish a successful cause of action against Dave for breach of the duty to procure insurance. If so, a court will impose liability on Dave as if he were Sue's insurer. Dave will be liable to Sue up to the limit of the $1 million insurance policy he was to have obtained on her behalf.

---

3. *Producer's duty to maintain coverage.* Producers also owe customers the duty to maintain coverage. Standing alone, a producer's status as an insurance agent or broker does not impose a duty to secure renewal of a customer's insurance or to advise the customer of an insurer's impending cancellation or nonrenewal. However, these duties can arise by agreement between the parties or by their past course of dealings.

A producer who simply arranged insurance on a customer's behalf has no duty to advise the customer of cancellation or nonrenewal. Usually, the insurer handles such notifications, and the producer can reasonably rely on this practice. If by agreement, however, the producer assumed the obligation to advise the customer of any impending lapse in coverage, the producer must discharge this obligation or be liable to the customer for loss resulting from cancellation or nonrenewal.

Additionally, a producer who has previously advised a customer of any coverage cancellation or nonrenewal might be liable for damages resulting from the failure to give notice at a later time. To succeed in such a suit, the customer must show that the producer assumed this duty and that a course of conduct sufficiently lengthy and consistent warranted the customer's reasonable reliance on the producer for notification. The producer's occasional reminder that a premium is due probably would be insufficient to prove the assumption of such a duty.

Example: Producer's Duty to Maintain Coverage

Dave purchases his personal insurance through Martha, an InsurCo agent. Dave has met Martha only once, three years ago, to arrange his insurance through her agency. Dave has always made coverage changes over the telephone, usually through Martha's secretary. Dave's car insurance lapses when he forgets to make a premium payment billed by InsurCo. He suffers a loss and claims he should have coverage because Martha failed to remind him when the premium payment was due.

Dave will probably not prevail in a lawsuit against Martha because she did not have an agreement with him to inform him of potential lapses in his coverage. Nor did any prior dealings between Dave and Martha support an argument that Martha caused Dave to rely on her to keep his coverage in force.

A second example involves the same factual situation, but with the following modifications. Dave has been insured through Martha's agency for ten years. Throughout that time he has always been late paying his premiums when billed by InsurCo. Martha has Dave's payment dates on her office calendar so she can call Dave to remind him to pay his premiums. Martha has told Dave, "I don't usually do this, but yours is a very good account, and I'll make sure your coverage won't lapse." Three times in the last ten years Martha has actually paid Dave's premium for him to prevent a lapse in coverage, collecting the premiums from Dave. On one occasion Martha fails to notice that Dave is late paying his premium. His coverage lapses, and he suffers a loss. Dave probably would prevail against Martha in a lawsuit for failure to maintain insurance based on Martha's agreement to keep his coverage in force and on a course of dealings between them.

---

4. *Producer's duty to place insurance with a solvent insurer.* The insurer's solvency should be one of the most important criteria for placing insurance business. Both the producer and the customer should seriously consider factors bearing on solvency in reaching the decision about where to place the customer's business. The producer should make reasonable attempts to inquire into prospective insurers' solvency and to disclose to the customer any information revealing a weak financial condition.

However, the producer is not liable for any loss to the insurance customer resulting from an insurer's insolvency. The producer is not the guarantor of the insurer's financial condition or solvency; yet the producer must use reasonable care in selecting or recommending a particular insurer.

Conversely, a producer might be liable for negligently placing business with an insurer when the producer either knew or should have known of the insurer's insolvency. Only a reasonable effort, not a perfect one, to remain informed of the insurer's financial condition is required. Clearly, the producer need not request a financial audit or examination of each insurer when contemplating placement of business. The producer can rely on public information, financial rating services, and any information available through a state department of insurance.

If a producer could have discovered, through reasonable means, indications of insurer insolvency or impending insolvency and places a customer's business while unaware of or unconcerned with this information, the producer might be liable to the customer. Producers always should be aware of the financial condition of insurers with which they do business. At a minimum, a producer should disclose any such information to the insurance customer and make an appropriate record of this disclosure.

A producer also should be careful in placing business with an insurer not legally admitted to do business in a state. All states have enacted excess and surplus lines (E&S) statutes that establish requirements for procuring policies from nonadmitted insurers. Examples of such requirements include the following:

- Only licensed producers can sell E&S insurance.

- E&S insurers must comply with minimum capital/surplus requirements.

- Producers must place E&S insurance only with an E&S insurer approved by the state as a nonadmitted insurer.

- Producers must appropriately notify the insured of the nonadmitted insurer's status.

In some states, if an insurer does not meet the requirements of the surplus lines statute, the agent or broker might be liable to the insured for any unpaid claims if the unauthorized insurer becomes insolvent.

5. *Producer's duty to advise.* Producers have the duty to advise their customers. Customers generally do not regard insurance producers as mere order-takers but seek out producers who are professional and knowledgeable about the insurance products they market. Many people rely extensively on their insurance producers' professional advice in selecting personal and commercial insurance coverages.

   Occasionally, an insured has either inadequate or no insurance coverage for an unanticipated event or one the insured incorrectly believed to have coverage for. In these situations, the insured might sue the producer, claiming that the absence of or shortfall in coverage resulted from the producer's failure to advise the customer correctly about insurance needs. Traditionally, courts have rejected claims based on a producer's failure to function as an expert adviser because the producer has no duty to advise, guide, or direct a customer after procuring the insurance for the customer. In most jurisdictions, status as an insurance producer alone does not require the producer to undertake the duty to counsel and to advise insurance customers about their loss exposures, available coverages, or the adequacy of insurance coverage limits.

Examples: No Duty to Advise

A court would find no duty to advise in cases such as the following examples:

- Allen chooses to obtain homeowners coverage through Maria, a producer, because he knows Maria and because he wants to save money on his insurance. The homeowners policy excludes watercraft liability, but Allen owns no watercraft at the time he obtains the policy. Later, he purchases a boat, thinking his policy covers it.

  Maria typically visits her customers at policy renewal time to determine whether they have acquired additional property requiring coverage. However, she does not inquire into the purchase of a watercraft in this case.

  Allen sustains a loss to his boat and then discovers that his homeowners policy excludes coverage for this loss. He asserts that his lack of coverage was the result of Maria's breach of the duty to advise.

  On these facts, no special or expanded producer-customer relationship exists because Allen had no long-standing relationship with Maria, and she did not give him expert advice on any other insurance coverage issues. Allen did not depend on Maria's professional judgment; Maria merely took an order for insurance and did not hold herself out as an expert or a consultant.

- Ming purchased a commercial property insurance policy through Ken, a producer, covering the contents in her place of business for up to $125,000. Three years later, Ming raised the coverage limit to $150,000, and two weeks after that, she sustained a loss. A dispute arises in the loss adjustment, and Ming asserts that she should have coverage for the full replacement cost of the contents, rather than for the actual cash value for which her policy provides payment. Ming claims that Ken breached the duty to advise her about the availability of coverage for the replacement cost of the contents.

  No special relationship between the producer and customer exists in this case. They had no previous dealings and only minimal contact over the years. Ming never consulted Ken about providing coverage but simply submitted an application for the coverage. Ming did not rely on Ken's expertise.

Applied strictly, this rule appears inconsistent with the concept of producer professionalism and customers' expectations. Accordingly, many jurisdictions have qualified this general rule, imposing liability on insurance producers for failure to advise their customers adequately if the facts show a special or expanded relationship between the producer and the customer. This relationship exists when a producer purports to be an insurance specialist, consultant, or counselor and has advised a particular customer about the customer's insurance needs on a long-standing basis.

Such a relationship would be, for example, a long-term producer-customer relationship in which producer and customer have discussed issues of coverage and the customer has come to rely on the producer's expertise. Evidence of the producer's acceptance of compensation for services apart from a commission received from an insurer, although not essential to establish the special or expanded relationship, supports the producer's duty to advise. A court might consider a number of factors in determining whether a special or expanded producer-customer relationship gives rise to an affirmative duty to advise the customer completely about insurance needs.

Examples: Duty to Advise

A court would find a duty to advise in cases such as the following examples:

- The insurance customer is a maritime construction company with a long association with the producer, a large commercial insurance brokerage that is expert in maritime insurance. The customer consults with the brokerage about buying a specific type of maritime insurance policy. The broker gathers extensive information about the customer's business to find the appropriate coverage. The customer leaves policy details to the broker to negotiate with insurers.

  The broker negotiates a maritime construction insurance contract that omits key language that would have provided the customer with coverage for "stand-down time," which includes costs for mobilized workers and equipment that must remain idle when a loss occurs. The insured sustains a covered loss but receives no compensation for "stand-down time."

  The producer has breached the duty to advise the customer in light of their special relationship. The brokerage is not merely an order-taker and order-placer because the following were involved:

  - Specialized line of insurance requiring unique knowledge
  - Producer's specific knowledge about the customer's business and insurance needs
  - Customer's clear reliance on the producer's expertise in a highly specialized field
  - Customer's ceding of responsibility to the producer to negotiate an insurance contract
  - Long-standing relationship between the customer and producer

- Simon obtains insurance for his farm through the producer, Louisa. The two have associated with each other for twelve years. Simon has purchased a farm liability policy through Louisa, protecting him from liability claims by any member of the public, but not covering farm employees.

  Simon tells Louisa that he plans to hire a part-time employee. However, Louisa does not tell Simon that the liability policy would not cover the employee and does not suggest other coverage that might be available for this situation. Simon hires the employee, who is injured on the job. The policy does not cover the injury.

  Because of the long-standing relationship, a special producer and customer relationship gives rise to Louisa's duty to advise Simon. Most important, however, Simon clearly relied on Louisa to evaluate his insurance needs and to assist him in obtaining the correct coverages. Simon consulted Louisa as an expert, and he depended on her advice.

Several important conclusions derive from case law dealing with the producer's duty to advise the insurance customer, including the following:

- The greater the producer's involvement in the customer's insurance matters and other matters bearing on insurance, such as the customer's business, the greater the chance that the courts will find a special or expanded producer and customer relationship.

- The more the producer leaves the arena of insurance order-taker or application conduit and begins to act as insurance adviser or counselor, the greater the chance that a court will find a special or expanded relationship.

- The more a customer relies on the producer's expertise and knowledge, the more likely that a court will find a special or expanded relationship.

- The greater the complexity of the insurance coverage sought, and the greater the level of specialized producer knowledge required, the greater the chance that a court would find the duty to advise on the producer's part.

Many producers are expanding their roles and offering more services, such as full insurance reviews, to their customers. As they do, they approach the line separating the standard producer and customer relationship from the special or expanded relationship. Accordingly, insurance producers face a greater risk of liability for breach of the duty to advise. Producers need to be aware that they must advise their customers carefully on insurance matters to make sure the information provided is complete. As with the discharge of other producer duties, producers should keep accurate written documentation of their advice to all insurance customers.

Defenses to Liability

The producer may have a defense to an allegation of breach of a duty owed to the customer. The producer can avoid liability by showing that his or her conduct was reasonable and appropriate or that factors not within the producer's responsibility caused the damage to the customer. Five of the defenses available to the producer are the five summarized here.

Producer's Defenses for Breach of Duty to Customer

1. The producer assumed no duty to the customer.

2. The producer did not breach a duty to the customer.

3. The insurance customer was partly at fault.

4. The insurance customer failed to read the policy.

5. Insurance was not available to the customer.

---

1. *The producer assumed no duty to the customer.* An insurance customer cannot force a producer to act on the customer's behalf. An agreement forms the basis of the producer-customer relationship, and the producer generally owes only duties that have been expressly or impliedly assumed. Therefore, a producer who has not agreed to obtain insurance for the client is not liable for breach of any duty to the client. When a customer alleges breach of the duty to maintain coverage, the producer who said or implied that the

customer's insurance would be kept in force has a valid defense. In cases alleging a breach of the duty to advise, the producer can defend on the basis that no special or expanded relationship ever existed between the producer and the customer and that, therefore, the producer did not expressly or impliedly assume an obligation to advise the customer on insurance coverage matters.

Frequently, the outcome of cases against producers turns on what, if anything, the producer promised to do for the insurance customer. Any conversations between the parties and any supporting documents are important in establishing this defense. The need for producers to retain good written documentation of transactions with insurance customers is apparent.

2. *The producer did not breach a duty to the customer.* If a customer can show that a producer agreed to do something, the next question is whether the producer carried out the agreement. If so, the producer has discharged the duty to the customer, has not breached the assumed duty, and is not liable to the customer.

    The producer who has followed clear instructions fully and completely or ambiguous instructions according to a reasonable interpretation of their meaning is not liable to the insurance customer. When allegations of failure to procure insurance arise, the producer has a valid defense if he or she acted reasonably and promptly on the customer's behalf and kept the customer informed about the progress toward obtaining the requested insurance coverage.

    In a claim for failure to advise the insurance customer appropriately, the producer's defense would be to show that the advice provided was reasonable and appropriate, even if not perfect. The producer need not anticipate all possible contingencies or give perfect advice on insurance matters. Producers comply with the duty to advise their customers when they provide the advice that a reasonable producer would give under the circumstances.

    Once again, documentation of producer transactions with insurance customers is important. Producers should be able to demonstrate what the customer asked them to do, what they did, and when they did it. A producer who accomplishes prompt, professional, and thorough work on the customer's behalf should have a valid defense to liability.

3. *The insurance customer was partly at fault.* Although insurance customers can generally rely on the producer's knowledge, care, and skill, they must also act reasonably regarding the insurance transaction. If the injury or loss to the customer occurred through the customer's fault in whole or in part, the producer can offer this conduct in defense to the customer's claim.

    Depending on the degree of the customer's fault, a court might reduce the claim against the producer either wholly or proportionately. For example, in a claim for an alleged breach of duty to procure insurance, the producer might offer the defense that the customer failed to cooperate in furnishing information that prospective insurers required.

In a claim for failure to advise an insurance customer appropriately, the producer might show that the customer did not present all of the facts necessary to allow the producer to give full and appropriate advice. For example, if a customer omitted essential details concerning a business operation in applying for broad, multi-peril coverage, the producer might not have had sufficient information to assess the various risks the exposure presented. If an uninsured loss occurs later and the customer sues, the producer can defend by showing that the customer's failure to provide essential information resulted in the lack of coverage.

In a claim for breach of duty to follow instructions, the insurance customer could be at fault because of having given vague, misleading, or erroneous instructions. A customer's inadequate instructions can defeat a claim or can result in reduced damages in proportion to the customer's own fault.

4. *The insurance customer failed to read the policy.* Historically, a producer could defend a lawsuit successfully because an insured failed to read the policy. The insured's behavior was measured against what a reasonable insured would do, and courts considered the insured's reasonable condut to be, at minimum, to read the insurance policy and verify the coverages requested. The general rule has been that an insurance customer's claim against a producer fails when an examination of the insurance policy would have revealed the absence of coverage or a term or condition that defeated coverage.

Example: Insured's Failure to Read Policy

Jane consults Al, a local insurance agent, regarding insurance for three business properties she owns and for a fleet of trucks used in the businesses. Jane explains that she wants full liability and physical damage coverage on the vehicles and that she wants the vehicles covered at all times. Al obtains the necessary information for the insurance applications and forwards them to CoverageCo, a large commercial insurer he represents.

CoverageCo issues a fleet policy that provides broad liability and physical damage coverage but contains an exclusion under the liability coverage for personal use of the vehicles by Jane's employees. The exclusion appears in large print and is readily discoverable upon even a cursory examination of the fleet policy. Three months after the CoverageCo issues the policy and forwards it to Jane, one of Jane's employees suffers a serious loss in a company truck during a weekend while on personal business. Jane sues Al when the insurer denies her claim, alleging that he failed to procure insurance or follow instructions.

In those states that allow the producer a traditional defense that the insured failed to read the insurance policy, Al will probably succeed in Jane's lawsuit against him. Jane was aware of the coverage she wanted and should have examined the policy when she received it to ensure that it included this coverage. The facts that the type of insurance was not highly specialized or technical and that the exclusion was clear and apparent in the policy would tend to strengthen Al's defense. Al might also have a defense that Jane's instructions were ambiguous and that he complied with a reasonable interpretation of them.

The strict application of the rule requiring that the insured read the policy has eroded. Some states do not recognize the rule at all, reasoning that the insurance customer has the right to rely on the producer's expertise in insurance matters. These courts also recognize that many insureds do not read their insurance policies and that policy language is often difficult for customers to understand. In these states, the producer cannot use the defense that the customer could have discovered the lack of coverage by examining the policy and then could have taken steps to secure coverage.

Courts that recognize the traditional rule have developed exceptions. A producer who has intentionally misrepresented policy provisions or coverage cannot use the defense because the producer's fault is greater then the simple negligent conduct of the insurance customer. Additionally, some courts, either implicitly or explicitly recognize this defense only when an examination of the policy reveals that exclusions, limitations, or conditions are clear without extensive analysis or interpretation. This line of reasoning requires only a reasonable examination of the policy, not an expert examination.

5. *Insurance was not available to the customer.* In most states, if a producer wrongfully fails to obtain insurance that actually is unavailable, the defense of "insurance not available" has been successful. The underlying concept is causation: If the producer cannot obtain insurance, the producer's alleged failure to act appropriately is not the true cause of the loss.

That the insurance was difficult to locate or would have required a great deal of effort to obtain is not a defense. That the insurance desired was more expensive than anticipated or was otherwise available on less favorable terms probably does not make it unavailable. In these circumstances, the producer must locate this insurance and advise the customer of its terms and price. Unavailability would be a defense, however, if the customer clearly specified that certain terms or a price limit were necessary in the desired policy, and no insurance was available within these limits.

Some jurisdictions have declined to recognize the defense of unavailability of insurance. They reason that the producer still has a duty to act appropriately and diligently on a customer's behalf and must advise the customer promptly that coverage is not available. The customer then can assess options and plan to manage loss exposures through other means.

Duties to Third Parties

Under general contract law principles, the parties to an agreement owe duties and obligations to each other, but not to third parties who might come in contact with either of them.

The principal and agent relationship is based on consent, whether express or implied. The producer-insurance customer relationship is one of principal and agent. Accordingly, third parties generally acquire no rights under this relationship. The breach of any duty a producer owes to a customer does not create any rights in third parties. A third party who intends to sue an insurance customer (typically in tort) cannot sue a producer who wrongfully failed to assist the customer in obtaining insurance coverage for the event that is the subject of the suit. Many courts have held that the producer owes a duty to act competently and appropriately only to the producer's principal and not to any third party. That a third party could have collected from the customer had the producer discharged all duties appropriately and arranged for insurance coverage, but now cannot collect, usually does not give the third party any rights against the producer.

Example: Third Party Suit Against Producer

Joe, owner of a moving company, obtains his business and personal insurance through Insurance Agency. Recently, he met with Darla, an Insurance Agency broker, to review his business insurance. Joe advised Darla that he will soon acquire two new trucks, and as of July 30 of this year he will need full liability coverage on these trucks. Additionally, Joe said that he needs coverage for any damage to his customers' property while in the custody of his company, regardless of whether any member of his company is at fault. Darla said that she will obtain this coverage.

Darla does not obtain the liability coverage that Joe requested. Later, one of Joe's new trucks is involved in a serious accident, destroying the household property of his customer, Pete. Pete had no insurance for this property. He relied on Joe's insurance during the move.

As the insurance customer, Joe would have an action against Darla for failure to follow instructions and for failure to procure insurance. However, any lawsuit Pete files against Darla probably would not be successful. Pete was not a party to Joe's and Darla's producer-customer relationship and therefore acquired no rights under their contract.

Some courts, however, have recognized a third-party right to sue an insurance customer's producer under similar circumstances. Generally, these cases are in the automobile insurance or workers' compensation area and are based on the contractual principle of third-party beneficiary rights. In some cases, the importance of drivers' liability insurance as a source of compensation for other drivers has resulted in conferring third-party beneficiary status on any driver who suffers loss from another driver's conduct. In other cases, injured drivers can sue negligent drivers' insurance producers if the negligent driver lacked liability insurance because of the producer's breach of a duty.

In workers' compensation or employer's liability situations, some courts have allowed third parties, such as injured workers or their families, to sue the producers who provided the employer's insurance for failure to discharge a duty regarding insurance coverage. Courts have recognized this third-party right to sue because of the importance of injured workers' receiving compensation and because, for most intents and purposes, workers are the intended beneficiaries of workers' compensation or employer's liability insurance.

In summary, the idea that third parties have the right to sue in cases involving insurance producers is relatively new and is still developing. In most cases, only the producers and customers have rights and duties with respect to each other, and third parties have none.

Duties and Liability to Insurer

In addition to the duties owed to the insurance customer, producers authorized to act on behalf of insurer principals must abide by a certain standard of conduct toward them. In many insurance transactions, a producer must represent both the insurer and the customer. Producers must, therefore, deal with insurers with care, skill, diligence, and loyalty. Breaches of duty to the insurer may make the producer liable for any resulting consequences.

Producer's Duties to Insurer

1. Duty to disclose risks

2. Duty to follow instructions

3. Duties of loyalty and accounting

4. Duty to transmit information properly

The producer has the following four duties to the insurer:

1. *Duty to disclose risks.* The producer's first duty to the insurer is the duty to disclose risks. In most cases, producers are the "eyes and ears" of the insurers they represent. They have the first contact with prospective insureds and at times know them personally. Frequently, the producer is directly involved in the underwriting process and might, in some cases, be responsible for obtaining all of the information upon which the underwriting decisions are based.

   Accordingly, producers owe a duty to their insurer principals to fully disclose any information material to the underwriting decision. Material information is that which would affect the decision about whether to issue an insurance policy covering the risk or that would at least affect the premium. The failure to disclose immaterial information probably will not subject the insurance producer to liability.

   An insurance producer who fails to fully disclose all matters concerning the risks and hazards of a prospective insured is liable to the insurer for damages resulting from the lack of full disclosure. If the insurer establishes that it would not have issued the policy had it received the appropriate information, the producer is liable to the insurer for the amount of the loss the insurer must pay to the insured.

   If the insurer would have issued the policy but with a higher premium, the producer would be liable to the insurer for the difference in the premium. For example, having noticed conditions on premises to be insured that place the property below the insurer's underwriting standards, the producer must advise the insurer of this or bear the consequences of any loss that the insurer would not have covered had it known the facts. Similarly, a binder would not be appropriate if the producer knew that a building was below the applicable underwriting standards. The producer owes a continuing duty to protect the insurer and cannot let coverage take effect if it is based on false or inaccurate information.

   The producer is not strictly responsible for information not known. For example, producers in some lines of insurance assist in obtaining completed applications and do not become further involved in the underwriting process. These producers must truthfully and accurately note the information they receive from the insurance customer. However, absent specific agreements with their insurer principals, they need not investigate the accuracy of the information they receive. If by agreement the producer assumes certain duties in the underwriting process, such as inspection of premises or examination of books and records, the producer must discharge these duties and must disclose any information material to the underwriting decision.

2. *Duty to follow instructions.* The producer owes the insurer the duty to follow instructions, which essentially mirrors the duty to follow the insurance customer's instructions. Producers must follow insurers' general statements of authority or specific directions. A producer who exceeds the authority given or who fails to comply with specific directions is liable to the insurer for resulting damages. For example, a producer who fails to disclose factors that could preclude underwriting a policy could be liable to the insurer for losses resulting from the nondisclosed information.

Example: Producer's Liability to Insurer

Martha is an insurance agent associated with InsurCo. Formerly, InsurCo gave Martha express binding authority regarding certain specified types of small commercial exposures. InsurCo has provided Martha with appropriate binder and application forms, as well as rating manuals and policy forms. For the last five years, she has issued binders for these type of exposures.

Recently, InsurCo underwriters have noted mounting losses in Martha's commercial book of business. InsurCo's underwriting department decides that a full review of Martha's accounts is necessary and withdraws Martha's binding authority for commercial business pending the review.

Paul meets with Martha two months later to discuss insurance for his small business. This exposure falls within the category of those for which Martha formerly could bind coverage. Martha believes that InsurCo would accept this risk, so, despite the absence of actual authority, she binds coverage. Three days later, during the binder term, Paul sustains a loss.

InsurCo must cover the loss, despite Martha's lack of actual authority to issue the binder. Martha was acting pursuant to apparent authority. However, InsurCo can sue Martha for breach of its express direction not to bind any commercial insurance coverage.

Cases involving breach of the duty to follow instructions arise in two areas. The first is in the improper use of binding authority. By agreement between the parties, insurers frequently grant producers the authority to bind coverage on the insurer's behalf, typically under a detailed statement outlining the circumstances under which the insurer can be bound. The doctrine of apparent authority can sometimes result in a producer's binding an insurer to cover certain risks beyond those authorized. If a producer binds coverage contrary to explicit insurer instructions, the insurer must cover the exposure but can sue the producer for the amount of the loss.

A second common situation involving breach of duty to follow instructions relates to an insurer's specific instructions to cancel, reduce, or otherwise limit coverage. A producer who has been instructed to cancel a certain policy and fails to do so is liable for the full amount of a loss that the insurer must cover. A producer who has failed to limit coverage as instructed is responsible for the difference between the coverage the insurer had to provide and the amount it would have paid had the producer followed its instructions.

A producer may have a defense against a lawsuit for failure to follow instructions if not given reasonable time to comply with the instructions, or if insurers' instructions were not clear. If the instructions were not clear, a producer who has acted according to a reasonable interpretation of the instructions would not be liable.

3. *Duties of loyalty and accounting.* The producer also owes the insurer loyalty and accounting. In many cases, insureds forward their premium checks to their insurance producer rather than directly to the insurer. Under the law, payment to a producer, with actual or apparent authority, constitutes payment to the insurer. For example, an insured who brings a premium check for the amount due to the producer's office one hour before coverage is to lapse is covered for a subsequent loss, whether or not the premium check ever reaches the insurer. The producer must receive and process premium payments on the insurer's behalf and transmit them to the insurer promptly. The producer also must keep accurate records of premiums received and verify receipt of correct compensation for coverage in force. A producer who causes any loss to an insurer because of failure to account appropriately is liable to the insurer for the financial consequences of the loss.

4. *Duty to transmit information properly.* The producer has the duty to transmit information properly to the insurer. As noted previously, producers must provide insurers with material information. One type of material information is the facts surrounding a loss involving an insured. When an insurance agent receives notice of a covered loss, typically in a report completed by the insured, it must be forwarded promptly to the insurer. A producer is liable to the insurer only if failure to forward such records results in adverse consequences or harm to the insurer. For example, a producer receives a report of an insured's loss shortly after it occurs but waits six months before advising the insurer of the loss. If the six months' delay has not prejudiced the insurer's ability to investigate and resolve any claims resulting from the loss, the insurer has no cause of action against the producer.

In some instances, the producer's failure to transmit important information promptly does cause loss to the insurer. For example, an insured who is being sued sends notice of the suit to the insurance producer for forwarding to the appropriate department of the insurer. Typically, an insured's answer to a complaint is due at the court within a specified period. If the insurer fails to appear in court or to answer a pleading on behalf of the insured,

Default judgment
An automatic judgment against a party to a lawsuit who fails to appear in court or to answer a pleading.

the result is a **default judgment** against the insured. That is, the insured automatically loses the lawsuit, and the insurer is liable to the insured for the consequences of this judgment. In this case, the insurer can sue the producer for failure to transmit notice of a lawsuit promptly.

The producer is liable to the insurer for any money the insurer had to pay in resolving the liability claim over the amount it would have had to pay had it received prompt notification of the loss. The producer might be liable for the entire loss if the insurer had a valid defense to the insured's liability that was not asserted because of lack of notice.

Errors and Omissions Coverage

An established rule of law is that liability should rest ultimately on the party at fault. This rule applies in the insurance context. Insurance producers bear the responsibility for any acts or omissions on their part that occur in the course of their insurance transactions. If any unreasonable conduct or breach of contract results in financial loss to any other party, the producer is responsible to that party for the full extent of the loss sustained.

As discussed previously, insurance producers can obtain errors and omissions (E&O) coverage for their exposure to loss resulting from harmful unintentional and wrongful acts they cause in their professional capacity. Insurers providing E&O coverage agree to indemnify covered insurance producers for financial loss resulting from claims for professional negligence, up to the limit of coverage the producer selects. Additionally, the insurers agree to defend the producers in lawsuits filed against them for covered acts.

Insurer's Liability for Producer's Acts or Omissions

Sometimes the insurer becomes liable for the producer's acts or omissions. In most instances, insurance customers file lawsuits alleging breach of a duty by a producer against the producer alone. Typically, the producer's errors and omissions insurer handles the case. However, the customer might include the insurer in the lawsuit, alleging that the producer acted on the insurer's behalf and that the insurer is, therefore, responsible for the producer's conduct. Insurers typically are included in customers' lawsuits when the producer either has no errors and omissions coverage or has coverage limits that are less than the loss claimed.

Actions against insurance producers typically allege either breach of contract or commission of a tort. Generally, an insurer is bound by any agreement between the producer and customer made within the producer's actual or apparent authority or ratified by the insurer.

Respondeat superior governs insurer responsibility for producers' tortious acts. In the insurance context, the insurer is responsible for producer negligence in insurance transactions with customers if a master-servant relationship exists between the insurer and the producer. If the producer is an independent contractor, liability rests with the producer only, not with the insurer.

Most insurance producers are independent contractors. Some insurers that are direct writers market their insurance products through employee sales representatives. Courts view these representatives as employees of the insurers; therefore, the insurers may be vicariously liable for the producers' tortious breach of duties and can be included in any lawsuit against the producer alleging such a breach.

Examples: Insurer's Liability for Producer's Act or Omission

- Dave, an independent insurance agent, is associated with seven insurers and writes both personal and commercial insurance. Bill, one of Dave's customers, directs Dave to obtain business interruption insurance for one of his businesses and to add two new buildings to those covered under his commercial property policy. Dave tells Bill that he will obtain the coverage through CoverageCo, which handles all of Bill's other commercial insurance. However, Dave neglects to obtain the insurance that Bill requests.

  Bill can sue Dave for failure to follow instructions and failure to procure insurance. Because Dave is an independent contractor, however, Bill has no action against CoverageCo.

- Assume the same facts, except that Dave is an employee marketing representative of CoverageCo with an office at CoverageCo's headquarters. Dave sells only CoverageCo insurance policies. Because Dave is CoverageCo's employee, Bill can appropriately include both Dave and CoverageCo in his action for failure to follow instructions and to procure insurance. CoverageCo is vicariously liable for Dave's negligent conduct.

CLAIM REPRESENTATIVES

Insurers typically act through claim representatives to resolve claims resulting from losses that their insurance policies cover. The insurance business now prefers the term "claim representatives" rather than "claim adjusters." Claim representatives verify coverage, investigate and determine the cause of loss and the amount of the damages, and conclude claims under the insurance policy promptly and professionally.

Claim management requires a great degree of care, skill, knowledge, and judgment. The claim representative has a responsibility to investigate and conclude claims consistent with company rules and procedures, legal requirements, and regulations of the state department of insurance.

Classification of Claim Representatives

The term claim representative describes the class of persons who participate in the adjustment and settlement of claims for losses covered by insurance. Claim representatives can be of different types, including the following:

- **Staff claim representatives** are salaried insurer's employees who handle claims for losses exclusively for their employer. Depending on the insurer's size and philosophy, they might handle claims in several types of insurance,

Staff claim representative
An insurer's salaried employee who handles claims for losses exclusively for that insurer.

or they might specialize in particular types of insurance or of claims. Staff claim representatives typically are assigned to particular claim offices. In sparsely populated areas, however, they might have scattered local offices or work out of local producers' offices.

Independent adjuster
An independent claim representative who provides claim handling services to insurers under contract for a fee.

- **Independent adjusters** provide claim handling services to insurers under contract for a fee. They contract with large or small independent insurers or self-insureds to adjust claims assigned to them. These adjusters are employees of adjusting firms and are independent contractors of the insurers. Independent adjusters are retained for a variety of reasons, including unanticipated heavy claim volume or storm activity, expertise in a particular line of insurance, or insufficient claim volume in a particular area to justify employing a full-time staff representative.

Public adjuster
An independent claim representative who provides claim handling services to insureds to assist them in presenting their claims to insurers.

- Insureds retain **public adjusters** to assist them in presenting their claims to their insurers. Generally, public adjusters receive their fees from the money their clients receive from the insurers. They are agents of the insureds retaining them, with no agency relationships with insurers. They are prevalent in some states and localities, but not in others.

Producers do not fall generally within the claim representative category but frequently have loss adjustment duties or otherwise might participate in the loss adjustment process. Some insurers authorize producers to settle certain types of losses, generally those that are not complex or do not exceed certain dollar amounts. Additionally, producers might assist in parts of investigations or in the preliminary handling of claims.

Claim representatives' acts can bind insurers even without authorization if the insurer subsequently ratifies the act. Usually, ratification occurs when the unauthorized act is beneficial to the insurer principal. Once the insurer ratifies the claim representative's conduct, it is bound by that ratification.

Example: Insurer's Ratification of Claim Representative's Act

Paula is an independent adjuster with no adjusting contract with CoverageCo, a national commercial insurer. Paula is aware that William has a large claim against CoverageCo because of the negligence of one of CoverageCo's insureds. Paula also knows that CoverageCo has denied liability to William on the grounds that its insured was not negligent and thus not responsible for William's loss.

Paula, seeking to impress CoverageCo and to secure an adjusting contract with the company, assists CoverageCo in resolving its dispute with William. Despite lack of authority, she meets with William, ostensibly on behalf of CoverageCo, and persuades him to settle for $5,000. Paula advises CoverageCo of this purported settlement, and CoverageCo's home office representatives ultimately decide that, although not authorized, the settlement is fair and proper. CoverageCo's representatives instruct Paula that the company accepts the settlement with William. CoverageCo then mails Paula a check for $5,000, payable to William, along with a release form and instructions to Paula to have William execute the release and formally conclude the settlement.

CoverageCo has ratified Paula's unauthorized settlement. Should it attempt to change its decision, claiming Paula's lack of authority as a defense, it would not succeed. Once an insurer ratifies an agent's act, it cannot disclaim that act as unauthorized.

Claim Settlement Authority

Claim representatives' authority follows the same general principles governing other principal and agent relationships: They have actual authority, which can be expressed or implied, and apparent authority. Acts within those types of authority can bind the insurer.

Actual Authority

Claim representatives' actual authority can be either express or implied. Each form of authority involves different forms of proof and, at times, different results. The claim representative acts pursuant to express authority when following instructions in an employment agreement, a company manual concerning claim management procedures, an insurer's memoranda or other directives, or verbal instructions from a supervisor. The claim representative who reasonably interprets the instructions and follows them acts appropriately pursuant to express authority.

Example: Claim Representative's Express Authority

An insurer has instructed a claim representative to resolve any covered claim up to $25,000. The claim representative does so in a particular case. The insurer later determines that the payment was too high under the circumstances presented. Absent more specific instructions regarding preapproval by the insurer or other limitations on the claim representative's authority, the claim representative acted appropriately with express authority.

If, in the same example, the claim representative settled a claim for more than $25,000 without the insurer's authorization, the act would be outside the express authority granted. This would even be true if the settlement is for a reasonable amount and is clearly in the insurer's best interest. The claim representative's instructions to resolve claims up to $25,000 were unambiguous.

Claim representatives also have the implied authority that a reasonable insurer would expect them to possess under the circumstances they encounter. The particular circumstances and the parties' prior dealings determine the scope of implied authority. If a claim representative reasonably believes that the insurer-principal wants him or her to take a certain action despite the lack of specific instruction, authority exists by implication.

In the previous example about the settlement of a claim beyond the claim representative's express authority, the facts might show that the act was appropriate under implied authority. This would be true especially if the claim representative had previously acted beyond the authority granted based on an interpretation of the principal's best interest, and the principal had not objected. Under these circumstances, the insurer had acquiesced to, or given unexpressed authorization for, the claim representative to settle claims above the authorized dollar amount when it appeared to be in the insurer's best interest.

A claim representative must have reasonable powers consistent with the duties assigned by the insurer, which generally are to investigate and dispose of claims as assigned. Implied authority can fill in any gaps in a claim representative's authority left by incomplete express authorization.

Example: Claim Representative's Implied Authority

David, a self-employed independent adjuster in a rural community, represents several insurers. David has a contract with InsurCo to adjust all losses assigned to him and that take place in his community. David's contract instructs him to "conclude all claims against InsurCo or its insureds" that are assigned to him "in the most expeditious fashion and in the best interests of InsurCo and its insureds." The contract also provides that InsurCo will reimburse David for all "reasonable claim adjustment expenses." Additionally, it instructs David to "effectuate any settlements and incur any reasonable adjustment expenses up to $5,000 without InsurCo's prior approval."

InsurCo has stated the express authority it has conferred upon David in general terms, giving him broad discretion to handle many types of claims, but little specific guidance on how to handle them. David probably has implied authority to do all of the following things, among others:

- Incur reasonable expenses (up to $5,000) for accident reports, photographs, technical expert fees (such as accident or loss reconstructionists and independent damage appraisers), independent medical examination fees, and defense attorney fees

- Make offers of settlement on InsurCo's behalf and bind InsurCo to these offers (up to $5,000)

- Take releases on behalf of InsurCo and its insureds

- Collect money in subrogation on InsurCo's behalf

- Dispose of salvage property on InsurCo's behalf

- Inspect and appraise property or hire others to do so on InsurCo's behalf

David's contract with InsurCo does not specifically enumerate these duties. The authority is implied authority because conducting these activities is essential to the discharge of the broader duties expressly stated in David's adjustment contract with InsurCo.

Apparent Authority

Just as for insurance producers, a claim representative who does not have actual authority to engage in certain conduct can have apparent authority. Apparent authority arises when a claim representative takes a certain action on the insurer's behalf, and third parties would reasonably believe that the claim representative had the authority to do so under the circumstances.

Apparent authority can be a broad basis on which to impose responsibility on an insurer-principal for a claim representative's acts. Insureds and third-party claimants with whom claim representatives deal are not responsible for knowing the insurer's customs, procedures, or levels of authority. Generally, a member of the public is reasonable in the belief that a claim representative has authority to take action relating to a claim. Thus, for insurance, if a claim representative without actual authority agrees to settle a claim for $100,000, the insurer must abide by that settlement. A third party could reasonably believe that a claim representative had authority to resolve the claim.

Many claim representatives' acts and statements can bind insurers. Generally insurer-principals are bound when claim representatives' words or conduct either result in the formation of contracts or cause the claimants or insureds to reasonably rely on them to their detriment. However statements such as "We'll handle your claim," "We'll take care of that damage," or even "We will pay your claim," ordinarily will not, without more, result in the insurer's liability to pay the claimant's claim. Such words do not usually result in an actual contract to settle the claim.

The insurer would be liable if a claimant acted on the claim representative's representation and as a result lost something of value. For example, the claimant might arrange for the repair of damaged property and spend a large sum of money to purchase repair parts based only on the claim representative's word that a claim would be paid. The claimant's reliance, however, must be reasonable.

Claim Representatives' Duties and Liability

As is the case with insurance producers, claim representatives owe duties to their insurers and to the customers they encounter, insureds and third-party claimants under liability policies. Claim representatives' duties are generally similar to those of producers, but they vary because of the different focuses of the respective positions.

Duties to Insurers

Claim representatives fulfill numerous insurance policy promises. Frequently, they deal with people during the most traumatic periods of their lives. For many insureds, claim representatives might be the only insurer representatives they encounter. Many people form their impressions of the entire insurance industry from their interactions with claim representatives.

Claim representatives' actions during the claim management process in most cases bind insurers to insureds and to third-party claimants. Claim representatives have this power, along with correlative duties to the insurer principals.

Claim Representative's Duties to Insurers

1. Duty to follow instructions
2. Duty of good faith and fair dealing
3. Duty to provide prompt, diligent, and professional service

The claim representative's duties to an insurer fall into the following three main categories:

1. *Duty to follow instructions.* A claim representative owes the insurer the duty to follow instructions. Because claim representatives' acts affect insurers so significantly, insurers regulate their conduct in advance in several ways. First, insurers typically have manuals and other written communications that set out appropriate procedures for claim management. Second, insurers routinely provide claim representatives a maximum dollar amount of settlement authority. Settlements for amounts in excess of this ceiling require insurer approval. Typically, local claim managers or home office personnel grant the insurer's approval to claim representatives for higher settlements. Third, claim managers give claim representatives they supervise specific instructions on individual claim files, addressing such matters as how to determine coverage for the loss, how to investigate the loss, how to evaluate the amount of the loss, and how to negotiate a settlement. Claim representatives owe their insurer principals the duty to comply with all of their instructions.

   A claim representative might breach this duty by, for example, exceeding the dollar amount of settlement authority. Whether the settlement agreement is with a third-party claimant or an insured, in most cases the insurer principal is bound for the unauthorized amount.

2. *Duty of good faith and fair dealing.* A claim representative owes the insurer the duty of good faith and fair dealing. To represent an insurer competently, the claim representative must be familiar with local case and statutory law, regulations of the state department of insurance relating to claim management, and insurance policy provisions pertaining to the loss adjusted.

3. *Duty to provide prompt, diligent, and professional service.* A claim representative has the duty to provide prompt, diligent, and professional service to the insurer. The insurer has the right to expect that its claim representatives will act promptly on claims made under insurance policies and will follow through with them, assisting insureds or claimants appropriately in moving the claims toward resolution. The insurer also has the legitimate expectation that a claim representative will exhibit good public relations skills and will act in a professional manner at all times.

Duties to Insureds and to Third-Party Claimants

The insurance transaction is one of utmost good faith and of substantial interest to the public. Accordingly, the law imposes duties applicable to the claim adjustment process to effectuate these broad principles. In general, any claim practice that is not in good faith or does not promote public policy is not appropriate.

Claim Representative's Duties to Insureds and Third-Party Claimants

1. Duty of fair and ethical claim adjustment

2. Duty to understand and comply with the law

3. Duty to provide prompt, diligent, and professional service

---

Claim representatives owe many individual duties to insureds or third-party claimants. These duties fall into the following three major categories:

1. *Duty of fair and ethical claim adjustment.* The duty of fair and ethical claim adjustment may be the most important claim representatives' duty because it is so fundamental to the claim management transaction. What is fair and ethical in all circumstances is difficult to state completely because of the breadth of these terms. State **unfair claim settlement practices acts** mandate minimum standards of ethical claim management conduct, and case law and administrative regulations further interpret the statutes. Each state's statute may differ, but most are similar in their major provisions.

   Many state laws are based upon the Uniform Claim Settlement Practice Act, developed by the National Association of Insurance Commissioners (NAIC). Under this model act the following are listed as prohibited claim settlement practices:

   - Misrepresenting policy provisions relating to the coverage at issue

   - Failing to acknowledge and act promptly on communications with respect to a claim

   - Failing to adopt reasonable standards for investigation of claims

   - Refusing to pay claims in some cases without conducting a reasonable investigation

   - Failing to affirm or deny coverage within a reasonable time after receipt of proof of loss

   - Failing to attempt to settle promptly and fairly when liability is reasonably clear

   - Compelling insureds to litigate by offering substantially less than the ultimate recovery

   - Attempting to settle for less than a reasonable person would expect from reading advertising material accompanying the application

   - Attempting to settle on the basis of an application altered without the insured's consent

   - Making payments without stating the coverage warranting payment

   - Coercing the insured to accept less than the arbitration amount by a policy of always appealing arbitration awards

Unfair claim settlement practices act
A law mandating minimum standards of ethical claim management conduct.

- Delaying the investigation by requiring both preliminary and final proofs of loss
- Failing to settle under one coverage when liability is clear to influence settlement under another coverage
- Failing to promptly provide a reasonable explanation of facts or policy provisions relied on to deny liability

Typically, the state department of insurance enforces a state's unfair claim settlement practices act. That agency learns of alleged violations of the statute by its own market conduct surveys, which involve examination of insurer claim files, or by consumer complaints. The agency conducts investigations into allegations of improper claim settlement practices and addresses any improprieties, as authorized by the state statute.

State insurance departments can impose fines and penalties in appropriate cases, under the applicable unfair claim practices statute. Some statutes allow for fines and penalties if the improper claim practices occur with sufficient frequency to be a pattern or practice. Some statutes or regulations authorize a fine or penalty for even a single act of unfair claim adjustment.

First-party bad-faith lawsuit
A lawsuit brought against an insurer by an individual insured or third-party claimant under a state unfair claim settlement practices act.

In some states, individual insureds or third-party claimants can file lawsuits against insurers based upon violations of the state unfair claim settlement practices act. Such suits are called **first-party bad-faith lawsuits**. Under such statutes, the consequences to the insurer can be significant because the insured might have the right to seek redress not only for compensatory damages, but also for damages for emotional distress and for attorney's fees. Courts might even award punitive damages in some cases when the insurer's actions merit punishment.

Third parties can also file lawsuits against insurers for unfair claim settlement practices. The third party sues the liable party's insurer seeking redress for alleged unfair claim settlement practices that occurred during the adjustment of the third party's liability claim.

State laws differ as to whether they authorize private lawsuits addressing unfair claim settlement practices. Some states allow only first-party suits or do not allow them at all. The rationale is that the legislature intended particular state unfair claim settlement practices act as an enforcement measure for the state insurance department's use and did not intend that every claimant and insured who alleges a single violation could sue under the act. This issue likely will continue to be the subject of debate, and state law likely will continue to vary. With the possibility of this type of lawsuit, however, the need for claim representatives to make sure they comply with applicable unfair claim settlement practices acts is apparent.

2. *Duty to understand and comply with the law.* A claim representative owes insureds and third party claimants the duty to understand and comply with the law. Compliance with the law falls within the subject of fair and ethical claim settlement conduct. The duty of good faith and fair dealing is not just a question of ethics and fairness, however, but also of the competence to process and resolve claims appropriately.

Example: Claim Representative's Duty to Understand Policy

Mary is a claim representative employed by MutualCo, a regional personal insurer. One month ago, MutualCo endorsed the section of its homeowners policy that provides for additional living expenses when a covered property loss occurs. The new endorsement provides that policyholders who qualify for additional living expenses, but who do not incur these costs, are entitled to a cash payment of $50 per day in lieu of these expenses.

Jane has a homeowners property loss that qualifies for additional living expense payments. She and her family temporarily move in with relatives, however, and incur no such expenses. Jane's claim representative, Mary, is unaware of the new endorsement and offers no cash payment in lieu of the additional living expenses.

Mary has breached the duty to understand and comply with applicable insurance policy provisions. If state law authorizes such a lawsuit, MutualCo can be liable in damages to Jane for Mary's failure to advise Jane of a benefit to which she was entitled.

Claim representatives must have sufficient knowledge of state statutory and case law, insurance department regulations, and insurance policy provisions to make correct payments to claimants and insureds under insurance policies. If a legal question is beyond the representative's knowledge, the representative should seek the advice of a lawyer who is expert in the matter. Claim representatives must advise insureds of all benefits to which they are entitled under the insurance policy that applies to the loss adjusted. This advice requires complete understanding of the various insurance policy provisions and any state case or statutory law that would affect insurance policy benefits.

Third-party claimants also have the right to fair and just treatment under the law. Although the insurer's primary duty is to its insured, the insurer must still refrain from explicitly or implicitly misleading the claimant as to matters relating to the law or insurance policy provisions.

Consistent with this requirement is the rule in many states regarding notifying claimants of the expiration of applicable statutes of limitations. In an insurance claim situation, for example, the third-party claimant's right typically is based in tort. State statutes of limitations provide that a plaintiff must file a tort lawsuit within a certain time, typically one to three years, or lose the right to sue. Many state laws provide that a claim representative who is on notice of a third party's tort claim, or who has been attempting to resolve such a claim, must notify that party of the applicable statute of limitations period. Some states require notice within a certain period of time. If the claim representative fails to comply with this notification requirement, the statute of limitations will toll, meaning that the clock stops running on the time for filing suit, preserving the claimant's right to sue for a reasonable time after notice is given.

In contrast to the duty owed to insureds, claim representatives are not responsible for advising claimants regarding all of the sums of money legally available to them as compensation in a liability claim. Indeed, the focus in the liability claim context is to protect the insured from claims of third parties by resolving them within the insured's coverage limits whenever reasonably possible.

Example: Notice of Statute of Limitations

Vic has submitted a bodily injury claim to InsurCo for injuries he received in an automobile accident that one of InsurCo's policyholders caused. Vic has been communicating with InsurCo since four days after the accident. An InsurCo claim representative concluded Vic's claim for damages to his car within six days after the accident. Vic has not been ready to settle his injury claim, however, because he claims that his injury has not healed and that he still needs treatment.

The state statute of limitations period within which Vic must file a lawsuit is one year from the date of the accident. That time period expires in two months. Vic says he is still not ready to settle his claim.

The InsurCo claim representative should advise Vic of the time when the statute of limitations period will expire and of the fact that, once it expires, InsurCo will honor no claim unless Vic or his representative has filed a lawsuit, either by telephone, or in person, and by a follow-up letter confirming the telephone conversation. State law might require such a letter and might require it to be sent within a minimum period before the statute of limitations period expires. If InsurCo does not comply with these procedures, Vic will probably have a valid claim even though the statute of limitations has expired.

Nearly every liability insurance policy has coverage limits that the insured selects when obtaining or updating coverage. A claim against an insured may be in excess of these limits. The insured in such situations has an **excess liability** loss exposure, a personal financial responsibility for any claim exceeding the limit of the insurance coverage.

Excess liability
Financial responsibility that exceeds the limit of insurance coverage for a claim.

Claim representatives must act reasonably to protect the insured from claims in excess of the liability coverage limits. If a claim representative engages in unreasonable conduct that results in an award to the claimant in excess of the liability coverage limits, the insurer will probably be responsible for the excess amount along with the limits of the liability coverage. The insurer is required to bear the financial responsibility because its unreasonable conduct resulted in an award implicating the insured's personal assets. Such unreasonable conduct might include a delay in processing the claim, poor investigation or defense of the claim, or poor judgment in contesting a claim that should have been settled.

Insurers, however, are not responsible for every claim in which an award is entered against an insured in excess of the policy coverage limit. The determining factor is whether the claim representative's conduct during the course of the claim was reasonable. If not, insurer liability in excess of the coverage limits may result.

Examples: Excess Liability Claims

- Martin is insured under a MutualCo personal insurance policy with liability coverage limits of $100,000 per accident. Martin has a loss covered by the policy in which Bill is seriously injured. Bill's claim, if Martin's liability can be demonstrated, is fairly evaluated at $500,000.

  MutualCo's claim representative, believing that Martin was not at fault for the accident, declines to make any settlement offer to Bill. The claim representative rejects Bill's settlement offer for the $100,000 coverage limit. The case proceeds to trial, and the jury awards Bill $700,000.

  MutualCo is responsible for the full $700,000 award, even though Martin has only $100,000 of liability coverage, if the claim representative's conduct was unreasonable. Given the amount of the award to Bill, such a showing probably is possible. MutualCo's claim representative will be accused of having unreasonably contested a claim that should have been settled when the opportunity presented itself.

- Jane is insured under a liability insurance policy issued by InsurCo. Jane has an automobile accident that Sue claims is Jane's fault. Jane believes, however, that Sue was at fault in the accident. Sue's car sustained minor damage, but she complains of a serious injury. Jane's liability insurance policy has coverage limits of $50,000 per accident.

  Sue makes a claim with Jane's insurer, InsurCo. Dave, the InsurCo claim representative assigned to the claim, discusses the accident with Jane briefly and concludes that it was clearly Sue's fault. Dave sends Sue a letter denying her claim without any further investigation.

  Five months later, Sue files suit against Jane. Dave hires an attorney to defend Jane in the lawsuit. The attorney recommends, among other things, the following to defend Jane in the lawsuit:

  - Depositions of Jane, Sue, the investigating police officer, and any witnesses to the accident

  - A thorough search for any witnesses to the accident

  - Sue's full medical record relating to her injury

  - An independent medical examination of Sue

  Dave refuses to authorize the lawyer to conduct this work, citing the need to control expenses and asserting that Jane was clearly not at fault for the accident, so that the work is unnecessary. The case goes to trial, and the jury finds that Jane is completely at fault and that Sue sustained a serious injury resulting in significant disability. It awards Sue $500,000.

  In all probability, InsurCo will be responsible for the full $500,000 judgment. Dave did not handle the claim against Jane reasonably. The investigation of the claim and the defense of the lawsuit authorized by Dave were far below the standard of effective claim adjustment required of insurers.

3. *Duty to provide prompt, diligent, and professional service.* A claim representative has the duty to provide prompt, diligent, and professional service to insureds and to third-party claimants. This duty gives effect to claimants' reasonable expectation that claim representatives will contact them promptly after they make claims and that claim representatives will act promptly and professionally in investigating and resolving claims. In many

states a rule of reasonableness applies to timely claim handling, with no set deadlines for any step in the claim process. In other states, statutes or insurance department regulations impose specific deadlines as to when various portions of claims must reach conclusion. For example, a statute or regulation might prescribe initial contact with the claimant or insured within fourteen days and a decision on whether to pay or deny a claim within sixty to ninety days. Other statutory time periods apply to acknowledgment of insureds' or claimants' communications or to status updates while investigations into claims are pending. Failure to comply with these deadlines can subject the claim representative's insurer to fines and penalties.

Claim Representatives' Personal Liability

Generally, actions alleging improper claim settlement practices are filed against insurers. This choice of defendant has both analytical and practical bases. Analytically, the insurer has made the promises contained in the insurance policy and must comply with the provisions of the state's unfair claim settlement practices act, so the insurer is the appropriate defendant for the lawsuit. Practically, the insurer also has much greater assets with which to pay a judgment than a claim representative who works for the insurer. Occasionally, however, claim representatives are the defendants along with insurers in lawsuits alleging unfair claim practices. The theory is that the representative committed the unfair practice and therefore is also an appropriate defendant in a lawsuit.

Most jurisdictions do not allow personal lawsuits against claim representatives for alleged unfair claim settlement practices unless the claim representatives' actions were willful, intentional, or reckless. The reasoning is as follows:

- The unfair claim settlement practices acts regulate insurers' conduct, and redress should be against the insurer.
- Only the insurer and insured have a relationship under the insurance policy that is the subject of the claim, and the claim representative is not a party to that agreement.

If, however, a claimant alleges that a claim representative has committed willful acts such as fraud, conspiracy, or theft, or has engaged in reckless or grossly negligent conduct, many jurisdictions allow lawsuits against them.

SUMMARY

This chapter examines the issues arising from the agency relationships that insurance producers and claim representatives have with their insurers. Insurance producers fall into three categories: producers, agents, and brokers. Producer is a generic term for anyone who can place insurance business with insurers. Agents, can be either general, special, or soliciting agents and represent insurers. Brokers represent insureds.

Producers may have actual authority, express or implied authority, or apparent authority. If a producer lacks authority to enter into an insurance transaction on an insurer's behalf, the insurer can bind itself to the producer's unauthorized acts by ratification.

General agents have the broadest authority of all insurance agents and can accept risks, agree upon and settle insurance terms, waive policy provisions, issue and renew policies, collect premiums, and adjust losses. Special and soliciting agents are limited to locating prospective insurance customers and presenting their applications for insurance to insurers for consideration. Brokers represent insureds and usually have neither actual or apparent authority to bind insurers. Instead, brokers bind insurance customers.

Producers must exercise a reasonable standard of care in the performance of their duties, deal with their customers in good faith, and exercise reasonable diligence on their customers' behalf. They must advise customers as to their coverage options, follow their instructions strictly, procure and maintain coverage, and place insurance with solvent insurers.

Producers have defenses against some allegations of breach of duty. For instance, a producer may not have been at fault or may not have assumed a particular duty. Insurance customers may share the fault. A customer's failure to read a policy, however, is not always a good defensive argument for a producer.

In general contract law, parties to a contract usually owe duties to each other, but not to third parties. Some courts, however, have recognized a third party's right to sue a producer. For example, an injured motorist may have a right to sue a producer for failure to obtain insurance for the negligent motorist causing the injury. Producers owe insurers the duties to disclose risks, follow instructions, and properly transmit claim information, as well as the duty of loyalty and accounting. A producer must not act contrary to an insurer's interests, particularly regarding receipt of premium payments.

Claim representatives investigate and determine amounts of losses, verify coverages, determine amounts of coverage, and conclude claims. Claim representatives can be staff claim representatives, employed by insurers; independent adjusters, who work for companies that contract with insurers or self-insureds to adjust claims; or public adjusters, whom claimants hire to assist them in presenting claims to insurers. Producers sometimes have loss adjustment duties.

Like producers, claim representatives may have actual authority, either express or implied, or apparent authority. Insurers also may ratify claim representatives' actions. Claim representatives owe duties to insurers to follow instructions, to understand and comply with the law, and to provide prompt, diligent, and professional service. Although they need not be lawyers, claim representatives must know the law as it relates to the claim management process. To insureds and third-party claimants, claim representatives owe duties to conduct fair and ethical claim management, to understand and comply with the law, and to provide prompt, diligent, and professional service.

Generally, complaining parties file actions alleging improper claim settlement practices against insurers directly, and most jurisdictions do not allow lawsuits against claim representatives personally for alleged unfair claim settlement practices unless the claim representatives' actions were intentional, or reckless. If, however, claimants allege that claim representatives have committed willful acts or have engaged in reckless or grossly negligent conduct, many jurisdictions allow lawsuits against the claim representatives personally.

Chapter 13

Direct Your Learning

Employment Law

After learning the content of this chapter and completing the corresponding course guide assignment, you should be able to:

■ Describe the employment-at-will doctrine and its exceptions.

■ Summarize the laws prohibiting discrimination on the basis of each of the following:

- Age

- Sex, race, color, religion, or national origin

- Disability

■ Describe the laws that protect people who have served in the military, or on juries, or who face garnishment of wages.

■ Summarize the laws governing labor-management relations, collective bargaining, and economic pressure used in the collective bargaining process.

■ Given a case, apply the laws that regulate employee safety and health, wages and hours worked, and employee benefits, and justify your answer.

■ Given a case, apply the laws that protect employee privacy, and justify your answer.

■ Define or describe each of the Key Words and Phrases for this chapter.

Develop Your Perspective

What are the main topics covered in the chapter?

United States common-law and statutory employment law are rapidly changing at both state and federal levels. This chapter provides the insurance professional with a background in the laws governing the employment relationship and the risks inherent in mismanaging that relationship.

Identify laws that prohibit discrimination.

- What individual factors can and cannot be used in employee selection?

Why is it important to learn about these topics?

Understanding employment law is crucial for everyone because they are invariably employees and many will also be employers or will represent their employers. U.S. employment law originated in the common law, but the twentieth century saw a rapid expansion of state and federal statutory and administrative law governing every aspect of the employment relationship. An organization's lack of expertise in human resources matters can indicate other problem areas and should put the insurance professional on guard. Failure to heed the legal environment of employment law can create a variety of employment-related and employment-practices liabilities.

Trace the development of the current employment laws.

- What rights are granted to employers and employees under the employment-at-will doctrine?
- What laws have been enacted to protect the continued employment of various individuals?

How can you use what you will learn?

Examine two or three federal laws governing employment and contrast how they might affect you as an employee and as an employer.

- What employment laws protect you specifically as an employee?
- What employment laws protect your employer?

Chapter 13
Employment Law

The law involving employer-employee relationships is one of the most rapidly expanding and changing areas of law. The employment relationship involves a complex web of common-law rights and obligations as well as federal and state regulation of virtually all of its aspects.

Insurance professionals, whether underwriters, claim representatives, producers, or others, must often evaluate organizations to decide whether to insure them or whether coverage applies. The insurance professional must make judgments about an organization's general character and evaluate overall managerial effectiveness. The extent of a firm's compliance with its legal obligations is an important clue about the quality of its management in general. For example, disregarding a legal requirement relating to workplace safety may suggest a careless attitude toward safety in general.

Organizations today require highly skilled human-resources management. Even small and medium-sized organizations have moved from using minimally staffed personnel departments, to human resources departments, either internal or external, with highly trained staff who have expertise in legal matters involving the employment relationship.

Lack of expertise in human resources matters, particularly in legal requirements, can indicate potential problem areas in an organization that could lead to higher risk exposure to a variety of employment-related and employment practices liabilities. This chapter provides the insurance professional with a background in the laws governing the employment relationship and the risks inherent in mismanaging that relationship.

The common law rarely interfered with employment relationships. The employer and employee agreed on the terms, and the employer could terminate the employee "at will"—for any reason or for no reason at all. In recent years, both Congress and state legislatures have enacted, with increasing frequency, laws regulating the respective rights and responsibilities of employers and employees. The result has been a dramatic rise in judicial and administrative claims in the area of labor and employment law.

Statutory law and the resulting case law affect many facets of employment and provide a variety of remedies to employees. Employers must stay informed of new legislation and legal developments at the federal, state, and local levels. Generally, the various federal statutes provide the minimum requirements employers must meet. State laws may provide higher standards.

A terminated employee may have several statutory bases for a lawsuit against an employer, as well as common-law bases, including contract claims, violation of public policy, intentional infliction of emotional distress, defamation, and invasion of privacy. Although at common law the doctrine of employment at will reigns, even common-law rules vary widely by state. In every case, an employer or employee must seek legal advice about the law of the applicable jurisdiction.

EMPLOYMENT-AT-WILL DOCTRINE

Employment at will
A legal doctrine under which an employer may terminate any employee at any time for any reason or for no reason.

With some limitations, most states apply the traditional doctrine of **employment at will**, under which an employer may terminate any employee at any time for any reason or for no reason. States usually make exceptions for terminations that are discriminatory or that involve employment subject to contract limitations on the power to dismiss or to a collective bargaining agreement. Under the employment at will doctrine, terminated employees who bring suits for breach of an employment contract or for tort, such as intentional infliction of emotional distress, defamation, and invasion of privacy, are not successful.

The common-law doctrine of employment at will has governed employer-employee relations in the United States since the late 1800s. Passage of the National Labor Relations Act (NLRA)[1] in 1935 first placed limits on employers' discretion to discharge employees. Even under that law, most labor contracts grant employers broad rights to discharge for cause, for example, for serious violations of work rules or employer policies.

While some states continue to apply the traditional employment-at-will doctrine, in the 1980s states began to pass employment laws that, among other things, limit the grounds for terminating an employee.

In addition, state courts have created several exceptions to the employment-at-will doctrine. The most common exceptions fall into the categories of claims for breach of express and implied contracts and for tort, including violations of public policy, intentional infliction of emotional distress, defamation, and invasion of privacy. Employees' lawsuits against employers for illegal termination are called **wrongful discharge** suits.

Wrongful discharge
A cause of action an employee may have against an employer for illegal termination of employment.

Courts continue to make exceptions to the employment-at-will doctrine, and at least one state, Montana, has abolished it by statute. Employment at will has been upheld in situations in which the employer has made it a written policy and has consistently referenced it in employee handbooks, personnel policy manuals, and forms.

If an employee suspects that his or her rights have been violated through a wrongful termination, two legal actions are possible. First, a claim can be made if a contract of employment has been formed between the employer and the employee. Second, a tort claim can be the remedy if specific causes of action are present.

Contract Claims

Breach-of-contract claims involve either express contracts or implied contracts. An express contract presents a relatively clear-cut case because the employer and employee have committed their intentions to writing and the contract has the same legal implications as any other contract.

State courts have found implied contracts of employers not to discharge employees without cause or to follow certain procedures before termination. Such a promise may be implied by an employer's written or oral communications or by a long-standing employment relationship. Written communications that create an implied contract include employee handbooks, memorandums to employees, and policy statements.

Tort Claims

An employee can sue under tort for termination of employment based on any of the following four causes of action:

1. Wrongful discharge
2. Intentional infliction of emotional distress
3. Defamation
4. Invasion of privacy

Many state courts recognize the tort action of wrongful discharge when the discharge is contrary to a strong public policy. For example, discharging an employee for refusing to commit an unlawful act or for whistleblowing may be a public policy violation. Also, discharging an employee in retaliation for exercising a legal right or privilege, such as filing a workers' compensation claim, may violate public policy even if the discharge does not violate an express provision in the applicable statute.

Although courts have awarded tort damages to employees for intentional infliction of emotional distress, to prevail on such a claim, an employee must prove the following:

- The employer's conduct was extreme and outrageous.
- The employer intentionally caused the employee to suffer severe emotional distress.
- The employee suffered emotional distress.

Defamation and invasion of privacy are also potential bases for awarding employees tort damages. They often arise as additional issues when an employee is discharged. A defamation suit usually stems from an allegedly false statement made by an employer about the reasons for discharging an employee. Such a statement is often made when a prospective employer contacts a former employer for a reference for the discharged employee. An employer is not generally liable for defamation based on negative statements in performance evaluations or negative job references unless the employer acted maliciously.

In the context of discharge, privacy claims can arise by virtue of unreasonable publicity of an embarrassing fact. An employer might be liable under the common-law theory of invasion of privacy if the employer's actions constituted an unreasonable intrusion into an employee's private affairs, for example, if an employer discloses private information about an employee's health or morality.

ANTIDISCRIMINATION LAWS

Laws prohibiting discrimination in employment affect all aspects of the employment relationship, from job application through termination. By expressly outlawing discharge on various grounds, these laws define a major exception to the employment-at-will doctrine. This section groups the numerous federal antidiscrimination laws according to the characteristic that each law protects.

Discrimination Based on Age

Two federal laws protect older workers from age discrimination: The Age Discrimination in Employment Act (ADEA)[2] of 1967 and the Older Workers Benefit Protection Act of 1990.[3]

Age Discrimination in Employment Act (ADEA)

The ADEA covers employers, unions, employment agencies, states and their political subdivisions, and governmental agencies. Employers that have twenty or more employees and that are engaged in an industry affecting interstate commerce are subject to the act. The ADEA forbids employment discrimination because of age against anyone age forty and over, and it bans mandatory retirement at any age. The original act prohibited mandatory retirement before age sixty-five, raised to seventy in 1979. No age limit has applied since 1986. The ADEA bars age discrimination in all aspects of the employer-employee relationship, including hiring; setting or applying wages, terms, conditions, and privileges of employment; and terminating employment.

The following employment practices regarding age are legal under the ADEA:

Bona fide occupational qualification (BFOQ)
The minimum qualification, under federal antidiscrimination laws, that an employee needs in order to be able to perform the duties of a particular job.

- An employer may put an age limit on employment if age is a **bona fide occupational qualification (BFOQ)**, that is, reasonably necessary to the normal operation of the business. A BFOQ is the minimum qualification, under federal antidiscrimination laws, that an employee needs in order to be able to perform the duties of a particular job. In any situation, a BFOQ is very difficult, and usually impossible, to establish.

- An employer may use preference in hiring, promoting, and paying employees if it is based on "reasonable factors other than age." For example, physical fitness might be a reasonable factor other than age that an employer may consider if a job is hazardous and requires a high degree of fitness. However, an employer cannot assume that every employee over a certain age is physically unfit to perform a particular job.

- An employer may hire, promote, pay, or dismiss employees according to a bona fide seniority system as long as that employer does not intend to evade the purposes of the act and does not require retirement of anyone based on age.

An employer may base mandatory retirement on age for the following two types of employees:

1. Executives in high policy-making positions who are over age sixty-five and entitled to a pension over a minimum amount a year.
2. Employees over age seventy who are serving under contracts of unlimited tenure at institutions of higher education.

The Equal Employment Opportunity Commission (EEOC) administers the ADEA. As a prerequisite to instituting a court suit, a person alleging age discrimination must file a charge either with an appropriate state agency or with the EEOC within a designated period after the complaint arose. The EEOC reviews the complaint; and, if it finds a violation of the ADEA, it may choose to proceed with administrative enforcement, which can include a hearing. The employee may not bring suit in court while this process continues. The EEOC can either file a lawsuit against the employer or issue a right-to-sue letter informing the complainant of the right to file a private lawsuit in court within a designated time.

Remedies for ADEA violations include back pay and reinstatement of the employee. Reinstatement means placing a person back to the position held before dismissal. The EEOC or court can order front pay, or prospective legal damages, when reinstatement would not be feasible. In the case of an intentional violation, the EEOC or court might order liquidated damages equal to the back pay award. According to court decisions, factors indicating willfulness include an employer's indifference to whether it was violating the ADEA or an employer's attempt to disguise the reason for termination.

Older Workers Benefit Protection Act

The Older Workers Benefit Protection Act amended the ADEA in 1990. Congress specifically intended this act "to prohibit discrimination against older workers in all employee benefits except when age-based reductions in employee benefit plans are justified by significant cost considerations." The act prohibits an employer from refusing to hire anyone over age forty to avoid adverse financial effects to an employee benefit or early retirement plan. For example, an employer can not refuse to hire an older employee in order to avoid an increase in health insurance premiums. Nor can an employer reduce or discontinue contributions to a pension plan on behalf of an employee who has reached a certain age. The act does allow bona fide employee benefit plans and early retirement incentive plans under certain circumstances.

Increasingly, employers are conditioning severance payments for discharged employees on their agreement to a general release of all claims against the employer and their agreement to leave voluntarily and not to seek reemployment with the employer. The Older Workers Benefit Protection Act of 1990 allows waivers of rights under the ADEA if they are knowing and voluntary. If the employee is given twenty-one days to consider the agreement before signing it and an additional seven days following its execution in which to revoke the agreement.

Discrimination Based on Sex, Race, Color, Religion, or National Origin

Since 1866, Congress has passed several laws prohibiting discrimination based on sex, race, color, religion, or national origin. They differ in coverage and remedies available. Plaintiffs suing under these laws can choose the legislation best suited to their cases. They may also have choices, or requirements, about whether they pursue remedies in courts, in administrative agencies, or both. This section offers a brief overview of what has become a very complex body of law.

Civil Rights Acts of 1866 and 1871

The first law prohibiting discriminatory employment practices was the Civil Rights Act of 1866,[4] more commonly called Section 1981. Congress passed this act shortly after the Civil War to give black citizens the same rights as all other citizens. The U.S. Supreme Court later interpreted Section 1981 as protecting not only blacks but all identifiable classes of persons who are subjected to intentional discrimination solely because of their ancestry or ethnic characteristics. However, Section 1981 does not apply to discrimination based on sex or religion.

While Section 1981 expressly protected only peoples' right to make contracts, the courts broadly interpreted the law as prohibiting discrimination in all aspects of private employment, including hiring, termination, terms and conditions of employment, and promotions. The Supreme Court narrowed this interpretation temporarily in 1989 by holding that Section 1981 did not prohibit on-the-job discrimination such as discriminatory harassment and discharge, but only discrimination in new employment contracts.

The 1991 Civil Rights Act again broadened the scope of Section 1981 to expressly encompass all facets of the employment relationship, including hiring, harassment, and termination. The 1991 Act also brings municipal, state, and local government units within the scope of Section 1981.

Unlike suits under Title VII of the Civil Rights Act of 1964 (Title VII), a suit under Section 1981 can be filed directly in the courts without first filing with the EEOC and undergoing a lengthy administrative process.

People suing under Section 1981 may recover compensatory and punitive damages in a potentially unlimited amount. The Civil Rights Act of 1991 amended Section 1981 to permit plaintiffs who win their suits to recover attorney fees as well as expert witness fees.

The Civil Rights Act of 1871[5] is a general antidiscrimination statute that applies primarily to state and local governing bodies.

Civil Rights Act of 1964 (Title VII)

The next major antidiscrimination act was the Civil Rights Act of 1964,[6] amended in 1991. The act extended the bases for protection against discrimination to religion and sex. The pertinent part of the act for purposes of this discussion is Title VII, titled "Equal Employment Opportunity." This broad act applies to employers, unions, and employment agencies and governs most employment discrimination actions, including the following:

- Employers subject to Title VII
- Prohibited employment practices
- Permissible employment practices
- Pregnancy discrimination
- Sexual harassment
- Sex-based insurance rates

Title VII applies to any employer that regularly employs fifteen or more persons in an industry that affects interstate commerce—most employers in the U.S. Even a small store with sixteen employees can affect interstate commerce when, for example, an out-of-state customer purchases an item. Title VII does not apply to the U.S. government or to any corporation wholly owned by the U.S. Nor does it apply to any religious group regarding employment of individuals of a particular religion to perform work connected with the group's activities, including educational institutions associated with it. It also does not apply to bona fide not-for-profit private-membership organizations, other than labor unions.

The EEOC is the federal agency that ensures compliance with Title VII. The usual procedure is for the aggrieved person to file a charge with the EEOC alleging discrimination. The charge must be filed within 180 days after the act occurred—or 300 days in a state with a state or local fair employment practices agency (deferral agency). That time limit does not apply to concealed facts from the other party.

Notification of the charge is served on the employer within ten days after receipt. The EEOC has exclusive jurisdiction for 180 days from the filing date, during which time it may make its own investigation. If the EEOC finds reasonable cause, it can arrange a fact-finding conference involving all those concerned to attempt to establish a settlement mutually agreeable to the parties. If no settlement has occurred within 180 days, the EEOC must issue a right-to-sue letter, notifying the complaining party that conciliation has failed. The complaining party may then institute a court suit, but must do so within ninety days after receiving the right-to-sue letter.

Title VII prohibits employers from failing or refusing to hire, terminating, limiting, segregating, classifying, or in any other way discriminating against employees or applicants for employment based on their sex, race, color, religion, or national origin.

Although religious discrimination can be subject to a BFOQ exception, Title VII requires employers to "reasonably accommodate" the religious practices of their employees unless they can demonstrate that doing so would result in "undue hardship" in the conduct of their business. The meanings of "reasonably accommodate" and "undue hardship" are questions of fact to be determined in individual cases. The burden is on the employer to show that the requested action would result in adverse economic effect involving the morale of other employees, effect on customers, plant safety, hygiene, or manner of operation.

A case of employment discrimination under Title VII may be based on either of two legal theories, disparate treatment or disparate impact, described as follows:

Disparate treatment theory
A legal basis for an employment discrimination complaint requiring the plaintiff to establish the employer's practice of intentionally treating individuals differently solely because of their sex, race, color, religion, or national origin.

1.   Under the **disparate treatment theory**, the employee must establish that an employer made it a practice to intentionally treat individuals differently solely because of their sex, race, color, religion, or national origin. An employment decision motivated in part by discrimination is unlawful, even if other factors also motivated the decision (a "mixed motive" case). However, if the employer can show that the same decision would have been made without the discriminatory motivating factor, the court's judgment is limited to declaring the parties' rights, attorney fees, and costs to the plaintiff, and damages cannot be awarded.

Disparate impact theory
A legal basis for an employment discrimination complaint requiring the plaintiff to establish that an apparently neutral employment practice or criterion, applied equally to all individuals, operated to exclude a disproportionate number of the protected class.

2.   Under the **disparate impact theory**, the employer's intent is not an issue. The employee must show that an apparently neutral employment practice or criterion that was applied equally to all individuals nevertheless operated to exclude a disproportionate number of the protected class. The 1991 Civil Rights Act altered the litigants' respective burdens of proof in disparate impact cases. The act permits a plaintiff to challenge the disparate impact of the employer's entire decision-making process as one employment practice and places the burden of persuasion (to persuade a judge or jury) on the employer to show that the challenged practice is job related and consistent with business necessity. Before the 1991 act, the plaintiff had to show specifically what practice of the employer led to the disparate impact and also had to prove that the employer did not have a legitimate business reason for the practice.

Title VII specifically permits discrimination on the basis of sex, religion, or national origin only when any of these characteristics is a BFOQ reasonably necessary to the normal operation of that business. Race or color, however, can never be a BFOQ. Proving that a BFOQ exists in any case is extremely difficult.

In the case of sex discrimination, the EEOC recognizes a defensible BFOQ if a person's sex is necessary for authenticity, such as, arguably, in the case of an actress or actor. In general, though, employers must consider individuals on the basis of their individual capabilities and not on the basis of their sex. For example, flight attendants can be male as well as female. The fact that coworkers, clients, or customers might prefer a certain sex is not a BFOQ.

Congress amended Title VII in 1978 to prohibit discrimination because of pregnancy, childbirth, or related medical conditions. The law provides that women affected by these conditions "shall be treated the same for all employment-related purposes, including receipt of benefits under fringe benefit programs, as other persons not so affected but similar in their ability or inability to work." Thus, the law protects a woman against such practices as discharge or refusal to hire solely on the basis that she is pregnant.

Another facet of sexual discrimination is sexual harassment. The EEOC defines this as any unwelcome sexual advances, requests for sexual favors, or other verbal or physical conduct of a sexual nature. The following two basic types of sexual harassment claims have emerged under Title VII:

1. **Quid pro quo sexual harassment**—when job advancement is conditioned on submission to sexual advances. Under the quid pro quo claim, the plaintiff's submission to sexual advances will not necessarily defeat his or her case. The question is not whether the plaintiff participated voluntarily, but whether the plaintiff indicated by conduct that the alleged advance was unwelcome.

2. **Hostile environment sexual harassment**—An employment discrimination claim in which the plaintiff alleges sexual discrimination because his or her refusal to submit to sexual advances resulted in abusive conduct or an otherwise hostile work environment. The Supreme Court has recognized the hostile environment claim even in situations in which the plaintiff cannot demonstrate an economic or tangible loss. An employee often commences a hostile environment case after resigning and claims the harassment amounted to constructive discharge. **Constructive discharge** is a situation created by an employer, through the conduct of a manager, a supervisor, or another employee that is so intolerable that an employee has no alternative but to resign.

The EEOC has issued guidelines on sexual harassment, which, while not dictating the decisions courts make in these cases, provide guidance to both courts and litigants. For example, the EEOC guidelines state that employers who knew or should have known about acts of sexual harassment and failed to take immediate corrective action are responsible for the acts of their employees, even if company policy specifically prohibits the acts.

Along with civil rights remedies, a plaintiff claiming sexual harassment may also have a tort claim for harassment under common law. Courts construe anti-harassment laws to prohibit harassment based on all protected categories. Employers increasingly see claims and suits alleging harassment based on age, disability, and race, and the breadth of anti-harassment laws appears to be expanding. Further, many harassment cases now hinge on the adequacy

Quid pro quo sexual harassment
An employment discrimination claim in which the plaintiff alleges that job advancement has been conditioned on submission to sexual advances.

Hostile environment sexual harassment
An employment discrimination claim in which the plaintiff alleges sexual discrimination because his or her refusal to submit to sexual advances resulted in abusive conduct or an otherwise hostile work environment.

Constructive discharge
A situation created by an employer, through the conduct of a manager, a supervisor, or another employee, that is so intolerable that an employee has no alternative but to resign.

of an employer's internal investigation of a harassment complaint. Thus, the adequacy of investigator training is often a key issue in dispute.

A similar issue is sex-based insurance rates. The use of sex-based actuarial tables in insurance has been subject to legal challenge.[7] In one case, the Supreme Court held that the use of such tables to calculate retirement benefits violates Title VII because it is related to employment. However, this does not prohibit the continued use of these tables for nonemployment-related decisions, such as determining rates for individual health and auto policies.

Civil Rights Act of 1991

The Civil Rights Act of 1991[8] contains key technical revisions to the following previously enacted discrimination laws:

- Title VII of the Civil Rights Act of 1964
- The Civil Rights Act of 1866
- The Americans with Disabilities Act of 1990[9]—to be discussed subsequently
- The Rehabilitation Act of 1973[10]—to be discussed subsequently
- The Age Discrimination in Employment Act of 1967

The 1991 Civil Rights Act also reverses parts of several Supreme Court cases that made it more difficult for plaintiffs to prevail in employment discrimination cases.

The principal changes in the area of employment discrimination that resulted from the 1991 Civil Rights Act include the following:

- The act amends Title VII and the Americans with Disabilities Act (ADA) to allow plaintiffs to recover compensatory and punitive damages in suits alleging intentional discrimination. These damages are subject to stated limits based on the employer's size, with a maximum recovery set at $300,000. In addition, courts can order such relief as back pay and reinstatement. Plaintiffs can also recover expert witness fees on the same basis as attorney fees.
- The act broadens the scope of the Civil Rights Act of 1866 to apply to all aspects of the employment relationship, including termination and harassment. As a result persons alleging intentional discrimination on the basis of race, color, ancestry, or ethnic characteristics (but not sex or religion) can recover potentially unlimited compensatory and punitive damages.
- The act changes the law regarding the burden of proof placed on each litigant in disparate-impact cases brought under Title VII and the ADA, making it easier for plaintiffs to prove their cases.
- Jury trials are available in cases in which plaintiffs seek compensatory or punitive damages under Title VII and the ADA.
- Prevailing parties can recover expert witness fees on the same basis as attorney fees.

Executive Order 11246

Employers with federal government contracts are subject to the civil rights acts as well as to Executive Order 11246,[11] of 1965, which bars job discrimination on the basis of sex, race, color, religion, or national origin. This order provides for some exemptions, most notably in the cases of employers with small federal contracts. Executive Order 11246 is also the source for federally mandated affirmative action plans for federal contractors and subcontractors. **Affirmative action plans** are employers' written plans for meeting hiring goals for groups the law protects.

Executive Order 11246 requires government contracts to include specific nondiscrimination provisions. Among these are provisions that the contractor will not discriminate against employees or applicants in protected groups and that the contractor will act affirmatively to ensure nondiscrimination and to offer employment opportunities to minorities, women, and veterans. The Office of Federal Contract Compliance (OFCC) of the Labor Department administers Executive Order 11246. Sanctions (penalties for noncompliance) include canceling the noncomplying employer's contract and forbidding future contracts with that contractor.

Affirmative action plan
A written plan that the federal government requires of employers with federal contracts, detailing how the employer will meet hiring goals for groups the law protects from discrimination.

Equal Pay Act

The Equal Pay Act (EPA)[12] of 1963 prohibits employers from paying lower wage rates to those of one sex than it pays to those of the other sex for work requiring equal skill, effort, and responsibility and performed under similar working conditions.

A wage differential is acceptable when it results from a seniority system, a merit system, or a system that measures pay by quality or quantity of production, or when it is based on factors other than sex, such as substantial differences in working conditions. Payment of different wage rates to temporary and part-time employees, new hires, and trainees is permissible if sex is not the real basis for the wage differential.

The EEOC administers the EPA. Civil remedies include back pay and an additional equal amount as liquidated damages. The act also provides for criminal penalties for willful violations. The act does not apply to employees exempt from legal minimum-wage provisions, except that it does apply to executive, administrative, and professional employees; outside salespeople; teachers; and academic administrative personnel.

Immigration Reform and Control Act of 1986

The Immigration Reform and Control Act (IRCA) of 1986[13] prohibits all employers and employee-referral services from hiring, employing, or referring aliens not authorized to work in the United States. The act also bars employment discrimination based on national origin and citizenship status. Although an employer cannot legally hire a person who is not authorized to work in the U.S., the employer also cannot legally discriminate against aliens who have obtained appropriate authorization to work in the U.S. IRCA requires employers to attest that they have verified the identities of their employees and their right to work.

Employers of unauthorized aliens are liable for civil penalties for each unauthorized alien for a first violation and a range of penalties for subsequent violations. They must require documentation and retain records of verification of citizenship from all employees. Verification and record-retention violations result in civil penalties, even if the person hired is a U.S. citizen. In addition, any employer who engages in a pattern or practice of violations of the act may face punishment by criminal fines for each violation, imprisonment, or both. Penalties for engaging in immigration-related employment discrimination practices include an order to the employer to hire the affected employee with or without back pay and to pay attorney fees. The Special Counsel's Office of the Justice Department enforces the act.

Discrimination Based on Disability

Two significant federal laws prohibit discrimination based on disability: the ADA and the Rehabilitation Act of 1973. This section summarizes each act.

Americans With Disabilities Act

In 1990, Congress passed the ADA, a sweeping reform measure affecting more than 43 million Americans with disabilities. The act became effective for most businesses in 1992 and prohibits discrimination against any qualified individual with a disability.

The ADA forbids discrimination against people with disabilities in all aspects of the employment process, including job-application procedures; hiring; advancement; termination; compensation; job training; and other terms, conditions, and privileges of employment. The act covers all employers (including governments and governmental agencies), employment agencies, and labor organizations. It defines "employers" as persons engaged in an industry affecting interstate commerce who have fifteen or more employees on each working day in each of twenty or more calendar weeks in the current or preceding calendar year.

As previously stated, the ADA bars discrimination against any qualified individual with a disability. The ADA defines disability as "a physical or mental impairment that substantially limits one or more of the major life activities of such individual," and "qualified individual with a disability" as an individual with a disability who, with or without reasonable accommodation, can perform the essential functions of the job the individual holds or desires. Infectious and communicable diseases, including AIDS, are disabilities within the ADA's terms, as are mental illness, drug addiction, and alcoholism.

The act requires employers to accommodate a physical or mental disability unless doing so would impose an undue hardship. Put another way, an employer may not deny a job opportunity or terminate the employment of an otherwise qualified employee simply because the employer would have to make an accommodation that is reasonable. Accommodations considered reasonable under the ADA include job restructuring, modified work schedules, and acquisition or modification of equipment or devices.

The factors to be considered in determining whether an accommodation will impose an undue hardship on the employer's business include the cost, the employer's financial resources, the type of business, and the effect that the accommodation would have on other employees' ability to perform their duties and on the facility's ability to conduct business.

Employers cannot use qualification standards, employment tests, or other selection criteria that might screen out individuals with disabilities unless they are job-related for the position in question and are consistent with business necessity.

The ADA prohibits employers from requiring job applicants to have medical examinations, although an employer may inquire into an applicant's ability to perform job-related tasks. Medical examinations are permitted only after an employer makes a conditional offer of employment and only if it is required of all those offered employment in the same job category. The post-offer medical exam may include a full physical examination as well as an extensive medical history. Any information obtained about an applicant's medical condition or history must be maintained on separate forms and in separate files and must be kept confidential, with limited exceptions.

An employer may require a medical examination of a current employee only if it relates to the employee's ability to do the job and is therefore a business necessity. For example, an employer cannot require an employee who has suffered a back injury to submit to a medical exam on return to work if the essential duties of the particular job do not involve activities requiring a strong back. Employers may conduct voluntary medical examinations and obtain voluntary medical histories as part of an employee health program.

Charges under the ADA must be filed with the EEOC, which investigates the charges and either sues or issues a right-to-sue letter allowing the plaintiff to file a court suit.

The 1991 Civil Rights Act amended the ADA to permit plaintiffs seeking relief for intentional discrimination to demand a jury trial and to recover compensatory and punitive damages, subject to limitations. Intentional discrimination can include failing to provide reasonable accommodation to the known disabilities of a disabled employee or applicant. The employer can avoid compensatory or punitive damages by demonstrating that it made good-faith efforts, in consultation with the disabled person, to identify and make a reasonable accommodation. The previously existing remedies of reinstatement, back pay, and attorney fees are also available to the plaintiff.

One recent trend in employment litigation is that the federal government is relaxing employment-related regulations while the states (and lower jurisdictions) are increasing their levels of regulation. This trend is particularly noticeable in the areas of anti-discrimination laws and wage and hour laws.

Because Title VII does not preempt local regulation at any level, many states and local jurisdictions have greatly expanded the list of protected categories as well as liability exposure. Common additions to the list of protected categories include political affiliation (outside of government-appointed positions), sexual orientation, transgender status, and appearance-related restrictions such as weight. Unlike Title VII (and the ADA/ADEA), many local jurisdictions, such as California, do not have any caps on potential damage awards.

Similarly, several jurisdictions, including California and Washington state, have much broader definitions of who is disabled than those applicable under the ADA. Employers and insurers are sometimes surprised to learn that they are liable for failing to accommodate conditions that do not qualify as disabilities under the ADA.

Rehabilitation Act of 1973

The Rehabilitation Act of 1973 prohibits employers with federal government contracts exceeding $2,500 from discriminating against disabled persons who are otherwise qualified to fulfill the contract. An otherwise qualified person is one who can perform the essential functions of the job either unaided or with reasonable accommodations made by the employer.

The accommodation is not reasonable if it imposes undue financial or administrative burdens on the employer or if it requires a fundamental change in the nature of the job. Employers with fifty or more employees and contracts of $50,000 or more must also prepare a written affirmative action program. The enforcement agency is the OFCC Programs of the Department of Labor.

Other Areas Affected by Antidiscrimination Laws

Antidiscrimination laws protect people in many situations. The following are three specific areas:

1. *Military Service.* The Vietnam Era Veterans' Readjustment Assistance Act of 1974[14] prohibits termination on the basis that the employee left employment to serve in the military, with certain exceptions. The act also gives employees who return from military service the right to immediate reinstatement to the same position or to a position of like status, seniority, and pay.

2. *Jury Duty.* Under the Jury Systems Improvement Act,[15] an employer cannot discharge, threaten to discharge, intimidate, or coerce any permanent employee who misses work because of jury duty. An employee can win reinstatement to the job or recover lost wages and benefits, and the employer may be fined $1,000 for each violation plus attorney fees.

3. *Garnishments.* The Consumer Credit Protection Act[16] prohibits discharge resulting from garnishment, or withholding, of an employee's wages for

indebtedness. Penalties include a $1,000 fine or imprisonment or both. In addition, each state has provisions for income withholding for child support and imposes a fine against employers that discharge, discipline, or refuse to hire individuals because of a withholding order for support.

LABOR-MANAGEMENT RELATIONS

Under the common law, an agreement among employees that tended to raise wages or alter hours, or for employees to unite to form such an agreement, was a criminal conspiracy. The modern trend of labor law has its roots in the 1930s. Since then, federal labor laws have aimed to protect individual workers by guaranteeing them the right to form associations and to form groups, or unions, to negotiate with employers.

The first modern labor law was the Norris-LaGuardia Act of 1932.[17] The main purpose of this law was to limit the use of the labor injunction, a court order to stop labor strikes. Norris-LaGuardia did not specifically require recognition of labor unions but prohibited any federal district court from issuing an injunction in a labor dispute until all efforts to resolve the issue through negotiation were exhausted.

The Norris-LaGuardia Act permits an injunction on a finding that unlawful acts may occur and may result in irreparable harm. The injunction is limited to the illegal acts and does not apply to the entire activity. The act also outlaws the so-called **yellow dog contract**, under which an employee, as a condition of employment, must promise not to join a union.

The Norris-LaGuardia Act was followed by the National Labor Relations Act (NLRA) of 1935,[18] which for the first time required recognition of labor unions and protected unionized employees from economic reprisal by employers. The NLRA has been amended several times since passage.

Collective-Bargaining Relationships

Collective bargaining is the process by which employees, represented collectively by a union, negotiate (bargain) with the employer on a labor contract dealing with wages, hours, and working conditions. The NLRA provides that a union becomes the exclusive bargaining agent when selected by a majority of the employees in a "unit appropriate for such purposes." What constitutes a "unit" is important because it helps determine the success or failure of a unionization drive. For example, if a majority of employees in one department votes for a given union but if the appropriate unit is the entire company, the employees might not have a majority. In determining what constitutes an appropriate unit, the National Labor Relations Board (NLRB) considers the similarity or dissimilarity of the employees' skills, duties, working conditions, and interests.

The usual starting point for obtaining recognition is for the union, usually without the employer's knowledge, to pass out authorization cards for the

Yellow dog contract
A labor agreement prohibited by the Norris-LaGuardia Act under which an employee, as a condition of employment, is required to promise not to join a union.

Collective bargaining
A process by which employees, represented collectively by a union, negotiate (bargain) with the employer on a labor contract dealing with wages, hours, and working conditions.

employees to sign. When employees return the cards, the union has the following two alternatives:

1. The union can make a direct request to the employer to bargain collectively. If the union has cards signed by more than 50 percent of the employees, the employer frequently proceeds to collective bargaining. If the employer refuses to recognize the union, the union can file an unfair labor practice charge. As a defense to the charge, the employer may challenge whether the union actually represents a majority of the employees.

2. The union can file a representation petition with the NLRB. The NLRB will then hold an election to certify the union as the authorized labor representative. The union must have cards signed by at least 30 percent of the employees before it can request an election.

Before an election, an employer will conduct a concerted campaign to influence the workers. The NLRA considers it an unfair labor practice for employers to interfere with, restrain, or coerce employees while they exercise their rights of self-organization. Generally, the employer can set forth any views, arguments, or opinions as long as it does not threaten reprisal, intimidate, or promise benefits. Conferring employee benefits while a representation election is pending, such as granting a pay raise or extra holidays immediately before an election, is unlawful. Threats of reprisal, such as a threat to move the plant or discharge workers, are also unlawful.

If a union receives certification, it then proceeds to bargain collectively with the employer, following mandated procedures.

Collective-Bargaining Process

The NLRA's basic premise is that collective bargaining is more likely to produce fair wages and good working conditions than would result if workers had to bargain individually with their employers. The act makes it an unfair labor practice for either an employer or a union to refuse to bargain collectively and in good faith.

While the statute does not specify what constitutes refusal to bargain, the NLRB and the courts have inferred a requirement that the representatives of both sides meet at reasonable times and confer in good faith regarding wages, hours, and other employment conditions. In determining whether a party has engaged in good-faith bargaining, the board considers the totality of actions the party has taken, including the employer's past labor relations.

The first question in determining good faith is whether collective bargaining is mandatory for the proposed subject matter. Alternatively, the subject matter might be an item that the parties can agree on but do not have to consider under the law. If it is a mandatory subject matter, then refusal to bargain shows bad faith. Conversely, neither party can move to a strike or a lockout because the other party refused to negotiate a nonmandatory item. Mandatory subject matter items under statute include the following:

- Wages, hours, and conditions of employment
- Merit wage increases
- Pensions
- Seniority rights
- Grievance procedures
- Management function clauses giving the employer certain prerogatives, such as the right to schedule work, to promote, and to discipline

Subject matter for which collective bargaining is not mandatory include the following:

- Right to subcontract work, unless it constitutes a departure from existing practices
- Ballot clause requiring a secret ballot of all employees (union and nonunion) to consider the employer's last offer before calling a strike

A take-it-or-leave-it approach by the employer from the time of the first bargaining conference is not good-faith bargaining. Another example of bad-faith bargaining occurs when an employer goes through a lengthy series of bargaining conferences without ever intending to enter into an agreement.

The NLRB's role is to act as an impartial guide during collective bargaining. Collective bargaining should result in a labor contract creating legally enforceable obligations between the parties that can be enforced by an injunction or a breach-of-contract suit.

Economic Pressure

If, following good faith bargaining, the parties cannot agree on a contract, they can use economic pressure to strengthen their positions. The economic tactics of the union are strikes, boycotts, and picketing.

The employees' right to strike is not absolute. For example, **sit-down strikes**, in which employees seize and occupy a part of the plant, are illegal. Employees cannot be on strike and at work simultaneously. They must be either subject to the employer's authority or off the job on a total strike. Thus, a refusal to work overtime or a slowdown to protest new piecework rates is an illegal strike.

Sit-down strike
The illegal seizure and occupation of a part of a plant by employees.

Boycott, or refusal to deal with an employer, is another economic tactic unions employ and can be either primary or secondary. A primary boycott is applied directly to the customers or service people dealing with the employer. Unionized employees apply a secondary boycott directly against one employer to induce the employer to stop doing business with another. Employees refuse to work on, or with, materials coming from, or going to, the second employer. The second employer is either engaged in a labor dispute or employs a non-union workforce. Similarly, the **sympathy strike** is a strike by union members who have no grievance against their own employer to support another union in a labor dispute.

Sympathy strike
A strike by union members who have no grievance against their own employer to support another union in a labor dispute.

The Taft-Hartley Act outlawed both secondary boycotts and sympathy strikes. In addition, the Landrum-Griffin Act makes it illegal for a union and an employer to evade the statutory prohibition against secondary boycotts by entering into an agreement under which the employer must refrain from using or transporting another employer's goods. Boycotts are often enforced by picketing, when union members stand or march outside an employer's premises.

Although the employer may not discharge an employee for striking, the employer may apply economic pressure by using replacement employees and lockouts. When the strike is economic because the parties have not been able to agree on labor contract terms, the employer can hire replacement employees and refuse to reinstate the striking employees. However, if the strike is because of unfair labor practices, wholly or partially, the employer must reinstate all the strikers, even if it requires dismissing the replacements. A refusal to do so makes the employer liable for full back pay.

In a lockout, the employer withholds work from the employees. Generally, an employer cannot, during bargaining negotiations, either lock out or threaten to lock out employees to gain a more favorable bargaining position. However, recognized exceptions to this rule exist. For example, a lockout is permissible to safeguard against loss, if the employer has reasonable grounds to believe that a strike is threatened or imminent, or if employees intend to stage a sit-down strike or to commit acts of sabotage.

REGULATION OF EMPLOYEE SAFETY AND HEALTH

Regulation of employee workplace safety and health falls under the Occupational Safety and Health Act (OSH Act) at the federal level and under various state job safety and health laws.

The Occupational Safety and Health Act[19] was signed into law in 1970 "to assure so far as possible every working man and woman in the Nation safe and healthful working conditions." The act encourages employers and employees to reduce workplace hazards and to institute improved safety and health programs.

State regulatory activity in industrial safety began long before the enactment of this act in the form of workers' compensation laws. Workers' compensation laws, now in force in all fifty states and the District of Columbia, provide for payment of medical expenses and some of the lost income of employees injured on the job. The workers' compensation system is a no-fault system in which the employer is strictly liable for work-related injuries and diseases. In return, the employee loses the right to sue the employer for common-law damages.

One of the main purposes of the workers' compensation system is to provide an incentive for employers and insurers to engage in workplace safety activities. Despite an overall reduction in occupational deaths and disabilities since 1911, when the first workers' compensation law was passed, in the 1960s the annual worker death rate was about 14,000 deaths and the disability rate was about 2.2 million. Many states provided erratic or no inspections of workplaces for occupational hazards. It thus became apparent that the various workers' compensation laws did not provide enough incentive for safety improvements in the workplace. For this reason, Congress enacted the national OSH Act.

The OSH Act is a comprehensive law that provides for safety and health standards for the workplace and employee protection. The consequences of noncompliance with the act include not only stringent penalties, but also shutdowns for employers that refuse to correct conditions following warnings by a federal inspector.

The act covers all persons engaged in a business affecting interstate commerce and who have employees. While the act does not directly apply to governments as employers, it requires federal agency heads to establish and maintain safety and health programs consistent with the standards applicable to the private sector under the act.

Congress created the Occupational Safety and Health Administration (OSHA) within the Department of Labor to administer the OSH Act. Since then, OSHA has been responsible for issuing and modifying the occupational safety and health standards applicable to businesses. Among OSHA's other responsibilities are to perform workplace inspections and investigations of working conditions, to certify and monitor state occupational safety and health programs, and to issue regulations requiring employers to record and report certain work-related injuries, illnesses, and death.

The OSH Act created also the Occupational Safety and Health Review commission, appointed by the president, to handle disputes arising from enforcing the act. The commission appoints administrative law judges, who hear all cases stemming from OSHA's issuance of citations.

The OSH Act also permits the Secretary of Labor to appoint advisory committees to help set standards under the act. Each advisory committee must consist of not more than fifteen members and must include, among others, equal numbers of persons qualified to present employers' viewpoints and of persons qualified to present employees' viewpoints.

Finally, the act created the National Advisory Committee on Occupational Safety and Health to advise, consult with, and make recommendations to the secretaries of Labor and of Health and Human Services on matters relating to the administration of the OSH Act.

The National Institute for Occupational Safety and Health (NIOSH), within the Department of Health and Human Services, performs activities such as research leading to the promulgation of new workplace safety and health standards, determining criteria for toxic materials and harmful physical agents, and publishing annual lists of toxic substances and the concentrations at which toxicity occurs. In addition, both OSHA and NIOSH provide training courses for federal and state compliance officers, industrial hygienists, and others in the industry responsible for workers' health and safety.

States may assume exclusive jurisdiction over their employees' health and safety conditions by developing and enforcing job safety and health programs that are at least as effective as those developed by OSHA under the act. Before assuming this jurisdiction, the state must obtain OSHA approval of the program.

Duties of Employers and Employees Under OSH Act

The OSH Act imposes duties on both employers and employees. It requires employers to comply with safety and health standards promulgated under the act covering workplace conditions and operations. It also imposes a general requirement on employers to maintain workplaces that are free from recognized hazards likely to cause death or serious harm to employees. This requirement, called the **general duty clause**, applies only to serious hazards not covered by a specific standard. The act requires employees to comply with safety and health standards and all applicable OSH Act rules, regulations, and orders.

> **General duty clause**
> An Occupational Safety and Health (OSH) Act requirement that employers comply with safety and health standards covering workplace conditions and operations and maintain workplaces free from recognized hazards likely to cause death or serious harm to employees.

With some exceptions, employers covered by the OSH Act must maintain records, including an annual log and summary, of employee work-related injuries and illnesses and must post them for the benefit of employees.[20] They also must keep a detailed record of each injury and illness and allow employees access to the log.[21] In addition, employers must verbally report to OSHA, within eight hours, any employee fatality and any accidents resulting in the hospitalization of three or more employees.

In general, employers must record only those work-related illnesses and injuries involving death, loss of consciousness, restriction of work or motion, transfer to another job, or medical treatment other than first aid. In addition, an employer might be subject to recordkeeping, reporting, and posting requirements under OSHA standards for particular hazards. Employers with no more than ten employees are exempt from most OSHA recordkeeping requirements.

Safety and Health Standards Under OSH Act

Safety and health standards adopted under the OSH Act govern general industry, such as stores, offices, and factories, as well as the construction, maritime, and agriculture industries. The standards contain specific requirements designed to protect employees against workplace hazards and cover such subjects as mandatory safety devices and equipment; training, protecting, and medically examining employees; and warning employees of hazards. The standards also mandate how employees must do their jobs safely.

An employer unable to comply with an OSHA standard may apply for a variance, that is, an order delaying the compliance requirement. Temporary variances are granted because personnel, materials, or equipment necessary to comply are not available to the employer or because the employer cannot build or alter facilities by the deadline for compliance. To receive a variance, the employer must demonstrate that all available steps have been taken to safeguard employees against the hazards covered by the standard and must submit a definitive plan for complying as soon as possible.

OSHA may grant a permanent variance if the employer can establish that its proposed practices will provide a workplace that is as safe and healthful as it would be if the employer complied with the standard. The employer must then comply with and maintain safety conditions specified by OSHA.

Enforcement and Penalties

The OSH Act is enforced through workplace inspections and investigations, generally conducted during regular working hours and without advance notice, by OSHA compliance officers. A representative of the employer and a representative authorized by the employees must have an opportunity to accompany the compliance officer during the inspection of any workplace. If the officer believes that the employer has violated any standard or its general duty to provide a workplace free from serious hazards, a citation is issued, and the employer has a reasonable time to correct the violation. OSHA then notifies the employer of the penalty, if any, and of the procedure and time within which the employer has (fifteen days) to submit notification of its intent to contest the citation or penalty.

The employer has the opportunity for a hearing before an administrative law judge. An employer may be able to establish that compliance with a particular standard is not required, for example, because the employees are not exposed to the hazard in question, because a more specific standard applies, or because compliance would result in a greater hazard than noncompliance. The Occupational Safety and Health Review Commission then issues an order. The act also provides for federal court review of these orders.

Violations of the OSH Act may result in stiff civil and criminal penalties. For example, willful or repeated violations may bring a civil penalty of up to a maximum dollar amount per violation. The act provides penalties for serious and for minor violations and penalties for failure to correct violations.

REGULATION OF WAGES AND HOURS

The federal government sets uniform standards for wages and hours through labor laws, regulations, and tax regulations. The Fair Labor Standards Act applies to most U.S. employers. Other federal acts set minimum wages of employers who work on various federal or federally-financed projects.

Fair Labor Standards Act

The Fair Labor Standards Act (FLSA)[22] establishes employment requirements relating to minimum wage, overtime compensation, child labor, and equal pay for men and women. Most states have their own wage and hour laws, which can set requirements exceeding the federal law.

The act covers employers engaged in interstate commerce, which includes most employers. The FLSA's overtime pay requirements also apply to governmental employers. Executive, administrative, and professional workers, certain agricultural workers, and outside sales employees are exempt from overtime provisions.

State laws—including those of California—can have much narrower exemptions than those found under the FLSA, inviting hundreds of state-level class action wage and hour suits in recent years. Under the FLSA, employees must "opt in" to multiple plaintiff suits, meaning that they must affirmatively become plaintiffs by choice. However, state class action laws often include "opt out" provisions, meaning that employees are assumed to be plaintiffs unless they choose not to be.

Minimum Wage, Overtime, and Hours of Work

Since 1997, the minimum wage has been $5.15 per hour. Minimum-wage requirements exclude casual babysitters and companions to disabled individuals.

The FLSA's overtime provisions apply to employees who are paid by the hour, called **nonexempt employees**. Under the FLSA, an employer must pay any nonexempt employee one and one-half times the employee's basic rate for each hour worked over forty hours a week. Executive, administrative, professional, and certain other employees are specifically exempt from the overtime provision and are therefore called **exempt employees**. Regulations issued by the Secretary of Labor define these categories of employees.[23] The entitlement of insurance claim representatives to overtime pay, for example, has been an area of some dispute and controversy.

Employers can require employees to work more than eight hours a day without overtime pay as long as they are not required to work more than forty hours in one week. Overtime pay must be computed weekly rather than on the basis of the employer's pay period. Thus, even if an employee works fifty hours in the first week and only ten hours in the second week of a two-week pay period, payment must be for ten hours of overtime earned during the first week. The workweek must consist of seven consecutive twenty-four-hour periods, but it is up to the employer to establish its own fixed, regularly recurring workweek.

The three exempt job categories are executive, administrative, and professional. For each job category, the regulations establish several characteristics that must apply to a particular employee's job duties to render that employee exempt from the act's overtime provisions. In addition, regulations effective in 2004, require that no employee receiving less than $425 a week can be classified as an exempt executive or administrative employee.

Compensable hours worked include hours worked for principal activities, required incidental activities (such as setting up equipment), rest periods of

---

Nonexempt employee
An employee who is paid by the hour and who receives hourly overtime pay.

Exempt employee
An employee who is paid a salary and who does not receive overtime pay.

less than twenty minutes, sleeping time for an employee on duty for up to twenty-four hours, training programs, and meetings (except if attended voluntarily outside regular working hours and not directly related to the employee's job). Meals of thirty minutes or more are not considered hours worked unless the employer restricts the employee's freedom by, for example, requiring the employee to sit at a desk and answer phones during lunch.

Posting and Recordkeeping Requirements and Enforcement

The FSLA requires employers to maintain certain employee data, including name, address, zip code, payroll records (including hours worked), pay rates, total wages, and deductions for at least three years. Additionally, employers must retain for at least two years all time records, wage-rate tables, work schedules, and records explaining the basis for any wage differentials paid to employees of the different sexes in the same establishment. Employers also must display in work locations the poster titled "Notice to Employees—Federal Minimum Wage."

The act requires employers to maintain records on exempt and nonexempt employees. Failure to maintain written time records can create a presumption that an employee's overtime claim is valid and thus could produce a large back-pay award and other liability. Willful falsification and destruction of records to avoid payment of wages are criminal offenses.

Under the FLSA, the Department of Labor's Wage and Hour Division investigates violations and gives employees the right to judicial enforcement of the act. Remedies in a suit brought by an employee include back pay equal to the underpayment to the employee and liquidated damages in the same amount as back pay, interest, attorney fees, and any other costs. The Department of Labor enforces remedies by injunction, back pay, or criminal sanctions.

Other Federal Minimum Wage Acts

Congress has passed specific acts to set minimum wages for employees working on federal or federally-funded projects. They include the following:

- The Davis-Bacon Act[24] establishes the minimum rate of wages for laborers and mechanics working on federal or federally financed construction, alteration, or repair projects. The act applies to employers with contracts of more than $2,000. Penalties for noncompliance include possible exclusion from future government contracts for three years.

- The Walsh-Healy Public Contracts Act[25] applies to employers with government contracts of more than $10,000 to manufacture or supply materials. The act requires covered employers to pay the prevailing minimum wage, plus time-and-a-half for hours worked in excess of forty per week.

- The Service Contract Act of 1965[26] covers employers with government contracts in excess of $2,500 to furnish services by use of service employees. Employers covered under the act must notify employees of statutory wage rights and must not pay less than the federal minimum wage.

Family Medical Leave Act (FMLA)

Employers are increasingly facing leave-related litigation under the Family Medical Leave Act (FMLA) and similar state and local laws. Many jurisdictions, such as California, Dade County (Florida), New Jersey, and Washington state, have local family medical leave requirements. Many such jurisdictions, including California, also have pregnancy-specific leave requirements in addition to those provided for by the FMLA and local family medical leave laws.

The FMLA applies to employers of fifty or more employees within a seventy-five-mile radius of the work location where the employee requests leave during twenty or more calendar workweeks in the current or proceeding calendar year. In calculating the number of employees, firms must use full-time, part-time, and temporary workers, as well as employees on leave.

To be covered under the FMLA, the employee must have worked for a covered employer for twelve months (not necessarily consecutively) and for at least 1,250 hours during the twelve-month period preceding the leave, and the employee must be employed at a worksite at which fifty or more employees work within a seventy-five-mile radius.

The FMLA covers absences for birth, adoption, and care for an employee's own serious health condition or that of his or her spouse, child, or parent. An employee need not invoke the term "FMLA" to be entitled to the law's protection. Employers bear the responsibility to decide whether the leave/absence qualifies and to document appropriately.

A serious health condition is any period of incapacity or treatment connected with inpatient care (that is, an overnight stay) in a hospital, hospice, or residential medical facility. Alternatively, it can also be a span of incapacity requiring absence of over three calendar days from work, school, or other regular daily activities that also involves continuing treatment by (or under the supervision of) a healthcare provider. Other qualifying situations occur during a period of incapacity because of pregnancy or for prenatal care; a period of incapacity because of or treatment for a chronic serious health condition (such as diabetes, AIDS, or epilepsy); permanent or long-term incapacity because of a condition for which treatment may not be effective (such as Alzheimer's, stroke, or terminal diseases); or any absences to receive and recover from multiple treatments for a condition that could result in incapacity of more than three consecutive days if left untreated (such as chemotherapy, physical therapy, or dialysis).

In terms of length of leave, the FMLA requires employers to provide up to twelve weeks of unpaid leave for covered events in a twelve-month period, calculated using one of four methods identified in the act. An employer should set forth which method it uses and notify employees of its methodology. If the employer does not explain its methodology, a court will apply the method that provides the most favorable result to the employee. Occasionally, the FMLA permits the employee to take intermittent leave or to work a reduced schedule.

The act specifies how employers must inform employees about their FMLA rights in posters, in writing, and in handbooks. Employees must be provided with the following information:

- Requirements for furnishing a medical certification for a serious health condition and the consequences for not doing so
- Employees' right to substitute paid leave and whether the employer will require substitution of paid leave
- Requirements for making any health premium payments, the consequences of failing to make timely payments, and circumstances under which coverage may lapse
- Requirements to submit a fitness-for-duty certificate to be restored to employment
- Information about whether the employee is a "key employee," one whose continued absence would result in the employer's significant economic detriment
- Employee's right to reemployment when the leave is completed
- Employee's potential liability if the employer makes the employee's health insurance premium payments while the employee is on unpaid FMLA leave and the employee fails to return to work

Workers who take FMLA leave must not experience a loss of any employment benefits accrued prior to the date of the leave. Generally, taking FMLA leave does not constitute a break in service for purposes of longevity, seniority under a collective bargaining agreement, or an employee benefit plan. An employer must maintain healthcare coverage under any group health plan for the duration of an FMLA covered leave at the same levels and under the same terms as if the employee had not taken the leave.

If an employee opts not to retain his or her group healthcare benefits while on leave, the benefits must be reinstated on the same terms as prior to the leave once the employee returns. Employers are required to maintain benefits other than group healthcare only to the same extent that benefits are provided by the employer's policy for other types of leave. Employers are required to restore employees to the equivalent of their pre-leave benefits and cannot require the employees to meet any new qualifications, such as a physical examination for life insurance.

REGULATION OF EMPLOYEE BENEFITS

The federal government, in an effort to correct practices that often left workers who were ready to retire with no pension and sick workers with no health insurance benefits, passed two laws that regulate these areas: ERISA and COBRA.

Employee Retirement Income Security Act (ERISA)

The Employee Retirement Income Security Act (ERISA)[27] of 1974 replaced a maze of state laws previously governing employee benefit plans and trusts. ERISA creates fiduciary duties for plan administrators, trustees, upper management, insurance brokers, and others regarding how they invest and distribute funds that support the plan and how they treat participants and beneficiaries, including an appeal process for denied claims.

ERISA does not require an employer to provide an employee benefit plan. An employer's obligations under ERISA arise only once the employer provides such a plan. ERISA preempts all state laws relating to employee benefits plans, except state laws that regulate insurance, banking, or securities. Self-funded employer retirement plans, for example, are generally not subject to state law.

Consolidated Omnibus Budget Reconciliation Act (COBRA)

The 1986 Consolidated Omnibus Budget Reconciliation Act (COBRA)[28] amends ERISA to require certain employers who sponsor group healthcare plans to offer employees and their dependents continuation of group health insurance coverage. It does not affect life insurance benefits provided under a group plan.

COBRA applies to group health insurance plans sponsored by employers with twenty or more employees (including part-time workers) on 50 percent of an employer's working days during the preceding calendar year. Plans sponsored by the federal government and religious organizations are exempt from COBRA.

Under COBRA, plan sponsors must provide each "qualified beneficiary" whose coverage would be lost because of a "qualifying event" with the chance to elect, within a specified time period, continuation coverage under the plan.

Qualified beneficiary
An employee who is covered under a group health insurance plan the day before a qualifying event occurs and the employee's spouse and dependent children if also covered under the plan.

Qualifying event
A termination of employment for any reason other than gross misconduct or a reduction in hours resulting in loss of coverage.

A **qualified beneficiary** is an employee covered under a group health insurance plan the day before a qualifying event occurs, as well as the employee's spouse and dependent children if also covered under the plan. A **qualifying event** is a termination of employment for any reason other than gross misconduct or a reduction in hours resulting in loss of coverage. Qualifying events for a covered employee's spouse and dependent children also include the employee's death, divorce from the employee, and the start of an employee's Medicare eligibility.

The act covers qualified beneficiaries for eighteen subsequent months if the qualifying event results from employment termination or from a reduction in hours. The beneficiaries are entitled to thirty-six months of coverage for any other qualifying event. If a second qualifying event, such as the covered employee's death, occurs during an eighteen-month continuation period, the spouse or dependent children may be entitled to an additional eighteen-month extension, for up to thirty-six months. The act also specifies certain events that will cause coverage to terminate before the expiration of the maximum time period.

For eighteen months after the qualifying event, the employer must offer the qualified beneficiary coverage identical to that provided before the qualifying event. If the health insurance plan changes benefits or premiums, COBRA coverage changes accordingly. The amount of the employee's premium for COBRA coverage cannot exceed 102 percent of the applicable group premium. This extra 2 percent covers the sponsoring employer's administrative expenses.

Under COBRA's notice requirements, once an employee's coverage under a group health insurance plan begins, the plan administrator must notify the employee and spouse of the rights provided under COBRA. Additional notification requirements arise once a qualifying event occurs that triggers the individual's right to continued coverage. The employer must notify the plan administrator within thirty days of the date of such an event. The administrator then has fourteen days to send a qualified beneficiary a written *election notice* of the beneficiary's rights under COBRA. The qualified beneficiary must elect or waive continuation coverage within sixty days of the later of either of the following dates:

- The date coverage terminates after a qualifying event
- The date an election notice is sent to the qualified beneficiary

If a qualified beneficiary waives continuation coverage, the coverage ends immediately. The beneficiary can revoke the waiver at any time within the election period but loses coverage for the time it was waived.

COBRA provides for stiff penalties for noncompliance. Any administrator who fails to meet the notice requirements may, at a court's discretion, be personally liable to the qualified beneficiary for up to $100 a day for each day a notice is not provided, plus other relief that a court may order.

EMPLOYEE PRIVACY

Federal statutes protect specific aspects of employee privacy. Common law often provides broader and more general protections to employee privacy. Employees may also bring common-law suits for invasion of privacy.

Employer Privacy Statutes

Federal laws protect employee privacy regarding drug, alcohol, and polygraph testing, and searches and surveillance.

Drugs and Alcohol

The Drug-Free Workplace Act[29] of 1988 requires employers who are federal contractors with a procurement contract for at least $25,000 and contract grantees to establish drug-prevention programs in the workplace and to track and report all drug-related employee convictions resulting from workplace activity. The government may suspend or terminate an employer who violates the act, or it may bar the contractor from federal contracts up to five years.

Courts have upheld the testing of employees by public-sector employers for drug and alcohol abuse when the employees were in positions for which safety and security were prime considerations. However, the courts have not conclusively decided the issue of whether drug-testing programs are permissible in the private sector.

Polygraph Tests

The Employee Polygraph Protection Act[30] of 1988 bars most private-sector employers, with limited exceptions, from requiring or even requesting employees or job applicants to take lie detector tests or from using or inquiring into the results of polygraph tests. The act also bars employers from discriminating against any employee or applicant who refuses to take a lie detector test. The act, however, grants employers a limited right to administer polygraph tests as part of ongoing investigations into employee theft, embezzlement, or industrial espionage. The act does not apply to government employers, nor does it prohibit the federal government from administering lie detector tests to contractors or other individuals, for purposes of national defense and security.

Act violations can result in civil fines of up to $10,000 per violation. An affected employee or applicant may bring a private civil suit against an employer who violates the act, and the employer may be liable for relief such as employment, reinstatement, promotion, payment of lost wages and benefits, and attorney fees. Also, the Secretary of Labor may seek an injunction to require compliance with the act.

Searches, Surveillance, and Background Checks

Employers are increasingly turning to sophisticated methods, such as computer and telephone monitoring, as well as using the more traditional method of physical searches, to oversee productivity and employee conduct.

Title III of the Omnibus Crime Control and Safe Streets Act[31] of 1968 and the Electronic Communications Privacy Act[32] of 1986 prohibit anyone from intercepting any wire or oral communication in a place of business engaged in interstate commerce. Interception of a communication is permissible, however, if one of the parties to a conversation has consented or if the monitoring occurs in the ordinary course of business. An example is monitoring customer service representative's phone conversations to ensure appropriate communication with customers.

Another burgeoning concern connected to employee privacy is employee background investigations. In addition to the Fair Credit Reporting Act (FCRA), out of the fifty states and District of Columbia, twenty-eight jurisdictions have no parallel laws, nine have laws which do not impose greater requirements on employers than the FCRA, and fourteen have laws imposing stricter requirements than those found in the FCRA. Additionally, important common-law privacy rights asserted often include disclosure of private facts.

Common-Law Invasion of Privacy

Employers' activities such as conducting polygraph tests, searches, and electronic monitoring have raised questions about the extent of an employee's right to privacy versus an employer's right to manage a business. State common law generally governs this area.

Employees are not entitled to an expectation of absolute privacy in the workplace. This rule applies to on-the-job sending and receiving of e-mail, instant messaging (IM), and Web surfing. Employers can monitor employee e-mails and Internet use with adequate notice to employees. However, an employer can be liable for invasion of privacy for making an unreasonable intrusion into an employee's private affairs that is highly offensive to the employee. An unreasonable intrusion either can be physical or might arise by an invasion into an employee's "emotional sanctum," such as into an employee's marital problems. Activities that may be unlawful intrusions include searches, surveillance, and mandatory polygraph tests.

Employees also can base claims of invasion of privacy on the disclosure of private facts. This basis requires showing unreasonable publicity, as well as evidence that the disclosure does not fall within the employer's legitimate business interests. For example, announcing an employee's mental condition to other employees might be an invasion of privacy if the disclosure is not limited to the employer's legitimate needs. Unlike defamation suits, truth is not a defense to a claim for invasion of privacy.

Employers also can face claims and suits by employees or former employees for defamation. For example, many states consider internal disclosures (those within the company or organization) of reasons for an employee's termination to be potentially actionable publications. Additionally, employer characterizations of reasons for an employee's termination in personnel records (such as "theft" as opposed to "violation of company expense reimbursement policies") can often lead to libel claims and litigation.

Health Insurance Portability and Accountability Act (HIPAA)

HIPAA is the acronym for the Health Insurance Portability and Accountability Act, enacted in 1996. The law's aim was to enhance the portability of health insurance coverage for workers, even in the event of job changes and unemployment.

Perhaps the largest effect of HIPAA has been in the realm of medical record privacy and confidentiality. HIPAA established new national standards for handling and accessing medical information. Before HIPAA, an individual's privacy rights regarding health information varied depending on the state of residence. Under HIPAA, healthcare providers, health plans and other healthcare services operating in all states must adhere to the guidelines established by the statute.

An individual state may enact legislation that gives consumers even greater degrees of privacy. However, states are barred from eroding or diluting any HIPAA-given rights. Some states may pass new laws to incorporate or strengthen HIPAA.

HIPAA grants all patients the right to see, copy, and request to amend their own medical records. Before HIPAA, only about half the states had laws mandating the right of patients to be able to see and copy their own medical records. Under HIPAA, patients can be charged for copies of the records, but HIPAA limits such fees.

Notice of privacy practices about how a patient's medical information is used and disclosed must now be given to the patient. For example, the first time they visit a doctor, patients typically will receive a notice informing them of their rights to medical records and information under the HIPAA. The notice must explain how to file complaints with the relevant healthcare provider and with the Department of Health and Human Services Office of Civil Rights.

HIPAA also mandates that healthcare providers account for disclosures of patients' health information. Consumers can learn the identity of those who have accessed their health records for the prior six years with exceptions. The requirement is waived when records are disclosed for purposes of treatment, payment, and healthcare operations.

Patients and consumers can lodge a complaint with their healthcare providers and/or with the DHHS if they believe a healthcare provider or health plan has violated their rights to privacy.

HIPAA encourages healthcare providers to accommodate special requests for confidential communications. HIPAA also creates a need for staff training, appointment of a privacy officer, and creating formal safeguards. These are part of the administrative requirements to which organizations must adhere under HIPAA Privacy Rules.

Patients now have a choice about having their names included in a hospital directory and about which immediate family members, close friends, or relatives may be privy to their medical information.

HIPAA authorizes both civil and criminal penalties if the government files a lawsuit for violations. HIPAA privacy rules have insurance and risk management implications with regard to possible claims for violating privacy of sensitive medical information. Statutory penalties not covered by insurance can be levied against entities that violate HIPAA rules. While these rules have prime relevance to healthcare providers, it is important to note that HIPAA creates exposures on the part of other entities, including insurers, which have reason to possess and procure medical information.

SUMMARY

Under the common-law doctrine of employment at will, an employer who was not limited by contract could terminate any employee at any time for any reason, or even for no reason. Laws and judicial decisions affecting the employment relationship have increasingly eroded this doctrine in recent years.

An employee who alleges wrongful termination may sue under several common-law remedies, including contract claims and tort claims. Employees in states that still adhere strictly to the employment-at-will doctrine may find it difficult to successfully sue based on contract claims in the absence of very explicit, formalized employment contracts.

Particularly as a result of laws prohibiting discrimination in employment, a big increase in claims against employers has occurred, as well as a rise in employers' potential loss exposure. These laws forbid discrimination against employees on such grounds as sex, race, color, religion, or national origin.

The Age Discrimination in Employment Act (ADEA) forbids employment discrimination on the basis of age against anyone age forty and over, and it bans mandatory retirement at any age in the absence of a "bona fide occupational requirement." The Civil Rights Acts of 1866, 1871, 1964, and 1991 focus, to varying extents, on discrimination based on sex, race, color, religion, and national origin.

Title VII of the 1964 Civil Rights Act is a broad antidiscrimination provision that applies to employers, unions, and employment agencies. Title VII governs most employment discrimination claims. The Equal Employment Opportunity Commission (EEOC) ensures compliance with the ADEA and with Title VII.

The 1991 Civil Rights Act provides the right to compensatory and punitive damages in cases of intentional discrimination. Plaintiffs in such cases also have the right to jury trials. Previously, plaintiffs in these cases had limited remedies, usually only reinstatement in jobs with back pay.

Employers with federal government contracts are subject not only to the civil rights acts but also to Executive Order 11246, which bars job discrimination on the basis of sex, race, color, religion, or national origin. This order is the source for federally mandated affirmative action plans for federal contractors and subcontractors.

The Equal Pay Act of 1963 (EPA) forbids discrimination in employment on the basis of sex in the payment of wages. The Immigration Reform and Control Act of 1986 (IRCA) prohibits all employers and employee-referral services from hiring, employing, or referring aliens not authorized to work in the United States but also prevents discrimination on the basis of citizenship. Both the Americans with Disabilities Act of 1990 (ADA) and the Rehabilitation Act of 1973 prohibit discrimination based on disability.

In an organized labor situation, the collective bargaining agreement regulates the employment relationship under the National Labor Relations Act of 1935 (NLRA), which has had several significant amendments. The NLRA sets forth specific requirements about what constitutes a collective bargaining unit, or union, and the collective bargaining process, as well as mandatory and nonmandatory subject matter for collective bargaining. Strikes, boycotts, and picketing are methods that employees can use to apply economic pressure to employers.

Other laws affect more specific aspects of the employment relationship. For example, the Occupational Safety and Health Act of 1970 (OSH Act) ensures employee health and safety, primarily by setting up safety and health standards for the workplace and providing for stringent penalties for employers who do not comply.

The Fair Labor Standards Act (FLSA) regulates wages and hours of work. The Employee Retirement Income Security Act of 1974 (ERISA) governs employee retirement benefits. The Consolidated Omnibus Budget Reconciliation Act of 1986 (COBRA), an amendment to ERISA and other statutes, requires the continuation of group health insurance to certain employees and dependents. Laws concerning drug and alcohol use, polygraph tests, and wiretaps, as well as court decisions in actions by employees for invasion of privacy, address issues concerning employee privacy.

CHAPTER NOTES

1. 29 U.S.C., § 151.
2. 29 U.S.C., § 621.
3. 29 U.S.C., § 626.
4. 42 U.S.C., § 1981.
5. 42 U.S.C., § 1983.
6. 42 U.S.C., § 2000e.
7. *Arizona Governing Committee v. Norris*, 463 U.S. 1073 (1983).
8. 42 U.S.C., § 12101.
9. 29 U.S.C., § 791.
10. S. 1745, P.L. 102-166, 105 Stat. 1071.
11. 30 F.R. 12319, 9-26-65.
12. 29 U.S.C., § 2.6d.
13. 8 U.S.C., § 1324a-b.
14. 38 U.S.C., § 2021.
15. 28 U.S.C., § 1875.
16. 15 U.S.C., § 1601.
17. 29 U.S.C., § 101.
18. 29 U.S.C., § 151.

19. 29 U.S.C., § 651.

20. OSHA Form No. 200.

21. OSHA Form No. 101.

22. 29 U.S.C., § 201.

23. 29 C.F.R., § 541.0.

24. 40 U.S.C., § 276a.

25. 41 U.S.C., § 35.

26. 41 U.S.C., § 351.

27. 29 U.S.C., § 1001.

28. Pub. L. Nos. 99-272—102-26 (codified as amended in scattered sections of U.S.C.; *see* 42 U.S.C., § 1395).

29. 41 U.S.C., § 701.

30. 29 U.S.C., § 2001.

31. Pub. L. Nos. 90-351—102-332 (codified as amended in scattered sections of U.S.C.).

32. 18 U.S.C., § 2510.

Chapter 14

Direct Your Learning

Business Entities

After learning the content of this chapter and completing the corresponding course guide assignment, you should be able to:

■ Given a case, apply the legal characteristics of corporate structure.

- Explain how incorporation provides limited liability to corporate stockholders and what exceptions reduce that protection.

- Contrast the role of state and federal laws in regulating corporations.

- Explain how an organization's corporate powers are defined.

- Explain who in the corporate structure is responsible for liability for torts and crimes.

- Explain how corporations are formed and how corporate ownership is created.

- Describe the rights, powers, and duties of corporate stockholders, directors, officers, and employees.

- Describe the procedures by which corporate existence can terminate through merger, dissolution, and reorganization.

- Describe foreign corporations and their limitations.

■ Given a case, apply the legal characteristics of a partnership.

- Describe the forms of partnerships.

- Describe the authority and liability of individual partners to one another and to third parties for contracts, torts, and crimes committed by or on behalf of the partnership.

- Explain how a partnership can terminate.

■ Describe the purposes and functions of limited partnerships, limited liability partnerships, and limited liability companies.

■ Define the purposes and functions of unincorporated associations.

■ Define or describe each of the Key Words and Phrases for this chapter.

Develop Your Perspective

What are the main topics covered in the chapter?

A vast amount of law governs business entities in the United States. This rapidly changing body of law encompasses the common law and statutory law at both state and federal levels.

Compare the types of business entities.

- How are investors in a corporation protected?

- Why might an individual wish to remain in operation as a sole proprietor?

Why is it important to learn about these topics?

An understanding of business entities law is fundamental to the exploration of loss exposures and interests in a business environment. The most basic forms of business are sole proprietorships, corporations, and partnerships. However, many other business entity variations exist in the U.S., which focuses more on private business relationships than most other industrialized countries.

Examine the laws that apply to various types of business entities.

- What are the advantages and disadvantages of the various forms of businesses?

How can you use what you will learn?

Analyze the common-law and statutory laws that apply to business entities.

- What are the federal and state statutes that apply to business entities in which you are involved?

- What are the responsibilities and liabilities that might affect the business entities in which you are involved?

Chapter 14
Business Entities

Business entities can be organized as sole proprietorships, corporations, partnerships, and unincorporated associations. Any individual can conduct a business as a sole proprietor. Corporations have a legal existence separate from their owners or managers. Partnerships enable individuals to combine their efforts for a particular business purpose. Unincorporated associations bring people together more informally for a common purpose.

In the context of insurance, the form of an organization is important for several reasons. First, the organizational form affects the insurability of the business. It determines who the owner is; that is, who has the legal responsibility for the organization's debts and its employees' actions. Owners' decisions can affect the acceptability of a risk for insurance coverage. An insurer's evaluation of an organization's owners is important because usually owners' interests are the ones that are insured. Moreover, owners can influence the frequency and severity of loss or can present moral or morale hazards that make an organization uninsurable.

Second, the form of organization directly influences the coverage provided by an insurance policy. For example, a policy will provide corporate stockholders some general liability coverage. Partners have coverage only for their actions as partners in the partnership named in the policy. Workers' compensation laws are specific about the coverage provided to executive officers of a corporation, partners, and sole proprietors.

Finally, the form of ownership to some extent determines exactly how the named insured should appear on the policy. Underwriters should look for any discrepancies between the wording of the name and the form of organization checked on the application. For example, the name can imply that the organization is a sole proprietorship (an individual in business), but partnership is checked on the application. With corporations, the policy should show all subsidiary corporations (and their operations). Many conglomerates have similar names for their various corporate subsidiaries, and it is easy to omit or incorrectly name one. Such a mistake could lead to later complications, in the case of a claim, for example.

Because corporations represent a significant proportion of business entities, and regulations apply to all aspects of their existence, value, and potential liabilities, this chapter addresses them first. Next, the chapter describes partnerships and limited partnerships. Finally, the chapter describes the unique characteristics of unincorporated associations.

CORPORATIONS

Corporation
A business entity organized under state law and entitled to the same rights as a person, distinct from its owners.

A **corporation** is a business entity, usually consisting of several individuals, organized under state law and entitled to the same rights as a person, distinct from its owners. Three main types of corporations are the following:

1. Governmental corporations, such as cities, counties, and states
2. Charitable or not-for-profit corporations, such as colleges, universities, hospitals, and religious institutions
3. Business for-profit corporations

The corporation is a separate, legally recognized entity that can sue, be sued, own property, hire employees, and enter into contracts in its own name and based on its separate legal identity. As a separate legal entity, the corporation affords protection from liability to its stockholders. The corporate charter and bylaws determine the corporation's reason for existence and its powers. The corporate structure defines methods of allocating and distributing assets, methods for stockholders to exercise their interests, rules governing actions of the board of directors and employees in the corporate interests, and procedures for transfer or dissolution of the organization.

Advantage of Incorporation

The primary advantage of incorporation is that it limits the owners' liability for the corporation's contracts and torts. For example, if the corporation goes bankrupt or if a tort claim consumes both the corporation's available insurance and its assets, the stockholders, who are the corporation's owners, are generally not liable for any remaining debt. In closely held and family corporations, however, loan contracts often bypass the stockholders' immunity from liability for corporate debts. Therefore, banks lending money to such corporations can demand from stockholders, as collateral, signed notes to secure the obligation with their credit, as well as with the corporation's credit.

Bypassing stockholders' immunity from tort liability is much more difficult than bypassing immunity from contractual liability. Therefore, a corporation or even individuals might incorporate a particularly hazardous business or part of a business separately to isolate loss exposures that might otherwise adversely affect the main enterprise.

Pierce the corporate veil
A court act of imposing personal liability on corporate officers, directors, and stockholders for the corporation's wrongful acts.

State laws make exceptions to corporate owners' limited liability. For example, several states hold stockholders liable for employees' wages and unemployment benefits earned but unpaid before a corporation's insolvency. Courts also make exceptions, that is, they **pierce the corporate veil**, by holding corporate officers, directors, and stockholders liable for the corporation's wrongful acts, for example, usually when a corporation was formed for an illegal purpose. For example, a court can permit a direct lawsuit against stockholders who have formed a corporation for the purpose of evading existing personal debts.

Similarly, if the stockholders themselves ignore their corporation's separate identity, the courts will also ignore it. For example, if a corporation is managed directly as though it were a sole proprietorship, with corporate and personal funds commingled and with no separate corporate records, a court will treat it as an individual enterprise or a partnership, making the stockholders liable for corporate actions.

"Thin financing" and inadequate capitalization also can defeat the limited liability of a corporation. Inadequate equity capital and excessive loans constitute "thin" corporate financing. Assume that a given amount of money is recognized as the minimum needed to ensure success for a corporation. The incorporating group invests 10 percent of that amount in shares of common stock (equity) and lends the corporation 90 percent. On insolvency, the 90 percent will receive treatment not as a loan, but as equity. A court treats the investors not as creditors but as investors for all of the money. Therefore, outside creditors will have priority in the corporation's assets; only after their full satisfaction will investors get anything.

Inadequate capitalization occurs when a corporation creates a subsidiary but attempts to avoid risking too much money, by providing it with insufficient equity capital to ensure success. If the subsidiary becomes insolvent, the courts ignore the separate legal identities of the parent and subsidiary and require the parent to pay the subsidiary's unpaid debts.

Federal and State Laws and Regulations

Federal law plays a large role in corporate operations under the constitutional power delegated to Congress in the Commerce Clause. Because most corporations are involved in interstate commerce, they are subject to Congress's power to regulate commerce among the states.

Congress charters certain types of corporations, such as public corporations, by special acts. Many federally chartered corporations compete with private business corporations. For example, in the insurance business, the federal government conducts the veterans and military insurance programs and the Federal Crop Insurance Corporation. Generally, however, federally chartered corporations implement federal government policies with only incidental business purposes.

State law governs the formation of corporations. In general, all states have laws that authorize corporate formation for any lawful purpose except insurance, banking, and the practice of a profession, and special acts cover some others. Business corporations can be held publicly or privately.

The public at large owns the stock of a **publicly held corporation**. The stock of a **privately held corporation** is held by one person or a small group of people, frequently family members, and is not traded in markets maintained by securities dealers or brokers. Privately held corporations are also called **close corporations**, or **closely held corporations**. Close corporations sometimes ignore formal corporate procedures, operate more like partnerships, and are, therefore, more vulnerable to attempts to pierce the corporate veil.

Publicly held corporation
A corporation with stock owned by the general public.

Privately held corporation, or **close corporation**, or **closely held corporation**
A corporation in which one person or a small group of people, frequently family members, own the stock and do not trade it in markets maintained by securities dealers or brokers.

Foreign corporation
A corporation formed in a state other than the state in which the corporation is doing business.

Alien corporation
A corporation chartered in a country other than the country in which the corporation is doing business.

A corporation is a citizen of the state that charters it, and that state is the corporation's domicile, or legal home. A corporation is a legal person or entity only in the state of incorporation. Therefore, if a corporation wants to do business in another state, it must comply with the other state's laws. A corporation formed in one state is a **foreign corporation** in any other state, and a corporation chartered in another country is an **alien corporation** outside that country. No state can give a corporation the right to operate in another state.

Interstate business competition has liberalized corporation laws because states want to attract new businesses. Delaware has led this competition for many years, and consequently many thousands of organizations incorporate in Delaware but have their principal places of business in other states. Delaware's corporation law favors management in several ways, including the following:

- It requires only one incorporator and allows a corporation to be the incorporator.
- Its courts construe corporate laws favorably for corporations.
- It has no minimum capital requirement.
- It has a favorable franchise tax.
- No corporate income tax applies for companies doing business outside of the state.
- It has no corporate sales, personal property, or intangible property tax.
- It does not tax nonresidents' stock and imposes no inheritance tax on nonresident holders.
- A corporation can keep all books and records outside the state.
- A corporation can maintain a principal place of business outside the state.

Some states apply their statutes, rather than those of the state of incorporation, if a substantial portion of the corporation's business is done in those states. These statutes are called **runaway corporation statutes**.

Runaway corporation statute
A state statute that applies to corporations doing business in the state that are incorporated in other states.

Corporate Law Provisions

A general corporation law contains provisions about the following corporate features and functions:

• Formation	• Reports	• Elections
• Powers	• Officers	• Directors
• Principal office and agent	• Stock	• Amendments
• Books	• Dividends	• Mergers and consolidations
• Certificates	• Meetings	• Dissolution and winding up

In 1950, the American Bar Association drafted the Model Business Corporation Act. Significant amendments later led to the Revised Model Business Corporation Act (RMBCA). Because of the RMBCA's nearly universal acceptance by the states, this chapter uses it as the base for discussion.

States have special incorporation laws for insurance, banking, railroads, telephone companies, savings and loan associations, and not-for-profit corporations. These special laws have unique features not shared by general business corporation law. State insurance laws, for instance, must provide for the incorporation of mutual insurance companies, which are for-profit corporations without capital stock. Federal statutes cover the incorporation of national banks.

General business corporation laws prohibit professionals, such as doctors, lawyers, and accountants, from incorporating because of the personal and confidential relationships they must form with their clients. However, many states have adopted special statutes authorizing **professional corporations (PCs)**. These statutes allow members of the same or associated professions to incorporate. Professional corporation members do not have limited liability for professional malpractice because professional ethics require personal responsibility for professional malpractice.

Professional corporation (PC)
A corporation formed under a statute that allows members of the same or associated professions to incorporate.

Corporate Powers

Corporation statutes define and limit the powers of corporations. Statutes require corporations to file a **corporate charter**, or **articles of incorporation**, that specifies their goals and objectives and the kind of business for which the corporation is being organized.

Corporate charter, or **articles of incorporation**
A document prepared during the formation of a corporation stating the corporation's goals and objectives and the kind of business for which the corporation was organized.

Traditionally, the corporate charter stated the corporation's precise purpose(s). Now, most states permit the stated purpose to be "for any lawful purpose." The RMBCA provides that "every corporation incorporated under this Act has the purpose of engaging in any lawful business unless a more limited purpose is set forth in the articles of incorporation."[1]

Because insurance corporation laws usually prohibit an insurance company from engaging in any other business, an insurance company's articles of incorporation specify the particular kinds of insurance the corporation will provide.

Typical Items Included in Articles of Incorporation

- Corporate name
- Duration (usually perpetual)
- Purpose
- Number, classes and par value of shares
- Provisions, if any, for the stockholders' right to purchase a proportionate share of a newly authorized stock issue
- Provisions, if any, restricting the transferability of shares
- Registered office or place of business and registered agent
- Number, names, and addresses of the initial board of directors
- Names and addresses of incorporators

In addition to the powers given by law and those stated in the charter, corporations have implied powers to do all things necessary or convenient to achieve the corporation's purpose. For example, historically the law has recognized the corporation's implied power to sue and be sued; to acquire, hold, and dispose of property; to have a corporate seal; and to adopt bylaws. The RMBCA recognizes fifteen implied powers.[2] The common law did not recognize some of these, such as the power to make donations for the public welfare and the power to be a member of a partnership. A corporation can exercise its powers, express or implied, only to further the organization's primary purpose.

Ultra vires
An act of a corporation that exceeds its chartered powers.

A corporation that exceeds its chartered powers acts **ultra vires**, or beyond its power. If a corporation has a restricted purpose clause, the stockholders can sue to enjoin (stop) the directors from engaging in *ultra vires* activities. If the corporation loses money in an *ultra vires* activity, the directors who authorized that activity are personally liable to the corporation for the loss. The attorney general of the state of incorporation can sue to enjoin any *ultra vires* activity or, in extreme cases that involve the public interest, sue to dissolve the corporation.

Liability for Torts and Crimes

A corporation, its directors, and its officers can be liable under both tort and criminal law. Under tort law, a corporation is liable as a principal or an employer under the doctrine of *respondeat superior* for all torts committed by its agents or employees within the scope of their agency or employment. Corporate officers and directors are not liable for an employee's or agent's torts unless they authorized or participated in the tort.

In addition to the corporation itself, the actual tortfeasor (employee) is always liable. For many types of negligence, however, the corporation's insurance policy covers the employee as well. Courts award compensatory damages for injuries resulting from negligence, but they can also award punitive damages for willful, wanton, or malicious torts.

Under criminal law, corporations can sometimes be guilty of a crime even with no specific criminal intent. For such crimes, often called absolute liability crimes, lack of intent is immaterial. This category of crime includes food and drug law violations and combinations in restraint of trade. The test of corporate criminal responsibility for absolute liability crimes is whether the responsible employee was acting within the scope of employment to benefit the corporation.

Other crimes, such as larceny, price-fixing, and obtaining money under false pretenses, require a specific criminal intent. The test for corporate responsibility is the same as that for absolute liability: whether the employee was acting within the scope of employment to benefit the corporation. A corporation can be responsible for an employee's criminal activity if it could have uncovered the activity through reasonable diligent supervision.

Officers and employees are personally responsible for their criminal acts. In addition, under statutes that impose criminal liability for unintentional acts, an officer can be criminally responsible for failure to ensure that subordinates comply with the statute.

Delaware and other states provide that a corporation can purchase and maintain insurance on behalf of any officer, director, agent, or employee against any potential liability arising out of the exercise of corporate powers. However, in response to the increasing number of lawsuits against corporate directors and officers in recent years, insurers have dropped coverage limits and increased premiums substantially. Meanwhile, prospective board members have demanded coverage with sufficient limits, and their refusal to serve without such coverage has made it difficult for many firms to obtain outside directors.

Corporation Formation

A corporation that confines its business to one state will usually find it advantageous to incorporate there. Choosing a different state might increase organizational and operational costs and taxes. For a corporation that operates in several states, the incorporators choose one state in which to incorporate. Some state statutes and courts are more favorable to management than others.

Promoters

A **promoter** is a person who brings a corporation into being. The promoter can be one or more persons, one or more corporations, or, particularly with nonprofit corporations, a paid organization. The promoter works to interest others in organizing a corporation, obtains their cooperation and assistance, and completes the legal and practical steps to create the corporation.

Promoter
A person who brings a corporation into being.

Legally, the promoter is not an agent because the corporation does not yet exist, and therefore there is no principal with which to form an agency relationship. Therefore, the promoter is legally a partner with fellow promoters. If the promoter's acts or contracts are to bind the corporation, the corporation upon its creation must adopt or ratify those acts or contracts. Promoters, like ordinary partners, have a fiduciary duty of the utmost good faith in dealing with one another and with the corporation they are organizing, but this relationship ceases when the corporation comes into existence.

Any contract entered into by the promoter on a proposed corporation's behalf binds only the promoter and the parties to the contract. Once created, the corporation can accept or reject the contract. Even if the corporation accepts the contract, in many states the promoter is still personally liable under the contract unless the other party consents to release the promoter. Some state laws imply a new contract, which relieves promoters upon the corporation's acceptance of the novation. Although this appears hazardous, as a practical matter, promoters usually become the corporation's original directors or officers and as such later ratify prior contracts.

Incorporation

Incorporator
One who signs the formal incorporation application that is filed in the appropriate state office.

The promoter can also be the **incorporator**, one who signs the formal incorporation application that is filed in the appropriate state office. There are usually three incorporators. New York allows only one person as the incorporator of a general business corporation but at least thirteen as incorporators of an insurance company.[3]

The certificate of incorporation includes the corporation's name. Corporate name selection is subject to statutory limitations. For example, some states specifically prohibit use of the words "insurance," "title," "bank," or "trust" in corporations' names other than those of regulated corporations organized under special statutes.

A business has a property right in its name. Therefore, a business cannot use a name resembling one used by another business in the same area.

Certificate of incorporation
A state-issued certificate that in some states signifies corporate existence.

State statutes require specific numbers of incorporators to sign the articles of incorporation, which are filed, along with fees, with the appropriate state office. Some states require proof of publication of the notice of incorporation, usually in a local newspaper or legal publication, to accompany the filing. The state then issues a **certificate of incorporation**. Under the RMBCA, corporate existence usually begins when the articles of incorporation are filed.[4] In some states, corporate existence begins when the certificate of incorporation is issued.

De jure (in law) corporation
A corporation formed in compliance with law.

De facto (in fact) corporation
A corporation formed in good faith and with a reasonable attempt to comply with the law, but failing to meet a minor requirement.

A corporation formed in compliance with law is called a ***de jure* (in law) corporation**. If, however, despite good faith and a reasonable attempt to comply with the law, there was a failure to meet some minor requirement, the corporation is a ***de facto* (in fact) corporation**. Only the state can legally challenge the existence of a de facto corporation.

If the corporation is neither de jure nor de facto—that is, it does not exist—individuals engaged in the business can be personally liable for its debts and contracts. However, a third party that has dealt with those individuals as a valid corporation might not be able to legally deny its corporate existence.

Innocent and inactive stockholders who have elected a board of directors and believe that a valid corporation has formed might not be personally liable, but those who are involved and are aware that no corporation was formed can be liable.

Organizational Meeting

Organizational meeting
The first meeting of a corporate board of directors, held to elect corporate officers, adopt bylaws, and take other actions to start corporate operations.

After the certificate is issued, the corporate **organizational meeting**, often the first meeting of the board of directors, takes place. If the articles of incorporation do not provide for the first board, the incorporators hold this meeting and elect the first board of directors. The board then meets to complete the organization by electing officers, adopting bylaws, accepting stock subscriptions, acting on pre-incorporation contracts negotiated by the promoters, and taking any other actions needed to start corporate operations.

Typical Corporate Bylaw Provisions

- Stockholders' meetings—date, place, proxies, conduct of elections, order of business
- Directors—term of office, compensation, meetings, loans, and authority to elect officers
- Officers—names and functions, appointment, removal, authority to sign checks and enter contracts
- Indemnification of directors, officers, and agents—provides for corporate reimbursement for individuals' liability
- Shares of stock—including issuance, transfer, record date
- Corporate seal and officers' signatures
- Amendment of bylaws

Bylaws are formal provisions for the corporation's structure, regulation, and operation. Statutes also govern many of these matters. The law holds officers, directors, and stockholders responsible for knowing the bylaws. Employees and the general public are not bound by the bylaws unless they have actual knowledge of them.

Corporate Ownership

Corporations raise funds by issuing two principal types of securities: debt securities and equity securities. A **debt security**, or **bond**, is a debt obligation issued by a corporation or government unit that promises to pay interest periodically at a stated rate and/or to pay the bond principal at a specified maturity date. An **equity security**, or **stock**, is a security used by a corporation to raise funds by granting stockholders an ownership share in the corporation. Bondholders are creditors of the corporation. Stockholders are its owners.

Equity securities are the corporation's capital stock and represent the stockholders' ownership of and equity, or financial interest, in the corporation. The corporation, as a separate legal entity, owns the corporate property. When a corporation dissolves, its property is the sole source of payment to creditors. Remaining funds after payment of all the corporation's creditors, if any, go to the stockholders in proportion to their ownership of stock.

Common stock is an ownership interest in a corporation that gives stockowners certain rights and privileges, such as the right to vote on important corporate matters and to receive dividends. It is ordinary stock with no preferences. Each share gives the stockholder one vote and dividends, if any. **Preferred stock** is generally nonvoting but has a priority over common stock, usually regarding dividends and capital distribution if the corporation ends its existence.

Voting rights may differ for different classes of stock. Suppose a corporation's promoters have authority to issue 400,000 shares of Class A common stock at $2 **par value** (face value), with shareholders in that class entitled to elect three directors. The promoters also have authority to issue 200,000

Debt security, or **bond**
A debt obligation issued by a corporation or government unit that promises to pay interest periodically at a stated rate and/or to pay the bond principal at a specified maturity date.

Equity security, or **stock**
A security used by a corporation to raise funds by granting stockholders an ownership share in the corporation.

Common stock
An ownership interest in a corporation that gives stockowners certain rights and privileges, such as the right to vote on important corporate matters and to receive dividends.

Preferred stock
Stock that is generally nonvoting but that has priority over common stock, usually regarding dividends and capital distribution if the corporation ends its existence.

Par value
The face value of stock.

shares of Class B common stock at $0.20 par value, with stockholders in that class entitled to elect four directors. By issuing Class B to themselves, the promoters obtain control of the corporation with a $40,000 investment (200,000 × $0.20) and the right to elect four directors, while the outside investors have minority representation on the board with an $800,000 (400,000 × $2) investment and the right to elect only three directors.

Dissolution
A corporation's termination.

The rights of common and preferred stockholders differ if the corporation dissolves. At **dissolution**, which is a corporation's termination, common stockholders share whatever remains after all corporate debts are paid. Preferred stock stockholders are usually entitled to a preference in corporate assets over common shares at dissolution and are entitled to their par value plus accrued dividends, if any, after debts are paid.

Stated capital
The total amount of capital contributed by stockholders to a corporation.

Stated Capital

Capital surplus
The difference between a stock's purchase price and its par value.

Stated capital is the total amount of capital contributed by stockholders. For par value stock, stated capital is the par value amount stated in the articles of incorporation. If the articles authorize issuance of 1,000 shares of $5 par value stock, and if all the stock is sold at par, the full amount received, $5,000, is stated capital. If the stock sells below par, say at $3 per share, the stock is "watered," or diluted, and the directors and stockholders are liable to unsatisfied creditors for the deficiency.

Stock right
A short-term option to purchase corporate shares.

Capital surplus is the difference between a stock's purchase price and its par value. If the stock sells above par at, say, $8 per share, then out of the $8,000 realized, $5,000 goes into stated capital and the remaining $3,000 becomes capital surplus. In general, capital surplus is a cushion against bad times. Capital surplus, however, can be transferred to stated capital by obtaining stockholder consent to amend the articles to increase the common share's par value from $5 to $8.

Stock warrant
An option to purchase corporate shares evidenced by a negotiable certificate (usually issued with preferred stock or bonds) that grants the holder the right to purchase a certain number of shares at a specified price on or before a specified date.

Stock Rights, Warrants, Options, and Preemptive Rights

Stock rights are short-term options to purchase corporate shares. They may be given to encourage present stockholders to purchase a proportional quantity of a new stock issue, often at less than market price. The usual procedure is to give so many rights per 100 shares of stock.

Stock option
An option to purchase corporate shares, often used to provide deferred compensation for executives and permitting executives to acquire a certain number of shares, usually relative to status or salary, at a stated price on or before a specified date.

Stock warrants resemble stock rights, except that they are evidenced by a negotiable certificate (usually issued with preferred stock or bonds) that grants the holder the right to purchase a certain number of shares at a specified price on or before a specified date.

Stock options are often used to provide deferred compensation for executives. They permit executives to acquire a certain number of shares, usually relative to status or salary, at a stated price on or before a specified date.

Preemptive right
The right of an existing stockholder to purchase the proportion of a new issue of stock that the stockholder's present holdings bear to the total outstanding shares of the same class of stock.

Preemptive rights, when given, are the rights of existing stockholders to purchase the portions of a new issue of stock that their present stockholdings bear to the total outstanding shares of the same class of stock.

If the market price of the shares rises, then rights, warrants, and options can be valuable. Each is worthless after the expiration date.

Redemption or Purchase by the Corporation

A corporation may reacquire issued securities by repurchasing them. This reacquisition is known as **redemption**. The original agreements between the corporation and purchasers of debt securities and preferred stock can include provisions making the securities redeemable at the corporation's option or providing for compulsory retirement of the security. Such agreements enable the corporation to reshape its financial structure at will when conditions change. A corporation might also provide for the redemption of nonvoting common stock. It cannot, however, provide for the redemption of all the common voting stock.

Redemption
A corporation's repurchase of previously issued securities.

A corporation can redeem stock only if its assets exceed its liabilities. Liabilities include any obligations to stockholders entitled to preferential treatment in dissolution proceedings.

Treasury stock is created when a corporation with sufficient surplus buys its own shares in the market and does not retire the shares. The shares may be held for reissuance at a higher price or for issuance to employees. As treasury shares, they are considered authorized and issued but not outstanding. These shares do not have voting or dividend rights. Redemptions usually result in the retirement of the redeemed shares. Upon retirement, the shares are considered unissued and are not classified as treasury stock.

Stock Certificates

The shares of a corporation are represented by certificates. Stock certificates are evidence of the stockholder's interest, of the value of the corporate securities. All types of corporate securities, including stocks, stock warrants, stock options, preemptive rights, and bonds, are negotiable instruments under the Uniform Commercial Code (UCC). The UCC and other state and federal laws can affect the parties' rights and obligations, such as those claimed by the owners of the instruments, as well as rights claimed by third parties.

A stock certificate is a negotiable instrument as long as it is outstanding. If a certificate is lost or stolen, the finder or thief has no title to it if it is properly endorsed. However, a later innocent purchaser of a lost or stolen certificate will have good title. If a stolen certificate is endorsed with a forged signature, an innocent purchaser for value will have no title to it.

If a stock certificate is lost, destroyed, or stolen, the owner is entitled to a new certificate, but must post a bond. The bond protects the corporation against the possibility that a properly endorsed certificate later can be presented for transfer by an innocent purchaser. Replacing destroyed certificates presents no problem. If a properly endorsed lost or stolen certificate is presented for transfer by an innocent purchaser for value, the corporation must record the transfer and issue another new certificate to the innocent purchaser. If the issue of a second certificate creates an overissue (more stock issued than the corporate charter permits), the corporation must pay the owner the stock's market value.

If a transfer agent inadvertently registers the transfer of a forged certificate presented by an innocent purchaser and issues a new certificate, the innocent purchaser has good title to that new certificate. The new certificate starts a new life and is untainted by the original certificate's forgery. For this reason, corporate transfer agents require the owner's signature as a guarantee of the certificate's authenticity.

Stockholders' Powers and Duties

Stockholders of most corporations delegate management powers to the board of directors. Stockholders have the power to elect board members, to remove them without cause in many states, and to approve changes in the articles of incorporation. The stockholders can make or amend bylaws and must often approve loans to the corporation's directors, officers, or agents. The board and the officers appointed by the board have the power to create and to implement business policy.

Stockholders can ratify board actions. A blanket shareholder resolution approving a board's actions for the past year is ineffective if the stockholders have no knowledge of the board's actions. If a board explains specific actions and then obtains stockholder ratification, however, an approving stockholder cannot later sue the managers regarding that action.

Shareholder derivative suit
A lawsuit filed on behalf of a corporation by stockholders against officers or directors for mismanagement.

The stockholders' ultimate recourse is to sue the directors for mismanagement. To exercise that right, the stockholders sue officers or directors on behalf of the corporation in a **shareholder derivative suit**, and any recovery goes to the corporation. For example, the Comprehensive Environmental Response, Compensation, and Liability Act (CERCLA) allows governments or private parties to recover environmental cleanup costs from those responsible for the release of hazardous substances. Although corporations are liable under the statute, CERCLA insulated individual officers and directors from liability unless they were directly involved in pollution incidents. However, individual directors and officers of companies incurring CERCLA liability can still be held liable through stockholder derivative suits that compel corporate boards to bring suits against individuals for harming the corporation.

Right to Information

Stockholders have a right to their corporation's financial statements, which they receive by mail at least annually. Stockholders also have the right to inspect certain books and records, such as some types of financial records, minutes of stockholders' and directors' meetings, and lists of stockholders' names and addresses.

Stockholders who hold either a specified percentage (commonly 5 percent) of the outstanding shares or who have been stockholders for a specified period, such as six months, can inspect these records for an appropriate purpose. The RMBCA gives certain inspection rights to any one stockholder "for a proper purpose,"[5] but stockholders can inspect correspondence files only under court order.

"Proper purposes" include seeking information to determine the value of corporate stock or the propriety of dividends or obtaining a list of stockholders' names to solicit their proxies, which are stockholders' written authorizations to agents to vote in their behalf. A **proxy** is an agent appointed to vote a stockholder's shares in the stockholder's absence. "Improper purposes" include obtaining a list of stockholders for the purpose of selling it to others, learning business secrets, aiding a competitor, or merely satisfying curiosity.

Stockholders' Meetings

Stockholders meet annually and also may hold special meetings. Corporations always call annual shareholder meetings. The holders of a certain percentage of the outstanding shares can call special meetings if permitted by statute, charter, or bylaws.[6] The articles or bylaws also can permit other persons, such as the president, to call meetings.

Most statutes require an annual meeting but leave it to the bylaws to specify meeting place and date. If no annual meeting occurs within a statutory time limit, a stockholder can apply to a court to order the meeting.

One purpose of annual meetings is to give stockholders, as the corporation's owners, the opportunity to vote on corporate matters. Statutes permit fixing a cutoff date before a meeting, called the **record date**, for determining which stockholders are entitled to vote. For example, if a meeting is to occur on February 25, the corporation might set a record date of February 5, and all stockholders who are owners of record on February 5 can vote at that meeting. That they might have sold their shares between February 5 and February 25 does not affect this right.

A written notice of a meeting, required by bylaws and by statute, must set forth the place, day, and hour. If, in addition to the election of directors, stockholders' approval is necessary for certain board-proposed actions, such as amendment of the articles, the notice must contain that information.

Any unnotified stockholder may have the meeting declared a nullity. Notice is waived if the stockholder either attends the meeting without protesting lack of notice or signs a written waiver before or after the meeting. Small corporations often dispense with notice and have all stockholders sign a waiver of notice.

To transact business lawfully at the meeting, a **quorum** is required, which is the proportion of outstanding shares of voting stock that must be represented at the meeting in person or by proxy. Once the meeting has a quorum, a stockholder's departure from the meeting has no effect. The rule is "once a quorum, always a quorum." The vote needed to accomplish a purpose is either a majority or more of the quorum, as set by statute, articles, or bylaws.

Proxy
An agent appointed to vote a stockholder's shares in the stockholder's absence.

Record date
The cutoff date before a stockholders' meeting for determining which stockholders are entitled to vote.

Quorum
The proportion of outstanding shares of voting stock that must be represented at a stockholders' meeting in person or by proxy.

A stockholder can vote by attending the meeting or by proxy. A proxy must be appointed in writing, and the writing is also called a "proxy." Proxies are subject to the law of the state of incorporation and, for corporations under its jurisdiction, to the federal Securities and Exchange Commission (SEC) rules and regulations. The SEC rules are designed to prevent fraud, encourage full disclosure, and make the proxy system available to people other than the corporation's managers. Because a proxy creates an agency relationship, the stockholder can revoke the proxy either by signing a later proxy appointing a different person or by attending the meeting in person.

Management of large corporations solicits proxies in notices of meeting mailings. Because stockholders of large corporations usually do not attend meetings, many of them sign and return the proxies. Consequently, meetings usually commence with sufficient proxies in management hands to control voting. If stockholders do not return sufficient proxies to constitute a quorum, a meeting cannot occur.

Whether voting by proxy or at the meeting, each stockholder usually has one vote per share owned unless the articles provide for more votes per share. Stockholders have no fiduciary relationship to their corporation; therefore, they can vote in their self-interests. Majority stockholders, however, must not manipulate corporate affairs to their advantage and to the disadvantage of minority stockholders. For example, majority stockholders cannot vote to redeem their own shares solely to provide themselves with needed funds with no valid corporate purpose.

Cumulative voting
A system for electing corporate directors whereby a stockholder can multiply his or her number of shares by the number of open directorships and cast the total for a single candidate or a select few candidates.

Some corporations' articles provide for **cumulative voting**, a system for electing corporate directors whereby a stockholder can multiply his or her number of shares by the number of open directorships and cast the total for a single candidate or a select few candidates. This provision facilitates minority representation on the board by allowing minority stockholders to elect at least one director. For example, if a stockholder holds 20 percent of a corporation in twenty shares and is voting on four positions on the board of directors, that stockholder holds eighty votes, all of which can be used to vote on one director position or can be spread among other directors.

Voting trust
An agreement among stockholders to vote their shares in a certain way.

Stockholders can join a **voting trust**, an agreement that they will vote their shares in a certain way or that one or more persons can vote their shares a certain way. Stockholders participating in a voting trust transfer their shares to a trustee, who then obtains new certificates in the trustee's name. The participants receive voting trust certificates that evidence their ownership of the shares held by the trustee and that entitles them to dividends as declared. The trustee votes the stock as owner. This arrangement provides voting unity by creating a voting bloc.

Stockholders can speak out at a meeting. They cannot initiate votes on issues that the board does not present to them. Although certain acts, such as amending the articles of incorporation, require stockholder approval, only the board can initiate and recommend such action. The stockholders have the right to a report of the meeting's proceedings and the right to select independent auditors of the corporation's books. If the board permits the stockholders to offer and vote on resolutions, it is not bound by the vote unless it affects stockholders' rights.

Stockholders' Actions

Stockholders have a choice of three types of civil lawsuits to file when they have complaints: class action suits, derivative action suits, and direct action suits. Stockholder suits are usually either class actions or derivative suits. The three types of suits are defined as follows:

1. *Class-action suits*. When one transaction damages many people, one or more people can file a representative suit, or a class action, on behalf of all, thus avoiding multiple suits on the same factual and legal questions. A common example is a lawsuit by a group of stockholders against the directors and officers for damages for fraud, such as failure to make a full disclosure in connection with a public stock offering.

2. *Derivative actions*. Under certain circumstances, one or more stockholders might also sue on the corporation's behalf in a derivative action. For example, if a corporation fails to sue a corporate officer who has diverted corporate assets for personal use, a stockholder can sue in a derivative action. Likewise, if an outside accounting firm has negligently audited the books to the injury of the corporation, a stockholder might file a derivative action. Monetary damages recovered in a derivative action go to the corporation, because the corporation was injured directly. Successful plaintiffs also receive reimbursement for reasonable litigation expenses.

3. *Direct actions*. Most civil lawsuits are **direct actions**, which seek remedies for direct harm. For example, a stockholder might sue for harm sustained while engaged in company business.

Direct action
A stockholder's civil lawsuit against a corporation.

Board of Directors

The board of directors makes two types of decisions. First, it decides the corporation's structure and form. Second, it decides business policy. The former requires stockholder approval; the latter does not.

Decisions requiring stockholder approval include any amendment of the articles, such as changes in the capital structure, purpose, or name, or preemptive right limitations. Stockholder approval is also necessary to enter a statutory merger or consolidation, to sell all or substantially all of the corporation's assets, or to dissolve the corporation. These decisions require stockholder approval because they change the terms of the contract between the stockholders and the corporation.

Business decisions that the board of directors can make without shareholder approval, subject to limitations in the articles of incorporation or statutes, include the following:

- Issuing stock or borrowing money
- Making policies for manufacturing and marketing
- Electing and assigning officer duties
- Declaring dividends
- Purchasing or selling property in the usual course of the business
- Making policies concerning insurance coverage
- Making all other policy decisions to continue for an indefinite term

The board elects officers to implement these policies.

Number and Qualifications

Statutes set the minimum number of directors required. Some statutes require a minimum of three directors; others require only one, if there is to be a board at all. In some states, the articles specify the number of directors; others allow the corporate articles to set a method of specifying the number of directors, such as through the bylaws.

Statutes also determine whether directors must be stockholders or residents of the state of incorporation. While most modern statutes have neither requirement, some state insurance statutes do have residency requirements.

Inside director
A corporate officer that serves on the corporation's board of directors.

Outside director
A member of a corporation's board of directors who is not a corporate officer and who may not necessarily be connected with the corporation.

Directors can be either inside or outside directors. An **inside director** is also a corporate officer; an **outside director** is not. Outside directors can be a corporation's commercial banker, lawyer, or consultants, or they might have no connection whatsoever with the corporation. Outside directors can provide perspectives on the corporation's activities that those involved in day-to-day management might not have.

The New York Stock Exchange encourages listed corporations to have at least two outside directors. They generally serve on a corporation's audit committee, where they can oversee corporate activities and regulate practices, watching for such actions as illegal payments at home and abroad. Upon accusation of mismanagement or impropriety, the officers can defend on the ground that independent outside directors approved their actions.

Directors can fix their own compensation unless the articles provide otherwise. This provision is necessary because of the widespread practice of electing outside directors.

Meetings

An individual director, whether inside or outside, has no legal right to act for or bind the corporation, and directors can make corporate decisions only when acting together in a meeting. An exception is that, if all the directors consent in a signed writing outside a meeting to an action, the consent has the same effect as a unanimous vote at a meeting.

Directors need not hold their meetings in the state of incorporation. If the bylaws state the date, time, and place of regular directors' meetings, additional notice is not needed unless the bylaws require it. Special meetings, however, always require notice. The notice need not contain an agenda of the business the directors are to transact, but good practice requires a complete agenda to preclude surprises and to allow the directors to prepare for the meeting.

The RMBCA defines a quorum as a majority of directors, unless otherwise specified in the articles or bylaws.[7] Because a director's duties are personal and nondelegable, proxy voting is prohibited.

Committees

The articles or bylaws can allow the board to elect an executive committee and other committees. Regular directors' meetings can occur as often as every other week, or as infrequently as every two or three months. The executive committee's authority to conduct business between meetings might be narrow or broad but cannot comprise all board powers.

Ordinarily, a board cannot authorize a committee to make long-term decisions that affect the corporation's ongoing business. For example, executive committees generally have no authority to propose amendments to articles, to adopt merger or consolidation plans, to fix directors' compensation, to amend or repeal bylaws, or to amend or repeal a prior board action that is not amendable or repealable.

Officers

Generally, the stockholders must approve actions about the corporation's nature, existence, purpose, and form. Directors are concerned with corporate structure and form as well as business policy. The officers implement the directors' policies in managing the corporation and in dealing with the outside world. Most statutes provide for the election of a president, one or more vice-presidents, a secretary, a treasurer, and other officers designated by the bylaws.

Officers generally have one or both of the following functions:

1. Managing the corporation's internal affairs
2. Dealing with persons outside the corporation

The principles of agency law govern an officer's right and power to deal with persons outside the corporation. An officer's actual authority comes from the articles, bylaws, or a board resolution. An officer's title is therefore not a certain indicator of that officer's authority. The president of a subsidiary, for instance, might have less authority than that of the parent company's vice-president.

For a corporation, the most important officer is often the **chief executive officer (CEO)**, to whom all other officers are subordinate. That officer is usually the

Chief executive officer (CEO)
The corporate officer to whom all other officers are subordinate.

Chief operating officer (COO)
The corporate officer responsible for the day-to-day running of a corporation.

President
The corporate officer who is or who has the powers of a chief executive officer, including the power to bind the corporation to any contract made in the corporation's ordinary course of business.

Vice president
The corporate officer whose implied authority derives from the related job function.

Treasurer
The corporate officer who receives and disburses corporate funds.

Secretary
The corporate officer in charge of the company's official records.

president but might be the chairman of the board or even have some other title. The corporation might also have a **chief operating officer (COO)** who reports directly to the chief executive officer.

The **president** either is presumptively the chief executive officer or has, by virtue of the presidency, the powers of a chief executive officer, including the power to bind the corporation to any contract made in the corporation's ordinary course of business. The **vice president** title is, by itself, meaningless. One might be a vice president in charge of sales, personnel, or some specific operation, and that officer's implied authority derives from the related function, not from the title. The **treasurer** ordinarily receives and disburses corporate funds.

The **secretary**, called the clerk in some corporations, is in charge of the company's official records and has no power, by virtue of that office, to deal with outsiders. There might be a secretary of the board and a separate secretary of the corporation, or both might serve. The secretary's statement that a document of the corporation is valid is conclusive evidence that the instrument is valid and reflects the board's full authority. These statements usually have the impress of the corporate seal, which further adds to the validity of the statement.

Duties of Directors and Officers

Because officers are agents, they have all the fiduciary duties of agents to their principal, the corporation. Directors are not the corporation's agents, but the law imposes on them similar duties.

Duties of Care and Loyalty

Officers and directors have a duty of care to the corporation. They must exercise the same degree of care that a reasonable officer or director would ordinarily exercise. They do not guarantee the profitability of the enterprise, and they need not even have special business skills.

Prudent officers and directors can disagree on a decision. The law therefore provides that a decision is proper if made within the range of reasonable "business judgment." Even if a given decision exceeds the bounds of business judgment, the officer or director is not liable for a loss unless lack of business judgment caused that loss.

The directors' minimum duty is to attend directors' meetings. A director cannot assert ignorance as a defense based on never having attended any meetings. In addition, a director should ask pertinent questions, should seek out information, and should not rely on management's unsupported statements. Accordingly, directors have the absolute right to inspect corporate books and records. However, directors have a right to rely on reports and written financial statements presented by officers or employees if the directors believe them to be reasonably reliable or competent; on lawyers, public accountants, and other outside experts; or on a board committee on which the director did not serve.

For instance, directors who vote for or assent to a dividend that is contrary to law are jointly and severally (individually and as a group) liable to the corporation for the amount of the illegal dividend. A director might avoid that liability only by voting against the dividend or by filing a written dissent. However, if in voting for the dividend, the director relies in good faith on a financial statement prepared by experts, the director can avoid liability.

In addition to the duty of care, directors and officers have a duty of loyalty to the corporation. The duty of loyalty exceeds the general duty not to defraud others. A fiduciary such as an officer or agent not only has a duty to avoid misrepresentation but also has an affirmative duty to disclose all material facts.

Transactions With the Corporation

In the course of business, directors and officers enter into transactions with the corporation. A corporation can benefit from business with one of its directors or with another corporation that shares some or all of the same people as directors. Some corporations have **interlocking directors**, that is, directors that are shared among corporations. The RMBCA provides that a contract between the corporation and a director or a firm with interlocking directors shall not be void or voidable because of the relationship, even if the director involved was present at the meeting and voted for the contract, if any of the following is true[8]:

Interlocking directors
Corporate directors who are shared among corporations.

- The material facts and relationship or interest were known or disclosed to the board, and the transaction was approved by sufficient votes without counting the interested director's vote.

- The material facts and relationship or interest were known or disclosed to the stockholders, and the stockholders voted for, or gave written consent to, the transaction.

- The contract or transaction was fair to the corporation.

Appropriation of a Corporate Business Opportunity

A director or an officer cannot secretly appropriate a business opportunity that belongs to the corporation. For example, if a director or an officer purchases a business that the corporation is seeking to acquire, the corporation can have a court declare that person a trustee, or temporary manager, of the purchased business on the corporation's behalf and require its transfer to the corporation upon reimbursement for the purchaser's cost.

Similarly, a director or an officer must not compete with the corporation. In the previous example, the corporation also can sue for profits it has lost because of the disloyal person's competition or can persuade a court to order a halt to the competition.

Officers and directors are privy to **insider information**, that is, material information about a corporation's affairs that could, if made public, change the value of the corporation's stock.[9] They cannot use such information to

Insider information
Material information about a corporation's affairs that could, if made public, change the value of the corporation's stock.

their own advantage, buying and selling stock, for example, to profit or to avoid loss. If they do, the stockholders from whom they purchased shares or to whom they sold shares can sue for damages.

This concept also applies to insiders other than officers and directors. For example, a mining engineer employed by the corporation, who knows of its major ore strike that has not been announced publicly may not buy that corporation's stock until after a public announcement. This rule also applies to people who receive tips about material, but undisclosed, information from insiders.

If a director, an officer, or an owner of at least 10 percent of the corporation's outstanding stock profits within a six-month period by trading that corporation's shares, then the corporation can take the profit.[10] Whether the party had inside information is immaterial. If inside and undisclosed material information was used in the transaction, the innocent person who dealt with the insider might also have an action for damages.[11] For example, an innocent person might make an important money-losing decision based on the inside information.

The Insider Trading Sanctions Act of 1984 imposes a civil penalty on anyone who deals in securities on the basis of "material, nonpublic" information, based not on a duty to the corporation's stockholders, but on a duty to the investing public. Information gained by legitimate research can be used freely. The information that cannot be used might come from such sources as a corporate insider, an investment house entrusted with such information for business purposes, or a law firm representing the corporation. The law imposes a penalty of up to three times the gain realized, or the loss avoided, payable to the United States Treasury.

Penalties for Insider Dealing

Corporate insiders who purchase shares of their own corporations based on material inside information face one or more of the following three penalties:

1. A court can award damages to the stockholder from whom the shares were purchased.

2. The corporation can take the profit if the stock is sold within six months of the date of purchase for a profit.

3. The U.S. Treasury, under the Insider Trading Sanctions Act, can take up to three times the profit.

Abuse of Minority Stockholders

Officers and directors cannot abuse minority stockholders. For example, particularly in closely held corporations, dividends might be withheld to "squeeze out" minority stockholders, excessive remuneration might be paid to favored individuals, insiders might receive shares to cement control, or a class of shares might be redeemed to provide funds for a favored stockholder.

The business judgment rule does not apply to decisions made for personal benefit and unjustified by a business purpose. A minority stockholder who sues on such a basis, however, has the burden of proving that the action was sufficiently arbitrary to constitute bad faith.

Officers and directors have duties imposed by the Employee Retirement Income Security Act (ERISA) of 1974. ERISA created fiduciary duties for employee benefit and pension plan administrators, trustees, upper management, insurance brokers, and others regarding how they invest and distribute funds that support such plans and the way they treat participants and beneficiaries. The law covers most employer- or union-established employee benefit plans, such as pension plans and other employee benefit programs, including sickness, accident, disability, death, unemployment, medical, surgical, and hospital plans; vacation plans; training programs; daycare; scholarship funds; prepaid legal services; and severance benefit plans.

A director or an officer who exercises discretionary control in such a plan's management or over its assets or who gives investment advice is a fiduciary under ERISA with certain statutory duties and liabilities. These duties include the obligation to act solely in the plan participants' interest, to exercise the care and skill of a reasonable person conducting a similar enterprise, to diversify investments unless it is clearly unreasonable to do so, and to act in accordance with the plan documents. Additionally, a fiduciary can be liable for another fiduciary's breach of duty if he or she knowingly participates in, conceals, or does not attempt to correct the breach. ERISA also specifically prohibits conflicts of interest such as transactions with interested parties or with the fiduciary's own personal account or interest.

A fiduciary who breaches these duties is personally liable for any resulting loss to the plan and can be subject to a civil penalty or to tax. A fiduciary can protect the plan from potential losses by purchasing errors and omissions insurance. If the fiduciary purchases the insurance with plan assets, the policy must enable the insurer to recover any loss payment from the fiduciary. Therefore, the insurance does not actually protect the fiduciary. To obtain personal protection, the fiduciary, employer, or employee organization must secure and pay for additional coverage separate from the basic errors and omissions policy.

Liability and Indemnification

Just as directors and officers owe duties to the corporation, so too does the corporation owe duties to the directors and officers. One such duty is indemnification. **Indemnification** in the context of corporate law refers to a corporation's right or duty to reimburse a director, an officer, or another employee for some or all of the expenses incurred in defending a lawsuit instituted or threatened against the person in his or her official capacity. It might include defense expenses, including attorney's fees, judgments, fines, and settlement amounts.

Indemnification
In the context of corporate law, a corporation's right or duty to reimburse a director, an officer, or another employee for some or all of the expenses incurred in defending a lawsuit instituted or threatened against the person in his or her official capacity.

Some indemnification statutes apply only to directors and officers. Others include employees and agents. Some prohibit reduction of statutory rights to indemnification, but others permit rights to be reduced by a provision in the articles of incorporation.

All states mandate indemnification, unless denied in the articles, when a person is found not liable in a civil case or not guilty in a criminal case. Even if a court imposes civil liability, a person might be indemnified at the company's discretion if he or she acted in good faith and reasonably believed that the conduct was in the company's best interests.

Dividends

Dividend
A portion of corporate profits paid to a stockholder.

Dividends are shares of corporate profits paid to stockholders. They are usually paid in cash rather than with shares of stock. A corporation might also declare a **property dividend**, which usually consists of shares of profits of another corporation that the declaring corporation has acquired. A **stock dividend** is declared in terms of additional shares of the issuing company. An extra dividend is a dividend in addition to the usual and expected regular dividend. Distribution of assets is not a dividend, because a dividend comes out of earnings. Therefore, distribution of assets is often called a **liquidating dividend** because the distribution is conducted during a reorganization of the corporation.

Property dividend
A portion of corporate profits consisting of the corporation's acquired shares of profits of another corporation.

Stock dividend
A portion of corporate profits issued as additional shares.

Some stockholders might prefer to plow profits back into the corporation and defer gains from profits, which are **capital gains**; others might want current dividends. Management decides whether to declare dividends in good faith and for a corporate purpose. To force dividend payments, the stockholders must prove bad faith, but courts have found bad faith in only a few cases.

Liquidating dividend
A distribution of assets conducted during a reorganization of the corporation.

The directors can defer (postpone) dividends and exercise bond call (redemption) provisions to provide expansion capital, develop an emergency surplus, or accomplish many other valid business actions. Preferred and common stock dividends can be deferred. Preferred stockholders might, however, have the right to vote for new directors if they do not receive dividends for a number of years.

Capital gains
Stockholders' gains from profits on their stock.

Once the board formally declares a dividend, the stockholders become creditors of the corporation to the extent of the dividend. If the corporation becomes insolvent before paying the dividend, the stockholders participate equally with other creditors to the extent of the dividend. Because declaration of a dividend creates a debtor-creditor relationship, the board cannot revoke a declared dividend. The corporation sends the dividend to the person who is the owner of the stock on a specified record date.

Treasury stock
A corporate stock issued as fully paid to a stockholder and subsequently reacquired by the corporation to use for business purposes.

A stock dividend can be paid in treasury stock or from authorized but unissued shares. As mentioned, **treasury stock** have been issued as fully paid to stockholders and subsequently are reacquired by the corporation to use for business purposes. If paid in shares of the same class, the stockholders' interest in the corporation remains the same but is represented by a greater number of shares.

In a **stock split**, a corporation divides its stock into multiple shares, reducing each share's value but increasing the number of shares each stockholder owns. For instance, a stockholder will receive two shares of $5 par value in return for one share of $10 par value. The stockholders of the class affected must approve a stock split. The usual purpose of stock split is to reduce the market value of each share, making the stock more marketable.

Stock split
The dividing of a corporation's stock into multiple shares, reducing each share's par value but increasing the number of shares each stockholder owns.

Merger and Share Exchange

Merger is one of three ways a corporation can end. The other two, discussed in the next section, are dissolution and reorganization. In a **corporate merger**, two or more corporations join to become another corporation. The newly merged corporation owns all assets and is subject to all liabilities of the merging corporations.

Corporate merger
The joining of two or more corporations into a single corporation.

Before a merger, the board of directors of each corporate party to the merger must adopt a plan of merger. The "disappearing" corporations' stockholders must approve the merger plan, but the new corporation's stockholders must approve the plan only if the number of voting or participating shares increases substantially.[12]

In a **share exchange**, a corporation acquires all of another corporation's outstanding shares in return for shares of the acquiring corporation. A share exchange plan must be adopted by the board of directors of the corporation and approved by the stockholders of the corporation whose shares are being acquired, but it does not need approval by the acquiring corporation's stockholders.

Share exchange
One corporation's acquisition of another corporation's outstanding shares in return for shares of the acquiring corporation.

Another way to complete a merger is for a corporation to sell all or most of its assets in return for the purchaser's shares, for distribution to the stockholders. This transaction constitutes a merger in fact, if not in law, and is therefore a *de facto* merger. Under the RMBCA, a sale of all or substantially all of a corporation's assets not in the usual course of business requires stockholders' approval in the manner of a statutory merger or consolidation.[13]

Stockholders are entitled to dissent to a merger, share exchange, or sale of all or substantially all of a corporation's assets not in the usual course of business. They are also entitled to have their corporations buy them out. If stockholders file a written dissent before or during the stockholders' meeting, they must receive a written notice after the action was taken giving them a period within which to file a payment demand.[14]

A corporation that owns at least 90 percent of another corporation's stock might merge that corporation into itself by board resolution without stockholder approval.[15] The corporation need send the merger plan only to the subsidiary's stockholders. Many insurance corporation laws require 95 rather than 90 percent ownership, and the state department of insurance must approve the merger.

Takeovers and Tender Offers

Takeover
The assumption of control by one corporation over another.

Mergers and share exchanges are friendly takeovers to which the corporations' boards agree. A **takeover** is the assumption of control by one corporation over another. When one corporation wants to control or acquire a corporation whose board does not agree, the acquiring company can attempt a hostile takeover.

One corporation can gain control over another by acquiring sufficient proxies from the other corporation's stockholders to elect its own board of directors or to vote for a merger. SEC rules and regulations govern proxy solicitation in these situations.

Tender offer
An offer by an acquiring corporation to purchase shares directly from the other company's stockholders.

One method of acquiring an unwilling corporation is for the aggressor corporation to purchase sufficient shares of that corporation to vote in its own board of directors. To purchase shares, the prospective acquirer will make an attractive **tender offer** to the target's stockholders. In a tender offer, the acquiring corporation offers to purchase shares directly from the other company's stockholders.

Any person or group that acquires, or intends to acquire, more than 5 percent ownership of a class of securities registered with the SEC must file a statement with the SEC and send a copy of the statement to each offeree and to the issuing company.[16] This information enables stockholders to make an intelligent decision on whether to sell.

Insurance Company Mergers

Because regulated corporations, such as insurance companies, can engage in only one kind of business, such businesses must be of the same kind to merge. Most states' insurance company merger laws mimic general corporation laws except that the state department of insurance must approve the merger.

On occasion, corporations with diverse interests have purchased controlling interests in insurance companies, ostensibly for investment purposes. The usual merger laws do not apply because the insurance companies continue as separate corporations. Several states have adopted insurance company laws that follow the National Association of Insurance Commissioners (NAIC) Model Insurance Holding System Regulatory Act. These laws restrict the takeover of insurance companies and require state department of insurance approval.

Dissolution and Reorganization

Dissolution, or termination, of a corporation can be either voluntary or involuntary. Each method follows a different procedure and has different repercussions for the parties involved.

Voluntary corporate dissolution begins with a board resolution to dissolve, approved by a majority of the stockholders. The corporation must also file a formal "statement of intent to dissolve" with the state. The corporation then proceeds with liquidation. If necessary, the corporation can apply for liquidation under court supervision. When liquidation is complete, the remaining assets go to the stockholders, and articles of dissolution are filed with the state, which issues a certificate of dissolution.

Involuntary dissolution occurs when the state of incorporation, the stockholders, or corporate creditors file for involuntary dissolution proceedings. State proceedings are unusual and occur only in cases of gross abuse of the corporate privilege or fraudulent acquisition of the articles of incorporation. A state might hold such a proceeding when a corporation has allegedly defrauded the public repeatedly.

Stockholders can ask a court for involuntary dissolution on the basis of the right to protect stockholders. The court can order liquidation of corporate assets and distribution of the proceeds after payment of debts to the stockholders. Grounds for stockholders' suits to dissolve a corporation include the following:[17]

- The directors are deadlocked, the stockholders cannot break the deadlock, and irreparable injury to the corporation either has occurred or might occur.
- The directors' or officers' acts are illegal, oppressive, or fraudulent.
- The stockholders are deadlocked in voting power and have failed to elect directors for two successive meetings.
- The corporate assets are being wasted or misapplied.

If a judgment for a creditor's claim is unsatisfied or the corporation admits insolvency in writing, the creditor can sue for dissolution of the corporation. The corporation need not be bankrupt; in other words, its liabilities need not exceed its assets. **Insolvency** means only that current liabilities (as opposed to total liabilities) exceed current assets. Thus, a corporation that cannot meet its current obligations is insolvent, even though its total liabilities are less than its total assets.

Because of the public interest in an insurance company's ability to pay its claims, courts usually designate the state department of insurance as the receiver in an insurance company dissolution proceeding.

Under Chapter 11 of the Bankruptcy Reform Act of 1978, a corporation may be placed voluntarily or involuntarily under federal bankruptcy court supervision for reorganization purposes. The bankruptcy court must appoint a committee of creditors and also might appoint a committee of stock security holders to work under its supervision. The court can permit the current managers to continue control of the business and may appoint an examiner to investigate and monitor the reorganization. The court can appoint a trustee to take control of the business if it finds management guilty of fraud, dishonesty, incompetence, or gross mismanagement or if it finds that the appointment of a trustee is in the interests of the creditors, stockholders, or other persons.

Insolvency
A situation in which an entity's current liabilities (as opposed to its total liabilities) exceed its current assets.

In the absence of a satisfactory reorganization or other plan, the bankruptcy court may convert the case to a regular bankruptcy liquidation proceeding under Chapter 7 of the federal bankruptcy law.

Foreign Corporations

A corporation created in one state is a citizen only of that state. In any state other than its state of incorporation, it is a foreign corporation.

Licensing to Do Business

To do business in another state, a corporation must be admitted and recognized by the state. For example, the RMBCA states, "A foreign corporation shall not transact business in this state until it obtains a certificate of authority from the secretary of state."[18] A corporation registered to do business in another state must have a registered office and agent there to establish a place for legal service of such papers as complaints in lawsuits.

Although a state can forbid or control activities of a foreign corporation in intrastate (within the state) commerce, the state cannot interfere with the interstate (between states) commerce of any corporation. The federal courts and Congress have consistently broadened the meaning of interstate commerce. For example, making a profit in a state does not necessarily mean that one is involved in interstate commerce.

Activities not considered interstate business include holding stockholders' or directors' meetings in the state, maintaining a bank account there, conducting an isolated transaction that is completed within thirty days, suing or being sued, and other transactions that are not completed for profit within the state of incorporation.

Laws governing insurance company admission are stricter than those for general business corporations. State laws can include requirements for deposits, reports, examinations, character reports on officers, and other requirements peculiar to insurance regulation. Out-of-state insurers generally apply to the state department of insurance rather than to the secretary of state.

Long-Arm Statutes

Long-arm statute
A law that enables a state's citizens to sue in their own state courts people or entities that are not physically present in the state but that have had minimum contacts there.

States have enacted **long-arm statutes** that enable their citizens to sue in their own state courts people or entities who are not physically present in the state but who have had minimum contacts there. For example, under a long-arm statute, a person who owns property in a state but who has never been there can be sued in that state by someone who is injured on the property. As another example, a corporation that syndicates a newspaper column in a state and that approves contracts and mails them from that state, can be sued there by a resident who claims libel in one of the columns published in that state.

Some long-arm statutes apply only to torts, others to contracts, and others to both. Some statutes are interpreted liberally and others narrowly. To sue a person or business entity, a plaintiff must effect **service of process**, that is, physical delivery of a complaint and summons to a defendant. Most states have passed a model Unauthorized Insurers Service of Process Act, which is essentially a long-arm statute for the insurance business. The act provides that service on a foreign insurer (one not licensed in the state) must go to the state department of insurance.

Service of process
The physical delivery of a complaint and summons to a defendant.

Corporation Characteristics Summary

- Formation—State and federal statutes provide for formation of corporations. Promoters form corporations.

- Limited liability—Corporations generally shield stockholders, directors, and officers from personal liability for torts and crimes.

- Corporate ownership—Stockholders own corporations. Types of stocks define ownership.

- Termination—Corporations can terminate by merger, dissolution, and reorganization.

Sarbanes-Oxley Act

In 2002, Congress passed the Sarbanes-Oxley Act, a response to a succession of corporate scandals that arose from discovery of gimmickry or fraud in certain companies' financial statements. These scandals raised fundamental questions about the model of corporate governance. Sarbanes-Oxley increased penalties for wrongdoing and created rules to prevent wrongdoing.

Key provisions of Sarbanes-Oxley, a long and complex law, help assure the credibility of financial statements with the following requirements:

- Creation of the Public Company Accounting Oversight Board to oversee and establish auditing, independence, ethics, quality control, and other standards for auditors of public companies

- Prohibition of certain activities by auditors

- Independence of the audit committee of a public company's board of directors

- Certification of corporate financial reports personally by the chief executive and chief financial officers

- Rapid, current, and transparent reporting

PARTNERSHIPS

The second form of legal ownership of a business entity is the partnership. Most states have adopted the Uniform Partnership Act (UPA) to govern partnerships. The UPA defines **partnership** as "an association of two or more persons to carry on as co-owners of a business for profit."[19] Mere co-ownership of property does not establish a partnership, even though the co-owners share the profits.

Partnership
An association of two or more persons to carry on as co-owners of a business for profit.

A business need not have physical assets but must have profit as its goal. Two or more persons who agree to work together in any line of activity and share the profits are presumed partners. However, a person who agrees to work for another in a business for a wage, salary, or commission, is an employee, not a partner. Partners share profits, although not necessarily on an equal basis. They also share losses in the same proportion as profits.

Partnership Formation

People form partnerships voluntarily, and they do not need government approval. Partnerships can arise by people's actions as partners, by an oral agreement, or by a written agreement. Sharing of the profits of the business is strong proof of a partnership. However, one can receive a share of profits and not be a partner if the profits were repayment of a debt, interest on a loan, wages, rent, an annuity to a deceased partner's widow or representative, or a payment for business goodwill or other property.[20]

If the partnership uses a fictitious name, which is a name other than all the partners' surnames, state law requires registration of the name in a public records office. The same requirement applies to an individual who chooses to conduct business under a fictitious name.

Joint Ventures

Joint venture
An unincorporated association of two or more entities established to conduct a single transaction or a series of related transactions.

A **joint venture** is an association of two or more entities established to conduct a single transaction or a series of related transactions, as compared with an ongoing business involving many diverse transactions. An example is a business established to operate a hotel under a long-term lease or to buy a single tract of land to subdivide it for sale to others.

The concepts of joint venture and partnership have virtually merged. Because a joint venture can range from an association for a single transaction to a complex, long-range association, joint ventures can differ more among themselves than they do from a partnership.

Some states prohibit corporations from joining partnerships on the theory that corporations would lose control of their operations in partnerships; legally, boards of directors must maintain control in managing businesses. In contrast, many courts have sustained corporate membership in joint ventures on the theory that these associations are single transactions with temporary partners. Today, however, most corporate joint ventures are incorporated and must adhere to corporate law.

Partnership by Estoppel

People who are not partners with one another also are not partners when it comes to dealing with third parties. An exception is partnership by estoppel, which protects innocent third parties who have relied on the appearance of a partnership.

A partnership by estoppel results if the following three elements are present:

1. A person purports to be a partner or permits others to think he or she is a partner.
2. The third party deals with the entity in justifiable reliance on a belief that it is a partnership or that the person who purports to be a partner is actually a partner.
3. The third party changes his or her legal position because of reliance on that belief, such as by entering into a contract.

Under these circumstances, the person who has permitted the appearances is liable to the third party to the same extent as an actual partner would be. In addition, the purported partner has the power to bind the partnership, just as an actual partner would. If all the partners consent to the representation, the apparent partner's transaction is a partnership act or obligation. If fewer than all the parties consent, the act is the joint obligation only of the consenting partners and not of the partnership itself.

A common risk of partnership by estoppel occurs when a partner has retired from a partnership but has not ensured appropriate notice of the retirement to people who previously knew of the partnership.

Partnership Liability

The common law did not consider partnerships legal entities. Therefore, for a partnership to sue or be sued, all the partners had to be joined individually in legal actions by or against the partnership. The case would be by or against "Adams, Burns, and Cunningham, partners trading as Helpful Adjustment Agency." A plaintiff suing a partnership would have to serve papers on each of the partners. The difficulties of serving papers on every party led some states to pass laws permitting suits against the partnership in its name. These **common name statutes** permit service of process on the partnership by serving any one of the partners. However, such laws also permit satisfaction of judgment only from the firm's assets and not from those of the individual partner who was served personally. When the partnership is the plaintiff, however, all partners must join in the suit.

> **Common name statute**
> A law that permits service of process on a partnership by serving any one of the partners.

In cases in which more than one person was at fault, the common law distinguished tort and contract liability. If two or more persons, such as partners, were liable on a contract, the liability was joint and a plaintiff had to sue all of those at fault. For tort cases, however, the liability was joint and several. The plaintiff could choose to sue all of the partners or any number of them.

Many states have changed this rule to make all obligations, contract as well as tort, joint and several so that fewer than all the partners could be sued. However, a judgment can be enforced only against the parties actually sued and served with process. In addition, the plaintiff cannot reach partnership assets unless the suit names the partnership itself.

Tort Liability

The laws of agency govern liability of a partnership and of the individual partners for torts committed by one of the partners. If a partner's act or omission in ordinary course of the partnership's business causes loss or injury to a third person, the partnership, that partner, and each of the other partners is liable, and the partners' private property can be used to satisfy the judgment. The acting partner is ultimately liable. If the partnership or any other partner is forced to respond in damages to the third party, theoretically the acting partner must reimburse the other partner or the partnership. In reality, however, insurance usually covers the liability.

Criminal Liability

Generally, a partnership is not responsible as a business entity for a crime, but the partners are responsible as individuals. However, statutes can make partnerships responsible for specific crimes. Vicarious liability does not exist in criminal law. Therefore, only a partner who has participated in a crime would be criminally responsible.

Partners' Relationships to One Another

The UPA, the partnership agreement, and general principles of contract and agency law govern the relationship among partners. Unless contrary to public policy, the partnership agreement can alter UPA provisions.

Financial Relationship

Unless otherwise provided, each partner shares equally in the enterprise's profits and in any surplus that remains on dissolution and after satisfaction of all liabilities. Unless the partnership agreement provides otherwise, each partner contributes to partnership losses in the same proportion as the partner shares profits, even when the partners' capital or service contributions are unequal.

Assume that Anne and Bob form a partnership. Of the total capital of $100,000, Anne contributes $90,000 in cash and Bob contributes $10,000 in cash. Bob also has a special skill the partnership will use. If the partnership makes a $10,000 profit in a given year, Anne and Bob are each, unless otherwise provided, entitled to $5,000. If the firm dissolves and $70,000 remains after all liabilities are paid, Anne and Bob must share the $30,000 loss unless the partnership agreement provides otherwise. Anne is entitled to $75,000 ($90,000 – $15,000, her original contribution minus half of the $30,000 loss). Therefore, Bob must provide Anne with $5,000 ($10,000 – $15,000, his original contribution minus his half of the $30,000 loss) to augment the partnership's remaining $70,000. Anne then receives the full $75,000, and Bob loses $5,000.

The partnership indemnifies each partner for payments made or personal liabilities incurred in the business when a partner has acted within the scope of his or her authority. A partner who must pay any court-assessed damages based on another partner's fraudulent business conduct, for instance, is entitled to indemnification. A partner who is guilty of gross negligence, fraud, or wanton misconduct that gave rise to damages, is solely liable and is not entitled to indemnification.

While a partnership is active, partners are not entitled to remuneration for services unless otherwise agreed. On dissolution, a surviving partner is entitled to reasonable compensation for services in winding up the partnership.

Fiduciary Relationship

Every partner has a fiduciary relationship with the other partners and the firm. A fiduciary's duties of mutual trust, loyalty, and good faith resemble those of an agent or a trustee. The fiduciary duties are implied in law, and no contract can waive them.

A partner who derives any personal benefit from any transaction connected with the partnership without the other partners' consent must account to the partnership for the benefit and hold any profits for the partnership as a trustee.[21] For example, Patsy and Paul are partners in buying and selling antiques. Paul learns that a valuable antique is for sale and buys it with his own money without informing Patsy, breaching his duty of loyalty. Patsy can demand that he turn the antique over to the partnership at his cost, and a court can declare him a trustee of the antique for the partnership's benefit. If he sells the antique, the partnership gets any profit he makes.

Partners are liable to the partnership for failing to render the services they originally agreed to perform. Most partnership agreements contain clauses requiring that the partners give the businesses full time and attention.

A partner is not liable to the partnership for ordinary negligence or for loss caused by errors in judgment. The partnership assumes the risk of ordinary poor judgment. A partner is, however, liable for gross negligence, fraud, or wanton misconduct.

Partnership's Books and Property

Unless otherwise provided, the partnership's books must be kept at its principal place of business. All partners have the right of access to the partnership's books for purposes related to the partnership.

Ownership of partnership property is not always clear. Traditionally, legal principles have limited ownership of property to persons or legal entities. Corporations qualify as property owners because they are created by law. Partnerships, as voluntary associations, do not have the same legal status as entities; they are merely aggregations of individuals.

The UPA resolves this problem by providing that partnership property might be held solely in the partnership's name. Property originally brought into the partnership or subsequently acquired by it is partnership property.[22] In general, when a partnership buys property, it takes title as follows: "Adams, Burns, and Cunningham, partners trading as the Excelsior Company." Under the UPA, however, title can be taken solely in the name of the Excelsior Company without naming the partners. When it is not clear whether the property belongs to the partnership, the law examines the partners' intentions at the time of acquisition.

Individual partners have an equal right with the other partners to use partnership property for partnership purposes, but not for any other purpose without the partners' consent.[23] It follows, therefore, that a partner has no interest in specific partnership property and cannot sell, mortgage, or bequeath such a portion. As a corollary, partnership property is not subject to attachment (formal seizure) by a partner's individual creditors.

When a partner dies, any right in specific partnership property belongs to the remaining partners. When the last partner dies, partnership property rights pass to his or her personal representative, who must liquidate the partnership and turn over any surplus to the heirs.

Assignment of Partner's Interest in Partnership

A partner's interest in the partnership is his or her share of the profits and surplus.[24] A partner can assign a financial interest in the partnership, but not the partnership status. Such an assignment does not give the assignee any right to interfere in management, to require information or an accounting, or to inspect the partnership's books. The assignee is entitled only to the profits assigned. On dissolution, however, the assignee is entitled to the assignor's interest and can require an accounting from the date of the last accounting agreed to by all the partners.

An assignment of one partner's financial interest in a partnership must be agreed to by the other partners, either in the original partnership agreement or when the assignment occurs. An assignment in itself does not dissolve a partnership, but, if not permitted in the partnership agreement, can be a ground for dissolution if the other partners desire it.

Types of Decisions and Consent Required

All businesses must make three types of decisions. The first is fundamental and involves the business's nature and structure. The second type consists of long-range policy decisions that set guidelines for business operations. The third consists of day-to-day operational decisions within the limits of general policy.

In a partnership, the first type of decision includes any alteration of the partnership agreement, including the addition of another partner, changes in capital contribution, and a change in the firm's principal place of business. Such decisions must be unanimous.

The UPA specifies that the following decisions must be unanimous:[25]

- Assigning partnership property in trust for creditors or in return for the assignee's promise to pay the partnership's debts
- Disposing of the partnership's goodwill
- Acting in any other way that would make it impossible to carry on the partnership's ordinary business
- Confessing (consenting to) a judgment
- Submitting a partnership claim to arbitration

The second type of decision, on long-range policy, requires a majority vote of the partners. The partners may, if they choose, appoint one or more managing partners to make all long-range policy decisions. Managing partners are common in insurance brokerage houses and large accounting firms. Any partner can make the third type of decisions, day-to-day decisions in the ordinary course of business, as long as the partnership agreement permits it.

Relationship of Partners to Third Parties

A partner has neither the right nor the power to bind the partnership by any contract with a third party that requires unanimous or majority consent. Third parties are at risk in dealing with partnerships if they are unaware of which partnership decisions require unanimous consent.

However, any partner acting alone can make ordinary day-to-day contracts involving third parties. Every partner is the partnership's agent for its business purposes,[26] so agency rules apply. A partner can have actual authority to bind the partnership (with express or implied authority or by ratification). Even without actual authority, a partner can bind a partnership under principles of estoppel.

Apparent Authority (Estoppel) of Partners

Apparent authority, also called authority by estoppel, arises when (1) the partnership, as principal, creates appearances that the acting partner has authority; (2) the third party is aware of those appearances; and (3) the third party then changes legal position in reliance on those appearances.

The existence of partnership itself creates the appearance that a partner has authority to act on behalf of the partnership. A third party might assume that all partners can act in the partnership's day-to-day business. If a partner lacks or has been denied authority to act, and a third party changes legal position because of the partner's actions, the partnership is estopped from denying that partner's authority.

For example, assume that Anne, Bob, and Carla are partners in the retail business of selling hunting and fishing equipment. Anne and Bob vote not to sell equipment for bow-and-arrow hunting, although Carla favors doing so. Other hunting and fishing equipment retailers in the area sell archery equipment.

Carla, despite the policy, contracts to purchase a quantity of bows and arrows from a supplier who is unaware of the restriction. The partnership is bound because the third party could have reasonably assumed that this partnership also sells such equipment. Carla, of course, is now at odds with her partners.

A third party also can assume that each partner is the partnership's agent for the purpose of its day-to-day business. Assume in the partnership of Anne, Bob, and Carla that Anne is to act only as bookkeeper, Bob as salesperson, and Carla as inventory purchaser. Anne then buys inventory from Terry, who is unaware of the division of labor. The partnership is estopped from denying Anne's authority to make the purchase.

Actual notice of a limitation on a partner's authority or a prior course of dealings may inform the third party of such a limitation. Suppose that Terry has, over time, sold goods to the partnership through Anne, a partner. The partnership has limited Anne to purchases of up to $1,000. Thus far, all of Anne's contracts with Terry have been under $1,000, but one day Anne orders $10,000 worth of goods from Terry. This deviation from the partnership's past practice might give Terry notice to investigate Anne's purchasing authority. If so, the contract would not bind the partnership. Anne, however, would be liable to Terry.

Acts Outside the Usual Scope of Business

The term "usual scope of business of the partnership" refers not only to what the partnership usually does, but also to what similar partnerships in the geographical area ordinarily do. These practices create appearances on which the third party might rely, thus estopping the partnership from denying liability. A partner's act outside the partnership's usual scope of business does not expose the partnership to liability because the partnership created no appearances. Instead, the third party merely relied on its own perceptions.

For example, suppose the partnership of Anne, Carla, and Bob is in the hunting and fishing equipment business. Carla enters into a contract to purchase a line of guitars. If neither this partnership nor like partnerships sell guitars, the partnership would not be bound to the contract unless Anne and Bob had given Carla this actual authority. The partnership is not bound even if Carla assured the supplier that she had authority to buy the guitars. Carla, not the partnership, created the appearance of her authority, and the partnership therefore can deny Carla's binding authority. The third party could sue Carla for breach of the implied warranty of authority that is given by all agents, including partners who act as agents.

Ability to Convey Real Property

The real property belonging to a partnership is held in the name of the partners and the partnership, such as in the name of "Adams, Burns, and Cunningham, partners doing business as The Excelsior Company." In such a case, all the partners must sign a deed to transfer legal ownership to a purchaser.

The UPA, however, allows a partnership to hold real property in the name of the partnership alone, such as in the name of "The Excelsior Company." Thus, any partner can transfer real property in the firm's name by signing a deed, and the partnership is bound unless the partner lacked actual authority to sell the property and the purchaser knew this fact. Even then, if the purchaser in turn sells the property to a third party who pays full value and is unaware of the lack of authority, good title to the property passes to the third party.

Partnership property might also be titled in the name of one or more partners without naming the partnership. Those partners are the property's "apparent owners." If a purchaser of the property gives full value and does not know of the partnership's interest in the property, good title passes on principles of estoppel.

The same principles apply to other types of property for which a written document indicates ownership, such as a bill of sale or an automobile title. Suppose a partnership buys an automobile with partnership funds and puts it on the partnership's books as partnership property, but takes title in an individual partner's name. If that partner, the automobile's apparent owner, sells it for value to a person who is not on notice of the partnership's interest in the vehicle, the purchaser obtains good title to the vehicle. Mere possession does not make the partner an apparent owner.

Spouses' Rights in Real Property

In some states, a spouse has an interest in individually owned real estate, effective at the death of the spouse who owns it. To transfer good title to realty in such states, the nonowning spouse's signature must be on the deed of conveyance.

The requirement of a spouse's signature would be intolerable in a partnership. Under the UPA, a partner's spouse has no claim to partnership real estate, and the signature of the partners alone will convey good title. Many lawyers nonetheless require partners' spouses to join in the transfer to avoid future difficulties if a spouse questions the partnership's existence.

Dissolution, Winding Up, and Termination

A partnership dissolves whenever any partner ceases to be associated in carrying out the business. Unless otherwise provided or agreed to, partnership affairs are then "wound up," or liquidated. When this process is completed, the partnership is terminated.

Rightful and Wrongful Dissolution

A dissolution is rightful if it is in accordance with the partnership agreement and is not any partner's fault. On rightful dissolution, the partnership is liquidated. If the partnership is solvent at the time of dissolution, the parties share in any surplus remaining after payment of debts and partners' equity. If it is insolvent, they share the losses.

If a dissolution is wrongful, however, the innocent partners have a choice. They can wind up the business and hold the at-fault partner liable for breach of contract damages. They also can choose to continue the business in the same name for the remainder of the partnership term. If so, they retain all partnership property for that purpose by posting a court-approved bond to secure payment of the wrongful partner's share of the remaining assets, less any damages the wrongful dissolution caused. The remaining innocent partners must then release the wrongful partner from all liability for existing debts. Creditors are not bound by this release and can still attempt to obtain payment from the wrongful partner. The bond protects the wrongful partner against possible action by creditors.

A partnership dissolves by operation of law if it becomes unlawful to carry on the partnership business or if the partnership becomes bankrupt. A wrongful dissolution occurs upon any partner's bankruptcy.

Rightful dissolution also occurs when the term of a partnership ends. The same result follows when (1) a partnership dissolves by one or more partners in a partnership without a term, which is a partnership at will, or (2) all the partners agree to dissolve even if the partnership has a term.

A rightful dissolution also can occur by a good-faith (fair) expulsion of a partner for a reason given in the partnership agreement. A wrongful dissolution occurs if a partner merely walks out on the partnership without justification and refuses to continue as a partner.

Courts also can declare dissolution. Any partner can apply to a court for a decree of dissolution in the following instances:

- A partner has been declared incompetent in any judicial proceeding or is shown to be of unsound mind (rightful dissolution).

- A partner has become otherwise incapable of performing his or her part of the partnership contract, for example, because of extended illness (rightful dissolution).

- A partner is guilty of conduct that harms the operation of the business (wrongful), such as competing with the partnership's business, embezzling the partnership's money, or breaching the partner's fiduciary relationship. Minor arguments or mere errors in judgment are not grounds for dissolution. This catch-all cause is usually combined with allegations in the next three categories.

- A partner willfully or persistently has breached the partnership agreement or has otherwise been guilty of business-related conduct making continuation of the partnership impracticable (wrongful).

- The partnership business can continue only at a loss (rightful).

- Other circumstances can render dissolution equitable. Depending on the circumstances, dissolution can be rightful or wrongful.

Winding Up the Partnership Business

A dissolved partnership can continue only in the following two circumstances:

1. Election of the innocent partners in a partnership that was dissolved wrongfully, as discussed previously
2. A continuation provision in the partnership agreement

A partnership agreement can provide that the partnership will not dissolve on any partner's death but will continue with the surviving partners. In legal terms, the partnership dissolves but is reformed immediately with the surviving partners as partners. This continuance provision usually includes the method of valuing the deceased partner's interest and a provision requiring life insurance for the partners, the proceeds of which enable the surviving partners to pay the deceased's estate the value of its interest.

If the partnership dissolves, liquidation of its business is necessary. The remaining partners or the last surviving partner's legal representative must wind up the partnership affairs. If the dissolution is by court decree, the court may either appoint an outside person, called a receiver or designate one of the partners to wind up the business.

Contracts may be necessary to enable the partnership to discharge prior contracts. For example, the liquidating partners might renew promissory notes to achieve a more orderly liquidation or enter into contracts necessary to perform prior existing contracts. Unless the partnership agreement provides otherwise, upon dissolution the partnership's assets are distributed in the following order:

1. Partnership creditors.
2. Partners' advances.
3. Each partner's capital. If partnership assets are insufficient, the loss of capital is deducted from each partner's capital contribution according to each partner's share of the profits.
4. Surplus to the partners. Any surplus remaining after payment of capital is divided in the same proportion as profits.

If the partnership has sufficient assets to pay creditors, partners' advances, and partners' capital contributions, there are few problems. Disagreements about the amount due any party can be settled by an audit pursuant to a court liquidation proceeding. If the partnership is insolvent, the partners have unlimited liability for partnership debts, and they must pay off the unpaid balance.

When not only the partnership but also all the partners are insolvent, the case goes into a bankruptcy court in liquidation proceedings. Federal bankruptcy law permits partnership creditors to enter the full amount of their claims against both the partnership assets and each individual insolvent partner's assets.

If one or more of the partners is solvent and their assets are sufficient to pay both their creditors and the partnership's outside creditors, they must do so.

Effect of Dissolution on Third Parties

Dissolution does not affect the rights of the partnership's existing creditors against the partnership, the partners, and the estates of deceased partners. If new contracts arise, as in orderly liquidation, the partnership, the partners, and the deceased partner's estate all are liable for these contracts.

A problem can arise if, after dissolution and without any authority, a partner enters into a completely new contract on the partnership's behalf. For example, Anne dies while on a trip, unknown to her partners Bob and Carla. Unaware of this dissolution of their partnership, Carla enters into a contract with Terry. Because Anne's death has dissolved the partnership, Carla lacks actual authority; however, she might have apparent authority. If Terry previously knew of the partnership, he is entitled to believe that it continues. If a third party has or should have had knowledge of a dissolution, the contract cannot be enforced. For example, if a partnership dissolves because continuation of the business becomes illegal, or if a partnership dissolves because one partner has gone bankrupt, third parties are held to have notice of such matters of public record.

If a partner without knowledge or notice of a dissolution enters into a completely new contract after dissolution, all the partners share any obligation the partnership incurs. If a partner knowing of a dissolution enters into a new contract, the partnership and the other partners might be bound, but they have rights against the partner who entered the contract.

If a contracting partner has no actual knowledge of a dissolution caused by a partner's death or bankruptcy but has received notice of a dissolution, as in a letter left unopened, the partner is solely responsible for a contract he or she entered into after dissolution.

A partner who has retired remains liable to third parties for obligations incurred while a member of the firm. Even the continuing partners' agreement to relieve the retiring partner of prior obligations does not change the third-party creditor's rights. To be relieved of these obligations, the retiring partner must obtain the third-party creditor's agreement to obtain payment only from the remaining partners. To avoid possible liability to new creditors who extend credit after a partner has retired, the partner must ensure proper notice of retirement. The term "retiring partner" includes a deceased partner's personal representative.

A new partner is not personally liable for debts incurred before joining the partnership; however the capital the incoming partner contributes is subject to prior creditors' claims. A new partner's personal liability starts with obligations the partnership incurs after admission. The new partner is entitled to a complete statement of the partnership's assets and liabilities.

Even if a partner retires or dies, the partnership still can continue. If the accounts between that partner, or his or her estate, and the partnership that continues are not settled, the retiring partner or estate can usually choose to receive either a continuing share of the profits or interest on the value of his or her share at the time of dissolution. In either case, however, the partner's claim against the partnership is subordinate to outside third-party creditors' claims.

Limited Partnerships and Limited Liability Partnerships

A **limited partnership** is a partnership of one or more persons who control the business and are personally liable for the partnership's debts, and one or more persons who contribute capital and share profits but who cannot manage the business and are liable only for the amount of their contributions. Only general partners can manage a business, and they have unlimited personal liability for its debts. If a limited partner exercises any control over the management, the limited partner might face an unlimited liability exposure. The firm can employ a limited partner, but this practice can raise difficult questions concerning when the limited partner's advice or review of management decisions becomes actual participation in management.

Despite limited partners' limited liability, federal income tax laws still treat a limited partnership as a partnership. The partnership itself is not taxed, and the income attributable to each partner is taxed at the partner's personal tax rate. To form a limited partnership, the partners must comply with a state statute and file a certificate of limited partnership with the appropriate public official.

In businesses with high up-front costs (such as theatrical productions) or with high depreciation allowances (such as some real estate developments), "paper losses" are attributable to each partner each taxable year. A paper loss is an unrealized loss. For example, stock valued at $20 dips to an $8 value. The stockowner who has not actually sold the stock realizes only a paper loss, not a real loss in cash.

Paper losses are particularly valuable to high-bracket taxpayers who, under some circumstances, can use these losses to offset other income. This offset reduces their taxable income while the limited partnership develops its business. A corporation would take those losses with no advantage to the investor.

Use of a limited partner's name in the partnership name can invite liability to outside creditors who are unaware of the limited nature of the partner's interest. Many states require the name of the limited partnership to contain either the words "Limited Partnership" or an equivalent abbreviation.

In general, the limited partnership is best suited to a temporary enterprise requiring a large amount of capital and having general partners who are good managers.

Some states recognize **limited liability partnerships**, which limit each partner's personal liability for acts or omissions of other partners. This limitation, however, usually does not apply to the following:

- Individual acts of negligence or wrongful acts by a withdrawing partner
- Debts or obligations of the partnership for which the withdrawing partner has agreed to be liable
- Debts and obligations expressly undertaken in the partnership agreement

Limited partnership
A partnership composed of one or more persons who control the business and who are personally liable for the partnership's debts and of one or more persons who contribute capital and share profits but who cannot manage the business and are liable only for the amount of their contributions.

Limited liability partnership
A partnership limiting each partner's personal liability for acts or omissions of other partners.

> **Partnership Characteristics Summary**
>
> • Formation—Partnerships are formed by two or more persons who agree to work together in any line of activity and share the profits.
>
> • Partnership liability—Partners are responsible for the partnership's torts and contracts under the laws of agency. Only partners, not partnerships, are responsible for crimes.
>
> • Ownership—Partners own all assets.
>
> • Termination—A partnership can be terminated by any partner's ending participation in the partnership.

Limited Liability Companies

Limited liability companies (LLCs) started in 1977 as a form of business entity combining some of the advantages of corporations and of partnerships. They are particularly appealing to real estate firms, high-technology start-up companies, and other entrepreneurial businesses with small numbers of active investors.

Two primary advantages of the LLC are the following:

1. They provide the limited liability of the corporation to all owners or members in the business.
2. They offer the tax advantages of a partnership, allowing the income to flow to each partner, or member, taxable at that individual's rate.

On the other hand, LLC disadvantages include the following:

• The Internal Revenue Service might treat an incorrectly set-up LLC as a corporation.

• An LLC must have at least two owners.

• In some states, professions (law, medicine, and accounting) cannot operate as LLCs.

• Courts have not decided many issues concerning LLCs.

UNINCORPORATED ASSOCIATIONS

The third form of legal business ownership is unincorporated association. An **unincorporated association** is a voluntary association of individuals acting together under a common name to accomplish a lawful purpose. An association can be for profit or not for profit. Although unincorporated, its form and organization resembles that of a corporation.

Unincorporated association
A voluntary association of individuals acting together under a common name to accomplish a lawful purpose.

Some corporations, particularly not-for-profit corporations, can be described as associations. Some state statutes provide for the incorporation of associations. For purposes of this discussion, the term "association" is used only in the sense of an unincorporated association.

An association resembles a partnership in many ways. Because an association is not a legal entity like a corporation, its members may be individually liable for the association's activities. Unlike a partnership, an association cannot hold title to real property or execute a lease in the association's name. A member's withdrawal does not cause a dissolution. Associations are the most common organizational form of not-for-profit institutions. An association, unlike a partnership, has formal articles of association or a charter and bylaws. Any expense-sharing or profit-sharing in an association is frequently other than per capita. Finally, an association's individual members do not have authority to participate directly in its day-to-day management. That power is usually vested in an elected board of directors or trustees.

The biggest difference between a corporation and an association is that an association is not a separate legal entity. It is formed under the common law right of contract, has no separate legal existence, and technically, does not have perpetual life.

Corporations can sue and be sued in the corporate name, but in most jurisdictions an association cannot. Associations are not subject to franchise, transfer, and other taxes commonly levied on corporations. They need not register in the states in which they do business or file various reports required of corporations. Associations, however, may have to comply with fictitious name statutes.

State Regulation of Associations

States have laws applicable to associations. The constitutional guarantee of freedom of assembly implies the right to form or join associations, and no legislation can eliminate that right. Any law affecting associations cannot unreasonably inhibit free speech or assembly, but may forbid activities that pose a clear and present danger to society.

A few states have statutes concerning many aspects of associations. Some states have laws that address specific matters, such as suits by or against associations in the association's name. Associations such as labor unions, insurance organizations, and credit unions are subject to any specific laws governing such operations.

Types of Associations

Because of the disadvantages of unlimited liability and the inability to hold title to property in an association's name, the number of unincorporated associations has declined recently in favor of corporations. The following are the six most significant types of unincorporated associations.

1. *Trade associations.* The more than 10,000 American trade associations comprise the largest group of unincorporated associations. These organizations foster their members' interests by exchanging and compiling information, lobbying, setting standards, and issuing publicity. They include boards of trade, chambers of commerce, and other business organizations.

2. *Labor unions.* The next largest group of associations is labor unions. The vagueness of organizational liability benefits this group. Association activities involve ambiguous liability, and the association form of organization further obscures both personal and group liability. Requiring incorporation, on the other hand, would make the lines of liability clear. Attempts to regulate unions by requiring them to incorporate raises questions concerning free speech and assembly rights and are therefore likely to fail.

3. *Benevolent and fraternal associations.* Fraternal and benevolent societies have long taken the form of associations. If these organizations provide insurance or credit for their members, they must conform to state laws on those subjects. Special statutes in many states regulate secret societies.

4. *Religious organizations.* Rules of churches or religious orders govern religious matters, but the same laws that apply to other associations govern secular matters.

5. *Clubs.* A club is an association of persons for some common objective, such as social purposes or the pursuit of literature, science, or politics. Clubs follow agency rather than partnership rules. A club member, therefore, is liable to pay money beyond the required subscription if that person expressly or impliedly authorizes a contract. The club's limitations on its agents bind third parties.

6. *Condominium owners' associations.* Most states have statutes regulating condominium association activities. Some condominium associations are incorporated, although statutes do not require incorporation. The acts usually specify limitations on the formation, powers, finance, and operation of condominium associations. All unit owners within the condominium are members, and the association is responsible for the condominium's operation and the care and preservation of the common areas, which are the shared areas of the property.

Formation and Financing

Associations can be either voluntary or involuntary. A voluntary association is usually formed by a group of individuals for some common lawful purpose and financed as they desire. An involuntary association is usually established by statute or regulation. Thus, for example, automobile insurance plans (assigned risk plans) are involuntary associations because, by law, all insurers that write automobile liability insurance in a given state must belong to that state's association. Furthermore, the statutes creating such associations frequently specify the means of formation, financing, and management.

Articles of Association and Bylaws

The contract of association is embodied in an instrument usually termed the "articles of association," "constitution," or "charter." Like a corporate charter, this instrument is the fundamental body of rules governing the association.

A voluntary association can adopt bylaws concerning internal procedures, members' rights and duties, and board and officers' powers. It also can adopt regulations concerning discipline, doctrine, or internal policy.

The association has the right to interpret and administer the bylaws and regulations, but courts will not enforce them if they compel a person to lose rights in accumulated assets or to forgo basic constitutional rights, or if they are illegal, immoral, or against public policy. For involuntary associations, the law establishing them can require that the articles or bylaws contain certain specified provisions.

Rights of Members in Association Property

Every voluntary association member has a property right in its assets. Because associations are not legal entities, any property an association ostensibly holds belongs jointly to its members as tenants in common. Therefore, common law gave members the right to dispose of the property at their joint pleasure. The articles of association, however, can give the right to control and dispose of property solely to the board of directors. Unless the articles or bylaws state otherwise, members lose whatever interest they have when their membership ends.

Dues and assessments paid by members become the association's property free from any individual right or claim. An individual member cannot prevent use of his or her dues for objectives to which a majority of the members agree.

Directors or Trustees

Association directors and trustees have legal rights and duties almost identical to those of corporate directors. One difference is that directors of not-for-profit associations do not have as high a standard of care as directors of corporations or associations engaged in business for profit because their positions in not-for-profit associations are often part-time and uncompensated. If they receive compensation, their standard of care is greater.

Liability of Members to Third Parties

Individual members can be liable for both torts and contracts arising from the association's activities.

Association members are jointly and severally liable for torts committed by the association's agents and employees acting within the scope of their employment. That the association, by law, might be sued in its own name does not eliminate the members' individual liability.

A member who has suffered damage to person, property, or reputation through the tortious conduct of another member or of an agent of the association cannot sue the association but can sue the other member or agent individually.

Absent statutes to the contrary, members of an association organized for trade or profit are individually liable for contracts made by an authorized officer or agent in the association's name or incurred in the course of business for which the association was organized. This liability exists even if the other party does not know the individual members' names. The existence of a law permitting suit against the association in its own name does not eliminate this individual liability.

Members of not-for-profit associations organized for social, moral, patriotic, political, or similar purposes and not for trade or profit do not have individual liability to third parties unless they join in authorizing a contract. Agency, not partnership, rules apply, and agency cannot be implied by the mere fact of association or paying dues.

Dissolution and Winding Up

Because no specific statutory provisions apply to the dissolution of associations, they can dissolve in a variety of ways, including the following:

- By members' vote
- By the death or withdrawal of substantially all the members
- By court action on application of creditors or members or for illegal conduct
- By the expiration of a period stated in the articles

Winding-up procedures, although not specified by statute, generally parallel those for partnerships. The person authorized to wind up association affairs liquidates the assets and pays all debts and obligations. That person distributes remaining assets pro rata (proportionately) among the members unless the articles provide otherwise. Sometimes the articles state that the remainder of the liquidated assets will go to a charitable or benevolent purpose.

Unincorporated Associations Characteristics Summary

- Formation—Voluntary: Group of individuals with common purpose. Involuntary: Established by statute or regulation.

- Ownership—Individual members have rights in the association assets.

- Liabilities—Individual members can be liable for both torts and contracts arising from the association's activities. Association members are jointly and severally liable for torts committed by the association's agents and employees acting within the scope of their employment.

- Termination—Unincorporated associations can terminate by membership vote, by the death or withdrawal of substantially all the members, by court action on application of creditors or members or for illegal conduct, or by the expiration of a period stated in the articles .

SUMMARY

Business entities can be sole proprietorships, partnerships, corporations, or associations, depending on their purposes. Each entity carries with it distinct legal implications, which directly influence insurance coverage.

The primary advantage of incorporation is the owners' limited tort and contract liability. A court might, however, "pierce the corporate veil" to hold stockholders liable, usually when a corporation has an illegal purpose. "Thin financing" and inadequate capitalization also can defeat limited corporate liability.

State laws generally govern corporations. The federal government charters special types of corporations, and federal law regulates corporate securities and interstate commerce activities. Corporate powers derive from corporate charters and bylaws, and corporations raise funds by issuing debt securities (bonds) and equity securities (stock).

Stockholders delegate management powers to the board of directors, who determine corporate structure and business policy and delegate daily management and outside dealings to officers. Officers and directors must exercise that degree of care that a prudent officer or director would ordinarily exercise but need not guarantee the corporation's profitability.

Corporations live forever unless they merge, dissolve, or reorganize. In a merger, two or more corporations join. Dissolution is a voluntary or involuntary termination of a corporation, and reorganization occurs when a corporation becomes bankrupt.

Partnerships are associations of two or more persons to carry on a business for profit. They form voluntarily and do not need government approval. Limited partnerships provide limited liability but offer tax advantages available to other partnerships.

Contract and agency law principles govern relationships between partners, including liability for torts and crimes. Every partner has a fiduciary relationship with the other partners and with the firm.

Partnership dissolution is rightful if it accords with the partnership agreement or is not any partner's fault, or if it occurs on a partner's death or the partnership business becomes unlawful.

Unincorporated associations are voluntary associations of individuals acting together to accomplish lawful purposes, either for profit or not for profit. They resemble corporations and partnerships but are not legal entities, so members might be individually liable to third parties for torts and contracts arising from association activities.

Common forms of associations are trade associations, labor unions, benevolent and fraternal associations, religious organizations, clubs, and condominium owners' associations.

Associations differ from partnerships in the following ways:

- An association cannot own realty or execute a lease.
- A member's withdrawal does not cause a dissolution.
- An association can be formed for profit or not.
- An association has articles, a charter, and bylaws.
- Expense sharing or profit sharing is frequently not per capita.
- Individual members do not participate in management.

Associations differ from corporations in the following ways:

- An association is not a separate legal entity.
- Corporations can sue and be sued in the corporate name, but in most jurisdictions associations cannot.
- Associations are not subject to franchise, transfer, and similar taxes.
- Associations need not register in states to do business.
- An association can more easily dissolve.

States can regulate associations but cannot violate constitutional guarantees of free speech and assembly. They can, however, forbid association activities that pose a clear and present danger to society.

No specific statutory provisions apply to dissolution of associations, and they can be dissolved in a variety of ways, including members' vote, death, or withdrawal; court action on application of creditors or members; or expiration of a period stated in the articles. Winding-up procedures generally parallel those for partnerships.

CHAPTER NOTES

1. Revised Model Business Corporation Act (RMBCA), § 3.01.

2. RMBCA, § 3.02.

3. 27 Cons. Laws of N.Y., Ann., § 1201(a)(1).

4. RMBCA, § 2.03(a).

5. RMBCA, § 16.02.

6. According to RMBCA, § 7.02(a), 10 percent of the outstanding shares are required to call a meeting.

7. RMBCA, § 8.25.

8. RMBCA, § 8.31.

9. Securities and Exchange Act of 1934, § 10(b)(5).

10. Securities and Exchange Act of 1934, § 16.

11. Securities and Exchange Act of 1934, § 10(b)(5).

12. RMBCA, Chapter 11.

13. RMBCA, § 12.02.

14. RMBCA, § 13.02, 13.21, 13.22.

15. RMBCA, § 11.04.

16. Williams Act of 1968.

17. RMBCA, § 14.30.

18. RMBCA, § 15.01.

19. UPA, § 6.

20. UPA, § 7(4).

21. UPA, § 21.

22. UPA, § 8.

23. UPA, § 25.

24. UPA, § 26.

25. UPA, § 9(3).

26. UPA, § 9(1).

Chapter 15

Direct Your Learning

The International Legal Environment of Insurance

After learning the content of this chapter and completing the corresponding course guide assignment, you should be able to:

- Summarize the history of international business and the growth of multinational companies.

- Given a case, recommend a method for a company to enter the international business markets based on foreign trade, foreign contractual relationships, and/or foreign direct investments.

- Describe the challenges and barriers facing international companies.

- Compare the predominant legal systems: civil law (Roman/French, German, Scandinavian [Nordic]), common law, Far Eastern, Hindu Islamic, and socialist/communist.

- Describe issues in public and private international law that affect international transactions.

- Describe the insurers and brokers leading the international insurance markets.

- Summarize the following financial considerations in international insurance:
  - Currency and foreign exchange markets
  - Expropriation
  - Accounting issues
  - Taxation issues (including the formation and benefits of tax havens)

- Explain how significant areas of the U.S. Internal Revenue Code (IRC), the Foreign Corrupt Practices Act (FCPA), and the Patriot Act influence international business and foreign investment.

- Summarize the roles and/or responsibilities of prominent multinational organizations and agreements in influencing the direction and development of world business.

- Define or describe each of the Key Words and Phrases for this chapter.

Develop Your Perspective

What are the main topics covered in the chapter?

The final chapter of this course turns to the international world of business and insurance, offering a basic understanding of the legal systems of other countries, as well as the issues the insurance industry faces in dealing with a global environment. The insurance industry has entered the international arena in a significant manner only recently, and insurance professionals are just beginning to study international issues. This chapter provides an overview of the international legal environment of insurance.

Identify risks facing an organization operating in an international market.

- What are the problems in entering international business markets?

- What challenges and barriers does a company face conducting business internationally?

Why is it important to learn about these topics?

After learning about the United States' legal environment of insurance, today's insurance student increasingly needs to understand the international legal environment of insurance.

Compare the advantages and disadvantages of other legal systems with that of the U.S.

- Which laws apply when there are conflicting U.S. and foreign laws?

- What multinational organizations or agreements influence the international legal environment?

How can you use what you will learn?

Examine your own organization's involvement in international business.

- What international contacts does your organization have today, or might it have in the future?

- What other systems of law might your organization encounter in today's world? Why?

Chapter 15
The International Legal Environment of Insurance

International business has been a major focal point of the United States economy for years, and more countries are coming to rely on it for growth and opportunities. International business presents opportunities to businesses of all sizes, along with legal and practical problems. International business is conducted within the framework of international law. In this framework, transactions between businesses of more than one country involve both of the following:

• Laws from the countries of both business parties to a transaction

• International legal doctrines

For example, an insurer might have to comply with the laws of its home country, the country in which it is doing business, an agreed-on country's legal system within a contract, or a multinational agreement. However, multinational agreements do not come into play that often in business transactions because individual business transactions are specific and do not always fall within the scope of international agreements.

When a U.S. company does business in a foreign country, the company must comply with both U.S. law and the national laws of the other country. Both bodies of law may be similar in some areas, such as antitrust, employment, tort, or environmental law. However, no two countries have identical laws. Foreign laws can present either an advantage or disadvantage to a company doing business in another country, whether they are laws affecting taxes, repatriation of income, or liability. For example, in Canada, punitive damages verdicts have just recently exceeded the $1 million threshold, while in the U.S. multimillion- and even multibillion-dollar punitive damages verdicts are common.

Additionally, if a U.S. business enters into a contract with a foreign company, the parties to the contract can choose which laws apply to that contract, including a specific state's contract laws, the foreign country's contract laws, international law within a United Nations Convention, or even the contract laws of a nonparty state.

Other, nonlegal factors can also have a great influence on the outcome of an international project. Factors such as cultural and language differences, time and distance problems, currency risks, differences in corporate structures and competition, and political differences all can affect international business dealings.

Overall, this chapter examines the various aspects of the international business environment, just as an enterprise considering a foreign venture might examine them. An underwriter reviewing an international organization's loss exposure might also consider these legal exposures in an account evaluation. This chapter examines the development of international business and the laws that help shape it, with particular attention to the insurance business. To aid in understanding the present state of the legal environment of international insurance, this chapter also explains the historic developments of international business and the challenges facing any company doing business in another country. These challenges can be legal, political, or cultural in nature.

THE MULTINATIONAL CORPORATION (MNC)

At the beginning of the twentieth century, trade between a few European countries, notably Great Britain, France, Germany, Italy, and Belgium, and their colonies, accounted for most of the international business economy. By the beginning of World War I, the number of companies involved in international business numbered a few thousand and were basically U.S.-based and western European-based. As the century progressed, the number of businesses operating multinationally grew.

World War II left much of European and Japanese production capacity in ruin. The U.S. industrial base not only survived intact, but certain technological and managerial advances during the war fueled the U.S. post-war economic expansion. U.S. companies expanded both domestically and internationally. U.S. businesses began seeking productive inputs such as raw materials and new markets for products. Those international markets grew rapidly, in part because the U.S. was the technological leader of the world, and corporate leaders embraced international expansion. The multinational corporation (MNC) became a largely U.S.-based phenomenon.

By the mid-1960s, MNCs were starting to form in Europe and Japan and, to a lesser extent, in the developing countries. These companies were growing and investing abroad, including in the U.S. From the 1980s on, some MNCs have evolved into truly global companies with revenue from foreign markets exceeding that of their domestic markets. The number of MNCs has increased to more than 63,000 parent companies, which control more than 820,000 subsidiaries around the world. However, most MNCs still are small, in terms of sales and number of employees, with the largest MNCs accounting for most foreign investments.

INTERNATIONAL BUSINESS

Businesses usually enter the international market with a single international investment, either exporting a single item to or importing it from another country. For insurers, this process could include insuring an insured's loss exposures in another country or expanding an insured's coverage to include opening a foreign operation.

The loss exposure in foreign markets depends on whether the operations are domestic and deal with foreign markets or are international. This section discusses the following three ways a company can participate in international business:

1. Foreign trade (imports and exports)
2. Foreign contractual relationships (product licensing and franchising)
3. Foreign direct investments (subsidiaries and joint ventures)

Foreign Trade

Foreign trade is the movement of a product from one country to another, or importing and exporting. Foreign trade is the most common way for a business to participate in the international market, and, compared to the others, it is the least risky and requires the lowest level of investment. **Business risk** is the possibility of loss or gain caused by economic variables, such as product demand or market competition. Business risk is risk associated with the unique circumstances of a particular company, as it might affect the price of that company's securities, and includes those risks that are inherent in the business's operation, such as lack of consumer interest in its products or services. Risk management professionals often refer to business risk as speculative risk and to the risk of accidental loss as pure risk or hazard risk.

Business risk
The possibility of loss or gain caused by economic variables, such as product demand and market competition.

Absolute and Comparative Advantage

The following two concepts are important to understanding countries' trade advantages:

1. Absolute advantage
2. Comparative advantage

A country has an **absolute advantage** when it specializes in goods or services it produces more efficiently and trades them for the goods and services it produces less efficiently. A country has an absolute advantage if it can produce a good at lower cost or with higher productivity than another country can. Absolute advantage compares industry productivities across countries.

Absolute advantage
The trade advantage that a country has when it specializes in goods or services it produces more efficiently and trades them for the goods and services it produces less efficiently.

All countries should apply the following two assumptions regarding absolute advantages:

1. They should specialize in the production of goods and services that use their inherent advantages to the greatest extent possible.
2. Through specialization and trade, they can become wealthier than if they do not engage in trade.

A country need not have an absolute advantage to benefit from trade. A simple comparative advantage yields similar benefits. A **comparative advantage** occurs when trading partners gain from trading with each other, even when one of the partners is more efficient in the production of all the produced goods and services.

Comparative advantage
The trade advantage that a country has when it gains from trading with other countries, even when it is more efficient in production of all the traded goods and services.

Absolute or comparative advantages do not, by themselves, explain all the reasons for engaging in trade, but they do form the historical basis for much of the public policy related to trade. A country can have an advantage in trade with its partners for several reasons. For example, a country can have a product or service that is exclusive. This product could be anything from a natural resource to a patented item or an educational advantage. As another example, a country could have low manufacturing costs as a comparative advantage.

U.S. Trade in the World Context

The U.S. is the largest trading nation in the world and has the largest gross domestic product (GDP) of any country. In 2003, for example, the U.S. imported goods worth approximately $1.3 trillion and exported goods worth $713 billion, resulting in a merchandise trade deficit of $547 billion for the year. However, in services trade, the U.S. exported $307 billion and imported only $256 billion, resulting in a trade surplus in services of $51 billion. The U.S. accounted for the following portions of the world's trade in 2003:

- 9.6 percent of merchandise exports
- 16.8 percent of merchandise imports
- 16.0 percent of service exports
- 12.8 percent of service imports

The single largest trading bloc of nations is the European Union (EU), accounting for approximately 37 percent of the world's exports and imports. The second largest trading bloc comprises the Asian countries, including Japan, with 26.4 percent of the world's exports and 22.8 percent of the world's imports. The North American Free Trade Agreement (NAFTA) countries (Canada, Mexico, and the U.S.) rank third with 19.5 percent of the world's exports and 25.8 percent of the world's imports.

The U.S. GDP exceeded $10.9 trillion in 2003, with the next six countries as follows:

1. Japan ($4.3 trillion)
2. Germany ($2.4 trillion)
3. U.K. ($1.8 trillion)
4. France ($1.75 trillion)
5. Italy ($1.5 trillion)
6. China ($1.4 trillion)

Foreign Contractual Relationships

The following two main types of foreign contractual relationships require and increase business risk and increase resource commitment:

1. Product licensing
2. Franchising

Product Licensing

Product licensing is permission granted by one company to another to manufacture its product or to use its distribution facilities or technology. The licensing of products between different countries can occur for three primary reasons, as follows:

1. A company may decide that it is not economically viable to sell its product in the second country because of labor costs, transportation costs, or regulations.

2. A company may decide that it does not have the time or resources to produce the product in another country.

3. A company may lack sufficient knowledge about the country's legal, political, social, and business environments.

Licensing technology includes granting the right to use, under specified conditions, the company's intellectual property, such as a copyright, trademark, or patent. One common license agreement provides for licensing computer software. A company does not buy the software program in a legal sense but buys the right to use the program and agrees to do so under set conditions. Just as software firms are concerned about the illegal use of their products, one of the major considerations for any firm granting a license to a foreign firm is protecting its assets. Before entering into any agreement, the domestic company assesses the trustworthiness of the foreign company it is dealing with and the foreign company's ability to meet the licensing agreement's financial requirements. Thoroughly understanding the foreign legal environment regarding copyright, trademark, and patent protection is necessary, and a company should consult a lawyer expert in the intellectual property field about intellectual property legal issues.

Product licensing
In international trade, the permission granted by one company to another to manufacture its product or to use its distribution facilities or technology.

Franchising

Franchising occurs when one company assigns to another the right to supply its products within a market. A franchise is a contract entered into for a specific time period. The franchisee (who receives the franchise) pays a royalty to the franchisor (who gives the franchise) for the rights assigned, in addition to other possible considerations. The franchisor provides training, technical assistance, specialized equipment, advertising, and promotion as stated in the arrangement. In franchising, the company image and its name are assets of the corporation involved. The franchisor allows the franchisee to use its image and certain assets. Much of the franchisee's success depends on the standardization of the firm's product or services. One of the most important aspects of franchising is the control over the use of the company's name and the quality of the product or service. For example, many franchisors keep control over all advertising and pricing of products in the markets.

Some companies control the risk of improper use of the corporate name or the risk of poor product or service quality by withholding vital technology or required component products. For example, a hotel chain can maintain

Franchising
One company's assignment to another company of the right to supply its products within a market.

control of its reservation system, or a grocery cooperative can maintain all consumer product distribution information.

Foreign Direct Investments

Foreign direct investment occurs when a company in one country acquires control over assets located in another country. This type of investment also anticipates managerial control of the assets acquired in the foreign market. This arrangement contrasts with **foreign portfolio investment**, which occurs when a company purchases foreign stocks, bonds, or other financial instruments. Foreign direct investment usually takes two forms: subsidiaries and joint ventures.

Subsidiaries

A **subsidiary** is a company owned or controlled by another company. A subsidiary might be subject to the parent company's complete or partial control. Generally, a company is not a subsidiary unless another company controls 50 percent or more of the shares, although a company can control another with less than 50 percent of the shares. Some countries do consider a company to be a subsidiary with less than 50 percent control, depending on the country and the market segment.

A distinguishing characteristic of a subsidiary, as opposed to a joint venture, is that a subsidiary issues stock. The stock can be 100 percent owned by the parent company, or some of the shares can be publicly traded in the foreign market. In fact, most joint ventures are subsidiaries with the partners each owning a percentage of the stock. In many foreign markets, the government requires a company to form a subsidiary to bring the parent firms and subsidiaries under the local laws of incorporation. These local laws can require both the subsidiary and the parents to comply with local financial reporting and disclosure.

The fully-owned subsidiary provides a company with the highest level of control over operations but presents the highest level of business risk, commitment of capital, and managerial control. With higher risk, a company expects to achieve higher returns. For a company experienced in international operations, this trade-off between risk and return can be acceptable and even desirable.

The time required for a company to enter a foreign market using a subsidiary varies, depending on the entry technique the company chooses or requires. Acquiring an existing company in the foreign market can usually occur relatively quickly. On the other hand, if a company develops its subsidiary from the ground up, it might take years to become a player in the foreign market. This latter approach probably gives the company the greatest control over the foreign affiliates because the parent company would develop its local management, distribution channels, and product mix. However, this approach also requires a larger investment of resources and time.

Foreign direct investment
A company's acquisition of control over assets located in another country.

Foreign portfolio investment
A company's purchase of foreign stocks, bonds, or other financial instruments.

Subsidiary
A company owned or controlled by another company.

Joint Ventures

In the international trade context, a joint venture involves shared ownership and control of a foreign operation. Joint ventures allow a company to enter either a geographic or product market and to acquire technology or revenue that would not otherwise be within reach. Joint ventures have high earnings and growth potential.

The most common joint arrangement involves a company's joining forces with a second company to operate a joint venture in the second company's country. In many countries, such as China, Russia, and the other former Soviet Union countries, joint ventures with the government or state-owned companies are common. Less common are joint ventures formed by companies from two different countries to operate in a third country. Additionally, companies rarely enter into joint ventures with more than two or three partners.

Like subsidiaries, joint ventures increase companies' business risk and commitment of resources. A company might have to invest substantial capital or share proprietary technology with its joint venture partners. On the positive side, however, the value of the joint venture can be greater than the sum of what the individual partners have contributed to the venture.

In some joint ventures, partner companies divide capital expenses among themselves and share the costs, depending on the market and the partners' preferences. Additionally, engaging in a joint venture requires a company to commit substantial managerial resources and might require considerably more time to enter a foreign market than that necessary to enter a domestic joint venture or acquire a subsidiary.

Perhaps the single most important aspect of forming a joint venture is choosing the right partner or partners. This choice is important because the companies share resources, managerial responsibilities, technology, and profits, among other things.

A company may choose foreign direct investment in lieu of trade (exporting and importing) for a number of reasons. Barriers to trade, both those occurring naturally (for example, transportation costs, language, and cultural differences), and other barriers (for example, tariffs, quotas, or political issues), contribute to a company's need to gain direct access to markets through direct investment. Companies seeking direct foreign investment fall into the following three general categories, defined for purposes of this text by how they relate to international trade:

1. **Resource seekers** are companies that enter a foreign market seeking that country's resources. For example, the U.S. not only produces oil but also seeks oil resources internationally. A U.S.-based company might invest capital in an oil-producing market to gain access to oil reserves. A German firm might enter a foreign market to gain access to lower-cost labor. The low cost of Chinese labor might be profitable in producing

Resource seeker
In the context of international trade, a country that enters a foreign market seeking that country's resources.

a product or even for making production possible. A resource-seeking company might also enter a foreign market to gain access to certain technology. For example, a Japanese company might build a research-and-development facility in the U.S. to gain access to engineers and scientists and to monitor its U.S. competitors.

Market seeker
In the context of international trade, a company that seeks new markets outside its own boundaries.

2. **Market seekers** are companies that seek new markets outside their own countries' boundaries. A company might find it more favorable to invest in a foreign country than to export, if the country has, for example, a desired natural resource or technological advantage. Companies also might seek markets for defensive purposes. For example, some companies have invested in China, Russia, and Eastern Europe knowing that they may not earn a profit for many years, but with the objective of being well established when the foreign country's internal market expands.

Market follower
In the context of international trade, a company that follows its customers into foreign countries.

3. **Market followers** follow their customers into foreign countries, a common trend in service industries such as insurance and banking. Many U.S. companies expanded into foreign markets in the first few decades after World War II, and U.S. banks followed them to service them abroad. Advertising agencies, accounting firms, and other service companies also followed their customers abroad. Several large U.S.-based insurers have made substantial commitments to world markets.

Despite substantial growth in the number and size of multinational corporations throughout the world, the U.S. is still home to the greatest number of, and the largest, MNCs. If WalMart, the largest U.S.-based MNC, with annual sales exceeding $256 billion in 2004 (and predicted to top $500 billion in five years), were a country, it would rank 20th in GDP in the world, placing it just behind Sweden and ahead of Austria. Additionally, four of the ten largest MNCs are U.S.-based in sales measurement, in addition to WalMart, listed as follows with ranks in parentheses:

*   ExxonMobil (2)
*   General Motors (3)
*   Ford Motors (6)
*   General Electric (9)

The rest of the top ten MNCs and their countries and ranks are as follows:

*   Royal Dutch/Shell, Netherlands (4)
*   British Petroleum, Great Britain (5)
*   DaimlerChrysler, Germany (7)
*   Toyota Motor, Japan (8)
*   Mitsubishi, Japan (10)

Challenges and Barriers

When a company engages in international business, either through trade or direct investment, it must be ready to adapt to specific national differences: to transact business in diverse locations with different cultures and languages and with legal and regulatory differences. Each company involved in the international market has different needs and requirements based on the type of business and the intended outcome of the business transactions. A company that exports surplus products has different needs and requirements from a company that intends to invest billions of dollars, pounds, yen, or yuan into a manufacturing facility in another country. Each company and each international transaction requires differing degrees of understanding of the other country's business environment.

All business transactions face both legal and practical challenges. A combination of the laws of two countries, along with the principles of international law, can compound the legal challenges that can arise from any transaction. The challenges also vary with the type of business transaction occurring, whether a sales contract, land purchase, merger, or acquisition. Each business transaction has specific and different factors that affect the possible outcome, and the laws affecting those transactions are of paramount importance.

Language

A language barrier can be the first challenge to a company in an international transaction. Although English has become the language of international business, skills with other languages are still necessary in most international transactions. In an international investment or sale of a product to a foreign market, numerous foreign language issues can arise, including interpretation of contracts, advertising, packaging information, product instructions, and warranties, as well as language issues regarding legal and regulatory compliance.

In many countries, it is common to speak more than one language—a possible advantage for international business in those countries. In the U.S. and Great Britain, less than two percent of English-speaking residents speak a second language, and the average number of languages spoken is one. In contrast, in Canada and Japan, the average number of languages spoken per person is two; in Belgium, France, Germany, and Sweden, it is three; and in the Netherlands, it is four.

The ability to speak multiple languages gives a businessperson an advantage, not only in direct business negotiations, but also in personal interactions. Language ability also prevents misunderstanding or mistranslation through a third-party translator.

Culture

The difference between cultures can be challenging to any business transaction. Many Asian and African cultures, for example, are very different from the U.S. culture. Differences in cultures can involve variations in manners, in body language, in religion, in family life and gender roles, and many other aspects of culture. For example, business travelers should consider interactions between business and family when planning business meetings and business socializing in some countries. Whether it is appropriate to invite a spouse to a business dinner or a family to a sporting event can vary by culture.

Time

Time differences between countries can make conducting international business challenging. For example, when it is 3:00 PM—an appropriate time for a conference call—in Philadelphia, it is 8:00 PM in London. Further, for companies communicating across the International Date Line, it can be Monday in London and Tuesday in Sydney, for example.

Additionally, different countries and cultures perceive time differently, and those perceptions can affect interactions within a business transaction. In many northern European countries, along with the U.S., people perceive time in a linear fashion. People at a business meeting in the U.S. might have a set agenda they follow closely, moving from one item to the next. In another country, such as Spain, people may perceive time less linearly and may tend to do many tasks at the same time. Some countries value the use, or quality expenditure, of time more highly than the quantity of time spent on any endeavor. One international business consultant refers to the following three types of time cultures[1]:

1. Data-based time countries run on the clock or calendar. People schedule appointments, jobs, and events at set paces or times, so as to use time efficiently. Data-based countries view actions as finite and place their achievement of goals, activities, and useful pursuits within a finite time frame.

2. Relationship-based time countries base their interactions on developing rapport among business associates. Companies are less concerned with meeting on set schedules or timelines to complete business deals. A company and its people in relationship-based countries are more concerned about getting to know each other, on the assumption that good business outcomes will result. This relationship-based system exists in many Middle Eastern countries, as well as in the multi-tasking countries listed previously.

3. Group-based time countries think of time as a long-term, big picture concept, with a past, present, and future. The group-based time countries are primarily Asian, such as Japan and China, which have centuries of cultural and religious beliefs that associate time with a sense of eternity.

Distance and Space

The physical distance between locations limits contact between individuals and influences the culture of both individuals and companies. New travel and communication technologies have helped to reduce some of the physical distance barriers to international transactions and have helped to unify the world into a single international market. Technology makes it possible to conduct international business around the world twenty-four hours a day.

Space also affects individuals and cultures. Each individual has a preferred personal space, and the size of a person's preferred personal space varies by culture. Personal space preference can relate to family structure and size as well as population density.

How people interact, as well as the circumstances under which they touch others, also differs within each culture. A kiss on the cheek is an appropriate greeting in some cultures, a handshake in others, a bow in others.

Types of Governments

Government structure is important to consider in all international business dealings. Changes in government can result in changes to the business and legal environment within a country. These changes can occur quickly or slowly, depending on the type of government in a country. Most countries in the world have one of the following six basic systems of government:

1. *Democracy*. Democracy takes many diverse forms, and the name of a government can be deceiving. For example, the Democratic People's Republic of Korea is the name of North Korea, a single-party communist dictatorship, and is not the name of South Korea, a democracy. **Democratic rule** is rule by the people through elected representatives. Modern democratic governments take the following forms:

Democratic rule
A form of government by the people through elected representatives.

Examples of Different Forms of Democracy

Nonparty Democracies	Parliamentary Democracies	Presidential Democracies	Multiparty Democracies
Kiribati	Australia	Brazil	Algeria
Micronesia	Canada	Egypt	Ethiopia
Nauru	Germany	Mexico	France
Palau	India	Philippines	Indonesia
Tuvalu	Japan	Russian Federation	Romania
Uganda	Turkey	South Korea	Taiwan
	South Africa	United States	

- A **nonparty democracy** is a form of government in which elected representatives have no political party affiliation.
- A **parliamentary democracy** is ruled by a prime minister and an elected parliament. Approximately sixty countries have had parliamentary democracies in recent years.
- A **presidential democracy** is governed by a president directly elected by the citizens. Approximately sixty countries have had presidential democracies recently.

Nonparty democracy
A form of government in which elected representatives have no political party affiliation.

Parliamentary democracy
A form of government involving rule by a prime minister and an elected parliament.

Presidential democracy
A form of government in which the citizens directly elect a president.

Multiparty democracy
A form of government in which representatives may be elected from several or many political parties.

Junta
A form of government by a group of military officers governing a country after seizing power.

Martial law
The assumption of control of a country by the military.

Monarchy
A form of government led by a hereditary chief of state with powers varying from absolute to ceremonial.

Absolute monarchy
A form of government led by a single ruler who selects advisers for assistance.

Constitutional monarchy
A form of government with a parliament, or a democratic legislative body, but with a monarch as a formal or ceremonial head of state.

Single-party government
A form of government that constitutionally permits only one specific political party.

Theocratic government
A form of government based on a religious doctrine and often led by religious leaders.

Transitional government
A temporary form of government used when a country is rebuilding its government, usually as a result of war.

- A **multiparty democracy** is a form of government in which representatives may be elected from several or many political parties. Many multiparty democracies have balancing roles of a prime minister and a president. Approximately thirty-five countries have had multiparty democracies in recent years.

2. *Military.* Military forms of government have occurred throughout history. Another term for these governments is **junta**, a group of military officers governing a country after seizing power. Military rule is commonly associated with single-party or transitional forms of government. By the late 1980s, military officers had overthrown civilian governments in 64 of 120 developing nations. Senior officers held all the key governmental positions and used martial law to maintain stability. **Martial law** is the means by which the military assumes control of a country, often because of a perceived need for military security or public safety.

   After World War II, almost all of the militarily ruled countries allied with either the U.S. or the Soviet Union. With the fall of the Soviet bloc, almost all countries that had been controlled by military authorities changed to democratic forms of government. Military-ruled governments have become less common in recent years.

3. *Monarchy.* A **monarchy** is a government that has a hereditary chief of state with powers varying from absolute to ceremonial. Monarchies can be kingdoms or dynasties over which one person rules for life. Individual monarchs can have titles such as king, queen, prince, emperor, czar, or sultan, among others. Two common forms of monarchy are absolute and constitutional. In an **absolute monarchy**, the leader rules alone and selects advisers for assistance. In a **constitutional monarchy**, a parliament, or democratic legislative body, replaces absolute monarchical rule. Many of the world's remaining monarchical governments had ended by the mid-20th century. Some countries, such as Great Britain, the Netherlands, Sweden, and Spain, still have kings and queens, but their powers are limited and often ceremonial, and democratically elected legislative bodies have the real power to govern.

4. *Single-party.* A **single-party government** usually has a constitutional requirement that only a specific political party can exist. Although these governments are not military, theocratic, or monarchical, most arose from those forms of government.

5. *Theocratic.* A **theocratic government** is based on religious doctrine, and religious leaders may govern. Throughout history theocratic governments have ruled countries such as Tibet and China and the Aztec, Incan, and Mayan empires in Latin America, as well as in many Islamic countries. Examples of theocratic governments today include Iran and the Vatican City.

6. *Transitional.* A country has a **transitional government** when it is rebuilding its government, usually as a result of war.

Examples of Different Forms of Government

Military Ruled	Monarchies	Single-Party	Recent Transitional
Congo	Cambodia	China	Bahrain
Myanmar	Jordan	Cuba	Iraq
Pakistan	Monaco	Laos	Liberia
Sudan	Nepal	Libya	Maldives
	Saudi Arabia	North Korea	Rwanda
	Swaziland	Syria	Somalia
	United Arab Emirates	Vietnam	

LEGAL SYSTEMS

Although no two countries have identical legal systems, many nations share legal approaches and concepts. This section contrasts various legal systems by grouping countries that use similar concepts and approaches. Although not all legal scholars agree as to the classifications, the classifications provided here probably reflect the most common views. Additionally, some countries classified within one system have incorporated legal concepts found traditionally within other systems. This section provides background information about the development of different legal systems to give the insurance professional a knowledge of the differences they might encounter in the international insurance and risk management environment.

In a majority of countries, the legal systems fall into the following two major categories:

1. Civil-law system
2. Common-law system

The civil-law tradition developed within the following three distinct subsystems:

1. Roman (and French)
2. German
3. Scandinavian (Nordic)

Some scholars consider the Scandinavian subsystem to be a separate major subsystem because of its distinct features. However, Scandinavian common law is of British origin.

The common-law countries give investors greater legal rights than civil-law countries. Within the civil-law countries, the Roman (French) system provides the weakest investor rights, followed by Scandinavian, and then German. However, the reasons for these differences vary, often reflecting historical development and corporate structure within the countries. Only Roman (French) civil-law counties have mandatory corporate dividend requirements, and German civil-law countries are the most likely to have legal reserve requirements for corporations.

Civil Law

Civil law, or Roman-Germanic law, uses comprehensive codes and statutes to form the backbone of a legal system. This system relies heavily on legal scholars to develop and interpret the law. The civil-law system is the most influential system in the world. More countries use its subsystems, in one form or another, than any other legal system. It is the dominant legal system of western Europe, almost all of Latin America, and parts of Africa and Asia. Additionally, the civil-law system can be found in parts of some traditionally common-law countries (for example, Louisiana in the U.S., Quebec in Canada, and Puerto Rico). However, these legal systems can vary a great deal from one country to another in their legal institutions, processes, and rules.

In the civil-law system, a judge is a civil servant whose function is to find the correct legislative provision within a written code of statutes and apply it to the facts presented in a case. Judges perform little interpretation of a code, and their opinions do not determine their thought processes on legal issues.

The civil-law courts usually are divided into two or more separate sets, each with its own jurisdiction over different issues, with a different hierarchy, judiciary, and procedures. The typical civil-law case usually is divided into the following three stages:

1. The preliminary stage involves submission of pleadings and appointment of a hearing judge.
2. At the evidence stage, a hearing judge takes evidence and prepares a written summary of the proceedings.
3. At the decision stage, the presiding judge decides the case based on the record provided by the hearing judge, the counsels' briefs, and arguments.

The civil law system does not have the common-law system's jury trial; instead, a series of isolated meetings, written communications, motions, and rulings help decide the case. Civil-law countries have varying time frames for these events; some countries' procedures proceed very quickly, and others proceed very slowly.

Roman-French Law

The French civil code of 1804 consolidated the contrasting concepts of law by decree and law by custom. Although a magistrate is the final arbiter of a private law dispute, a court can rely on appointed experts, who have wide-ranging powers to investigate and present evidence to support an opinion rendered by a court. A magistrate usually will not reject an expert's opinion.

However, in France and Italy, a party can appeal a primary court's opinion, although courts in those countries tend to have extremely heavy backlogs. Under these circumstances, the examination of detailed factual or legal issues can be difficult because, with the passage of time, memories fade and some witnesses become difficult to find.

The French civil code was the basis for codes in the Netherlands, Italy, Portugal, and Spain. Haiti also adopted the French Code, and Bolivia and Chile adopted it for the most part. In turn, Ecuador, Uruguay, Argentina, and Colombia used the Chilean code as the model for their own legal systems. Puerto Rico and the Philippines used the Spanish code as their legal systems' model.

German Law

Germany's location in the center of Europe has greatly influenced its political and social history. Germany has the third largest economy in the world (after those of the U.S. and Japan). Many scholars consider the German civil law system as the most developed and influential of all the civil-law subsystems.

The German private law, or *Bürgerliches Gesetzbuch* (BGB), is the civil code that took effect in 1900. Unlike the French Code, which was designed for laypersons to read, the BGB was developed for legal professionals to read and was too technical for laypersons. The German civil law influenced the U.S. legal education system; the American Law Institute's (ALI) restatements, or authoritative treatises, on law; and the development of the Uniform Commercial Code (UCC).

The original German code emphasized the rights of people to enter into contracts freely and dealt with the enforceability of all kinds of contracts. Similarly, the German code requires a finding of fault on the part of a wrongdoer in a tort suit. Although some elements of those concepts still exist, the availability of insurance as a risk- and damage-spreading mechanism has caused the German code to expand individual obligations and potential culpability. Compensation for damages without culpability has effectively created a "cradle-to-grave" safety net as part of a wide social compact in Germany. For example, German statutes grant compensation for certain types of accidents, regardless of culpability, including railway, traffic, aircraft, electrical, gas, and nuclear power station accidents.

The German and Swiss codes, along with the French code, influenced code developments in Brazil, Mexico, pre-communist China, and Peru. Additionally, Japan used the German code in the development of its own code, and Turkey used the similar Swiss code in developing its legal system.

Scandinavian Law

The Scandinavian (Nordic) legal system is both a civil-law system and an independent system. The legal systems in the Scandinavian countries are based neither on large bodies of codified regulations, like those of the French and German systems, nor on case (common) law.

The Scandinavian legal systems evolved from a long-established history of customary law. Elements of law by decree developed as a result of Germanic and Russian influences. Additionally, the Scandinavian countries have codified historical business practices as statutes. In tort law, as distinguished from contracts, damages contain a punitive element beyond just and fair compensation.

The development of a virtually distinct legal system in Scandinavian countries resulted from the historically close links among those countries. For example, Finland was part of Sweden for hundreds of years until it became part of Russia, then eventually gained independence. Norway, now independent, was part of Denmark.

Common Law

In the common-law legal system, a judge interprets the facts of a case, examines precedents (prior judicial rulings in similar cases), and makes a decision based on the facts in the current case. Precedents are guides, not rigid frameworks for all decisions. This system tends to be fact-intensive, relying on the judge's reasoning for a final decision.

England and most of the former British colonial countries, including Australia, Canada, India, and the U.S., use the common-law system. Japan's law combines the civil- and common-law systems, particularly relating to corporate law, which resulted from U.S. influence in post-World War II Japan. The Far Eastern legal systems also influenced Japan's legal system. Other examples of blended common-law systems are Canada and the U.S. Both the province of Quebec and the state of Louisiana have state legal systems based on French civil law.

Far Eastern Law

The Far Eastern legal system is not a "system" in the same sense as the civil- or common-law systems. The Far East is a regional group of countries that fall within other legal systems but that have a common background profoundly influencing their legal developments over the centuries. In the Far Eastern system, China has a dominant presence. Although both Korea and Japan have different legal systems, they both reflect the Chinese influence. Additionally, legal systems of some Far Eastern countries have been influenced by religion.

Until the 19th century, Japan's civil code was based on the developing German civil code. However, this imported legal code did not supplant the local customary law already existing in Japan. Even today, a tradition of informal compromise, contrasted with individual parties' asserting their rights in negotiations, remains a strong characteristic of the Far Eastern countries' approach to contract disputes. Japan today has relatively few attorneys, judges, and lawsuits.

Other Asian countries have relied on both civil and common law to vary-
ing degrees. French colonialism influenced the legal systems of the southeast
Asian countries Laos, Cambodia, and Vietnam for many years. By contrast,
England's common-law system influenced the legal systems of Singapore,
Malaysia, and Brunei. U.S. influence was prevalent in post-World War II
Japan and in the Philippines after the Spanish-American War.

Hindu Law

Hinduism provides religious and philosophical rules in India and some
surrounding countries. The Hindu legal system is perhaps the oldest in
the world. The customs and laws of Hinduism have applied separately and
distinctly to the members of four major caste groups: Brahmans (priests),
Kshatriyas (warriors), Vaishyas (tradesmen), and Sudras (servants and
artisans). Movement from one caste to another historically was not permitted,
even with professional or political success, although laws have attempted to
eliminate the rigid caste system. Legislation in India has voided all the rules of
the caste system when they conflict with social justice.

By the early 1800s, most of India was under the control of the British, whose
policy in settling colonies was to retain existing law, allowing Hindu law to
become the official system for the Hindu population. The effect of British rule
on Hindu law was the development of legislation, the judiciary, and the legal
education system. A statutory code of commercial, criminal, and civil procedure has replaced the Hindu law of contracts and property. However, India's
legal system still reflects remnants of the caste system.

Islamic Law

The Islamic legal system is used in countries whose citizens are almost
entirely followers of the Islamic religion. This legal system is based on
the foundations of the *Book of the Qur'an* (*Koran*) and includes almost all
of the countries of the Middle East and northern Africa, southern Asia,
southeastern Europe, and parts of southeast Asia. More Islamic countries are
members of the United Nations than countries whose majorities follow any
other religion. Islam is the second most prevalent religion in the world with
approximately 1.2 billion followers.

With the end of World War I and the collapse of the Ottoman Empire,
Europeans regained control of most the territories that Islamic warriors had
captured in previous centuries. In the decades following World War II, many
Islamic peoples attempted to gain their independence, often from European
countries. Internal debates, still ongoing, centered on whether states should
be theocracies or should be secular states that follow Islamic law.

The primary system of law within the Islamic countries is the *Shari'ah*, with a
secondary system of jurisprudence called the *fiqh*. The *Shari'ah* consists of the
two primary sources of Islamic law from which all legal principles derive, the

Qur'an and the *Sunnah*. The *fiqh*, or Islamic jurisprudence, is the process of applying *Shari'ah* principles to both real or hypothetical cases.

The *Qur'an*, the highest source of law within Islam, gives followers of Islam the authority to make law and render opinions. The *Sunnah* forms a second tier of the *Shari'ah* and mandates the standard of conduct people are to follow to comply with the *Qur'an*.

The *Qur'an* is a religious book, not a legal code or book of law, but it serves as the foundation for the Islamic legal system. It contains specific precepts about ethics, crime, business transactions, domestic relations, inheritance, and war. The *Qur'an* differs from a code of law in that it does not mention the legal consequences of the disregard of its rules.

The *faqh* refers to the body of laws developed from the *Shari'ah*. These principles are considered infallible and not subject to amendment. Five schools of *faqh* (*faqh madhhabs*) exist today. Four are within the *Sunni* sect of Islam. The fifth school is within the *Shai* (*Shiite* or *Shiah*) sect of Islam. At times, conflict has divided the different *faqh madhhabs*. Identifying with a different school or attempting to change affiliation can be considered heresy. Additionally, at times judges prohibit intermarriage between the different *faqh madhhabs*.

Approximately 90 percent of all Muslims identify themselves as *Sunni*, with the balance being *Shai*. The *Shai* live primarily in Iran, southern Iraq, Syria, and Lebanon and believe that the leader of the Islamic religion should be a direct descendant of Muhammad. *Sunni* Muslims do not have this requirement. A significant difference between *Shai* and *Sunni* is that *Shais* also believe that individual reasoning (*ijtihad*) is a legitimate source of Islamic law.

Socialist-Communist Law

The socialist system originated with the Marxist overthrow of czarist Russia in the October Revolution in 1917, which created the Soviet Union. Before the revolution, Russia was a civil-law country. The result of the Marxist takeover was the imposition of socialist ideology over the civil-law system that already existed. The central idea of the system was the emphasis on the state's interest over that of individuals. Russia developed new codes that reflected the Marxist ideas that the laws should serve the interests of socialism.

Private-sector business legal principles, such as contracts, commercial law, torts, property, and bankruptcy, are of little use within a socialist system. Public law replaces private-sector legal principles. For example, because the government owns all property and production, all contract law is public. In a socialist country, the socialist political party controls and influences the entire legal system, including the courts. All decisions from the courts, although independent in nature, are subject to party control or revision.

Western civil- and common-law systems heavily influenced the law in Russia. Asian socialist-communist countries discovered problems applying the Soviet-style legal principles in their societies. The communist People's

Republic of China, for example, abandoned the legal principles introduced to them by the Soviets and developed a more informal system more similar to Far Eastern traditions.

With the fall of the Soviet bloc in the 1990s, former eastern European bloc countries abandoned the socialist-communist legal system in favor of a civil-law system. Many changes were profound, with legislatures endorsing basic free market principles. The actual changes varied by country. Today Russia is a civil-law country. However, the Russian government often changes the legal applications of civil law with regard to individuals and businesses.

Several other communist-ruled or communist-influenced countries, such as Cuba, North Korea, Vietnam, and the People's Republic of China, still use the Soviet-based legal system. The People's Republic of China now permits a private economy and has adopted it as part of the Constitution of the People's Congress. China's dominant constitutional principles still require observance of socialist doctrine. China also has adopted civil-law type of codification, the General Principles of Civil Law, and is developing an ever more extensive codification.

INTERNATIONAL LAW

International law is the body of legal principles governing relationships among nations. That definition has expanded to include relations between international organizations and states, among international organizations, and between states or international organizations and individuals.

International law
The body of legal principles governing relationships among nations.

Those resolving international disputes between individuals or corporations first apply any international agreement or treaty (public international law) that governs the dispute. If no treaty or international agreement applies, then any laws of involved countries that apply directly to the dispute (private international law) are considered

Public international law concerns the interrelation of nation states and is governed by treaties and other international agreements. **Private international law** involves disputes between individuals or corporations in different countries and is also referred to as conflicts of law. It involves questions about which laws apply in settling the disputes and how they apply. It determines which jurisdiction's law applies to the business transaction in question, which country's court hears a dispute, and whether other countries will enforce the foreign decision.

Public international law
A law that concerns the interrelation of nation states and that is governed by treaties and other international agreements.

Private international law
A law that involves disputes between individuals or corporations in different countries.

International treaties agreed to by a business's country of origin govern some international business transactions. These treaties may be between two countries, or they may be multilateral treaties among many countries. The North American Free Trade Agreement (NAFTA) is a trilateral treaty governing all business interactions involving Canada, Mexico, and the U.S. Other treaties, such as the World Trade Organization's (WTO) General Agreement of Tariffs and Trade (GATT), involve more than one hundred countries as signatories. These international agreements affect member countries by requiring that they amend their national laws to comply with the agreements' requirements. For example, countries that signed GATT agreed to adjust their tariff rates on imported goods from other GATT member countries. However, these agreements are not limited to trade and tariffs. NAFTA includes investment provisions, and the recent WTO's Trade-Related Aspects of Intellectual Property Rights agreement ensures that the laws of member countries set basic standards for the protection of intellectual property (copyrights, trademarks, and patents).

In any legal dispute arising between parties from different countries, the following two issues must be considered:

1. Whether a court in one country will recognize the decision of another country's court (comity)
2. Whether the court has the right to hear the legal dispute (jurisdiction)

These issues are important in all international transactions, and the previous actions by a court in a particular country are important to know about when conducting international transactions.

Comity
The courtesy by which one country recognizes, within its own territory or in its courts, another country's institutions.

The **comity** of nations is the courtesy by which one country recognizes, within its own territory or in its courts, another country's institutions. This recognition can also apply to the rights and privileges acquired by a citizen in a country. Many experts believe that comity is the basis for all private international law.

Just as in domestic cases, one of the basic questions of international law is whether a court has the right (jurisdiction) to preside over a particular case. Like domestic courts, courts in international cases must determine if they have jurisdiction over the person or entity (*in personam* jurisdiction) and over the subject matter (*in res* jurisdiction) and if they have jurisdiction to render the particular judgment in the case. In international cases, personal jurisdiction is based on whether the person or entity is present in the country or has committed the act in question in that country.

A significant issue frequently arising in international law is whether one country's courts have jurisdiction over either another country's citizen or a corporation with its place of business in another country. Jurisdictional issues are increasing in importance and complexity as governments try to control the increase in international business. For example, one country's jurisdiction over Internet commerce originating in another country raises complex jurisdictional questions. Other cases involving jurisdictional issues include the U.S.'s attempt to prevent U.S. residents from purchasing prescription drugs from other countries, China's claim to all Chinese-language domain names and its blocking of certain Web sites, and some European courts' claiming authority over Web sites from outside their countries' borders.

The Hague Conference on Private International Law has drafted an international convention (agreement) to help determine in which court plaintiffs can sue foreign parties and on which occasions countries must recognize foreign courts' judgments. The Preliminary Draft Convention on Jurisdiction and Foreign Judgments in Civil and Commercial Matters (the Hague Convention) was adopted in 1999. It requires domestic courts of those countries that enter into the agreement (signatory countries) to enforce foreign judgments that meet the treaty's standards. In effect, the proposed agreement standardizes the enforcement of foreign judgments. This agreement could significantly affect international business because it gives corporations and individuals a transnational mechanism for redress for violations of their contract or tort rights and increases the possibility that a plaintiff can collect a foreign court's judgment.

Negotiations and discussions continue on this draft of the convention as countries raise areas of individual concern. For example, U.S. companies are concerned that foreign courts will levy judgments against them that would not be required under U.S. law, while parties with claims against corporations want to limit the corporations' ability to choose jurisdictions most favorable to them for litigation. To further illustrate, the U.S. recognizes the fair use exceptions to copyright law, while most other countries have more restrictive copyright laws. The Hague Convention would allow intellectual property rights holders to determine the forums to hear their disputes, thus subjecting U.S. consumers to other nations' more restrictive laws.

The drafted Hague Convention does not require that any country's law apply in any given dispute, but merely lays the groundwork for which jurisdiction (court) might hear a case. However, generally, the United States' courts would apply U.S. law; the French courts, French law; and the British courts, British law, so the choice of forum actually does influence the outcome of a case.

INTERNATIONAL INSURANCE MARKETS

The international insurance industry is divided into two segments: life insurance and nonlife insurance. In the U.S., the two segments are designated life/ health insurance and property-casualty insurance.

In 2003, the total insurance premium for all insurance worldwide was $2.94 trillion, an 11.8 percent increase over 2002's $2.63 trillion. A Swiss Re *sigma* study, "World Insurance in 2003,"[2] examined the insurance markets of 152 countries, making explicit reference to 88 countries in the survey of world insurance premiums, an increase from 69 in 1994. To be included in the survey, a country must have had reliable data and direct premiums of over $100 million from 1994 to 1998, over $150 million from 1999 to 2002, and at least $200 million in 2003.

In 2003, nonlife insurance premiums rose 15 percent to $1.27 trillion, while life insurance premiums rose 9 percent to $1.67 trillion. Industrialized nations generated just under 90 percent of the premium volume, with emerging market countries accounting for approximately 10 percent of the world market.

The Players—Insurers

The U.S. insurance industry, like those almost everywhere else, began as a series of international business ventures. Following the pattern set by Lloyd's of London, insurers around the world first formed to provide coverage for ocean cargo and merchant shipping. This business resulted in the location of insurance centers in cities with major ports or on major rivers, such as Hartford, New York, San Francisco, and Shanghai.

Providing international insurance became a specialty. Although U.S.-based insurers responded to an increased demand for international coverage during World War II and during the subsequent rise in multinational corporations based in the U.S., relatively few insurers are heavily involved in insuring international operations, and only a few are multinationals in their own right.

Insurers have several reasons for not having expanded into international business for many years. The primary reason is that they have been preoccupied with their domestic insurance markets, focusing on the expanding domestic economies, the development of new products such as multiperil forms, and the demand for increasing liability coverage.

Additionally, few senior managers were aware of either the opportunities or the problems associated with international operations. The requisite international knowledge and experience were not widely available within the industry. Regulatory restrictions have made some of the most rapidly expanding and potentially most profitable markets difficult for many insurers to enter. The time and managerial resources necessary to enter international insurance markets have often been too high compared with the perceived rewards.

Global competition is now a factor in virtually every industry, and insurance is no exception. As governments continue to deregulate industries, as more countries turn to market-based economies, and as trade barriers continue to lower, global competition in all industries will continue to increase. International mergers and acquisitions, both by U.S. insurers abroad and by those entering the U.S. market, have increased significantly. Many insurers, agents, and brokers are finding that even the small companies they insure have at least incidental international loss exposures. Companies with international loss exposures are seeking coverage for their entire operations, both domestic and international. Many companies want a single source to address all their needs. The insurance industry must be prepared to handle the expanding international loss exposures of international business.

The Players—Insurance Brokers

Brokers face enormous demands for their services as the types of risks their business clients face increase and become more complex. This demand has resulted in the evolution of the broker's role into one of service provider for all risk-related issues. Many insurance brokers use sophisticated risk-modeling techniques in combination with market knowledge to develop complete

World Life and Nonlife Insurance Premiums, 1994–2003

(Direct premiums written, U.S. $ millions)

Year	Nonlife[1]	Life	Total
1994	$ 846,600	$1,121,186	$ 1,967,787
1995	906,781	1,236,627	2,143,408
1996	909,100	1,196,736	2,105,838
1997	896,873	1,231,798	2,128,671
1998	891,352	1,275,053	2,166,405
1999	912,749	1,424,203	2,336,952
2000	926,503	1,518,401	2,444,904
2001	969,945	1,445,776	2,415,720
2002	1,098,412	1,534,061	2,632,473
2003	1,268,157	1,672,514	2,940,671

1. Includes accident and health insurance.

Source: Swiss Re, *sigma*, various issues.

The World's Leading Insurance Countries, 2003

(Direct premiums written, U.S. $ billions)

Rank	Country	Nonlife Premiums[1]	Life Premiums	Total Premiums		
				Amount	Percent Change From Prior Year	Percent of Total World Premiums
1	U.S.[2]	$574.6	$480.9	$1,055.5	4.9%	35.89%
2	Japan[3]	97.5	381.3	478.9	7.4	16.28
3	U.K.	91.9	154.8	246.7	4.2	8.39
4	Germany	94.1	76.7	170.8	25.8	5.81
5	France	58.2	105.4	163.7	30.8	5.57
6	Italy	40.1	71.7	111.8	33.0	3.80
7	South Korea	17.8	42.0	59.8	5.4	2.03
8	Canada[4]	36.3	22.8	59.1	22.1	2.01
9	Netherlands[5]	24.9	25.4	50.3	26.4	1.71
10	Spain	27.0	20.0	47.0	3.5	1.60

1. Includes accident and health insurance.
2. Nonlife premiums include state funds; life premiums include an estimate of group pension business.
3. April 1, 2003–March 31, 2004.
4. Life business is expressed in net premiums.
5. Nonlife premiums are gross premiums, including a small amount of reinsurance premiums.

Source: Swiss Re, *sigma*, No. 3, 2004.

risk-management programs for their clients. Insurance brokers also have expanded the services they provide to clients to include such things as actuarial consulting, asset management, claim administration, employee benefits, human resources consulting, and risk management.

Throughout the 1990s, the insurance broker business went through a period of consolidation in the U.S. and Europe, resulting in a highly concentrated market. In 2002, global commercial brokerage revenues were estimated at approximately $27 billion, more than half of which was consolidated within the two largest brokerage firms, Marsh & McLennan and Aon Corporation.

However, the broker sector remains fragmented. Outside the major consolidation at the top, the insurance brokerage business has many small niche firms. Today, further consolidation is starting to occur among both medium-size brokers and regional brokers. An attempt to fuel revenue growth and expansion into additional markets is driving this second round of consolidations.

The development and usage of insurance brokers vary widely by country and region. Brokers play an important role in the U.S. and U.K., and their use is increasing within the European Union. Additionally, brokerage firms have strong positions in Latin America and Southeast Asia but are virtually nonexistent in the Asian markets of Japan, South Korea, China, and India. With the liberalization of these markets and the growth of the emerging markets, brokers providing insurance products to their clients should see new growth opportunities around the world.

FINANCIAL CONSIDERATIONS IN INTERNATIONAL INSURANCE

An important reason, if not the most important reason, for an organization to enter the international market is to generate revenue. Possible financial risks and opportunities are, logically, of concern. Financial considerations in the international insurance market include the following:

- Currency and foreign exchange markets
- Expropriation
- Accounting issues
- Taxation issues

Currency and Foreign Exchange Markets

A business operating in the international market must consider both currency and foreign exchange markets because sales, profits, or investment can increase or decrease in value based merely on the change in the value of the other country's currency.

A currency is a unit of exchange, facilitating the transfer of a good or service between individuals, companies, countries, or a combination of these entities.

A country or region has a specific currency that is the dominant medium of exchange for goods and services. Exchange rates are prices at which currencies, goods, and services can be exchanged for each other, and they facilitate trade between countries.

Almost every country has a single currency. Some countries share the same name for their currencies. For example, Canada, Hong Kong and the U.S. all name their currencies "the dollar." Some countries share the same currency (such as the Euro), and some countries declare the currency of another country to be legal tender. For example, Panama and El Salvador have declared U.S. currency to be their legal currency. If the value of the currency is **pegged currency**, the government in question maintains its value at a fixed rate relative to the other currency. For example, the Hong Kong dollar (HK) is pegged to the U.S. dollar at an 8:1 ratio, meaning that $8 HK is equal to $1 U.S.

Pegged currency
A currency based on the fixed exchange rate of another country's currency.

The exchange rate (foreign exchange rate or FX rate) between two currencies shows how much one currency is worth in terms of the other. For example, an exchange rate of 120 Japanese yen to the U.S. dollar means that ¥120 is worth the same as $1. If a country's currency is appreciating, it becomes more valuable, and the exchange rate increases. Conversely, if the country's currency is weakening, the exchange rate decreases.

If a country's currency is allowed to float freely, its exchange rate against other countries varies, and it changes constantly within the financial markets around the world. A currency tends to become more valuable whenever demand for it is greater than the available supply and less valuable whenever demand is less than available supply.

An increase in demand for a specific currency results from either an increase in transaction demands for currency or an increase in speculative demand for the currency. The transaction demand for money is highly correlated to the country's level of business activity, gross domestic product (GDP), and employment levels. The greater the number of people who are unemployed, the less the public as a whole spends on goods and services.

Central banks typically have little difficulty adjusting the available money supply to accommodate changes in the demand for a currency resulting from business transactions. Speculative demand for money is much harder for central banks to accommodate. However, central banks try to accommodate this demand by adjusting domestic interest rates, thus allowing an investor to choose to buy a currency if the interest rate generates a high enough return for the investment. The higher a country's interest rates, the greater the demand for that currency.

When a corporation is involved in international business, it must be concerned that its international assets will retain their value in the future. A company does not want investments or income that will devalue in the future. A currency tends to lose value, relative to other currencies, if that country's inflation level is relatively high, if the country's level of output is expected to decline, or if a country is troubled by political uncertainty. In the foreign exchange markets, rate fluctuations usually are linked to the world economy or significant events in a specific national economy.

Expropriation

Expropriation
A government's lawful acquisition of property without the owner's consent.

When dealing in another country, a business must be aware of the possibility that the government will expropriate its assets. **Expropriation**, in its legal sense, means a government's lawful acquisition of property without the owner's consent. The government acquires property rights and the owner loses them. The term usually refers to a government's takeover of private property, often without fair compensation, but usually with a legal assertion that the government has a right to do so.

The power of eminent domain is a government's power to confiscate private property for public use. Most governments use eminent domain when they require property for the completion of a public project such as a road, and the owner of the property is unwilling to negotiate a price for its sale.

The exercise of eminent domain is not limited to real estate but can also involve personal property. Governments can also condemn the value in a contract, such as a franchise agreement. For this reason, many franchise agreements stipulate that, in condemnation proceedings, the franchise itself has no value. Owners' rights vary by country. The U.S. Constitution requires payment of just compensation upon use of eminent domain. In France, the Declaration of the Rights of Man and of the Citizen mandates giving just and preliminary compensation to the property owner.

Accounting Issues

A demand for and supply of capital transcending national boundaries often drive international business transactions in today's capital markets. High-quality accounting standards are a necessary element of a sound capital-market system. Companies use different forms of accounting to determine their financial situations. However, with the increase in cross-border capital-raising and investment transactions comes an increasing demand for a set of high-quality international accounting standards that companies could use as a basis for financial reporting worldwide. In the U.S, for example, domestic firms that are registered with the Securities and Exchange Commission (SEC) must file financial reports using U.S. generally accepted accounting principles (GAAP). Foreign firms filing with the SEC can use U.S. GAAP, their home country GAAP, or international standards. However, if they use their home country GAAP or international standards, foreign companies must provide a reconciliation to U.S. GAAP.

The Financial Accounting Standards Board (FASB) is the designated organization in the private sector for establishing standards of financial accounting and reporting in the U.S. Those standards govern the preparation of financial reports, and the SEC and the American Institute of Certified

Public Accountants (AICPA) officially recognize them as authoritative. Such standards are essential to the economy's efficient functioning because investors, creditors, auditors, and others rely on credible, transparent, and comparable financial information.

The London-based International Accounting Standards Board (IASB), organized in 2001, is developing a single set of high-quality global accounting standards that require transparent and comparable information in general-purpose financial statements. The IASB receives funding from the major accounting firms, private financial institutions, industrial companies, central and development banks, and other international and professional organizations throughout the world.

In 2002, the FASB and the IASB issued the Norwalk Agreement, a memorandum of understanding that marked a significant step toward formalizing their commitments to the convergence of U.S. and international accounting standards. Work continues on the project. As of 2005, the EU required that all EU-listed public companies prepare their consolidated financial statements using IASB Standards.

Taxation Issues

Corporations involved in international business must deal with issues of taxation in their home country jurisdictions as well as in the foreign country in which they conduct business or invest.

In today's business environment, many countries seek to attract investment by offering a "tax holiday," ranging from a partial to a total exemption from corporate income tax to an exemption for a number of years. At the end of the tax exemption period, a normal corporate tax rate applies to the corporate earnings of the investment. Some countries have placed conditions on tax holidays, requiring that the corporation agree not to close down operation at the expiration of the tax holiday. Countries impose this requirement because many corporations have discovered that it is profitable, at expiration of the tax holiday, to close operations and relocate to a different country, often a country offering another tax holiday.

Countries use different approaches, including the following, to tax corporations' earnings in the context of international commerce:

- **Territorial tax systems** tax all companies only on the economic activity that occurs within the country's geographic boundaries, regardless of the location of the company's incorporation or operations. For example, Ireland does not tax an Irish company on profits earned through sales in the U.S. However, both U.S. and Irish firms pay taxes on profits they earn through the sale of products in Ireland.

- A **worldwide tax system** taxes domestically incorporated companies on their total earnings from both domestic and international activities. Foreign companies are taxed on their economic activity within the

Territorial tax system
A revenue collection scheme that taxes all companies only on the economic activity that occurs within the country's geographic boundaries, regardless of the location of the company's incorporation or operations.

Worldwide tax system
A revenue collection scheme that taxes domestically incorporated companies on their total earnings from both domestic and international activities.

country's geographic boundaries. For example, a U.S. company pays taxes on profits earned through its sales in the U.S. and in Ireland. An Irish company pays taxes in the U.S. on profits it earns only on sales in the U.S.

Border tax adjustment (BTA)
Tax rebates on exported goods and taxes on imported goods, used by a government to establish a "tax-neutral" setting for international trade and investment.

- **Border tax adjustments (BTAs)**, rebates on exports and taxes on imports, are instruments governments use to establish a "tax-neutral" setting for international trade and investment. The General Agreement on Tariffs and Trade (GATT), which defines the scope of international BTAs, recognizes only consumption taxes (taxes applying directly to goods and services) as eligible for BTAs. A Value Added Tax (VAT) is BTA-eligible, but corporate income taxes are not.

Earnings stripping
A process by which a company reduces its overall tax liability by moving earnings from one taxing jurisdiction, typically a high-tax jurisdiction, to another jurisdiction, typically a low-tax jurisdiction.

- Corporations can use several processes to reduce their tax liability relating to international commerce. **Earnings stripping** is a process by which a company reduces its overall tax liability by moving earnings from one taxing jurisdiction, typically a high-tax jurisdiction, to another jurisdiction, typically a low-tax jurisdiction. Earnings stripping arrangements usually involve the extension of debt from one corporate affiliate to another. The debt accumulates within the corporation's high-tax jurisdiction, which allows it to deduct interest payments from its taxable income in the high-tax country.

Inversion, or **expatriation,** or **reincorporation**
The process by which a corporate entity established in a low-tax country purchases the shares and/or assets of a domestic corporation.

- **Inversion**, or **expatriation**, or **reincorporation** is the process by which a corporate entity established in a low-tax country purchases the shares and/or assets of a domestic corporation. The domestic company's share-holders typically become the new foreign parent company's shareholders. This process allows the domestic company to change its legal location and become a foreign-based corporation. An inversion typically does not change the company's operational structure or physical location; however, it does change the parent company's tax structure. A corporation may accomplish an inversion by setting up a foreign company and then reverse-engineering a merger to move the company's legal location. Large companies calculate each of their divisions' profits and losses separately.

Transfer price
The price one part of a company charges for products and services it provides to another part of the same company.

The **transfer price** is the price one part of a company charges for products and services it provides to another part of the same company. Under tax laws, companies are required to charge another affiliate or division the same price it would demand in an "arm's-length transaction," that is, a transaction between two unrelated entities. Different countries have different transfer pricing laws, a subject of concern for all who do international business. Many experts believe transfer pricing is the most important international tax issue facing MNCs. Most countries impose strict transfer pricing rules on international transactions. Noncompliance can lead to pricing adjustments and large penalties.

Tax haven
A country whose regulations offer financial and business incentives encouraging organizations from other countries to do business there.

In many countries, regulation imposes high costs on domestic businesses. Consequently, many companies seek **tax havens**, or countries whose regulations offer businesses financial advantages. To move a business or division of a corporation offshore to operate in a pro-business climate usually requires nothing more than forming an offshore corporation in a tax haven country and transferring assets from the domestic corporation.

One of the reasons companies "go offshore" is to reduce corporate taxes. Many tax havens impose few or no taxes on foreign companies and have strict privacy laws. Corporations' decisions about tax havens are based on the advantages for the particular international investment project. A business should consider the following when establishing a subsidiary in an offshore tax haven:

- The country's tax structure
- The country's level of enforcement of its privacy laws
- The country's language
- The type of judicial system the country has
- The country's political stability
- The country's independence from the parent company's home country
- The costs of establishing the new subsidiary in the country

Tax havens are typically countries that have no taxes of any kind, whether personal or corporate income tax, capital gains tax, foreign investment tax, withholding tax, estate tax, sales tax, value added tax, and so forth. They have no financial reporting requirements. Generally, a tax haven requires a yearly registration fee of under $500. Some examples of well-known tax havens are Antigua, the Bahamas, Belize, the British Virgin Islands, the Isle of Man, Luxembourg, Nevis and St. Kitts, and the Turks and Caicos.

To understand the precise role of tax havens, it is important to distinguish between two types of income: return on labor and return on capital.

Income from labor derives from work: salary, wages, fees for professional services, and the like. Income from return on capital is the return on an investment: dividends on shares of stock; interest on bank deposits, loans and bonds; rental income; royalties on patents. Most corporations seek to use tax haven benefits for income derived from the return on capital and income from an investment portfolio. When a corporation forms a subsidiary or a trust in a tax haven, return on capital can be almost tax free, or at least taxed at a very low rate.

A tax haven country may have one of the following four types of corporate tax structures:

1. *Low or minimum taxes.* Some tax haven countries impose low or minimal taxes on all corporate income, wherever earned. Many countries with this system have double-taxation agreements with the high-tax countries that might help reduce the withholding tax imposed on income derived from the high-tax countries by local corporations. Double taxation arises because of competing claims of tax authorities of a home corporation's home country and the country of the source of income. Generally, the income source country gives way to the home country, with exceptions.

Both the British Virgin Islands (BVI) and Cyprus are examples of low-tax haven countries. However, BVI no longer has a tax treaty with the U.S.

2. *No corporate taxes.* Some tax haven countries have no income, capital gains, or wealth (capital) taxes. They allow companies to incorporate and/or form trusts. These countries primarily charge small fees when a corporation files incorporation documents, on issuing of shares, and on annual registration fees. Any income these governments derive from corporations is not related to corporate income. No-tax haven countries include the Bahamas, Bermuda, and the Cayman Islands.

3. *No taxes on foreign income.* Some tax haven countries impose income taxes, both on individuals and corporations, but only on locally derived income. These countries exempt from tax any income earned from foreign sources that involve no local business activities. Often, these countries do not tax income derived from the export of locally manufactured products. The countries that have no tax on foreign income fall into two different groups:

    *   Countries that allow a corporation to do business both internally and externally but that tax only the income derived from internal sources

    *   Countries that tax a corporation for income derived from local business but do not tax income derived from external business. Some companies would conduct only foreign business and thus be exempt from taxation.

    Countries applying both these types of no tax on foreign income include Gibraltar, Guernsey, Isle of Man, Jersey, Liberia, and Panama.

4. *Special tax concessions.* Some tax haven countries impose all or most of the usual taxes, but either provide concessions to special types of companies or permit some special corporate structure allowing for lower taxes. Some special tax haven countries give tax exemptions on shipping or to movie production companies, for example. Examples of special tax haven countries are the Netherlands and Austria.

Tax haven countries also offer corporations some advantages relating to privacy of stock information. These tax haven countries allow for the issuance of **bearer shares**, stocks that are owned by the holder, the one who has possession of the share certificate. No one but the bearer of the shares knows who owns stock in the corporation. The ownership remains private, and shares can be bought, sold, or exchanged in complete privacy. In contrast, most jurisdictions (such as the U.S., Canada, and Great Britain), require shares to be registered with a government agency. With **registered shares**, the government and other parties know who owns a corporation's shares and the selling and buying prices for the shares.

For example, International Business Corporation (IBC) is incorporated in a tax haven and authorized to do business anywhere in the world except in that country. Just like U.S. corporations, the same person can act as a stockholder,

Bearer share
A corporate share that is owned by the holder of the share certificate and is not registered; therefore, ownership remains private.

Registered share
A corporate share on which records are kept indicating the share's owner and its selling and buying price.

a member of the board of directors, the president, an agent, or any other officer within the company.

Another privacy advantage that tax havens offer to corporations results from their laws forbidding financial institutions, such as banks, brokerages, and insurance companies, and advisers, such as brokers, accountants, attorneys, and investment advisers, from divulging information about clients or accounts to any third party. These privacy laws apply to all third parties, including individuals, companies, and governments.

U.S. LAW

The most significant U.S. federal legislation influencing international business and foreign investment are the tax code (Internal Revenue Code), the Foreign Corrupt Practices Act, and the U.S. Patriot Act. Each of these laws affects an organization's earnings and practices in relation to international trade and business.

Tax Code

Within the U.S. tax code (Internal Revenue Code, or IRC),[3] a number of sections specifically address international business and foreign investment. These sections can either help or hinder international investment and trade. For example, the current IRC allows a U.S. company to claim a credit against its U.S. taxes for taxes paid in other countries. These credits help avoid the double taxation of earnings that arise from the U.S.'s worldwide tax system. Foreign tax credits are limited to the U.S. corporate tax rate. The U.S. federal corporate income tax code contains six marginal rates ranging from 15 to 39 percent. The majority of corporate income is taxable at a 35 percent marginal tax rate. The marginal tax rate refers to the highest published tax rate at which a taxpayer's last dollar earned is taxable. With a corporate tax rate at this level in the U.S., many companies form subsidiaries in tax haven jurisdictions and even move their incorporation to another country.

Currently, U.S. companies must divide their foreign earnings into nine categories, or "baskets," and a company cannot use any credit it earns in one basket to offset earnings in another basket. Additionally, IRC Section 163(j) places a number of restrictions on a company's use of earnings-stripping techniques.

Repatriation of earnings is the process by which a U.S. parent company moves earnings from its foreign-based affiliates back to the U.S. to the parent company or to its stockholders. In the U.S., the Internal Revenue Service (IRS) levies corporate income tax at the time earnings are repatriated. IRC Subpart F codifies the federal government's system of "anti-deferral" rules, which lead to the taxation of certain kinds of foreign-source income in the year the company earned it, even though the U.S. parent company did not repatriate those profits during the year.

Repatriation of earnings
The process by which a U.S. parent company moves earnings from its foreign-based affiliates back to the U.S. to the parent company or to its stockholders.

Foreign sales corporation (FSC)
An organization that U.S. law permits export-intensive corporations to create in order to reap tax benefits from exports.

Since the early 1960s, the U.S. has maintained a series of export-related tax benefits for export-intensive corporations called **foreign sales corporations (FSC)**. Under IRC Section 922(a), an FSC is defined as a corporation that has met all of the following rules:

- It must be a corporation created or organized under the laws of a qualifying foreign country or any U.S. possession other than Puerto Rico.

- A qualifying foreign country is a foreign country that meets the IRC's exchange of information rules.

- It had no more that twenty-five shareholders at any time during the tax year.

- It had no preferred stock outstanding at any time during the tax year.

During the tax year the FSC must do the following:

- Maintain an office in one of the qualifying foreign countries or U.S. possessions listed in the section

- Maintain a set of permanent books of account (including invoices) at that office to sufficiently establish the amount of gross income, deductions, credits, or other matters required to be shown on its tax return

- Have at least one director, at all times during the tax year, who is not a resident of the U.S.

- Have elected to be an FSC, and the election must have been in effect for the tax year

While designed to spur U.S. exports, these provisions appeared to be a way of leveling the playing field with countries that use "border tax adjustments" by removing the cost of Value Added Tax (VAT) from the price of the exported products before shipping them abroad. In 1997, the EU challenged the legality of U.S. FSC rules before the WTO. A WTO panel eventually agreed with the EU and struck down the FSC arrangement, which the U.S. replaced with the **Extraterritorial Income (ETI)** arrangement in 2000.

Extraterritorial Income (ETI)
A mechanism to subsidize U.S. exporters unable to take advantage of border tax adjustments because the U.S. has an income tax rather than consumption tax like Europe's value-added tax (VAT).

ETI was a mechanism to subsidize U.S. exporters unable to take advantage of border tax adjustments because the U.S. has an income tax rather than consumption tax like Europe's value-added tax (VAT). In 2002, a WTO Appellate Body ruled that the ETI was also prohibited and later ruled that if the U.S. does not comply with the decision, the EU could impose more than $4 billion worth of sanctions on U.S. exports, a matter continuing in dispute in the ensuing years.

Foreign Corrupt Practices Act

U.S. companies, including insurers, planning to do business in foreign markets must be familiar with the Foreign Corrupt Practices Act (FCPA).[4] In general, the FCPA prohibits payments to foreign officials to obtain or keep business.

Passage of the FCPA was a result of an SEC investigation in the mid-1970s in which more than 400 U.S. companies admitted making questionable or illegal payments in excess of $300 million to foreign government officials, politicians, and political parties to secure or maintain business. The payments ranged from bribery of high-ranking officials to secure a favorable action by a foreign government to facilitating payments to make sure that basic government ministerial or clerical duties were completed. Congress enacted the FCPA to stop these acts and to restore public confidence in the integrity of the U.S. business system.

The FCPA also requires companies who list their securities in the U.S. to meet certain accounting provisions. These accounting provisions operate in tandem with the anti-bribery provisions, requiring a company to keep accounting records that accurately reflect all the company's transactions and to maintain an adequate system of internal accounting controls.

The FCPA has had an enormous effect on how U.S. companies conduct international business. Several companies that paid bribes to foreign officials have been the subject of criminal and civil enforcement actions, resulting in large fines and suspensions and debarment from federal procurement contracting. Additionally, some of these companies' employees and officers have gone to prison.

Following the passage of the FCPA, Congress became aware that U.S. companies were operating at a strategic disadvantage to foreign companies that routinely paid bribes and that, in some countries, could even deduct the cost of these bribes as business expenses from their taxes. In 1988, Congress directed the Executive Branch to start negotiations in the Organization of Economic Cooperation and Development (OECD) to obtain agreements with the U.S.'s major trading partners to enact legislation similar to the FCPA. In 1997, the U.S. and thirty-three other countries signed the OECD Convention on Combating Bribery of Foreign Public Officials in International Business Transactions. Since 1998, the U.S. has also applied FCPA to foreign companies and individuals who perform any act to further a corrupt payment while in the U.S.

The U.S. Department of Justice is responsible for all criminal and civil enforcement of anti-bribery provisions regarding domestic and foreign companies and nationals. The SEC is responsible for civil enforcement of the anti-bribery provisions regarding issuers.

Any person or company violating the FCPA can be barred from doing business with the federal government, and an indictment alone can lead to suspension of the right to do business with the government. Furthermore, any conduct that violates the anti-bribery provisions of the FCPA also can create a private cause of action under the Racketeer Influenced and Corrupt Organizations Act (RICO Act) or under other federal or state laws.

The Patriot Act

Congress enacted The Patriot Act of 2001[5] as a reaction to the terrorist attacks on the World Trade Center in New York City and the Pentagon in Washington, D.C., on September 11, 2001. The law's stated purpose is "to deter and punish terrorist acts in the United States and around the world, to enhance law enforcement investigatory tools, and for other purposes." The Patriot Act increases the surveillance and investigative powers of U.S. law enforcement agencies in several far-reaching ways, in addition to changing the following U.S. laws:

- Wiretap Statute (Title III)
- Electronic Communications Privacy Act
- Computer Fraud and Abuse Act
- Foreign Intelligence Surveillance Act (FISA)
- Family Education Rights and Privacy Act
- Pen Register and Trap and Trace Statutes
- Money Laundering Act
- Immigration and Nationality Act
- Money Laundering Control Act
- Bank Secrecy Act
- Right to Financial Privacy Act
- Fair Credit Reporting Act

The Patriot Act's implications for online privacy are considerable. It extends the government's ability to gain access to personal financial information and student information without any suspicion of wrongdoing, simply by certifying that the information likely to be obtained is relevant to an ongoing criminal investigation. Additionally, several sections of the law apply directly to business, including those that track and invest internationally including the following:

- Section 209 enables law enforcement to seize voice-mail messages via a search warrant, instead of a Title III wiretap order. This section overturns case law that requires the government to apply for a Title III warrant before it can obtain unopened voice-mail messages (but not e-mail messages) held by a service provider.

- Section 215 revises the Foreign Intelligence Surveillance Act (FISA) provisions governing access to business records for foreign intelligence and international terrorism investigations. The Patriot Act broadens the FBI's ability to obtain business records pursuant to a court order. Previously, section 501 of FISA (50 U.S.C. section 1862) had subjected only common carriers, public accommodation facilities, physical storage facilities, and car rental facilities to FISA business record authority. The Patriot Act eliminates these categories and allows the FBI to issue subpoenas to any person, including Internet service providers, banks, and any other business within the reach of business record authority.

- Subtitle B (Sections 351-366) amends the banking and finance laws to permit the government access to information from banks that might relate to terrorism. Section 351 gives the institutions and their directors, officers, employees, and agents protection from liability for reporting suspicious activities. The section also applies to securities brokers and dealers regulated by the Securities and Exchange Act of 1934 and consumer reporting agencies governed by the Fair Credit Reporting Act.

- Additionally, Section 351 allows the Secretary of the Treasury to impose sanctions, including cutting off all dealings with U.S. financial institutions or banks in foreign nations whose bank secrecy laws deny information to U.S. agencies. Foreign banks maintaining correspondent accounts in U.S. banks must designate someone in the U.S. to receive subpoenas related to those accounts and their depositors. If those subpoenas are not answered, the accounts can be ordered closed. This section also empowers the Treasury Secretary to require U.S. banks to exercise enhanced due diligence to find out who their private banking depositors are if they come from nations that will not assist U.S.

- Section 352 prohibits financial institutions from knowingly becoming involved in unlawful financial transactions with suspected terrorists and requires that companies establish and maintain written, anti-money-laundering programs that, at a minimum, do the following: (1) incorporate internal policies, procedures, and controls based on the company's assessment of its money-laundering risks; (2) designate a compliance officer; and (3) establish ongoing employee-training programs as well as independent audit functions to test programs.

- The act applies anti-money-laundering requirements to insurers offering products with investment features or features of stored value, such as annuities and life products. These rules exclude property-casualty insurers from specific sections of the law aimed at detecting terrorists' money-laundering schemes within financial institutions because property-casualty insurers do not establish, maintain, administer, or manage private bank accounts and do not keep premium for investment purposes for policyholders.

- Section 815 provides a new defense to civil or criminal liability under FCPA for service providers who preserve stored data at the request of a law enforcement official under 18 U.S.C. section 2703(f). This section specifically provides a defense to private lawsuits for unauthorized access to or disclosure of stored data under FCPA.

MULTINATIONAL ORGANIZATIONS AND AGREEMENTS

Several prominent international organizations and agreements affect practically all international business dealings. They also can influence the direction of world business developments.

United Nations (UN)

In 1944, representatives of China, the Soviet Union, the U.K., and the U.S. met to propose a new international organization, the United Nations (UN). They signed the UN Charter in 1945. Over the years, the number of UN member states has grown to 191 countries.

Under the UN Charter, the UN's purposes are as follows:

- To maintain international peace and security
- To develop friendly relations among nations
- To cooperate in solving international economic, social, cultural, and humanitarian problems
- To promote respect for human rights and fundamental freedoms
- To be a center for harmonizing the actions of nations in attaining these goals

The five principal UN bodies include the following:

1. General Assembly
2. Security Council
3. Economic and Social Council
4. International Court of Justice
5. Secretariat

The UN entity, however, is much larger than these five bodies, actually encompassing some fifteen agencies and several programs and bodies.

The General Assembly is the UN's deliberating body and comprises representatives of all the member states. Decisions on important questions, such as those involving peace and security, the admission of new members, and budgetary matters, require a two-thirds majority vote for passage, while a simple majority vote can decide other matters.

Under the UN Charter, the functions and powers of the General Assembly include the following:

- To consider and make recommendations on the principles of cooperation in the maintenance of international peace and security, including the principles governing disarmament and arms regulation
- To initiate studies and make recommendations to promote international political cooperation; the development and codification of international law; the realization of human rights and fundamental freedoms for all; and international collaboration in economic, social, cultural, educational and health fields
- To elect, jointly with the Security Council, the judges of the International Court of Justice
- On the recommendation of the Security Council, to appoint the secretary-general

The Security Council's primary responsibility is to maintain international peace and security. It functions continuously with representatives of each of its members present at all times at the UN Headquarters in New York City. When a complaint concerning a threat to peace comes before it, the Security Council's first action usually is to recommend to the conflicting parties that they try to reach agreement by peaceful means and then, in some cases, to investigate and mediate.

When a dispute leads to armed conflict, the Security Council's first concern is to end it as soon as possible. The Security Council also authorizes the UN to send peacekeeping forces to help reduce tensions in troubled areas, keep opposing forces apart, and create calmer conditions in which peaceful settlements might result. The Security Council also can decide on other enforcement measures, economic sanctions, or collective military action.

The UN General Assembly elects the Security Council's fifty-four member governments for overlapping three-year terms. These seats are allocated based on geographical representation, as follows:

- Fourteen to African countries
- Eleven to Asian countries
- Six to Eastern European countries
- Ten to Latin American and Caribbean countries
- Thirteen to Western European and other countries (including the U.S.)

The UN's Economic and Social Council (ECOSOC) is responsible for promoting higher standards of living, full employment, and economic and social progress through many other UN agencies. ECOSOC is also responsible for the following:

- Identifying solutions to international economic, social, and health problems
- Facilitating international cultural and educational cooperation
- Encouraging universal respect for human rights and fundamental freedoms

ECOSOC's responsibility extends to over 70 percent of the human and financial resources of the UN organization system. In carrying out its mandate, ECOSOC consults with academicians, business sector representatives, and more than 2,100 registered non-governmental organizations (NGOs).

The International Court of Justice (ICJ), located at the Peace Palace in The Hague (Netherlands), is the UN's principal judicial organ. The ICJ has the following dual role:

1. To settle, in accordance with international law, the legal disputes that countries submit to it
2. To give advisory opinions on legal questions that duly authorized international entities and agencies refer to it

The ICJ comprises fifteen judges elected to nine-year terms by the UN General Assembly and Security Council. The ICJ cannot include more than one judge of any nationality. Judicial elections take place every three years, for one-third of the seats, with rules allowing reelection of judges. ICJ judges do not represent their national governments but act as independent ICJ magistrates.

ICJ judges must have the qualifications required in their respective countries for appointment to the highest judicial offices or must be jurists of recognized competence in international law. The ICJ's composition also reflects the principal legal systems of the world. When the ICJ does not include a judge representing a country that is party to a case, that country can appoint a person to sit as an *ad hoc* judge only for that case.

The ICJ can hear disputes in one of the following ways when a concerned country has accepted jurisdiction:

- By the conclusion of a special agreement between parties to submit the dispute to the ICJ.
- By virtue of a jurisdictional clause, typically, when the countries in question are parties to a treaty.
- Through the reciprocal effects of declarations the countries have made under a law providing that each has accepted the jurisdiction of the ICJ as compulsory in the event of a dispute with another country that has made a similar declaration. More than sixty countries have such a declaration in force. However, a number of these declarations are subject to the exclusion of certain categories of dispute.

The Secretariat is the UN's international staff, working around the world to carry out the UN's daily operations. The General Assembly appoints the secretary general, who heads the Secretariat on the Security Council's recommendation for a renewable five-year term.

World Trade Organization (WTO)

The World Trade Organization (WTO) deals with trade rules among nations. The WTO's existence depends on agreements that most of the world's trading nations have negotiated and ratified. The WTO's goal is to help producers of goods and services, exporters, and importers conduct their business. The organization has nearly 150 members, accounting for over 97 percent of all world trade. Additionally, about 30 other nations are negotiating for membership. The entire membership makes the WTO's decisions, by consensus.

In 1997, WTO members agreed on telecommunications services, with 69 governments agreeing to wide-ranging liberalization measures. In the same year, 40 governments successfully concluded negotiations for tariff-free trade in information technology products, and 70 governments concluded a financial services deal covering more than 95 percent of trade in banking, insurance, securities, and financial information. In 2000, WTO members started discussion of agriculture and services.

WTO members operate a non-discriminatory trading system. Each country receives guarantees that its exports will receive fair and consistent treatment in other countries' markets, and each country promises to do the same for imports into its own market. The WTO system gives developing countries some flexibility in implementing their commitments. Over three-quarters of the WTO member states are developing, or less developed, countries. These countries have longer time periods to implement agreements and commitments, opportunities to increase trade, and support to help them build an infrastructure for WTO work, handling disputes, and implementing technical standards.

In the WTO, no board of directors or WTO executive has power to run the organization. WTO members negotiated among themselves to impose discipline on member countries. Members enforce all decisions and rules under agreed procedures that they themselves have negotiated, including the possibility of trade sanctions. Sanctions imposed are authorized by the membership as a whole. In this respect, the WTO is different from some other international organizations, such as the World Bank and International Monetary Fund (IMF), which have bureaucratic structures in place to enforce actions.

Reaching decisions by consensus among approximately 150 WTO members can be difficult. However, the primary advantage of consensus is that such decisions are more acceptable to all members.

WTO agreements are the legal groundrules for most international commerce. They guarantee member countries important trading rights. The three primary WTO agreements include the following:

1. The General Agreement on Tariffs and Trade (GATT)
2. The General Agreement on Trade in Services (GATS)
3. The Agreement on Trade-related Aspects of Intellectual Property Rights (TRIPS Agreement)

The General Agreement on Tariffs and Trade (GATT) began with trade in goods. From 1947 to 1994, GATT was the basis for negotiating lower customs duty rates and other trade barriers. Since 1995, the updated version of GATT has become the WTO's umbrella agreement for trade in all goods. It has annexed dealings with specific sectors, such as agriculture and textiles. It has also annexed dealings with specific issues, such as state trading, product standards, subsidies, and actions taken against **dumping**, the act of selling a large quantity of goods at less than fair value, including selling goods abroad at less than the market price at home. The implementation of the GATT agreement is the responsibility of the Council for Trade in Goods (Goods Council) which comprises representatives from all WTO member countries. The Goods Council has eleven committees dealing with specific subjects, such as agriculture, market access, subsidies, and anti-dumping measures. These committees

Dumping
The act of selling a large quantity of goods at less than fair value, including selling goods abroad at less than the market price at home.

consist of all member countries, and the Goods Council receives all reports from the Textiles Monitoring Body, the working party on state trading enterprises, and the Information Technology Agreement (ITA) Committee.

The General Agreement on Trade in Services (GATS) sets forth the principles that allow banks, insurance firms, telecommunications companies, tour operators, hotel chains, and transport companies wanting do business abroad to enjoy the same principles of free and fair trade that originally applied to trade in goods. WTO members have also made individual commitments under GATS, stating which of their services sectors they are willing to open to foreign competition and how open those markets will become.

The Agreement on Trade-related Aspects of Intellectual Property Rights (TRIPS), the WTO's intellectual property agreement, sets forth rules for trade and investment in ideas and creative work. TRIPS states how all intellectual property, including the following, should be protected in international business and trade:

- Copyrights
- Patents
- Trademarks
- Geographical names used to identify products
- Industrial designs
- Integrated circuit layout designs
- Undisclosed information, such as trade secrets

North American Free Trade Agreement (NAFTA)

The North American Free Trade Agreement (NAFTA) is a comprehensive regional trade and investment agreement that Canada, Mexico, and the U.S. entered into in 1994 to improve all aspects of doing business in the North American market.

The objectives of this Agreement, as elaborated more specifically through its principles and rules, including national treatment, most-favored-nation treatment and transparency, are to do the following:

- Eliminate barriers to trade in, and facilitate the cross-border movement of, goods and services between the territories of the parties
- Promote conditions of fair competition in the free trade area
- Substantially increase investment opportunities in the territories of the parties
- Provide adequate and effective protection and enforcement of intellectual property rights in each party's territory
- Create effective procedures for the implementation and application of the agreement, for its joint administration, and for the resolution of disputes
- Establish a framework for further trilateral, regional, and multilateral cooperation to expand and enhance the benefits of this agreement

NAFTA eliminated nearly all tariffs between the U.S. and Canada by 1998 and is to eliminate nearly all tariffs between the U.S. and Mexico by 2008.

NAFTA also removes many of the non-tariff barriers, such as import licenses, that have helped to exclude U.S. goods from the other two markets, particularly Mexico. NAFTA ensures that restrictive government policies will not coerce investment and that U.S. investors receive treatment equal to domestic investors in Mexico and Canada. At the same time, NAFTA's extensive easing of cross-border services rules ensures that U.S. companies need not invest in another country to provide their services if they do not wish to do so.

NAFTA establishes a mechanism for settling disputes between NAFTA countries over the interpretation and application of the agreement. It also contains separate dispute resolution mechanisms for antidumping and countervailing duty matters, as well as for specific sectors, such as investment and financial services.

For a U.S. product to be eligible for lower tariff rates when entering Mexico or Canada, the product must be produced in the U.S. entirely of NAFTA component parts; or, if the product consists of foreign component parts, a substantive transformation from the foreign component part to the final product must have occurred. Since NAFTA, trade among the three countries has increased more than 200 percent.

European Union (EU)

The European Union (EU) is a group of European democratic countries committed to working together for peace and prosperity. The EU is unique in that each member state delegated some of its national sovereignty so that decisions could be made on specific matters of joint interest democratically. This EU pooling of sovereignty is called "European integration."

The Treaty of Maastricht (1992) introduced new forms of cooperation between the EU member state governments; for example, on defense and in the area of "justice and home affairs." By adding this intergovernmental cooperation to the original "European Community" system, the Treaty of Maastricht created the European Union (EU). All EU decisions and procedures are based on EU treaties, to which all member countries agree.

In the early years, much of the cooperation among EU countries centered on trade and the economy, but now the EU also deals with other issues, such as citizens' rights; ensuring freedom, security and justice; job creation; regional development; and environmental protection.

The following five EU institutions play specific roles:

1. The European Parliament, elected by the people of the member states
2. The Council of the European Union, representing the governments of the member states
3. The European Commission, the executive body

4. The Court of Justice, the judicial body
5. The Court of Auditors, which manages the EU budget

These institutions are flanked by the following five other important EU bodies:

1. The European Economic and Social Committee, which makes recommendations relating to economic and social issues
2. The Committee of the Regions, which represents regional and local authorities
3. The European Central Bank, responsible for monetary policy and managing the common EU currency, the Euro
4. The European Ombudsman, who deals with citizens' complaints about administration by any EU institution or body
5. The European Investment Bank, which finances EU investment projects

Common Market
The European Union's member countries' single, unified market in which goods, services, people, and capital can move freely across borders.

The member states over time removed all barriers to trade among them and turned their **Common Market** into a genuine single market in which goods, services, people, and capital could move freely across borders. The single market was formally completed at the end of 1992, though the EU countries still have more to accomplish to complete the Common Market, such as creation of a genuinely single market in financial services.

Euro
A single European currency managed by the European Central Bank.

Additionally, in 1992, the EU decided to go forward with an economic and monetary union (EMU), involving the introduction of a single European currency, the **euro**, managed by the European Central Bank. The euro became a reality in 2002, when euro notes and coins replaced national currencies in twelve of the fifteen countries of the European Union (then Belgium, Germany, Greece, Spain, France, Ireland, Italy, Luxembourg, the Netherlands, Austria, Portugal, and Finland).

Association of Southeast Asian Nations (ASEAN) and ASEAN Free Trade Area (AFTA)

Five member states (Indonesia, Malaysia, Philippines, Singapore, and Thailand) established the Association of Southeast Asian Nations (ASEAN) in 1967. Later, Brunei Darussalam, Vietnam, Laos, Myanmar, and Cambodia joined ASEAN.

ASEAN's purposes are twofold, as follows:

1. Accelerating the economic growth, social progress, and cultural development in the region through joint endeavors in the spirit of equality and partnership to strengthen the foundation for a prosperous and peaceful community of Southeast Asian nations
2. Promoting regional peace and stability through respect for justice and the rule of law in the relationship among countries in the region and adherence to the principles of the United Nations Charter

ASEAN members have made significant progress in lowering intraregional tariffs through the Common Effective Preferential Tariff (CEPT) Scheme of the ASEAN Free Trade Area (AFTA) agreement.

The ASEAN region has a population of approximately 500 million, a total area of 4.5 million square kilometers, a combined gross domestic product of $737 billion, and a total annual trade of $720 billion.

Asia-Pacific Economic Cooperation (APEC)

Asia-Pacific Economic Cooperation (APEC) began in 1989 as a loose organization of countries set around the Pacific Ocean. APEC has attempted to facilitate economic growth, cooperation, trade, and investment in the Asia-Pacific region. Since its inception, APEC has worked to reduce tariffs and other trade barriers across the Asia-Pacific region, creating efficient economies and increasing exports. The key to achieving APEC's vision is what is referred to as the Bogor Goals (adopted in Bogor, Indonesia, in 1994), which call for free and open trade and investment. Member countries aim to achieve these goals by 2010, with developing country members achieving these goals by 2020.

APEC is the only inter-governmental body that operates on the basis of non-binding commitments, open dialogue, and equal respect for the views of all participant countries. Unlike the WTO or other multilateral trade bodies, APEC has required no treaty obligations of its participants. APEC members reach all decisions by consensus and undertake commitments totally on a voluntary basis.

APEC has twenty-one member states, including, among others: Australia, Canada, Japan, the U.S., the People's Republic of China, Hong Kong, and Mexico. APEC's member states account for more than one-third of the world's total population (2.6 billion), approximately 60 percent of the world's GDP (with the U.S.'s $19.254 trillion), and approximately 47 percent of all the world's trade. The APEC member states also represent the most economically dynamic region in the world, having generated nearly 70 percent of the global economic growth in its first 10 years.

SUMMARY

Organizations involved in international business before World War I numbered a few thousand. Following World War II, the U.S. industrial base spurred international growth as businesses sought raw materials and new markets for products, and some businesses, predominantly in the U.S., began forming multinational corporations (MNCs). By the mid-1960s, MNCs were forming in Europe and Japan. After the 1980s, MNCs evolved into truly global companies with their foreign revenue exceeding their domestic revenue.

A country involved in international trade may have (a) an absolute advantage, created when a country specializes in goods or services more efficiently and trades them for the goods and services it produces less efficiently, or (b) a comparative advantage, created when trading partners gain from trading with each other. A company, based on the advantages it seeks, can participate in international business in the following three ways:

1. Foreign trade
2. Foreign contractual relationships
3. Foreign direct investments

Any organization conducting international business must weigh potential challenges and barriers of such ventures according to the types of transactions the organization requires. These challenges and barriers include language, culture, time, distance and space, and types of government.

Countries share legal approaches and concepts, which can be grouped into predominant families of law. In general, countries adopt legal systems that are either civil-law systems, which include Roman-French law, German law, and Scandinavian law; or common-law systems, which include Far Eastern law, Hindu law, Islamic law, and Social Communist law. In general, common-law countries give investors greater legal rights than civil-law countries.

International law comprises public international law, which governs the interaction of nation states; and private international law, which governs disputes between individuals or corporations in different countries. Together these form the body of legal principles that an MNC operates within.

International insurance segments include life/health insurance and property-casualty insurance in the U.S. and the life insurance and non-life insurance segments outside the U.S. The primary players in the international insurance markets include insurance companies and brokers.

An organization enters the international market to generate revenue, but faces corresponding financial risks relating to the following aspects of international business:

1. Currency and foreign exchange markets
2. Expropriation
3. Accounting issues
4. Taxation issues

The most significant areas of U.S. law influencing international business and foreign investments include the tax code (Internal Revenue Code), which governs repatriation of earnings, foreign sales corporations, and extraterritorial income; and the Foreign Corrupt Practices Act, which prohibits payments to foreign officials to obtain or keep business. The USA Patriot Act, seeking to deter and punish terrorist acts, has also had a significant effect on U.S. international business transactions.

Some prominent multinational organizations and agreements that affect practically all international business dealings are described as follows:

- The United Nations (UN) seeks to maintain international peace and cooperation while promoting human rights and fundamental freedoms.

- The World Trade Organization (WTO) seeks to help producers of goods and services, exporters, and importers conduct their business by dealing with trade rules among nations.

- The North American Free Trade Agreement (NAFTA) was formed in 1994 between Canada, Mexico, and the U.S. to improve trade across their borders.

- European Union (EU) is a group of European democratic countries working together for peace and prosperity.

- Association of Southeast Asian Nations (ASEAN) and ASEAN Free Trade Area (AFTA) is composed of five member states that seek to accelerate economic growth, social progress, and cultural development while promoting peace and stability.

- Asia-Pacific Economic Cooperation (APEC) seeks to facilitate economic growth, trade cooperation, and investment in the Asia-Pacific region.

CHAPTER NOTES

1. Hick, *Global Deals*, pp. 67–72.
2. "World Insurance in 2003," *sigma*, No. 3/2004, Swiss Reinsurance Company
3. U.S.C., § 26 et seq.
4. U.S.C., § 15 et seq.
5. Public Law 107-56.

Index

Page numbers in boldface refer to definitions of Key Words and Phrases.